Blackwell Companions to Literature and Culture

This series offers comprehensive, newly written surveys of key periods and movements and certain major authors, in English literary culture and history. Extensive volumes provide new perspectives and positions on contexts and on canonical and post-canonical texts, orientating the beginning student in new fields of study and providing the experienced undergraduate and new graduate with current and new directions, as pioneered and developed by leading scholars in the field.

A COMPANION TO

THE MODERN
AMERICAN NOVEL
1900–1950

EDITED BY

JOHN T. MATTHEWS

WILEY-BLACKWELL

A John Wiley & Sons, Ltd., Publication

This paperback edition first published 2013
© 2013 Blackwell Publishing Ltd

Edition history: Blackwell Publishing Ltd (hardback, 2009)

Registered Office
John Wiley & Sons Ltd, The Atrium, Southern Gate, Chichester, West Sussex, PO19 8SQ, UK

Editorial Offices
350 Main Street, Malden, MA 02148-5020, USA
9600 Garsington Road, Oxford, OX4 2DQ, UK
The Atrium, Southern Gate, Chichester, West Sussex, PO19 8SQ, UK

For details of our global editorial offices, for customer services, and for information about how to apply for permission to reuse the copyright material in this book please see our website at www.wiley.com/wiley-blackwell.

The right of John T. Matthews to be identified as the author of the editorial material in this work has been asserted in accordance with the UK Copyright, Designs and Patents Act 1988.

Wiley also publishes its books in a variety of electronic formats. Some content that appears in print may not be available in electronic books.

Designations used by companies to distinguish their products are often claimed as trademarks. All brand names and product names used in this book are trade names, service marks, trademarks or registered trademarks of their respective owners. The publisher is not associated with any product or vendor mentioned in this book.

Limit of Liability/Disclaimer of Warranty: While the publisher and author(s) have used their best efforts in preparing this book, they make no representations or warranties with respect to the accuracy or completeness of the contents of this book and specifically disclaim any implied warranties of merchantability or fitness for a particular purpose. It is sold on the understanding that the publisher is not engaged in rendering professional services and neither the publisher nor the author shall be liable for damages arising herefrom. If professional advice or other expert assistance is required, the services of a competent professional should be sought.

Library of Congress Cataloging-in-Publication Data

A companion to the modern American novel 1900–1950 / edited by John T. Matthews.
    p. cm. – (Blackwell companions to literature and culture)
  Includes bibliographical references and index.
  ISBN 978-0-631-20687-3 (cloth) – ISBN 978-1-118-49208-6 (pbk.)
    1. American fiction–20th century–History and criticism–Handbooks, manuals, etc.
2. Modernism (Literature)–United States.   I. Matthews, John T.
  PS379.C63 2009
  813′.5209–dc22

                        2008036226

A catalogue record for this book is available from the British Library.

Cover image: Edward Hopper, *Nighthawks* (detail), 1942, oil on canvas, 84.1 × 152.4 cm. Friends of American Art Collection, 1942.51, The Art Institute of Chicago. Photograph by Robert Hashimoto. Reproduction © The Art Institute of Chicago.
Cover design by Richard Boxall Design Associates

Typeset in 11 on 13 pt Garamond 3 by Toppan Best-set Premedia Limited
Printed in Malaysia by Ho Printing (M) Sdn Bhd

1   2013

Contents

Notes on Contributors

Donna Campbell is Professor of English at Washington State University. She has written *Resisting Regionalism: Gender and Naturalism in American Fiction, 1880–1915* (1997), and has published widely in scholarly journals on American literature. She writes the annual "Fiction: 1900 to the 1930s" chapter for *American Literary Scholarship*. Her next book will be a study of women writers of naturalism.

Edward P. Comentale is Associate Professor of English at Indiana University. His first book was *Modernism, Cultural Production, and the British Avant-Garde*, and he is now at work on a monograph treating modernism, regionalism, and popular music entitled *The State I'm In: Modernism and American Popular Music*. Recent articles deal with the modernist Midwest, William Faulkner, country music, and the Coen brothers.

Susan V. Donaldson is the National Endowment for the Humanities Professor of English and American Studies at William and Mary College. She has written *Competing Voices: The American Novel, 1865–1914* (1998), and coedited, with Anne Goodwyn Jones, *Haunted Bodies: Gender and Southern Texts* (1997). Current projects include books on the politics of storytelling in the US South and on William Faulkner, Eudora Welty, Richard Wright, and the demise of Jim Crow.

Leigh Anne Duck teaches at the University of Memphis, where she is Associate Professor of English and an affiliate of the Benjamin L. Hooks Institute for Social Change and the Center for Research on Women. Her book, *The Nation's Region: Southern Modernism, Segregation, and U.S. Nationalism*, appeared in 2006, and she has begun a new cross-cultural project on literature of the US South and South Africa.

Mark Eaton specializes in American literature, African-American literature, American ethnic literature, postmodernism, and film studies at Azusa Pacific University, where he Professor of English. He is coeditor, with Emily Griesinger, of a volume of essays called *The Gift of Story: Narrating Hope in a Postmodern World*

(2006) and has published widely on American literature and culture in scholarly journals.

Susan Edmunds is the author of *Out of Line: History, Psychoanalysis and Montage in H. D.'s Long Poems* (1994) and *Grotesque Relations: Modernist Domestic Fiction and the U.S. Welfare State* (2008). She is a professor of English at Syracuse University, where she specializes in twentieth-century American literature and culture, African-American studies, modernism and the avant-garde, and experimental fiction.

Barbara Foley is Professor of English at Rutgers University-Newark, where she teaches Marxist theory, US literary radicalism, and African-American literature. Her books include *Telling the Truth: The Theory and Practice of Documentary Fiction* (1986), *Radical Representations: Politics and Form in U.S. Proletarian Fiction, 1929–1941* (1993), and *Spectres of 1919: Class and Nation in the Making of the New Negro* (2003). She is currently working on a book about politics, history, and the making of Ralph Ellison's *Invisible Man.*

Richard Godden is Professor of English at the University of California at Irvine, where he teaches courses in twentieth-century American literature, literature of the American South, and the relation between economic and literary forms. He is the author of *Fictions of Capital: Essays on the American Novel from James to Mailer* (1990), *Fictions of Labor: William Faulkner and the South's Long Revolution* (1997), and *William Faulkner: An Economy of Complex Words* (2007).

Matthew Pratt Guterl is Associate Professor of African American and African Diaspora Studies at Indiana University, where he also directs the American Studies Program. He has written *American Mediterranean: Southern Slaveholders in the Age of Emancipation* (2008) and *The Color of Race in America, 1900–1940* (2001), and coedited, with James T. Campbell and Robert Lee, *Race, Nation, and Empire in American History* (2007).

George B. Handley is Professor of Humanities at Brigham Young University. His books include *New World Poetics: Nature and the Adamic Imagination of Walt Whitman, Pablo Neruda, and Derek Walcott* (2007), *Postslavery Literatures in the Americas: Family Portraits in Black and White* (2000), *Caribbean Literature and the Environment: Between Culture and Nature* (2005) (ed.), and *America's Worlds and the World's Americas* (2006) (ed.).

William R. Handley is Associate Professor of English at the University of Southern California. Past President of the Western Literature Association, he is the author of *Marriage, Violence, and the Nation in the American Literary West* (2002), and coeditor, with Nathaniel Lewis, of *True West: Authenticity and the American West* (2004). He has also published essays on Virginia Woolf, Toni Morrison, LA freeways, and Mormonism, among other topics, and is the editor of a forthcoming book on the film *Brokeback Mountain.*

Hsuan L. Hsu has recently been appointed Assistant Professor of English at the University of California at Davis. He is completing a manuscript entitled *Scales of Identification: Geography, Affect, and Nineteenth-Century U. S. Literature*, and has published on contemporary literature, Asian-American literature, film, regionalism, and the theory of space and cultural production.

Rita Keresztesi is Associate Professor of English at the University of Oklahoma, where her research and teaching focus primarily on twentieth-century American literature and culture, with an emphasis on issues of ethnicity, race, and class. Her book, *Strangers at Home: American Ethnic Modernism between the World Wars*, was published in 2005. She is currently working on a new book that examines the cultural and intellectual exchanges between African-American and Afro-Caribbean artists and thinkers.

Delia Konzett is Assistant Professor of English and Cinema/American/Women's Studies at the University of New Hampshire. She is the author of *Ethnic Modernisms: Anzia Yezierska, Zora Neale Hurston, Jean Rhys, and the Aesthetics of Dislocation* (2003) and is currently working on a new project on war and Orientalism in Hollywood WWII film. Her teaching interests include modernism, cinema, film theory, ethnic writing, and the representation of race in film and literature.

Andrew Lawson teaches American literature of the nineteenth century through the present in the School of Cultural Studies at Leeds Metropolitan University. He is the author of *Walt Whitman and the Class Struggle* (2006) and is completing a book to be called *Downwardly Mobile: American Realism and the Lower Middle Class*. He has also published on Mark Twain and Stephen Crane.

Christopher Looby teaches at the University of California at Los Angeles, where he is Professor of English, specializing in United States literature of the eighteenth and nineteenth centuries, and Gay/Lesbian/Queer Studies. He is editor of *The Complete Civil War Journal and Selected Letters of Thomas Wentworth Higginson* (2000) and author of *Voicing America: Language, Literary Form, and the Origins of the United States* (1996).

Heather Love is the M. Mark and Esther K. Watkins Assistant Professor in the Humanities at the University of Pennsylvania. Her interests include gender studies and queer theory, the literature and culture of modernity, affect studies, film and visual culture, psychoanalysis, race and ethnicity, and critical theory. She is the author of *Feeling Backward: Loss and the Politics of Queer History* (2007), and is working on a project on Erving Goffman called *The Stigma Archive*.

John T. Matthews is Professor of English and American Studies at Boston University. He is the author of *The Play of Faulkner's Language* (1982), '*The Sound and the Fury': Faulkner and the Lost Cause* (1990), and the forthcoming *William Faulkner: Seeing Through the South* (2009). He is currently completing a book on the US South and modern fiction called *Look Away, Look Awry: The Problem of the South in the American Imagination*.

Justus Nieland is an assistant professor of English at Michigan State University. He works in modernism, the avant-garde, and film studies, and is the author of *Feeling Modern: The Eccentricities of Public Life* (2008). He is writing a book on David Lynch for the Contemporary Film Directors series at the University of Illinois Press, and coauthoring a book, with Jennifer Fay, on film noir and the cultures of globalization.

Patrick O'Donnell is Professor of English at Michigan State University, where he specializes in modern and contemporary American literature, postmodern literature and theory, and literature and film. He is the author of *John Hawkes* (1982), *Passionate Doubts: Designs of Interpretation in Contemporary American Fiction* (1986), *Echo Chambers: Figuring Voice in Modern Narrative* (1992), and *Latent Destinies: Cultural Paranoia in Contemporary U.S. Narrative* (2000). He is writing *The American Novel Now: Contemporary American Fiction Since 1980* for Wiley-Blackwell.

Jeanne Follansbee Quinn is Director of the Program in History and Literature at Harvard University. She has coedited, with Ann Keniston, *Literature after 9/11* (2008) and is completing a book entitled *Democratic Aesthetics: Popular Front Antifascism.*

Eric Rauchway is Professor of History at the University of California at Davis. The author of *Blessed Among Nations: How the World Made America* (2006), *Murdering McKinley: The Making of Theodore Roosevelt's America* (2003), and *The Refuge of Affections: Family and American Reform Politics, 1900–1920* (2001), he is currently working on a book entitled *The Gift Outright: The West, the South, and America, 1867–1937.*

Charles J. Rzepka is Professor of English at Boston University. He is the author of *Detective Fiction* (2005), *Sacramental Commodities: Gift, Text, and the Sublime in De Quincey* (1995), *The Self as Mind: Vision and Identity in Wordsworth, Coleridge, and Keats* (1986), and numerous articles on British Romanticism and detective fiction. He is coediting, with Lee Horsley, the *Blackwell Companion to Crime Fiction.*

Jani Scandura is Associate Professor of English at the University of Minnesota. She is the author of *Down in the Dumps: Place, Modernity, and American Depression* (2008) and coeditor, with Michael Thurston, of *Modernism, Inc.: Body, Memory, Capital* (2001). She is working on a new book entitled *Suitcase: Fragments on Memory, Matter, and Motion.*

Michelle Stephens published *Black Empire: The Masculine Global Imaginary of Caribbean Intellectuals in the U. S., 1914–1962* in 2005. She is at work on a second project provisionally entitled "Black Acts: Race, Masculinity and Performance in the New World." Associate Professor of English at Colgate College, she specializes in American, African-American, and Caribbean literatures.

Michael Trask writes on the intersections of queer theory and feminism, high and low culture, and social theory and traditional literary criticism, and teaches in the Department of English at the University of Kentucky. He is the author of *Cruising*

Modernism: Class and Sexuality in American Literature and Social Thought (2003) and is currently working on a book called *Camp Stories: Mass Culture, School Culture, and the New Social Movements*.

Nancy Woloch teaches history at Barnard College, Columbia University. Her publications include: *Women and the American Experience* (4th edn, 2006), *The American Century: A History of the United States Since the 1990s* (6th edn, 2008), *The Enduring Vision: A History of the American People* (6th edn, 2008), and *Early American Women: A Documentary History* (2nd edn, 2002). She is working on a book on protective labor laws, 1890s–1990s.

Jeremy Yudkin is a professor of Music at Boston University and Visiting professor of music at Oxford. He is the author of eight books on various aspects of music, including *Music in Medieval Europe* (1989) and *Understanding Music* (1996). He has recently published two books on jazz, *The Lenox School of Jazz: A Vital Chapter in the History of American Music and Race Relations* (2006) and *Miles Davis, Miles Smiles, and the Invention of Post Bop* (2007).

List of Figures

Preface

When I first agreed to edit this collection of essays on the modern American novel, I thought immediately of the sorts of pieces I wished I'd been able to send my students to through the years. A number of excellent resources for teaching modern literature have appeared recently, almost all of them designed to provide concise but comprehensive coverage of standard literary topics and movements in the period and genre of study. The best do an excellent job of locating and relating individual works and authors, and helping readers understand where given literary elements fit in the broader accounts of major developments. The series of Companions in which this volume appears, however, in allowing a greater number of essays and more flexible organization, invites attention to other pedagogical purposes. Over the past two decades, modernist studies has enjoyed a burgeoning of exciting new historical, theoretical, and cultural scholarship. This innovative work has at least complicated, and sometimes even called into question, almost every accepted assumption of our field.

One of the objectives of this Companion is to reflect the directions of such new scholarship: not only do many of the essays propose fresh descriptions of familiar novels of the period, or new descriptions of freshly (re)discovered ones, they also root their reformulations in contemporary theoretical speculation and historical research that ought to stimulate advanced students (and nonspecialist teachers) to their own explorations of the field and its underlying conceptual questions. The bibliographic sections that follow the essays include titles suggested for further reading. We can imagine many ramifications, some beyond the bounds of what gets said here: the continued reconfiguration of courses to allow comparison of texts from other national traditions around the globe, from underrepresented literatures within hemispheric America, and from minority traditions within the continental US; writing assignments that ask students to work historically with modernity while thinking analytically of modernism; the study of modernism as conceptually intertwined with the experience of postmodernity and postmodernism. This collection brings together established literary scholars who have set new agendas in the study of the modern

American novel, and younger scholars who have begun to publish the next generation of cutting-edge work. It also includes articles by a number of historians, who provide invaluable accounts of the material and intellectual environments occupied by novelists and their readers during the first half of the twentieth century.

We hope to have met a standard of authoritative originality throughout the essays. They have been conceived to furnish readers with a variety of tools: to provide concise studies of relevant economic, social, and cultural contexts; to rethink traditional accounts of familiar topics like realism, naturalism, and regionalism with respect to modernism; to complicate the origins and purposes of modernism; in fact, to extend an idea proposed by Peter Nicholls that we should be thinking more in terms of a plurality of modernisms, including a range of ethnic and mass-cultural varieties; and to question some of the received categories for study of the nation's fiction during this period, including those upon which the volume's self-definition rests: the novel, America, modernism, and modernity. The luxury of a book like this is that so many of our essays aim to incite reconsideration, inquiry, and speculation, as well as provide information.

The first set of essays recreates the habitat for literary activities between 1900 and 1950. Eric Rauchway's essay on economic history addresses many central topics: urbanization, immigration, speculation and consumption, labor and the New Deal, and postwar recovery. Each of these sets backdrops for much of the period's fiction, particularly in the interwar years, when some kinds of modernism sought refuge in aesthetic opposition to the economic and social transformations attendant to modernity, and subsequent tendencies toward political literature during the Depression insisted on representing such conditions to national audiences. Rauchway's chapter enriches numerous essays that follow here, including those on realism and capitalism, the proletarian movement, Southern literature, and regionalism. Nancy Woloch provides a concise, comprehensive account of major changes in women's lives over the period. Her essay furnishes much useful empirical data about the conditions affecting women – data about employment and education, for example – that will help students of literature read the novels of this era with a usable sense of what was happening, and how different writers both reflect and intervene in these trends (or in some cases ignore or oppose them). The essay keeps the distinct stories of various groups of women in mind, and shows how differences in class and race affected opportunity and the decisions women could make. Readers will be able to see how the artistic ventures of women writers of the Harlem Renaissance, for instance, grew out of the broader effects of migration to northern cities, and the distinctive employment pattern of African-American women. In the next essay, Matthew Guterl recounts the broader history of modern African-American life through the lens of literary perceptions of it. His essay charts distinct phases of black experience and mentality, from the horrors of Jim Crow segregation, through the "New Negro" Renaissance, the Great Depression, and on to the horizon of the civil rights movement, each phase put in dialogue with influential cultural reflections like those of Thomas Dixon, Jr. or W. E. B. Du Bois.

Guterl's essay offers several points from which subsequent essays may be seen to launch out. Reading through the example of Richard Wright's short story "Long Black Song," from *Uncle Tom's Children,* Jeanne Follansbee Quinn distinguishes an aesthetics for fiction of the period that is drawn from pragmatist philosophy, such an aesthetics defining and enjoining the problem of progressivist art rather than insisting upon theoretical solutions. The essay maps the poles of modernist epiphany and proletarian conversion, then shows how pragmatism complicates, without expecting to solve, the step from aesthetic vision to political action. Wright's story becomes an epitome of the incommensurability of aesthetics and politics that troubled much other fiction of the 1930s. Woloch's piece gives the reader a context for Michael Trask's contention that the modern novel embraced (with productive ambivalence) a revolution in sexual mores, with its possibilities for individual emotional and even economic growth. His argument vivifies and expands the idea of the modern in the many novels he treats. Sex and ethics are pried apart in a way that suggests just how profound the shifts of modernity were; Trask restores some of that sense of newness, particularly now that scholars have begun to accept views that emphasize the continuities of modernism with earlier periods, or stress some of the conservative implications of modernist treatments of modernity. Readers will want to note Trask's analysis of Gertrude Stein's wayward style (or styling of waywardness) from the standpoint of sexual vagrancy, as well as his fresh discussions of frequently taught works like *Sister Carrie, The House of Mirth, My Ántonia, Winesburg, Ohio, The Great Gatsby*, and *Grapes of Wrath*.

The two following pieces pursue the interplay between American fiction and two distinctive modern art forms: jazz and cinema. Jeremy Yudkin offers a documentary account of changing attitudes toward jazz from its inception to its canonization by mid-century. The essay's historical survey helps readers appreciate the flux of contemporary debates about this innovative kind of music, and invites them to explore the record of controversy themselves. The cultural nexus of the "American arts" of jazz and a jazz-inflected American literary style inspires Yudkin's suggestive discussions of Langston Hughes, Ralph Ellison (who wrote extensively about jazz), and Norman Mailer. Justus Nieland explores the international cultural and political circumstances that led French intellectuals to appropriate American modernist literary style in order to invent a "visual humanism" after the two World Wars. Nieland shows how the 1940s French cultural critic Claude-Edmonde Magny translates modernist experimental technique in the novel into a style of film, one devoted to the sort of ethics that transcend individual subjectivity. The essay bends received delineations of textual and cinematic fiction by using interdisciplinary methods across the media (in this case prompted by Magny's own insistence on the common purposes crossing modern film and fiction). Nieland also opens up a transatlantic context for the cultural reception and value of the modern American novel.

The next group of essays reconsiders familiar categories of modern American literature: late nineteenth-century realism, literary naturalism, and modern realism. Andrew Lawson develops a line of inquiry into the realistic aesthetic of Henry James, William

Dean Howells, Mark Twain, Stephen Crane, Theodore Dreiser, and the early Edith Wharton that concentrates on the opposition between mass culture and elite forms of literary production. Lawson's analysis illuminates the shifting material circumstances of writing fiction – the economics of producing imaginative goods for a rapidly developing literary market – as it also provides the basis for a key family trait of early realist modernism: its self-consciousness about representational practice. The divide between high and low culture, now understood to have been more fluid and murky than critics once believed, provoked the kinds of equivocation Lawson charts; it also anticipates the assumptions grounding later essays in the Companion on subsequent phases of modernism such as the fiction of high modernism or the Hollywood novel. Donna Campbell thinks about what makes American naturalism a kind of protomodernism by employing a definition of modernism that emphasizes its addressing of modernity. Campbell's thesis disturbs a simple chronological sequence from naturalism to "classic modernism," showing instead that the two may mostly be different spaces of continuing engagements with modernity. The essay provides concise yet thorough analyses of main exemplars of naturalism like Frank Norris, Stephen Crane, Kate Chopin, the later Dreiser, Jack London, and Anzia Yezierska, while suggesting broader affiliations with a range of other writers (such as Wharton and Paul Lawrence Dunbar, for example). Richard Godden examines labor and production history in the period of high capitalism during the American 1920s to excavate economic preoccupations in Ernest Hemingway, Wharton, and F. Scott Fitzgerald. Godden's essay demonstrates how imaginative work resisted assumptions being posited by modern capitalism: the dominance of industrial production, the myth of liberal individualism, the confidence in gratification through the consumption of commodities. Godden suggests how forms of modernism emerged to counter these dominant features of modernity – what Godden considers a (false) *capitalist* realism: in Hemingway producing a sensitivity to the way the consumption of commodities encouraged amnesia toward labor; in Wharton leading to a sort of hyperrealistic attention to objects that challenges the forgetfulness of reification; and in Fitzgerald exposing the fictionality of self-made men like Gatsby as those who have forfeited their own material reality.

Several essays take up the idea that, as Campbell suggests, alternative modernisms occupy simultaneous spaces during the early century. Leigh Anne Duck unfolds modernism's concern with negotiating the temporal changes of modernity by treating them through spatial and demographic segregation. Drawing on Bakhtin's analytical category of chronotope (pertaining to time and space in a narrative), Duck shows how progressive capitalist time contrasts in modern literature with personal eccentric forms that resist it. Duck's analysis allows for a more explicitly materialist explanation of why modernist art gravitates toward the spatialization of experience, and she ranges across a wide variety of examples: Sherwood Anderson, Nathanael West, Du Bois, Gertrude Stein, the Native American writer John Joseph Mathews, Faulkner, and Ellison. The essay also suggests how the urgencies and anxieties of modernism extend into contemporary permutations of global modernity, anticipating a number of essays in the volume that explore the intertwining of modernism and postmodernism. Hsuan

Hsu also centers economic factors in his account of regionalism. Hsu distinguishes separate moments and kinds of regionalism: a turn-of-the-century form of regionalism associated with the local color movement and exemplified by Hamlin Garland, Charles Chesnutt, and Sarah Orne Jewett, for example, as opposed to a newer regionalism of the 1920s. That regionalism – instanced in Anderson, Sinclair Lewis, Edgar Lee Masters, and the Southern Agrarians – performed the cultural work of *producing* regions for modern national-level capitalist development. Hsu's closing section on ethnic regionalism demonstrates how labor exploitation based on racial subjugation was transmuted into the cultural differences of place, and how writers like Zitkala-Sa (Gertrude Bonnin), Américo Paredes, Jean Toomer, and Carlos Bulosan questioned such conventions of representation. Ed Comentale offers an original reformulation of Midwestern modernism through Giorgio Agamben's theory of potentiality. Comentale suggests that the Midwest is inevitably associated with national potential. But potentiality necessarily swings between a condition of general sadness or disappointment that accompanies any specific materialization of an ideal (it's never what's dreamt of) and a resource for more critical resistance to the specific *kind* of materialization embodied in urban industrial capitalism, with its emergent culture of consumption (life could always be better, in ways symbolized by regional habitation). Comentale considers Midwestern writers like Ruth Suckow, Willa Cather, Sherwood Anderson, and Dreiser, but also turns to the painters Grant Wood and Thomas Hart Benton to amplify his thesis. Susan Donaldson picks up on Hsuan Hsu's inclusion of Southern authors in modern regionalist writing by seeking the origins of modernist narrative self-consciousness in the violent abruption of modernity on the South by the Civil War. Donaldson documents the upheavals brought to all Southern groups by the collapse of the Confederacy, showing how African-American writers like Julia Anna Cooper, Ida B. Wells, and Frances Ellen Watkins Harper explored new ways of telling stories in order to consolidate new social and political narratives. Donaldson incorporates most of the prominent post-Reconstruction through early twentieth-century Southern novelists into her innovative account of an indigenous Southern modernism – from George Washington Cable through Charles Chesnutt, James Weldon Johnson, Allen Tate, Faulkner, Frances Newman, Eudora Welty, Richard Wright, and Ellison.

My essay on high modernism corresponds with Donaldson's by arguing that the confrontation with a Southern past was central to modernism's engagement with the realities of modernity. At the cusp of the new century, the nation's uneasy denial of its relation to the peculiar social and economic history of the South finally had to be addressed when the federal government began to act toward new foreign colonial territories as it had formerly acted toward its Southern region. Debates about racial subjugation, neoplantation agricultural empire, and an increasingly strong federal state all figured into modern literature's anxious recognition that the South had always been integral to the national project and prosperity, based as it was on hemispheric plantation colonialism. Many principal American modern novelists were Southern in essential ways, and this essay suggests how habits of denial might be traced through a figure surprisingly common to many high modernist texts: the colonized black male body. Michelle Stephens explores the ways African-American artists sought to realize the opportunities for racial self-expression offered by modern social realities such as migration to Northern cities and increased access to cultural organs like the stage and magazines. She chronicles phases in the difficult attainment of a separate black modernism, beginning with an insistence on racial visibility in popular theatre and early film. Stephens valuably links the later, more self-possessed modernist art of the Harlem Renaissance to Caribbean anticolonialist culture of the 1920s, showing how the African-American modern novel must include hemispheric Americans like Eric Walrond and George Lamming. The essay's final turn follows out the challenge to a largely masculinist New Negro African-American modernism by other writers of color: conspicuously Zora Neale Hurston, but also Jean Toomer (who writes sympathetically of women's oppression in the plantation South).

More combatively, Rita Keresztesi challenges the hegemony of high modernism as an aesthetic formation that guarded ethnic privilege. She contends that canonical modernism reinforced social practices that policed ethnic populations during the migratory movements characterizing modernity. The essay insists that there is a politics involved in formulating modernism as essentially "high," and that there is a variety of "ethnic" writing that ought to be counted as modernist, not all of it characterized by formal experimentalism or designed for consumption by educated elites. The essay arcs from the emergent modernism of *The Confidence-Man* to a residual form in *Invisible Man.* Writers like Nella Larsen and Hurston are positioned as examples of one kind of modernism, while Native American writers like Mourning Dove, D'Arcy McNickle, and John Joseph Mathews appear as practitioners of another, and Jewish-American ones like Anzia Yezierska and Henry Roth of still another. Barbara Foley reprises a thematic taxonomy of proletarian fiction in her essay, listing scores of titles treating each of the genre's five principal subjects: strikes, race and antiracism, nonclass-conscious workers, the development of class consciousness, and everyday working-class life. Foley then moves to a consideration of formal classification, and in particular two subgenres, that she finds more illuminating to proletarian purposes: the single-protagonist novel of development, and the collective novel. In addition to remarks about a host of proletarian novelists from these standpoints, Foley also suggests how Richard Wright and John Dos Passos exemplify the appropriation of modernist formal techniques for proletarian novelistic objectives. A contrasting kind of progressivist fiction appears in Susan Edmunds' account of the modern sentimental novel. Edmunds argues that the modern sentimental tradition, far from functioning as a distraction from political imagination, actually associated domestic life with the possibility of social revolution. Edmunds reads a remarkable array of writers – Edith Wharton, Nella Larsen, Edna Ferber, Yezierska, Walter White, Meridel Le Sueur, Richard Wright, Faulkner, Toomer, Djuna Barnes, Tillie Olsen, Nathanael West, Flannery O'Connor – as drawing terms from the discourse of home life to represent debates about the formation of the US welfare state.

The next set of essays recuperates a number of former "minority" traditions of the American novel from the first half of the century now being reconceptualized as fully central to modernism. Heather Love complicates the category of lesbian fiction by noting the ambivalence generated by the emergence of lesbianism under social and medical disciplinary impulses: the formation of lesbian identity cannot be separated from its pathologization. Love's readings begin with Henry James's *The Bostonians*, then take up Sarah Orne Jewett, Gertrude Stein, Hilda Doolittle (H. D.), Nella Larsen, Gale Wilhelm, Djuna Barnes, Jane Bowles, and Patricia Highsmith; they describe a trajectory toward more explicit affirmation of same-sex affection between women. The analytical subtlety of the essay foregrounds aspects of textual unrepresentability – kinds of opacity, strains of searches for the language of inchoate new social relations and forms of affectional attachment. Christopher Looby detects a similar concern with matters of formal representation in observing the inseparability of reflection on story-telling itself and the question of homosexual desire. Looby traces a preoccupation in gay fiction with the question of whether the queer novel might be possible at all given the snug ideological fit between traditional novelistic plots of self-realization and narratives of heterosexual romance and marriage. Looby's essay focuses on early instances like Charles Warren Stoddard's *For the Pleasure of His Company* (1903) and Edward Prime-Stevenson's *Imre: A Memorandum* (1906) to explicate the historical, theoretical, and artistic quandaries constraining gay writers at the turn of the century. The essay goes on to survey a range of gay fiction during subsequent decades, linger-ing particularly over neglected works by "Blair Niles," Dawn Powell, and Charles Henri Ford and Parker Tyler, and ending with a reflection on Carson McCullers' *A Member of the Wedding*.

William Handley's essay is one of three to address modern popular subgenres, in his case the Western. Handley raises numerous provocative questions about the his-torical significance of the Western, as well as its current timeliness: the essay looks at issues of high versus popular culture, gender and genre, market demands versus resistance to commodification, and the Western's typical engagement with myths justifying the domestication of the land. The essay focuses on that ur-Western, *The Virginian* (1906), and the best-selling author of them all, Zane Grey, but also gives ample space to lesser-known artists and, very valuably, to women writers of Westerns. Handley also detects the pressure of the Western on more canonical works by Cather and Fitzgerald. Charles Rzepka maps the chronological development of detective fiction during the first half of the century, covering all the usual suspects: Dashiell Hammett and Raymond Chandler during the interwar years of the hard-boiled form; Horace McCoy and James M. Cain from the postwar noir period; Mickey Spillane and Chester Himes principally as Cold War instances; and, growing out of earlier tradi-tions of "alternative" detective fiction, more contemporary feminist and gay/lesbian, postmodernist, and high cultural parodic versions (the last in Vladimir Nabokov and Thomas Pynchon, for example). Mark Eaton pursues the relation of hard-boiled detec-tive fiction to the Hollywood novel, not only establishing in helpful detail the familiar hostility of "serious" writers to their reliance on periodic indenture to the film studios, but more surprisingly showing that Hollywood was actually indispensable in other ways. For one thing, studio contracts subsidized authors who wouldn't have been able to get any writing of their own done otherwise; Eaton looks at the exemplary career of Faulkner in this regard. But as an object of fascination for modern America, Hollywood also provoked a huge number of novelistic treatments of itself as phenomenon, and Eaton's essay goes on to survey those Hollywood-themed novels – many by lesser writers, along with notable ones by Dos Passos, Fitzgerald, Horace McCoy, and Nathanael West.

The closing cluster of essays probes the limits of the definitions enabling our collection. Delia Konzett challenges the usual positioning of Asian-American fiction within postmodernism, making a compelling case that what drives Asian-American writing is a "belated modernist project"; Konzett identifies the roots of post-World War II Asian-American writing in the experience of migration and displacement – principal features of modernity. The essay joins a number of earlier ones here that spell out the plurality of modernisms the field has come to recognize, expanding the set of literary responses to modernity far beyond what Konzett sees as the experimental techniques tending to distinguish "high" modernism. Patrick O'Donnell isolates strains in modernism that come forward in the light of postmodernism. The essay steers clear of the period-model of evolution and rupture for the succession of modernism by postmodernism, undercutting the whole notion of temporal contiguity, and showing the challenge to linear temporality as a central modernist/postmodernist problematic to begin with. Readers will appreciate O'Donnell's account of key debates, with its summaries of principal schools of interpretation and theories of postmodernism. Readings that focus on Stein, Barnes, and Faulkner illustrate key purposes of modernism (the destabilization of knowledge and identity through their spatialization into the language of process in Stein; the destabilization of gender/identity binarism in Barnes; and the textualization of genealogy, history, and consciousness in Faulkner). George Handley begins his essay by positioning American modernism – especially of the regional and racial minority varieties – within the hemispheric movements of anticolonialism, under which common efforts were made to affirm the value of indigenous rural cultures against the incursions of imperialist modernity. Handley mounts a trenchant argument against treating US literature as exceptional, maintaining that it shares with other New World nations three fundamental conditions: the effects of widespread diaspora, often violently forced; the genocide of indigenous populations; and the degradation of the environment. Against the forgetfulness of imperialist powers toward such history, across the hemisphere, the modern novel offers the work of countermemory.

Jani Scandura concludes our book with a rumination on the afterlife of modernism. Scandura makes something of a deconstructive turn against modernism's desire for and exaltation of the thing *itself* – its apparent longing for an end to (as transcendence of) figurative language. This desire she reads as fetishistic, harboring an equivocation that ends up revealing the figural within the literal, and making the remnant/ the leftover/Derrida's *le reste* internal to the thing. Scandura manages to weave this theoretical meditation on the status of things in modernism with a very particular social history: the implications of modern technological food preservation. The longing to preserve leftovers immediately becomes a Freudian dream in Scandura's hands, one that's related to the remnant figure of a relocated Japanese-Canadian woman in Joy Kogawa's novel *Obasan* (1981). Taking up a dream that one of Freud's patients has, in which the dreamer confuses an oven with a refrigerator, Scandura translates the functions of these modern kitchen appliances to correspond to the psychological processes of introjection and melancholy by which individuals either succeed or fail to overcome trauma. Introjection involves incorporating and eventually working through threatful experiences; melancholy is the consequence of refusing to process grief: you get stuck with unusable leftovers. I can say only that Scandura fuses the psychoanalytic, ideological, and historical here, insisting that readers think hard about what's been left out of traditional ways of preserving both modernity and modernism – internal ethnic populations, to begin with. The insistence on these theoretical and historical phenomena contextualizes the modern American novel in a new conceptual way; the focus on Kogawa's novel – even as it breaks the frame of the 1900–50 boundaries – presses the idea of the incomplete, perhaps incompletable, project of modernism, its haunting of postmodernism as itself leftover modernism; and it hints at a certain absence discovered and installed at the heart of modernism that persists into postmodernism, though perhaps with increasingly explicit attention to the ethics or acceptance of absence.

Acknowledgments

For over three decades now I have taught a course in the modern American novel at Boston University. I've been remarkably fortunate in the intelligence, sense of adventure, and industry that students have brought to these classes. I want to dedicate this book to the undergraduate and graduate students who have made my course in the modern American novel a lifetime joy, and who have managed to make it a distinct intellectual challenge and achievement each semester. Many of you remain vividly memorable to me; I thank you for the countless observations and questions that have contributed to the evolution of my thinking about modern fiction, about contemporary American culture, and about why literature matters in the first place. I also wish to thank Melanie Benson for serving as a graduate research assistant during the preliminary phase of this book; as ever, her work for it was insightful and meticulous. My embarrassment at how long it's taken finally to complete this project is tempered a little by the pleasing fact that her own book will beat it to publication. I also wish to thank Boston University, particularly College of Arts and Sciences Deans Jeffrey Henderson and Virginia Sapiro, for research funds these past two years that helped in the preparation of the book for press. I want to thank as well the contributors to this Companion. I knew many of them professionally before this project began, but more of them were – and quite a few remain – only written voices on the other side of the screen. I've been gratefully astounded at their generosity toward this project, the originality of their conceptions for these essays, as well as the exactitude of their scholarship, and their seemingly inexhaustible capacity to indulge the ravings of an editor on the edge of a nervous breakdown. It took a long time for the nearly 30 of us finally to sprint, jog, tumble, inch backwards, or get dragged across the finish line, and so I want to thank our editors at Wiley-Blackwell, particularly Andrew McNeillie, who urged me to undertake this project, Emma Bennett, Rosemary Bird, and Hannah Morrell, for the confidence and patience that sustained me through the years we worked on this book. I do wish I'd done this sooner, but I suppose that's true for almost everything else in life too.

Edward Hopper, *Nighthawks* (detail), 1942, oil on canvas, 84.1 × 152.4 cm. Friends of American Art Collection, 1942.51, The Art Institute of Chicago. Photograph by Robert Hashimoto. Reproduction © The Art Institute of Chicago.

1

An Economic History of the United States 1900–1950

Eric Rauchway

In 1900 Americans still counted as a country people, and for most of them the rhythms of rural life shaped their ideas about past, present, and future. They shared memories of cultivation and scheduled their work in anticipation of the seasons and obedience to the weather. But before the twentieth century had half passed, the American city grew to overshadow the farm. Business cycles displaced seasons at the center of Americans' forecasts, and while weather still played its capricious part in determining how fully an investment might come to fruition, a host of other factors, epiphenomena of the industrial world, joined storm, drought, and flood as the unpredictable masters of fate. Americans who lived through this shift from rural to urban life often complained that the regimentation and complexity of the industrial world robbed them of their independence. At the same time, the shift to modern modes of production turned the United States into the most nearly independent national actor on the world's stage, at the center of an international economy Americans had little experience managing or even imagining. Only through the wrenching of war and depression did they come even to a tentative reckoning with the way the world worked now, and their place in it.

The Move to the Cities, 1900–1920

The shift from farm to city occupies a central place in the developmental theories of economists and the developmental histories of those nations fortunate enough to make it. By shifting resources out of agriculture and into industry, a people make possible greater specialization in production and begin to learn how to manufacture goods for which they can earn higher profit margins than they can for agricultural commodities. The shift to cities requires more elaborate networks of connections extending not only from farm to mill to market, but from steel town to rubber town to manufacturing center.

The movement of the American people from farm to city thus entailed the extension of American influence throughout the continent, as railroads and telegraphs made the riches of the interior available to the manufacturing centers on the coasts. While the balance of the population shifted to cities and went to work on the assembly lines of factories, a smaller but still significant share of the populace moved into the remoter parts of the nation's territory. As the population concentrated itself in cities, its frontier outposts grew more numerous and farther-flung.

The mobility of the American people thus meant not only a shift to cities, but also the extension west and south of the urban economy. Movement west meant wars with the indigenous peoples of the continent, and it meant the reshaping of American politics to admit the peculiar interests of those underpopulated western states. Extension of the modern American economy to the South also meant the end of the South's traditional isolation from urban life and culture. All these shifts and changes provoked profound political and cultural changes in the American people. As they became a more urban nation, they began to think of themselves in new ways.

In the summer of 1893 the historian Frederick Jackson Turner seized on a landmark pronouncement by the US Census to mark an epoch in US history:

> In a recent bulletin of the Superintendent of the Census for 1890 appear these significant words: "Up to and including 1880 the country had a frontier of settlement, but at present the unsettled area has been so broken into by isolated bodies of settlement that there can hardly be said to be a frontier line. In the discussion of its extent, its westward movement, etc., it can not, therefore, any longer have a place in the census reports." This brief official statement marks the closing of a great historical movement. Up to our own day American history has been in a large degree the history of the colonization of the Great West. The existence of an area of free land, its continuous recession, and the advance of American settlement westward, explain American development. (Turner 1920: 1)

In 1910 Turner elaborated on this theme: "A new national development is before us, without the former safety valve of abundant resources open to him who would take. Classes are becoming alarmingly distinct . . ." (Turner 1920: 280). His pronouncements captured the imaginations of many Americans seeking for an explanation of why their country plunged repeatedly into depression, why so many Americans found themselves out of work through no evident fault of their own, why the ladder upward from wage-work to self-employment seemed to have gone, and why working Americans now joined unions and struck against the national welfare. They had used up all the free land, and with it went the outlet for discontented labor radicals, who had no choice but to congregate in cities and clamor for expropriation of the comfortable classes' wealth. By 1920, Turner's story seemed to have reached a logical peak, as a year of strikes and police raids culminated in the Census's dry confirmation that half the American population now lived in officially urban areas (Haines 2006).

These two census bookends, 1890 and 1920, offer a useful cartoon sketch of American urbanization at the start of the twentieth century, and Turner's gloss on these occurrences gives us an excellent starting point for what such changes might have meant for the United States. But they provide only a starting point, and stopping with them often occasions erroneous conclusions constituting what we might call the nationalist fallacy, which has two components. First, it incorrectly creates the picture of a uniform country. Not only was the United States a large and diverse republic at the turn of the century, and unevenly economically developed, but it had then as it has now a highly federalized system of government, with a considerable degree of local control over policy. Second, it omits mention of the international influence on American affairs, which was particularly significant in the decades before World War I.

The end of the frontier and the move to cities did not mean the end of Americans' mobility, but it meant that the pattern of their movement followed a different course than the one Turner outlined, and became discernibly part of an international movement of peoples.[1] Turner thought the move to cities would mean an end of the United States's peculiar character as a frontier nation, believing that as Americans crowded into cities they would become more and more like the European peoples from whom they had seceded, miserable in their proximity and riven by class. But as the social scientist Charles Beard wrote in 1912, a close observer might have reason to believe that even as Americans became a city people they would become a city people quite unlike any other: "In addition to the unhappy working and living conditions which characterize modern urban centers generally, the American city has special problems of its own on account of the large percentage of foreigners embraced in its population . . . Our larger cities are in fact foreign colonies" (Beard 1912: 22–4).

In the first decade of the twentieth century, annual net immigration to the United States increased dramatically from about 288,000 in 1901 to about 818,000 in 1910 (Carter, Gartner, Haines, Olmstead, Sutch, and Wright 2006: series Aa13). Foreign immigration accounted for as much as half the population growth in the US during this period (Barde, Carter, and Sutch, 2006).

While it is certainly possible to overstate the importance of immigration to US history, it is not possible to overstate it by much, especially for the early twentieth century. On the one hand, the US was only one among a set of New World nations that received immigrants in the late nineteenth and early twentieth centuries, when tens of millions of Europeans sought work and residence overseas. If the US was a nation of immigrants, so were Canada, Argentina, Brazil, Australia, and others. And because those nations had smaller populations than the US did, foreign-born people accounted for a much larger share of their population. For example, in 1911 immigrant arrivals in Canada amounted to about 5 percent of the total population, while in the US at about the same time, they accounted for only 1 percent of the total population, so we might want to say that immigrants had five times the impact in the further north of North America than they did in the United States (Mitchell 2003: series A8 and A1). And if both countries had completely integrated national labor markets, then this might be true strictly as an assessment of the economic impact of additional labor.

But to suggest as much entails two errors. The first is another application of the nationalist fallacy to the United States. Immigrants did not arrive in America evenly dispersed over the landscape; if they had, they might indeed have assimilated, little noticed, into the population. Rather, they landed in a few select locations and often stayed there. The federal character of American politics then translated this uneven local impact of immigration into national conflicts over policy. The second is a sin specific to social science: the idea that an immigrant is only one unit of a quantifiable mass – which might be so if all foreign migrants came from some single source country named, perhaps, Foreignia. But immigrants came potentially from a wide variety of places, spoke a wide variety of languages, and worshiped a wide variety of gods – if, that is, we are speaking of immigrants to the United States: the US received not only more, but more kinds of immigrants than other New World nations in the age of mass migration. Immigrants from Britain and Ireland accounted for the largest share of the sojourners streaming to Canada and Australia, immigrants from Spain dominated the migration to Argentina and those from Portugal the newcomers to Brazil, but immigrants to the United States came from all over, and no single country of origin dominated.

Immigrants to the United States made up a diverse population before they even began to mix with the already resident Americans. In the playwright Israel Zangwill's rather unflattering language, they constituted "a hodge-podge of simultaneous hordes" (cited in Rauchway 2006: 67). The numerous nationalities encouraged some enthusiastic observers to invent American multiculturalism: as Randolph Bourne wrote, "We have needed the new peoples – the order of the German and the Scandinavian, the turbulence of the Slav and Hun – to save us from our own stagnation" (cited in Rauchway 2006: 67). But to more Americans, the many kinds of immigrants mattered for their economic impact (see Rauchway 2006: 65–9 for further discussion).

Inasmuch as immigration increased the labor supply, it threatened workers with competition, and so one would expect employers to favor immigration more than employees would. The added element of cultural difference gave employers an increased incentive to employ immigrants: a shop foreman could prevent unionization by deliberately hiring a workforce drawn from not only different but traditionally antagonistic populations: Catholics and Protestants, Japanese and Chinese, Germans and Poles, Irish and English, and so forth; the world's bitter history presented many possibilities. Members of a multicultural workforce looked less likely to talk to one another, let alone organize and unite behind common interests. At the time and ever since, many observers have essentially agreed with Karl Marx's coauthor Friedrich Engels, who wrote that American laborers divided into "the native-born and the foreigners, and the latter into (1) the Irish, (2) the Germans, (3) the many small groups, each of which understands only itself; the Czechs, Poles, Italians, Scandinavians, etc. And then the Negroes . . . The dissimilar elements of the working class fall apart" (cited in Rauchway 2006: 66).

Labor activists opposed immigration for just these reasons. As the sometime political candidate and theorist Henry George wrote, the new immigrants, "believed to be imported, or at least induced to come, for the express purpose of reducing wages and making employers independent of their men . . . have naturally been regarded with dislike and dread" (cited in Rauchway 2006: 69).

Amid this dislike and dread, some Americans simply moved. One study finds that for every 10 immigrants that arrived in an American city, four residents left to find a home somewhere else in the country (Hatton and Williamson 1998: 168; see also Eldridge and Thomas 1964: 71–5 and Goodrich et al. 1936: 679–85.) But this migration worked differently from Turner's safety valve: where his idea of the western movement had discontented American factory workers moving west to settle on the free land and find release from modern conditions, the migration of the early twentieth century saw discontented American factory workers moving from eastern industrial employment to western industrial employment, finding perhaps higher wages, but no relief from industrial conditions or indeed from foreign competition for their jobs: some western factory towns had proportions of immigrant labor as high as or higher than eastern cities (Overton 1946).

Other Americans, and increasingly union leaders, began to oppose immigration. A member of the Machinists' Union said in 1902, "every thinking man in the ranks of organized labor is wondering how long the United States can supply work to the illiterate hordes of Eastern Europe if they continue to come in unchecked." The President of the United Mine Workers supported immigration restriction in 1909 by arguing, "the first duty of a community is to give its own members the opportunity of being employed at decent wages." Samuel Gompers, President of the American Federation of Labor, wrote in 1911 that immigration should slow because it was "to a very large extent induced, stimulated artificial immigration . . . for the exploitation of the ignorant classes" (Lane 1984: 7, 10).

While an influx of immigrants competing for workingmen's wages generally increased support for restriction of immigration, it had other effects too. On average, and allowing for the influence of other factors, American cities with rising numbers of immigrants began spending more of their tax dollars on public health. Explanations for this increase abounded at the time. Some observers, like Jane Addams, attributed a general increase of interest in social problems to the concerns of immigrant communities who themselves had to endure such problems. Others attributed it to the xenophobia of native-born Americans convinced that swarthier populations must carry disease. Irrespective of the cause, the development of even a modest, local program of social spending gave taxpaying Americans an increased worry that immigrants might come to the United States to drain the public purse.

With middle-class Americans worried that immigrants might cost them tax dollars, and working-class Americans worried that foreign competition might do them out of a job, or at least lower their wages, and with all Americans' susceptibility to xenophobic appeals accentuated in 1917 by the imminence of war, Congress passed – over President Woodrow Wilson's veto – an immigration restriction bill that forbade immigrants who could not pass a literacy test, along with those previously blocked (as most Chinese and Japanese immigrants were) and migrants coming from a newly defined Asiatic barred zone. In 1921, amid a postwar depression, Congress followed with an Emergency Immigration Act establishing quotas for immigrants of various nationalities, and in 1924 with the National Origins, or Johnson–Reed, Act. These laws dramatically reduced immigration to the United States, and other New World nations followed suit, breaking up what had been something like a global market for labor and insulating American workers from some foreign competition.

If, rather than staying in cities and opposing immigration, American workers had wanted to move to the countryside, they would have found it increasingly difficult up to World War I. Over the decade after 1900 the price of farmland rose 6 percent a year on average, its speediest rise in American history to date (Lindert 1988: 54). Rates of farm tenancy increased, as it became more difficult to buy a farm outright (Wright 1988). Only after the war did the price of farmland begin to fall, as the introduction of tractors reshaped American agriculture and increased the flow of Americans to cities.

With the introduction of tractors, American farming changed dramatically. The amount of farmland devoted to the feeding of horses and mules, the draft animals who provided the principal, nonhuman, premechanical source of horsepower in the fields, peaked in 1915. Tractors put animals out of jobs, and men too, as machines replaced hands in the harvesting of crops. As farmers needed fewer draft animals, they needed fewer acres devoted to feeding their livestock, and so more land became available for feeding people. Farms grew fewer, while those that remained grew larger (Olmstead and Rhode 2001).

The American shift to urban life entailed a shift not only in the way Americans lived and worked but in the way many Americans envisioned themselves. It became less possible, as Turner worried, for Americans to imagine themselves as a hardy people dependent only on their own resources. As they took jobs in factories and worked at the whim of managers, as they lived in rented apartments, as they bought food that once they would have prepared for themselves, they depended more on one another. The American cities, affected as they were by global migrations of people, also gave evidence that the US depended on other nations.

Americans continued to move to their cities, even as they resisted the implications of their new lives. Through their Congressmen, they opposed immigration, and eventually succeeded in restricting it. As the cities continued to grow, the US Congress dragged its feet in letting this economic and cultural shift affect American politics: after the 1920 Census showed more Americans in cities than not, the legislators failed in their constitutional duty to reapportion the House of Representatives. As one scholarly observer noted:

> The House is still organized according to the census of 1910, so that the recent great shifts of population, notably to California and the centers of the automobile industry, remain disregarded in Congress, and in the Electoral College as well. In many states the situation resulting from neglect or unfair discrimination in the demarcation of legislative districts is perhaps even worse. (Chafee 1929: 1015–16)

The popular press gave such concerns blunter expression, as when the *American Mercury* ran an article complaining of "Government by Yokel" (Chafee 1929: 1016, n. 3). Modernizing countries generally retain nostalgia for their lost rural past. But the United States had structural institutions like the Senate (which apportions two Senators to each state, however underpopulated) and incidents like the failure to reapportion after 1920 that ensured a more profound lag in letting the shift toward city life affect national economic policy.

The Prosperity Decade

Over the course of the 1920s American motor vehicle bureaus showed an increase of automobile registrations from an average of one for every three households to one per household. By 1929 the 123 million Americans owned 23 million cars, which meant that, at a tight fit, the whole country could go on the road at once.

The growth of the automobile industry signified an increase of factory production, which meant an increasingly urban laboring class; it drew on glass, iron, steel, rubber, timber, and other industries. It drove the construction of roads and roadside attractions. It also indicated the increasing importance of consumer debt. Henry Ford's motor company made it possible for more Americans to own cars, by building the standard Model T and reducing its price constantly, and were Ford's the whole story of the car industry, credit would scarcely enter it. But General Motors (GM) changed the car market by introducing planned obsolescence, with regular new models, and began extending credit through its General Motors Assurance Corporation (GMAC).

With new car models and with other durable goods, like radios, boilers, and domestic appliances, advertising helped Americans learn how much they needed color and color style: "every free-born American has a right to name his own necessities," the industry journal *Advertising and Selling* proclaimed (Marchand 1985: 160). Consumer debt doubled over the course of the decade (Carter et al. 2006: series Cj889 and Ca10).

Global credit, too, had extended as a result of the war, and the United States was at the center of the world network of debt. Belligerent nations borrowed money from the US to wage war. Unlike the money Americans had borrowed from Europe in the nineteenth century, wartime borrowing went to destructive purposes. Through the 1920s the crippled countries struggled to recover from the damage they had inflicted on each other, and to pay back their debts. Continued American lending kept them afloat for much of the decade.

Both at home and abroad, the smooth continuation of economic affairs depended on this new tendency to borrow. If money significantly slowed its flow overseas before other countries had recovered from their injuries, an international crisis might ensue, as nations failed to repay debts. If American consumers significantly slowed their borrowing, a domestic crisis might ensue, as manufacturing firms depending on consumer credit to fuel their output slowed or even stopped. In the event, both crises occurred in relatively quick succession.

Not until the end of the decade did Americans begin to worry much about such possibilities. For much of the 1920s, policy affecting economic affairs looked like nineteenth-century law. Republican administrations raised tariffs in 1921, 1922, and 1930, helping to reduce international trade. They restricted immigration in 1921 and 1924, introducing quotas that cut immigration to the United States in half. Both laws inspired other countries to restrict trade and immigration in turn. The world economy gradually slowed, and as the barriers to the movement of goods and labor went up, economies lost their ability to adjust to crises.

Meanwhile, the New York stock market went up and up, driven evidently by still more borrowing. Americans of the era distinguished between investment and speculation, believing that investment reflected careful study and a long-term commitment to business prospects, while speculation reflected judgment about other people's investment decisions. And speculation looked like it was on the increase. Not only were Americans speculating more in the stock market, they were taking increasing risks by borrowing money from their brokers to do it. At last the Federal Reserve System decided it could countenance such frivolous use of its credit no longer. Noting in 1928 "an unprecedented volume of transactions on the exchange and a continued rise in security prices," while "brokers' loans reached a record figure . . . and continued to increase," the Federal Reserve began "withdrawing funds from the money market" and making it more expensive to borrow money (*Federal Reserve Bulletin*, cited in Rauchway 2008: 17).

With higher interest rates in the United States, New York's foreign capital issues halved after 1928. And countries that depended on money from America slid into default: Germany, Argentina, Brazil, Australia, Canada, and Poland all began to falter (Eichengreen 1992: 223). In 1929, the New York stock market crashed. American consumers, uncertain about what might happen next, paused in their buying and their borrowing to buy. Within a few months of the crash, new car registrations fell by a quarter of their precrash number. In the next year, spending on consumer durables fell by a fifth. Banks failed, factories closed, and unemployment began a sickening climb to its peak, in 1932, at slightly under 25 percent of the American workforce.

Americans had a folk tradition of returning to the countryside when the cities entered a slump, and in 1932 and 1933, the share of Americans living on farms rose – the only time in the first half of the twentieth century it would do so (Carter et al. 2006: series Da2). Even so, the American economy had become an urban economy, and with the coalition of voters behind Franklin D. Roosevelt's victory in 1932, its politics would become more urban too.

The New Deal

When Roosevelt accepted the Democratic nomination for President in the summer of 1932, he pledged himself to "a new deal for the American people." In that speech he promised public works, working-hours legislation, reforestation, agricultural price supports, mortgage support for home-buyers, publicity in corporate accounting and securities issuing, and the restoration of international trade. All these measures responded to the current crisis, but all had also long been demands of various constituencies styling themselves populist or progressive, and all derived from the recognition that Americans had become at last a people who could not do without their cities, and must begin to think of themselves accordingly. As Roosevelt put it, "this nation is not merely a nation of independence, but it is if we are to survive, bound to be a nation of interdependence, town and city, and North and South, East and West" (*New York Times*, July 3, 1932: 8). Drawing on this understanding, Congress implemented all these requests and more, adding in Roosevelt's first term alone watershed management, legalization of labor unions, federal deposit insurance, and a strengthened Federal Reserve System.

At Roosevelt's election, unemployment stood at near 25 percent, and real GDP at under three-quarters of its 1929 level. Over the course of the New Deal, GDP grew between 8 and 11 percent a year, and unemployment fell to around 10 percent. Roosevelt's first two terms in office thus present the picture of an economy recovering from the disaster of 1929–32, without fully returning to normal. On balance, the New Deal did not prevent this process of recovery, and some of Roosevelt's policies – particularly, perhaps, reflation of the currency, and relief programs like the Works Progress Administration (WPA) – provided some employment and dignity to American citizens as well as stimulus to the economy. At the same time, some New Deal programs may have slowed the recovery – particularly, perhaps, the National Recovery Administration (NRA), which allowed industry cartels to fix prices. But NRA ran for less than two years before the Supreme Court invalidated it early in 1935, while the meliorative effects of relief and currency devaluation operated into the start of World War II.

The most important and lasting changes the New Deal wrought in the US economy had little to do with resolving the immediate crisis, instead seeking to change the way the American marketplace worked. By giving groups, regions, or individual persons within the American economy more autonomy in negotiating, the New Deal sought to create what the economist John Kenneth Galbraith (1952) called "countervailing power," on the assumption that through the nineteenth and into the twentieth century, the federal government had used laws such as tariffs to increase the power of corporations. As Senator Lewis Schwellenbach (Democrat of Washington) explained, Turner's independent frontiersman was a myth:

> Don't let anyone tell you that government bounties were not being given in those days. . . . The railroads got their sections of land in each township. . . . Vast tracts of timber lands were available for . . . the timber operators. . . . A protective tariff system was maintained by which hidden taxes were removed from the pockets of everyone who labored in industry and agriculture. . . . There were [government] bounties galore. But the people who worked, and who bought and consumed our products never got in on them. (cited in Smith 2006: 120–1)

For example, the Wagner Act, or National Labor Relations Act of 1935, offered legal protections to labor unions so they could bargain more effectively with corporate managers on behalf of workers. The Tennessee Valley Authority (TVA) and Public Works Administration (PWA) began to modernize the economies of the South and West to afford them more independence from the Northeast. The Social Security Act of 1935 established basic protections of unemployment, old-age, and disability insurance to American workers (though it did not provide healthcare), thus rendering them somewhat less dependent on their employers. All these laws operated on the principle of countervailing power rather than direct state intervention to redistribute wealth, which served the purpose of keeping the federal government relatively small. As Senator Robert Wagner (Democrat of New York) explained, such measures provided "the only key to economic stability if we intend to rely upon democratic self-help by industry and labor instead of courting the pitfalls of an arbitrary or totalitarian state" (cited in Jacobs 2005: 145). The concept of countervailing power allowed New Dealers and scholars afterward credibly to claim they had preserved American capitalism. For all that the New Deal did, it left the essential marketplace functions of commerce largely intact.

The War and After

Mobilization for World War II brought the end of the New Deal but a massive increase of government spending. In 1943, unemployment fell below its 1929 level. By the end of the year, Congress had ended WPA and many other New Deal agencies. At the same time, it increased federal spending from 8 percent of GDP in 1938 to 40 percent in 1943. The remaining unemployment from the Great Depression vanished in the war.

Mobilization of industrial resources brought Americans flooding back into factory cities, to plants like Henry Ford's Willow Run in Michigan, a mile-long assembly line that at its peak could produce a B-24 bomber in just over an hour from start to finish, or Henry Kaiser's Richmond, California shipyards. Such facilities vacuumed up workers from the regions where they languished, and put them to work on the materiel of war. The munitions-makers included women as well as men; 40 percent of the welders at the Richmond Kaiser plant were women (Kennedy 1999: 647–55).

The rush of Americans to manufacturing plants during the war appeared to complete a process begun with the transformation of the countryside. Farming became ever more a government-assisted minority pursuit, rather than the ordinary way of life for most Americans. The war also allowed the federal government to attack racial segregation more directly than the New Deal ever had. Roosevelt's Executive Order 8802, banning discrimination in federal employment, helped bring African Americans in large numbers out of the South to work in port and manufacturing cities for the war effort. At the same time defense contracting and manufacturing brought rapid industrialization and modernization to the South and West, creating new industrial areas and new manufacturing specialties in the once backward or frontier regions (Schulman 1994).

The Postwar Settlements

The end of mobilization brought the fear that depression might return. Policymakers created postwar global institutions to manage international trade and finance at the 1944 Bretton Woods conference, spawning the International Monetary Fund (IMF) and the International Bank for Reconstruction and Development (better known as the World Bank). Both operated on the philosophy that an interdependent world economy, managed cooperatively through international institutions, would more easily create prosperity and peace (Borgwardt 2005).

The newly reindustrialized nation reached new accommodations between labor and management after the war. Strikes and postwar inflation created political opportunities for Republicans, who won a congressional majority in 1946 and passed the Taft–Hartley Act in 1947, allowing states to prohibit closed shops, among other limits on labor organization (Lichtenstein 1989).

With the labor movement curbed, the New Deal's countervailing powers largely intact, a limited form of social insurance in place, and the war's mobilization efforts over, the shape of America's urban economy briefly settled – but not before the generous veterans' benefits for home ownership as passed in the Servicemen's Readjustment Act of 1944 (better known as the GI Bill) began to create a suburban America and a set of policies and attitudes meant to promote a consumers' economy (Cohen 2003).

NOTE

1   Historians continue to debate whether Turner's safety valve ever actually existed. See, e.g., Ferrie (1995), Goodrich and Davidson (1935, 1936).

REFERENCES AND FURTHER READING

Barde, Robert, Susan B. Carter, and Richard Sutch. (2006). International migration. In Susan B. Carter et al. (eds), *Historical Statistics of the United States* (vol. I, pp. 523–652). New York: Cambridge University Press.

Beard, Charles A. (1912). *American City Government: A Survey of Newer Tendencies*. New York: The Century Co.

Borgwardt, Elizabeth. (2005). *A New Deal for the World: America's Vision for Human Rights*. Cambridge, MA: Belknap Press of Harvard University Press.

Carter, Susan B., Scott Sigmund Gartner, Michael R. Haines, Alan L. Olmstead, Richard Sutch, and Gavin Wright (eds). (2006). *Historical Statistics of the United States, Earliest Times to the*

Present, Millennial Edition, 5 vols. New York: Cambridge University Press.

Chafee, Zechariah, Jr. (1929). Congressional reapportionment. *Harvard Law Review* 42, 8: 1015–47.

Cohen, Lizabeth. (2003). *A Consumers' Republic: The Politics of Mass Consumption in Postwar America.* New York: Alfred A. Knopf.

Eichengreen, Barry. (1992). The origins and nature of the great slump revisited. *The Economic History Review* 45, 2: 213–39.

Eldridge, Hope T. and Dorothy Swaine Thomas. (1964). *Demographic Analyses and Interrelations*, ed. Simon Kuznets, 3 vols. Vol. 3, *Population Redistribution and Economic Growth.* Philadelphia: American Philosophical Society.

Ferrie, Joseph P. (1995). Up and out or down and out? Immigrant mobility in the antebellum United States. *Journal of Interdisciplinary History* 26, 1: 33–55.

Galbraith, John Kenneth. (1952). *American Capitalism: The Concept of Countervailing Power.* Boston: Houghton Mifflin.

Goodrich, Carter and Sol Davidson. (1935). The wage-earner in the westward movement I. *Political Science Quarterly* 50, 2: 161–85.

Goodrich, Carter and Sol Davidson (1936). The wage-earner in the westward movement II. *Political Science Quarterly* 51, 1: 61–116.

Goodrich, Carter et al. (1936). *Migration and Economic Opportunity.* Philadelphia: University of Pennsylvania Press.

Haines, Michael R. (2006). Population characteristics. In Susan B. Carter et al. (eds), *Historical Statistics of the United States.* Available online at <http://hsus.cambridge.org>.

Hatton, Timothy J. and Jeffrey G. Williamson. (1998). *The Age of Mass Migration: Causes and Economic Impact.* New York: Oxford University Press.

Jacobs, Meg. (2005). *Pocketbook Politics: Economic Citizenship in Twentieth Century America.* Princeton, NJ: Princeton University Press.

Kennedy, David M. (1999). *Freedom from Fear: The American People in Depression and War, 1929-1945.* New York: Oxford University Press.

Lane, A. T. (1984). American trade unions, mass immigration and the literacy test. *Labor History* 25, 1: 5–25.

Lichtenstein, Nelson. (1989). From corporatism to collective bargaining: Organized labor and the eclipse of social democracy in the postwar era. In Steven Fraser and Gary Gerstle (eds), *The Rise and Fall of the New Deal Order, 1930-1980* (pp. 122–52). Princeton, NJ: Princeton University Press.

Lindert, Peter H. (1988). Long-run trends in American farmland values. *Agricultural History* 62, 3: 45–85.

Marchand, Roland. (1985). *Advertising the American Dream: Making Way for Modernity.* Berkeley: University of California Press.

Mitchell, B. R. (2003). *International Historical Statistics: The Americas, 1750-2000*, 5th edn, 3 vols. Basingstoke, UK: Palgrave Macmillan.

Olmstead, Alan L. and Paul W. Rhode. (2001). Reshaping the landscape: The impact and diffusion of the tractor in American agriculture, 1910-1960. *The Journal of Economic History* 61, 3: 663–98.

Overton, Richard C. (1946). Westward expansion since the Homestead Act. In Harold F. Williamson (ed.), *The Growth of the American Economy: An Introduction to the Economic History of the United States* (pp. 338–65). New York: Prentice-Hall.

Rauchway, Eric. (2006). *Blessed Among Nations: How the World Made America.* New York: Hill and Wang.

Rauchway, Eric. (2008). *The Great Depression and the New Deal: A Very Short Introduction.* Oxford: Oxford University Press.

Schulman, Bruce J. (1994). *From Cotton Belt to Sunbelt: Federal Policy, Economic Development, and the Transformation of the South, 1938-1980.* Durham, NC: Duke University Press.

Smith, Jason Scott. (2006). *Building New Deal Liberalism: The Political Economy of Public Works, 1933-1956.* Cambridge, UK: Cambridge University Press.

Turner, Frederick Jackson. (1920). *The Frontier in American History.* New York: Henry Holt and Company.

Wright, Gavin. (1988). American agriculture and the labor market: What happened to proletarianization? *Agricultural History* 62, 3: 182–209.

2

The Changing Status of Women 1900–1950

Nancy Woloch

"They are all social workers, or magazine writers in a small way," an observer wrote of young women at a Greenwich Village gathering in 1913. "They are all decidedly emancipated and advanced, and so thoroughly healthy and zestful. . . . They shock you constantly. . . . They are of course all self-supporting, and independent, and they enjoy the adventure of life." The engaging young women praised by journalist Randolph Bourne, a Columbia College graduate of 1912, represented the "new woman" of the early 1900s, who he thought would be "a very splendid sort of person" (Cott 1987: 34–5). Few achieved the cutting-edge status of the Greenwich Villagers Bourne described, but many types of "new women" met the challenges of the new century. Vital themes of women's history from 1900 to 1950 include: the continual movement of women into the workforce, the expansion of women's rights, the salience of race, and the dynamic growth of the middle class.

Workers, Migrants, and Immigrants

By the start of the twentieth century, industrialization had changed the nature of work and women had surged into the labor force. In 1900, one out of every five women worked and women made up nearly 20 percent of all employees. Of five million women wage-earners, one fourth worked in manufacturing, where they constituted 17 percent of employees; five times as many women worked in industry as they had three decades earlier. South or North, women made up much of the textile workforce; they crowded the labor pool in clothing and food production; they formed the bulk of employees in canning plants and commercial laundries; they took jobs in print shops, bookbinderies, and cigar and tobacco factories. White-collar work beckoned, too. Introduction of the telephone and typewriter transformed the office world. By World War I, women stenographers, typists, and telephone operators dominated clerical work. Women also moved into retail sales and into teaching; by 1900, three out of four teachers were women, and even more in cities.

For women workers, domestic service remained a major job category, as it had always been. Among the million women in domestic service in 1900 – maids, laundresses, cooks, companions, waitresses, and nurses, whom the Census classified as domestic workers – 26 percent were native-born, 19 percent daughters of immigrants, 28 percent foreign-born, and 27 percent African-American. Women who had a choice spurned domestic service because of the lack of free time, drudgery, boredom, and especially the low status associated with it. A Massachusetts report of 1902 claimed that women preferred jobs in factories, stores, or restaurants to domestic work, even if they earned less; an employer responded to a survey published a few years earlier that the native-born woman who took such work "loses caste at once." Immigrants, such as young Scandinavian women in the Midwest, became domestic workers, as did, in the Far West, Mexican-American women, who also worked as canners and farm laborers.

African-American women played a prominent role among women wage earners. In 1890, almost a million black women were employed – 37.8 percent in agriculture, 30.83 percent in domestic service, 15.5 percent in laundry work, and a tiny 2.76 percent in manufacturing. In 1900, when about one out of five white women worked for pay, two out of five African-American women did; over one-quarter of black working women were married, compared to 3.26 percent of white women workers. Like white counterparts, however, black women in the labor force were likely to live in or move to cities. Most black migrants who left rural areas moved to southern cities, where a surfeit of black labor filled domestic jobs for low pay. Even before the massive African-American migrations of the World War I era, the lure of jobs drew black women to northern cities in greater numbers than black men. Black women migrants, unlike men, could always find jobs, as cooks, laundresses, scrubwomen, maids; in New York in 1910, four out of five employed black women held domestic jobs. In southern cities, domestic work was often the only option. As New York social worker Mary White Ovington observed in 1911, the African-American woman took "the job that the white girl doesn't want."

Many young working women were immigrants, most likely "new" immigrants from Southern or Eastern Europe. In immigrant families, married women rarely held jobs outside the home, though they might take in piecework or boarders. Daughters of immigrants, in contrast, became wage-earners; they took whatever type of work was near their homes – factory work, mill work, domestic work. In Chicago in 1900, half of Italian women aged 15 to 19 worked for pay outside the home. The garment industry in eastern cities relied on the low-paid labor of young, single daughters of immigrants. Twenty thousand young working women participated in New York's great shirtwaist strike of 1909–10. In March of 1911 a fire broke out on the top lofts of the Triangle shirtwaist factory, a building with locked doors between floors and no fire escapes. Spreading from floor to floor, the fire trapped many of Triangle's 500 workers and 146 women burned in the flames or leaped out of windows to their deaths.

"We have tried you good people of the public and we have found you wanting," labor leader Rose Schneiderman told a public meeting after the fire. New York's Factory Investigating Committee, organized in response to the Triangle disaster, ultimately recommended safety laws for factories and other protective measures.

Young women in the Progressive-era workforce often served as bridges between American culture and immigrant families. They also developed their own culture, one that involved fashion, film, and fiction as well as dance halls, amusement parks, and the custom of "treating," or dating. Consumer culture among young women workers, historians contend, represented independence, fostered assimilation, defied authority, and shaped identity.

Middle-Class Women: Education, Career, and Social Reform

"No longer is a college course considered so unusual an experience for a woman as it was ten, or even five years ago," wrote Barnard senior Virginia C. Gildersleeve in an essay of 1899. "No longer does ambition alone bring girls to academic life. They come now more as the majority of men enter – drifting direct from school, largely as a matter of course, because it seems a natural thing to do, because their families wish it, or because they themselves have a notion that four years at college is an amusing experience" (Woloch 1992: 467). Gildersleeve, by 1911 Dean of Barnard, identified one source of the rising number of women college students at the turn of the century: well-off entrants were joining the middle-class scholarly types. The numbers of both surged through the 1920s.

Higher education for women had made strides in the late nineteenth century. The founding of eastern women's colleges and coordinate colleges, the admission of women to several private universities, and women's acceptance at large state universities in the Midwest and West all transformed campus life. The college experience still reached only a small proportion of college-age women (or men) but the number of women enrolled grew rapidly after 1870, as did their share of college populations. By 1900, the 85,000 women who attended college constituted 37 percent of all college students; by 1920, when 283,000 women went to college, they constituted 47.3 percent. "While the education of men has outgrown the old college system, . . . " a president of Vassar explained, "that for women has but just grown up to it" (Woloch 2006: 275). Still, rapid feminization of student populations evoked ire. Some Progressive-Era colleges took steps to curtail the trend: by ending the admission of women, as at Wesleyan; limiting women's enrollment, as at the University of Chicago; or segregating women in sex-typed programs such as home economics, as at many state universities.

Women students in 1900 justifiably voiced concern with the question: "After college – what?" Many entered professions dominated by women, such as teaching, social work, or librarianship. Those who chose law or medicine often worked for women's organizations or as public employees, rather than as self-employed entrepreneurs. Women college graduates also filled the ranks of women's pressure groups and reform associations. By 1900, middle-class women had long-established footholds in voluntarism and civic affairs. They had joined temperance societies and women's clubs; national alliances such as the Women's Christian Temperance Union (1873) and the General Federation of Women's Clubs (1892) boasted huge memberships. African-American women's clubs united in the National Association of Colored Women's Clubs (1896). Turn-of-the-century women with progressive inclinations formed groups with overtly political purposes, such as the National Consumers' League (1899), to promote protective laws for women workers; the National Women's Trade Union League (1903), to forge alliances with and promote unionization among working women (the New York branch was prominent in New York's shirtwaist strike of 1909–10); the National Child Labor Committee (1904), to attain laws to end the employment of children; or the women-dominated National Association of Settlements (1911).

Women's activism in Progressive-Era public life often had roots in settlement work. As at Hull House, founded in Chicago by Jane Addams and Ellen Gates Starr in 1889, women typically constituted the majority of residents. Social settlements, Jane Addams explained, provided opportunity for the educated woman to do something worthwhile with her training. They also enabled women with advanced degrees in the social sciences to assume prominent roles in scholarship and social reform. Cornell graduate Florence Kelley, first a Hull House resident, became Illinois's first factory commissioner and subsequently general secretary of the National Consumers' League (NCL), from which base she promoted protective laws for women workers relating to maximum hours, minimum wage, and night work; the Supreme Court endorsed maximum hours laws in *Muller v. Oregon* (1908). Mount Holyoke graduate Frances Perkins, first a settlement worker, became an NCL activist, labor commissioner of New York State and later, during the New Deal, the nation's Secretary of Labor.

Women also achieved notice on the radical edge of the women's movement. Feminist voices on the left included Charlotte Perkins Gilman, feminist author and theorist; Crystal Eastman, pacifist, suffragist, and activist; Emma Goldman, anarchist and inspirational lecturer; and birth control pioneer Margaret Sanger, who declared in her short-lived publication of 1914, the *Woman Rebel*, that "women cannot be on an equal footing with men until they have full and complete control over their reproductive function" (Woloch 2006: 369). Gilman and Eastman belonged to the exceptional feminist association Heterodoxy, which began in Greenwich Village in 1912; by 1920 the group had 60 members – artists, writers, socialists, anarchists. Lively meetings, run by founder Marie Jenney Howe, often heard guest lecturers including Goldman and Sanger. Heterodoxy was "the easiest of clubs," wrote member Inez Haynes Irwin. "It entailed no dues or obligations. . . . Everything we said was off the record" (Schwarz 1982: 13). Heterodoxy members – no doubt the subject of the observation by Randolph Bourne that began this essay – included anthropologist Elsie Clews Parsons, progressive educator Elisabeth Irwin, psychologist Leta Hollingworth, author Fannie Hurst, radical Elizabeth Gurley Flynn, and Mary Ware Dennett, advocate of sex education and free speech. Exuding confidence, Heterodoxy members embraced a range of causes from reproductive freedom to sexual emancipation to woman suffrage. Left or center, organized women provided an arena where the suffrage movement could claim or recruit a constituency.

Winning the Vote

"A city is in many respects a great business corporation, but in other respects it is enlarged housekeeping," Jane Addams declared in 1907. "May we not say that city housekeeping has failed partly because women, the traditional housekeepers, have not been consulted as to its . . . activities?" New industrial and urban conditions, Addams contended, necessitated the enfranchisement of women. The very complexity of city government, she argued, "demands the help of minds accustomed to detail and variety of work, to a sense of obligation for the health and welfare of young children, and to a responsibility for the cleanliness and comfort of others" (Addams 1907: 180). In Addams's argument – typical of her generation's suffrage movement – woman suffrage was not an issue of women's right, but rather a solution to contemporary problems, for the benefit of all.

The Progressive-era woman suffrage movement that Addams supported had entered a new phase. Between 1869, when post-Civil War woman suffrage organizations had formed, and 1890, the movement had been split into two rival wings: the National Woman Suffrage Association, New York-centered, worked for a federal woman suffrage amendment; the American Woman Suffrage Association, Boston-based, strove only for state victories. In 1890 the rival factions united in the National American Woman Suffrage Association (NAWSA), which campaigned solely on the state level. Now united, suffragists no longer urged radical causes such as divorce or women's economic emancipation from men. Rather than challenge traditional ideas about woman's place, suffragists urged an extension of woman's sphere and stressed the good works that women could accomplish once enfranchised.

By 1896 only four western states had endorsed full woman suffrage: Wyoming, Utah, Colorado, and Idaho. Despite energetic campaigns, not a single state followed between then and 1910. But NAWSA profited from rising membership. During these years, woman suffrage became a national movement, with strong contingents in all regions, including the South. The suffrage movement also profited from the rise of other women's organizations – from the temperance movement and the women's club movement – and from the progressive climate. Woman suffrage finally benefited from new leaders: Anna Howard Shaw, minister, physician, and orator, who led NAWSA from 1904–15, and Carrie Chapman Catt, the talented strategist of state campaigns, who served as president from 1900–4 and again from 1915–20.

In 1910, the state of Washington enfranchised women, and in 1911 a crucial California victory followed. Other western states fell into line. By 1914, Oregon, Arizona, Kansas, Nevada, and Montana had endorsed woman suffrage; in 1913 the Illinois legislature, which had granted women partial suffrage, approved their right to vote in federal elections. By the time Carrie Chapman Catt assumed leadership in 1915, NAWSA was poised for victory. Catt planned next to win the critical backing of New York State, which NAWSA accomplished in 1917 (the suffrage movement's first victory in an eastern state); push through the long-delayed federal amendment; and achieve ratification by the states.

Unexpected developments intervened. A dissident faction had been mobilizing within NAWSA. Under the leadership of Alice Paul, a young Quaker activist, dissidents formed their own group, the Congressional Union, to press for a federal amendment. Leaving NAWSA in 1915, the CU joined with western women voters to form the National Woman's Party in 1916. The NWP gained attention in 1917 when Paul and her followers began to picket the White House to condemn the "party in power" for failing to produce a woman suffrage amendment. Following the model of British suffragists, American counterparts faced jail and self-imposed hunger strikes.

United States entry into World War I in 1917 also affected the suffrage campaign. Many suffragists, including Jane Addams and Carrie Chapman Catt, had been pacifists and had formed a Women's Peace Party in 1915. US entry into war broke pacifist ranks; a small remnant, including Addams, remained active in pacifism but most suffragists dropped the cause of peace. For them World War I presented an opportunity. Catt, who converted President Woodrow Wilson to the cause in 1916, demanded passage of woman suffrage as a "war measure." It was unjust to deprive women of the vote, she claimed, just when the nation needed their loyalty and support.

With President Wilson's support, Congress – which had just passed a prohibition amendment – finally approved a woman suffrage amendment in June 1919. On August 26, 1920, the 36th state, Tennessee, ratified the woman suffrage amendment. Victory reflected the highly charged momentum of the final years, Catt's skill, and the pressure generated by war. In the presidential election of 1920, 26 million new women voters participated; they had been transformed, said Catt, from "wards" of the state to "free and equal citizens" (Chafe 1991: 21). Victory, culminating a 70-year crusade, represented a monumental achievement. It also increased fragmentation among proponents.

The 1920s: Jazz Age and Harlem Renaissance

"The pioneer feminists were hard-hitting individuals, and the modern young woman admires them for their courage," wrote journalist Dorothy Dunbar Bromley in *Harper's Magazine* in 1927. "But she does not want to wear their mantle." The up-to-date young women in their twenties and thirties who Bromley presented in her article, "Feminist – New Style," were "the truly modern ones, those who admit that a full life calls for marriage and children as well as a career." Shedding the cooperative spirit of the Progressive era, young women of the 1920s professed "no loyalty to women en masse," Bromley wrote. Rather they were "moved by an inescapable compulsion to be individuals in their own right" (Ware 2002: 128). Seeking personal fulfillment and freedom from old-fashioned goals, the new generation of 1920s women had a self-absorbed and apolitical cast.

Politicized women began the decade with grand hopes. Catalyzed by the triumph of woman suffrage in 1920, many expected the leverage to achieve reform and improve political life. Enfranchisement did not gratify their hopes; still, it represented a significant advance. In the 1920s, for the first time, nationwide, women ran for public office; political parties welcomed women on their national committees, and politicians competed for the women's vote. In 1921 Congress passed the Sheppard–Towner Act, an innovative healthcare plan, which offered matching funds to states that established maternal and childcare clinics. But by 1925, no "women's vote" had evolved. Women did not vote as a bloc, legislators lost interest in them, and former suffragists assessed why their worthy goals had foundered. Historians suggest that their sense of failure was exaggerated and that they accomplished more than they realized.

Meanwhile, new issues divided the women's prewar movement. In 1923 the National Woman's Party (NWP), a small group of suffrage veterans, proposed an Equal Rights Amendment (ERA) that would erase sex as a legal classification. The proposal failed to gain ground in Congress. But the majority of activists in the women's movement voiced alarm, among them leaders of the Women's Trade Union League, the NCL, and the Women's Bureau of the Department of Labor, formed in 1919 to safeguard the interests of women in industry. An ERA, claimed its foes, would upset protective laws that curbed the exploitation by employers of women workers. Once united for suffrage, politicized women now debated a new question: would legal equality jeopardize working women? Did statements in law on gender difference imperil women's rights? To *The Nation* in 1928, conflict was inevitable: the "sex struggle" and the "class struggle" had converged.

Quarrels among its members aside, the postwar women's movement faced a less friendly political climate: the progressive mood had grown conservative; moreover, enthusiasm for women's causes was fading. Women's organizations of the pre-World War I era persisted through the 1920s but activist women found new directions. Some former suffragists joined the new League of Women Voters, a training ground for civic involvement; others turned to party politics, a revived peace movement, or the campaign for birth control. Still others shifted their energy from social reform to personal or professional goals. "I no longer work on movements," a former suffragist declared. "My energies are bent on achieving an income which will enable me to write realistic novels" (Showalter 1989: 57).

Some ambitious women of the 1920s turned to vocation, career, and the goal of "economic independence." Middle-class women surged into white-collar jobs, the business world, and the professions. Modern women, said *Nation* editor Freda Kirchwey, were "out in the world, in contact and in competition with men" (Showalter 1989: 14). Many hoped to merge marriage with career, as did one in five professional women in 1920, one in four in 1930, and more thereafter. Preoccupied with shedding tradition and inhibition, young women – like Bromley's "Feminist – New

Style" – sought "individualism" and "equality" in their private lives. The defiant flapper symbolized young women's change in style. "Breezy, slangy, and informal in manner," as an observer described her (Slosson 1994), the prewar flapper had been an upper-middle-class phenomenon. In the 1920s, her flamboyance and competitive zeal reached a larger constituency. Consumerism, too, defined the flapper. She *was* what she bought: her cloche hat, raised hemline, cigarettes, make-up, and bobbed hair. In the 1920s, beauty parlors multiplied; production of cosmetics soared; and young women learned style and attitude from the movies, where stars like Clara Bow exuded sex appeal.

Innovators of the 1920s included birth control campaigners. In the pre-World War I era, Margaret Sanger had opened a birth control clinic, courted arrest, lectured across the country, and generated an avid response. Women were "awakening up all over the nation," a St Louis woman wrote to Sanger in 1916, "and waiting for someone to lead the way" (Gordon 1974: 230). During the war, Sanger moved away from her left-wing roots and won support among well-off women. In 1917 she started the *Birth Control Review*; in 1921 she founded the American Birth Control League; and for the rest of the 1920s defended the cause with eugenic arguments ("more children from the fit and less from the unfit"); sponsored clinics in big cities nationwide; courted support among doctors; and strove to change the laws so that physicians could legally supply contraception to healthy (married) women. Birth control remained a controversial cause, one that neither wing of the women's movement endorsed; it also rested on a shaky foundation until legalized by a federal court decision in 1936.

Another group of innovators in the 1920s were women participants in the Harlem Renaissance. Many were migrants to Harlem. Author and anthropologist Zora Neale Hurston, born in 1891 in Eatonville, Florida, arrived in New York in the 1920s to matriculate at Barnard. A graduate student of Franz Boas at Columbia, she embarked in 1927 on a field trip to southern Florida to collect African-American folklore, a project intended to invalidate racial stereotypes. Jessie Redmon Fauset, a Cornell graduate of 1905, came from Philadelphia's black middle class. Her novels of the 1920s and 1930s, written in New York, centered on middle-class women and problems of class. Nella Larsen, part Danish and part African-American, became a nursing student and librarian in New York. Best-known for her novels of the 1920s, Larsen dealt with women's status in a male-dominated society. Women novelists of the Harlem Renaissance focused on questions of race, gender, and class, and in instances sought to transcend the notion of race. For creative black women as for white counterparts, the exuberant thrust of the 1920s was short-lived. Once depression struck, a need for security trumped the quest for individualism.

The Great Depression and the New Deal

"I am sitting in the city free employment bureau," wrote reporter Meridel Le Sueur in 1932 from St Paul, Minnesota. "It's the women's section. We have been sitting here now for four hours. We sit here every day, waiting for a job. There are no jobs. . . . Most of the women who come here are middle aged, some have families, some have raised their families and are now alone, some have men who are out of work" (Ware 2002: 146). Le Sueur's article on "Women on the Breadlines," published in *New Masses*, reflected the depths of the Great Depression. By 1933, one-quarter of workers were unemployed, middle-class families fell from security to panic, and migration to cities halted or reversed itself, as urban areas became pits of unemployment.

Depression's onset quenched women's expectations. As the economy contracted, job opportunities disappeared, hopes of "economic independence" faded, career aspirations drooped, and feminist goals sank. New trends emerged in 1930s family life: the marriage rate dropped, desertion rose, and the birthrate, which had been in decline through the 1920s, fell yet further. Still, hard times underscored the significance of women's traditional roles. When male "breadwinners" lost their jobs and family income diminished, housewives compensated by "making do" – with meatless recipes, hand-me-down clothes, home industry, and household businesses. Sociologists who studied the families of the unemployed reported that men "cut adrift from their usual routine" succumbed to helplessness. But "the women's world remained largely intact and . . . became if anything more absorbing" (Lynd and Lynd 1937: 179).

Women's role in the workforce changed, too, not always in expected ways. When unemployment rose, government, the labor movement, and public opinion polls urged an end to the hiring of married women, who, many thought, deprived male providers of jobs. Women's groups objected; they opposed the Economy Act of 1933, which in effect fired wives of federal employees from government posts. They also protested other inequities such as those National Recovery Act (NRA) codes that provided lower wages for women than for men doing the same work and the exclusion of many women workers from the benefits of New Deal laws, which did not cover farm workers or domestic workers. African-American women voiced their complaints independently; over half of black female workers had lost their jobs during the Depression, yet government relief programs rarely accepted them.

But hard times brought some surprises in the labor market. Despite public antagonism to working wives, women overall were less likely than men to lose their jobs: the depression hit heavy industry harder than the service sector, in which most women worked and which recovered faster. For the same reason, women entered the labor force with more ease than men. The number of employed women in the 1930s rose 25 percent and the number of working wives surged by an astounding 50 percent. The married woman worker – in part due to hard times – was a major new woman of the decade.

Women of the 1930s also assumed prominent roles in public life. When New York governor Franklin D. Roosevelt became president in 1933, women with backgrounds in suffrage and social welfare won appointments to high-level government jobs. Secretary of Labor Frances Perkins, a former social worker who had served as FDR's industrial commissioner in New York State, became the first woman cabinet member. Perkins took an active role in the passage of some of the New Deal's most significant measures, including the Social Security Act of 1935 and Fair Labor Standards Act of 1938. Both laws provided benefits for which women reformers had long campaigned. Many other activist women left their marks on New Deal politics. Ellen Woodward, a Mississippi suffragist, headed women's work-relief programs under CWA and WPA; Mary W. Dewson, another veteran of social welfare, led the women's division of the Democratic party and helped lead FDR's 1936 campaign. Mary McLeod Bethune, educator and friend of Eleanor Roosevelt, headed "Negro Affairs" at the National Youth Administration from 1935 to 1943 and served as a leader of FDR's "Black cabinet."

Eleanor Roosevelt, who personified women's contributions to the New Deal, capitalized on a decade of experience in women's organizations to reach unprecedented prominence in public life. Tireless campaigner, political strategist, presidential advisor, syndicated columnist, radio personality, and whirlwind of activity, the First Lady promoted women's activities in her columns and at her all-women press conferences, started in 1933 to aid the careers of women journalists. She also crusaded for her favorite causes, such as the federal homestead program, an antilynching law, and work-relief camps for women. In her advice tract on coping with the Depression, *It's Up to the Women* (1933), Eleanor Roosevelt urged her readers to assert themselves as "inspirations of the home," as activists in civic affairs, and in paid work as well. A woman's "first duty is to her home," the First Lady wrote, but that "must not of necessity preclude her having another occupation" (Roosevelt 1933: 145).

Women and World War II

"I had friends whose mothers went to work in factories," Dellie Hahne, a retired Los Angeles teacher, told interviewer Studs Terkel for his oral history of World War II, *The Good War*. "For the first time in their lives, they worked outside the home. They realized that they were capable of more than cooking a meal." At one Sunday dinner during the war, Hahne heard women she knew "talking about the best way to keep their drill sharp in the factory. . . . It was just marvelous. I was tickled." That wartime opportunity was temporary dismayed Hahne: "We were sold a bill of goods." Even so, she found great value in women's wartime employment. Women, she concluded, "had a taste of freedom, they had a taste of making their own money, a taste of spending their own money, making their own decisions. I think the beginning of the women's movement had its seeds right there in World War II" (Terkel 1984: 119).

Urged to leave the workforce in the 1930s, women found new options in World War II. As the nation's supply of manpower shrank, federal agencies such as the War Manpower Commission and the Office of War Information appealed to women to take war jobs. About six million women joined the workforce during the war. The number of women workers rose by over half and the proportion of women who worked leapt from 27 to 37 percent. Defense industries experienced the biggest influx. Women migrated to war production centers, such as Detroit and Seattle; they moved into well-paid jobs in shipyards, steel mills, and ammunition factories; they ran cranes and lathes, repaired engines, cut sheet metal, and made instrument panels. In auto production, one of four workers was female. The number of women union members more than tripled; 9.4 percent of unionized workers in 1940, women constituted 21.8 percent in 1944. Race discrimination continued, but many African-American women left domestic work for better-paid jobs in the service sector or defense production. The domestic workforce fell by 400,000, and the number of African-American women on the federal payroll, some in white-collar jobs, tripled. Overall, war changed the composition of the female workforce: three out of four new women workers were married, an omen of future developments.

The war worker was not the only "new woman" of the war era. Housewives coped with food shortages and rationing. Almost 400,000 women served in the armed forces, where they constituted 3 percent of military personnel. Japanese women, with their families, experienced evacuation and internment when the federal government sent 110,000 West Coast Japanese to "relocation" centers in desolate inland areas from 1942–5; the government considered all Issei (first generation Japanese) enemy aliens. Crowded into one-room apartments and eating at camp mess halls, Japanese families experienced generational strife between American-born children (Nisei), who were US citizens, and Issei parents; traditional family relations fell apart. Of four legal challenges to internment to reach the Supreme Court, the last, and most successful, came from a young California Nisei, Mitsuye Endo, of Sacramento, who disputed the legality of detaining loyal citizens without due process of law. The decision in her favor, *Ex Parte Endo* (1944), helped end internment camps.

The impact of the war emergency failed to alter long-held beliefs about women's "place." To the public, women's labor in defense industry was a temporary expedient, acceptable only "for the duration" of the war. Government propaganda urged women to join the workforce by emphasizing traditional roles. Women exerted little influence on public policy, even in the area of labor relations. The Women's Bureau issued directives on the fair treatment of new workers, but no laws forced employers to follow them. Childcare facilities never caught up with the need for them. In contrast, public opinion linked the working mother with wartime hazards such as family break-ups, rising divorce rates, child neglect, juvenile delinquency, and teenage immorality. War did not boost the cause of sexual equality. Rather, the scarcity of men increased their value, just as wartime disruptions fueled desire for traditional ways of life.

"We can expect the flood tide of women in the labor force to recede rapidly with the coming of peace," wrote Mary Anderson, head of the Women's Bureau, in 1944 (Litoff and Smith 2000: 269). At the war's end, plans to demobilize women workers and make room for returning veterans took effect swiftly. When defense plants closed or converted to civilian production, most women lost their jobs. The Women's Bureau claimed that women did not want to advance "at the expense of veterans," although they hoped to retain "some if not all the gains" of the war years. The end of the war only briefly halted the long-term growth of the female labor force, as the decades ahead would prove.

World War II's impact on women, historians suggest, took varied forms. The war provided unprecedented job opportunities, higher wages, an easing of some occupational restrictions, and public recognition of women's efforts. These changes did not endure. Even as they occurred, traditional attitudes persisted. Hostility to married women workers survived the war and fostered anxiety afterward. Still, married women's numbers as workers, which had increased incrementally throughout the century, continued to rise.

Postwar Women: Mixed Messages

Writer Betty Friedan remembered 1949 as "the year the feminine mystique hit us." A recent college graduate, Friedan was part of the generation that felt most severely affected. "In 1949, nobody had to tell a woman that she wanted a man, but the message certainly began bombarding us from all sides," Friedan recalled. Injunctions to find "feminine fulfillment" and "domestic bliss" had insidious appeal, she contended. "The feminine mystique made it easier to retire smugly, avoiding conformity and competition as men could not" (Friedan 1976: 7, 16). Friedan did not speak for all women of the late 1940s; historians now question the pervasiveness of the postwar domestic stereotype Friedan analyzed and challenge her generalizations about women's consequent oppression, dependence, and desperation. Still, unquestionably, in the late 1940s, women's roles were in flux and many factors promoted domesticity.

Revived interest in private life drew heavy federal support. The GI Bill of Rights, or Servicemen's Readjustment Act (1944), provided returning veterans (98 percent men) with extensive benefits, including subsidies to continue their educations or learn new skills; about half, some six million, grasped the opportunity. The Veterans Administration also helped ex-service people buy homes, and home ownership – which reached about 45 percent of the population from 1890 to 1945 – began to climb. Throughout the postwar era, helped by highway construction and low-rate mortgages, suburbs mushroomed. Levittown, a development of 17,500 identical homes, built by teams of workers at minimal cost, arose in Hempstead, Long Island; when Levittown's sales office opened in 1949, prospective buyers stood in line for five days. In southern California, communities sprang up in the San Fernando Valley to house families of (male) aircraft and auto workers. Suburban growth catered to young families. In 1946 more marriages occurred than in any previous year; by 1950, the average marriage age for women had fallen to 20, and more women wed between 15 and 19 than in any other age group. In 1947 the birthrate began to accelerate. This began a postwar "baby boom" that did not peak until 1957 and continued into the 1960s. The first edition of Dr Spock's child-rearing guide (1944) could not have been better timed. The book reached a million readers a year between its first edition and 1960.

Women's higher education in the postwar era promoted domesticity, too. By 1947, veterans constituted half of college enrollments and reduced women's share of campus populations. Women's enrollment in fact rose. In 1942, 585,000 women attended college (41.6 percent of the college population); by 1950, 727,270 women attended college (31.6 percent). College fostered upward mobility among GIs; women, more likely than men to drop out, sought upward mobility through marriage, especially early marriage; among African-American women, an exception, 90 percent of college entrants graduated. Home economics programs proliferated; advisors urged young women of the late 1940s to attend college to gain training as homemakers and to have "something to fall back on." Faculty thought that women's aspirations declined. "I felt increasingly that something had gone wrong with our young women of college age," recalled an English professor at the University of Illinois, discussing the late 1940s and early 1950s (Rosen 2001: 41).

As domesticity gained cultural support, the women's movement faded. When war began, endorsement of an ERA seemed to be gaining strength. The Republicans in 1940 and the Democrats in 1944 supported equal rights planks in their party plat-forms, though not necessarily a constitutional amendment. The ERA won the support of the General Federation of Women's Clubs and made progress in the House but in 1946 failed to attain a two-thirds majority in the Senate, needed to start any ratifica-tion procedure. In 1944, foes of ERA mobilized a National Committee to defeat the Unequal Rights Amendment, comprising a dozen labor groups and women's organi-zations. Intensified discussion of ERA drew support for an equal pay bill. A wartime campaign for equal pay foundered in 1946 when Congress failed to move on a pro-posed equal pay bill (it would be passed in 1963, when the clause providing equal pay for "comparable work" was changed to "equal work"). States revived exclusionary and limiting protective laws from the pre-World War II era, as well as measures that discriminated against married women workers.

Before the war ended, the Labor Department issued recommendations to sever women from wartime jobs, provide work for returning veterans, and ensure a smooth transition. As war production plants closed and large industries like aircraft and shipbuilding laid off workers, the presence of women in heavy industry declined; women's share of the labor force in auto production plunged from 24 percent in 1944 to 7.5 percent in mid-1946. By the end of 1946, two million women had left the labor force and another million had been laid off. African-American women, the last line of emergency workers hired during the war, were hard hit after it. The proportion of women who worked sank from 37 percent at the war's end to 28 percent in 1947. High pay and new options that had attracted women to the wartime workforce vanished.

But retreat from the workplace was temporary: working women were the wave of the future. As early as 1952, the number of employed women reached its wartime high and just kept climbing. The new woman worker of mid-century, unlike her counterpart early in the century, was likely to be married, middle-class, and middle-aged. By mid-century, married women made up half the female workforce and each year their proportion rose. With each year that passed, as well, working wives were more and more likely to be mothers with children under 17 at home. In 1940 only 15 percent of married women worked, but in 1950, 21 percent, and 10 years later,

30 percent. The ranks of older women workers grew. The largest segment of new women workers after the war were in their forties or older; and women from middle-class families entered the workforce faster than any other group. Unlike war workers, new women workers from the late 1940s on entered sex-typed occupations – the garment trades, sales and office work, teaching, and nursing. After World War II, professional and managerial fields grew so rapidly that the proportion of women in them fell. But the number of women in these fields grew steadily. Thus, although the baby boom would eventually fade, the movement of wives and mothers into the workforce continued and accelerated. The postwar working mother was as representative of her contemporaries as the suburban housewife – and the trend to which she contributed more enduring.

Should women have careers or devote themselves to their families? The late 1940s offered two messages. Women "would do well to recapture those functions in which they have demonstrated superior capacity . . . in general, the nurturing functions around the home," declared a mid-century bestseller, *Modern Woman: The Lost Sex* (Lundberg and Farnham 1947: 368). Frieda Miller, head of the Women's Bureau, in contrast, defended aspiration: "Intermingled . . . with the necessity for self-support is the need to make a contribution to society in a field adapted to one's individual personality," wrote Miller in an article of 1947 that looked toward the future. "Pursuing a career," she contended, was no longer "an act of heroism," nor restricted to single women: "It may well be that we are approaching a period when for women to work may be an act of conformism" (Chafe 1991: 161).

The new working woman of the late 1940s justified her role with a traditional rationale: she worked to augment family income – to enable her family to maintain a middle-class lifestyle. Thus she contributed to a major trend in postwar America: the expansion of the middle class. The middle class had grown in the century's first three decades until stopped short by depression; after World War II, it soared to twice the size it had been in the 1930s. The postwar middle class, wrote journalist Agnes Meyer in 1950, had been "augmented by seepage from above due to the decline of big fortunes and by seepage from below, due to the rise of wages, the improvement of educational opportunities, and technological progress" (Woloch 2006: 499). Class, to a large extent, shaped women's options and aspirations at mid-century. Many postwar women, whether housewives or working mothers, in suburbs or cities, had probably recently stepped upward into the middle class. Looking back at their earlier years, amid the uncertainty of depression and war, they looked forward to stability and security, prosperity and affluence.

African-American Women at Mid-Century

"I was just glad the war was over," declared Fanny Christina Hill, an African-American migrant from Texas to Los Angeles in the 1940s. Hill had found work as a riveter in 1943 with North American Aircraft; when she took a pregnancy leave, the war ended – as did her job. "I didn't feel bad because my husband had a job and he also was eligible to go to school with his GI bill," Hill recalled. She did domestic work and factory work until, in 1946, her old job unexpectedly became available: "When North American called me back, was I a happy soul!" she exclaimed. "It was better than anything else because you had hours to work by and you had benefits and you came home at night with your family. So it was a good deal" (Gluck 1987: 41–2).

To be rehired in 1946 at an aircraft plant was uncommon among black or white women. Fanny Christina Hill's role as a migrant better typified African-American experience. Mass migration transformed black history in the 1940s. The mechanical cotton picker cut the need for southern field labor; sharecropping ebbed as a way of life; and from 1940 on, waves of African-American migrants left the rural South for northern cities; by mid-century at least a third of black Americans lived outside the South, some lured by wartime job openings. Those who remained in the South often became migrants to urban areas as well; both types of migrations continued into the postwar era. Nationwide, as white Americans moved to suburbs, African Americans moved to cities. In this way, as in others, the history of African-American women after World War II diverged from that of the white majority and followed another trajectory.

Young women migrants to cities after the war might find work on the margins of the urban economy. Ruby Daniel Haynes, whose story journalist Nicholas Lemann (1991) tells in his study of postwar migration, moved from Clarksville, Mississippi to Chicago in the late 1940s. In the next two decades, she worked in a janitorial job, laundry, awning factory, and as a barmaid, hotel maid, and office cleaner. She also raised eight children, sometimes with the aid of welfare. In 1950, 60 percent of black working women held service jobs, like Ruby Haynes, and 42 percent were domestic servants, unaffected by federal labor law or union contracts. African-American women sought paid employment in higher proportions than women in general; they worked more continuously throughout their lives; and like Ruby Haynes, in her sporadic jobs, and Fanny Christina Hill, in her well-paid job, fused paid employment with child-rearing. As among white women, the roles of wives and mothers in the workforce increased. In 1950, three out of ten African-American wives worked, compared with 19 percent of white married women.

African-American working women at mid-century earned half the income of their white counterparts. However, change in the black female workforce occurred: the proportion of black women in professional and white-collar work rose. In 1950, African women constituted half of black college graduates and 58 percent of black professionals, mainly because the preponderance of black teachers were women. Professional women's income fostered the growth of the black middle class in postwar America. Middle-class women were the mainstays of black women's organizations, such as the National Council of Negro Women, a federation of black women's groups formed in 1935 and first led by Mary McLeod Bethune.

Urban migration of the 1940s and after had mixed impact on black communities, according to sociologists who studied them. One was an "excess" of women, or imbalanced sex ratios, in urban areas, which made stable family life elusive and left women at a social disadvantage. "Most low-income women have to take love on male terms," contended two African-American scholars in their 1945 study of Chicago's black community (Drake and Cayton 1945/1970: 584). Sociologists also pointed to the origins of the black urban female-headed family at around mid-century. The numbers of such families declined in rural areas, studies found, but rose 50 percent in cities. Between 1947 and 1962 (the much-touted era of family "togetherness," according to *McCalls* and other women's magazines), the rate of births to unmarried mothers among African Americans doubled. Urban migration also had positive effects on black communities. City residence clearly fostered women's prominence in the early Civil Rights movement. Black women had long been active in groups such as the NAACP and Urban League, and this commitment led to new ones. Rosa Parks, a seamstress in Montgomery, Alabama, had been a long-time NAACP member and local activist before her role in her city's bus boycott in 1955. Ella Baker, granddaughter of slaves and graduate of Shaw University in North Carolina, moved to New York City in 1927, worked subsequently for the federal WPA and the NAACP. Heading her local NAACP branch during World War II, Baker was positioned for a leading role in the Civil Rights movement in the 1950s.

Looking Ahead

The lives of American women in 1950 differed in crucial ways from those of counterparts in 1900. Enfranchised, women were now candidates for public office and active members of political parties. The proposed ERA remained a controversial issue at mid-century, but dispute over it had faded to the margins. Beneficiaries of birth control and its widespread availability, women had gained some leverage to shape their reproductive lives. Growing numbers of women had access to higher education, and their proportions of college populations were again on the rise, as they had been earlier in the century. In 1900, when under 4 percent of college-age Americans went to college, women were just under 36 percent of college populations; in 1950, when 27 percent of college-age Americans were enrolled, women constituted almost 30 percent. The numbers of women workers, most notably married women workers, had increased steadily and continued to rise. In 1900, 5.6 percent of married women were wage-earners, and in 1950, 23.8 percent. Over the 50-year span, women had gained political rights, reproductive rights, and educational opportunity, and had vastly expanded their roles in the labor force. Elements of continuity persisted: women at mid-century still saw their primary roles as family members and still operated in a gendered workplace. Also, the experience of minority women in some ways diverged from that of the white majority; most recently, migration to cities had brought both liabilities and opportunities.

At mid-century lying immediately ahead was an era of economic growth, in which the GNP soared, credit expanded, income inequality ebbed, median family income doubled, upward mobility beckoned, and middle-class membership mushroomed. New or once-scarce consumer goods flooded the market, from cars to televisions to home appliances and frozen food. Increased buying power gave postwar women unprecedented roles as consumers, which many welcomed. But consumption alone did not define women's history in the 1950s, nor did the domestic stereotype: the growing workforce, unionization, civic activism, and civil rights organizations would also play important parts.

References and Further Reading

Addams, Jane. (1907). *Newer Ideals of Peace.* New York: The Macmillan Co.

Bailey, Beth L. (1988). *From Front Porch to Back Seat: Courtship in Twentieth Century America.* Baltimore: Johns Hopkins University Press.

Chafe, William H. (1991). *The Paradox of Change: American Women in the 20th Century.* New York: Oxford University Press.

Cott, Nancy F. (1987). *The Grounding of Modern Feminism.* New Haven, CT and London: Yale University Press.

Drake, St. Clair and Horace R. Cayton. (1945/1970). *Black Metropolis: A Study of Negro Life in a Northern City.* Chicago: University of Chicago Press.

Fass, Paula S. (1977). *The Damned and the Beautiful: American Youth in the 1920s.* New York: Oxford University Press.

Friedan, Betty. (1976). *It Changed My Life.* New York: Dell Books

Gluck, Sherna (ed.). (1987). *Rosie the Riveter Revisited: Women, the War, and Social Change.* Boston: Twayne Publishers.

Gordon, Linda. (1974). *Woman's Body, Woman's Right: Birth Control in America.* New York: Penguin Books.

Jones, Jacqueline. (1985). *Labor of Love, Labor of Sorrow: Black Women, Work, and the Family from Slavery to the Present.* New York: Vintage Books.

Kessler-Harris, Alice. (2001). *In Pursuit of Equity: Women, Men, and the Quest for Economic Citizenship in 20th-Century America.* New York: Oxford University Press.

Lemann, Nicholas. (1991). *The Promised Land: The Great Migration and How it Changed America.* New York: A. A. Knopf.

Litoff, Judy Barrett and David C. Smith (eds). (2000). *What Kind of World Do We Want? American Women Plan for Peace.* Wilmington, DE: Scholarly Resources.

Lundberg, Ferdinand and Marynia F. Farnham. (1947). *Modern Woman: The Lost Sex.* New York and London: Harper & Brothers.

Lynd, Robert A. and Helen Merrell Lynd. (1937). *Middletown in Transition: A Study in Cultural Conflict.* New York: Harcourt Brace.

Meyerowitz, Joanne (ed.). (1994). *Not June Cleaver: Women and Gender in Postwar America.* Philadelphia: Temple University Press.

Roosevelt, Eleanor. (1933). *It's Up to the Women.* New York: Frederick A. Stokes.

Rosen, Ruth. (2001). *The World Split Open: How the Modern Women's Movement Changed America.* New York: Penguin Books.

Rosenberg, Rosalind. (2008). *Divided Lives: American Women in the Twentieth Century*, 2nd edn. New York: Hill and Wang.

Ruiz, Vicki L. (1998). *From Out of the Shadows: Mexican American Women in Twentieth-Century America.* New York: Oxford University Press.

Schwarz, Judith. (1982). *Radical Feminists of Heterodoxy: Greenwich Village, 1912-1940.* Lebanon, NH: New Victoria Publishers, Inc.

Showalter, Elaine (ed.). (1989). *These Modern Women: Autobiographical Essays from the Twenties.* New York: The Feminist Press.

Slosson, Preston William (1994). "The flapper grew bolder": Changing roles for young women. In Linda R. Monk (ed.), *Ordinary Americans: U.S. History Through the Eyes of Everyday People*

(p. 175). Alexandria, VA: Close Up Foundation Publishing.

Terkel, Studs (ed.). (1984). *The Good War: An Oral History of World War II.* New York: Ballantine Books.

Ware, Susan. (1981). *Beyond Suffrage: Women in the New Deal.* Cambridge, MA: Harvard University Press.

Ware, Susan (ed.). (2002) *Modern American Women: A Documentary History.* New York: McGraw-Hill.

Woloch, Nancy (ed.). (1992). *Early American Women; A Documentary History.* Belmont, CA: Wadsworth Publishing Company.

Woloch, Nancy. (2006). *Women and the American Experience.* New York: McGraw-Hill.

3
The Status of African Americans 1900–1950

Matthew Pratt Guterl

Winslow Homer's darkly iconic painting, *Gulf Stream* (1899), features a black man, wearing only a tattered pair of pants, lying supine on the deck of a listing and battered sailboat. Though the bulk of the painting is in shadow, a single shaft of daylight illuminates the boat, drawing the viewer's attention to a few twisting cane stalks, a crumpled sail, and a broken mast, all scattered across the deck and around "the Negro." The man is not resting comfortably. The blue waters surrounding the craft are filled with crazed sharks, gnashing their teeth and hungering after his flesh. A waterspout sits in the near background, and angry clouds are only a few miles away. A distant schooner is headed in the opposite direction and cannot bring him to salvation.

Gulf Stream was an unusual piece for Homer, a New England painter whose heroic portraits of hardy sailors, their families, and the seafaring life were thought to be quintessentially "American." Indeed, Homer's patrons worried about the unnamed black, and pressed the artist to offer a positive interpretation of the troublesome image, a request he refused or ridiculed. His sequel, *After the Hurricane* (1899), featured a black body, lying in the sand next to an upside-down, crushed boat, and offered little solace to those who hoped to find the black sailor alive and well. Despite the concerns of Homer's patrons, *Gulf Stream* reflected the artist's long-standing liberal convictions about race relations and a growing concern about the twists of fate that had transformed the racial dynamic in America. That unnamed man's voyage, we can assume, began under calmer skies and under better circumstances. Adrift somewhere in the Gulf Stream, lacking food, water, and strength, he faced greater challenges than ever before in the dawning twentieth century. His plight neatly encapsulated the situation confronting African Americans, when the progress made after Reconstruction seemed to have been completely undone, and threats to the safety of "the Negro" were everywhere.

As the reaction to Homer's troubling portrait suggests, most white Americans at the turn of the century thought "the Negro" was a unique sort of social, political, and racial "problem" whose ultimate solution was elusive. Liberals or Progressives offered the benefits of "full citizenship," but at a great social distance and with insufficient attention to enforcement or protection, especially in the South. Hard-edged advocates for Jim Crow policies argued that such a problem required draconian controls to limit mixture, to control social intercourse, and to restrain the "impulses" and "instincts" of African peoples in the United States. "The Negro," they argued, was not (and might never be) ready for full citizenship, and should be legally confined to menial labor by an industrial color bar until such time as the race either died out or had advanced far enough to be reconsidered as members of polite society. At the same time, African Americans and their allies hoped that "the Negro problem," once addressed properly, would illuminate the country's explicit commitment to group progress and individual advancement. In pushing back against the architects of Jim Crow, they generated crucial, if gradual, progress towards civil rights.

These two narratives – the mobilization of the African-American community around rights and the ascension of the idea of "the Negro" in the American mind as a "problem," or threat – often ran off in different directions. They did not, in other words, affect the "status" of African Americans in the same way. But they did some-times converge. "The Negro," in the end, was a creation of American fantasy, a fiction of advertisement, film, and the minstrel stage, and a much needed shadow man whose rejection, surveillance, policing, punishment, and generally loutish behavior could hold together, or lend coherence to one of the largest, newest, and most heterogeneous countries in world history. Unhappily bound to this cartoonish concept, African Americans found their struggles for citizenship and social justice set against a terribly racialized backdrop. The growing significance of the black image in American film, literature, and mass culture could, then, work directly against the interests of the fledgling civil rights movement of the early twentieth century, especially when those images featured only buffoonish stereotypes and racist caricature. Middle-class uplift organizations formed in the Progressive Era would, for instance, stage their first dra-matic public protests against D. W. Griffith's film, *Birth of a Nation* (1915), which portrayed "the Negro" as a rapist and social terrorist. But if African Americans loathed these representations, mainstream American culture loved them. *Birth of a Nation* was a smash hit. Immigrant populations found relief from their own pitiful circumstances in the image of "the Negro" as an eternal inferior, against whom they could positively measure their own ascent up the social ladder. It was better and easier for American society in the end if poor and dirty European immigrants, laboring in factories, should note their own progress in relation to black America, than that they should take heed of the growing distance between themselves and the Vanderbilts or Rockefellers.

What is the history of this image of "the Negro"? What does it tell us about the place of African Americans in the United States? Focusing on three key moments in twentieth-century African-American history – the Nadir, the Renaissance, and the Depression – this essay plots the shifting status of "the Negro" and the push for civil rights from the turn of the century up to the end of World War II. It identifies those moments when black American activists, artists, novelists, and filmmakers struggled to gain some control over the most public representations of "the Negro," or where they labored to find room within American culture for a varied, textured, complex black humanity. Alongside a narrative history of African-American and American political formation, this essay also considers – over the first 50 years of the twentieth century – the unusual historical convergence of factors that gave "the Negro" extraordinary cultural status, or prominence, even as the social, economic, and political positions of African Americans were worn down and artificially depressed.

The Nadir

At the turn of the twentieth century, the status of African Americans was shaped by emerging institutions of domination and control – known collectively as Jim Crow – that could sometimes make freedom seem as onerous as slavery. In the wake of the Civil War, the nation's commitment to a unique, Christian "mission" had spurred the reforms of Reconstruction, but by the end of the century North and South were united in a sense that the fate of the country was to be determined not by its pursuit of full citizenship for everyone, but by its consolidation of whiteness and Christianity in the service of a new nationalism. America, it was assumed, was a white Christian nation. In the legal realm, the possibilities for African Americans – once broadened by emancipation and Reconstruction – were likewise increasingly narrowed by the emergence of Jim Crow and a series of dramatic setbacks. The abolitionists who had once raised the uncomfortable moral questions related to chattel bondage, and the liberal radicals who had hoped to extend basic civil rights and civic privileges to the freedmen, were no longer in a position to influence public policy. Some, like Wendell Phillips, were dead. Others, like Phillips's long-time sympathizer, Frederick Douglass, were too old or too isolated to do anything. The few remaining political supporters of "the Negro" had been voted out of office, a consequence of new, more conservative feelings on this issue. The entire South was now populated with Negrophobes, who were convinced that "the Negro," once removed from the institution of slavery, with its paternal governance and social controls, was a natural criminal. Almost everyone agreed with the plantation nostalgist, Thomas Nelson Page, that African Americans posed a problem – "the Southerner's problem" – that should be left to the region that understood it best.

The proliferation of city spaces and new modes of public transport after slavery required new laws to govern the conduct between whites and blacks. The bulk of those new laws, of course, were local ordinances or state regulations, and in this manner, Jim Crow was built on a smaller, more intimate scale than South African apartheid, with its national legal codes, would later be. Where these laws were challenged, the result revealed not the enduring strength of the civil rights amendments of Reconstruction, but their comparative weakness in the American imagination. When, for instance, Homer Plessy, an "octoroon" with mixed heritage, challenged Louisiana's segregationist Separate Car Law in 1892, he did so at the request of a concerned civil rights group, composed of African Americans and Creoles. The use of the train was itself a reflection of the significance of public transportation and public space in the struggle for social equality. It was just as significant that Plessy was light-skinned enough – indistinguishable from most Europeans, by the visual standards and observational techniques of the day – that his legal troubles began not when he boarded the "white" car, but when he later identified himself as "colored" to a surprised conductor. Hoping to overturn the state's emerging laws governing racial space and defining appropriate physical proximity, Homer Plessy lost his court case in Louisiana, and, more tragically, lost his appeal to the United States Supreme Court, which generated a long-lasting legal rationale for the whole of the nation when it came to isolating people of African descent, giving them a color-coded name, and assigning a "place" for them in the world. "Separate but equal," as Justice Henry Billings Brown concluded in the 1896 decision, *Plessy v. Ferguson*, was to be the law of the land for three generations.

The *Plessy* decision, though important, was a surface reflection of deeper, more widely shared concerns. For the Alabama educator Booker T. Washington, who was born into slavery and raised in the deep South, those concerns were worth addressing, if only to advance his own position on things. Speaking at the 1896 Atlanta Cotton State's Exposition, to a crowd composed of anxious planters and New South propagandists, Washington strove to say exactly what these men wanted to hear, and to say it in such a way that they would approve wholeheartedly. "The masses of us," he confessed humbly in his "Atlanta Compromise" speech, "are to live by the productions of our hands . . . it is at the bottom of life we must begin, and not at the top." Having ceded "modern" industrial labor and machine work to white America, and having claimed servile labor for his people, Washington proceeded, as well, to eschew any right to shared public space, turning segregation into a "positive good." "In all things that are purely social," he concluded, "we can be as separate as the fingers, yet one as the hand in all things essential to mutual progress" (Washington 1901/1965: 147, 148). Washington's grand concession, coming during a massive wave of immigration, was meant to preserve some kind of economic opportunity – no matter how limited – for African Americans at a moment where, all things being unequal, most people might prefer to hire poor whites, even for the dirtiest and most menial tasks. It certainly gained him great fame and, for a short while, a virtual stranglehold over philanthropy directed towards "the Negro." The cost of this agreement, though, was a tacit capitulation to the fears of the Negrophobes of the deep South, who suggested that "the Negro" was, first and foremost, a "beast," whose mere presence threatened everything. White fear made Booker T. Washington famous.

The most popular expression of this prevailing fear of racial contamination and the corruption of the republic came in Thomas Dixon's novel, *The Leopard's Spots*, first published in 1902. Like many of his contemporaries, Dixon had developed a remarkably coherent, all-encompassing critique of Reconstruction, offering the supposed "failure" of the 1860s – the "reign of terror" as he called it – as a cautionary tale for the South and for the nation, and ridiculing those idealists who had once lobbied for immediate equality and full citizenship for "the Negro." Turning the politics of Harriet Beecher Stowe's *Uncle Tom's Cabin* on its head, Dixon offered Simon Legree as a survivor of the war, transformed into a "violent Union man" and a schemer for black rule. Legree's fictional coconspirator, Tim Shelby, was a "full-blooded negro," a former slave and guerilla campaigner during the late stages of the war. Shelby, as Dixon described him, "kept his kinky hair close," and when he smiled his ears moved "up and down like a mule." He kept a "tiny moustache which he tried in vain to pull out in straight Napoleonic style." His image, produced for the novel as a part of its *faux*-historicism, can be read in any number of ways, but Dixon, who understood late nineteenth-century racial science quite well, framed the image with his story so that readers would gaze at the curve of the lip, the slope of the nose, and the shape of the eyes – conveniently focused on middle space, and not gazing directly at the viewer – and see not a man or a citizen but a "beast" (Dixon 1902: 85, 89).

Dixon, a child of the postbellum South, and a former lawyer, actor, and preacher, infused his narrative of Reconstruction with a spiritual authority, creating a literary "encyclopedia" of the fear of race-mixing (Williamson 1986: 99). Federal troops in the South, as Dixon tells it, were protecting postbellum marriages across the color line, intimate metaphors for the forced union of "black republicans" and the white South. At the novel's emotional climax, set in the heyday of "Negro rule" in the postwar South, the wedding of Tom and Annie, a 17-year-old bride, complete with fiddle-playing, is interrupted by a "black shadow" – "a big negro trooper," with a "broad grin, and his eyes bloodshot with whiskey." Accompanied by six "negro troopers," the gang steals away with Tom's bride. As the black men make off with the white woman, "laughing and yelling," Tom pleads with his wedding guests to fire into the woods, despite their fear that Annie might be shot – "My God, shoot!" he cries, "There are things worse than death." "Like young tigers," Dixon writes, the heroic white South, embodied by those vengeful wedding guests, "sprang across the orchard toward the wood." At the end of it, Annie lay dead, but she was also "saved from them brutes." It was better that she should die, Dixon assumed, than that she should unwillingly breed with the "big negro trooper." One protagonist later concludes "You cannot build in a Democracy a nation inside of a nation of two antagonistic races. The future of America must be an Anglo-Saxon or a Mulatto." The South, then, was the front line of the struggle against mixture, impurity, and devolution, a desperate struggle, as Dixon imagined it, between "white" and "black" (Dixon 1902: 124–6, 383).

Dixon's twinned portrait of "the Negro" as a threat to the South, and of "the Mulatto" as a challenge to the future of the republic, did not go unmet. "How does it feel to be a problem?" asked Harvard-educated New Englander W. E. B. Du Bois, in his transformative collection of essays, *The Souls of Black Folk* (1903). Born after slavery and raised in liberal New England, Du Bois was of a younger generation than Booker T. Washington, with a different approach to racial issues. Few African Americans in the South would have heard such a question, but for the egocentric Du Bois, his comparatively fortunate life was the story of "the race" writ large, and his deeply philosophical and interior questions, no matter how obscure, could illuminate the plight of the poor and uneducated children of slaves in the deep South. His meditations on "the Negro problem," Dixon would surely have noted, were deliberately laced with discussions of mixture and hybridity, a reflection of Du Bois's own "mulatto" background, his veneration of light skin, and his awareness of prevailing theories of "hybrid vigor." He answered his question: "being a problem is a strange experience, – peculiar even for one who has never been anything else." As a social outcast in the South, "the Negro" was defined by "twoness," a split sense of self resulting from the effects of racism, and the impossibility under difficult circumstances "to merge his double self into a better and truer self." Du Bois maintained:

> He would not Africanize America, for America has too much to teach the world and Africa. He would not bleach his Negro soul in a flood of white Americanism, for he knows that Negro blood has a message for the world. He simply wishes to make it possible for a man to be both a Negro and an American, without being cursed and spit upon by his fellows, without having the doors of opportunity closed roughly in his face. (Du Bois 1903: 2–3)

This, at least, was how Du Bois understood the "problem." At the heart of Du Bois's response to the Negrophobes, then, was an eloquent defense of hybridity, and a challenge to all those who would separate "the Negro" and "the Anglo-Saxon," blackness and whiteness.

Du Bois also offered a parallel response to Booker T. Washington, the guileful architect of the "Atlanta Compromise." By 1903, Washington had become a tight-fisted dispenser of patronage, who had dined at the White House, and whose approval could sway Andrew Carnegie and others to support or ignore particular African Americans. Furthermore, the "compromise" offered by the enigmatic "boss" of the "Tuskegee Machine" to the New South had been graciously and quickly accepted. Washington's political organization swallowed up black-owned newspapers, devoured the careers of independent African-American educators, and funneled financial support to close allies. Historians have struggled to make sense of a man who could sound like a black separatist, but who routinely told "darky" jokes to white audiences, and who tolerated segregation in print while secretly funding legal challenges to Jim Crow. Biographer Louis Harlan (1986), for instance, has stressed Washington's hunger for power, and his willingness to do or say whatever was needed to accumulate more authority and control. Literary critic Houston Baker, in slight contrast, had once stressed Washington's "masterful" appropriation of white stereotypes, but now worries that he was an "imperialist educator" in the service of Jim Crow (Baker 1989: 36, 2001: 63). For Du Bois, it made little sense to suggest that racial progress could flow from a public acceptance of social apartheid. He accused Washington, a very powerful man, of "hushing" his critics, and of uncritically embracing "a gospel of Work and Money" while throwing out "the higher aims of life." "Mr. Washington's programme," Du Bois summed, in one of *Souls'* most powerful sections, substituted "submission" for "manly self respect," and Washington himself "practically accepts the alleged inferiority of the Negro races." Such an argument could not really hurt Washington, whose reputation appeared unassailable, and who was insulated by the favors of white men in power, all of whom hoped that Du Bois was right. But it could most certainly establish Du Bois as the chief alternative, and as an aggressive advocate for that variant of the liberal tradition in America that hoped to extend full citizenship rights to "the Negro" (Du Bois 1901: 33, 36).

For Du Bois and for others, that liberal tradition was at its zenith when the setting was integrated across racial lines and segregated by class, with well-educated whites, mulattos, and blacks coming together to discuss matters of great social import. Such gatherings were, of course, extraordinarily rare. Rare, that is, until a series of riots swept across the urban South and upper Midwest, culminating in the 1907 Springfield riot, in the richly symbolic hometown of "the Great Emancipator," Abraham Lincoln. Moved by the spirit of "progressivism" – an often inchoate jumble of "moral uplift" ideologies that sought, at different times, various reforms related to the betterment of society – Du Bois, William English Walling, Jane Addams, and a handful of "neoabolitionists" were swept together in the formation of the interracial National Association for the Advancement of Colored People. In these early years, the NAACP, with Du Bois editing its journal, *The Crisis*, engaged in hard-nosed journalistic muck-raking, lobbied for an antilynching law, and protested against racism wherever it was found. Its counterpart was the National Urban League (NUL), which pressed for an "uplift" of poor migrants and better social conditions. Where the law seemed to exclude African Americans, the NAACP sent Moorfield Storey, Clarence Darrow, or some other famous figure, to argue its points. When D. W. Griffith's film, *Birth of a Nation*, revealed itself to be a popular celebration on lynching and white supremacy, the NAACP mobilized a national protest against the film's distribution. If Booker T. Washington sought to soothe white anxieties by sanctioning racial separation, then the NAACP proclaimed tolerance, equalitarianism, and integration to be better markers of "progress" in modern America. In the age of Jim Crow's ascendancy, this was a lonely fight.

The great irony, of course, was that both the formation of the NAACP and the refinement of Jim Crow drew strength from the same spirit of progressivism. Progressives, Michael McGerr reminds us, hoped "to change other people." That broad goal, though, was shared by a richly variegated social and political movement that also hoped, at times, to "end class conflict," or "control big business," or "segregate society." Segregation, in this context, was a means to an end, a legislative solution to a social problem, and the goal was to produce a more peaceful, harmonious, empathetic social order, an alternative to the rapacious capitalism and social Darwinism of the Gilded Age. For Southern progressives, Jim Crow was, then, a kinder alternative to "race war" or "expulsion." For many Northern progressives, too, strictly drawn racial lines in public spaces or in neighborhoods served an important social purpose. Indeed, in most cases, segregation was assumed to be the surest route to prevent "contamination" or the spread of disease into white areas, and to minimize the great

chance of racial friction "along the color line," while still allowing for the incorpora-
tion of black labor and the inclusion of African Americans as demi-citizens. Most
Americans still had deep reservations about the future of "the Negro" in the United
States, and only a few believed – as Du Bois did – that the limits imposed on the
lives of black people were not a product of nature, but an expression of human will.
The NAACP thus offered men and women like Du Bois a propitious solidarity with
other appropriately middle-class reformers at a time when "black Americans," as
McGerr puts it, "had little reason to place their faith in state power and little reason
to believe they could gain it" (McGerr 2003: 183, 201).

Renaissance

The Great War brought wrenching change to American society, and opened up new
opportunities for African Americans. The United States had emerged from the war as
an undisputed world power, a rival to France and Britain. The search for wartime
unity had led to the creation of "superpatriotism," and the general distrust of immigrants who clung to their "ethnic" pasts, or who manifested divided loyalties. The
tools of an emergent mass culture had been refined and sharpened, and had served the
propaganda needs of a nation-state at war. European immigration had slowed to a
thin trickle. And to replace the masses from Ireland, Germany, and Italy, to fill the
factories, mills, and slaughterhouses on which the war effort and American life
depended, tens of thousands of rural black people had migrated into cities and towns
across the South and, most dramatically, into the urban North, where the scale and
pace of the influx echoed the worst years of "the alien menace." When, in the aftermath
of the war, the federal government had come to see dissenters and immigrants and
Bolsheviks as serious threats to national security, African Americans – always "alien"
– suffered their own excessive surveillance, and were assumed to be potential subver-
sives, even where they, like Du Bois, encouraged loyalty during a time of war. It
would have been hard, in the context of this untrusting nationalism, to predict a
"renaissance" of any sort, let alone one that featured "the Negro" as an object of deep
and profound sympathy.

   The immediate postwar context was also charged by the arrival of Marcus Garvey,
a Jamaican immigrant with a fondness for the self-help ideologies of Booker T.
Washington and the radicalisms of Bolshevism and Irish nationalism. Setting himself
at Liberty Hall in New York, Garvey created a "Black Scare" overnight with his rabble-
rousing speeches, his penchant for inciting a race war, and his establishment of what
was, in essence, a pan-African state-in-exile, complete with uniforms, titles, and even
a Provisional President. His Universal Negro Improvement Association operated both
as a cult of personality – with Garvey as "the Negro Moses" – and as a global commercial and political organization, pursuing a black capitalism that hoped to connect
black producers in the Caribbean and Africa with black markets everywhere. Garvey
– short, dark-skinned, and color-conscious in a West Indian fashion – also attached

an interest in racial purity to Washington's segregationist policies, so that isolation could stave off "race suicide." Arguments like these were aimed directly at men and women who, like Du Bois, were integrationist and light-skinned. When coupled with an economic agenda, they could sound powerfully populist to the vast group of subscribers to the *Negro World*, the remarkable global newspaper of Garveyism. The interracial and integrationist NAACP, which had seemed so radical in 1910, looked like a collection of "Old Negroes" and untrustworthy whites when compared to Garvey's "race first" ideologies and newer, more dangerous organization.

Garvey's meteoric rise coincided with the birth of the second Ku Klux Klan. The national organization that emerged in the early 1920s, distantly related to the Klan of the 1870s, balanced "respectability" and "malice," and could argue against the consumption of alcohol even as it spurred a sunset lynching in the countryside. It was extraordinarily popular – with as many as five million members (MacLean 1994: xi). The "new" Klan was suspicious of modernity, its rhetoric laced with what historian Nancy MacLean has called "reactionary populism," bringing together "anti-elitism" with "the commitment to enforce the subordination of whole groups of people." Distrustful of Jews and Catholics, the rich and the poor, it saved its most potent venom for "the Negro," assumed to be either lazy, corrupt, or predatory. At its worst, it urged troubled communities to use lynching as a means to an end. Lynching, one Klansman suggested, was merely a response to "loafing." It is clear, however, from the numerous photographs taken of burning, dangling corpses, surrounded by smiling white faces – men and women, boys and girls – that lynching was a deeper part of the social fabric of the Klan, and that it helped to establish an "American" identity for its members (MacLean 1994: xiii, 140; see also Allen, Lewis, Litwack, and Als 2000). Curiously, the Klan could knowingly echo Marcus Garvey's call for race purity. Indeed, by 1924, Garvey had voiced support for the Klan, which pursued, as he saw it, parallel social policies. "A black man who advocates racial integrity," argued Earnest Sevier Cox, a Virginian and white supremacist, "cannot be opposed by a white man who advocates racial integrity . . . they fight in a common cause" (cited in Martin 1976: 344). Even as the integrationist leadership class of black America worked to get rid of the troublesome "black Moses," the Klan offered Garvey its support.

But the Great Migration changed everything. It brought African Americans out of the South, and concentrated them in communities where they enjoyed some slightly greater measure of liberty. It brought "Negro" music – blues and jazz – up the Mississippi and across the North, and bound together black and white musicians. It brought Josephine Baker – briefly – to the New York stage, and landed literary talents Wallace Thurman, Langston Hughes, Zora Neale Hurston, and Jean Toomer among others in the rich surrounds of the "Negro metropolis." And it inflamed white fears and concerns, sparking race riots and new regulations controlling patterns of black settlement and experience. The decade of the Klan and Garvey was, then, also the decade of the Harlem Renaissance. Centered in the cosmopolitan cores of Chicago and New York, the Jazz Age seemed ripe with possibilities for the advancement of African Americans. A growing interest in African-American music, art, and literature offered the leadership class of the NAACP and the National Urban League a chance to marshal their resources in pursuit of an unusual agenda. If the road to economic progress and full citizenship was closed by Jim Crow and racism, Du Bois, Charles Johnson, James Weldon Johnson, Alain Locke, and others reasoned, perhaps success in the arts could remove the roadblocks. It was a peculiar argument. But there were few options. Similar movements, self-described as "renaissances" to emphasize a return to a former state of grace and success, had worked before, in Ireland, for instance, where a literary revival had laid the foundation for widespread nationalism, international attention, and an independent nation-state. And, even as the United States wrestled with its new status as a world power, there were parallel attempts to define American culture and to stake an aesthetic claim quite distinct from the Old World. If African-American art – and individual black "geniuses" and creators – could sit at the center of this new national culture, there was a slim chance that white folks might come to a new, more respectful opinion of their darker fellow citizens.

But the role of mainstream, middle-class civil rights organizations in shaping this Jazz Age strategy cannot be underestimated. Indeed, in their gentle competition with each other, and their shared eagerness to put the proletarian chauvinisms of the Garvey movement behind them, the NAACP and the NUL, though quite different, were often on the same page. Both organizations used their monthly magazines – aptly titled *The Crisis* and *Opportunity* – as venues for emerging and "discovered" African-American poets, short story writers, and dramatists. Both offered awards or prizes, and sought to link individual writers and artists with wealthy patrons, philanthropic organizations and foundations. All strove to cultivate talent and "genius" and, once it matured, to package and advertise it as a marker for the success of "the race." This was a fairly oblique, consumerist approach to the general concerns of poor African Americans, who preferred jobs, clean water, access to education, and safety to a handful of novels and paintings, and whose lives would not have been improved by the ascending reputations of Langston Hughes or Aaron Douglas. It was also an entirely unnatural phenomenon, and was hardly the evolutionary outgrowth of the migration of these same impoverished African Americans from the rural deep South to the urban North, where their concentration, increased social stratification, and closer proximity to higher culture would, as if by the laws of nature, produce a new "folk" literature. It was, instead, "artifice imitating likelihood," an ambitious advertisement masquerading as a finished product (Lewis 1979: 120).

In exploring the political thrust of the Renaissance, some historians have argued that some "New Negroes" – and especially Alain Locke, the Howard University philosopher and aesthete – had broader ambitions for the movement. George Hutchinson's *Harlem Renaissance in Black and White*, for instance, describes the African-American arts and letters movement as an expression of cultural pluralism, with a new social radicalism bridging the gap between the "lyrical left" of white New York and the avant-garde of black Harlem. White and black activists and artists believed in the power of literature, painting, poetry and drama to change the world, and they hoped, working together, to create a space for "the Negro" at the

American table. Black and white together fostered "egalitarian interracial efforts, intimacies, and commitments," Hutchinson argues, and if those networks and relationships "fell short of ideological purity," this is "less significant than that they would work at all in a culture so patently hostile to their existence" (Hutchinson 1995: 27). In Hutchinson's telling, then, the Harlem Renaissance was a rare opportunity for something close to a free and fair exchange of ideas, with lasting consequences for the interrelations of American culture. It would be impossible, after this rich dialogue, for anyone to imagine American culture without thinking of the African-American element.

The productive synergies of white and black artists did not, however, take place in a vacuum. Indeed, despite the best efforts of Locke and others, the intended purpose of "New Negro" art was not so perfectly understood by its primary consumer audience. It was true that the distinctiveness of black culture – a result of racism and oppression – was also its unique selling point, and its contribution to a truly *national* culture. White audiences, however, seemed to care far more about what black culture could mean for *them*, for their tortured psychologies and yearnings for "authentic" and "primitive" releases. In this context, some of the message so carefully envisioned by the NAACP, the NUL, and other organizations was eclipsed by other cultural transformations. As David Levering Lewis writes: "the new religion of Freudianism, with its sexual trapdoor under the ordered mind, transformed the Afro-American's perceived lack of cultural assimilation from a liability into a state of grace" (Lewis 1979: 99).

To further complicate matters, the black leadership class struggled to keep their precious and talented stable of artists "on message." The original political intent of the Renaissance was to show black people at their middle-class "best" in order to gain respectability and, through that, increased access to civil rights. But while Hughes, Claude McKay, Thurman, Rudolph Fisher, Hurston, and their "generation" may have disliked the enthusiasm for tropical "darky" caricatures, they also chafed at the controls of their elders. Most of these younger writers experimented with dazzling playfulness with storylines and subjects that seemed vulgar and apolitical, and that, when read without care by white audiences, could slide backwards into mean stereotype. There was no room to understand the subtlety of these works, only a "stampede for the exotic and forbidden" by "frantically stimulated whites" (Lewis 1979: 165). If white pluralist radicals and New Negro artists "shared a major premise" and were "bound together symbiotically," it was also true that the two movements drew diametrically opposite conclusions from that convergence; "in the Village," Lewis concludes, "bohemia was a value; in Harlem it was a strategy" (Lewis 1997: xvi). The pluralist potential of the Renaissance, so wonderfully described by Hutchinson, was steadily undermined by this divergence, and by the new, emergent obsession with "the Negro," a colorful id or provocative anticitizen.

It was far more important, in 1925, to set "the Negro" as an antipode for what it meant to be an "American." Twenty-five years earlier, African Americans were still largely confined to the South, with Jim Crow providing a *cordon sanitaire* for the nation. The first waves of the Great Migration – the source of the Renaissance – had, in the end, established "the Negro problem" as a national issue. By 1927, Lothrop Stoddard, a popular writer on racial subjects, could describe a national focus on "the Negro" as the best chance for the *"Re-Forging of America,"* or the "welding" of a decidedly heterogeneous European population into a single racial unit (Stoddard 1927). The hue and cry of partisans like Stoddard was complemented by an increased attention to redlining, spatial segregation, and the violent policing of intercity borders, a result of growing black populations in Northern cities. At the national legislative level, the passage of a massive immigration reform bill in 1924, limiting the number of European immigrants, effectively put an end to the "alien menace," at least where that supposed "menace" concerned "dingy white" Catholics and Jews from the Old World, but it also encouraged the American social science corps to shift some of its attentions to this newly enlarged concern for African Americans. Arriving new immigrants, their numbers now reduced to a fraction, found the passage to whiteness made easier by the national interest in "the Negro problem." Southern and Northern approaches to race were coming together in unexpected, often powerful ways. One year after the Johnson–Reed Immigration Act had passed, Madison Grant, one of the foremost nativists of New England and a long-time advisor on immigration issues, offered his help to a Virginia white supremacist. Together they would author the Virginia Racial Integrity Act of 1925, which reduced many generations of Southern thinking on race, rights, and miscegenation down to its simplest expression: the "one drop rule," which rendered anyone with one drop of black blood (in so far as such things could be determined) a "Negro."

The interest in defining blackness as a sweeping and unchanging thing, as a cornerstone of American mass culture, and in reimagining "the Negro" as a national problem, had a deeper social purpose, as well. In a nation of immigrants, most of them from Europe, the new cultural significance of black folks could make it easier for the "dingy whites" of Italy, Ireland, and Germany to imagine themselves as superior, as first-class citizens in a republic. Progress up the social ladder was not so quick as many immigrants assumed. And nativism (the assault on immigrants as "foreigners" and "outsiders") was still a concern, still a source of great friction, and still a part of the platform of the Klan. But the anxieties of the Great War and the Red Scare about "hyphenate" Americans quickly gave way, in the 1920s, to the interest in whiteness as a source of connection and solidarity. Alain Locke may well have imagined Harlem as "Dublin" for African Americans, but the broader transformation of the American racial landscape made these sorts of immigrant analogies far less powerful (Locke 1925/1992: 7). Indeed, for far too many white Americans, Harlem seemed much closer to Africa than it was to Manhattan, and a journey up above Central Park to the Cotton Club or some other segregated dance hall was like crossing the Atlantic to go on safari. Conversely, poking fun at "the Negro" at a local amusement park, or laughing at *Birth of a Nation*, could help to align the interests of working people – many of them European immigrants – with their "betters." All in all, one can watch blackness and whiteness, Africa and America, slide further and further apart in this decade, even while "New Negroes" worked, against all odds, to bring them closer together.

The great concerns of the Renaissance, though, included not just blackness but mixture and its consequences. In the close wake of the Garvey movement, with its deep disgust for light skin and high brows, there was much to talk about. The great irony of the slaveholding South, as so many noted, was its public insistence on white supremacy and its obvious, if private, enthusiasm for rape and concubinage. Out of this came extraordinary physical and visual diversity within the slave population, and within free African populations during and after slavery. "Mixed bloods," summed Charles S. Johnson of the National Urban League, "they are suspended between two races – mulattoes, quadroons, musters, mustafinas, cabres, griffies, zambies, quatrivis, tresalvis, coyotes, saltaras, albarassadores, cambusos – neither white nor black" (Johnson 1925). For some, the newness of the "New Negro" was a literal expression of an emerging racial type – now comfortable, after two or more generations of freedom, in their brownness, and not seeking to escape their blackness or seek whiteness through marriage, or hair-straightening gels or skin bleaches. Such expressions ran, intriguingly, parallel to the contemporary arguments of Mexican nationalist, José Vasconcelos, who conceived of *"la raza cosmica"* as the quintessential expression of a new Mexico (Vasconcelos 1925). For others, the crystallization of a "biracialist" sensibility served as a backdrop for a discussion of the tragedy and pathos of "passing," using one's light skin, straight hair, and "good" features to surreptitiously cross the color line into whiteness. For Nella Larsen, the stylish author of *Passing* (1929) and *Quicksand* (1928), who was also half Dutch, there was an autobiographical element in this discussion, one that was obliterated by the fixation on whiteness and blackness. (Only recently has the truth of Larsen's claims been recognized. See Hutchinson 2006.) George Schuyler, one of the great satirists of the day, parodied the whole interest in "passing" by offering a science fiction story, wherein a black scientist creates a process through which all "Negros" could become "Caucasians." In the ensuing effort to unveil those black folks masquerading as "ofays," many prominent whites are shown to be mixed themselves. In the end, Schuyler's new "mulattoes" flee to Mexico, where they assume a better reception. Winhold Reiss's *Harlem at Night*, a monochromatic portrait of stylized "black" life in all its libidinous variety stands, then, in obvious contrast with the artist's portrait of the "Negro woman" Elise Johnson McDougald, whose light caramel-colored skin is accentuated by her white dress, an off-white background, and her black hair, swept back behind her head. "Mongrelism" may well have been, as Ann Douglas (1996) suggests, a metaphor for the relationship between white and black literary culture and white and black authors in the 1920s, but it was also a very "real" thing, troubling those very categories, and offering a serious social subject for thoughtful commentators like Reiss and the great bulk of African-American artists, novelists, and activists.

For W. E. B. Du Bois, who was either disgusted or outraged by the fictions of "the younger generation," mixture could be revolutionary. The Renaissance, Du Bois feared by the end of the decade, had become apolitical, its artists engaged in "arts for art's sake" rather than social or economic critique. Having long fancied himself a novelist, Du Bois thus offered *Dark Princess*, published in 1928, as a corrective for the Renaissance, hoping, once again, to yoke serious literature to serious politics. The protagonist, Matthew Townes, a Pullman porter, becomes embroiled in a global conspiracy against "the white Leviathan," and is allied (and romantically involved) with a renegade Indian princess and her Japanese, Chinese, and African comrades. Such a novel played, of course, on the widely prevalent fears of a "rising tide of color," and it evoked a sense that the darker world could, by recognizing that race and class had become conflated on a global scale, overturn decades of imperialism and racial supremacy. Pointedly, the novel ends not with a color-coded Armageddon, or a clash of the races, but with the birth of Townes's son, a hybrid "Messenger and Messiah to all the Darker Worlds," with skin the color of "gold." "Madhu," as the Princess calls him, is greeted by three wise men, by a "pageant" of men "clothed in white with shining swords," and by the "silver applause" of trumpets (Du Bois 1928/1995: 307, 310–11). There is precious little ambiguity here. Still, even this rather transparent argument about the rich and possible synergies between "miscegenation" and revolution was misunderstood by a mainstream American culture that had come, instead, to prize the simplicity and utility of the "one drop rule."

By the end of the 1920s, the nation's conception of race had changed. For the first time, it was developing a *national* sense of race, with the white-over-black dyad at its core. Older distinctions – the variations of European peoples, or the skin color spectrum of African America – were increasingly lost. This was a social revolution of sorts – a revolution in the way the nation-state, through culture, science, and policy, could organize bodies and shape experience. And few felt the different pressures of this moment more acutely that did Jean Toomer, the light-skinned, handsome novelist whose prose poem, *Cane*, was such a troublesome text. Toomer was the grandson of P. B. S. Pinchback, a Gilded Age racial chameleon who raised his grandson in a world where it was possible to trace one's lineage to distant Africa and still be something other than black. *Cane*, published in 1923, was, in many ways, the embodiment of the pluralist project conceived by Alain Locke and described by George Hutchinson. Toomer imagined the book, at one point, as a complement to Waldo Frank's *Our America* (1919), which had ignored the contributions of "the Negro." But, though he "featured the Negro" in *Cane*, Toomer never thought that he could be limited to that identity. Almost everyone who read the book, though, described Toomer as a "Negro," even Waldo Frank and Alain Locke. In the end, Toomer never published another book, having never managed to convince anyone of his own, increasingly anachronistic, racial position. As Toomer later put it, the "new people" – Americans of "mixed blood" – were forced to use the "dominant, which is to them alien, language" of blackness and whiteness, and could no longer "find . . . words with which even to talk of themselves." "All was closed," he summed, "and sealed tight" (Toomer n.d.). Words like "black" and "white" have complicated histories, Toomer reminds us.

No matter how eloquent it was, Jean Toomer's utopian introspection might well have been lost on the great bulk of African Americans. For most, it wasn't all rosy up North, but it was surely better than it had been down South. At the close of the 1920s, black people had moved north in greater numbers than ever before. They had been beaten during race riots, and subject to unreported acts of day-to-day violence. But they were able to vote, if in small numbers, and to participate in city politics in some fashion. They had been concentrated in racially segregated neighborhoods, where property values were stagnant or sinking, and where most of the businesses were owned by outsiders. But they had access to streetcars, and the local policemen were sometimes black. They were poor, and often excluded from the best jobs, and the highest wages. But they were no longer subject to Jim Crow, and had escaped the medieval brutalities of the deep South. White people were convinced that "the Negro" was a feral, sexual creature, and crowded into Harlem to gain access to its tropical delights. But the new prominence of black people in literature – even if derived from these stereotypes – offered a fuller pride in "the race," and a sense that "the Negro" could produce works of art or be named a "genius." The important question, in the end, was whether the Renaissance's reaction to Garveyism's social message, and its focus on the creation of a distinctly "black" art and culture – in lieu of a pursuit of home ownership, small business development, and economic advancement – had adequately prepared African Americans for the challenges that lay ahead.

Depression

When the Great Depression arrived in 1929, it altered the racial dynamic in the United States and the world. Across the Atlantic, Josephine Baker's fabulous celebrations of excess and abandonment suddenly seemed stale and irrelevant, forcing "the Black Pearl" to reinvent herself as a more versatile performer, as the embodiment of France. In the United States, the Depression did not, as some suggest, bring the Harlem Renaissance to an end, but it did shift cultural production away from snazzy Jazz Age portraits of Harlem dance halls, rent parties, and flappers – away, in other words, from a high-end consumer capitalism where "the Negro" was the rarest product for sale. It foregrounded, instead, "the least of the citizens," including – sometimes – those African Americans bound to rural, backward spaces by social class, tradition, and poverty. In Harlem, the devastation was so breathtaking, so sudden, that there was hardly enough time to look back upon the much ballyhooed Renaissance of the 1920s, to wonder, indeed, at the extraordinary naivety that had led many of the brighter minds of the African-American intelligentsia to believe "that race relations in the United States were amenable to the assimilationist patterns of a Latin country" (Lewis 1979: 306). There was only time to turn, once again, against racism, and to keep searching for crawlspace, for light, for hope.

African-American literature and culture in the Depression and during World War II featured folklorish portraits of rural black speech, and emphasized (with the partial exception of Richard Wright) the dignity of ordinary African Americans performing hard labors in the field and the factory. In doing so, black culture reflected the interests of American culture more generally, as the nation struggled to rebuild its central myth of inevitable success around something other than consumption, accumulation, and excessive display. Coming, as it did, after a decade of NAACP and NUL investment in the concerns of the black middle class, this interest in poor, rural blacks, with all their faults and irregularities, as an appropriate subject for novelists, painters, social scientists, and "intellectuals" was a great reversal. The recovery of the African-American "folk," complete with its valorization and humanization of ordinary people, radically expanded the civil rights philosophies of the early 1920s: no longer was it just a question of whether well-educated, middle-class blacks could *acquire* some aspects of civilization, and could demonstrate that acquisition through the authorship of fine literature, careful painting, and florid rhetoric; it was now a question of whether the standards of civilization themselves could be expanded to include the everyday wisdom, struggles, and earthiness of the most ordinary, uneducated, poorest people in the United States.

The struggles of black artists and activists were not, however, one and the same with those of the nation as a whole. For most Americans, the New Deal was a dim light in the darkness of the Depression. Roosevelt's agencies and programs offered relief but not welfare, and focused on the luckless small property owner or floundering small business owner, men and women rather like George Bailey in Frank Capra's *It's a Wonderful Life* (1946). Its public works programs were vast, technologically sophisticated, and modernist, demonstrating a control over nature and an indomitable spirit. Its general reformist ethos focused on the emergent power of the white American consumer, invariably styled as mainstream, lower-middle-class, from a small town and aspiring to a better life. It did not attempt to "improve" Americans, as had the Progressive moment, but assumed, instead, that they were already fundamentally decent people who had hit a big rough patch that was not of their own making. It was neither a form of moral capitalism nor simple window dressing. For these reasons, and for others, it was attacked by some libertarians and populists as an overreaching affront to "the littlest guy," and reviled by others for leaving the basic framework and inequities of the national economy unreconstructed. Where the New Deal "celebrated the decency, honesty, and patriotism of ordinary Americans" (Gerstle 200: 153) few whites would have included "the Negro" in that category of "ordinary." Rural blacks in the deep South, many of them sharecroppers, were, of course, completely crushed by the Depression. And some of the well-intentioned liberals in FDR's employ did, in fact, address the pervasive discrimination that affected the distribution of relief. But the broader plight of "the Negro" was a consequence of things beyond the scope of Roosevelt's administrative solutions. Indeed, if Africans Americans featured in some of the policies of the New Deal – and most especially Roosevelt's later symbolic executive order creating a Fair Employment Practices Committee – they rarely occupied the center stage in the bigger, national discussions about the federal response to the Depression.

This is not to say, of course, that they did not try to do just that. Indeed, African Americans exploited every advantage they gained and refused to accept New Deal apathy as the right public policy wherever they found it. Walter White and Mary McLeod Bethune, for instance, lobbied Eleanor Roosevelt, schooling her in the plight of black Americans, and serving as an informal switching point, or "Black Cabinet," between her White House connections and their links to the civil rights activism of A. Philip Randolph and others. Bethune, once a follower of Booker T. Washington, may well have lobbied, picketed, and orated against the perpetuation of racism, but, as Harvard Sitkoff observes, "Within the government, she fought for the same causes, masking her militancy with homespun homilies and appeals to those in power based on a sense of fair play for all" (Sitkoff 1978: 81). There were, too, countless other less public examples of political mobilization, like the effort to unionize sharecroppers in the deep South, or the continued push for an antilynching bill. Emboldened by the color-blind liberalism of a few New Deal officials, they relentlessly pressed for attention, relief, respect, and change, generally within the framework of American nationalism, as reformers dedicated to minor modifications of the culture of capitalism and not at radicals determined to break it apart. In doing so, they pitted themselves against the radical tradition – against Marxism and socialism. If, like Du Bois, many mainstream African-American activists imagined the New Deal to be a "second Reconstruction," an expansion of the nation-state's administrative power aimed not at the empowerment of racism but at the protection of basic civil liberties for all, it was also true that few in the Black Cabinet shared the older man's desire to completely remake the social contract.

Despite these efforts of the NAACP, the Black Cabinet, and other "respectable" organizations, the most sustained discussion of "the Negro problem" in the Depression was colored by the old accusations of rape, ignorance, and predation. It came out of Scottsboro, Alabama, with the arrest in 1933 of nine young black men and boys. Like many poor, wandering folks in the Depression, these "Scottsboro boys," as they were called, had all hitched a ride on a slow train crossing one corner of the deep South. There were several poor whites on the train as well, including a few sojourning women with murky, promiscuous pasts. When the train was stopped, and police discovered these "boys" – unsupervised and ungoverned – in close proximity to the presumed object of their lust (two white women), a cascading series of assumptions (that all black men were natural rapists, that the presence of unattached white women would inflame the ardor of "the Negro," and that a crime must have occurred) led to their arrest and trial for rape. The middle-class NAACP, fearful that its image would be tarnished, dragged its feet and worried that the boys might be guilty. This procrastination, in turn, opened the door for the Industrial Labor Defense, associated with the Communist Party of the United States, to defend all nine. By the time the decade was over, "the Scottsboro Boys" had become a global *cause célèbre*, and the CPUSA had proven itself to be an aggressive, if marginal, force for equality. The NAACP, the nation's largest and most reputable civil rights organization, had by this point turned away from advocating the kind of economic reform that would generate real social change, and continued to focus on middle-class concerns, echoing the New Deal, or on legal challenges to segregation that appealed to the integrationist, bourgeois core of the group. In an age where the New Deal had pulled a deeply conservative nation a bit to the left, and where public conversation about the Depression was suffused with sympathy for the plight of the common people, only the CPUSA and the ILD had the courage to defend nine impoverished and uneducated young black men, all of them improperly accused of rape.

Despite the slight leftward tilt of American political culture, Depression-era American politics was also strangely apathetic, suffused with "inaction," "passivity," and "traditionalism." Once the world turned upside down, Americans might have overturned the nation's political framework, or marched in the streets for revolution. Eschewing a radical critique, American mass culture chose, instead, to privilege the enthusiastic, optimistic narrations of a first generation Sicilian immigrant like Frank Capra, featuring an emotional "identification with patriotic images and heroes" (Gerstle 2001: 173), and emphasizing the role of corrupt character and reform through example. In *It's a Wonderful Life* (1946), for instance, the lean, tough circumstances of the Depression could be a blessing in disguise, revealing what was supposed to be truly important. Capra's other films, historian Lawrence Levine reminds us, were often about the interplay between good and bad, small towns and big cities, honest rural folk and less trustworthy city slickers, and relied on "formulaic" endings to resolve the ambiguity between the American dream and the realities of the Depression. There was little room in these stories for poor black folk (Levine 1993: 252–4).

In part, this focus on the upside of economic downturn, or the wholesomeness of the rural, was a consequence of the New Deal's efforts to reframe the history of the United States as a history of middling, everyday Americans, eschewing the 1920s focus on celebrity, accumulation, and fame for the lives of bankers, family farmers, and small business people. Still, there was, in fact, an anthropological interest in hardscrabble, working-class people, for out-of-work bellhops, miners, farmers, and others. This probing search for "the folk" in American culture manifested itself in these years in a number of different ways, ranging from James Agee and Walker Evans's *Let Us Now Praise Famous Men* (1940) to John Steinbeck's *Grapes of Wrath* (1939). And it was driven by the state, which sought relief from the threat of social revolution, and not by emerging aesthetic conventions or cultural taste. Works Progress Administration programs kept artists out of the poor house, and put them to work painting murals or small-scale representations of "the everyday." The Federal Writer's Project, another WPA program, also employed talented writers in the service of this new national narrative, encouraging them to get close to the poor, to gain their confidence, and to take copious notes on the real-life experiences they shared over a beer or a lemonade on someone's front porch or at the kitchen table.

If, however, the reality of working-class America was diverse – with whites and blacks and Mexicans and Asians working together or apart in different places – the iconography of the New Deal was largely focused on white men and women, and celebrated the hard work or iron-jawed suffering of both. The New Deal's foundation,

Gary Gerstle argues, was a "progressive civic nationalism" that "affirmed the social rights of the American people to economic security" and also "welcomed into the national community a great variety of Americans." There were limits, though, to that "great variety." "The invitation," Gerstle continues, went "most strongly to Jews and Euro-American Catholics, especially those from southern and eastern Europe who had been the target of the 1924 immigration law." The rapt attention of photographers to white faces captured on film in the documentary style – like Dorothea Lange's "Migrant Mother" (1936) – conveyed a powerful message to a "nation of immigrants." Even Frank Capra, who popularized many of the central myths of the New Deal, buried his Sicilian past, and especially the story of his brother's "descent" into blackness, in a "flood of white Americanisms" (Du Bois 1903: 3, Gerstle 2001: 153–4, 174–5).

Where it touched upon the lives of blacks, this Depression-era interest in "the folk" could bring with it a lingering, if troubling curiosity about slavery. Federal Writer's Project folklorists, for instance, sojourned across the South and the Midwest in search of former slaves to interview, sometimes capturing the voices, songs, and stories of the few remaining Americans to have crossed the line from slavery to freedom (see Berlin, Favreau, and Miller, 1998). Often, this curiosity had a certain, fundamentally racial politics. W. E. B. Du Bois's radical argument in *Black Reconstruction of Democracy*, published in 1935, was meant as a cautionary tale for the New Deal, urging closer attention to the poor black sharecroppers of the South and to their capacity for collective action and full citizenship, during and after slavery. But Du Bois's social scientific text, with its focus on the "general strike" and its exposition on race and class, had little purchase in American popular culture. One of the most popular radio programs of the day, *Amos 'n' Andy*, featured two bumbling "black" characters (in reality, two white vaudeville actors) who were entirely overmatched by their urban lifestyles. In even starker contrast, Margaret Mitchell's romantic *Gone with the Wind* (1936), published one year after Du Bois's history, was a complete blockbuster. The life story of a young Irish American woman, the child of a first generation slaveholder, suggested that a crumbling social order can bring out the best in some people, allowing for their individual triumph over adverse circumstances, and their return to "those enduring values they had lost sight of in better times" (Levine 1993: 218). For Scarlett O'Hara, of course, this "triumph" over the wartime privations of the Old South was enabled by her trustworthy slaves, all of them simple stereotypes, embodying docility, strength, flightiness, and mothering. Scarlett's perseverance was dependent upon the labors of blacks, none of whom would think to conduct a "general strike." "Tomorrow is another day," she reminds herself at the end of the novel, transforming the story of Civil War into a metaphor for the Depression, a reflection of the crisis that white America needed to endure and overcome (Mitchell 1936/1999: 1037). Black Americans – slaves, noncitizens, and beasts – were not participants in this struggle. In all too many of the movies produced in Hollywood's "Golden Age," the escape into a narrative of success in the face of daunting odds included the regular and comedic, if brief, "Negro" appearance, often as a waiter, a house-servant, or a maid, and usually including the word, "Yessir." For

Mitchell, and for many, many others, "the black poor" were, then, a uniquely unrevealing *lumpenproletariat*, an internal caste of subterranean others, socially and culturally located, in all cases, below or beneath even the poorest whites around and lacking any sort of group consciousness. Mitchell's happy portrait of black obedience, tellingly, does not match the noisy, radical protests of the era described by historians Robin D. G. Kelley, Patricia Sullivan, and others.

African-American artists and writers, often employed by the WPA, worked in Margaret Mitchell's context, and struggled to portray "the Negro" as capable of progress and advancement, or as deserving of sympathy. New Deal muralists like Aaron Douglas, once the *wunderkind* of the 1920s, had a vast canvas on which to unveil the future of "the race." "Aspects of Negro Life," Douglas's remarkable series from 1934, traces the history of Africans in America, from slavery through Reconstruction, with an emphasis on heroism, valor, and positive evolution. In *Aspiration* (1936), Douglas foregrounds three African-American figures — clutching an architect's compass, a square, a chemist's vial, and an open book — as they progress towards a nearby modern city on a hill. Beneath them, in darker shadows, we see only raised arms with manacles, a reference to the past centuries of slavery. Progress, embodied by the city of the future, seems not so far off. Few other representations of "the Negro" from this period feature this element of technological sophistication, which had served as a constant and clear marker of racial status in American history. Amos and Andy, for instance, could hardly be confused with these figures, nor would either know what to do with an architect's compass. Nor, in truth, could Douglas's trio be confused with "Prissy" or "Mammy" from Mitchell's *Gone with the Wind*.

In portraiture, African-American visual artists likewise attempted to portray ordinary, working-class black Americans as complex, interesting, and introspective — and entirely unlike the simple-minded slaves who populated the American imagination. Jacob Lawrence, for example, was affiliated with the Harlem Art Workshop, which was, in turn, sponsored by the WPA. Small groups such as this left their stamp on many African-American writers and artists in the 1930s, cultivating a particular kind of social consciousness. On the surface, and taken one at a time, Lawrence's small paintings are disturbing images, featuring extraordinarily dark, crudely shaped bodies, with few or no facial features, and only remedial emotional capacity. *They were very poor*, produced between 1940 and 1941, foregrounds two figures, a man and a woman, with shoulders slumped, hands idle, seated in front of two empty bowls in a room devoid of any furnishings beyond a practical iron pot — not in use but hanging from the wall — and a plain wooden table. The title of the painting, rendered in the past tense, is implicitly archival, suggesting a possible change in status after the portrait was created, either through self-improvement or, one supposes, death. But there is something else in the painting. The dark, inscrutable visage of each figure might reflect "the Negro" as something lacking individual consciousness, but this technique also refuses the traditional, overly sentimental focus on the two most damning, and oft-stereotyped facial features — the eyes and the lips — both of which appear in numerous Depression-era films. There is little cause, within the tan borders of the painting, for optimism: there is only the room, their posture, the empty bowls, and the sad, rough-hewn expression on their faces. Little cause, that is, until the image is seen in its context, as one snapshot in the "Migration" series, as a part of Lawrence's "visual ballad," with "each image a stanza-compressed, like the blues, to the minimum needs of narration" (R. Hughes 1997: 456). His striking, Depression-era work imagines black America in this same fashion, as a serial story rather than singular, frozen diorama. His most famous, Depression and World War II era works, the series which we know as "Toussaint L'Ouverture," "Frederick Douglass," "Harriet Tubman," "John Brown," and, of course, "Migration," are composed in multiple frames, allowing their subjects to evolve, develop, mature, and change.

Lawrence's younger contemporary, Eldzier Cortor, approached the same problem – that of individual African-American identity in the United States, where the bulk of the white population refused to believe such a thing was possible – in a slightly different fashion. His early work of portraiture *Peeling Potatoes* (1939) is of a piece with the broader, wide-ranging fetish with "the folk" and echoes some of the details of *They were very poor*. It could be set in Chicago, or Mobile, or anywhere. A small potbellied stove sits in the background, and a cast-iron pot half full with peeled potatoes sits at the foot of a black man seated in a plain wooden chair and wearing a rumpled suit and hat. The man smokes a cigarette, which is nearly finished, and is bent awkwardly, holding a small paring knife in his right hand and a potato in his left. A small, spiral peel drifts downward into the pot. Like the man and woman seated at Lawrence's spare table, the subject of Cortor's study looks off into the middle space; an indecipherable expression matches the unknowable object upon which his gaze is affixed. His eyes are solidly black, with no iris and no pupil – reminiscent of Lawrence's refusal to come close to stereotype – and the finer details of his face are captured in careful shadings. Cortor chose a light brown paper for the painting, so the question of skin color is addressed at a great distance. There is something in the man's furrowed brow, his pursed lips, his softened eyes, and tilted head that suggest sadness, or melancholy. The artist went to extraordinary lengths here to render this man's face in great detail, and without a hint of jubilation, contentment, or satisfaction. Strikingly reminiscent of Lange's *Migrant Mother*, *Peeling Potatoes* is, then, a reminder that great sadness, personal disillusionment, and quiet, manly suffering, attributes that were often not thought possible for "the Negro," are the surest evidence of individual humanity.

These artists worked in a strange, tumultuous moment in American history, where older patterns of racism existed alongside new possibilities. Despite the pervasiveness of racism in the Depression era, the New Deal, as an expression of an expanding nation-state, offered basic liberties and rights to ever larger numbers of citizens and, in doing so, offered African Americans some small measure of hope that they might be next in line. Indeed, as federal patronage, the New Deal was a welcome, if entirely unreliable means of support. For talented artists, work with the WPA could open the door for a new series of murals, a steady paycheck, and even professional training. For sharecroppers in the deep South, it could mean little, if anything, as resources were allocated federally to the specific "alphabet soup" agencies, but distributed on a local level by men who were often unsympathetic to "the Negro." But it was surely better than nothing. In terms of nationalism, with its "race-based notions of belonging" (Gerstle 2001: 178), African Americans were largely left out of the American family. When one surveys all of Frank Capra's documentary efforts to boost the war effort, it doesn't take long to note that only African Americans found their contributions shuffled off into a separate, segregated film, *The Negro Soldier.* But at least the film was made. If Franklin Delano Roosevelt was a genteel patriarch for the troubled United States, it was also true that he avoided photo opportunities that featured him in a warm handshake, or friendly embrace, with black people. But most African Americans knew that Walter White, Mary McLeod Bethune, and others had regular, if informal, access to the President and his advisors. And his wife, Eleanor, and some in his political party seemed to care an awful lot about civil rights. After 40 years in the desert, a glass of water – even when only half full – could make all the difference.

Harvard Sitkoff once wrote that "all revolutions begin with a trickle" (Sitkoff 1978: 58). That trickle, in this case, flowed North. Over the 1920s and 1930s, the Great Migration had brought larger numbers of African Americans into cities, where long-standing political machines, many of them associated with the Northern wing of the Democratic Party), were used to court diverse groups of voters segregated into small ethnic enclaves. In 1928, former New York Governor Al Smith's campaign for President drew quietly upon the support of black leaders, establishing a beachhead that would be expanded in the next election. Roosevelt's predecessor, Herbert Hoover, may have beaten Smith at the ballot, but he had also alienated African Americans during the early years of the Depression, and had seemed to have no interest in improving race relations. In 1932, disgusted with the results of loyalty to Hoover, Robert Vann, the influential editor of the black newspaper the *Pittsburgh Courier,* reached out to the Democrats, and urged his readers to give up their "blind partisan-ism and patriotism" (quoted in Weiss 1983: 14). Once in office, Roosevelt labored, in carefully choreographed New Deal concessions and through the work of his wife, to show that his administration and his party were more attentive to the needs of "the Negro" than were the Republicans, who may well have been the "party of Lincoln," but who had just as clearly come to take the black vote for granted. The Southern wing of the Democratic party was, of course, a backer of Jim Crow, and so Roosevelt had to move carefully to press for the New Deal reforms above all else. By the end of the New Deal, though, it was possible for some in the Democratic party to imagine African Americans as an important swing vote, with practical group needs that could be addressed by a tolerant, liberal nation state. Thus, even as audiences clucked over Prissy's comedic squeals on the silver screen, and enjoyed laughter at Mammy's expense, partisans in the Democratic Party were listening to the Black Cabinet, dispensing administration officials to the deep South to mediate disputes between Negrophobes and sharecroppers, and conceiving of "the Negro problem" as a serious national political issue, worthy of attention and supervision by the federal government.

Conclusion

At the advent of the American Century, then, "the Negro" had become an "American Dilemma" rather than "the Southerner's Problem" (Myrdal 1944/1962). World War II had created a demand for even more labor in the North, and sparked a second Great Migration, accelerating the establishment of new loyalties, settlement patterns, and cultural dynamics across the country. The change in location over the first half of the twentieth century, or the national outmigration from the South, had brought blackness to the center of American culture. It had also prepared African-American activists for the battles yet to come, and given the black community mastery of the very tools – the law, social science data, and the arts – that had once been used only to justify repression and control. Indeed, in their experience with the Democratic Party, with the Communist Party, and with emerging struggles over their role as citizens in a republic imperiled by the Depression, African Americans gained some small amount of hope for the future, and tangible organizing skills for the coming civil rights movement. Out of the deep South, where Communists had fought to unionize black sharecroppers, came a history of quiet, determined solidarity across rural spaces, a lasting precedent for voter registration drives. Out of the North came other, more conflicted, lessons. There was, famously, Roosevelt's "Black Cabinet." There was a renewed sense of political power and patriotism, best captured in the work of African-American activists to equate fascism with racism, and Nazism with Jim Crow, in a "Double V" campaign designed to win the war abroad and the fight against racism at home. And in 1941, when A. Phillip Randolph organized the March on Washington Movement – threatening to march thousands of angry African Americans into a predominantly Southern city – he also extracted from Roosevelt a promise of a Fair Employment Practices Committee, establishing a model for domestic diplomacy between the leadership classes of the races, one that would be used and reused over the next 25 years.

The other side of hope, of course, was despair. In 1943, when rumors spread like wildfire through Harlem that a black GI had been killed by the police, the resulting devastating race riot presaged the later violence of Watts, Detroit, and Newark. Newly integrated cities featured rigidly segregated neighborhoods, deteriorating social conditions, and deepening class divisions, a "ticking time bomb," as Thomas Sugrue calls it,[1] for the postwar violence of the North and the simultaneous creation of a suburban safety valve for disaffected whites, who hoped to better themselves by moving out of the newly blackened cityscape. Warfare along the color line was brutal, and often deadly. Out of these tragic circumstances – out of "the horror of Negro life in the United States" – came men and women like Richard Wright's "Bigger Thomas," representatives of the grimmer side of blackness, "dense" and "heavy," as Wright put it, "shadows athwart our national life" (Wright 1940/1988: 461, 462). At its very worst, black life in the United States – whether rural or urban, North or South – would remind thoughtful Americans of the attempted extermination of the Jews, which followed their confinement into the ghettos of Europe, leaving the nation open to the charge that it cared little about civil rights, and even less about the emerging conception of human rights. At mid-century, then, it was unclear whether the Bigger Thomases of the dystopian North – let alone the "better classes" of black America – could ever enjoy the benefits of full citizenship and fair play, or whether the long-dreamed-of integration of law schools, workplaces, and social clubs would offer them a chance at a better life, or a better world for their children.

NOTE

1   This is the title of the second chapter in Sugrue (1996).

REFERENCES AND FURTHER READING

Allen, James, Jon Lewis, Leon Litwack, and Hilton Als (eds). (2000). *Without Sanctuary: Lynching Photography in America.* Santa Fe, NM: Twin Palms Publishers.

Anderson, Carol. (2003). *Eyes Off the Prize: The United Nations and the African American Struggle for Human Rights.* New York: Cambridge University Press.

Baker, Houston. (1989). *Modernism and the Harlem Renaissance.* Chicago: University of Chicago Press.

Baker, Houston. (2001). *Turning South Again: Re-Thinking Modernism/Re-Reading Booker T. Washington.* Durham, NC: Duke University Press.

Berlin, Ira, Marc Favreau, and Steven F. Miller (eds). (1998). *Remembering Slavery: African Americans Talk About Their Personal Experiences of Slavery and Emancipation.* New York: New Press.

Blum, Edward. (2004). *Reforging the White Republic: Race, Religion, and American Nationalism, 1865-1898.* Baton Rogue: Louisiana State University Press.

Dixon, Thomas Jr. (1902). *The Leopard's Spots, a Romance of the White Man's Burden.* New York: Doubleday, Page, & Co.

Douglas, Ann. (1996). *Terrible Honesty: Mongrel Manhattan in the 1920s.* New York: Farrar, Straus, & Giroux.

Du Bois, W. E. B. (1903/1989). *The Souls of Black Folk.* New York: Bantam.

Du Bois, W. E. B. (1928/1995). *Dark Princess: A Romance.* Jackson: University of Mississippi Press.

Fireside, Harvey. (2005). *Separate and Unequal: Homer Plessy and the Decision that Legalized Racism.* New York: Carroll & Graf.

Gerstle, Gary. (2001). *American Crucible: Race and Nation in the Twentieth Century.* Princeton, NJ: Princeton University Press.

Guterl, Matthew Pratt. (2001). *The Color of Race in America, 1900-1940.* Cambridge, MA: Harvard University Press.

Harlan, Louis. (1986). *Booker T. Washington: Wizard of Tuskegee, 1901-1915.* New York: Oxford University Press.

Hughes, Langston. (1996). Cora unashamed. In *Langston Hughes: Short Stories*, ed. Akiba Sullivan Harper (pp. 40–9). New York: Hill & Wang.

Hughes, Robert. (1997). *American Visions: The Epic History of Art in America.* New York: Alfred A. Knopf.

Hutchinson, George. (1995). *The Harlem Renaissance in Black and White*. Cambridge, MA: Harvard University Press.

Hutchinson, George. (2006). *In Search of Nella Larsen: A Biography of the Color Line*. Cambridge, MA: Harvard University Press.

Jacobson, Matthew Frye. (1998). *Whiteness of a Different Color: European Immigrants and the Alchemy of Race*. Cambridge, MA: Harvard University Press.

Johnson, Charles S. (1925). The vanishing mulatto. *Opportunity* October: 291.

Kelley, Robin D. G. (1990). *Hammer and Hoe: Alabama Communists During the Great Depression*. Chapel Hill: University of North Carolina Press.

Levine, Lawrence. (1993). *The Unpredictable Past: Explorations in American Cultural History*. New York: Oxford University Press.

Lewis, David Levering. (1979). *When Harlem Was in Vogue*. New York: Alfred A. Knopf.

Lewis, David Levering. (1993). *W. E. B. Du Bois: Biography of a Race, 1868-1919*. New York: Henry Holt.

Lewis, David Levering. (1997). Preface to the Penguin edition. *When Harlem Was in Vogue*. New York: Penguin Press.

Locke, Alain. (1925/1992). Foreword. *The New Negro* (pp. xxv–xxvii). New York: Touchstone.

MacLean, Nancy. (1994). *Behind the Mask of Chivalry: The Making of the Second Ku Klux Klan*. New York: Oxford University Press.

Martin, Tony. (1976). *Race First: The Ideological and Organizational Struggles of Marcus Garvey and the Universal Negro Improvement Association*. Dover, MA: Majority Press.

McGerr, Michael. (2003). *A Fierce Discontent: The Rise and Fall of the Progressive Movement in America, 1870-1920*. New York: Free Press.

Mitchell, Margaret. (1936/1999). *Gone with the Wind*. New York: Warner Books.

Myrdal, Gunnar. (1944/1962). *An American Dilemma: The Negro Problem and Modern Democracy*. New York: HarperCollins.

Oshinsky, David. (1997). *Worse than Slavery: Parchman Farm and the Ordeal of Jim Crow Justice*. New York: Free Press.

Page, Thomas Nelson. (1904/1970). *The Negro: The Southerner's Problem*. New York: Johnson Reprint.

Sitkoff, Harvard. (1978). *A New Deal for Blacks: The Emergence of Civil Rights as a National Issue: The Depression Decade*. New York: Oxford University Press.

Stoddard, Lothrop. (1927). *Re-Forging of America*. New York: Charles Scribner's Sons.

Sugrue, Thomas J. (1996). *Origins of the Urban Crisis: Race and Inequality in Postwar Detroit*. Princeton, NJ: Princeton University Press.

Sullivan, Patricia. (1996). *Days of Hope: Race and Democracy in the New Deal Era*. Chapel Hill: University of North Carolina Press.

Toomer, Jean. (n.d.). America and problems. Jean Toomer Papers, Bieneke Rare Book and Manuscript Library, Yale University.

Vasconcelos, José. (1925/1997). *La Raza Cosmica*. Baltimore, MD: Johns Hopkins University Press.

Washington, Booker T. (1901/1965). *Up From Slavery*. In *Three Negro Classics*, ed. John Hope Franklin. New York: Avon Books.

Weiss, Nancy J. (1983). *Farewell to the Party of Lincoln: Black Politics in the Age of FDR*. Princeton, NJ: Princeton University Press.

Williamson, Joel. (1986). *A Rage for Order: Black-White Relations in the American South Since Emancipation*. New York: Oxford University Press.

Wood, Peter H. (2004). *Weathering the Storm: Inside Winslow Homer's Gulf Stream*. Athens: University of Georgia Press.

Wright, Richard. (1940/1998). How Bigger was born. In *Native Son* (pp. 433–62). New York: Perennial Classics.

4
Pragmatism, Power, and the Politics of Aesthetic Experience

Jeanne Follansbee Quinn

In the culminating scene of "Long Black Song," the third and central story in *Uncle Tom's Children*, Richard Wright's 1940 collection of stories,[1] Sarah watches helplessly from a knoll above her house as a lynch mob seeks retribution for her husband's murder of a white gramophone salesman. As the cars approach, Sarah experiences a moment in which she senses a still-inchoate link between the black and white men who are poised to kill each other.

> Somehow, men, black men and white men, land and houses, green cornfields and grey skies, gladness and dreams, were all a part of that which made life good. Yes, somehow, they were linked, like the spokes in a spinning wagon wheel. She felt they were. She knew they were. She felt it when she breathed and knew it when she looked. But she could not say how; she could not put her finger on it and when she thought hard about it it became all mixed up, like milk spilling suddenly. Or else it knotted in her throat and chest in a hard aching lump, like the one she felt now. (Wright 1940/1993: 154)

The scene captures a stunning contradiction between Sarah's vision of natural racial harmony and the "old river of blood" enacted in the violent conflict between her husband, Silas, and his white adversaries (p. 154). The abstract image of black and white men interconnected like the spokes of a wagon wheel stands in stark contrast to the knot in her throat as she witnesses Silas's murder played out with shotguns and flames below. Wright's use of the figurative "knot" to describe the tightening in Sarah's throat conjures up the literal knots around the necks of lynching victims and suggests that Sarah's *body* registers her sympathy with Silas even as she *imagines* a "link" between the adversaries below. In spite of the image of racial harmony, Sarah's knotted throat destabilizes rather than affirms a clear sense of connection between the races. Her moment of epiphany produces a multiplicity of feelings and only the most vague awareness of "that which made life good." Instead of "*claritas*" (the term Stephen Dedalus uses in Joyce's *A Portrait of the Artist* to describe the radiant wholeness of aesthetic effect), Sarah's moment of intense aesthetic perception unravels into a chaotic mass of contradictory thoughts and feelings. Although she at first responds to the harmonies of natural color – among men, among fields and skies – and fashions a simile to capture her intuition of order, she ultimately cannot articulate "how" the men she watches might be interconnected in a good life. Not only does the answer escape her grasp; the attempt to formulate an answer results in increased complexity, not clarity of vision. Thoughts become "mixed up"; ideas get upturned "like milk spilling suddenly"; feelings become "knotted" and "hard," like a rope around her throat.

Sarah's vision dramatizes her oscillation between two unsatisfactory conceptions of social connection: liberal universalism and "blood" politics. While Sarah longs for brotherhood – she conjoins the races just as she links "land and houses," "green corn-fields and grey skies" – the simile of the spinning wagon wheel remains an abstract and impotent image when juxtaposed with nooses, flames, and real blood spilled in violent confrontations between the races. Wright represents Sarah's moment of aesthetic perception as a moment of paralysis born of her inability to escape an impossible choice: to identify with her vision of interracial brotherhood is to deny the violent deaths of Silas and other black men and women; to identify with Silas is to reproduce the conditions of his annihilation. It is Sarah's inability to resolve the contradiction between abstract and blood kinship that leads to the deconstruction of clarity in her moment of aesthetic perception.

Sarah's moment of aesthetic confusion dramatizes a central preoccupation for writers in the 1930s: what role does aesthetic experience play in the social world? And, by extension, what kind of cultural work does literature – as a spur to aesthetic experience – do to promote social and economic justice? "Long Black Song" connects a story about the devastating effects of racism and the consequences of racial solidarity with a self-conscious exploration of the efficacy of aesthetic experience. In so doing, Wright acknowledges the intricate connections between representation and social power. "Long Black Song," like the other stories in *Uncle Tom's Children*, suggests that the "truth" about race is not biological but social: "Race" emerges through the institutionalized enforcement of certain differences (but not others), which, in turn, produce a social script that naturalizes and reproduces those boundaries. Wright represents the constraints of the social script as inexorable and inevitable. In story after story, a black male protagonist is annihilated either literally or symbolically in brutal confrontations with white vigilantes who "police" racial boundaries. Wright explicitly links the violent destruction of these black men to his own experience of "living Jim Crow," establishing a continuum between the symbolic violence of his confrontation with racist antagonists in "Ethics" and the mob violence that destroys black protagonists like Bobo, Mann, Silas, and Johnny Boy in the ensuing stories.

By characterizing "living Jim Crow" as a dangerous but always scripted drama, Wright depicts "race" as a *representation* enacted through social roles that have material consequences. Distinguishing race as a sociocultural representation does not make it any less real, and, in fact, the stories are relentlessly pessimistic about the possibility of change. Still, if representations are ultimately (linguistic) "fictions," does this mean that they may be malleable? In short, can "race" be "rewritten"? I see "Long Black Song" – and Sarah's subjectivity in particular – as a self-reflexive moment of exploration in which Wright considers the sociocultural effects of his own practice as a writer. Sarah's rapturous engagement with the natural world and with the gramophone music precipitates the bloody confrontation between Silas and the lynch mob, suggesting the dangers of aesthetic experience. But it also generates Sarah's dawning sense that her paralysis comes from the ongoing cycle of violence she has imbibed and the broader implication that *reimagining* relations between the races might be the place to begin reshaping society.

Wright's depiction of Sarah's moment of perception offers an extended consideration of the somatic and political effects of aesthetic experience – and identification – in the context of cultural debates in the period about the efficacy of literary representation. The "work" of identification shaped this debate, as critics explored, expounded on, and exchanged theoretical and practical accounts of the mechanics, as well as the effects, of aesthetic experience. While the discourse of aesthetics long precedes these debates, the economic and social crisis of the 1930s produced a concurrent crisis in representation that provoked renewed interest in the ethical dimensions of aesthetic discourse. As Kenneth Burke observed about criticism in the 1930s, "a large portion of it was written . . . during a period of stress that forced upon all of us the need to decide exactly wherein the work and efficacy of a literary work reside" (Burke 1953: x). At stake in these extensive and often contentious debates was a contest over the ontological properties of "art." Most critics agreed that "art" produced "identification" – which Burke defined as "one's mental and material ways of placing oneself in groups" (Burke 1941/1973: 227) – and that identification offered a means for producing new structures of feeling. The tricky question for critics centered on the meaning and social significance of those new habits of thought.

Wright's dramatization of aesthetic experience in "Long Black Song" provides a means for reconstructing a portion of the critical debate on identification. In addition, the story's exploration of aesthetic experience makes visible a desire for, and an attempt to construct, an alternative to the unsatisfactory politics of liberalism and Marxism. Representations of aesthetic experience proliferate in *Uncle Tom's Children*, but it is in "Long Black Song" that Wright most explicitly grapples with alternatives to the modernist epiphany and the proletarian conversion as modes of identification. Sarah's moment – with its emphasis on confusion, its rejection of blood politics, and its grappling for new words to describe alternative social relations – reflects Wright's engagement with pragmatist aesthetics and politics, which he absorbed through his association with Kenneth Burke and his relationship with other black intellectuals. Pragmatism coalesced around a set of practices, rather than principles, that challenged fixed categories of intellectual and political identity, particularly binaries. By privileging multiplicity, irresolvability, "remainders," and, most crucially, human agency, pragmatism offered Wright a strategy for negotiating the formal limits of socialist realism for representing black experience. Pragmatist aesthetics, like pragmatist politics, recognized difference, assuming *identification* without insisting on *identity*.

By making the subject of aesthetic experience black, however, Wright challenges and complicates pragmatist conceptions of "nonidentity" and justice by showing the effects of power on the construction of black subjectivity (Posnock 1992: 37). Sarah's doubly marginal position – as black and female – garners only ambivalent sympathy from Wright. She emerges as both pitiful and dangerous, as both marginal and as a projection of black male disempowerment. Yet she remains: an unaccounted-for remnant of racial conflict in the Jim Crow South. Most critics have read Wright's depiction of Sarah as evidence of his misogyny and his anxiety about the impossibility of black manhood in a racist society. However, I want to suggest that Sarah represents Wright's complex – and self-conscious – engagement with his own social position as a black male writer. The construction of gender in the story, then, reflects both Wright's view of the effects of racism on the male subject and his anxiety about the feminization of aesthetic experience and the marginalization of the black writer.

Art's Special Knowledge: Identification and the Aesthetics of Cognition

For Wright and other writers, interest in the cultural work of identification occurred in the wake of I. A. Richards's empirical investigation of psychological responses to poetry and in the context of English translations of Western Marxists like Lukács, both of which first appeared in the United States in the late 1920s. Writers in the 1930s were preoccupied with identification *because* they were critical of post-Crash economic and social conditions. If authors could make readers identify with particular people or interests, the thinking went, they might promote action on behalf of interests not their own. But Sarah's paralysis points, in particular, to the limitations of both liberal universalism and identity politics, positions that correlate with the aesthetic "poles" Alfred Kazin (1942/1982: 402) associated with formalism and Marxism. In dramatizing Sarah's rejection of both *political* options, Wright points to the existential impasse of the black subject and to an essentialism common to both *aesthetic* projects. Moreover, it demonstrates Wright's engagement with contemporary debates about identification. The work of identification in "Long Black Song" emphasizes the role of feeling over cognition in the construction of subjectivity, a position that distances his representation from the mimetic forms of representation championed by both formalist and Marxist theories of the "work" of art.

By dramatizing the *limitations* of cognition and the *power* of irrational habits of thought, Wright challenges critics at both ends of the political spectrum – Agrarian John Crowe Ransom and *New Masses* editor Mike Gold – and carves out an aesthetics and a politics that *use* alienation and lack of clarity as tools, to paraphrase Ralph Ellison, for slipping the yoke (Posnock 1998a: 63–4). For both Ransom and Gold, identification was a *cognitive* experience – an incorporation of art's special knowledge – that occurred when people recognized and absorbed a set of values conveyed through typical characters and situations. According to Ransom, who developed his aesthetic theory in a series of essays collected in *The World's Body* (1938), literary works helped individuals develop a "new kind of knowledge," which equipped them to resist the "instinctive necessity" to acquire and consume (Ransom 1938: 45, 44). Ransom assigned literary forms the cultural work of disciplining "natural" human instincts and training individuals to participate in "civilization" (p. 42). Like the Romantic cultural critics who preceded him, Ransom asserted that culture stood against economic liberalism run amuck. According to Ransom, identification produced a metaphorical disembodiment which altered the mind so that "when we come back to our own world there begins in us a different style of consciousness altogether" (p. 70). Where Ransom looked to identification to help people discover enduring human values, Mike Gold argued that identification could trigger a conversion experience that would transform an unself-conscious working class into a self-conscious proletariat. In outlining the tenets of proletarian realism in a 1930 *New Masses* essay, Gold argued that literature would represent workers' experience with "technical precision," thus allowing more direct access to that experience (Gold 1930: 5). Gold rejected literature that distorted reality, calling instead for "facts": "Facts are the new poetry. The proletarian writer . . . will work with facts. Facts are his strength. Facts are his passion. . . . Facts create their own form" (Gold 1931a: 13). If proletarian literature did its work, identification would help rebuild a more just society by rebuilding the affective structures of the working class. Class solidarity could be born when readers identified with authentic representations of workers' experience in order to be infused "with the emotional habits of Communism" (Gold 1931b: 12).

Ransom and Gold held distinctly different conceptions of subjectivity, yet their work reveals surprisingly similar views on the *process* of identification. For Ransom, identity was an *a priori* human attribute. He assumed autonomous individuals who possessed the freedom necessary to oppose capitalism and freely choose the traditional, precapitalist society he favored. Thus, for Ransom, identification entailed recognizing a dissonance between the organization of the modern world and the truth about human beings and their lives. Gold, on the other hand, argued that the subject was through and through a product of economic structures. While this perspective implies that subjects are malleable constructions of external conditions, Gold's notion of aesthetic identification reflects a similar underlying essentialism. Both see identification as a process for uncovering a concealed identity, thus making visible the previously invisible organization of the world. For Ransom, identification helped people recognize fundamental truths about human experience. For Gold, identification revealed the truth about experience as well, but that truth centered on workers and the experience of the working class. Both argued that accurate representations of contemporary life facilitated the criticism of current economic and social structures. Moreover, both positions asserted that art produced a special kind of knowledge. In short, both positions reflected a commitment to *mimetic* rather than *hortatory* forms of representation.

While I argue that these critics shared a commitment to mimesis – and, I would add, to criticizing capitalism – I do not claim that their aesthetic projects did the same work. In fact, Ransom's and Gold's *politics* pointed them toward very different roles for mimesis. Where Ransom imagined imitating nature as a means for recovering what had been previously (and, perhaps, irrevocably) lost, Gold, following Lukács, imagined mimesis as a means for generating catharsis. For Ransom, mimesis allowed the revelation of "human value" and of "love," which he associated with resistance to any idealizing or rationalizing impulse (Ransom 1938: 207, 208). Gold, on the other hand, embraced Lukács's formulation of socialist realism, in which viewers, who perceived the real conditions of modern life, mimetically (and dialectically) represented, experienced a catharsis that " 'suspend[ed]' everyday life" and allowed a new perspective on the world (quoted in Fekete 1977: 225). This catharsis could not be produced by abstract doctrine or by "tendentiousness," but only through the dialectical representation of reality (Lukács 1934: 44). For both critics, identification occurred by stripping away dangerous illusions to reveal the underlying structures that organized the world. Both positions required the exchange of a flawed or incomplete view of the world for another, more complete, view that occurred by activating a latent sense of identity in readers, a realization of their "true" human nature or class position. For both critics, aesthetic experience precipitated the alignment of subjects with already known, already established categories of social experience.

Identification Without Identity: Pragmatism and the Aesthetics of Contradiction

As Sarah's experience suggests, there is no singular truth to be embraced. While poised to witness Silas's inevitable immolation, she felt *both* the possibility of human brotherhood *and* the pull of racial identification. Wright's depiction of Sarah's confusion, of her *lack* of clarity, speaks not only to the limitations in theories of aesthetic experience I've outlined above, but also to the idea that aesthetic experience is not universal, but is grounded in historical specificity. The experience of white supremacy generates both the somatic knot in Sarah's throat and the organization of Sarah's vision, which Wright depicts through a series of pairings that proceed from the originating opposition of "black men and white men." Her experience as a farmer's wife provides the specific imagery – the "green cornfields and grey skies," "the spinning wagon wheel," the spilled milk – while her role as witness to a lifetime of vigilante violence against black men produces the sense that "men killing and being killed" has all happened before (Wright 1940/1993: 155). While Wright's essentialist construction of gender seems to belie the historicity of his depiction of race, his representation of female desire works metaphorically to figure the violation – or impossibility – of black subjectivity. Sarah's confusion, then, points to the racial bias of both Ransom's and Gold's theories. Ransom's ahistorical universalism cannot account for the specificity of aesthetic experience or the structuring effect of differences in power. Gold's theory, while it recognizes the historical construction of subjects, cannot negotiate the effects of *racial* experience on the production of class consciousness.

Because Wright depicts this moment from Sarah's point of view, the narrative structure positions readers as witnesses to Sarah's response as well as to events occurring below. We are invited to share Sarah's horror and confusion as we figuratively witness the violence through her eyes, helpless, like Sarah, to intervene as we watch the conflagration below. Wright's narrative strategy dramatizes the convergence of the aesthetic and political experiences of identification, where the *aesthetic* experience of affinity with the characters and situations in literature maps onto the *political* experience of allying oneself with a particular set of social or economic interests. We, like Sarah, see the impossibility of choice, while, simultaneously, the situation invites our outrage at the injustice we witness. I say "we" here meaning readers, but let me clarify by saying that the "we" who read *Uncle Tom's Children* when it was published in 1938 and again in 1940 were largely white and middle-class, despite the significant attention the book received in the black and radical presses (Fabre 1993: 161–2). In fact, Eleanor Roosevelt mentioned the book in her regular newspaper column, prompting a surge in sales (Fabre 1993: xviii). Wright admitted later, in "How 'Bigger' Was Born," that the ease with which white readers deflected his critique of racism in *Uncle Tom's Children* troubled him, but "Long Black Song" seems to anticipate the impotence of its representation of racial violence, and it reflects Wright's ambivalence about the transformative power of aesthetic experience.

The story's expressionism distinguishes "Long Black Song" from the other stories in *Uncle Tom's Children* that employ a more characteristically naturalist style. While the representation of Silas's decision to fight back fits within the trajectory of the volume's depiction of the development of a collective multiracial class consciousness, the lyrical depiction of Sarah's consciousness reveals the influence of modernist writers from Stein to Joyce. Wright's decision to fuse the socialist realism he learned as a member of the John Reed Club with modernist expressionism points to Wright's awareness that socialist realism alone might not produce social action. The story's expressionism – located in Wright's representation of Sarah's consciousness – opens up an exploration of the role of aesthetic experience in the production of the subject. More broadly, I suggest that the eclecticism of Wright's aesthetic here reveals his growing disenchantment with the limitations of socialist realism for depicting black experience, as well as his evolving materialist conception of language as an agent for *reorienting* as well as *representing* the world. Wright's polemical impulse finds expression, I claim, through his engagement with pragmatism.

Wright's pragmatism reveals his debt to black intellectuals' incorporation of pragmatist ideas about culture and language, as well as Wright's own contact with works by William James, John Dewey, and Kenneth Burke. Pragmatist ideas circulated through a network of personal and professional affiliations in the first half of the twentieth century, but this network is best understood not as a "school" or "genealogy," but rather as a constellation of overlapping, related, but nonidentical interests. Black intellectuals, beginning with Alain Locke and W. E. B. Du Bois, who studied with James at Harvard, embraced pragmatism's nonessentialist stance as a strategy for challenging racism. Pragmatism's historicism, its skepticism of the logic of identity – philosophical and social, its emphasis on future-looking, creative improvisation, and its embrace of mixture, context, contingency, and "transitions," offered a means for constructing an anti-imperialist, antiracist, democratic politics. For Locke and Du Bois, James's pluralism, with its celebration of "no complete generalization, no total point of view, no all-pervasive unity, but everywhere some residual resistance to verbalization, formulation, and discursification" suggested the malleability of social conditions and the possibility for social change (James 1987: 1312–13). Both Locke and Du Bois absorbed pragmatism's emphasis on the histori-cal contingency of cultural formations to critique biological theories of race and to locate racism in the social practice of racial distinction. As Wright was to say later, in *White Man, Listen!*, "Negroes are Negroes because they are treated as Negroes" (Wright 1957/1995: 108). This view was amplified by Wright's exposure to the cultural relativism of Boasian anthropology, which similarly rejected fixed biological and cultural categories.

Franz Boas's work influenced a generation of social scientists, including Chicago School sociologist Robert E. Park, who studied with Dewey at Michigan and, later, with James at Harvard (Hutchinson 1995: 51–2). Chicago sociologists Louis Wirth and E. Franklin Frazier, both friends of Wright's, helped shape Wright's view of black experience and his conception of the social role of the black writer (Fabre 1993: 232, 1985: 192, Cappetti 1993: 266). Wright's engagement with the Chicago School included his Introduction to St. Clair Drake and Horace R. Cayton's 1945 study of black life in urban Chicago, *Black Metropolis*, where he quoted *Principles of Psychology*. Drawing on James's account of the production of the "social self" through the reci-procity of social relations, Wright highlighted James's condemnation of the " 'fiendish punishment' " of " 'going unnoticed' " or "being 'cut dead' " to describe the experience of racial segregation (Wright in Drake and Cayton 1945/1993: xxxii).

The pragmatist orientation towards culture emphasized representation, exploring the *usefulness* of ideas in practice rather than their *truthfulness* as propositions. The pragmatist resistance to identity produced a concomitant view of language, which similarly resisted identity – or fixed meanings – and privileged linguistic skepticism, preferring "transitions," "unreconciled diversity," and "what is left over" (James 1987: 1181, Dewey 1994: 41, 48). Rather than viewing language as identical to the modes of thought it represented – a view that conceived of language as a form of knowledge rather than a tool – pragmatists recognized the lability of language, and thus the contingency of interpretations of social relations. Moreover, pragmatists explored the potential of nonlinguistic and prelinguistic somatic experience for shaping language. In these "transitional" moments of bodily, noncognitive perception, pragmatists laid the groundwork for their view of culture as always becoming (though not necessarily always evolving) and, hence, as always revisable. Locke and Du Bois grasped the social potential in these ideas, while American literary modernists, including James's former student Gertrude Stein, grasped their aesthetic potential. Stein's experiments with language and the representation of black vernacular speech in her 1909 story "Melanctha" galvanized Wright and influenced his expressionism, particularly in "Long Black Song."

Pragmatism's conception of language – and, therefore, its conception of aesthetic experience – proceeded from its rejection of the notion of the "autonomous" subject as well as its belief in the possibility of human agency. By rejecting the notion of autonomous subjects in favor of what Burke called "the realistic position . . . that treats *individuals as members of a group*," identification became an expression of "both positive and negative responses to authority" and the range of "material interests" possible among complex social actors (Burke 1941/1973: 226, 227). According to John Dewey, in "Individualism Old and New," the modern subject, unlike the Lockean liberal subject, was shaped in a "collective age" and constituted by a reciprocity between self and society (Dewey 1930/1981: 57). In *The Public and Its Problems*, Dewey insisted: "The idea of a natural individual in his isolation possessed of full-fledged wants . . . is as much a fiction in psychology as the doctrine of the individual in possession of antecedent political rights is one in politics" (Dewey 1927: 102). The complexity of multiple, overlapping, and even contradictory identities was the result of the ideological production of the subject. As Burke observed, "*in this complex world, one is never a member of merely* one '*corporation.' The individual is composed of many 'corporate' identities. Sometimes they are concentric, sometimes in conflict*" (Burke 1941/1973: 307). For Burke, the subject was simultaneously the product of these identities and never wholly determined by any of them. Though constituted by ideology – or through what Burke called "allegiance" to "*symbols of authority*" (p. 305) – subjects' multiple "identities" allowed the possibility of human agency, particularly during "*highly transitional eras, requiring shifts in allegiance to the symbols of authority*" (pp. 305, 307). Individuals' experience, as subjects, at the intersection between unconscious ideological formation and conscious affiliation or alienation, necessitated identification (or "allegiance") as "equipment for living" (p. 293).

Pragmatist identification did not require an *identity* of experience, but its *reorientation*. As Dewey argued in *Art as Experience*, "the interests . . . of another become an *expansion* of our own being" (Dewey 1934: 334). When "limiting prejudices melt away," we don't inhabit another's experience, nor do we abandon our own. Instead, new perspectives are, as he claims, "built into our own structure" (p. 336). Dewey's emphasis on *process* – on seeing, hearing, building – suggests the fluidity of identity and identification. Unlike liberal conceptions of identification based on the notion of a common humanity, or Marxist conceptions based on recognizing oneself as a member of a class, pragmatists insisted that identifications were necessarily partial, overlapping, and strategic. Experience could be reoriented by those who were like us as well as by those who were not. In fact, identification, as Burke argued, marked social division, not identity. According to Burke: "In being identified with B, A is 'substantially one' with a person other than himself. Yet at the same time he remains unique . . . at once a distinct substance and consubstantial with another." Identification forced people "to confront the implications of *division*," Burke claimed, for identification "is compensatory to division" (Burke 1952: 21, 22). While misgivings about social, ethnic, and economic "divisions" preoccupied Burke and Dewey (as well as Randolph Bourne and Horace Kallen), black intellectuals understood "division" as the product of systems of rationalization that legitimated – and obscured – the unequal distribution of social and economic power. For Du Bois and for Wright, attacking the assumed logic of social inequality meant targeting the systems of rationalization that made segregation seem like a commonsense answer to racial "division."

Sarah's devolution into irresolvable and "mixed up" thoughts and feelings speaks not only to the intricacies of interracial social relations and the brutality of interracial violence. Wright's representation of Sarah's intense aesthetic perception also suggests that the truth of her vision resides precisely in its irresolvable complexity. As Burke points out, "'poetic' meaning . . . derive[s] its vision from the maximum *heaping up* of . . . emotional factors, playing them off against one another, inviting them to reinforce and contradict one another, and seeking to make this active participation itself a major ingredient of the vision" (Burke 1941/1973: 148). Wright "heap[s] up" the contradictions in the story, a tactic that also allows him to explore the social efficacy of aesthetic perception. Sarah's moment captures some of the inexplicability of racism, but it also challenges the impulse towards clarity – aesthetic and political. Wright implies a parallel between moments of aesthetic clarity and political solutions that entail abstracting out ambiguity and simplifying complex relationships. His aesthetic emphasizes the fluid, the "nonidentical," over the "fascist," which Wright associates with a "social order [conceived] as changeless and eternal" (quoted in Miller 1990: 179). In "Long Black Song," Wright seems to privilege Sarah's aesthetic experience precisely because it resists simplification.

Associating aesthetic simplification with a fascist social order reveals a broader context for Wright's exploration of aesthetic experience in the widespread anxiety about the encroachment of European fascism, "Southern style." "Fascism" proved a capacious accusation for leftist critics: their concerns clustered around antidemocratic, antiliberal, antilabor, and nativist activities with excessively militaristic, nationalistic, or racist components. The South, in particular, was accused of "brewing a [fascist] poison composed of equal measures of anti-New Deal, anti-union, anti-leftist, anti-Semitic, and anti-Negro bigotry" (Sitkoff 1978: 122). For if any region in the US seemed ripe to produce a fascist-style "dictator," it was the South, home of the "Dixie demagogue." In a region shaped by paternalism, a tradition of racial scapegoating, a disposition toward capital rather than labor, and a post-Reconstruction history of single-party rule, spell-binding speakers with iron-fisted control over state and local politics like Mississippi's Theodore Bilbo, Georgia's Gene Talmadge and, especially, Louisiana's Huey Long seemed poised to take the South toward fascism. Accusations of fascism Southern-style circulated liberally, from W. J. Cash's anatomization of the "mind of the south" (1941/1991: 338) to Grace Lumpkin's charge in her exchange with editor Seward Collins (published in the *New Republic*) that Allen Tate and the Agrarians promulgated a form of fascism (Sunny Side of Fascism 1936: 132). Simultaneously, as Stark Young's 1931 essays on fascist Italy reveal, fascism's vision of an ordered and orderly society offered conservatives a sociopolitical model preferable to a contemporary South roiling with challenges to the paternalism of capital and the hierarchy of race. As Wright knew, the populist appeal of fascism – in Europe and among Southern conservatives – emerged, in part, from the fascists' canny manipulation of cultural representations (Fabre 1993: 245–6).

According to Burke, the problem of fascism stemmed from a political strategy that converged with an aesthetic strategy. In "The Rhetoric of Hitler's Battle," his speech for the 1939 Writers' Congress, Burke warned of the dangers of identification, dangers that Wright expresses in his sympathy with the aesthetic complexity of Sarah's vision. Burke argued that Hitler's rise to power was largely due to his successful rhetoric of identification. The power of *Mein Kampf* lay in Hitler's ability to use compelling tropes from Christian and liberal culture to subjugate others. The problem of fascism stemmed from a political strategy which was also an aesthetic strategy: Hitler insisted on "complete identification" between himself and the German people. For Burke, "complete identification" led to a totalizing "unity," which he depicted metaphorically as a reduction of all social discourse to Hitler's "one voice" (Burke 1941/1973: 198, 205, 207). In contrast to the monologism of German fascism, Burke posited a "'babel' of voices," which he associated, in this speech and elsewhere, with the multiple and competing voices of "the *parliamentary*," a public – and textual – space where identification was always partial and provisional (pp. 200, 199). Identification provided the necessary common ground for "discourse" without requiring the erasure of all social differences. In fact, Burke insisted on acknowledging the existence of "necessary" "factions" and of differences in political power as a way of explaining the idiosyncrasies of aesthetic and political response and as a defense against the totalizing potential of univocal discourse (p. 313).

Pragmatism and the Limits of Justice

Wright understood racial essentialism – even in the form of black solidarity – as a univocal discourse that underwrote white supremacy. Yet he also recognized the political necessity of racial solidarity if blacks were to challenge institutional racism. Hence "Long Black Song" captures both Wright's criticism of racism and his ambivalence about how to escape racial essentialism. In addition, the story challenges pragmatism's aesthetics of "nonidentity." By demonstrating the limits of irresolvability as a strategy for social intervention, Wright explores the gap between awareness of injustice and the construction of a "political technology" for combating it (Dewey quoted in Eldrige 2004: 20). "Heap[ed] up" contradictions allow Wright to depict the complexity of racism and the paralysis of the black subject, but the story also asks us to consider whether depicting injustice ameliorates it. On the one hand, Wright seems committed to the instrumentalism of mimesis, that is, to the notion that mimetic representation (socialist realism) itself exemplifies "symbolic action." Yet the story's depiction of Sarah's ineffectual paralysis (which anticipates the same paralysis in readers) suggests that Wright remains pessimistic about pragmatism's "instrumental reason." While other critics – Burke included – shared Wright's pessimism about pragmatism's capacity to produce a coherent politics, both Burke and Wright grasped the potential of pragmatism to articulate *resistance* to the politics of identity even if it failed to articulate an alternative social vision. By acknowledging the contingency of human experience – aesthetic and otherwise – pragmatism recognized the possibility of loss and the unequal distribution of social and political power, thus opening a sliver of space for the construction of a radical democratic politics.

Wright sets up the problem of the efficacy of aesthetic experience by locating the story's point of view in Sarah rather than Silas. The narrative structure invites us to sympathize with Sarah's restless longing and her loneliness. We feel bewitched – with her – by the miraculous music coming from the white salesman's gramophone. But we also feel uneasy. Wright represents the dangers of aesthetic experience by associating it with illicit sexual desire and with the desire for consumer goods. His depiction of Sarah's aesthetic pleasure suggests sexual climax, making the moment of aesthetic engagement a foreshadowing of her sexual engagement with the salesman. Moreover, the ambiguity of their sexual encounter is central to understanding Wright's ambivalence here. Sarah isn't exactly raped, but she isn't exactly a willing partner either. Wright depicts her resistance, the salesman's insistence, her escape and his pursuit, but Wright makes it unclear whether Sarah surrenders to her desire, or gives in out of fear – or some combination of both – compounded by loneliness and the effect of the gramophone music.

But when Silas returns, he reads Sarah's desire as a betrayal that threatens his patriarchal right to be the sole proprietor of his property. At this moment, the story's point of view shifts to Silas, who insists that female desire must be contained and that his assertion of male prerogative must take precedence even when the racial politics of the situation mean his certain death. Sarah's desire becomes one of a constellation of desires produced by the structuring effects of capitalism: Silas's desire to be a "man," signified by dominating his wife and protecting his property; Sarah's desire for consumer goods; the white gramophone salesman's desire to make a sale, and the lynch mob's desire for vengeance. Wright seems to suggest that aesthetic experience – coded here as illicit desire – can destroy; therefore, it must be disciplined to prevent the violence it will inevitably produce. However, when Sarah watches Silas's immolation from the hill, Wright emphasizes the *dis*connection between aesthetic perception and direct action. Here, even though Sarah *imagines* brotherhood, she is powerless to enact it. Sarah's inability to act at this moment would seem to confound the earlier suggestion that aesthetic experience can precipitate violence and destruction.

How do we reconcile the apparent impotence of Sarah's moment of revelation at the end of the story with Wright's representation of the violent consequences of her aesthetic response to the gramophone music? And what do we make of Wright's sympathy for the complexity of her final vision? At the most fundamental level, the story's multiple perspectives on aesthetic experience exemplify the contradictory character of pragmatist identification. However, by making us privy to Sarah's subjective grappling for a way to understand what she sees below her, Wright invites us to associate Silas's assertion of male prerogative with the racial hierarchy that destroys him. That is, in this moment, Wright seems to represent a continuity between Silas's white patriarchal values and the exercise of white supremacy that spells his inevitable doom. In this moment, then, Sarah's aesthetic experience corresponds to the narrative's criticism of racial violence and correlates with the narrative's abstract desire for justice.

As a category of experience, the aesthetic has been invoked as a defense against the encroachment of industrial culture, and we can see an echo of this position in the way that Sarah's experience reveals the devastating effects of capitalist desire. Simultaneously, Wright seems to condemn the hedonistic pleasure Sarah feels in response to nature and the gramophone music, which suggests a variation on the position that aesthetic experience is unforgivably irresponsible. But both of these views maintain a separation between aesthetic experience and other experience. While the first view positions aesthetic experience *outside* culture, the second assumes that aesthetic experience is an *escape* from culture. In contrast, pragmatist aesthetics, by refusing the separation of aesthetic from everyday experience, makes aesthetic experience the impetus for social justice. In *Art as Experience*, Dewey argues for the "aesthetic quality of moral action" (1934: 39), just as Burke insists that aesthetic forms offer "*strategies* for dealing with *situations*" (1941/1973: 296). For pragmatists, then, aesthetic experience is implicitly ethical, and aesthetic forms are explicitly diagnostic. As Burke points out, literary forms are "symbolic actions"; they "are answers to questions posed by the situation in which they arose" (p. 1).

Going back to the story, we see that Wright locates the genesis of the violence in "Long Black Song" in Sarah's response to the gramophone music, coming, as it does, when she's feeling particularly lonely and vulnerable. I agree with critics who claim that "Long Black Song" blames Sarah for Silas's death and who see the story as an example of Wright's misogyny. However, I think a more complex dynamic is at work here. If, as Abdul JanMohamed argues, the story pits Silas's "hardness" against Sarah's "soft" "non-resistance" (JanMohamed 2005: 60), how do we account for Wright's apparent critique of the economy of revenge precipitated by Sarah's surrender to the white salesman? The white salesman dies to re-establish Silas's dominance over his wife; Silas dies to pay for challenging the white man's "right" to take a black woman. But what about Sarah? In the story's scale of justice, she's what James called an "unclassified residuum" (quoted in Posnock 1998a: 58). Sarah survives, but we know nothing of what becomes of her after Silas's cataclysmic death. Yet, by depicting Sarah's *subjective* response to what she sees, Wright reveals the hierarchies of power that shape the inevitability of the plot, and he presents hers as a consciousness open to new structures of feeling.

Wright shapes Sarah's moment of perception as a process of making connections, which he signifies by using the conjunction "and." The word "and" levels distinctions between the linked elements, a strategy that works, in Sarah's imaginative vision, to erase hierarchy and naturalize racial equality. Sarah's sense that "black men *and* white men" belong together "somehow" precedes her ability to articulate "how" that might happen in light of the history of killing that has fashioned her consciousness and circumscribed her life. But the language itself, by refusing hierarchy even while remaining unable to articulate a specific vision of racial harmony, opens the space for something different. Moreover, Wright's syntax emphasizes the active process Sarah experiences while grappling with an idea she cannot express linguistically. At this very moment, her "idea" is still a feeling, a somatic experience that remains at the margin of her consciousness where "she could not put her finger on it."

Wright's use of language reveals a tension between a mimetic view of language, which assumes that language emerges from and reproduces what already exists, and a pragmatic view, which sees language as a "form of action" that names and organizes, but also "conveys possibility" (Dewey 1994: 152, 1934: 242). Wright's conjunctions represent what William James described as "transitive consciousness." Operating in the shadow of existing relations and habits of expression, "transitive consciousness" is that state of consciousness in which new relations can be grasped and can begin to be articulated in language (James 1977: 36). By emphasizing the *process* of Sarah's imagination, Wright dramatizes the *inception* of Sarah's perspective on racial relations, highlighting the active, *creative* work of perception as it performs in relation to already existing habits of thought and action.

Sarah's moment of insight exemplifies an alternative – and radical – pragmatist aesthetic, which emerges through Wright's rewriting of the conventions of modernist epiphany and proletarian conversion. Sarah's moment produces neither the clarity of vision and perception of truth characteristic of the modernist epiphany, nor the recognition of identity with a class or race characteristic of the proletarian conversion. Moreover, Sarah's consciousness, represented as a vivid and fluid entity, becomes the place where the aesthetic and political dimensions of pragmatism converge. By "heaping up" contradictions and emphasizing irresolvability, Sarah's moment challenges aesthetic notions of organic unity. Similarly, her sense of the limitations associated with both universal brotherhood and blood politics points to a skepticism towards any totalizing political approach to identity. By depicting Sarah's insight emerging through an active process of perception – rather than presenting it as an identifiably discrete and complete event – Wright explores the role of consciousness in conceptualizing new forms of political and social solidarity. Sarah's incomplete and processual way of grasping new ideas suggests the reciprocity of her consciousness with a world characterized by its openness, multiplicity, and resistance to "unities" of all kinds. By placing us with her on the hill and privy to her thoughts, Wright invites us to absorb that emergent, but fragile possibility.

"Long Black Song" never loses sight of the material effects of power. Its pessimism is clear. As events unfold, they suggest that desire inevitably incites violence and death. Sarah's fragile vision has no power to change what happens. If we view these final events from Silas's point of view, the story points to the impossibility of black men possessing anything – even their wives – in a racist society. From this perspective the irony lies in the fact that Silas dies at the hands of the white patriarchy he has tried so hard to imitate in all the years of accumulation and "uplift." But most of the story occurs from Sarah's point of view, and we would be remiss to forget that hers is the central consciousness here. I suggest that locating the narrative in Sarah's point of view for most of the story disrupts the seamlessness of Wright's account of black male violation. Sarah's vision demonstrates the limits of identification in an economic system that racializes class differences and emasculates black men, and it reveals Wright's ambivalence about his own practice as a writer.

At the end of the story, Sarah is literally and figuratively "left over," a position that allows her an alternative perspective on the effects of power without granting her agency to affect it. Because Sarah, as a *subject*, exists outside of the economy that destroys Silas, her vision offers a momentary position from which to critique the economy of desires that shape and destroy Silas. While Silas's death illuminates the impossibility of black men entering the economy, the story concentrates on the injustice of his *exclusion* rather than on the injustice of the economy itself. In contrast, Sarah's longing for an alternative place of identification provides a brief counterpoint. Even as it contains her longing in an ultimately impotent vision of racial harmony, Sarah's vision exists *outside* the patriarchal economy. Wright's treatment unequivocally marginalizes her vision, revealing his own pessimism about the efficacy of aesthetic experience. Yet this moment implies a pragmatic impulse by suggesting that imagination – exemplified in Sarah's consciousness – represents currently unrealized potential as a radically democratic practice.

NOTE

1 *Uncle Tom's Children* was originally published in 1938 as a four-story collection. In 1940, Wright reissued the book, adding an opening autobiographical essay, "The Ethics of Living Jim Crow," and a fifth and final story, "Bright and Morning Star." "Long Black Song" appeared in both volumes.

REFERENCES AND FURTHER READING

Aaron, Daniel. (1992). *Writers on the Left: Episodes in American Literary Communism*. New York: Columbia University Press.

Alexander, Thomas. (1992). *John Dewey's Theory of Art, Experience, and Nature: The Horizons of Feeling*. Albany: SUNY Press.

Bernstein, Richard J. (1993). *The New Constellation: The Ethical-Political Horizons of Modernity/Postmodernity*. Cambridge, MA: MIT Press.

Brinkley, Alan. (1983). *Voices of Protest: Huey Long, Father Coughlin and the Great Depression*. New York: Vintage.

Burke, Kenneth. (1941/1973). *The Philosophy of Literary Form*. Berkeley: University of California Press.

Burke, Kenneth. (1945). *A Grammar of Motives*. Berkeley: University of California Press.

Burke, Kenneth. (1952). *A Rhetoric of Motives*. New York: Prentice-Hall.

Burke, Kenneth. (1953). *Counter-Statement*. Los Altos, CA: Hermes.

Cappetti, Carla. (1993). Sociology of an existence: Wright and the Chicago School. In Henry Louis Gates, Jr. and K. A. Appiah (eds), *Richard Wright: Critical Perspectives Past and Present* (pp. 255–72). New York: Amistad.

Cash, W. J. (1941/1991). *The Mind of the South*. New York: Vintage.

DeCosta-Willis, Miriam. (1986). Avenging angels and mute mothers: Black Southern women in Wright's fictional world. *Callaloo* 28 (Summer): 540–51.

Denning, Michael. (1996). *The Cultural Front: The Laboring of American Culture in the Twentieth Century*. London: Verso.

Dewey, John. (1925/1994). *Experience and Nature*. Chicago: Open Court.

Dewey, John. (1927). *The Public and Its Problems*. Athens, OH: Swallow Press.

Dewey, John. (1930/1981). Individualism, old and new. In *The Later Works, 1925–1933*, ed. Jo Ann Boydston (vol. 5, pp. 41–143). Carbondale: University of Illinois Press.

Dewey, John. (1934). *Art as Experience*. New York: Perigee.

Diggins, John. (1972). *Mussolini and Fascism: The View from America*. Princeton, NJ: Princeton University Press.

Drake, St. Clair and Horace Cayton. (1945/1993). *Black Metropolis, a Study of Negro Life in a Northern City*. Chicago: University of Chicago Press.

Eagleton, Terry. (1986). *Against the Grain: Essays 1975–1985*. London: Verso.

Eldridge, Michael. (2004). Dewey on race and social change. In Bill E. Lawson and Donald F. Koch (eds), *Pragmatism and the Problem of Race* (pp. 11–21). Bloomington: Indiana University Press.

Fabre, Michel. (1985). *The World of Richard Wright*. Jackson: University Press of Mississippi.

Fabre, Michel. (1993). *The Unfinished Quest of Richard Wright*, trans. Isabel Barzun. Urbana: University of Illinois Press.

Fekete, John. (1977). *The Critical Twilight: Explorations of the Ideology of Anglo-American Literary Theory From Eliot to McLuhan*. London: Routledge.

Foley, Barbara. (1993a). The politics of poetics: Ideology and narrative form in *An American Tragedy* and *Native Son*. In Henry Louis Gates, Jr. and K. A. Appiah (eds), *Richard Wright: Critical Perspectives Past and Present* (pp. 188–99). New York: Amistad.

Foley, Barbara. (1993b). *Radical Representations: Politics and Form in U S. Proletarian Fiction, 1929–1941*. Durham, NC: Duke University Press.

Fraser, Nancy. (1998). Another pragmatism: Alain Locke, critical "race" theory, and the politics of culture. In Morris Dickstein (ed.), *The Revival of Pragmatism: New Essays on Social Thought, Law, and Culture* (pp. 157–75). Durham, NC: Duke University Press.

Gold, Mike. (1930). Notes of the month. *New Masses* 6, 4 (September 30): 3–5.

Gold, Mike. (1931a). Art is a weapon! Program of the workers' cultural federation. *New Masses* 7, 3 (August): 11–13.

Gold, Mike. (1931b) Toward an American revolutionary culture. *New Masses* 7, 2 (July): 12–13.

Hakutani, Yoshinobu. (1996). *Richard Wright and Racial Discourse*. Columbia: University of Missouri Press.

Hutchinson, George. (1995). *The Harlem Renaissance in Black and White*. Cambridge, MA: Harvard University Press.

Iser, Wolfgang. (1974). *The Implied Reader: Patterns of Communication in Prose Fiction from Bunyan to Beckett*. Baltimore, MD: The Johns Hopkins University Press.

James, William. (1977). *The Writings of William James*, ed. John J. McDermott. Chicago: University of Chicago Press.

James, William. (1987). *Writings 1902–1910*. New York: Library of America.

JanMohamed, Abdul R. (1995). Negating the negation as a form of affirmation in minority discourse: The construction of Richard Wright as subject. In Arnold Rampersad (ed.), *Richard Wright: A Collection of Critical Essays* (pp. 107–23). Englewood Cliffs, NJ: Prentice Hall.

JanMohamed, Abdul R. (2005). *The Death-Bound Subject: Richard Wright's Archaeology of Death*. Durham, NC: Duke University Press.

Kazin, Alfred. (1942/1982). *On Native Ground*. San Diego, CA: Harcourt.

Lewis, David Levering. (1993). *W. E. B. DuBois: Biography of a Race, 1868–1919*. New York: Holt.

Lukács, Georg. (1934). Propaganda or partisanship? Abridged and trans. Leonard F. Mins. *Partisan Review* 1, 2 (April–May): 36–46.

Lumpkin, Kathryn DuPre. (1940). *The South in Progress*. New York: International.

Michie, Allan A. and Frank Rylick. (1939). *Dixie Demagogues*. New York: Vanguard Press.

Miller, Eugene E. (1982). Richard Wright and Gertrude Stein. *Black American Literature Forum* 16, 3: 107–19.

Miller, Eugene E. (1990). *Voice of a Native Son: The Poetics of Richard Wright*. Jackson: University Press of Mississippi.

Murphy, James. (1991). *The Proletarian Moment: The Controversy Over Leftism in Literature*. Chicago: University of Illinois Press.

Pells, Richard. (1973). *Radical Visions and American Dreams: Culture and Social Thought in the Depression Years*. Middletown, CT: Wesleyan University Press.

Poirier, Richard. (1992). *Poetry and Pragmatism*. Cambridge, MA: Harvard University Press.

Posnock, Ross. (1992). The politics of nonidentity: A genealogy. *Boundary 2* 19, 1: 34–68.

Posnock, Ross. (1998a). *Color and Culture: Black Intellectuals and the Making of the Modern Intellectual*. Cambridge, MA: Harvard University Press.

Posnock, Ross. (1998b). Going astray, going forward: DuBoisian pragmatism and its lineage. In Morris Dickstein (ed.), *The Revival of Pragmatism: New Essays on Social Thought, Law, and Culture* (pp. 176–89). Durham, NC: Duke University Press.

Poulet, Georges. (1980). Criticism and the experience of interiority. In Jane P. Tompkins (ed.), *Reader-Response Criticism: From Formalism to Post-Structuralism* (pp. 41–9). Baltimore, MD: Johns Hopkins University Press.

Ransom, John Crowe. (1938). *The World's Body*. New York: Scribner's.

Rideout, Walter. (1992). *The Radical Novel in the United States, 1900–1954*. New York: Columbia University Press.

Rorty, Richard. (1989). *Contingency, Irony, and Solidarity*. New York: Cambridge University Press.

Shusterman, Richard. (1992). *Pragmatist Aesthetics: Living Beauty, Rethinking Art*. Oxford: Blackwell.

Sitkoff, Harvard. (1978). *A New Deal for Blacks: The Emergence of Civil Rights as a National Issue*. New York: Oxford University Press.

The sunny side of fascism. (1936). Correspondence between Seward Collins and Grace Lumpkin. *New Republic* 87 (June 10): 131–2.

Walker, Margaret. (1988). *Richard Wright, Daemonic Genius: A Portrait of the Man, a Critical Look at His Work*. New York: Amistad.

Warren, Nagueyalti. (1988). Black girls and native sons: Female images in selected works by Richard Wright. In C. James Trotman (ed.), *Richard Wright: Myths and Reality* (pp. 59–77). New York: Garland.

West, Cornel. (1989). *The American Evasion of Philosophy: A Genealogy of Pragmatism*. Madison: University of Wisconsin Press.

Westbrook, Robert. (1991). *John Dewey and American Democracy*. Ithaca, NY: Cornell University Press.

Williams, Sherley Anne. (1995). Papa Dick and sister-woman: Reflections on women in the fiction of Richard Wright. In Arnold Rampersad (ed.), *Richard Wright: A Collection of Critical Essays* (pp. 63–82). Englewood Cliffs, NJ: Prentice Hall.

Wright, Richard. (1940/1993). *Uncle Tom's Children*. New York: Harper Perennial.

Wright, Richard. (1957/1995). *White Man, Listen!* New York: HarperPerennial.

Young, Stark. (1931). Notes on fascism today I, II, III. *New Republic* 68 (July 22 and 29, August 5): 258–60, 281–3, 312–14.

5

Class and Sex in American Fiction: From Casual Laborers to Accidental Desires

Michael Trask

It is habitual for critics of American literature to posit the naturalist turn around 1900 as the moment when the novel shrugged off its high-realist mantle and began to assume the rather different attire of modernist fiction, with its resolute emphasis on topics that the civilized novel of manners had typically defused and dispatched. In this essay I will be concerned to track the novel's change through two of these topics, sexual desire and class difference, by first observing that these too underwent a cultural metamorphosis around 1900. Whereas the novel traditionally depicted class and sex as things that had to be normalized and rectified through the marriage plot, which set desire on the path toward conjugality and thereby mitigated its hazards via the harmonic realignment of social hierarchy, the novel around 1900 began to lose interest in this long-established narrative pattern and to focus instead on sexual competition and material wants as motive forces unchecked by moral stays or cultural mandates. In the American literary tradition, where the commitment to the marital plot had always been relatively weaker than that of its European counterpart, the insistence on thwarting the narrative of marriage and its formal teleology became an imperative that shaped the genre of American realism, which represented its moral and aesthetic program as an assault on the romantic illusions of conjugality.

The great nineteenth-century realists, William Dean Howells and Henry James, thus composed novels at the *fin de siècle* that not only repeatedly flout the courtship romance (in James's *The American*, say) but also dramatize divorce, the antithesis of the marriage plot (in books like *A Modern Instance* and *What Maisie Knew*). This is to say nothing of James's fascination with the adultery plot, which had long underwritten his fiction's interest in what we might call the narrative of conjugal estrangement (developed in *Portrait of a Lady* and perfected in *The Golden Bowl*), yet became more pronounced in the new century when his novels began to use adultery as a pretext for exploring more interesting erotic geometries than the dyad or love triangle (witness *The Sacred Fount*, a virtual primer in partner-swapping well ahead of that craze's 1970s heyday). James may have been spurred to such plots in part because of his interest in attracting an audience. In his view, novel reading had expanded as a pastime because of "the innumerable women who, under modern arrangements, increasingly fail to marry – fail, apparently, even, largely, to desire to" (James 1899/1984: 101). And while none of these dissenting alternatives to the marriage plot may have been unique to the period, nor even particularly American, their prevalence at the turn of the twentieth century not just in James's but in many novels helps us to see that novelists were less interested in getting either sex or class straight than in exploring the ways that both sexual desire and class relations inevitably turned out wrong "under modern arrangements" – or, at the very least, were far less stable and more open to reconfiguration than many people writing fiction had apparently cared to acknowledge.

Two overlapping examples will serve to measure the sea-change in attitudes about desire and class that I am describing. In Theodore Dreiser's *Sister Carrie* (1900), the title character cohabits in quick succession with two different men, neither of whom is her husband and one of whom, Hurstwood, is already married. After she has taken up with Drouet, the first of her two lovers, Carrie hears what Dreiser calls the "voice of the people" (Dreiser 1900/1994: 89), who tell her: "Look at those who are good. How would they scorn to do what you have done. Look at the good girls; how will they draw away from such as you when they know you have been weak. You had not tried before you failed" (p. 90). This is the voice of traditional morality, of course, and its cadences are as well-known in the pulpit – "the voice of God" (p. 89), as Dreiser also calls it – as in the long tradition of sentimental fiction in American history, which decrees that the fallen woman must be made to suffer for her weakness, not simply by her mortification for being unlike "those who are good" but more often than not by dying for that lack of virtue. But in Dreiser's book, as Carrie's career demonstrates, exactly the opposite occurs. Carrie's erotic misadventures do not damn her so much as they launch her rather brilliant arrival in society. Women, even "good" married ones, do not draw away from her; they befriend her – a vast improvement over the isolation she faces in the "conservative round of toil" (p. 14) of her sister and brother-in-law's flat. Far from signaling a failure, Carrie's accession to Drouet's and then Hurstwood's extramarital largesse precipitates her own startling worldly success as first an amateur and then a professional stage actress. In spite of what the "voice of the people" may tell her, then, we might say that sleeping around is the best thing that ever happened to Carrie. Extramarital dalliance is equivalent not just to Carrie's socialization but to an unprecedented rise in income and status.

The sort of vice that makes Carrie better rather than worse and rise rather than fall figures crucially in my other example: the case of Lily Bart in Edith Wharton's *The House of Mirth* (1905). If a common way of reading these two novels against each other is in terms of changing class dynamics –the lower-class nobody Carrie Meeber becomes the celebrity Carrie Madenda, just as the well-born Lily Bart ends up little more than the type of "dingy woman" she pities and loathes (Wharton 1905/1999: 12) – one might add to this dual cultural narrative of elite anxiety and social mobility a rarely noted rationale for Lily's lapse in status: her steadfast refusal to sleep her way to the top. Throughout Wharton's novel, Lily is overcome by powerful moments of scruple that interfere with her otherwise blithe commitment to flirtation. It is when the flirtation turns into something other than desire at a distance that Lily recoils in horror from the prospect of a frankly opportunistic sexuality whose obvious intent even the greenest undergraduate can spot from the distance of a hundred pages but to whose brutality Lily herself never fails to react with endless reserves of surprise. When the lecherous Gus Trenor seeks payback for his generosity toward a woman he has been treating as a mistress, for example, or when Simon Rosedale offers Lily the "plain business transaction" (p. 294) of the vulgar but appetizing prospect of his hand in marriage and the fortune that attends it if only she will exercise her power over the eminently blackmailable Bertha Dorset, Lily seems incapable of mustering any other affect than shock.

While for this reason readers may not be able finally to credit Lily's astonishing naivety, Wharton seeks to demonstrate something different in her protagonist from cut-and-dried verisimilitude or psychological nuance. She wants to show us that Lily's real tragedy is precisely her prudishness. As someone who cannot bear to look behind the surfaces of things for fear of losing faith in a world that has at any rate cast her out, Lily ends up a martyr to a cause that has few if any true believers. When she rejects Gus Trenor's advances or burns Bertha Dorset's compromising letters to Selden, she thinks she is following Dreiser's "voice of the people" and behaving like "those who are good." In the well-worn ethical reading of this novel, of course, this is exactly right: she is good, even as precious little good comes of her valiant, self-sacrificing acts. But there is every reason to believe that this ethical reading is one from which Wharton would have demurred, and not merely because Wharton was a sexual adventurer who lacked the erotic reservations with which she saddles her protagonist. Partly because of her own sexual opportunism, Wharton had very little patience for her culture's immemorial equation of morality and sexual continence. And in this impatience she is indicative of a society that, at least in some quarters, was eager to sever the seemingly innate link between ethics and erotics, especially where women were concerned. It might be too much to say that Lily should have taken a page out of Carrie's playbook and slept with Trenor or any of the other men in her life, if it were not the case that she does borrow at least one of Carrie's strategies for success by appearing on stage, on display, in the celebrated "tableau vivant" (1905/1999: 132) where she portrays Joshua Reynolds's Mrs Lloyd. But even there, we must acknowledge, Lily does not fully embrace the part of the actress. Lily (unlike Carrie) gets on stage in a private home, not in a commercial theatre; her performance (unlike Carrie's dancing and speaking) is one of stasis and inaction; and though her compelling stature seduces men in public, she (unlike Carrie again) does not take them into her bed. From this standpoint, in which Carrie's success might be understood as something to emulate, Lily has her priorities all wrong. Resisting the commercialization of herself as vulgar, she fears making a misstep (and so the only way left to her is down); continually misconstruing the private sphere as something that will shelter her, she fails to realize that it is precisely her commitment to female sanctity that destroys her.

In other words, Lily thinks that by saving her sexual virtue she will protect her class status – a version, albeit with higher stakes, of the situation Carrie faces in Dreiser's novel. But as we have seen, Carrie's loss of virtue results in a dramatic increase in caste. Perhaps as a result of Carrie's having less to lose by losing her virtue, she has more to gain. But the lesson of Wharton's novel seems to be that Lily's declassing is not incidental to her insistence on sexual purity. Since everyone already believes her guilty of sexual indiscretions she has not committed, Lily really does have nothing left to lose. Indeed all she has left by the novel's end is her perpetual sense of shame. And it is this shame, finally, that Wharton marshals to make her story less tragic than pathetic. If Lily had been a little more shameless, one suspects, she might have stood a better chance. Chance is the operative word here, for I have been reading these characters and their trajectories in tandem in order to make the point that their creators, separated by enormous divides of money, taste, disposition, and outlook, might be understood to meet on the peculiar terrain of sexual opportunism. In very different kinds of novels – one the epitome of a celebrated if short-lived American naturalism, the other more or less the culmination of the Gilded Age novel of manners – Dreiser and Wharton begin to imagine a world in which sex is not the abject limit to social belonging but in fact a wholly conventional if not quite legitimate means to achieving a higher class.

This is not exactly a hegemonic opinion in the first half of the twentieth century. But my point is less that novelists valorize sex for its capacity to make one a better person than that sex at the turn from the nineteenth to the twentieth century comes to be detachable from valorization itself. Once sex is divorced from ethics, it starts to pose new kinds of problems for a culture in which numerous other kinds of divorce (including marital divorce itself) become prominent, even as the older moral or ethical dilemmas around sexuality never quite recede from view. The most pressing problem sex poses for moderns – its contradictory status as both an inalienable part of one's self-identity and an eminently contractual, supremely public experience – is one to which the traditional recourse to marriage and children does not answer. And while many writers continue to treat sexual conduct as the foundation of an ethics, their work also evinces a strong disincentive to follow out this grounding of morality in desire. The major novelists of the first half of the twentieth century seem averse to any claim on sexuality's causes or consequences. It remains throughout the period a source of accident, a kind of random variable of the social world on which characters seek to impose narrative logic at their own peril.

In Willa Cather's *My Ántonia*, for example, Jim Burden sleeps with the dangerously attractive Lena Lingard while he is an undergraduate at the University of Nebraska. As the figure in the book most associated with leading men on, which is to say with forcing men to make the wrong moves, Lena's seductiveness recalls the temptation of the serpent, a figure with whom Jim has already done battle and emerged victorious earlier in the novel. Her walk is "undulating," and at one point she "sidles" up to Jim

(Cather 1918/1994: 151, 172). "To dance with Lena," Jim tells us, "was like coming in with the tide." As a result of their affair, as Jim puts it, "I was drifting" (p. 166). It is somewhat difficult to locate the nature of the danger Lena poses to Jim, unless it is precisely the danger of drifting itself. But Cather seems to imply that a certain amount of "drifting" is necessary, even salutary, for bucking the straight and narrow paths that the world ordains and thus for getting ahead at all. Lena "never tried to hinder or hold me back" (p. 223), Jim tells us after their affair. This is a peculiar declaration, since it is Lena who tells Jim she plans never to marry (because she wants to "be accountable to nobody," p. 216) and who finds Dumas's *Camille* maudlin and implausible; and it is Jim who, when we are introduced to him in the novel's intro-duction, has a wife. Jim's statement reveals a predictable obedience to the time-honored gender ideology whereby men roam and women settle down. Cather's novel treats this ideology as not only naive but readily falsifiable, since it is the unmarried Lena and her equally unattached friend Tiny Soderball (the proprietor, so we are led to infer, of a brothel in the Klondike) who travel the farthest and change their lives the most. But Jim's view of marriage and women of course is not entirely mistaken. After all, the astonishingly fecund Ántonia, with her husband and many children, has not only failed to move forward in the world of Cather's novel but also, at least as Jim renders her, regressed to a kind of unaltered state.

Even as she entrusts the story of Ántonia to Jim, we would be wrong to assume that the distance between Cather and her narrator is negligible or, for that matter, that Jim's narration of the lives of the various women in his own life is unmotivated. We can measure the real divide between author and character by observing that unlike Cather, who neither welcomes nor resists change but instead admits its necessity, Jim views change as identical with compromise and debility. Jim embodies a powerful nostalgia that Cather portrays as less conservative than destructive, in so far as its desire to preserve the world at all costs in a more or less frozen state ends up sacrific-ing anything like vitality. To change, in Jim's view, is to weaken or lose power (a threat of degeneration that informs the preference found in a later Cather protagonist, Godfrey St. Peter in *The Professor's House*, for his beloved Tom Outland to have died young rather than to have lived into an inevitably disappointing maturity). Thus whereas early on it is Jim's fear of the changes in Ántonia that keeps him away from her, it is his discovery that she in fact hasn't changed that occupies him in the last part of the book. In "Shimerda's Boys," the novel's last act, Jim acquires an acute case of selective memory syndrome when he envisions "a succession of pictures fixed there like the old woodcuts of one's first primer" (Cather 1918/1994: 258) in his reunion with Ántonia, who "lent herself to immemorial human attitudes which we recognize by instinct as universal and true." "No wonder her boys were so tall and straight," he declares. "She was a rich mine of life, like the founders of early races" (p. 259). That phrase "tall and straight" is a revealing one, since throughout the book Cather gives us very few positive images of rectitude, of the world showing itself at its best when it is, so to speak, straightened out. In calling Jim's memory selective, I mean to draw attention to the fact that Jim forgets how distressed he used to be by Ántonia's flexible identity – and the gender confusion it seemed to precipitate. He tells us that when Ántonia worked the fields, "her arms and throat were burned as brown as a sailor's" (p. 93). "I like to be like a man" (104), she tells Jim in rebuttal to his clear dislike of her sliding into this role. These views of her are literally distasteful to Jim; hence the importance Jim bestows on the fact that the Cuzak family eats "*kolaches*" (p. 248), not because of the kind of food it is but because of the name Cather chooses to give it. By not translating "kolaches," which is just a Czech word for pastry, or by having Jim not translate it, Cather signals Jim's investment in having Ántonia return to her native tongue and her native identity (not to mention gender). Having lost her English, Ántonia regains her feminine role as mother to a race. From Jim's standpoint, not being assimilated saves Ántonia from changing too much, if at all. And marriage turns out to be the signal mechanism for that preservation of identity, just as Lena's indifference to the marriage plot secures her ability to transform herself, by way of the "casual Western" (p. 211) city of Lincoln and then of San Francisco, from immigrant farm girl to cosmopolitan fashion designer.

In referring Lena's sexuality to the "casual" locales she inhabits, *My Ántonia* helps us to see that a decisive subplot in the major novels of American modernism concerns the effort to fix sexual desire that has become rampant or misdirected, to transform into causal terms an erotics distinguished largely by its casualization. And such casualization is hardly incidental to the casualization of class relations and of labor that was a prominent feature of American society in the first half of the twentieth century. In *My Antonia*, Jim Burden's efforts to impose meaning onto sex and its consequences produce a distorted account of Ántonia, yet one that, by writing Ántonia into an idealized narrative of reproduction and identity, has the value of glossing over the equally disorienting sexuality Jim encounters in Lena Lingard's embrace. In a sense, Ántonia is made to submit to a gender discipline that the unanchored Lena will not abide. This deflective strategy arises elsewhere in the novels of Cather's contemporaries, where it draws on the same nostalgia that motivates Jim Burden's desire to rationalize or narrate sex back into the social text. This is the dominant affect that modern novelists are keen to parse, even as their work sometimes shares in that nostalgia itself. The puzzlement induced by the sexually irregular is all the more baffling – and thus all the more susceptible to violent expulsion – because it occurs in the midst of a social order that seems uninterested in shoring up traditional moral viewpoints with the traditional moral institutions of marriage and family. It is as if the social text and the literary text have each confronted and succumbed to the hegemony of casual relations without putting up much of a fight.

In "Melanctha," for example, the middle story of Gertrude Stein's *Three Lives* (whose placement at the book's center might be understood to signal Stein's commitment to driving a wedge between the conventional categories a woman can occupy as either the spinster "Good Anna" or the hausfrau "Gentle Lena"), desire is a matter of drifting and surplus. "Too complex with desire," Stein writes, Melanctha Herbert is "less sure" about where things go and how they fit in the world than, say, her comfortably married friend Rose Johnson (Stein 1909/1990: 61). And so she moves outward, toward the margins of her social world, the "railroad yards" and "the shipping docks" (p. 71), as if in frequenting such venues she might find a material appositive for her migrant eros in the casual laborers who work these particular lines. "Melanctha had not found it easy with herself to make her wants and what she had, agree," Stein writes (p. 62). Desire – what one "wants" – is precisely the feature of the self that will not submit to equivalence in Stein's story, despite not only Melanctha's efforts but also her lover Jeff Campbell's implorations on her behalf. Jeff finally abandons Melanctha because of her "way of not being ever equal in your feeling to anybody real": "You never can be equal to me" (p. 136), he writes to her in a farewell letter. He means not equality in the political sense but the fact that he cannot make Melanctha, who "was too many for him" (p. 124), add up correctly and without remainder. This surplus clouds the version of love that matters to Jeff, the "always living good and being regular" (p. 86) he promotes as the goal for "the colored people." Distinguishing between "kinds of love" (p. 87), Jeff (who happens to be a physician) asserts the scientific view that desire can be harnessed or tamed, made "right" or "regular," by domestication (where domesticity serves as a sort of control environment for calibrating lust or passion). In keeping with this staunchly utilitarian view, Jeff also believes that desire can be reduced to necessity – a condition he demands of Melanctha before his break with her. Because her desire is "too much," its surplus always liable to gravitate toward other and different objects, it subverts Jeff's requirement that Melanctha "need" his love, rather than (what he cannot tolerate) merely choosing to be with him. Melanctha's problem, according to Jeff, is that her desire is too profuse to be compassed by the laws of property. It doesn't know where to stop and it doesn't know where it rightfully belongs. And the main consequence of Melanctha's "too complex" desire for Jeff Campbell is that it stands in the way of his own class aspirations.

One way of understanding the discontinuous text of *Three Lives* in both its whole and its parts – characters come into relationships, fall out of relationships, return to relationships – is to see its aleatory pattern as the rough draft for the main plot of Stein's later work. Even in a novel as accessible as *The Autobiography of Alice B. Toklas*, narration proceeds fundamentally through a series of digressions and disconnects: first this guest came to the Rue de Fleurus, then the next one, then the next ("Everybody brought somebody," Alice tells us. "It was an endless variety. And everybody came and nobody made any difference. . . . and there were the endless strangers who came and went," p. 124). Stein's world is virtually an ecology of random and episodic encounter. Problems arise when characters like Jeff Campbell or the good Anna imagine an alternative to a social world in which affinities are less a matter of chance or impulse than of hallowed necessity. In this respect, Stein's stylistic experimentalism redoubles something like a social experiment or utopian imagining. Whereas Wharton, Cather, and Dreiser can merely hint at a society in which casual ties might have a privileged (albeit beleaguered) place, Stein takes such casualness to be the norm. If in the late work of Henry James, to whom Stein professed discipleship, the predominant mode of relationship is one of perpetual rearrangement of partners, in Stein partnership seems almost beside the point. It is this feature of her work that critics have the hardest time assimilating to our customary views of what makes for proper social bonds.

This is only to say that even as novelists may recognize the increasing prevalence of casual ties in both sex and class, their work often does its best to turn such casualness to account. In the work of her own disciple Ernest Hemingway and her friend Sherwood Anderson, for example, we discover not only a commitment to the vignette characteristic of Stein's work but also, and somewhat differently, an ago-nistic stance toward the episodic nature of desire that Stein's work generally omits. Like *Three Lives*, Hemingway's *In Our Time* is more anthology than sustained long-form narrative. Its individual stories are punctuated by a series of "chapters" that ostensibly form a sustained narrative in their own right but serve if anything to distort the status of long-form narrative beyond recognition. This is a book filled both formally and thematically with indefiniteness and lack of closure, with belated and mistimed encounters; characters understand themselves at "the end of some-thing" or "out of season," to borrow two of Hemingway's own titles, without the consolation of knowing where they should be or what should come next. The jumpy, preemptive quality of many of this book's stories mimics at the level of style the subject matter with which these stories deal: the inability of reproductive sexuality to confer continuity or stability on the social order. These are stories, after all, filled with stillbirths, abortions, fathers who commit suicide even as their wives deliver babies. They are also stories, like "Mr. and Mrs. Elliott," replete with the failure of reproductive sexuality – "Mr. and Mrs. Elliott tried very hard to have a baby," presumably without success (Hemingway 1925/1996: 85) – in which an alternative to conjugal heterosexuality comes uneasily to take its place (as when Mrs Elliott spends her days and nights in bed with her "girl friend" while Mr Elliott "lived apart in his own room," p. 88).

More often than not in Hemingway, however, the reaction to the failure of conjugal heterosexuality is not Mr and Mrs Elliott's unorthodox arrangement but something much closer to trauma. This is most literally the case with Jake Barnes in *The Sun Also Rises*, a man who, castrated during the war, can neither have nor relinquish the woman he loves. Less overtly though no less insistently than *In Our Time*, *The Sun Also Rises* manifests an extreme indifference to causal narration. Its characters' move-ments from Paris to Spain occur in the absence of any discernible motivation apart from touristic whim. Like *In Our Time*, this is a book governed by familiar yet con-tinually thwarted itineraries, both sexual and social. The fact that Jake never goes anywhere he hasn't been before implicitly tells us that his path is governed by a sort of repetition-compulsion. Yet even as Jake's destinations are preset, Hemingway's settings – hotels, campsites, barrooms, cafés, taxi cabs – are all transient and resolutely unstable spaces, the nexus of chance encounters and missed rendezvous. As a prose stylist famous for his solidity of place and detail, Hemingway has a rather contradic-tory habit of filling his work with floating or portable spaces – like Horton's Bay in *In Our Time*, a "lumbering town" whose parts are "carried away" until the town itself vanishes (1925/1996: 31). It is in one such place that at the beginning of *The Sun Also Rises*, and quite by accident, Jake runs into Brett Ashley accompanied by a phalanx of dancing gay men. These men make Jake "very angry" despite his awareness that "they are supposed to be amusing and you should be tolerant." It is their "superior, simpering composure" that makes him want to "swing on one" (Hemingway 1926/2003: 28); yet it is not merely homosexual panic that motivates Jake in this instance. For "superior" is a term of contempt that Jake also uses to describe the "boxing champion" (p. 11) Robert Cohn (who actually does throw a swing at Jake later in the novel). In both cases, the "composure" Jake abhors seems to reside in the ease with which men without any "aficion" (p. 136) for Brett – like the gay men, like Cohn – can nonetheless perform as if they loved her: "She had been taken up by them," Jake notes. "I knew then that they would all dance with her. They are like that" (p. 28). Here "superiority" assumes the shape of an elaborate play-acting of desire without substance, and Jake's inferiority becomes a badge of honor of sorts, a way of distinguishing himself from poseurs like the gay men or the virile and sexually active Cohn. Whereas all these men can enjoy Brett's body without consequence or commitment, Jake feels all the consequences and commitments of passion without the ability to consummate it.

In Hemingway the casualties of war serve as the objective correlative for the trauma inflicted by a world of casual, nonprocreative sexuality and ties lightly cast off, which is only to say that even though Hemingway enjoins us to imagine a world with little in the way of sacral commitments to hold it together, he does not wish us to approve of it. Sherwood Anderson has by contrast as ecumenical a view of sexual variance as one is likely to encounter in an American writer, although his pluralism is tempered by a strong conviction of the divide between the normal and the aberrant. His 1919 novel *Winesburg, Ohio*, in which the stories are so loosely tethered to one another as to make the book a novel in name only, begins with an episode in which Wing Biddlebaum, a former schoolteacher, "worked as a day laborer in the fields, going timidly about and striving to conceal his hands" (Anderson 1919/1996: 13). Biddlebaum's desperate attempt to control these "forever active, forever striving" hands results from their having been implicated in his pederastic embrace of "a half-witted boy of the school" who "became enamored of the young master" (pp. 10, 12). Reduced from the relatively plush status of "master" to that of field laborer as well as forced to change his name (from Adolph Meyers), Wing condenses several features of the casualization of sexuality and class to be found among twentieth-century novelists. The most notable is that while from one perspective his actions admit to escape (through the alias of "the name . . . he got from a box of goods at a freight station as he hurried through an eastern Ohio town," p. 13), from another perspective his mobility can only be downward – a declension inseparable from his erotic disgrace. Wing's "hurried" flight from scandal and his alias recall the clandestine, anonymous movement along freight lines at the center of the casual laborer's existence. It is as if he has embarked on the trip that Stein's Melanctha, with her irresolute visits to the rail yards, merely contemplates.

"A few years before" writing *Winesburg, Ohio* in a Chicago boarding-house, Anderson tells us in his memoirs, "I had been a laborer. I was myself, at that time, filled with all sorts of strange lusts" (cited Anderson 1919/1996: 152). Whereas Wing's lapse into a life of manual labor is precipitated by his "strange lusts," Anderson suggests in his own commentary that this pattern is commutative; laboring itself might be conducive to strange lusts and the "somewhat strange relations going on about me" in the urban milieu of his tenement (p. 152). And this is so because both casual labor and casual sex substitute innovation and dynamism, the winged migration, as it were, of the former Adolph Meyers, for security and stability. That erotic promiscuity and informal or unsteady, seasonal work habits were reciprocal vices was an assumption basic to the early twentieth-century social imagination. And even as Wing's story records his continual paranoia at being caught out, the episode itself establishes the centrality of erotic chance and concealment for the novel as a whole. The licentious Elizabeth Willard, who "had had half a dozen lovers before she married Tom Willard," for example, "was forever putting out her hand into the darkness and trying to get hold of some other hand" (p. 125). Anderson forges an intimacy between the overactive hands of the restlessly libidinous casual laborer and the most ostensibly decorous of his book's characters. If his mother "sought blindly, passionately, some hidden wonder in life" (p. 125) under the guise of an unhappy if proper marriage, then George Willard will end the novel by escaping from his small-town fate on a train. George "did not think of anything big or dramatic," Anderson tells us on the novel's last page, he "thought of little things" (p. 138). In this inconclusive conclusion, the novel recapitulates the emphasis on discontinuity and episodic desire with which it sets the pattern in Wing Biddlebaum's story. The implication of George's thoughts as he leaves Winesburg is that such desire is incompatible with grand narrative unity, much less finality.

One of the oddest features of Anderson's book is its very loud pronouncement that it withholds judgment on the sexual predilections of its characters even as it simultaneously insists that the ostracism or lapse in standing that results from these predilections is more or less indelible. It is as if for Anderson the life of the casual laborer or the erotic pervert is one that cannot be shed lightly if at all. The "danger of becoming a grotesque" (1919/1996: 6), it would seem, is that one is fated to remain a grotesque. If in *The Sun Also Rises* Jake Barnes advances the ceremonial majesty of the Spanish fiesta as a means to recover a world of authenticity and belief, and construes bona fide "afición" as a way out of threadbare sexual customs to which no one in the expatriate circle pays heed, in *Winesburg, Ohio* the work of identity fills the vacuum threatened by a world of total casualness and its perpetual transformations. "It was the truths that made the people grotesques" (p. 6), Anderson writes in the novel's prologue – a sentence we might slightly rephrase to suggest that for Anderson the grotesque becomes the sort of truth rendered unavailable by the labile and anarchic perversities that loom so large in this text. Grotesqueness provides a rebuttal to the fantasy of self-transformation – of desire without consequences – to be found in Wing Biddlebaum's alias and flight. But even this gloss does not capture the complexity of "truth" for Anderson, since it is not truth in itself but undue adherence to it that turns one into a grotesque. If someone "took one of the truths to himself, called it his truth, and tried to live his life by it," Anderson writes, "he became a grotesque and the truth he embraced became a falsehood" (p. 7).

To get at the sense of this fairly abstract "theory concerning the matter" (p. 7), one might take one's example not from Anderson but from his contemporary, F. Scott Fitzgerald, whose *The Great Gatsby* provides us with a sort of textbook study in the dangers of too much belief in what should remain pragmatic or instrumental fictions of the self. For if Gatsby's great talent is his improvisational skill, which allows him to finesse his past and concoct a whole persona by virtue of the anomic nature of the social order whose rhythms he has quickly come to master, then his great failing would have to be his tenacious and self-destructive commitment to "repeat the past" (Fitzgerald 1925/2004: 110) and thus, or so he hopes, to change it. What is most striking about this desire for a new past is its nostalgic commitment to an ideal of conjugal felicity, a kind of latter-day marriage plot in which it becomes imperative for Gatsby not just to have the wealth and status of a rich man or to have the girl he loves but to have both simultaneously, one as a necessary corollary of the other. In this commitment to commitment, Gatsby differs somewhat from his creator, who was much more at ease with both self-invention and – if his college drag acts are any indication – with sexual improvisation than Gatsby himself. The syncopation of the music that gives the Jazz Age its name, and which has provided Gatsby with the means to navigate Daisy's world through its capacity both to improvise and to entertain discordance, yields finally to a fatal devotion to synchronicity, in which Gatsby seeks to insert himself into a courtship plot whereby his wealth and station, not to say his other genteel merits, alone recommend him to Daisy's approval. Daisy's "rich, full life" (p. 149) attracts Gatsby in equal measure to her physical charms; "gleaming like silver, safe and proud above the hot struggles of the poor" (p. 150), Daisy, in granting Gatsby her hand, will transform him thus, in a version of the frog-prince fairytale, into someone "from much the same stratum as herself" (p. 149).

If Gatsby's desire to legitimize his sexual relation with Daisy by rewriting his past is understood as a delusion and a mistake, it is worth noting that both Tom and Nick are just as dedicated as Gatsby himself to understanding the past as the arbiter of the present. Hence Tom's "little investigation" into Gatsby's "affairs" (p. 133) confirms his suspicion that Gatsby is "Mr. Nobody from Nowhere" (p. 130); and hence Nick's final epiphany reveals that however much they strive to overcome its dispositive effects, persons are "borne back ceaselessly into the past" (p. 180). And if the most acute correction of Gatsby's misplaced interest in legitimacy comes from Daisy herself, who tells him that they "can't help what's past" and that her current love for him should be "enough" (p. 132), it is because women in this novel seem much more willing than the men around them to acknowledge the past as past and to leave it behind. This recognition Fitzgerald treats as inseparable from his female characters' more sanguine attitude toward unaccustomed and certainly looser sexual arrangements.

No female character, for example, suffers the "appalling sentimentality" (p. 111) about erotic fidelity that Gatsby himself feels. Indeed Daisy's admission of her ability to imagine herself loving both Tom and Gatsby at once is an intolerable state of affairs to Gatsby, who insists that such a dissonant condition be denied. Acknowledging her "mistake" in marrying George Wilson (who deceives her by coming to their wedding in a borrowed suit), Myrtle Wilson takes a page out of Wharton's foreclosed playbook for Lily Bart and assumes that by taking Tom as her "sweetie" (p. 35) she can in fact sleep her way to a higher class and station in life. That she is equally mistaken about Tom's interest in leaving Daisy for herself does not vitiate the strategic willingness she entertains in abandoning her husband so much as it confirms Tom's own snobbery and hypocrisy. And the fact that Jordan Baker is "too wise ever to carry well-forgotten dreams from one age to another," mirrored in her reckless "movements between hotels and clubs and private homes" (pp. 135, 155), at first provokes in Nick a "tender curiosity" (p. 57) with respect to her "incurably dishonest" "dealing in subterfuges" (p. 58) but later induces him to see her condescendingly as a product of the same artificial culture of "magazines" and "advertisement" (pp. 66, 119) that has given rise to Gatsby: "I remember thinking she looked like a good illustration" (p. 177), Nick notes of Jordan in their last encounter. Indeed if Nick is "one of the few honest people [he has] ever known," this "cardinal virtue" (p. 59) comes at the expense of a certain repression, a need to gloss over those unsavory lapses in erotic decorum he would rather not confront, like his presence in McKee's room after Myrtle Wilson's party: ". . . I was standing beside his bed and he was sitting up between the sheets, clad in his underwear, with a great portfolio in his hands" (p. 38). Nick's ellipsis tries to render elliptical – even while it draws attention to – the likely erotic transgression that has occurred in this room between these two men. As these examples suggest, women in *The Great Gatsby* appear much more tolerant of erotic seriality and the accidents of desire than the men around them. Jordan says as much when she tells Nick that she likes him because he is not "careless" (p. 58), thus leaving her all the more at liberty to be so herself. And it is Gatsby who feels compelled to turn the "colossal accident" (p. 149) of his affair with Daisy in Louisville into something closer to fate. But in Gatsby's case (as in, say, that of Thomas Sutpen in Faulkner's *Absalom, Absalom!*), accidents can never really be rectified or reckoned with. They merely give way to more accidents – like the car crash that kills Myrtle and, as a result of Wilson's grief and Tom's manipulation of it, precipitates the events that kill Gatsby too.

Sutpen's is if anything a more extreme version of Gatsby's futile effort to revise the past, as "if he could," Fitzgerald writes, "return to a certain starting place" (p. 110), in order to legitimize his present desires. A "Nobody from Nowhere" like Gatsby, Sutpen also understands sexual respectability and class position to be coincident; and like Gatsby, his efforts to forge this coincidence in his own career are undone by events beyond his anticipation or control. Yet if Gatsby's problem is that he doesn't follow Daisy's advice and leave the past well enough alone, Sutpen's is that his past seems always doomed to catch up with him and foil his best-laid plans (as when his son Charles Bon becomes engaged to his daughter Judith). Like Gatsby, Sutpen suffers from the monomania that characterizes Anderson's "grotesques"; in his case it is the desire to have a proper son and heir, an identical copy of himself. It is telling, then, that the son who proves most intractable to his father's vision, Bon, is also the novel's most sexually ambiguous figure. Already but not exactly married (to a mulatto in New Orleans, with whom he has a child) when he becomes engaged to Judith, Bon repeats the father's actions (Sutpen's first wife is also mixed-race, which is why he abandons her) but not the father's intentions. Bon's intentions remain as ambiguous in this novel as his sexuality; what Bon desires, we might say, is as hard to decipher as his own mysterious appeal.

The urbane and exotically sensual Bon is of course, as critics have long noted, the most if not the only attractive character in Faulkner's novel, equally alluring to his brother and his sister as well as to their aunt Rosa, who has never met him but whose fantasy life is much enriched by the idea of him. And he attracts Quentin Compson, of course, whose goal it is to solve the mystery of this wholly, promiscuously elusive figure. That Bon cannot be pinned down, either racially or otherwise, that he eludes or at least confuses categorization (as both brother and lover), that even in death he continues to dominate the environs of Sutpen's Hundred, suggests how erotic accident itself haunts and discredits not only the particular ideal of dynastic purity to which Sutpen is devoted but also the general economy of erotic propriety that the South, as Quentin's roommate Shreve nastily points out to him on repeated occasions, at any rate has long since abandoned. Shreve's continual taunt that Rosa is Quentin's "aunt" captures exactly the sense that an overzealous purity crusade will always beget its most perverse antithesis in the culture of incest that Shreve, no less than Faulkner himself, construes as endemic to Southern culture. Control (of familial integrity, of racial distinction) will always yield to the unavoidable accidents of desire.

Among the various other examples one might produce of the period's fascination with casual sexuality or perverse desires as a surrogate for modernity's other forms of casualization and the anxieties that attend them, perhaps the most vivid such instance is to be found in the Joad family's displacement from settled farmers to migrant workers in Steinbeck's *The Grapes of Wrath*. Their declassing, after all, occurs alongside the family's desperate effort to preserve the sanctity of the domestic unit and the failure of that preservation on various fronts: in Connie's slipping away from the pregnant Rose of Sharon in the dead of night, for example, or in the intimate suckling of an anonymous stranger that Rose of Sharon herself performs in a boxcar during the novel's dramatic finale. While Steinbeck is on record as having arrived at this scene even before composing his novel – indeed, as having essentially written *The Grapes of Wrath* in order to write this ending – one might wonder exactly what drew him, aside from its sentimental power, to such a moment. The ambiguity of this scene, which reverses the order of things on any number of levels (adult/child, stranger/intimate) is of course richly suggestive. Yet this scene also condenses and highlights a feature of Steinbeck's work not often discussed in criticism of this novel. Whereas it is customary for readers to praise the strength of her character, it has rarely occurred to them that Ma Joad's maternal prowess might be seen as coercive pressure, despite the fact that she induces Rose of Sharon to nurse the starving man – "I knowed you would. I knowed!" she tells her daughter after their silent exchange (Steinbeck 1939/1997: 453), just as it has been Ma all along who has fought against both reason and practicality to keep the family intact. Notwithstanding his compassion for Ma Joad, I want to propose the counterintuitive suggestion that Steinbeck may very well want us to find fault with her insistence on the sacralization of the family at all costs – a preservation that here, in the boxcar, assumes its most unnerving consequences. In the informal, piecework world of intimate strangers that the Joads have entered, Steinbeck's novel suggests, the family is something of a luxury best left behind. As with Sutpen's fixation on purity of blood and class, which Faulkner reveals as the ground of its own destruction, *The Grapes of Wrath* both maintains a complete commitment to the centrality of the family and shows how perverse or damaging such a commitment is.

The Grapes of Wrath thus takes us full circle, but with important differences, from the world envisioned by the novelists of the early twentieth century with whom I began this essay. For if a central theme of Dreiser and Wharton was the opportunistic, amoral nature of the erotic world, such writers nonetheless preserved a space for a more or less utopian vision of conjugal and erotic harmony – what Lily, contemplating Nettie Struthers's happy marriage, envisions late in *The House of Mirth* as "the solidarity of life," compared to "the wild centrifugal dance" and "disintegrating influences" of her Darwinian social orbit (Wharton 1905/1999: 314). Such a vision is not simply unavailable in writers like Steinbeck but plainly out of place. For Steinbeck, the utopian alternative to the casual and mercenary world of migrant servitude that the Joads have entered is not the peaceable family but the government camp – the space, as Michael Szalay has argued, of better (because institutionalized) "detachment and impersonal charity" (Szalay 2000: 167). But if American novels of the modern period neglected to concern themselves with what Christopher Lasch (1995) calls a "haven in a heartless world," they manifested even less interest in the exploration of individual consciousness that had been a staple of the realist novel since Flaubert and that persisted, albeit in rather attenuated form, through the work of Wharton and Dreiser. Whereas Wharton's narrator often treats "Miss Bart" as by turns a distant acquaintance and a cautionary tale, and whereas Dreiser's narrator often wants us to see Carrie as a case study in the inevitable victory of environment over will, both characters nonetheless retain the shape of the private and special individual, the enabling fiction of realist fiction itself. But even as he impels us to empathize with the suffering of the Joads, Steinbeck is under no illusion that this is anything other than one interchangeable family among others.

Indeed our empathy derives in no small part from the fact that we are meant to assume that their situation is not unique but transpersonal and symptomatic. And if this tendency toward typicality does not exactly herald the death of the subject, it comes rather close to burying the romance of individualism that had long buttressed the novel and that is inextricable from the primal romance of conjugal heterosexuality. As confidence in that romance itself begins to wane in the culture of modernism, and as the normative account of erotic experience shifts from "the idea that sexual behavior is involved with the whole of the individual's character," as Lionel Trilling put it in a 1948 review of the Kinsey report, to what he censoriously identified as "the tendency to divorce sex from the other manifestations of life" (Trilling 1948/2000: 132, 122), so too does the development of individualized character, with its trajectory from unawareness to rich inner life, cease to count as the catalyst for novelistic narrative.

This tendency toward the displacement of sexual experience onto surface contacts and the concomitant hollowing out of the substantive individual are readily apparent in the interwar epic novels of John Dos Passos. While there was perhaps nothing new about the sort of omnibus technique Dos Passos practiced, with its layered plots and multiple characters, there was certainly something unusual in Dos Passos's willingness to forgo, to a degree that would have been unrecognizable to the composers of Victorian triple-deckers, any hint of depth or dimension in the characters whose narratives he charts in *Manhattan Transfer* and the *USA* trilogy. The devices Dos Passos employs – the camera eye, the newsreel, and, in the case of *USA*, the frequent unmediated jumps between them and the collage of narratives in the trilogy itself – insert an irreducible distance between readers and characters, a disorientation that marks these novels throughout as a definitive instantiation of the paratactic and chance-driven *Gesellschaft* that provides the *mise-en-scène* for Gertrude Stein's work. The jagged and preemptive style of *USA*'s not quite intertwined stories, to which we return and from which we depart virtually without transition or mediation, dictates that characters in the *USA* trilogy remain strangers to us not only when we meet them but also when we leave them, as well as virtual strangers to one another even in the midst of close attachment. After a sexually adventurous cross-country trip with Ike Hall, for example, during which they have each sworn a fraternal loyalty to the other, Fainey (Mac) Macreary fails to jump the freight train that Ike has already boarded, leaving Dos Passos to note only that "That was the last [Mac] saw of Ike Hall" (Dos Passos 1929/2000: 61).

At its most extreme, Dos Passos's narrative style withholds coherence or stability from any particular character at the same time as it forces us to attribute such inconsistency itself to an erotic promiscuity that has become hegemonic. Take the example of *Manhattan Transfer*'s Ellen Thatcher, whose name and identity are as fungible as the marriages and affairs she regularly contracts. Ellen is characterized from birth as a slippery figure: "They've oiled her" at the hospital, where even then she cannot be "told apart" from other babies (Dos Passos 1925/1983: 7). Ellen's inborn variability is the motor that drives her perpetual desire to engage in illicit relations even with strangers. From "Elaine" in her marriage to Oglethorpe to "Helena" in her marriage to Herf, Ellen is singularly defined by a willingness "to shift things around" in order to maximize the distribution of herself (pp. 134, 238, 260). "I don't want to be had by anybody," she tells the lawyer George Baldwin at one point (p. 226), precisely because she wants to be had by everybody. In this regard she forms the prototype for the *USA* trilogy's Eleanor Stoddard, Ellen's near-namesake, a woman who decorates houses for a living (a career she comes to by way of set design in the theatre) and who, like Ellen, is subject to continual flirtations and erotic overtures from the men around her. Such overtures are endemic, it would seem, to the modern workplace, as Alice and Janey in *The 42nd Parallel* acknowledge when discussing "the danger of staying in an office alone with a man" late at night, when "a man had just one idea" (Dos Passos 1929/2000: 122). Yet unlike Alice and Janey, who respond to male harassment by taking up with each other (in an affair that ends, as almost all bonds do in this novel, when each of them moves on to a different job), Eleanor sees men's unsolicited sexual advances in the same novel as less threatening than welcome. For Eleanor, such advances mean social advancement because sexuality in Dos Passos's vision means circulation. This is why he assigns pride of place in the preface to *The 42nd Parallel* to two figures who will find their epitome in Eleanor Stoddard and who will in crucial ways preside over his trilogy as a whole: the "street walker" who "fidgets under an arclight" and her counterpart, "the dummy girl in a red evening dress" placed "in a showwindow" by "two sallow windowdressers" (p. xiii). If the dummy is lifeless and still while the prostitute "fidgets," both are nevertheless imagined as the dynamic agents as well as products of an innovative economy where erotic desire appears the global form of currency – a feature of the novel borne out soon enough by Mac's work with Dr Bingham, a traveling salesman who peddles pornography in the sticks.

While the Dos Passos of the 1920s and 1930s has long been regarded as perhaps the premier American novelist of dissent, and while this opinion has long informed those aspects of his trilogy – its anomie, its will to disorientation – in which critics have wanted to see him as the chronicler of a society in danger of losing all ethical grounds, one can hardly overlook the fact that Dos Passos has as much respect for the instrumentalist culture he so vividly realizes in this fiction as he has contempt for its dehumanizing consequences. In the world of the *USA* trilogy, all relations have become public relations (which happens to be the job that Eleanor's lover J. Ward Moorehouse invents for himself). Eleanor and Ward thrive in this world because they manipulate both relations and designs; they are at home in the culture of image and desire, of the epiphenomenal and informal, that Dos Passos recognizes as inevitable. It is not insignificant that their match – an adulterous romance between a PR consultant and an interior decorator – should serve to displace from consideration the matrimonial romance whose representational monopoly has waned in tandem with the producer culture that throughout the first half of the twentieth century was experiencing its own death throes. That their relationship is less a matter of clandestine secrecy than of public meetings, more a business partnership than a union of souls, points to an account of erotic experience that has exchanged intimacy for publicity, inner life for engrossing spectacle. What attracts Eleanor to Ward, of course, is precisely his directorial finesse. When she is standing in his house confronting his wife about the "horrible rumors" regarding her carryings-on with Ward, Eleanor is overcome by "emotion" because she finds the occasion "like a play, like a Whistler, like Sarah Bernhardt" (Dos Passos 1929/2000: 282). We might say that for Eleanor it is the act or the artifice that holds the most appeal, over and above any substantive depths of feeling or meaning such artifice may embellish.

To be sure, Dos Passos aims a great deal of irony at such captivation by surfaces and set-pieces, and it would be a mistake to underestimate the ambivalence with which he and the other novelists I have surveyed here approach modernity and its new rules. It is a truism of American modernism that it flowered out of a sustained and irreversible revolt against – as Alfred Kazin dryly sums up this particular cliché – "a period of dark ignorance and repressive Victorian gentility" (Kazin 1942/1995: xxi). Yet such a view does not do justice to the complex and ambiguous attitudes one discovers among a host of modernist figures who regarded the American past, Puritan or otherwise, from the vantage of an uncertain present. From Gertrude Stein's pronouncement in *How to Write* that "the oldest country is the United States of America" (1931/1975: 72) to Cather's view, in the prefatory note to *Not Under Forty*, that "the world broke in two in 1922 or thereabouts" and that it can reasonably be divided into those "backward" persons born before 1882 and everyone else, American modernists were as keen to scrutinize the past as they were to bury it. But this is only to say that, however progressive their viewpoint might be at a given moment in time, no writers are uniformly forward-looking. Modernist writers clearly felt they were living in a moment of drastic transition, and their work registered such transition with both experiment and nostalgia, enthusiasm and ironic detachment. And this dialectical attitude prevailed in those areas of social life, namely sex and class, that – subject to the most tenacious ideological assumptions – underwent the most dramatic of struggles toward redefinition.

Modern American novelists, we might say, were committed in equal measure both to this process of redefinition and to the preservation of inherited assumptions. The latter commitment manifests itself most strikingly in the narrative tension to be wrung out of the nonnormative or queer figures who populate so many of the novels between 1900 and 1950. As the case of Sherwood Anderson demonstrates, while "the revolt from the village" shaped the basic mission of his project, nonetheless the village remains intact at the end of *Winesburg, Ohio* even though George Willard ends up fleeing it. The world as Anderson presents it does not so much accommodate the "grotesques" he delineates as it uneasily suffers their presence. In very little writing of the first half of the twentieth century do we approach anything like a utopian impulse with respect to social change (the great era of utopian fiction having ended with the Gilded Age writers, like William Dean Howells and Edward Bellamy, from whom modernists resolutely distanced themselves). In fact in a culture where both class relations and erotic assumptions underwent striking upheavals, very few of the most significant writers of fiction saw fit to elaborate these movements as other than problems or symptoms, and almost always of each other. But in directing their energies toward such a problematic concern by means of floating persons, casual encounters, and episodic lust, American modernists both sustained the novel's long preoccupation with desire's sociability and irrevocably laid bare that sociability's limits.

REFERENCES AND FURTHER READING

Anderson, Sherwood. (1919/1996). *Winesburg, Ohio*. New York: Norton.

Cather, Willa. (1918/1994). *My Ántonia*. New York: Vintage.

Cather, Willa. (1936/1988). *Not Under Forty*. Lincoln: University of Nebraska Press.

Dos Passos, John. (1925/1983). *Manhattan Transfer*. Boston: Houghton Mifflin.

Dos Passos, John. (1929/2000). *The 42nd Parallel*. Boston: Houghton Mifflin.

Dreiser, Theodore. (1900/1994). *Sister Carrie*. New York: Penguin.

Faulkner, William. (1936/1990). *Absalom, Absalom!* New York: Vintage.

Fitzgerald, F. Scott. (1925/2004). *The Great Gatsby*. New York: Scribners.

Hemingway, Ernest. (1925/1996). *In Our Time*. New York: Scribners.

Hemingway, Ernest. (1926/2003). *The Sun Also Rises*. New York: Scribners.

James, Henry. (1899/1984). The future of the novel. In *Literary Criticism, Volume 1: Essays on Literature, American Writers, English Writers*, ed. Leon Edel (pp. 100–10). New York: Library of America.

Kazin, Alfred. (1942/1995). *On Native Grounds: A Study of Modern American Prose Literature*. New York: Harcourt.

Lasch, Christopher. (1995). *Haven in a Heartless World*. New York: Norton.

Stein, Gertrude. (1909/1990). *Three Lives*. New York: Penguin.

Stein, Gertrude. (1931/1975). *How To Write*. New York: Dover.

Stein, Gertrude. (1933/1990). *The Autobiography of Alice B. Toklas*. New York: Vintage.

Steinbeck, John. (1939/1997). *The Grapes of Wrath*. New York: Penguin.

Szalay, Michael. (2000). *American Literature and the Invention of the Welfare State*. Durham, NC: Duke University Press.

Trilling, Lionel. (1948/2000). The Kinsey Report. In *The Moral Obligation to be Intelligent: Selected Essays*, ed. Leon Wieseltier (pp. 120–36). New York: Farrar Straus Giroux.

Wharton, Edith. (1905/1999). *The House of Mirth*. New York: Modern Library.

6
Jazz: From the Gutter to the Mainstream

Jeremy Yudkin

In the first half of the twentieth century – for reasons of intellectual snobbery, the American cultural inferiority complex, associations with "low life," racism, and misunderstanding – jazz and practitioners of jazz experienced a general miasma of disdain mixed with gradually increasing glimmers of appreciation. This gradual change in the acceptability of jazz as a topic of serious interest over the first half of the twentieth century can be demonstrated by a survey of music history books, journals, and articles in both specialized and popular magazines over that period. The change was also no doubt due to a growing respect among the white population for African-American intellectual and cultural figures and to a growing familiarity with the music. Jazz experienced a roller-coaster ride in the annals of American respectability and acceptance over the first half-century of its existence, but the trend was gradually upwards, and in the 1950s jazz entered the mainstream of American intellectual life.

General histories of music published in the US were very slow to show interest in any American music, let alone in jazz. From 1870, when the first general music history book (*The History of Music* by Frédéric Ritter) was published in the United States, and for many decades thereafter, American music received no mention. This pattern was followed until the early 1940s. Implicit in all these books (and indeed in concert and artistic life through most of the country during those years) was the view that significant and civilized culture belonged to Europe, with its over 2,000-year history of art and poetry and documented music making, and that America would become cultivated only in proportion to its emulation of the European tradition (Hitchcock 1986).

Even when American music was the subject of a specialized history book, most authors were interested only in "high-art" or European-influenced classical music. Ritter, the author of the first general history of music, turned in 1883 to the American scene. His book, *Music in America,* discussed classical music exclusively, as did Louis Elson's *The History of American Music* (1904) and William Hubbard's *History of*

American Music (1908). In 1916 the musicologist, librarian, and scholar Oscar Sonneck urged historians to deal with the actuality of music making in America and to focus on what was characteristic about American music rather than on its similarities to music from Europe. Sonneck's suggestions were only partially adopted by John Howard, whose *Our American Music* of 1931 was the first to include a discussion of folk music in America. But Howard's view was still informed by that of earlier scholars: America was a wilderness, needing to be civilized by the ancient musical traditions of Europe (Hitchcock 1986, Matthews 1986, Newsom and Hitchcock 1986).

The first published appearance of the word "jazz" seems to have been in an article in the sports pages of a San Francisco newspaper in 1913, which reported that a local baseball team had hired a band to entertain the players, and that the musicians had plenty of "jazz," which the writer defined as "pep" or "enthusiasm" (Collier 1988: 6). In 1917, the year of the first jazz recordings, in one of the earliest published articles on jazz, Walter Kingsley was of two minds about the qualities of jazz (and the nature of its practitioners):

> Jazz music is the delirium tremens of syncopation. It is strict rhythm without melody. To-day the jazz bands take popular tunes and rag them to death to make jazz. . . . [On the other hand] jazz is based on the savage musician's wonderful gift for progressive retarding and acceleration guided by his sense of "swing". (Kingsley, quoted in Walser 1999: 6–7)

(To "rag" a tune meant to play it in syncopated rhythm. Note the mixture of disdain and admiration in the description.) However, the first recordings soon became best-sellers, and the band that made them, the Original Dixieland Jazz Band, soon became extremely popular (and very highly paid) and spawned several imitators. A dance journal wrote in 1917, "The jazz band idea is sweeping the country. . . . Wherever you go, you hear jazz music" (quoted in Collier 1988: 7–8).

But views on this music were decidedly mixed. Even the local newspaper in the birthplace of American jazz, the *New Orleans Times-Picayune*, declared in an editorial of 1918 that jazz performances were "manifestations of a low streak in man's tastes" (quoted in Collier 1988: 5).

A year later, however, the Swiss conductor Ernest Ansermet wrote a (deeply patronizing) appreciation of the Southern Syncopated Orchestra and especially its clarinetist Sidney Bechet:

> There is in the Southern Syncopated Orchestra an extraordinary clarinet virtuoso . . . [His solos] are admirable equally for their richness of invention, their force of accent, and their daring novelty and unexpected turns. . . . what a moving thing it is to meet this black, fat boy with white teeth and narrow forehead, who is very glad one likes what he does, but can say nothing of his art, except that he follows his "own way" – and then one considers that perhaps his "own way" is the highway along which the whole world will swing tomorrow. (quoted in Walser 1999: 11)

But in 1920 *Living Age* magazine described jazz as producing "a sound more indicative of Hell than of Heaven" (quoted in Collier 1988: 9).

During the so-called "Jazz Age," many people deplored the sounds and the social consequences of the music. In 1921 the town of Zion, Illinois, banned jazz, having determined that, together with alcohol and tobacco, it was a sin (Pearson 1994: 52, n.1).

In 1924 Marion Bauer, an American musicologist, wrote about jazz for a French music journal:

> "Jazz" is the true child of the age; but one shouldn't forget that it is also the child of the dregs of the civilized world and that it comes from the lower classes of society. The dances that have penetrated everywhere, in our salons, in our ballrooms, were created in a quarter of San Francisco . . . where one finds the outcasts of ports, the scum of all nations and all the races; it would take the alchemy of magicians to turn material from such vile origins into a true masterpiece! (quoted in Porter 1997: 131)

A number of clever and derisive definitions of the word jazz were reported in a 1925 editorial by Charles S. Johnson in *Opportunity*:

> There is a new international word – Jazz. . . . The Etymological Dictionary of Modern English defines it as "a number of niggers surrounded by noise. . . ." . . . Horatio Parker, an American composer of note . . . calls it "naked African rhythm, and no more." . . . Henry Van Dyck . . . referred to it before the National Education Association as "a species of music invented by demons for the torture of imbeciles." . . . [One intellectual remarked:] "Some happy day, we shall beat our swords into ploughshares and our jazz bands into unconsciousness." (quoted in Porter 1997: 122)

One unusual clergyman, Rev. Charles Stelzle, was moved in 1925 to wonder about the positive significance of jazz. "Jazz is not necessarily the gateway to hell," he wrote. "It may be the portal to life eternal" (quoted in Meltzer 1993: 53). But the Baptist pastor Dr John Roach Straton was moved to invoke the same metaphor when he was interviewed about jazz in an article in the *New York Times* in May 1926. The article, entitled "Straton Says Jazz is 'Agency of Devil,'" suggests that Dr Straton regarded the growth of jazz as synonymous with a general tendency towards an overall collapse of civilization:

> "If I were asked to answer in a single sentence, 'what shall we do about jazz,' I would reply that we ought to consign it to a hotter place than this earth," said Dr Straton. "I have no patience with this modern jazz tendency, whether it be in music, science, social life or religion. It is part of the lawless spirit which is being manifested in many departments of life, endangering our civilization in its general revolt against authority and established order. Jazz music is just as much a revolt against the standards of modesty and decency as is the jazz tendency in dress.

"Jazz, with its discord, its appeal to the sensuous, should be stamped out. The jazz hound is an outlaw and a musical bandit. Like the gunman, he is running amuck and should be relentlessly put down. . . ." (quoted in Porter 1997: 143–4)

Even black journalists compared jazz unfavorably with classical concert music. In 1929 in the black newspaper *The Chicago Defender* Dave Peyton advised the musicians among his readers to make sure that they practiced assiduously: " . . . if you are in a jazz band do not give up proper study on your instrument. You may be called upon to render real service and to play *good* music. . . . Jazz is on the wane, and the better class of music is coming back into favor with the critical public" (quoted in Walser 1999: 58–9, my italics).

Some black writers began to see jazz as the proud manifestation of a separate and worthy culture. Novelist, essayist, critic, and poet Langston Hughes was a member of the circle of black writers and musicians whose work contributed to the phenomenon known as the Harlem Renaissance. He wrote poetry to be accompanied by jazz and poems that tried to capture "the meanings and rhythms of jazz." His first book of verse was entitled *The Weary Blues* (1926). In an essay, "The Negro Artist and the Racial Mountain" in *The Nation* in 1926, he wrote: "Jazz to me is one of the inherent expressions of Negro life in America" (quoted in Walser 1999: 56).

And in the 1920s jazz began to attract serious and enthusiastic attention both in the United States and abroad. In 1926 the self-styled "jazz missionary" and bandleader Paul Whiteman published a book called simply *Jazz*, about the music (and himself) (Whiteman and McBride 1926: 295). And in the same year Henry Osgood's *So This Is Jazz* appeared, a book the author regarded as "the first attempt to set down a connected account of the origin, history, and development of jazz music" (Osgood 1926: vii). The English writer Robert Mendl's book *The Appeal of Jazz* was published in London in 1927. Mendl wrote, "I find in [jazz] an abundance – sometimes a superabundance – of vigor; a rhythmic verve so exhilarating that one can hardly keep one's feet still . . ." (Mendl 1927: 65).

By the end of the 1920s the mastery of one particular jazzman, Duke Ellington, was beginning to be noticed in the white press. An article in *The Bookman* in 1929 commented:

> Duke Ellington's Orchestra (also known as The Washingtonians), especially when playing its leader's own dance-tunes, is dogmatically pronounced to be supreme in this field. . . . There is more and better melody in one of the dances of this astounding Negro than in ten of the pallid tunes of the average operetta . . . (quoted in Porter 1997: 157)

Ellington's work was also praised by an English writer, Constant Lambert, who was himself a composer and a conductor. In his book *Music Ho!*, published in 1934, Lambert seemed genuinely enthusiastic about Ellington's work (though he patronized both Ellington and blacks in general and was a vicious anti-Semite):

The best records of Duke Ellington . . . can be listened to again and again because they are not just decorations of a familiar shape but a new arrangement of shapes. Ellington, in fact, is a real composer, the first jazz composer of distinction, and the first negro composer of distinction. (quoted in Porter, 1997: 155, 153–4)

General appreciation of the music, however, was still tempered by the persistence of old attitudes. In 1934 the satirist and social commentator H. L. Mencken excoriated the sounds of jazz as "unpleasant," "crude banalities," its beat as "monotonous," and its tunes as "rubbish fit only for tin whistles" (*Baltimore Evening Sun*, September 3, 1934).

Much of the early writing on jazz came from Europe. In 1932, the Belgian Robert Goffin published *Aux frontières du jazz*, a personal appreciation (never translated into English) that distinguished between the whitened, concertized version of jazz as purveyed by arrangers such as Paul Whiteman (whom Goffin cleverly called his "bête blanche") and the real thing (Feather 1966: 722). In 1934, the same year as the Englishman Lambert's book, the French writer Hugues Panassié, who was one of the founders of the famous Hot Club de France and editor of the journal *Jazz hot*, wrote another of the early books that made a serious study of jazz. In *Le jazz hot* (1934) translated in 1936 as *Hot Jazz: The Guide to Swing Music*, the author praised the special characteristics of jazz and tried to identify those elements that made it "hot," "authentic," and "true" as opposed to "sweet" or "imitation." The book features a brief foreword by Louis Armstrong, Panassié's "greatest of all hot soloists" (Panassié 1936: 19, 291, 51). In the same year as Panassié's book, Armstrong himself published a brief anecdotal autobiography, not always in his own words, entitled *Swing That Music*, which contains some important recollections about the earliest years of jazz (Armstrong 1936). The insightful introduction is by Armstrong champion and famous crooner Rudy Vallee. And yet not all Europeans were enthusiastic about jazz. Georges Duhamel, in his fear of the Americanization of his country, wrote in 1931 that jazz was "a triumph of barbaric folly" (Duhamel 1931: 121).

A significant but often overlooked indicator of the slowly growing popularity of jazz was the publication of jazz discographies. The earliest of these were also published in Europe. In 1936, Charles Delaunay's *Hot Discography* appeared in Paris and a few years later was reprinted in New York. Delaunay was the cofounder, with Panassié, of *Jazz hot*, and seems to have coined the word "discography" (Atkins 1982). And in the same year another jazz discography, *Rhythm on Record*, by Hilton Schleman, who was a record company publicist, was printed in London.

One American writer, Helen Kaufmann, a self-described "music-lover," wrote what she called a "cheery bird's-eye view" of American music in 1937. Her *From Jehovah to Jazz* refers often to the European enthusiasm for jazz and suggests that Americans might learn from it ("Jazz is said in Europe to be the distinctive contribution of America to music, an assertion resented with some justice in serious musical circles here, for [jazz] has long been regarded askance as the cheap and vulgar outlet of the uncultured." "In Europe it is taken seriously as a valuable addition to musical literature, although in America, outside of its own amusement realm, it has not yet attained any such recognition"). Her writing is strongly colored by contemporary patronizing attitudes towards "negroes" and others, but she covers early psalm singing, the music of American Indians, folk music, spirituals, school songs, ballads, amateur music making, minstrel shows, blues, ragtime, and swing, and she speaks enthusiastically of Gershwin, Armstrong, Tommy Dorsey, Ellington, and the Goodman Quartet, with Teddy Wilson, Lionel Hampton, and Gene Krupa (Kaufmann 1937: ix–x, 270, x). In the same year, Waldo Frank suggested that jazz was an echo of the Industrial Revolution. "This song is not an escape from the Machine to the limpid depths of the soul. It is the Machine itself! It is the music of a revolt that fails. Its voice is the mimicry of our industrial havoc." And in a startlingly suggestive metaphor he wrote: "Jazz is a moment's gaiety, after which the spirit droops, cheated and unnurtured" (Frank 1937: 119).

By the end of the 1930s, swing bands had turned jazz into a widely popular phenomenon. An editorial in *Opportunity*, published in the summer of 1938, described the scene:

> A few Sundays ago upwards of twenty thousand people, according to press reports, attended a "swing" carnival at Randalls Island, New York City. . . . It remained, however, for Duke Ellington and his orchestra to send the crowd into such rapture that for a few minutes it appeared that a riot was imminent as thousands of swing-crazed young men and women broke over the barriers and attempted to storm the bandstand. (quoted in Porter 1997: 159–60)

More books on jazz were beginning to be published, and jazz musicians were beginning to be taken seriously. Two jazz concerts were given at the shrine of classical music performance, Carnegie Hall, in 1938. Benny Goodman was invited to speak and teach at the most prestigious institute for classical music in the country, the Juilliard School of Music in New York (Porter 1997: 162). In the late 1930s Goodman became famous for playing classical music as well as jazz. In 1938 he released a recording of the Mozart Clarinet Quintet (with the Budapest String Quartet) and appeared in a classical music recital at Town Hall in New York. In 1939 Goodman performed in Carnegie Hall a new work he had commissioned from Béla Bartók. That same year Goodman published an autobiographical book, *The Kingdom of Swing*, about jazz and his life in it, culminating with his recent triumphs.[1] In 1939 Alain Locke, a professor of philosophy at Howard University, wrote in *Opportunity*:

> The music season just closing has been one grand crescendo for Negro music, with almost too many events and too wide an up-swing to be adequately chronicled in a single article. . . . But the predicament is a pleasant one, since it does vindicate our title ["Negro Music Goes to Par"] as a fair and honest assessment of the musical situation. This year Negro music has really gone to par. (quoted in Porter 1997: 163)

In 1939 Charles Edward Smith and Fred Ramsey published *Jazzmen: The Story of Hot Jazz Told in the Lives of the Men Who Created It*, an important early anthology of writing about the musicians of jazz. Smith later went on to become one of the founding members of the Institute for Jazz Studies.

A serious discussion of American music in a general book on music history first came in 1940, when Howard McKinney and William Anderson published their *Music in History: The Evolution of an Art*. In addition to some passing mentions of Gershwin and Copland, *Music in History* devotes the last 18 pages (out of about 900) to "American Hopes." This book was one of the first general music history books to consider jazz seriously. The authors adopt the (for the time) revolutionary approach of dividing American music into three (implicitly equal) streams: folk music, "serious" music, and "popular" music, the last of which includes the songs of Stephen Foster, comic operas, Sousa marches, ragtime, the blues, and swing. Popular music offers "the one outstanding contribution which America has made to twentieth-century music," and of particular importance in this contribution are "jazz and swing" (used more or less synonymously) (McKinney and Anderson 1940: 854). In 1941, Paul Henry Lang's influential *Music in Western Civilization* also discussed American music, but the subject receives barely six pages out of 1,100 and in a chapter entitled "Peripheries of Nineteenth-Century Music" (Lang 1941: 933–88). And in the same year a book on teaching music in high schools warned against incorporating jazz into the curriculum, for "Swing music . . . is primarily physical. . . . To use such music in the school as a substitute for serious music is to cheat youth of a highly important experience which has the possibility of assisting in the development of spiritual resources" (Dykema and Gehrkens 1941: 455).

In addition to scholarly histories and textbooks two types of popular writing about jazz began to appear in the late 1930s and early 1940s: books and articles by amateur enthusiasts of the music, who wished to proselytize about their passion, and books or articles containing interviews with performing musicians. The new magazine *Down Beat* helped provide a forum for these discussions as well as to historicize the music. Two controversies added to the sense of "style periods" and the perception of historical depth in jazz in the late 1930s and in the 1940s. First there were those who felt that the popularity of swing indicated a dilution in the immediacy and authenticity of the music. They advocated a return to "traditional" jazz, namely the simultaneous improvisation and small-group sound of the New Orleans style that had marked the music of the 1920s. The second was the controversy over bebop.

In the early 1940s, just as jazz, in the form of swing, reached unprecedented levels of popularity, a self-consciously intellectual, antipopulist movement known as bebop began to alienate audiences. Harry Henderson and Sam Shaw reported in *Collier's* in 1948 that dance-hall managers decried the new music for "killing the goose that laid the golden egg" (quoted in Porter 1997: 173).

Bebop was deliberately demanding. "You have to be an extremely accomplished musician to attempt bop," wrote one critic (quoted in Porter 1997: 174). Another asserted, "It's a difficult music to play and understand. That's why our young musicians, better schooled than yesterday's swing men, are turning to it once they find that swing is a pushover" (Bill Gottlieb in the *New York Herald Tribune*, quoted in Porter 1997: 176). Looking back on the bebop era from many years later, Dizzy Gillespie, one of its major figures, wrote in 1979:

> For a generation of Americans and young people around the world, who reached maturity during the 1940s, bebop symbolized a rebellion against the rigidities of the old order, an outcry for change in almost every field, especially in music. The bopper wanted to impress the world with a new stamp, the uniquely modern design of a new generation coming of age. (quoted in Walser 1999: 170)

Gillespie was also quoted (by Stephanie Barber, in an unpublished interview in 1987) defining bop as follows: "It's variations on a theme never stated." As a symbol of its intellectual content, boppers borrowed licks and chords from contemporary classical composers, especially Stravinsky, who was then living in Los Angeles (Porter 1997: 179–80).

The arguments over bebop continued throughout the decade. Louis Armstrong, by then one of the best-known and most respected figures in jazz, was quoted and (according to him) misquoted on both sides of the issue: "Don't you know I'm crazy about that 'Re Bop' stuff?"; "Mistakes – that's all bebop is"; "It's all just flash" (quoted in Porter 1997: 182, 184, 185).

By 1948, Armstrong said that he was tired of the controversy: "They're always misquotin' me so I don't like to discuss it no more" (Porter 1997: 185). However, in 1953 Armstrong was still speaking out against bop. In a newspaper interview he said, "It's just one of those crazes that makes a big hit overnight and then fades right out of the picture. It's crazy stuff – lots of discords and solo interpretation that just doesn't make sense" (King 1953). Leonard Feather tried to explain the music in 1949 with *Inside Be-bop*, but it took a while for bop to become widely understood and acceptable. As late as 1953 Benny Goodman complained to the *New York Times*, "Maybe bop has done more to set music back for years than anything. Basically, it's all wrong. It's not even knowing the scales. The results have got to be bad. What you hear in bop is a lot of noise" (Firestone 1993: 354). It was natural that the old-timers were threatened by it. Somebody once asked Eubie Blake what bop was, and he answered, "Nothin', man, nothin'" (quoted by Stephanie Barber in 1987 interview).

More discographies appeared in the 1940s. *The Jazz Record Book* of 1942 by Charles Smith et al. was a brief guide for collectors, but Orin Blackstone's comprehensive *Index to Jazz* was published in four volumes from 1945 to 1948. Also in 1948, Delaunay's discography was revised, edited by Walter Schaap and George Avakian, and significantly expanded, as the *New Hot Discography*. The following year, the first volume was published of a complete alphabetical discography, compiled, again, by Europeans. English jazz enthusiasts Dave Carey and Albert McCarthy were so thorough with their *Directory of Recorded Jazz* that they could only publish a few letters at a time. It took them eight years and six volumes to get to "L," by which time the publishers gave up on them.

Jazz education took an important step in the 1940s, when Robert Goffin, the author of *Aux frontières du jazz* and an enthusiastic supporter of the music, and the writer and critic Leonard Feather gave a 15-part lecture series on jazz at the New School for Social Research in New York in 1942 (Feather 1996: 722–38), and jazz writer Rudi Blesh (jazz critic for the *San Francisco Chronicle* and later for the *New York Herald Tribune*) gave a series of lectures at the San Francisco Museum of Art in 1943 (Hasse and Kernfeld 2002).

In 1943 *Esquire* magazine began featuring a poll, in which a panel of experts voted for an "all-star" group of jazz musicians. The resulting band played at the first jazz concert ever given at the Metropolitan Opera House in New York on January 18, 1944 (Feather 1996: 728). As the 1940s continued, more and more writing on jazz appeared in the popular press, and the arguments about swing versus traditional and bebop versus swing became more and more heated. Phrases such as "real jazz," "real American jazz music," and "true cultural values" were set against "nonsense," "damage," and "flashy virtuosity"; "phonies" were trying to "pervert" jazz, "professional vipers" such as Dizzy Gillespie were aiming to "cut the heart out of the real main line jazz" (Carter Winter in "An open letter to Fred Robbins" in *The Jazz Record* 50 (November 1946): 12), and "fascists" were frustrated at their "inability to foist their idiotic views on the public" (Leonard Feather in *Metronome* 61 (September 1945): 16), Goffin continued his criticism of saccharine jazz and Paul Whiteman-style playing in *Jazz: From the Congo to the Metropolitan* (1944) but praised Benny Goodman's band, named true jazz "the real music of America" (Goffin 1944: 240), and called for jazz to be taught in conservatories, and jazz archives to be established. Rudi Blesh published his history of jazz, *Shining Trumpets*, in 1946. In it he analyzed those traits of jazz that he believed to be direct descendants of African music and told the history of the music. But even this book helped to perpetuate the jazz wars, for Blesh praises the "authenticity" of the music of the 1920s over the "commercialism" of swing, which he condemns as "the music of defeat," "salon music," "not jazz," "reactionary," "anti-jazz," "nihilistic," "destructive," and "rabble-rousing" (Blesh 1946: 262, 266, 270, 289–91). Also in 1946 the brilliant and argumentative Winthrop Sargeant, who was music critic for the *New Yorker* for 25 years, from 1947 to 1972, and wrote about both classical music and jazz, published a revised edition of his book *Jazz, Hot and Hybrid* (which had first appeared eight years earlier) (Smith 1986). Before becoming a music critic Sargeant had played violin in the New York Symphony.

In his book Sargeant severely criticized jazz for its limitations and praised it for its vitality. On the one hand he called jazz a kind of folk music that was not susceptible to the kind of analysis commentators often deployed for it; its creators were humble and uneducated and depended upon "impulse" and "instinct"; the music was primitive, formulaic, and limited: "in poetic resources it is about as rich as pidgin English."

On the other hand Sargeant delighted in the "excitement" of jazz: "Melodically, jazz is often strikingly beautiful and original"; "It has the quality of vitality that characterizes music designed to fill a real and thirsty demand"; "There can be no doubt that the world is richer for it" (Gottlieb 1996: 763–73). Racism and reverse racism were not far below the surface (and sometimes on the surface) of many of these debates about the qualities of jazz. The *Esquire* poll came in for its share of criticism on both sides. And the black-owned trade magazine *Music Dial* directly addressed topics such as discrimination in hiring practices and racism in the musicians' union (Tucker 2002).

In 1947 the writer and commentator Ralph de Toledano published a collection of essays about jazz that had appeared in *Downbeat*, *Swing Music*, *Saturday Evening Post*, and *Fortune*, through which he wished to demonstrate the history and importance of jazz. The collection was called *Frontiers of Jazz* and the articles focus on the roots and early inventors of the music and trace its gradual growth through the decades. In 1948 the prolific bandleader and banjoist Eddie Condon published his memoirs, which are full of entertaining stories about jazz musicians.

In the late 1940s ambivalent feelings about jazz in general were still in evidence among traditional scholars. In 1947 Marion Bauer, who had written so scathingly about jazz in the 1920s (see above), was now a professor of music at New York University. In a revised edition of her book *Twentieth Century Music*, her own deprecating attitude towards jazz was abundantly clear. Although she obviously felt obliged to consider the phenomenon in her book, her chapter on "Jazz and American Music" began with the following sentence: "Jazz, for better or for worse, is a twentieth century American product." Other comments included the following: "Whether we like it or not, Europe considers jazz the one original contribution that American has made to modern music"; "[Jazz] has beaten its insidious rhythms into every corner of the globe" (Bauer 1947: 316–17). But in the same year, from January to October, author and lecturer Rudi Blesh presented a series of programs on jazz on the radio (Hasse and Kernfeld 2002).

Ambivalence about jazz was strongly evident in the book on American popular music by Sigmund Spaeth, prolific author, music critic, and journalist. In the same chapter of *A History of Popular Music in America* he described jazz in terms of its "distortion of the conventions of popular music," "decadence," "creativ[ity]," and "underlying aesthetic significance" (Spaeth 1948: 415, 421, 424). But the late 1940s also saw jazz become the focus of a scholarly article in the most prestigious American academic journal of musical analysis and musicological study. The *Journal of the American Musicological Society* in 1948 published Richard Waterman's "'Hot' Rhythm in Negro Music," which attempted to trace the influence of African rhythm on American folk music and jazz and contained transcriptions of West Indian songs and jazz solos. In the same year the Marxist scholar and critic Sidney Finkelstein published an articulate and passionate claim for the importance of jazz as the music of an oppressed people in his book *Jazz: A People's Music*. He discusses blues and folk music, engages closely with the social and racial issues behind the music, and, in remarkably prescient passages, makes two important predictions for the future of jazz. First, he said, jazz would bring American music to a time "when the artificial distinction between 'classical' and 'popular' will disappear . . . and the only questions to be asked will be, is it good music or bad? Is it honest music or dishonest?" Second, he hoped that one day Americans would recognize jazz as "a prized cultural treasure" (Finkelstein 1948: 19–20). The first prediction is slowly being fulfilled, and in 1990 the United States Congress passed a resolution declaring jazz "a rare and valuable national American treasure."

On the whole, however, as a study by Morroe Berger published in 1947 in *Journal of Negro History* showed, jazz was regarded with suspicion and distrust for the first four decades of its history. White (and a few black) ministers and educators were worried about its feeling of abandon and lack of restraint; classical musicians disliked it because it was played by musicians without formal training (cited in Stearns 1956: 309).

Significant and widespread public and intellectual acceptance of jazz both as a vital current presence on the American scene and as a phenomenon worthy of historical and musical analysis belongs to the 1950s. The now-famous Institute of Jazz Studies at Rutgers University was founded in 1952 by Marshall Stearns, who was a professor of English literature but also taught jazz at New York University and at Hunter College. The Institute was established as a research center and an archive of jazz materials, including books, recordings, photographs, and jazz memorabilia. Another important archive of jazz was established in the cradle of jazz by William Russell in 1954: the Tulane University Archive of New Orleans Jazz, which numbers among its holdings an important collection of oral histories (Zager and Kernfeld 2002, Berger 2002).

The 1950s experienced an enormous upsurge in the number and quality of books and articles written on the subject of jazz. Guthrie Ramsay (2003) writes, "The growth of formal criticism – *writing* about jazz – supplied a crucial impetus for the elevation of the music's status" (p. 121). Again a significant proportion of them were first published in Europe, by means of which English, French, and German writers helped to show Americans the importance of their music. Out of 13 surveys, stylistic studies, and histories of jazz published in the 1950s, six were published in Europe. The first survey, simply entitled *Jazz*, was published by Rex Harris in London in 1952, and *Modern Jazz: A Survey of Developments since 1939* by Alun Morgan and Raymond Horricks (1956) also came out in London. *Jazz* surveys the music from the roots of jazz in West Africa, to "the great individualists" Armstrong, Bechet, and Morton, to swing (discussed in the chapter "American Commercial Exploitation"), to the influence of jazz on classical composers, and includes a chapter on jazz in England. *Modern Jazz* is beautifully written and contains sensitive and thorough discussions of performances and recordings as well as a chapter on jazz in England, Sweden, Germany, and France. Two books by French authors in the 1950s were translated into English: André Hodeir's *Hommes et problèmes du jazz* (1954) appeared in New York two years later as *Jazz: Its Evolution and Essence*; and *Jazz* by André

Francis appeared in French in 1958 and in English in 1960. Another small French book, which was not translated, was Lucien Malson's *Les maîtres du jazz* (1952), which had chapters on the major figures of American jazz, including King Oliver, Louis Armstrong, Duke Ellington, and others, and was influential in spreading the word on the continent about jazz – France's "enfant adoptif." Joachim-Ernst Berendt's *Das Jazzbuch: Entwicklung und Bedeutung der Jazzmusik* (The Jazzbook: Development and Meaning of Jazz Music) was published in 1953, but did not arrive in the United States in English until 1962 as *The New Jazz Book: A History and Guide*. Ultimately this book was translated into 16 languages and is believed to have sold more than a million copies (Lindenmaier 2002).

Berendt, who was also a concert and festival organizer and record producer, wrote two other books about jazz in the 1950s, *Jazz-optisch* (1954) and *Variationen über Jazz* (1956), neither of which was translated into English. These books and others solidified the view of jazz as a subject worthy of historical study, as was appropriate for an art now entering its fifth decade. Barry Ulanov, who had written on both Mozart and Bing Crosby and Duke Ellington in the 1940s, but spent his career as an English professor and author of books on religion and psychology, published the extremely thorough *A History of Jazz in America* in 1952 and *A Handbook of Jazz* in 1957. In 1954 Louis Armstrong followed up his brief 1936 autobiography with more detailed reminiscences in *Satchmo: My Life in New Orleans*.

An important stage in the historicizing process was reached in 1955, when the jazz writers and music producers Orrin Keepnews and Bill Grauer, founders of the record label Riverside, published *A Pictorial History of Jazz: People and Places from New Orleans to Modern Jazz*, an invaluable photographic survey of jazz and its musicians from slave ships and Storyville (the red-light district of New Orleans) to the charmingly youthful André Previn, Gerry Mulligan, and heartthrob Chet Baker. But the book is more than a photographic record: it is arranged chronologically in chapters, each of which is opened by a thoughtful historical introduction, and the photos themselves are accompanied by lengthy informative captions.

Also published in 1955 was Nat Hentoff and Nat Shapiro's *Hear Me Talkin' to Ya*. This book is subtitled *The Story of Jazz by the Men Who Made It*. This was the first book of jazz history in which the story was told in the words of the musicians themselves. Contributors included Louis Armstrong, Hoagy Carmichael, Stan Getz, Freddie Greene, Bunk Johnson, Anita O'Day, Charlie Parker, Oscar Peterson, Billy Taylor, Fats Waller, and Lester Young.

One of the most active writers on jazz in the 1950s was the English-born Leonard Feather, who had taken part in the lecture series on jazz in New York in the 1940s. Feather was a composer and arranger and a prolific author, who published many books and numerous articles on jazz. His *Encyclopedia of Jazz* came out in 1955, *The Encyclopedia Yearbook of Jazz* in 1956, and *The New Yearbook of Jazz* in 1958. In 1957 he released an interesting new book on the elements that make jazz what it is, focusing on the instruments, the sounds, the performers, the types of combos and bands, the composers and arrangers, and the nature of improvisation (*The Book of Jazz: A Guide to the Entire Field*). It also includes an eloquent and heartfelt chapter on "Jazz and Race."

It was the 1950s that produced an important American music history book that dealt seriously with the vernacular traditions of American music. Gilbert Chase's (1955) *America's Music: From the Pilgrims to the Present* brought the rich traditions of all kinds of performed music under the legitimate gaze of historians of American music and included discussions of spirituals, ragtime, American Indian traditions, popular song, folk music, Sousa marches, blues, and jazz. Chase denounced the "genteel" and "respectable" attitudes of the past and aimed to provide a picture of American music in all its pluralistic variety. Jazz was accorded a chapter of its own ("Jazz: Tradition and Transformation"), in which the history of jazz is sketched, from its "cradle" in New Orleans to swing. There is also a separate 15-page chapter on the blues. Chase clearly understood that jazz was central to America's musical history and indeed one of its most characteristic forces. Chase placed a quotation from Anaïs Nin's diary at the head of his chapter: "Jazz is the expression of America's self, its sensual potency, its lyrical force."

Literary writers on jazz in the 1950s included Langston Hughes and Ralph Ellison. In 1939 Hughes had collaborated with the jazz pianist and composer James P. Johnson on an opera called *De Organizer*. The rhythms of jazz also influenced his 1951 *Montage of a Dream Deferred* — a book-length poem in five sections depicting the African-American urban experience using history, poetry, and music. In 1958 he made a recording with the Henry "Red" Allen band. Hughes also wrote a series of books for children about important black figures in American history, among which were two books about jazz and jazz musicians: *The First Book of Jazz* and *Famous Negro Music Makers* (both 1955). The latter includes chapters on Jelly Roll Morton, Bessie Smith, Duke Ellington, and Louis Armstrong. The *First Book of Jazz* is beautifully written for children — lucid and informative, with history lightly woven into tales and a few easily assimilable chapters on elements such as improvisation and syncopation. And as part of his pedagogical work in jazz, in 1954 Hughes released an LP entitled *The First Album of Jazz for Children*. It was narrated by the author, who also supplied program notes, and it discussed the music from its beginnings to New Orleans, ragtime, and the blues through to Dizzy Gillespie and Lennie Tristano, with many recorded musical examples.

Ralph Ellison (1914–94) was a musician and student of jazz before he became a writer. He wrote widely and prolifically on jazz for more than 50 years, including profiles of famous musicians such as Charlie Parker, Jimmy Rushing, Charlie Christian, Mahalia Jackson; reviews of recordings; a homage to Ellington on his 70th birthday; and an analysis of how the blues contribute to the quality and tone of Richard Wright's autobiographical *Black Boy*. His articles appeared in *The Saturday Review*, *The Antioch Review*, *High Fidelity*, and *Esquire*, among other places. Jazz and the processes of making jazz also permeate his fiction, as Robert O'Meally's compilation of some of Ellison's jazz writing shows. In both *Invisible Man* and *Juneteenth*, for example, blues and jazz musicians appear as guides and central figures. "My basic sense of artistic form is musical," Ellison wrote in 1974 (Ellison 2001: ix). He also famously stated that the three American institutions were the Constitution, the Bill of Rights, and jazz (p. xi). O'Meally writes that "Ellison is known by jazz scholars and aficionados as an original and incisive music critic whose specialty was jazz" and that taken together, his musical writings "are among the most eloquent works ever written about jazz" (Ellison 2001: x).

Audiences for jazz, both live and recorded, also grew markedly in the 1950s. "The audience for authentic jazz is enormous," reported Howard Taubman in the *New York Times* of August 7, 1955. Clubs, such as those along 52nd Street in Manhattan, flourished; and record companies began to sign lucrative contracts with top jazz musicians such as Dave Brubeck and Miles Davis.

The personalities of jazz musicians began to reflect the times. Davis, for example, was regarded as an icon of cool in the 1950s. His elegant suits, his Ferrari, his big house, and his *sprezzatura* on the stage put him in the company of the beautiful people of the decade: Marlon Brando, James Dean, Elizabeth Taylor, and Ava Gardner. In Europe he counted Juliette Greco and Jean Paul Sartre among his friends. He was the subject of feature articles in *Time* magazine (January 20, 1958) and *Life International* (August 11, 1958). Quincy Jones has said that Davis was "hip and cool . . . It was a way to be dignified and proud and individualistic" (Early 2001: 42).

1956 was a particularly productive year for published work on jazz. *The Story of Jazz* (1956) by Marshall Stearns was written under a Guggenheim Fellowship and became a widely used historical survey of jazz in the 1950s. It includes two important chapters on Afro-Cuban music and expressiveness in jazz, and a thoughtful and nuanced chapter on race. The mainstream Music Educators National Conference recognized jazz as an appropriate educational field for the first time in 1956. And starting in 1956 Leonard Bernstein began writing about jazz in popular magazines such as *Vogue* and producing television shows explaining the music to huge audiences. Distinguished writers and educators such as Billy Taylor illuminated the pages of journals and magazines with thoughtful discussions about the social and cultural implications of the music. Woody Woodward, who was a general manager for Pacific Jazz Enterprises, told the story of jazz and sketched the biographies of many jazz musicians (and compiled a discography of 10 thousand recordings) in his *Jazz Americana* of 1956.

Also in 1956 the pioneering work of jazz criticism by André Hodeir became available in English. André Hodeir's *Jazz: Its Evolution and Essence* was thorough and serious. A performer, arranger, and composer, Hodeir applied the careful analysis that had until that time been reserved for classical music to jazz. His detailed discussion of Ellington's 1940 recording "Concerto for Cootie" was perhaps the first technically adept analysis of a jazz performance, taking into account formal structure, phrase length, thematic variation, harmony, orchestration, timbre, tempo, rhythm, and expression, among many other considerations. Hodeir pronounced the work a "masterpiece." The book was both comprehensive and sophisticated, containing a history of jazz from its beginnings to the new "cool" school as well as thoughtful discussions on harmony, melody, different rhythmic foundations, the phenomenon of swing feel, and insights into the incompatibility of jazz and classical music.

William Grossman and Jack Farrell published *The Heart of Jazz* in 1956, a wonderfully thorough and idiosyncratic view of the music, including chapters on the Christian element in New Orleans jazz; on the role of different instruments in the music; on Bunk Johnson, Jelly Roll Morton, and Kid Ory; on "Renaissance" jazz groups; on "Progress, Novelty, and Dave Brubeck," "The Apostasy of Louis Armstrong," and many other topics. Grossman was a professor at New York University and Farrell a writer who specialized in books and articles on steam locomotives and edited the *Locomotive Quarterly*. In the same year bandleader Eddie Condon brought out *A Treasury of Jazz*, a collection of articles by other writers on jazz, rescuing some from potential obscurity.

In the 1950s jazz came into its own as an academic subject on college campuses in and around New York. The files of the Institute of Jazz Studies at Rutgers contain a syllabus for a course in jazz history at New York University for 1950 given by Marshall Stearns (reproduced in Walser 1999: 195–9). (Guest lecturers included Edmond Hall, Louis Armstrong, Duke Ellington, Benny Goodman, Count Basie, Dizzy Gillespie, George Shearing, and Lennie Tristano.) Stearns also helped organize jazz courses at several other universities and colleges in the New York area during the 1950s (Walser 1999: 195–6). Rudi Blesh was hired to teach jazz history at Queens College of the City University of New York and later also at NYU (Hasse and Kernfeld 2002).

The curriculum of mainstream classical music history, however, was very slow to take jazz into its fold. One of the most influential books of music history, Donald Jay Grout's *A History of Western Music*, whose first edition came out as the 1950s came to an end, devotes five lines to jazz (and two and a quarter pages to American music in general – out of 742).

In the 1950s jazz even showed up in the psychoanalytic literature. In three articles psychiatrists discussed jazz in terms of cultural conflict, theories of psychology, and, in terms of trombone playing, "the pleasure connected with . . . sublimated anality [which] is derived not only from a throwing off of super ego taboos, but also comes about through a sudden momentary release of the energy needed to repress the aggressive impulses" (see Miller 1958, Esman 1951, Margolis 1954).

In 1957 Nat Hentoff and Nat Shapiro followed up their first book featuring performers with a second, entitled *The Jazz Makers*, in which they presented written portraits of 21 musicians whom they felt were among the "significant enrichers of the jazz tradition." David Ewen's *Panorama of American Popular Music* contains three chapters on ragtime, the blues, Tin Pan Alley, and jazz. And in 1957 the *New York Times* reported on an appeal to the Vatican by the Italian Jazz Federation for an "authoritative Roman Catholic pronouncement" on the purity and religious feeling in jazz. The appeal came in response to a condemnation of jazz by a militant lay organization known as Catholic Action (quoted in Walser 1999: 238–9).

In the 1950s jazz became a secret weapon in the Cold War. The *New York Times* of November 6, 1955, reported on its front page: "America's secret weapon is a blue note in a minor key."[2] In the late 1950s the Voice of America, which was beamed to countries in the Communist bloc, reached 80 million listeners with its jazz program, which was supposed to show the world that jazz symbolized American freedom, racial harmony, and individual achievement (Walser 1999: 240). As further evidence of this, the US State Department sponsored international tours of Louis Armstrong and his band. This did not stop the normally cautious Armstrong from speaking out strongly against segregation at home and even from canceling one of his tours. As President Eisenhower dithered over his decision to send federal troops to Arkansas to enforce civil rights, Armstrong, who was by now in his late fifties and one of the best-known black Americans in the world, pulled no punches in an interview with the *New York Post* in September of 1957:

> Louis (Satchmo) Armstrong charged today that President Eisenhower was a "two-faced" man with "no guts" who was letting Gov. Faubus of Arkansas run the federal government. Explaining in Grand Forks, N.D., why he canceled a good-will trip to Russia, Armstrong said: "The people over there ask me what's wrong with my country. What am I supposed to say?" He added, "It's getting almost so bad a colored man hasn't got any country." (quoted in Walser 1999: 247)

The irony of asking a maligned minority to travel the world showing off the open-mindedness of American society was not lost on any of the traveling musicians.

The jazz tours began in 1956 with a band led by Dizzy Gillespie and continued over the next 20 years, featuring many of the American masters of jazz, including Gillespie, Armstrong, Benny Goodman, and Duke Ellington (see Von Eschen 2005, and review by Dickstein 2005). (Ellington and his orchestra continued these exhausting worldwide trips until a few months before he died in 1974). The death of Stalin in 1953 had led to a slight warming of East–West relations and to a slight loosening of state censorship in the Soviet Union. Jazz bands tapped into an underground enthusiasm for the music behind the Iron Curtain. But American jazz musicians also traveled to many other countries around the world, including those in Africa, the Middle East, the Far East, Latin America, and South Asia. The summons by their government to represent their country abroad also represented a significant breakthrough in terms of the music's acceptance at home.

In 1958 jazz critic Ralph Gleason published an anthology of articles about jazz entitled *Jam Session*. In it he printed a representative selection of published pieces on what he called the "jazz culture" – personalities and musicians, styles new and old, definitions of the music, and contemporary reportage – as well as poems, interviews with musicians, and a couple of new articles of his own on jazz poetry and the economics of jazz. The latter is particularly revealing of the burgeoning jazz business in the 1950s, and it is worth reproducing some of the results of his research. Gleason reports that at that time (1958) the number of record companies had expanded to include more "majors" and several dozen minors, that these were issuing 600 jazz LPs a year, that jazz represented 9 to 12 percent of the total retail market, and that the top jazz records would be featured "in every record store, right alongside Toscanini, Rosemary Clooney and Elvis Presley" (Gleason 1958: 268). Hundreds of radio programs and 75 magazines were featuring jazz or record reviews. Professional jazz musicians who could hardly live by their music in previous years could make a decent living from royalties from compositions, recordings, and radio play. Many could survive (at least in New York or Hollywood, the centers of recording) solely on the income they derived from recording dates, and others supplemented their income by playing in clubs, writing arrangements, and taking part in well-managed tours. (The Jazz at the Philharmonic tour, for example, paid high salaries and included travel in first class.) Gleason concluded "Jazz is big business today. There's no denying it" (1958: 242, Owens 2002).

Gleason's conclusion is supported by other data, suggesting that jazz, mostly undiluted by commercial elements, was now able to exist on its own terms. Some of the bebop players and members of the "cool school," such as Dave Brubeck, Gerry Mulligan, and the Modern Jazz Quartet, were financially quite successful, and the bands of Ellington and Basie continued to make profits despite the high costs of travel and maintaining a large group of players. There were jazz clubs not only in New York but also in most major cities across the US. And jazz historian James Lincoln Collier estimates that "in the 1950s pure jazz had an audience that probably numbered millions" (Collier 2002).

One new phenomenon of the 1950s in America was the jazz festival.[3] These included the Newport Jazz Festival and the Music Inn in Lenox, Massachusetts, where a distinguished jazz performing series was begun in 1955 (at the so-called Music Barn), featuring performers of the caliber of Duke Ellington, Louis Armstrong, and Count Basie. Another important component of jazz in Lenox was the School of Jazz, which was directed by John Lewis every summer from 1957 to 1960 (see Yudkin 2006). This school featured a stellar roster of teachers that included Lewis and the other members of the Modern Jazz Quartet, and Jimmy Giuffre, Bob Brookmeyer, Jim Hall, Dizzy Gillespie, Bill Evans, and Oscar Peterson, as well as lecturers on the history and styles of jazz and many other jazz topics. Important figures such as jazz educator David Baker, pianist and composer Ran Blake, and the iconoclastic duo Don Cherry and Ornette Coleman, were students at Lenox. Indeed it was at the Lenox School of Jazz in 1959 that Coleman first came to spectacular public attention. The foundation of this school and its brief flourishing (it ran into financial difficulties after four years) were important symbols of the rapidly increasing acceptance of jazz as a subject worthy of serious study.

The Newport Jazz Festival was first organized in 1954 by wealthy socialites Louis and Elaine Lorillard and directed by George Wein, who was then the owner of the

Storyville Club in Boston. In that year it was held on the lawn of the Newport Casino and later in various locations around Newport. In 1956 the Festival was the occasion of a major boost for the sagging fortunes of the Duke Ellington Orchestra, when the audience went wild for a long saxophone solo in Ellington's "Diminuendo and Crescendo in Blue." In 1958 the festival was the subject of the film *Jazz on a Summer's Day*, which shows the palpable excitement of the event and the new (and sometimes uncomfortable) association between the jazzers and the well-dressed, well-heeled, yachting and tennis crowd. The New York Jazz Festival was founded on Randall's Island and the Monterey Jazz festival in Monterey, California in 1958, and the Playboy Jazz Festival in Chicago in 1959.[4]

Beginning in the 1950s, jazz was also featured at some classical music festivals or other arts festivals. In 1957, for example, Brandeis University commissioned six new jazz works for its Festival of the Arts (Hentoff and McCarthy 1959: 232). The significance of these festivals was that, unlike in most other venues – like nightclubs, dances, and shows – the audience was there primarily to listen to the music (Anon. 2002).

This new attitude is symbolized also by the popularity of jazz concerts in traditional concert halls, such as those at Carnegie Hall and other venues across the country. The Jazz at the Philharmonic band, whose changing personnel had begun playing in the Philharmonic Auditorium in Los Angeles, was by the mid-1950s touring to concert halls across the US and Canada as well as Europe, Australia, and Japan.

In the 1950s jazz made frequent appearances on television and movie screens as the subject of documentaries. Three-minute filmed performances by jazz players and singers, such as Count Basie, Nat "King" Cole, Red Nichols, George Shearing, Duke Ellington, and Sarah Vaughan were offered by the Snader Telescriptions Corporation to television stations across the country to be strung together as entire programs. In 1954 the movie *Jazz Dance* featured two dancers demonstrating dance steps to the playing of contemporary musicians. During the 1950s a Sunday afternoon television series on music, entitled *Omnibus* and written, narrated, and performed by Leonard Bernstein, was broadcast by CBS. The program "The World of Jazz" was aired on October 16, 1955. And in 1956 an LP with Bernstein, entitled *What is Jazz?* was released. It featured parts of the television broadcast soundtrack, appearances by Coleman Hawkins, Buck Clayton, Miles Davis, Red Garland, and John Coltrane, as well as part of a concert with the New York Philharmonic, Louis Armstrong's Sextet, and Dave Brubeck's Quartet. Bernstein's missionary work for jazz had a very powerful influence among mainstream musical audiences in the 1950s (Chambers 1998, vol. 1: 238).

In 1956 CBS broadcast the documentary *Music of the South*, which explored the roots of jazz. A wonderful movie tribute to Louis Armstrong, *Satchmo the Great* (1957), features Louis Armstrong and his All Stars on tour in Europe and Africa and Armstrong playing "St. Louis Blues" with the New York Philharmonic conducted by Leonard Bernstein. From December 30, 1957 to January 7, 1959, CBS put on four one-hour "All Star Jazz Shows," which squeezed in several groups playing for a few minutes each. A historic television program was taped in 1957, when Billie Holiday, Lester Young, Coleman Hawkins, Count Basie, Doc Cheatham, Thelonious Monk, and many others made *The Sound of Jazz* for CBS, in which they play in front of a small audience in an informal studio setting. Two important series on jazz were broadcast nationwide in 1958: *The Subject is Jazz*, which ran for 13 weeks on National Educational Television, and *Art Ford's Jazz Party* (13 weeks, WNTA-TV). In 1959 Miles Davis was the subject of *The Sound of Miles Davis*, in which his sextet performed "So What," from the album *Kind of Blue*, and Davis played three pieces from the album *Miles Ahead* with the Gil Evans orchestra. Also released in 1959 was the powerful *Cry of Jazz*, a movie about the black experience in America and its influence on the music (Smith, Ferko, Rye, Kernfeld, and Gabbard 2002).

Jazz also served as the basis for many film and television soundtracks in the 1950s. Teddy Buckner, Benny Carter, Ziggy Elman and others play the music for Elia Kazan's *Panic in the Streets* (1950). Alex North wrote the jazz score for *A Streetcar Named Desire* (1951), Leith Stevens for *The Glass Wall* (1953) and *The Wild One* (1954), and Leonard Bernstein for *On the Waterfront* (1954) and *The Man with the Golden Arm* (1955). Well-known performers played or wrote scores for movies. French directors loved the American feel of jazz. Miles Davis improvised the soundtrack for Louis Malle's *Ascenseur pour l'échafaud* (1957), and John Lewis wrote the score (and the Modern Jazz Quartet played on the soundtrack) for Roger Vadim's *Sait-on jamais* (also 1957). In 1958 the movie *I Want to Live* featured a Johnny Mandel score and *Touch of Evil* a menacing score by Henry Mancini. In 1959 jazz soundtracks for movies reached a climax, with John Lewis's score for *Odds against Tomorrow*, Charles Mingus's for *Shadows*, and Duke Ellington's for *Anatomy of a Murder*. In the late 1950s television dramas also began to feature jazz themes and jazz soundtracks, particularly on detective or crime series. The trend started in 1957 with Pete Rugolo's music for *Richard Diamond, Private Detective*. In 1958 Henry Mancini wrote the music for *Peter Gunn*, a crime series based in a jazz club. The background theme was nominated for an Emmy award, and the soundtrack album became a hit. These were followed by Count Basie's theme for *M Squad* (1958), Elmer Bernstein's score for *Johnny Staccato* (1959), and Mancini's score for *Mr. Lucky* (1959) (Smith et al. 2002).

The 1950s also saw a considerable expansion in the amount and variety of jazz recordings. New record labels specializing in jazz, such as Prestige, New Jazz, Verve, Riverside, Pacific, Fantasy, and Contemporary, were founded; older jazz labels such as Clef, Savoy, and Blue Note flourished; and bigger labels like Columbia, Vanguard, and Atlantic began turning their attention to jazz or founding new jazz series, such as Vanguard's Jazz Showcase. More discographies appeared to try to keep track of all these new records. Discographies of individual musicians began to appear, many of them published in Denmark. By the end of the decade discographies of Louis Armstrong, Benny Goodman, Billie Holiday, Jelly Roll Morton, King Oliver, Charlie

Parker, and Jack Teagarden were available (Atkins 1982: 2). Delaunay once again weighed in with a new *Hot discographie encyclopédique* (1951–2), and Albert McCarthy produced a nearly 300-page volume of new recordings and reissues released in the year 1958 alone.

Towards the end of 1958 a new and serious magazine, *The Jazz Review*, was founded. It appeared monthly until the beginning of 1961 and was the means of distribution for a great deal of thoughtful writing about jazz. In the first issue Gunther Schuller, who was to become an influential jazz scholar, composer, and performer, presented a detailed analysis of a Sonny Rollins solo on record. The analysis evoked Mozart, Shakespeare, and Rembrandt, and made a passionate argument for the importance and power of jazz. Also for the first issue William Grossman wrote the first of what turned out to be a series of articles on jazz history. Other contributors included Lawrence Gushee, then working on his PhD at Yale and later a professor of musicology; Nat Hentoff, critic and writer, who was cofounder of the magazine, co-author of *Hear Me Talkin' to Ya*, and associate editor of *Down Beat*; composer-arrangers Bill Russo and Quincy Jones; and saxophonist Cannonball Adderley. In 1958 the Ford Foundation provided a grant of $75,000 to Tulane University to study the history of jazz in New Orleans. And as another mark of the acceptance and financial viability of jazz, in 1958 the famous classical-music impresario Sol Hurok added Erroll Garner to his list of concert attractions (Hentoff and McCarthy 1999: 333). By 1958 even the *New York Times* regarded jazz as having achieved "respectability." In an article entitled "Jazz Makes it up the River," the *Times* conveyed the news that jazz's "long voyage from New Orleans barrelhouse to public respectability [has] end[ed] in a triumph" (Hentoff and McCarthy 1999: 327).

By 1959 jazz had become sufficiently established in the mainstream of American intellectual life that several collections of essays were published undertaking to consider the music from an objective and contemplative viewpoint. Three important collections were published in that year. The first was an anthology of essays edited by Martin Williams, cofounder of *The Jazz Review* and jazz critic for the *New York Times*. Williams was to become known to generations of young students of jazz as the editor and compiler of the *Smithsonian Collection of Classic Jazz*, a multirecord selection of representative recordings of jazz through the ages. The 1959 anthology, entitled *The Art of Jazz*, brought together essays by most of the best-known scholars and critics of the time (including Marshall Stearns, André Hodeir, Lawrence Gushee, and Williams himself) on topics ranging from ragtime to the latest Hard Bop movement. The arrangement of the essays projects a historical overview. Also in 1959 a single-author collection by the lyrical and insightful jazz writer Whitney Balliett appeared. *The Sound of Surprise* contains 46 essays, three from the mid-1950s and the majority published in the *New Yorker* during the period 1957 to early 1959. Balliett's writing is pure, original, and often revelatory. He homes in on important truths when he describes Ella Fitzgerald's "clear, scrubbed voice" as "sometimes so finished that it takes on a blank perfection" (Balliett 1959: 72–3) or, in a piece on Miles Davis, speaks of the "remarkable distillation" of his playing, during which "what comes out of his horn miraculously seems the result of the instantaneous editing of a far more diffuse melodic line" (p. 128). The drummer Max Roach has "an intense, mosquitolike touch on his instrument" (p. 221); a new example of Third Stream music (music that mixed classical and jazz) was "a perfect, and totally unconvincing, tour de force" (p. 162). (See also Balliett 2003.) In the same year a third book of essays, simply entitled *Jazz*, was published by Nat Hentoff and Albert McCarthy, with contributions by a dozen authors, including Williams, Schuller, and Hentoff himself. Like the Williams collection, this one conveys historical perspective, as the articles range from "The Roots of Jazz" through "Boogie-Woogie," "Chicago," a thorough analysis of the style and materials of Ellington, to bebop, the re-emergence of traditional jazz, and a thoughtful essay on "Jazz at Mid-Century." In this last piece Hentoff writes that in the late 1950s jazz has "achieved a depth and range of content . . . that does merit – and reward – serious attention. . . . never before has jazz had so large an international audience, and never before has so much been written about it throughout the world" (Hentoff and McCarthy 1999: 327).

Two other books were published in 1959 in London. One of them contained essays by both English and American writers. It was called *These Jazzmen of Our Time* (Horricks 1959) and it had chapters on Brubeck, Davis, Gil Evans, Monk, Mulligan, Rollins, and several other contemporary figures in jazz. Horricks wrote eight of the chapters himself. The other book did not make its way to the United States until the following year, but it was an important contribution to intelligent writing on jazz. The book was *The Jazz Scene* by Eric Hobsbawm under the pseudonym Francis Newton. This was a marvelously erudite and thoughtful encomium to the value and difference of jazz, written by one of Britain's most distinguished historians.

Finally, in the 1950s, jazz became a metaphor for life, for a sense of the possible. Jazz was sexuality, freedom, individuality, courage, belief, feeling. Jazz was the emblem of the Beat poets, the symbol of the counterculture. And no one expressed this more forcefully than Norman Mailer, author of the World War II novel *The Naked and the Dead* (1948), editor of the intellectual magazine *Dissent* from its founding in 1954 until 1963, and cofounder of the iconic *Village Voice* in 1955. For Mailer jazz was a powerful symbol in a post-Holocaust, post-Hiroshima age. In a 1957 essay Mailer used jazz as a representation of all that was "hip," a symbol of "communication by art," and lauded the music as a means to "open the limits of the possible for oneself," for "to swing is to communicate . . . " (Mailer 1959: 341, 354, 350).

NOTES

1 Goodman later appeared with orchestras all over the country, performing the Mozart, Weber, and Nielsen concertos, and works by other composers, including Copland and Hindemith, from whom he commissioned new concertos.

2   During the 1950s many aspects of American
and European culture were used as propaganda. The English intellectual magazine
Encounter, which began publication in 1953,
was funded by the CIA. The CIA also provided
funds in the same year to keep the (left-wing,
anti-Communist) American journal *Partisan
Review* afloat. The Eisenhower administration
sent musicals (*Oklahoma!*), operas (*Porgy and
Bess*), ballets, and art exhibits abroad to demonstrate the individuality and freedom of
American composers and artists. Abstract
painting was regarded as the ideal expression
of American artistic autonomy. See Menand
(2005).

3   Jazz festivals abroad had begun in the late
1940s, including in Australia and in Nice and
Paris (all founded 1948).

4   Also in 1959 the International Jazz Jamboree
Festival began in Warsaw.

References and Further Reading

Anon. (2002). Festivals. In Barry Kernfeld (ed.),
The New Grove Dictionary of Jazz, 2nd edn
(vol. 1, pp. 753–9). New York: Grove's
Dictionaries.

Armstrong, Louis. (1936/1993). *Swing That Music.*
New York: Da Capo.

Armstrong, Louis. (1954). *Satchmo: My Life in New
Orleans.* New York: New American Library.

Atkins, Jerry. (1982). Magnificent obsession: The
discographers. *Jazz Journal International* (Novem-
ber-December), expanded in *IAJRC Journal*
(Winter 1989–90). Available at <www.
jazzdiscography.com/Essays/obsess.htm>.

Balliett, Whitney. (1959). *The Sound of Surprise: 46
Pieces on Jazz.* New York: Dutton.

Balliett, Whitney. (2003). *Collected Works: A Journal
of Jazz, 1954–2001.* New York: St. Martin.

Bauer, Marion. (1947). *Twentieth Century Music:
How It Developed, How to Listen to It*, revised edn.
New York: Putnam.

Berendt, Joachim-Ernst. (1953). *Das Jazzbuch:
Entwicklung und Bedeutung der Jazzmusik.* Frankfurt am Main: Fischer. English translation
(1962) *The New Jazz Book: A History and Guide*,
trans. Dan Morgenstern. New York: Hill and
Wang.

Berger, Edward. (2002). Institute of Jazz Studies.
In Barry Kernfeld (ed.), *The New Grove Diction-
ary of Jazz*, 2nd edn (vol. 2, p. 326). New York:
Grove's Dictionaries.

Blackstone, Orin. (1945–8). *Index to Jazz*, 4 vols.
Fairfax, VA: Record Changer.

Blesh, Rudi. (1946). *Shining Trumpets: A History of
Jazz.* New York: Knopf.

Carey, Dave and Albert J. McCarthy. (1955–63).
*The Directory of Recorded Jazz and Swing Music
(including Gospel and Blues Records)*, 6 vols. Ford-
ingbridge, UK: Delphic.

Chambers, Jack. (1998). *Milestones: The Music and
Times of Miles Davis*, 2 vols in one. New York:
Da Capo.

Chase, Gilbert. (1955). *America's Music: From
the Pilgrims to the Present.* New York:
McGraw-Hill.

Collier, James Lincoln. (1988). *The Reception of Jazz
in America: A New View*, I.S.A.M. Monographs
27. New York: Institute for Studies in American Music.

Collier, James Lincoln. (2002). Jazz (i), V, 8. In
Barry Kernfeld (ed.), *The New Grove Dictionary
of Jazz*, 2nd edn (vol. 2, p. 381). New York:
Grove's Dictionaries.

Condon, Eddie. (1948). *We Called It Music.* New
York: Henry Holt.

Condon, Eddie and Richard Gehman (eds). (1956).
Treasury of Jazz. New York: Greenwood.

Delaunay, Charles. (1936). *Hot Discography.* Paris:
Corrêa.

Delaunay, Charles. (1948). *New Hot Discography:
The Standard Directory of Recorded Jazz*, ed.
Walter E. Schaap and George Avakian. New
York: Criterion.

Delaunay, Charles with Kurt Mohr. (1951–52).
Hot discographie encyclopédique, 3 vols. Fontenay-
aux-Roses: Editions jazz disques.

De Toledano, Ralph. (1947). *Frontiers of Jazz.* New
York: Oliver Durrell.

Dickstein, Morris. (2005). Diplomatic bands. *The
Times Literary Supplement* (April 15): 22.

Duhamel, Georges. (1931). *America the Menace:
Scenes from the Life of the Future.* London: George
Allen and Unwin.

Dykema, Peter and Karl Gehrkens. (1941). *The Teaching and Administration of High School Music.* Boston: Birchard.

Early, Gerald (ed.). (2001). *Miles Davis and American Culture.* St Louis: Missouri Historical Society Press.

Ellison, Ralph. (2001). *Living with Music: Ralph Ellison's Jazz Writings,* ed. Robert G. O'Meally. New York: Modern Library.

Esman, A. (1951). Jazz – a study in cultural conflict. *American Imago* 8: 219–26.

Ewen, David. (1959). *Panorama of American Popular Music.* Englewood Cliffs, NJ: Prentice Hall.

Feather, Leonard. (1949). *Inside Be-bop.* New York: Robbins.

Feather, Leonard. (1956). *The Encyclopedia Yearbook of Jazz.* New York: Horizon.

Feather, Leonard. (1957). *The Book of Jazz: A Guide to the Entire Field.* New York: Horizon.

Feather, Leonard. (1958). *The New Yearbook of Jazz.* New York: Horizon.

Feather, Leonard. (1987). *The Jazz Years: Earwitness to an Era.* New York: Da Capo.

Feather, Leonard. (1996). Goffin, *Esquire* and the Moldy Figs. In Robert Gottlieb (ed.), *Reading Jazz* (pp. 722–38). New York: Pantheon.

Finkelstein, Sidney. (1948). *Jazz: A People's Music.* New York: Citadel.

Firestone, Ross. (1993). *Swing, Swing, Swing: The Life and Times of Benny Goodman.* New York: Norton.

Francis, André. (1960). *Jazz,* trans. Martin Williams. London: Grove.

Frank, Waldo. (1937). *In the American Jungle (1925–1936).* New York: Farrar and Rinehart.

Gleason, Ralph (ed.). (1958). *Jam Session: An Anthology of Jazz.* New York: Putnam.

Goffin, Robert. (1944/1975). *Jazz: From the Congo to the Metropolitan,* trans. Walter Schaap and Leonard Feather. New York: Da Capo.

Goodman, Benny and Irving Kolodin. (1939). *The Kingdom of Swing.* New York: Stackpole.

Gottlieb, Robert (ed.). (1996). *Reading Jazz: A Gathering of Autobiography, Reportage, and Criticism from 1919 to Now.* New York: Pantheon.

Grossman, William L. and Jack W. Farrell. (1956). *The Heart of Jazz.* New York: New York University Press.

Grout, Donald Jay. (1960). *A History of Western Music.* New York: Norton.

Harris, Rex. (1952). *Jazz.* Harmondsworth, UK: Penguin.

Hasse, John Edward and Barry Kernfeld. (2002). Blesh, Rudi. In Barry Kernfeld (ed.), *The New Grove Dictionary of Jazz,* 2nd edn (vol. 1, pp. 238–9). New York: Grove's Dictionaries.

Hentoff, Nat and Albert J. McCarthy (eds). (1959). *Jazz.* New York: Rinehart.

Hentoff, Nat and Nat Shapiro (eds). (1955). *Hear Me Talkin' to Ya: The Story of Jazz by the Men Who Made It.* New York: Rinehart.

Hitchcock, H. Wiley. (1986). Histories. In H. Wiley Hitchcock and Stanley Sadie (eds), *The New Grove Dictionary of American Music* (vol. 2, pp. 399–402). New York: Grove's Dictionaries of Music.

Hitchcock, H. Wiley and Stanley Sadie (eds). (1986). *The New Grove Dictionary of American Music,* 4 vols. New York: Oxford University Press.

Hobsbawm, E. J. [as Francis Newton]. (1960). *The Jazz Scene.* New York: Monthly Review.

Hodeir, André. (1956). *Jazz: Its Evolution and Essence,* trans. David Noakes. New York: Grove.

Horricks, Raymond (ed.). (1959). *These Jazzmen of Our Time.* London: Gollancz.

Hughes, Langston. (1955). *The First Book of Jazz.* New York: Franklin Watts.

Hughes, Langston. (1955). *Famous Negro Music Makers.* New York: Dodd, Mead.

Kaufmann, Helen L. (1937). *From Jehovah to Jazz: Music in America from Psalmody to the Present Day.* Port Washington, NY: Kennikat.

Keepnews, Orrin, and Bill Grauer. (1955). *A Pictorial History of Jazz: People and Places from New Orleans to Modern Jazz.* New York: Crown.

King, Brian F. (1953). Bop on wane, blues back says exposition headliner. *Springfield Sunday Republican* September 27.

Kingsley, Walter. (1917). Whence comes jass? Facts from the great authority on the subject. *New York Sun,* August 5.

Lang, Paul Henry. (1941). *Music in Western Civilization.* New York: Norton.

Lindenmaier, H. L. (2002). Berendt, Joachim-Ernst. In Barry Kernfeld (ed.), *The New Grove Dictionary of Jazz,* 2nd edn (vol. 1, pp. 193–4). New York: Grove's Dictionaries.

Mailer, Norman. (1959). The white negro: Superficial reflections on the hipster. In *Advertisements for Myself* (pp. 337–58). New York: Putnam.

Malson, Lucien. (1952). *Les maîtres du jazz*. Paris: Presses Universitaires de France.

Margolis, N. (1954). A theory of the psychology of jazz. *American Imago* 11: 263–90.

Matthews, Ramona H. (1986). Howard, John Tasker. In H. Wiley Hitchcock and Stanley Sadie (eds), *The New Grove Dictionary of American Music* (vol. 2, pp. 344–5). New York: Grove's Dictionaries of Music.

McCarthy, Albert J. (1958). *Jazz Discography*. London: Cassell.

McKinney, Howard and William Anderson. (1940). *Music in History: the Evolution of an Art*. New York: American Book Company.

Meltzer, David. (1993). *Reading Jazz*. San Francisco: Mercury.

Menand, Louis. (2005). Unpopular front: American art and the cold war. *The New Yorker* (October 17): 174–9.

Mendl, R. W. S. (1927). *The Appeal of Jazz*. London: Philip Allan.

Miller, Miles D. (1958). Jazz and aggression. In Robert Walser (ed.), *Keeping Time: Readings in Jazz History* (234–39). New York: Oxford University Press.

Morgan, Alun and Raymond Horricks. (1956). *Modern Jazz: A Survey of Developments since 1939*. London: Gollancz.

Newsom, Jon and H. Wiley Hitchcock. (1986). Sonneck, Oscar G(eorge) T(heodore). In H. Wiley Hitchcock and Stanley Sadie (eds), *The New Grove Dictionary of American Music* (vol. 4, p. 262). New York: Grove's Dictionaries of Music.

Osgood, Henry. (1926). *So This Is Jazz*. Boston: Little, Brown.

Owens, Thomas. (2002). Jazz at the Philharmonic. In Barry Kernfeld (ed.), *The New Grove Dictionary of Jazz*, 2nd edn (vol. 2, pp. 394–5). New York: Grove's Dictionaries.

Panassié, Hugues. (1936). *Hot Jazz: The Guide to Swing Music*, trans. Lyle and Eleanor Dowling. New York: Witmark.

Pearson, Nathan W., Jr. (1994). *Goin' to Kansas City*. Urbana and Chicago: University of Illinois Press.

Porter, Lewis. (1997). *Jazz, A Century of Change: Readings and New Essays*. New York: Schirmer.

Ramsay, Guthrie P., Jr. (2003). *Race Music: Black Cultures from Bebop to Hip-Hop*. Berkeley: University of California Press.

Schleman, Hilton. (1936). *Rhythm on Record: A Complete Survey and Register of All the Principal Recorded Dance Music from 1906 to 1936, and a Who's Who of the Artists Concerned in the Making*. London: Melody Maker.

Shapiro, Nat and Nat Hentoff (eds). (1957). *The Jazz Makers*. New York: Grove.

Smith, Charles Edward et al. (1942). *The Jazz Record Book*. New York: Smith and Durrell.

Smith, Charles Edward and Fred Ramsey, Jr. (eds). (1939). *Jazzmen: The Story of Hot Jazz Told in the Lives of the Men Who Created It*. New York: Harcourt Brace.

Smith, Ernie, Josh Ferko, Howard Rye, Barry Kernfeld, and Krin Gabbard (2002). In Barry Kernfeld (ed.), *The New Grove Dictionary of Jazz*, 2nd edn (vol. 1, pp. 784–801). New York: Grove's Dictionaries.

Smith, Patrick J. (1986). Sargeant, Winthrop. In H. Wiley Hitchcock and Stanley Sadie (eds), *The New Grove Dictionary of American Music* (vol. 4, p. 145). New York: Grove's Dictionaries of Music.

Spaeth, Sigmund. (1948). *A History of Popular Music in America*. New York: Random House.

Stearns, Marshall W. (1956). *The Story of Jazz*. New York: Oxford University Press.

Tucker, Sherrie. (2002). Historiography. In Barry Kernfeld (ed.), *The New Grove Dictionary of Jazz*, 2nd edn (vol. 2, pp. 249–55). New York: Grove's Dictionaries.

Ulanov, Barry. (1952). *A History of Jazz in America*. New York: Viking.

Ulanov, Barry. (1957). *A Handbook of Jazz*. New York: Viking.

Von Eschen, Penny M. (2005). *Satchmo Blows up the World: Jazz Ambassadors Play the Cold War*. Cambridge, MA: Harvard University Press.

Walser, Robert (ed.). (1999). *Keeping Time: Readings in Jazz History*. New York: Oxford University Press.

Whiteman, Paul and Mary Margaret McBride. (1926). *Jazz*. New York: Sears.

Williams, Martin (ed.). (1959). *The Art of Jazz: Essays on the Nature and Development of Jazz*. New York: Oxford University Press.

Woodward, Woody. (1956). *Jazz Americana: The Story of Jazz and All-Time Jazz Greats from Basin Street to Carnegie Hall*. Los Angeles: Trend.

Yudkin, Jeremy. (2006). *The Lenox School of Jazz: A Vital Chapter in the History of American Music and Race Relations*. Lenox, MA: The Lenox Library Association.

Zager, Daniel and Barry Kernfeld. (2002). Stearns, Marshall W(inslow). In Barry Kernfeld (ed.), *The New Grove Dictionary of Jazz*, 2nd edn (vol. 3, p. 653). New York: Grove's Dictionaries.

7

French Visual Humanisms and the American Style

Justus Nieland

The pathos of modernity's mechanical image stems from the way moderns know it to be essentially inhuman but so often ask it to bear a universal humanity. Formed automatically, seemingly devoid of will and intention, photography and cinema exposed modernists to a stratum of perceptual reality heretofore unavailable to the paltry, unassisted eye. In this sense, film, like photography, became a modernist "meta-technology: a medium whose constant subject-matter was the limits of the human" (Trotter 2006: 239). Shaking their confidence in naked human perception by revealing its constitutive gaps, repressions, and patterns of attention, such technologies posed a real challenge to modernists, who were anxious about the ways the new media furthered the pervasiveness of mechanism in the social order, and yet were aware that these visual technologies – by destroying the so-called "reality" of the senses – could in fact become a powerful weapon in their battle against mimetic realism. For moderns, part of the alluring modernity of camera vision lay in its role as an inhuman supplement to human seeing, cracking staid codes of vision and opening them to the perceptual experimentation and radical subjectivity we have come to associate with modernism. And yet the modernist inhumanity of the visual media, further eroding the vanishing modern faith in a transparent, objective, and disembodied subject of vision, existed in a kind of dialectical tension with another promise whispered by the new media – the fantasy that the photograph, and later the cinema, might perfectly record the script of nature and thereby provide a universal language transcending boundaries of age, race, class, religion, gender, and nationality (North 2005, Hansen 1991).

My essay explores a more local version of how modernism and its inhuman visual technologies were called to respond to the broad challenge to the human posed by the global forces of modernization. I do so by examining the place of the modern American novel in the particular cluster of mid-century visual humanisms operating in France in the postwar context, and by telling a story of how and why a form of modernist style, and its cinematic visuality, became read as the sign of a new, international humanism. Recent studies of literary modernism's visual culture have encouraged us to consider the role of modern literature in the emergence and production of new kinds of modern observers – *modern* because they reflect newly skeptical philosophical discourses of vision, or the nascent visual epistemologies of emerging social sciences like anthropology and sociology, or the influence of new visual technologies like photography and film (Jacobs 2001). Drawing upon this style of thinking, my essay considers what kinds of observers French intellectuals produced in their reading of modern American fiction, how this kind of vision is shaped by humanism, and why the particular visuality of the modern American style would lend itself to a form of humanistic witnessing.

I approach these questions through a close reading of French literary critic Claude-Edmonde Magny's fascinating 1948 study, *The Age of the American Novel*. Magny's work, best known today as one of the first sustained attempts to describe the influence of cinema on the technique of authors like Dos Passos, Faulkner, and Hemingway, also stands as an unruly archive of mid-century humanisms inflected through the philosophical traditions of phenomenology and existentialism (Magny was, in fact, a student of Jean-Paul Sartre's). An eloquent example of the conscription of the modern American novel in the service of humanistic seeing, Magny's text is all the more striking in an intellectual context dominated by rising concerns about the very inhumanity of America's new, postwar hegemony on the continent. In what follows, then, I aim to reconstruct the heady visual culture of Magny's humanism in the context of postwar France, showing how the style of the modern American novel becomes – in the work of Magny and others – both a new, and newly impersonal grammar of the human being and a form of postwar internationalism. I then conclude by considering Magny's reading of modern American style in dialogue with current critical returns to the politics of modernist style that find in it, as Magny did, a cosmopolitan metaphysic.

The Age of the American Novel

Magny's study, which initially appeared as a series of articles in 1944 and 1945, is generally understood as an example of French intellectuals' postwar Americanophilia – their enthusiastic reception and willful reinvention of American culture in keeping with local philosophical currents. Bored with the bloodless, bourgeois novel of psychological introspection à la Proust and Gide, the French had developed a taste for the modern American novel as early as 1928, with French expatriate Maurice-Edgar Coindreau's translation of Dos Passos's *Manhattan Transfer* for Gallimard Press in Paris. In the 1930s, Coindreau would go on to translate the work of all of the authors who became known as *les cinq grands* (Dos Passos, Hemingway, Caldwell, Steinbeck, and most importantly, William Faulkner), sparking a publishing craze for the American novel that went underground during the German Occupation, when American fiction (like its films) was banned and the practice of reading them became, in Jean-Paul Sartre's terms, a "symbol of resistance" (Sartre 1945: 115). What Magny calls "The Age of the American Novel" peaked in the years immediately following the Liberation, which saw the 1944 launch of Marcel Duhamel's influential series of hard-boiled crime novels, *la série noire*, largely comprising translated works of American pulp fiction, and the publication of a number of book-length French critical studies of the American novel, including Magny's own. The vogue had begun to wane by the end of the decade, when the imported technical charms of *le style américain* – as the experiments of the American novel were commonly known – could no longer be separated from the cultural work of Americanization on the continent. But during the Occupation and the immediate postwar period, *le style américain* was a telling barometer of France's vision of the postwar face of the United States, as, in Sartre's terms, "tragic, cruel, and sublime" (Sartre 1945: 114).

A kind of modern realism, the hallmark of *le style américain* was a new mode of poetic objectivity that eschewed intellectual analysis for journalistic concreteness and reportage, modeling a nonpsychological, behavioristic approach to character that privileged spontaneous and often violent action over soulful navel-gazing, gesture over interiority. Tailor-made for France's reigning existentialist aesthetic, the American novelistic style was, much like the American *film noir*, an invention of the French that tells us plenty about the kind of sentimental primitivism through which many French critics saw their postwar American imports. For this reason, Magny's study, the first attempt in France to "fuse the literary and philosophical interest in American fiction and culture with the grass-roots popularity of the movies" (Elsaesser 2005: 242), tends to be read as typical of a certain mode of highbrow appropriation and refashioning of American pop culture. With its twinned taste for modernism and mass-cultural form, Magny's *The Age of the American Novel* anticipates French film critics' later discovery of the vernacular modernism of Hollywood movies in the pages of *Cahiers du Cinéma* in the 1950s.

Without denying the romantic limitations of Magny's view of the American novel or forgiving its occasional slumming in the pulpy American grain, I want to suggest that Magny's text be read as an example of the visual humanisms operating within – and a kind of anxious response to – the horizon of Americanization in postwar Europe. Magny suggests something along these lines near the conclusion of the first portion of her study, which deserves to be quoted at length:

We are here concerned with a new convergence of the same kind as that which has already been discussed – a convergence between the results of psychoanalysis, behaviorism, and sociology and *the new vision of the world* that the movies and the novel communicate to us almost unconsciously, by virtue of their technique alone. It is no longer a question of a kinship between two forms of the same genre, or of two neighboring arts, but of one between the abstract themes that haunt contemporary thought and the conclusions that are suggested by the evolution toward an epoch of purely aesthetic techniques belonging to the domain of the emotions rather than of the intellect. This is a partial explanation of the growing vogue for the American novel in France . . . But this is not the only reason for its success: it also gives us a more simple and direct, and therefore a more universal, vision of man than that proposed by our traditional literature. Through its masterpieces we glimpse *the promise of a new humanism*. If its major importance is its content, however, why is it that its technique is the most imitated? To use Sartre's apt phrase, it is because the technique is pregnant with a whole metaphysic. (Magny 1972: 100–1, my emphasis)

In the literary and visual culture in which her study emerges, Magny's appeal to the "promise of a new humanism" echoed a volley of similar calls, since in France's reconstruction period, humanism was in fact "the dominant ideological tendency" for roughly 15 years following World War II (Kelly 1989: 103). Having served as an ideological umbrella for antifascism during the Resistance, "humanism" reemerged as the watchword of a defensive postwar consensus among socialists and Catholics, offering a common ideological reference point for the nascent Fourth Republic that soldered wartime divisions within the nation while also conveniently excusing the collaborationist positions of many traditional Catholics. Indeed, in 1945 and 1946, it seemed everyone in France claimed to be a humanist, from the Catholic perfectionists of Emmanuel Mounier's Personalist movement; to the socialists, whose resurgent humanism was spurred by the recent publication of Marx's early, and deeply humanist, 1844 Paris Manuscripts; to the Gaullists, to the French Communist Party. Even Sartre got into the act, giving a well-attended lecture titled "Existentialism is a Humanism" in 1945. The cresting humanist tide within the nation would soon be affirmed internationally with the 1948 adoption of the Universal Declaration of Human Rights by the General Assembly of the United Nations. But of course, with the 1946 passing of the Blum–Byrnes agreement, which reopened French movie screens to American markets, with the arrival of Marshall Plan aid in 1948, and with the Franco-American NATO alliance in 1949, international humanism became inextricably connected to the emerging bipolar world of the Cold War, and to the global reach of Americanization and its cultural products. In a 1945 interview with André Malraux published in the British arts journal *Horizon*, Malraux made clear that the "new humanism" defining the postwar orientation of European culture was in fact, indicative of salutary "convergence" between America and Europe – a "harmony of sensibilities" – that would produce a new "Atlantic culture" (Malraux 1945: 238).

While Magny's analysis often speaks in Malraux's Atlanticist idiom of humanistic cultural "convergence" rather than American "influence," her study also appears a year after the French communist press had begun to turn against *le style américain*, finding in the novels of William Faulkner or Henry Miller a despairing and reactionary pessimism and an unwelcome reminder of Yankee imperialism (Smith and Miner 1955). For humanism at this moment was also the contested ideological terrain on which "neutralist" leftist intellectuals like Sartre, Simone de Beauvoir, or Maurice Merleau-Ponty would attempt to defend Marxist revolutionary humanism from Stalinist terror, and to carve out a political "third way" by aligning themselves neither with the false promises of American-style liberal democracy or a revolution that seemed to exacerbate a bloody dictatorial apparatus in the USSR. In *Humanism and Terror* (1947), Merleau-Ponty described precisely this tough spot:

> Thus we find ourselves in an inextricable situation. The Marxist critique of capitalism is still valid and it is clear that anti-Sovietism today resembles the brutality, hybris [sic], vertigo, and anguish that already found expression in fascism. On the other side, the Revolution has come to a halt . . . It is impossible to be an anti-Communist and it is not possible to be a Communist. (Merleau-Ponty 1947/1969: xxi)

Thus, whatever Magny means by the "new humanism," her call for it in an analysis of Franco-American cultural exchanges is overdetermined by her fractious intellectual culture, divided between Gaullist Atlanticism and leftist neutralism.

The contours of this humanism, Magny insists, are limned in the particular technique linking the American novel and the movies, which is to say, in the so-called cinematic "objectivity" or "realism" of *le style américain*. Magny does *not* propose an expressivist reading of style, one that would read the objective technique as narrowly national, an expression of what those wild Americans do, or how they feel or act. Rather, the American style is the vessel of "a whole metaphysic" – a philosophical idea, an ethical perception of experience – crossing media and national boundaries, haunting the postwar cosmopolitan ether. Moreover, Magny locates this technique in the domain of the "purely aesthetic." Later in the study she clarifies that she means *aesthetic* "in the etymological sense of the word" – that is, as a form of *sensual perception* (1948/1972: 57). The "objectivity" shared by the American novel and film, rather than cool and detached, is a visual mode throbbing with human feeling. No sterile thing, technique carries the seed of metaphysical warmth. In other words, Magny's book attempts to square postwar humanism with a certain form of emotive *impersonality*. This may seem odd for students of modernism, since we are accustomed to think of impersonality – the "external method" of Wyndham Lewis, say, or the Eliotic "escape from personality," or the satiric types of Nathanael West – as an expression of modernist antihumanism. But in the context of Magny's visual culture, this idea – that technique is most human when it is most objective – has a real currency, consistent with existentialist, phenomenological, Marxist, and Christian humanisms, and their various points of intersection.

Magny's argument that the convergent changes in the modern French and American novel stem from "the imitation, conscious or unconscious, of the techniques of the film," depends upon her sense of deeper affinities between these media (Magny 1948/1972: 3). There is, she argues, a "triple relationship – psychological, sociological, and aesthetic" between them from the start (p. 4). Psychologically, films and novels are *empathetic* media – they "satisfy the same basic need – our desire to live a different life for a moment, to identify temporarily with the nature or emotion of another human being. In short, they satisfy man's curiosity about other men" (p. 4). Unlike theatre, which for Magny was currently working to prevent identification, the novel and the film "systematically seek out all means leading to the emotional fusion of character and audience." They "must lay bare the human heart and face," and they do so primarily through their typical constructions of personhood – characters and stars (p. 8). Following André Malraux's argument in "Equisse d'une psychologie du cinéma" (Sketch for a Psychology of the Moving Pictures) that the face of the star "expresses, symbolizes, incarnates a collective instinct" (Malraux 1958: 326), Magny claims that the identificatory myths of stars, like novelistic characters, depend on their being like us and bigger than us, universal and particular, an "ideal being" brought down to "the level of average humanity" (Magny 1972: 13).

Strangely, though, while films and novels minister to a human need for empathy and identification, their sociological essence is a fundamental solitude. So, although it is common to think of a novel reader as honeycombed in privacy and the cinemagoer as a member of a public experience, for Magny, the cinema at its best is, like the novel, addressed "to those things that are deepest and most solitary in man" (Magny 1948/1972: 18). Although the experience of cinema unfolds collectively, once the story begins, "each person returns to the solitude of his own perception" (p. 18). "Emotional contagion," Magny avers, "is minimal at the movies, maximal at the theatre," and this relative immunity from infectious sentiment means that "it is incomparably easier to maintain one's freedom of judgment in a movie house than in a playhouse" (p. 19). This difference between the cinematic and theatrical experience, which joins cinema to the novel, stems from the fact "that the aesthetic essence of theatre is spectacle" – a perception simultaneously apprehended and mutually conditioned by the audience members, and thus a collective witnessing that performatively reconstitutes community in mode of Greek tragedy. The movie, on the other hand, is "only slightly – or not at all – a spectacle; it is much more – like the novel – a story" (p. 19). The crucial aesthetic affinity between the cinema and the novel, then, is that they are both *narratives*, and as a result, feed individual, rather than collective, perception: the film, rather than external to its spectators, is "the very stuff of their dreams – materialized, enriched, made incarnate" (p. 20).

The stakes of this fleshy mode of perception shared by the novel and film are high for Magny. These art forms are "exactly suited to modern consciousness and its needs" because they embody

what distinguishes contemporary society from a more primitive society: the simultaneously particular and personal relationship of the individual to the collective soul in the former, as opposed to that individual's more diffuse participation in the community in the latter. With the same danger: the barely conscious descent into absolute solitude and the loss of all objectivity by the substitution of what one wants for one what actually *is* – in short, the concrete equivalent of the attitude philosophers call solipsism. Modern man is alone in the movie house, though he is surrounded by a thousand spectators similar to himself. They too are lost in their own dreams, they too are hypnotized by the screen and what is happening on it – but each is for the moment a stranger to the others. One thousand consciousnesses become impervious to their neighbors, divided by what seems to unite them. (Magny 1948/1972: 20–1)

In these existentialist terms, the cinema and the novel always share a visuality torn between empathetic participation in human community and radical solitude. Their sociological situation is framed, on one side, by a compensatory psychological essence (empathy) that satisfies "man's curiosity about other men," and on the other, by an aesthetic essence (narrative) that threatens to dissolve the objective world in the desiring imagination of a voracious subject. This perceptual mode is especially timely in a postwar social environment newly skeptical of the dangers of "the collective soul," and yet aware that reactionary individualism may fall prey to a similar threat – the loss of objectivity and, indeed, of the self. "In the life of societies, Magny observes, "there are undoubtedly periods when the collective conscious is integrative and others when it is disintegrative" (1948/1972: 15). Wary of "the individual's more diffuse participation in the community," contemporary society is defined by the "disintegrative" character of collective consciousness that, Magny hypothesizes, may even explain the "star crisis" of the movies (p. 15). As "powerful collective instinct[s]" wane, so too the stars that embody them (p. 15). Mythic personhood thus gives way to the more uncertain modes of impersonality – neither fully collective feeling nor onanistic solitude – that Magny attempts to square with the "principles of a new humanism" and finds articulated in the specific "film aesthetic" of American fiction. "The Age of the American Novel," then, is not an era in which the lymphatic body of French intellectual culture gets a transfusion of vital American sap, but a "period of transformation and disintegration," where the glamorous and transcendent personalities of novel and screen – and the convergence of mass desire they organize – are supplanted by "neutral detectives without personality," by heroes that "melt into" the story (pp. 15–17). Such minimal heroes testify to a pervasive characterological vagrancy symptomatic of a broader postwar concern about heroic personality and the novelistic "art of narration itself," which ceases to be the story of a "personal destiny" or "a collective entity" and becomes instead a quasi-documentary "description" of action within dispersive situations (pp. 169–70).

For Magny, the "extreme modernity" of the modern American novel lies in two major technical innovations borrowed from the film: first, "absolutely objective" narration, "pushed to the point of behaviorism," in which characters and events are "described only from the outside, with neither commentary nor psychological interpretation"; and second, "the more specifically technical innovations" of varied points of view – novelistic fades, superimpositions, crosscutting, close-ups – "made possible by the extension to the novel of the principle of changing the position of the camera, the discovery of which transformed the cinema by making of it an art" (Magny 1948/1972: 39). Magny's humanistic trick is to connect these two techniques – to show that the subjective pole is just another modality of externalized description and that behaviorism, rather than narrowly deterministic, is something like a technology of human freedom itself. As a manifestation of psychological behaviorism, objective technique reduces the psychological reality of a person or thing to what can be perceived by an external observer, to a succession of acts and gestures, to "'conduct' in a given situation" (p. 40). Eschewing the transcendent narrative perspective Magny associates with the nineteenth-century novel, this "aesthetic of the stenographic record explains nothing and limits itself to placing the facts before us in all their ambiguity" (p. 42). Emotion isn't felt inside so much as it is witnessed externally by the reader and by a world of others in which the characters act; they "exist so strongly that they can dispense with having an inner life" (p. 43).

Magny's discussion of "the behavioristic view of man," with its idiom of psychological "facts" and "acts" of characters within ambiguous "situations," is clearly indebted to her mentor, Sartre, and also picks up on contemporaneous efforts to yoke behaviorist psychology, phenomenology, and cinematic perception. In his 1945 *Atlantic Monthly* essay, "American Novelists in French Eyes," Sartre opposes the outmoded novel of intellectual analysis to "a psychology of synthesis which taught us that a psychological fact is an indivisible whole. [The analytical novel] could not be used to depict a group of facts which present themselves as the ephemeral or permanent unity of a great number of perceptions" (Sartre 1945: 119). Moreover, Sartre claims, the shortcomings of the analytical novel are political:

> All around us clouds were gathering. There was war in Spain; the concentration camps were multiplying in Germany, in Austria, in Czechoslovakia. War was menacing everywhere. Nevertheless analysis – analysis à la Proust, à la James – remained our only literary method, or favorite procedure. But could it take into account the brutal death of a Jew in Auschwitz, the bombardment of Madrid by the planes of Franco? Here a new literature presented its characters to us synthetically. It made them perform before our eyes acts which were complete in themselves, impossible to analyze, acts which it was necessary to grasp completely with all the obscure power of our souls. (Sartre 1945: 119)

What can American literature possibly have to do with the death of a Jew in Auschwitz? Sartre's assumption seems to be that nonanalytical style is better equipped to account for brutal political realities because it locates the human in a space of action and the reader in an arena of witnessing. When Hemingway or Caldwell present a character who lives but doesn't contemplate, the reader "sees them born and formed in a situation which has been made understandable to him"; when Faulkner or Dos Passos describe their heroes from the outside, the reader "is only the witness of their conduct. It is from their conduct that we must, as in life, construct their thought" (1945: 119). *As in life*. Objective technique, for Sartre, is a tool for living – an instrumental gizmo that builds before the reader's eyes a stylized form of lived experience consistent with the open, ambiguous present and unforeseeable futurity of existential action. In fact, his "Existentialism is a Humanism" lecture defends existentialism against the charge of subjectivism in similarly *moral* and *visual* terms. In action and behavior, we "create an image of man as we think he ought to be"; when we choose ourselves, we choose all of humanity, "everything happens as if all mankind had its eyes fixed on us and were guiding itself by what he does" (Sartre 1945/1995: 37, 39). So, while we tend to think of Sartrean seeing as the condition of being fixed by the mortifying gaze of another (Jay 1993), the "Humanism" lecture redefines action as a kind of situated moral conduct bound to the gaze of a universal humanity created and affirmed in particular human acts and choices. And this is not, Sartre insists, a human *essence* but a human condition – those *"a priori* limits which define man's condition in the universe. Historical situations vary . . . What does not vary is the necessity for him to exist in the world, to be at work there, to be there in the midst of other people, and to be mortal there" (Sartre 1945/1995: 52). Explicitly opposed to an "absurd" humanism that would – like the Kantian morality Sartre seems to invoke – take "man as an end and as a higher value," existentialism sees the human as always in the making. Constantly "outside himself," projecting himself into the future, Sartre's human is properly ecstatic and impersonal (pp. 60–1).

Sartre's claim for the American novel as a perceptual mode best suited to the political realities of the time depends both upon his existentialist morality and on the "psychology of synthesis," a psychology which understands a psychological "fact" as an indivisible whole, grasped in action and gesture – in conduct before the eyes of others. This is a mode of Gestalt psychology central to the early phenomenology of Maurice Merleau-Ponty, Sartre's friend and then coeditor of *Les Temps Modernes.* Merleau-Ponty's lecture "The Film and the New Psychology," delivered in March of 1945 at l'Institut des Hautes Etudes Cinématographiques, France's state-sponsored film academy, echoes the terms of Sartre's account of objectified emotion and perceptual situatedness, while implicating the cinematic presentation of the human as a privileged way of being in the world. Rejecting classical theories of perception that understood the visual field as the sum of sensations to be deciphered by the intelligence, Merleau-Ponty followed the Gestaltists in proposing a more primordial mode of seeing, that more complete (and more obscure) "grasp" described by Sartre above: "I perceive in a total way with my whole being; I grasp a unique structure of the thing, a unique way of being, which speaks to all my senses at once" (Merleau-Ponty 1945/1964: 50). Importantly, this new psychology "brings a new concept of *the perception of others"* predicated on the rejection of both introspection and the notion that the meaning of emotion is readily available to inner observation (Merleau-Ponty 1945/1964: 52, my emphasis). Citing directly Sartre's own 1939 essay on the emotions, an experiment in phenomenological psychology, Merleau-Ponty insists that anger, shame, or hate are not "psychic facts hidden at the bottom of another's consciousness: they are types of behavior or styles of conduct which are visible from the outside. They exist *on* this face or *in* those gestures, not hidden behind them" (p. 52). Following Sartre's theory of the emotions as purposive acts and ways of constituting the meaningfulness of the world, Merleau-Ponty argues that emotion is not "a psychic, internal fact but rather a variation in our relations with others and with the world that is expressed in our bodily attitude" (Sartre 1938/1995, Merleau-Ponty 1945/1964: 53). We see others, others become manifest to us, as behavior, because the human is defined by "a commerce with the world and a presence to the world that is older than intelligence" (Merleau-Ponty 1945/1964: 52). If the new psychology reveals the human as a being "thrown into the world and attached to it by a natural bond," then cinema is the instrument of a phenomenological humanism, a technology of intentional consciousness (p. 53). Films are not sum totals of images, words, or noises, but temporal or sensory gestalts irreducible to their component parts, primordially given to perception, and thus the aesthetic exaggeration of our lived experience of the tiniest perceived thing:

> A movie is not thought; it is perceived. That is why the movies can be so gripping in their presentation of man: they do not give us his *thoughts*, as novels have done for so long, but his conduct or behavior. They directly present to us that special way of being in the world, of dealing with things and other people, which we can see in the sign language of gesture and gaze and which clearly defines each person we know. (Merleau-Ponty 1945/1964: 58, original emphasis)

In these 1945 essays, both Sartre and Merleau-Ponty turn away from the novel of introspection towards a phenomenological humanism – one predicated on a visual objectivity that bears witness to "the inherence of the self in the world and in others" (Merleau-Ponty 1945/1964: 58). Sartre locates this objectivity in the perceptual mode of the American novel, Merleau-Ponty in the cinema's way of seeing.

Magny's study marshals both insights in her account of the humanistic objectivity that links the technical experiments of the novel and cinema. Objective description produces a gestural universalism – "the universality of mimicry" stretching from Steinbeck and Dos Passos to Charlie Chaplin – that restores

> a certain idea of *man*, independent of the accidents of class and condition. Truly classic in spirit – classic in the same way as Chaplin's movies, which make people laugh in Shanghai as well as in Romorantin – it is more nearly universal than our eighteenth-century literature because it truly encompasses all races and all classes. It is coextensive with the planet. It demonstrates the principle of a new humanism. (Magny 1948/1972: 45)

At the risk of conflating important differences between the phenomenologies of Sartre, Merleau-Ponty, and Magny, I want to underscore their shared sense that objective technique entails a visual idiom of gesture, action, and conduct that beggars analysis or intellection, given instead to aesthetic – sensuous – perception. Chaplin's gestural mutism, which Magny will link to Dos Passos's elliptical technique, is "truly international" because it is "apprehended rather than understood, it can affect men of all ages, of all classes, of all nations, and – especially – of all intellectual levels" (Magny 1948/1972: 58). These humane gestures, like those of the protagonists of the American novel described by Sartre or those that, for Merleau-Ponty, define our everyday way of being in the world, are both *sensual* and *situated*, embedded in a scene and always subject to the gaze of others.

The humanistic backdrop of Sartre and Merleau-Ponty thus helps to explain how, for Magny, the objective narration, which places the perceiver *in a situation*, and among others, is so suited to the second major technical innovation – multiple points of view – that, by her logic, the modern novel borrows from the film. Every scene in a movie is perforce photographed from a certain location, which means that the aesthetic essence of the film is to fragment reality into a "disconnected series of appearances": the vision of the world offered by cinema refuses clinical disinterestedness and "'pure' vision, a vision of someone who would not have a point of view" (Magny 1948/1972: 88). Rather, the technique of the movies is "fundamentally *engagé*, inherently incapable of giving us . . . any image that is abstractly impersonal" (p. 88). Magny explicitly borrows Sartre's contemporaneous phenomenology of engaged literature (*littérature engagée*). Writing, Sartre argues, is action that reveals human situatedness: "If you name the behavior of an individual, you reveal it to him; he sees himself. And since you are at the same time naming it to all others, he knows that he is *seen* at the moment he *sees* himself" (Sartre 1947/1965: 16, original emphasis). Having "given up the impossible dream of giving an impartial picture of Society and the human condition," the engaged writer understands the word as a "a pact of generosity between author and reader" (pp. 17, 49). Such generosity requires the creative faculties and situatedness of both parties, and thus dialectically discloses the human freedom of each while underscoring the nature of art itself as "for and by others" – a subjective project completed outside the self, in the objectivity of an other's act of reading (p. 37). In these terms, what Magny calls "objectivity" is another mode by which the cinematic novel acknowledges its place in the world, the situation in which it finds itself. Eschewing the godlike and disembodied abstraction of Cartesian perspectivalism, the objective technique of the American novel is *concretely* impersonal, humane, and committed.

The Grammar of the Human: Ellipses and Adjectives

I now want to explore more specifically the impersonal grammar of commitment spoken by the American novel, as Magny understands it, and to show how her suggestive reading of style draws on contemporary ideas in French visual culture about humanistic vision. Magny's study is divided into two parts: the first, "The American Novel and the Movies," which I've described above, sets forth her general meditations on the aesthetic affinities between the novel and the film, as well as her discussion of the technical innovations borrowed by the novel from film; the second, "Time and Impersonalism in the American Novel," offers a series of author-specific analyses of impersonal technique in the work of Dos Passos, Hemingway, Steinbeck, and Faulkner. As the title of the second part indicates, Magny now subordinates a focused discussion of the cinematic qualities of this style to its various modes of impersonalism, though this understanding of impersonality is everywhere enabled by vision, its technological agents, and their manipulations of temporality.

This is most evident in her best chapters – searching discussions of impersonality in Dos Passos and Faulkner. I approach these readings through the stylistic hallmarks that most interest her in these authors, ellipses and adjectives, respectively. A "kind of nonsubjective impressionism," novelistic ellipsis is a manner of presenting events not "as no one except possibly God himself could ever have seen," but "only as any given spectator might have seen it . . . a certain kind of ellipsis thus appears as a direct consequence of the objectivity that forbids the artist to show the public anything that could not have been seen by a recording apparatus" (Magny 1948/1972: 50). Magny's two governing assumptions about ellipses – that the novel and the film are each, essentially, an "art of ellipsis," and that the ellipsis is not just a formal strategy but one serving "to cloak a metaphysical meaning as well" – are endemic to a particular postwar moment in French film criticism known today as the *nouvelle critique* (Magny 1972: 49, 51). Buoyed by the post-Liberation renaissance of French film culture, and voiced by critics like Roger Leenhardt, André Malraux, Alexandre Astruc, and most importantly, André Bazin, this new critical line was marked by the belief that cinema was essentially a narrative medium, with close ties to the novel and the theatre; by the conviction that cinema was a fundamentally popular, indeed, commercial, art; and by a turn away from the dazzling formal strategies of the cinematic avant-gardes of the 1920s, as well as their recondite position within culture at large. Cinematic modernism, by carving into, shaping, or otherwise aestheticizing reality through its various montage experiments, was out, and increasingly seen as an aesthetic deformation of the real. "Realism" was back in, and with it a resurgent respect for the "profilmic" – that elusive chunk of lived reality preceding the imposition of the camera – and for editing strategies that would themselves find ways to preserve the spatiotemporal continuity of reality. One can understand Magny's freighted appeal to the metaphysical dimension of ellipsis in this critical climate: in narrative ellipsis, cinema finds itself confronted with its own inevitable interruption of spatiotemporal continuity, with the vexing gap between representation and "the real." Film is elliptical at heart.

In these terms, the challenge of ellipsis is phenomenological, and the question of editing ethical: how to cut into the dense texture of reality in a way that preserves its fundamental richness? It was, of course, the great film critic André Bazin, founding editor of the film journal *Cahiers du Cinéma* and godfather of the French New Wave, whose lifelong championing of cinematic realism offered the most complete meditations on this question, and for whom the question of ellipsis was always a metaphysical and humanist one. These concerns are most evident in two of Bazin's famous essays on Italian neorealism, "An Aesthetic of Reality: Neorealism" and "De Sica: Metteur en Scène." The first, published in 1948 like Magny's study, aims to describe the realism of this new, post-Liberation Italian school of cinema, and to argue for its international importance. The essay is especially interesting for our purposes because it claims that "the aesthetic of the Italian cinema . . . is simply the equivalent on film of the American novel," and because it finds in this cinema, and in its technical properties, an exemplary humanity:

> What is a ceaseless source of wonder, ensuring the Italian cinema a wide moral audience among the Western nations, is the significance it gives to the portrayal of actuality. In a world already obsessed again with terror and hate, in which reality is scarcely favored

any longer for its own sake but is rather rejected or excluded as a political symbol, the Italian cinema is certainly the one which preserves, in the midst of the period it depicts, a revolutionary humanism. (Bazin 1948/1971: 39, 20–1)

While Bazin owes the opposition here between "humanism" and "terror" to Merleau-Ponty's study, the notion of humanism he defends is rather different (Merleau-Ponty 1947/1969). We experience this revolutionary humanism in the Italian films' relationship to reality: refusing to instrumentalize the real, to "treat this reality as a medium or a means to an end" or to foreclose reality by converting it into a political symbol, they remind us "that the world *is*, quite simply, before it is something to be condemned" (Bazin 1948/1971: 21). So too do these films attempt to restore to a moral audience of human beings who watch them something of their presymbolic, phenomenological *thereness*: "Nobody is reduced to the condition of an object or a symbol that would allow one to hate them in comfort without having first to leap the hurdle of their humanity" (p. 21).

The humane work of returning us to the world, and to ourselves, requires giving the spectator "as perfect an illusion of reality as possible," and for Bazin, the more cinema follows its general "evolutionary trend" towards realism, the more it "comes ever closer to the novel" (1948/1971: 26). No naive realist, Bazin insists that realism can only "be achieved in one way – through artifice," and he identifies as the two most significant events since 1940 in the evolution of realist artifice Orson Welles's *Citizen Kane* (1941), and Roberto Rossellini's *Paisà* (1946), two films that, for Bazin, bear the stylistic imprint of the modern American novel (1948/1971: 26). Rather than using montage to abstract from reality, signifying it in advance by dividing it into "a series of either logical or subjective points of view of an event," Welles's signature deep-focus photography "takes in with equal sharpness the whole field of vision contained simultaneously within the dramatic field," and thus allows the mind of the spectator to encounter the visible continuity of reality as structured by the frame much as we do in life, making our own perceptual choices within the dense fabric of the sensible (p. 28). Bazin's discussion of Welles here condenses many of the same points he made in his earlier essay, "The Technique of *Citizen Kane*," published the year before in *Les Temps Modernes*. In that piece, Bazin had connected *Kane*'s newsreels and the novels of Dos Passos and read this link as a sign of the "mutual influence that literature and cinema have on each other," one which "does not diminish the uniqueness of their respective means of expression" (Bazin 1947/1997: 236). But there, as he does in the "Aesthetic of Reality" essay, and as he will do again later in his 1952 essay "In Defense of Mixed Cinema," Bazin attempts to change the terms of the conversation altogether – away from "influence" or facile technical copying and towards the convergence, across media, of a common purpose, a metaphysic: "Rather than an influence one on the other, it is an accord between cinema and literature, based on the same profound aesthetic data, on the same concept of the relation between art and reality" (Bazin 1948/1971: 40).

In one of the most astonishing passages of "An Aesthetic of Reality," Bazin explores this accord by connecting the elliptical narrative technique of Rossellini's *Paisà* to the objective technique of the modern American novel – for him, the very apotheosis of style, where form becomes something like a force of nature:

> The objective nature of the modern American novel, by reducing the strictly grammatical aspects of its stylistics to a minimum, has laid bare the secret essence of style. Certain qualities of the language of Faulkner, Hemingway, or Malraux would certainly not come through in translation, but the essential qualities of their styles would not suffer because their style is almost completely identical with their narrative technique – the ordering in time of fragments of reality. The style becomes the inner dynamic principle of the narrative, something like the relation of energy to matter or the specific physics of the work, as it were. This is what distributes the fragmented realities across the aesthetic spectrum of the narrative, which polarizes the filings of the facts without changing their chemical composition. A Faulkner, a Malraux, a Dos Passos, each has his personal universe which is defined by the nature of the facts reported, but also by the law of gravity which holds them suspended above chaos. (Bazin 1948/1971: 31)

In the modern American novel's objectivity, Bazin finds a nearly perfect identity between grammatical style and the temporal structuring of reality's "facts," an idealized management of the ineluctable ellipticality of the visible. If a "fact," as Bazin later defines it, is "a fragment of concrete reality in itself multiple and full of ambiguity," then objective style amounts to an ethical regard for the facts, where narrative assumes the purity of physics, artfully arranging the filings of reality without defiling their integrity (p. 37).

In a later essay on neorealism, "De Sica: Metteur en Scène" (1952), Bazin clarifies that Rossellini's use of ellipsis is a moral "way of seeing" manifested in his "exterior approach," which "offers us an essential ethical and metaphysical aspect of our relations with the world" (Bazin 1952/1971: 62). We can understand this as yet another example of the tendency in France to read American objectivity as a technology of human locatedness. Whereas "ellipsis in classic montage is an effect of style," in Rossellini's films it is "a lacuna in reality, or rather in the knowledge we have of it, which is by its nature limited" (p. 66). In the "Aesthetic of Reality" essay, Bazin explores more carefully how the narrative ethics of elliptical style – whose formal transparency allows it to pass as *non*style – at once nurtures the mental activity of spectators and guides them to an awareness of their human limits. Like the American novel, *Paisà*'s fragmented narrative "reveals enormous ellipses – or rather, great holes," and Rossellini's strength as a filmmaker lies in the way his elliptical technique allows the scattered facts of the real to enter into relationships with each other, and thus to take on meaning in the mind of the spectator in a noninstrumental fashion (Bazin 1948/1971: 35). Facts become meaningful "not like a tool whose function has predetermined its form," but "only after the fact, thanks to other imposed facts between which the mind establishes certain relationships (pp. 36, 37). Images, themselves "just a fragment of reality existing before any meanings," are also "image facts," brought by the mind of the spectator into centrifugal networks of significant relationships that testify to, as they recreate, the "concrete density" of reality itself (p. 37). In this rich phenomenal web, "man himself is just one fact among others, to whom no pride of place should be given *a priori*" (p. 38). Human being and mechanical image – both are concrete, *situated* facts, and Bazin insists that is the special gift of Italian filmmakers to portray human "action without separating it from its material context and without loss of that uniquely human quality of which it is an integral part" (p. 38). It is this sensitivity to human situatedness, and to the limitations of human vision's total purchase on reality, then, that aligns ellipsis in Italian neorealism to "the very fabric of the narrative, the law of gravity that governs the ordering of the facts, in Faulkner, Hemingway, and Dos Passos" (p. 39).

This is not quite the end of the story, since the concluding section of Bazin's essay, "The Realism of the Italian Cinema and the Technique of the American Novel," ends with a meditation on the very compatibility of these styles, and these nations, in the context of America's postwar occupation of Italy. For Bazin, *le style américain* is so naturally suited to the Italian national context because of "the exceptional affinity of the two civilizations as revealed by the Allied occupation. The G.I. felt himself at home at once in Italy, and the *paisan* was at once on familiar terms with the G.I., black or white" (Bazin 1948/1971: 40). Transcending boundaries of nation and race, this stylistic fit embodies a perfect cultural marriage in a culture of occupation, of a piece with the "widespread black market and the presence of prostitution, wherever the American army went" – economic realities of the postwar period Bazin takes for humanistic exchanges, and "by no means the least convincing example of the symbiosis of two civilizations" (p. 40). Informed by a rosy Atlanticism that would do Malraux proud, Bazin's analogy makes clear that the American army is as at home in the world as the American style, itself a force of nature. For how can we fail to read this stylistic compatibility politically, as either an index of American economic aggression or as the naturalization of America's status as always at home in the world?

Bazin's refusal to do so, his insistence that this stylistic affinity follows from a surfeit of basic human intimacy, is in fact consistent with his generally apolitical – or better, his prepolitical – reading of neorealist style. His essay on Vittorio De Sica, for example, credits the filmmaker with a persistent tenderness that consists in allowing humans and things "to exist for their own sakes, freely; it is in loving them in their singular individuality" (Bazin 1952/1971: 69). De Sica's work contains a reservoir of "unattached love" irreducible to partisan politics; so, while both the Communists and the Christian Democrats have instrumentalized De Sica's films to support their political platforms, bending its affect to their purposes, the very fact that "each party can with equal plausibility lay claim to being the proprietor of it" means that "much authentic and naive love scales the walls and penetrates the stronghold of ideologies and social theory" (p. 71). This, because for Bazin, there is an inexhaustible residue of human need that can never be alleviated or produced by a "given historical institution" or a "particular economic setup"; politics may promote the "objective conditions necessary for human happiness," but not the subjective ones, which stem from "the congenital indifference of our social organization, as such, to the fortuitousness of individual happiness" (p. 74). In this idea that human feeling – happiness as well as suffering – stems from a metaphysical alienation, we see Bazin's own Christian brand of existentialism, one that departs crucially from Sartre, an important early influence on Bazin's aesthetic theory. Whereas Sartre's atheist humanism retooled emotion as a form of action within the world fully compatible with his increasingly radicalized partisan politics in the 1950s, Bazin sees human feeling as finally irreducible to political instrumentality. This explains Bazin's intentionally paradoxical formulation of neorealism as a "revolutionary humanism" in "An Aesthetic of Reality." Its humanism inheres in what Bazin calls its prepolitical "communicative generosity," which shows us not humanity in a mass, but as one fact among others in a dense thicket of reality, a human within "concrete social realities" freed of the "apriori values of politics" (pp. 21–2).

Magny's reading of Dos Passos depends similarly on the metaphysics of ellipsis, but its understanding of elliptical technique is rather more "polymorphous" than Bazin's. Like Bazin, though, Magny will strip the impersonal humanism of Dos Passos's style from a specific political agenda. On the one hand, Dos Passos's ellipsis is linked to the "aesthetic imperative of discretion and taciturnity" borrowed from the cinema, where words would burn with the sensual immediacy of images, and act more directly on their reader's "sensitive soul" (Magny 1948/1972: 49, 60). In this sense, elliptical technique would reintroduce into literature "some purely *aesthetic* elements the functions of which are neither discursive nor narrative" (p. 59). By focusing on the harmonious timbre of voice rather than semantic content, the laconic "polyphony" of Dos Passos would be "resolutely nondiscursive," part of "a total art addressing itself to man as a whole – not only to the most intellectual, the most lucid, and yet the most limited part of his being" (p. 60). Even more oddly, Magny locates the potential nondiscursivity of Dos Passos's style in his very "aesthetic of redundancy," the way key themes from the character-based narratives in *USA* (of Charlie Anderson, Margo Dowling, J. Ward Morehouse, and the like) are musically echoed in the Newsreels and Camera Eye sections so that the trilogy as a whole lends itself to an "absentminded reading," where the reader doesn't so much *understand* the novel's themes as "hear" them accrue, intuitively, almost unconsciously (p. 115). Ellipsis in these terms would function as a kind of nondiscursive, sensory image addressing a "total" rather than narrowly rational human being. And yet on a more sustained level, Dos Passos's ellipses are linked to a host of literary strategies testifying to pervasive characterological impersonality in the *USA* trilogy: "consciousness without solidity"; "emotions, desires, and wishes" that don't belong to a self; as "vacillating" or "drifting" "beings without inner consistency"; in sum, "the novel of a people dispossessed of themselves" (pp. 118–23). Here, ellipsis is "the only technique adequate to the experience of nothingness" (p. 63). Thus, Magny understands ellipsis as at once the communicative means of addressing a fuller human being and the literary expression of the very abdication of the human condition. Ellipsis, we might say, is the dialectical technique of a humanity that would, in the act of reading, find its essence affirmed in proportion to its alienation from it.

The "profound truth" of Dos Passos's novel of objective technique is "the nonexistence of the psychological," an evacuation of the inner life of the human that Magny observes in some of *USA*'s most famous features (Magny 1948/1972: 67). Its experimental "visual" techniques, the Newsreel and Camera Eye sections, work in conjunction with the narratives to blur the personal and the public, the particular and the anonymous. In the scraps and fragments of Dos Passos's Newsreel montages, Magny hears "the completely impersonal monologue of the collective unconscious," and in the impressionistic Camera Eye segments she sees this disembodied monologue alight for a moment in an anonymous individual (p. 113). The narrative traffic between character narratives of named individual characters and these more experimental visual sections only further underscores the nullity of the inner life, since the characters' "personal" feelings are mockingly doubled in the Camera Eye sections just as the jingoistic clichés, scraps of popular song, or bits of adspeak so artfully juxtaposed in the Newsreels insinuate themselves into the thoughts and utterances of the characters, who, much like Nathanael West's characters, talk in headlines.

Here and elsewhere, Magny's reading of impersonality in Dos Passos follows the lead of Sartre, who, in a suggestive essay on *1919*, noted how speech in *USA* "comes from afar . . . It is as if there were a Platonic heaven of words and commonplaces to which we all go to find words suitable to a given situation" (Sartre 1938/1962: 100). The problem of utterance and authenticity, for Sartre, is the problem of time, which is fully reified and deterministic in Dos Passos: "Each event is irreducible, a gleaming and solitary *thing* that does not flow from anything else, but suddenly arises to join other things" (p. 96). Like Sartre, Magny observes how Dos Passos's curious use of the preterit, normally "the best tense for expressing things in the process of happening," allows characters to narrate events of their lives as if they were never possessed, but always already dead (Magny 1948/1972: 117). Characters describe themselves "objectively, a little as if [their lives] were being projected on a screen," but this narration is not "entirely objective," since characters have access to their "feelings," however clichéd and ready-made they may be (p. 117). The "recording apparatus – which is, instead of ordinary introspection, a 'lens' in the true sense of the term – is in [their] consciousness," and as a result characters can never be intimate with themselves (pp. 117–18). As such, the preterit in Dos Passos is "terrible," deadening events as soon as they happen so as to prepare us for the trilogy's main character, Time, "the inexorable and monstrous time of capitalist society as it incoherently unwinds in the Newsreels" (pp. 127, 128). As for Bazin, Magny's understanding of time is explicitly Bergsonian: Dos Passos's characters are deprived of time's "organic rhythm, the dense continuity of living tissue," moving instead in the "dead" time of "Society – objective, inexorable, and spatialized" (pp. 129–30).

Stripping the human of its constitutive elements – freedom, dignity, expressive authenticity – and reducing it to "the triple determinisms of hunger, sexuality, and social class: Pavlov, Freud, and Marx," Dos Passos's elliptical technique "proposes a completely different conception of man, and thus it is scandalous" (Magny 1948/1972: 67–8). Magny insists that Dos Passos's radical impersonality be seen as "a revolt against the essence of the human condition rather than against this or that form of society. It is Man, or Being, and not Capitalism or American society that is taken to task" in his novels (p. 67). In a historical and intellectual climate dominated by fears about the new American economic hegemony on the continent, and of globalization under the rubric of Americanization, how should we understand Magny's insistence that Dos Passos's critique of capital is really a critique of Being? The subsumption of a nation-state's specific mode of economic aggression by a general metaphysics, or a canny awareness of Americanization's global reach and violence, despoiling Being itself? Magny suggests the latter, I think, when she observes that "the inexorable pulsation at the heart of Dos Passos's work is that of the basic, regular rhythm of the transmission belt in the heart of a factory – invisible, omnipresent, all-powerful. The rhythm of the modern world itself" (p. 130). If the subsequent impersonality is a form of "metaphysical satire," then one might reasonably assume that Dos Passos would value, in negative fashion, some normative humanness absent in the world of *USA*. But Magny insists that Dos Passos cannot judge because judgment presupposes "some organized system of positive norms," whereas Dos Passos "offers nothing positive, nothing affirmative." Instead, "he is just angry, that is all. Very simply, he says *no*" (p. 139). And yet in this passionate negativity, Magny finds Dos Passos's technique the apogee of a novel that "will have made itself so impersonal that it will no longer be a work of fiction, a work of imagination perhaps capable (who knows?) of transforming the world" (p. 143).

But how would such a transformation be brought about, and why must it be impersonal? This claim, that in Dos Passos total impersonality becomes a mode of Sartrean committed writing, only makes sense in light of earlier claims about the *communicative* potential of ellipsis – its sensual address to a fuller, more total humanity. Magny is, in short, invested in two interrelated modes of elliptical impersonality in Dos Passos: a characterological impersonality that is the global, metaphysical product of American capitalism and its inexorable temporality, and a readerly or, if you will, spectatorial impersonality that happens in acts of communicative generosity like reading or watching movies. The former impersonal mode registers a kind of dehumanization; the latter activates, in a phenomenological sense, the human faculties of a witness that involves the reader in the world. Magny again follows Sartre in the way she measures the alienated essence of the total human being – like Bazin's, situated in an organic continuity of living tissue, experiencing the eventfulness of lived, personal time – by its distance from the vagrant beings of the *USA* trilogy. Sartre's reading of Dos Passos hinges on a fine description of the act of reading his fiction that anticipates his literary phenomenology in *What is Literature?* Sartre proposes that in the act of reading Dos Passos our very freedom comes into relief through an emotional encounter with inhumanity, a "hybrid creature, an interior-exterior being" whose "vacillating, individual consciousness" wavers and is diluted in the "collective consciousness" (Sartre 1938/1962: 102). If, in Bazin's reading of De Sica, the affective yield of our spectatorial encounter with the human is an abundance of prepolitical, unattached love that inheres in the human being's singular individuality, our encounter with Dos Passos's creatures, for Sartre, produces disgust, revolt, and indignation at their "statistical determinism" (p. 102). Reading Dos Passos's work, the reader experiences a strange impersonality in which he or she becomes at once a member of an anonymous, public "they" (what Heidegger calls "the everyman" of the public realm) hostile to individual possibility and its critic:

> In order to understand the words, in order to make sense out of the paragraphs, I first have to adopt [the everyman's] point of view. I have to play the role of the obliging chorus. This consciousness exists only through me; without me there would be nothing but black spots on white paper. But even while I am this collective consciousness, I want to wrench myself away from it, see it from the judge's point of view, that is, to get free of myself. This is the source of the shame and uneasiness with which Dos Passos knows how to fill the reader. I am a reluctant accomplice (though I am not sure I am reluctant), creating and rejecting social taboos. (Sartre 1938/1962: 101)

Following, then, the Sartrean logic of committed reading and writing that Magny assumes, the more we encounter the "passionate negativity" of Dos Passos's revolt against the human condition, the more fully we experience our humanity in the communicative act of reading.

Magny puts this sort of readerly phenomenology to practice in her fascinating reading of William Faulkner, one rooted in the stylistic production of *fascination* itself, and in its etymological sense – as a magical phenomenon, a kind of sacred spell or enchantment cast upon the reader. For fascination is the fruit of Faulkner's style, seemingly perverse in its linguistic obscurity: its tendency to begin stories at their ending, or to tell at least two stories at once, or to occlude the shadowy events of the past that seem to lock his characters in their tragic obsessions, or to surround his fulsome, inexorable, imponderable nouns with a dense thicket of adjectival qualification. This neuromancy of style, for Magny, is the essence of a narrative method that is *"enveloping* and implicative rather than developmental and discursive" (Magny 1948/1972: 181, original emphasis). Faulkner's adjectival excess is a technology of envelopment that turns the reader into an "involved witness," establishing a crucial parallel between the scene of reading and a narrative whose order of events tends to be reconstituted by a spectator of the drama (like Horace Benbow in *Sanctuary* or Quentin and Shreve in *Absalom, Absalom!*) (p. 195). Like the enveloped reader, the textual witness "is at first external and indifferent to it but . . . quickly becomes immersed – and by the end of a few pages, implicated – in these affairs that do not in any way concern him" (p. 193). Encroaching on the limits of discursivity, the superabundance of adjectives is sensual. When we lose ourselves in Faulkner's sentences, "we literally get *entrammeled,"* and as a result, "we end by *seeing* much less distinctly those things that the author believes himself to be describing, but we *feel* them better" (pp. 198, 197).

This entrammelment is humanistic, and contrasted to the technology of the photograph:

> An adjective is not a photograph or a mold; it cannot in any way claim to explain the essence of something (a role semantics reserves to the substantive). A beach is not in itself "desolate" (as in Gracq) or a September afternoon "weary" (or "dead" or "long") – except through the intermediary of a human consciousness. Even the fact that something is blue or red implies at least the presence of a retina. To charge "things" with more "qualities" than current language can bear is simply to provide them with so many *handles* by which we can, when we wish, catch them, control them, make them serve our own ends. It is obvious that a certain kind of writer might use epithets to present things to the reader in a magical way, to *suggest* them rather than truly to describe them – in short, *to force them to appear*, which is the strict meaning of the word "evoke." (Magny 1948/1972: 199, original emphasis)

Adjectives, unlike photographs, are tools of human agency, extending "our power over things, things that are re-created by us in our image, things that are given particularities that make no sense except in relation to ourselves" (p. 198). Magny's comparison implies her awareness of Bazin's famous claim for the "essentially objective character of photography" in "The Ontology of the Photographic Image" (1945/1967): "For the first time, between an originating object and its reproduction there intervenes only the instrumentality of a nonliving agent. For the first time, an image of the world is formed automatically, without the creative intervention of man . . . All the arts are based on the presence of man, only photography derives an advantage from his absence" (Bazin 1945/1967: 13). Against photography's inhuman purchase on things, Magny credits the adjective for precisely the sort of sympathetic linguistic anthropomorphism whose rejection, 10 years later, will ground the novelistic antihumanism of the French *nouveau roman*. Alain Robbe-Grillet, for example, will substitute the humanist work of metaphor and analogy and its attendant metaphysics for a "sense of sight" that refuses to appropriate a world of things, but is instead "content to take their measurement . . . without attempting to penetrate them since there is nothing inside, without feigning the least appeal since they would not answer" (Robbe-Grillet 1958/1989: 52–3). Magny insists that the experience of adjectives produces a double reversal: things become human, but human consciousness, plunged into syntactical darkness, also "congeals and becomes more obscure, tends towards the opaque, blind, and totally self-oriented mode of existence, which is doubtless that of the inorganic, of the thing . . . To use Sartre's language, the '*en-soi*' and the '*pour-soi*' exchange their characteristics in Faulkner" (Magny 1948/1972: 198–9).

The point of this "magical exchange" between the consciousness of beings ("*pour-soi*") and the inner matter of things ("*en-soi*") produced in the matrix of adjectival fascination is the human communication it enables across the radical gap between imagination and the material world. Across this break, novels can't communicate any *things* at all but only their "human significance – that is, the impression they have produced, the emotion they have given rise to . . . in short, the contents of [the author's] own consciousness" (Magny 1948/1972: 201). And this emotional transfer happens through a structure of shared fascination: "the Witnesses, the Mediators, are charged with the task of communicating to us, by a kind of contagion, what they feel. It is because *they* are fascinated that we will see with their eyes and be fascinated in turn" (pp. 205–6). For Magny, the way Faulkner's adjectives produce humanistic involved witnessing is a powerful example of his desire for a "total identification" with his reader (p. 206). In effect, the adjective is the engine of a "truly 'Marxist' and cooperative literature" in which the reader is a producer, implicated in the structure of mutual responsibility that, as Sartre argues in *What is Literature?*, constitutes the very objectivity of the literary object (Magny 1948/1972: 207).

Perhaps most striking is Magny's implicit claim for the role of Faulkner's modernist style in the reciprocal event of reading, since the more convoluted or opaque Faulkner's style – given as it is to the "indispensable shadow" of meaning, to the "element of madness" or the "inkiness" of narrative events – the more it envelops the reader in a sensual, nondiscursive mode of narrative (Magny 1948/1972: 208–9). In other words, Faulkner's modernism attaches the reader to the density of the phenomenological real that so obsessed Bazin, while avoiding the rhetorical violence Bazin associated with certain forms of cinematic modernism: his style "keep[s] reality from being attenuated and eroded by the very means used to describe it – discursive narration, which is necessarily analytical" (p. 210). Faulkner's sentences "are like webs, like nets thrown over a too-rich reality that the novelist has no right, lest he betray it, to analyze or sift" (p. 218). Magny's Bazinian idiom becomes even more clear when she compares the complexity of Faulkner's narration to Welles's deep-focus reformation of cutting: reacting against "everything analytical and dissociative that is necessarily part of both narrative and speech," both offer us "a vision not so much of an absurd world as of a universe in which everything coexists, in which all beings are simultaneously perceived" (p. 219). In doing so, the adjective becomes a path to the "total world" of the *terra Faulkneriana*, a "synthesized universe," a "whole bloc of humanity" where plot prevails over character, events over humanity. If for Bazin, the revolutionary humanism of neorealism understands humanity, impersonally, as "one fact among others," so too for Magny, the real hero of Faulkner's work is "a social entity of which men and women are constituent elements" (p. 219).

Le Style Américain and the New Cosmopolitanism

Through the supposed nondiscursivity of narrative, Faulkner's style forges a world community that joins readers and characters in an enveloping fascination with the past "*Abbild*," the image of a "great immobile Event that hangs heavily over their heads and has made, so to speak, a hole in the monotonous succession of similar days" (Magny 1948/1972: 221, 222). Magny's conception of a captivated humanity is eschatological: the traumatic hole in time which the characters experience "can in no way be different until, with the Incarnation . . . the marriage of Time and Eternity takes place" (p. 223). Faulkner's fascinated community is thus a fallen one, sinners all, but by sketching, in negative fashion, the conditions for salvation, Faulkner's fiction participates in "the reconstruction of a Church" (p. 232). And yet it can be no historical accident that Magny's best examples of this "malady of the modern spirit" are the "Negroes of the Southern plantations" and "the entire Jewish people" (p. 222). So, while Magny's rapt humanity may indeed be holding out for a messianic event to restore the human into a meaningful temporal continuum, it is also poised on the other side of historical catastrophe – both the recent Holocaust and America's long history of racial violence – and thus, while waiting, bears witness to the traumatic exclusions from the human community.

At stake here is the relationship between Magny's conception of history and the version of cosmopolitan humanism she offers. In some ways, her Christian idiom of Eternity and her citizenship within the total, "synthesized universe" of Faulkner's world seem bound to a Hegelian notion of historical progress as the teleological unfolding of human destiny, and appear to echo a familiar reading of the Faulknerian human as a Cold War hero. In the conservative mid-century domestication of the avant-garde, when the New Critics and the New York intellectuals enshrined an aesthetics of difficulty and so made bad modernism good, Faulkner became America's reigning postwar moralist. His reputation burnished by the postwar liberal consensus, Faulkner, much like Jackson Pollock, was read as exemplary of the freedom of the individual under capitalism, and of the power and plight of human will amidst a lapsed modern world of social and moral decay (Schwartz 1988, Guilbaut 1983). Faulkner's humanism of suffering and enduring, like Pollock's expressionist vitality, thus became a sign of the moral virtues of American-style capitalism over the inhuman depredations of communist totalitarianism. Lawrence H. Schwartz, who has told this story well, sees the French existentialist reading of Faulkner, and Magny's in particular, as of a piece with that of American critics like Malcolm Cowley and Robert Penn Warren. Like the Americans, Schwartz claims, the French celebrate the same heroic "literature of freedom" and the same heroic "fundamental man," albeit inflected through a local tradition of Resistance humanism that values individual dignity, justice, and the conquering of despair and nihilism (Schwartz 1988: 142–8).

However, Magny's visual culture, as I have argued above, allowed her to find in *le style américain* a rather different version of humanism, and used it to imagine an impersonal observer skeptical of Americanization rather than its literary avatar. Magny turned to the so-called "objective" and cinematic technique of the modern American novel to construct a properly cosmopolitan observer, for whom cosmopolitan human-ism informs both a communicative and epistemological ideal. As a communicative ideal, the visual objectivity of the American novel convokes a moral audience of seers in which human action, emotion, and behavior is always subject to the eyes of others, always seen by other involved witnesses; at the same time, objectivity enacts a sensual or nondiscursive mode of address to what is most human in that audience. As an epistemological ideal, visual objectivity requires a way of seeing oneself, impersonally, as situated in the world, of seeing one's point of view as limited and partial rather than transcendent or universal, and of seeing one's human actions as located in a dense phenomenological texture in which everything coexists and in which acts of political instrumentality and decisionism will always cut violently into the coimplicated order of things. Amidst rising concerns on the continent about America's role in the world, Magny refashions American style as a form of humane vision that would be subject to a global moral community, and that would act modestly in that world, seeing itself as a contingent historical actor in an ever more proximate and interconnected global stage. If the modern American style, in France, is less a formal fetish than an anxious hope for a more humane and cosmopolitan superpower, then Faulkner's fascinated community – traumatized by historical violence, awaiting a more humane order, and looking anxiously at America – is but a novelistic microcosm of a broader global wish image.

In the service of a postwar cosmopolitanism, the French retooled a cool modernist technique, warmed it up, and asked it to speak a visual esperanto. That this strange episode seems less odd today probably owes something to the resurgence of calls within the academy for a new and improved humanism, as well as the rising prestige of modernist style in critical returns to a humane cosmopolitanism. Shortly before his untimely death, Edward Said, for example, called for a "different kind of humanism" that would be "cosmopolitan and text-and-language bound" (Said 2004: 11). Freed from its Eurocentric and imperialist misappropriation, humanism, so Said hoped, might be restored to its role as a fundamentally "*modernist* theory and practice of reading and interpreting" – a technology of uncertainty and ongoing critique (p. 55). Rather than consolidate or affirm the always known, humanism, as a modernist "technique of trouble," enjoys a constitutive relationship with the new, the alien, and the innovative, and serves as a "means of questioning, upsetting, and reformulating so much of what is presented to us as commodified, packaged, uncontroversial, and uncritically codified certainties" (pp. 77, 28). Drawing both on Said's own discussions of modernism and on Sartre's theories of reading and writing as acts of human recognition, another critic has recently explained the experimental forms of modernist novels as models of democratic community built on nonconsensual reciprocity and the exchange of difference, models that turn reading into a political training ground for cosmopolitan citizenship (Armstrong 2005). Perhaps most suggestive in this regard is Rebecca Walkowitz's new study, *Cosmopolitan Style* (2006), which finds in the hallmarks of modernist narrative a practice of "critical cosmopolitanism" (p. 2). By critical, Walkowitz means, first, a general skepticism about political instrumentality and collective agency that finds stylistic expression in challenges to violent purposiveness, heroic agency, and nationalistic teleologies of history; and second, a welcome "suspicion of epistemological privilege," a kind of self-conscious modernist *thoughtfulness* about thought that understands knowledge claims as always contingent and historically located (p. 2).

What contemporary critics find ethical about modernist form, of course, looks a lot like what Magny, at mid-century, found so promising about the cosmopolitan objectivity of modern American style. Now as then, modernist style becomes good, becomes downright necessary, when it puts a human face on the real inhumanity of globalization and its economic engine, liberal capitalism in *le style américain*. Rather than marking the end of the spell cast upon the American academy by the French theoretical tradition of so-called antihumanist thought, our new modernist humanism testifies to that tradition's most crucial insight – that humanity and its freedoms are structured by global forces, powers, and forms of political instrumentality that operate in excess of human agency or will. If there is a lesson to be drawn from the historical parallel between the postwar "Age of the American Novel" and our own critical moment, it is that we find the more human and cosmopolitan modernism we need in the gap between America's actual action in the world and what we would like it to be. And this critical pathos is especially acute today, when, once again, the American global footprint seems far too large and too certain.

REFERENCES AND FURTHER READING

Armstrong, Paul B. (2005). *Play and the Politics of Reading: The Social Uses of Modernist Form*. Ithaca, NY: Cornell University Press.

Bazin, André. (1945/1967). The ontology of the photographic image. In *What is Cinema?: Vol. 1*, ed. and trans. Hugh Gray (pp. 9–16). Berkeley: University of California Press.

Bazin, André. (1947/1997). The technique of *Citizen Kane*. In *Bazin at Work*, trans. Alain Piette and Bert Cadullo, ed. Bert Cadullo (pp. 231–9). London: Routledge.

Bazin, André. (1948/1971). An aesthetic of reality: Neorealism (Cinematic realism and the Italian school of the liberation). In *What is Cinema?: Vol. 2*, ed and trans. Hugh Gray (pp. 16–40). Berkeley: University of California Press.

Bazin, André. (1952/1971). De Sica: metteur en scène. In *What is Cinema?: Vol. 2*, ed and trans. Hugh Gray (pp. 61–78). Berkeley: University of California Press.

Elsaesser, Thomas. (2005). Two decades in another country: Hollywood and the cinephiles. In *European Cinema: Face to Face with Hollywood* (pp. 233–50). Amsterdam: Amsterdam University Press.

Guilbaut, Serge. (1983). *How New York Stole the Idea of Modern Art: Abstract Expressionism, Freedom,* and the Cold War, trans. Arthur Goldhammer. Chicago: University of Chicago Press.

Hansen, Miriam. (1991). *Babel and Babylon: Spectatorship in American Silent Film*. Cambridge, MA: Harvard University Press.

Jacobs, Karen. (2001). *The Eye's Mind: Literary Modernism and Visual Culture*. Ithaca, NY: Cornell University Press.

Jay, Martin. (1993). *Downcast Eyes: The Denigration of Vision in Twentieth-Century French Thought*. Berkeley: University of California Press.

Kelly, Michael. (1989). Humanism and national unity: the ideological reconstruction of France. In Nicholas Hewitt (ed.), *The Culture of Reconstruction: European Literature, Thought and Film, 1945–50* (pp. 103–19). London: Macmillan.

Kuisel, Richard F. (1993). *Seducing the French: The Dilemma of Americanization*. Berkeley: University of California Press.

Magny, Claude-Edmonde. (1948/1972). *The Age of the American Novel: The Film Aesthetic of Fiction Between the Two Wars*, trans. Eleanor Hochman. New York: Frederick Ungar Publishing Co.

Malraux, André. (1940/1958). Sketch for a psychology of the moving pictures. In Susanne Langer (ed.), *Reflections on Art: A Source Book of*

Writings by Artists, Critics, and Philosophers (pp. 317–27). Baltimore, MD: Johns Hopkins Press.

Malraux, André. (1945). An interview with Malraux. *Horizon* 12: 70, 236–44.

Merleau-Ponty, Maurice. (1945/1964). The film and the new psychology. In *Sense and Non-Sense*, trans. Hubert L. Dreyfus and Patricia Allen Dreyfus (pp. 48–59). Evanston, IL: Northwestern University Press.

Merleau-Ponty, Maurice. (1947/1969). *Humanism and Terror: An Essay on the Communist Problem*, trans. John O'Neill. Boston: Beacon Press.

North, Michael. (2005). *Camera Works: Photography and the Twentieth-Century Word*. Oxford: Oxford University Press.

Robbe-Grillet, Alain. (1958/1989). Nature, humanism, tragedy. In *For a New Novel*, trans. Richard Howard (pp. 49–76). Evanston: Northwestern University Press.

Said, Edward W. (2004). *Humanism and Democratic Criticism*. New York: Columbia University Press.

Sartre, Jean-Paul. (1938/1962). John Dos Passos and *1919*. In *Literary and Philosophical Essays*, trans. Annette Michelson (pp. 94–103). New York: Collier Books.

Sartre, Jean-Paul. (1938/1995). The emotions: Outline of a theory. In *Essays in Existentialism* (pp. 189–254). New York: Citadel Press.

Sartre, Jean-Paul. (1945). American novelists in French eyes. *The Atlantic Monthly* 178: 114–18.

Sartre, Jean-Paul. (1945/1995). The humanism of existentialism. In *Essays in Existentialism* (pp. 31–62). New York: Citadel Press.

Sartre, Jean-Paul. (1947/1965). *What is Literature?*, trans. Bernard Frechtman. New York: Harper & Row.

Schoonover, Karl (forthcoming, 2009). Neorealism at a distance. In Temenuga Trifonova (ed.) *European Film Theory*. New York: Routledge.

Schwartz, Lawrence H. (1988). *Creating Faulkner's Reputation: The Politics of Modern Literary Criticism*. Knoxville: The University of Tennessee Press.

Smith, Thelma M. and Ward L. Miner. (1955). *Transatlantic Migration: The Contemporary American Novel in France*. Durham, NC: Duke University Press.

Trotter, David. (2006). T. S. Eliot and cinema. *Modernism/Modernity* 13, 2: 237–65.

Walkowitz, Rebecca. (2006). *Cosmopolitan Style: Modernism Beyond the Nation*. New York: Columbia University Press.

8

Early Literary Modernism

Andrew Lawson

If the subject matter of the late realist text is typically the testing of character under the pressures of environment and circumstance, then it's perhaps not surprising that the realist novel becomes increasingly preoccupied with its own containing structures of narrative form and point of view. A sustained focus on the fate of character in relation to context runs parallel, in the novels of Henry James, William Dean Howells, Mark Twain, Stephen Crane, Edith Wharton, and Theodore Dreiser, with a self-conscious meditation on the formal constraints and possibilities of narrative. Following Perry Meisel, we might call this heightened sense of structural limits *reflexive realism*, a form that "takes the tale it (re)presents, not as immediate, self-sufficient, and available to mimesis, but as a distinct and analogous function of the conventions of its own narration" (Meisel 1987: 6). This is a self-conscious fiction, one that communicates an awareness of its own partial and constructed grasp of "reality" to its readers. These are novels which won't let us forget that we are reading novels, novels that can't quite be sure about what, in late capitalist society, reading novels might mean.

What gives rise to this reflexive awareness is the antagonistic relation of the literary novel to its debased, commercial form in the mass publishing market. By the 1880s, the reading public had both expanded and become fragmented by mass immigration, as well as regional and class divisions, producing what Henry James described as "our huge Anglo-Saxon array of producers and readers," a cis-Atlantic spectacle of "production uncontrolled, production untouched by criticism, unguided, unlighted, uninstructed, unashamed" (James 1905/1972: 56–7). A host of new magazines – *McClure's*, *Cosmopolitan*, the *Ladies' Home Journal*, *The Saturday Evening Post* – sought to attract readers with sensational stories in easily digestible form: stories that concerned "queer characters, accidents, romantic incidents, snowings-up, threatened starvation, adventures with wild animals" (Howells 1977: 110). At the same time, publishers increasingly rationalized production and attempted to anticipate market trends in search of "bestsellers" to match Lew Wallace's *Ben Hur* (1880), or George du Maurier's *Trilby*

(1894) (Anesko 1986, Borus 1989). If James continually presents his characters and his readers with a choice between those "objects, subjects, [and] contacts" of a "thin" and those of a "rich association," then it is with the mordant sense that the majority have already chosen the "thin" – that the popular effusions of the Harriet Stackpoles of this world have a wider constituency than the polished productions of the Master (James 1966a: 277). The late realist novel is produced under circumstances of considerable "friction with the market" (Anesko 1986).

What happens to the novel in the "age of realism" – what defines its modernity – is a wholesale renegotiation of the contract between author and reader. The author is led to distance himself or herself from readers who now take on the unknowable character of the mass, appearing to the literary artist as consumers, hacks, and voyeurs – diverse, far-flung, polyglot. The novelist develops a new concern with fictional artifice, as if announcing that he or she is no longer prepared to be always at hand as the reader's trusted friend and guide, intervening in the narrative to offer sage judgments, carefully adjudicating moral issues, or preparing the ground for crises and revelations. In the novel of the 1880s and 1890s, the "friendly" author figure is replaced by what Henry James called in the Preface to *The Golden Bowl* the "impersonal" author, an aloof and coolly professional figure, "everywhere felt but nowhere seen" (James 2001: 19). The polite fiction of the author as a reliable mediator between reader and character is dissolved as though by the corrosion of an ancient trust (Hochman 2001: 11–28). The fatal contaminants are the alienating conditions of a market society in which authors can no longer write in the simple faith that they have "readers" in the first place.

Henry James

Early in his career, James showed a determination to break with the traditional realist novel. In a review of George Eliot's *Middlemarch*, James declares that Eliot's work, "vast, swarming, deep-coloured, crowded with episodes," sets a limit to "the development of the old-fashioned English novel" (James 1873/1971: 354, 359). But for James, *Middlemarch* is burdened by too much realistic detail: there is too dense a reconstruction of the social life of a provincial town, and not enough "design and construction" (p. 354). James took Eliot's subject, that of an "ardent young girl" who, in "yearning for a larger moral life than circumstance often affords," ends up "soiling her wings" by marrying a man of "hollow pretentiousness and mouldy egotism" (pp. 354, 358). Eliot's Dorothea Brooke and Edward Casaubon become the Isabel Archer and Gilbert Osmond of James's *The Portrait of a Lady* (1881). But James set himself the task of surpassing the limits of the realist novel set by Eliot. James tells us in the Preface to the New York edition of the novel how he decided he would forgo "comic relief and underplots," and would place "the centre of the subject in the young woman's own consciousness" (James 1966a: xii, xiii). In doing so, James seeks to produce "some direct impression of perception of life," making the reader comprehend Isabel's "individual vision," the "pressure" of her "individual will" (pp. viii, ix). James wants his reader to weigh a specific "amount of felt life," to feel "the impress that constitutes an identity" (pp. viii, x). This reader will have to work hard, therefore, in accompanying Isabel on her journey from innocence to experience, from dazzling light to interior gloom – sharing her moments of both blindness and insight.

What James communicates by adopting Isabel's limited point of view is the sense that she is a stranger to herself, and to the real nature of her desires. He informs us that "the depths of this young lady's nature were a very out-of-the-way place, between which and the surface communication was interrupted by a dozen capricious forces" (James 1966a: 35). This interruption between depth and surface is ironic in that Isabel's "deepest enjoyment was to feel the continuity between the movements of her own soul and the agitations of the world" (p. 35). The irony is that an aesthetic, contemplative nature that seeks to develop itself through self-culture blinds itself to the material realities determining that development, to what Isabel's friend Madame Merle calls the self's "shell," or "envelope," its "cluster of appurtenances" (p. 201). Isabel cannot see that Osmond is not a cultivated man but a shallow dilettante who marries her for her money, and for the fortune she will bring the daughter he has fathered by her confidante. James's achievement is to make the reader share in Isabel's ignorance, and in the suspense of her dawning realization. The nature of what Isabel perceives as the "tie binding these superior spirits" is made all the more obscene for being repressed by the narrator, its horror left unspoken (p. 245).

In the 1890s, James experimented with limited point of view and narrative ellipsis, withholding vital information from the reader. In the short novels, *What Maisie Knew* (1897) and *In the Cage* (1898), we are dependent on focalizing characters with a dramatically attenuated grasp of their situation: a young girl condemned "to see much more than she at first understood" (James 1966b: 21) about her parents' divorce, and a female telegraphist who struggles to piece together the details of an adulterous affair from the messages she receives. James's late novels deal with similarly restricted points of view, presenting characters who struggle to place themselves against endlessly ramifying relations and obscurely menacing circumstances. *The Wings of the Dove* (1902) is the story of a writer in the mass market that also allegorizes the work, and the effects, of writing. Merton Densher writes with "deplorable ease" for a "wretched public," occupying "a mere inky office-table" at a Fleet Street newspaper (James 1965: 45, 59). Kate Croy sees the chance of escaping lower-middle-class banality by attaching Densher to an American heiress, Milly Theale, who falls, first of all, for Kate's "English," "eccentric," "Thackerayan character" (p. 115). Milly's companion, Susan Stringham, "a contributor to the best magazines," sees Milly as "one of her own New England heroines" (pp. 73, 133). At dinner, at the house of Kate's rich Aunt Maud, the guests talk of Densher's knowing Milly as if "he had publicly paragraphed a modest young lady" (p. 219). But Densher eventually contrives a way of eluding the pervasive publicity and puerility of mass-market fictions. Although he figures his affianced relation to Kate as a "subscription," and sees her as "an uncut volume of the highest, the rarest quality," he tires of "reading the romance of his life in a cheap edition" – the effect produced by playing Kate's game (pp. 236, 340, 311). Surrounded by other people's fictions, Densher can preserve his individuality, his "margin" of freedom, only by refusing to read the "sacred script" of Milly's last letter to him, bequeathing him her fortune (p. 444). What he cherishes is her "freshness and delicacy," uncontaminated by publicity: he winces at the thought that the details of the bequest might be "published" (pp. 450, 455). This insistence on aesthetic purity and privacy causes Densher to sever his links with the feminine world of fiction in which he has been enmeshed: a recovery of autonomy and manhood purchased at the cost of celibacy and silence.

In *The Ambassadors* (1903), another writer, Lambert Strether, inwardly contemplates his sense of failure and remorse at 55, and confesses openly to Maria Gostrey his dependence, as editor of "the Review," on the largesse of Mrs Newsome, to whom he is engaged. This largesse, in turn, has its obscure foundation in her late husband's American factories. Strether cannot bring himself to reveal the "article produced" there: as if "unpopular" art is debased by the margin of freedom advanced capital grants it (James 1973: 40–1). In his failing struggle to lead Chad, prodigal heir to the Newsome fortune, back from Paris to his "definite material reward" in Woollett, Massachusetts, Strether writes letters home which he considers "worthy of a showy journalist" in "beating the sense out of words" (pp. 40, 214). But Strether discovers, through Chad, a new, aesthetic approach to the art of living, refreshing his mind's "rather grey interior" with the "cool special green" of the environs of Paris (pp. 126, 343). "Live all you can," he tells Chad's friend, Bilham, "it's a mistake not to" (p. 140). Yet Strether plays for time, for the "postponement" of any "final reckoning" with Woollett, and its literally unspeakable material base (p. 372).

The Ambassadors shows how the aesthetic life, and the writing of novels, remains grotesquely dependent on capital. In James's last novel, *The Golden Bowl* (1904), aesthetic terms reverse into monetary ones. The "appreciation" by Maggie Verver of her fiancé, the Prince, connotes both desire and an assessment of his value as a *morceau de musée* to add to her millionaire father's collection of European art. The novel depicts a world in which sexual and commercial values are inseparable, a world dominated by the exchange of commodities. There is really no difference between the acquisition of valuable objects and of persons; and while people remain silent in this novel, guarding their secrets, objects speak. The cracked bowl the Prince and his lover, Charlotte Stant, consider buying as a wedding gift is purchased by Maggie, and her husband's affair is thereby revealed (Charlotte has, meanwhile, married Maggie's father, adding to the incestuous entanglements of the plot). Maggie keeps her knowledge of the affair from Charlotte, who is thereby placed in the characteristically Jamesian condition of hermeneutic suspense, terrorized by her fragmentary, incomplete grasp of the situation.

Shedding her "American" innocence, Maggie acquires an authorial power over the other characters, watching them from a distance and coolly directing their fates.

Maggie turns the English country house into a panopticon, placing its inhabitants under her surveillance. Jean-Christophe Agnew sees James as identifying with Maggie's authorial power, her ability to script social performances: and with her exercise of "the magic power of the commodity form" (Agnew 1994: 203), which turns Charlotte and the Prince into "human furniture" (James 2001: 574), as she and her father take a last inventory of their possessions. But it's more likely that James shares Charlotte's terror at the imperial sweep of the Verver gaze. It is this terror that lies behind the Jamesian ellipsis: this is a novel that refrains from plumbing its own depths, its economic and sexual abysses (Pearson 1972). Just as we never learn the source of Verver's wealth, we are kept in the dark about the state of the novel's two marriages and the reasons for their failure. All of James's stylistic tricks of abstractness, vagueness, and allusiveness are here placed in the service of one last strategy of postponement (Chatman 1972). A willingness to track down every last mote of consciousness is combined with a withering reticence, as James's narrator hints at, but refuses to confront, the obscure sources of shame.

William Dean Howells

Like James, Howells pitted literary fictions against popular forms. *The Rise of Silas Lapham* (1885) begins with Bartley Hubbard of *The Events* newspaper interviewing the eponymous hero in order to create a "human interest" story for his "Solid Men of Boston" series. The interview places both paint-manufacturer and journalist in a critical frame, allowing us to witness the paint-manufacturer's self-satisfaction, and Hubbard's automatic reliance on the stock phrases of the rags-to-riches story. At the same time, Howells makes us dependent for our first view of Lapham on Hubbard's "sincere reporter's rhetoric" (Howells 1986: 5). When Hubbard writes that Lapham "did not dwell on his boyhood trials," but spoke of them with "an abiding sense of their reality," we are made aware of the difficulty in deciding, in such a densely mediated, doubly ironic context, on what differentiates reality from rhetoric (p. 5). The narrator points out that Lapham receives a check for his story, a commercial interest Hubbard's "sincerity" beguiles him into forgetting. It is out of such chance collisions of interest and sentiment that the story of Lapham's rise and fall is woven. Howells's theme is how difficult it is to be sincere, to be true to one's self, in a society that is both governed by automatic responses and subjected to the chance operations of the marketplace. But the narrator of Lapham's story is extremely reticent on this theme. (Lapham's daughter Penelope, who is reading *Middlemarch*, wishes Eliot would "let you find out a little more about the people for yourself," p. 88.) Rather than undertake direct comment, Howells relies on repetitions of key words and tropes, on the deft manipulation of multiple ironies.

The central event of Lapham's life is his father's accidental discovery of a paint-mine on his Vermont farm, "in a hole made by a tree blowing down" (1986: 7). His life is saved in the Civil War when the bullet he thinks of as meant for him instead kills another man. Lapham's fortune is eroded by speculation in a falling market, and his new home destroyed by a fire he accidentally starts himself. His younger, beautiful daughter, Irene, believes she is being courted by Tom Corey, the scion of a Boston Brahmin family, when she receives a newspaper article about his friend's Texas ranch; but it turns out to have been sent by the friend, not by Corey, who is in fact in love with the elder, and plainer, daughter, Penelope. Howells laboriously underscores this effect of the aleatory by repetitions of a key word: Lapham refers to his sacking of his partner as "a business chance" (p. 47); Penelope complains that people aren't allowed a "chance" to behave reasonably in stories (p. 217); the ruined Lapham admits he has missed his last "chance" (p. 350). Howells has Corey declare, in support of Lapham, that "character . . . must go for something. If it's to be the prey of mere accident and appearance, then it goes for nothing" (p. 293). But when he is asked at the close whether he has any regrets about what he has done, Lapham replies "it don't always seem as if I done it . . . a hole opened for me, and I crept out of it" (p. 365). If the lesson of James's fiction is that we come late to ourselves, then Howells's more "realist" but no less reflexive fiction suggests we are not spared enough by the automatic workings of the social structure to hold on to any sense of a fixed identity (Seelye 1991).

In his most ambitious novel, *A Hazard of New Fortunes* (1890), Howells attempts to map the shifting social space of the modern metropolis, to make sense of its blurred demarcations, distracting details, and unknowable others (Kaplan 1992). This effort at social representation puts considerable pressure on both the shaping, containing function of the narrative, and on the authorial voice. Written in the aftermath of the Haymarket Riot of 1886, which raised for Howells the specter of open class conflict, the novel is plotted around the launch of a New York magazine, *Every Other Week*, by a modern manager, Fulkerson, and an aspiring capitalist, Dryfoos, who together hire an uprooted Bostonian, Basil March, and a German socialist, Lindau, as writers. The novel records the efforts of March to move beyond a conception of literary art as a "sacred refuge" (Howells 1971: 26) resembling the refined sanctuary of his Boston home, a position that prevents him from completing any of the sketches of urban life he makes on his peregrinations around New York in search of an apartment. March and his wife, Isabel, value their rides on the elevated train for the "fleeting intimacy" these afford with tenement-dwellers glimpsed through their windows.

A sense of "the striving and suffering" of the working classes develops beneath March's "whimsical, or alien, or critical" attitudes, but he remains committed to the point of view of the detached, "philosophical observer" (pp. 306, 412). Because of his lack of direct engagement with social realities March can only see "phases of low life" as either "picturesque" or else vaguely threatening. He is unable to go beyond what the narrator calls a "dreamy irony" (p. 65).

Howells vacillates in his handling of the narrative, once class conflict, in the form of a streetcar strike, has disrupted the smooth, containing surface provided by March's aestheticism. The novel entertains a variety of possible resolutions: marriages across class and sectional lines, the deaths of Lindau and Dryfoos's son, Conrad, and March's opportunity to buy the magazine, interspersed with homilies on Christian ethics, and earnest disquisitions on "this economic chance-world in which we live" (p. 436). These uncertain attempts at narrative closure indicate that Howells has lost confidence in the ability of the realist novel to safely encompass and defuse the social tensions it sets out to represent, and in the universalizing, authorial voice (Kaplan 1992). When March declaims against the rule of chance in the economic arrangements of American society, his wife draws attention to his own particular circumstances and motivation: his fear that, as she puts it, "Dr. Dryfoos may give up being an Angel and Mr. Fulkerson may play you false" (p. 438). The voice of the author is exposed as the voice of the contributor, the man of letters as "hireling," nervously shaping his words to suit the demands of editor and owner (p. 353). *A Hazard of New Fortunes*, a novel about a group of men who start a mass-circulation magazine, first appeared in the pages of a mass-circulation magazine, *Harper's Weekly*, a material circumstance that haunts its ambitions to stand as an autonomous literary artifact.

Mark Twain

If James was the highbrow adornment of the publishing house of Harper in the 1890s, then its most lucrative author was Mark Twain. Twain sold more books than either James or Howells, but he was no less subject to the ordeals of authorship. Samuel Clemens first appended his pseudonym "Mark Twain" to the tourist literature of *The Innocents Abroad* (1869) and *Roughing It* (1872), before producing his first novel proper, *The Adventures of Tom Sawyer* (1876), tapping a market demand for boys' fiction and child-rearing advice. Twain's career as a novelist is built on an exploration of the cultural authority of language and a dissection of its registers, opening authorship itself up to critical inspection, through burlesque, parody, and ventriloquism (Lowry 1996).

Twain's reflexive realism works, in *The Adventures of Huckleberry Finn* (1885), by the ventriloquizing of a range of debased popular discourses that have the power to produce a world for those skilled in their vocabulary and susceptible to their ideological persuasion. After a single, parodic appearance in a "notice" to the reader abjuring any moral sense, the "author" disappears, to be succeeded by his delegated representative, an illiterate, 13-year-old "river-rat." (Huck obscurely acquires the ability to write at some point in the story: at the close, he grumbles about what "a trouble" it is to "make" a book [Twain 1985: 369].) Huck listens to the verbal performances he witnesses and reproduces them for us, apparently innocently, usually without direct criticism. Twain makes his points by placing a heavily ironic accent on words with ideological charms. Twain's main target is the romantic Southern discourse of "aristocracy," paternalism, and "chivalry," a discourse that creates a world of gentlemanly plantation owners in white linen suits and nervous, refined women like the dead poetess, Emmeline Grangerford. The chivalrous South is the conscious invention of Southern historians and writers attempting to set the record straight in the post-Civil

War period: bestselling novels such as *Gabriel Conway* by Bret Harte (1875) and *Kate Beaumont* by J. W. De Forest peddled the image of an Old South of feuds and star-crossed lovers, while Joel Chandler Harris's Uncle Remus stories presented stubbornly persistent images of faithful Uncle Toms, and kindly Mammies. The most avid consumers of this kind of literature were middle-class Northerners, who read romantic, nostalgic tales of the fallen South to appease a vague sense of guilt, to thrill at the poetic and melancholy spectacle of a world, in historian Wayne Mixon's words, "so irrevocably and satisfyingly lost" (quoted in Gray 1989: 90). Northern capital sought to preserve a patina of Southern glamour in order to bolster its own claims to cultural legitimacy and distinction. Twain mocks the Southern myth by presenting it through the naive viewpoint of Huck and adding his own ironic commentary. Huck tells us that Col. Grangerford's suit was "so white it hurt your eyes to look at it" (Twain 1985: 164); Twain throws in the casual side: "each person had their own nigger to wait on them" (p. 165).

The major burden of the narrative is Huck's developing friendship with the escaped slave, Jim: a relationship that involves a complex mixture of condescension, affection, pleasure, and dread. Critics have struggled to comprehend Twain's ethical purpose in the novel's ending, when Tom Sawyer needlessly prolongs Jim's imprisonment so that he can enact the prison escapes he has read about in romantic fiction. In these profoundly disturbing chapters, Jim becomes the hapless victim of a white child's schemes and fantasies, with Huck reduced to the role of passive spectator. The uncertain tone might be read as reflecting Twain's own guilt and outrage at the plight of black people in the post-Reconstruction South: denied constitutional rights, exploited as hard labor under both the convict-lease and sharecropping systems, their freedoms legally curtailed by Black Codes (Nilon 1992). Jim's predicament reflects the dilemmas of African-American history: the condition of being "half-slave, half-free" (Schmitz 1971). But the charade of the ending might also be read as reflecting the frustration of the Northern middle class that Twain had effectively joined on moving, as a celebrated author, to Hartford, Connecticut: an impatience at the expense and difficulty of reconstructing the South. These tensions and ambiguities have helped to guarantee the novel its position at the center of the American literary canon and of continuing critical controversy (Arac 1997).

Twain's next novel, *A Connecticut Yankee at King Arthur's Court* (1889) is a palimpsest of overlaid tales and texts, in which authorship is again a problematic business. A nameless narrator describes meeting a "curious stranger" at Warwick Castle, who tells him of the "transmigration of epochs" (Twain 1986: 33). The narrator then reads, and quotes extensively, from Malory's legends of King Arthur. The stranger tells the narrator about his origins in Hartford, Connecticut, his job as superintendent of an arms factory, and a fight with a worker in which he is knocked unconscious and wakes to find himself in the sixth century at Camelot. The stranger hands the narrator a parchment manuscript which the narrator then reproduces for us. Authorship is thus parodied and disavowed through a series of false starts and framing devices. This will become one of the familiar literary devices of modernism: the relativizing of narrative "truth" by revealed artifice, the reader made aware of his or her dependence on a particular voice and perspective. But the framing device and the distancing effect of the parody also suggest an author dealing with material that he cannot take direct responsibility for, material he is anxious about bringing before the public.

The curious stranger, Hank Morgan, is scathing about the "gilded minority" of aristocrats and priests at Camelot who lord it over "the actual Nation" of "small, 'independent' farmers, artisans, & c." (Twain 1986: 125). Morgan uses nineteenth-century knowledge to create factories producing soap, sewing machines, newspapers, melodeons, and barbed wire, as well as a clandestine system of schools or "man-factories" that will "turn groping and grubbing automata into *men*" (p. 159). But Morgan's dream of republican virtue is continually frustrated by the feudal habit of deference to authority. Camelot represents an anarchic production reminiscent of Gilded Age America: Morgan discovers that even the holy water business has its "financial panics" (p. 187). Camelot's backwardness allows Twain to give free rein to his modernizing spirit, his enthusiasm for Yankee inventions, as well as his probing of the complex interfaces between the biological and the technological, between the human body and "machine culture" (Seltzer 1992). Hank recalls a lost love from a "vague dim time," the operator girl from "Hello-Central," whose voice comes over the telephone wire in the "soft summer mornings" (pp. 137, 143). Twain's fascination with phonetic texture, the connection between character and voice, produces a complex nostalgia for a human presence made poignant by its technological mediation. Modernity allows human essence to be both embodied and alienated in the machine: a situation that also relates to the pleasures and anxieties of authorship. Hank starts a newspaper in Camelot purely for the pleasure of seeing his authorial voice appear in print, only to find that his factotum has interposed his own inventions. Hank's original message gets lost in the machinery of publication.

More troubling feelings emerge at the climax of the narrative, when Morgan decides to pitch "hard unsentimental common sense and reason" against "the life of knight-errantry" (p. 355). In the chaos that ensues after Arthur and Lancelot go to war over Guenever, Morgan constructs a fortress of electrified fences and hidden dynamite, and proclaims a republic. Awaiting the knights' assault, he occupies himself in writing, in "turning my old diary into this narrative form" (p. 391). Disenchanted by the population's stubborn allegiance to kings and priests, Morgan reflects on the "folly" of "such human muck" (p. 392). In the final battle, men are turned, not into self-governing republicans, but "homogeneous protoplasm" by the combined effects of his electrical currents, high explosives, and Gatling guns (p. 396). Morgan's lieutenant, Clarence, supplies a postscript telling of his presumed death at the hands of the rival magician, Merlin; a "FINAL P. S. BY M. T." informs us only that Merlin's magic has sent Morgan to sleep until the nineteenth century. The suppression of the mediating author allows Twain to disguise his voice and his feelings: or rather, to admit to powerfully ambivalent, conflicted feelings about modernity and human nature. But it also condemns him to perspectivism, the sense that every take on reality is arbitrary and fictive, both self-conscious and self-canceling.

Stephen Crane

A similarly ironic sense of perspective shadows Stephen Crane's fictional productions. Crane's first novel, *Maggie, A Girl of the Streets* (1893), appealed to a contemporary interest in the plight of the urban poor already signaled in Jacob Riis's pioneering work of sociology *How the Other Half Lives: Studies Among the Tenements of New York* (1890). But the novel also launches an attack on outmoded literary conventions and elaborates a new aesthetic credo of mimetic truth and sensory immediacy. The attack comes in the summary of Maggie's view of her bartender suitor, Pete: "Maggie perceived that here was the beau ideal of a man. Her dim thoughts were often searching for far away lands where, as God says, the little hills sing together in the morning. Under the trees of her dream-gardens there had always walked a lover" (Crane 1979: 19). Maggie appears absorbed in the bestselling genre of domestic or sentimental fiction, epitomized by Maria Susanna Cummins's *The Lamplighter* (1854), which was republished in the early 1890s: the story of an orphan of the slums, Gerty Flint, who endures a series of trials with Christian fortitude, resists the wiles of an upper-class seducer, marries her childhood sweetheart, and ends up established in a substantial, middle-class house. Maggie's emotional absorption in the language of Christian sentiment is all the more ironic in that she is destined for the collar and cuff factory and a career as a prostitute.

What ought to be a thoroughly conventional story of the slums, sanctioned by the example of reformers like Riis, is littered with extraordinarily self-conscious images: Maggie eats "with side glances of fear of interruption . . . like a small pursued tigress" (Crane 1979: 9); Jimmie runs to the hall of the tenement "shrieking like a monk in an earthquake," and later becomes "immured like an African cow" (pp. 9, 15); Maggie encounters a man in evening dress who "wheeled about hastily and turned his stare into the air, like a sailor with a search-light" (p. 52). The last simile jolts because it crosses a vast discursive distance, its "like" signaling unlikeness, as it maps the polarities of aristocratic nonchalance and uniformed labor, the human and the mechanical, the leisurely and the compulsively activated. Crane's stylistic effects are deployed against a reified, mass-market language which has acquired the taint of the mechanical, in a compulsive defiance of cliché.

In *The Red Badge of Courage* (1895), Crane tests the abstractions of cliché and convention against the experience of a novice Civil War soldier, Henry Fleming, adopting his point of view as the basis for his narrative. Henry has "dreamed of battles all his life," and has read of "Greeklike struggles" (Crane 1998: 5). On this basis, he prepares "certain sentences" that he imagines will contribute to a "beautiful scene" of farewell with his mother (p. 6). But rather than talk, like a Spartan woman, of Henry "returning with his shield or on it," his mother sits "doggedly peeling potatoes" and tells him to be sure to send his socks home when they need darning (p. 6). A yawning gap opens between preformed "sentence" and recalcitrant experience (Bell 1993: 145).

Henry often thinks more like a writer than a soldier: reminding us that *The Red Badge of Courage* is an exercise in style, the work of a man who had never seen battle (and who, following a recurrent pattern, only did so after writing about it). Henry notices that the soles of a dead soldier's shoes have been "worn to the thinness of writing paper," and the image recurs at Henry's moment of triumph, when, joining the battle, he realizes that he has mastered his fear and that obstacles have "fallen like paper peaks" (Crane 1998: 22, 86). He is now "what he called a hero," even though he has not been "aware of the process. He had slept and, awakening, found himself a knight" (p. 86). Henry wakes to find himself honored and famous, the fulfillment of every writer's dream.

Henry's attainment of heroism at the end of the novel has perplexed critics, unable to agree on whether Crane is sympathetic to Henry's moral growth or shows him to be self-deluded by deploying his habitual irony (Solomon 1967, Brooke-Rose 1986). The novel certainly appeals to the 1890s cult of heroic masculinity which, linked to imperial conquest and a sense of racial superiority, was epitomized by Theodore Roosevelt's celebrated charge up San Juan Hill in the Spanish–American War (Kaplan 1990). Crane's text echoes this imperial hubris when Henry imagines "peoples" secure "in the shadow of his eagle-eyed prowess" (1998: 5). On the other hand, Crane's narrative has relentlessly skewered the mythology of war, showing war to be a chaotic affair run by largely incompetent generals, one of whom surveys the battle with "the appearance of a businessman whose market is swinging up and down" (p. 39). Written in the aftermath of the 1892 Panic, in which industrial production was disturbed by yet another cycle of boom and bust, Crane's novel draws ironic parallels between militarism and corporate capitalism. Small wonder, given these inconsistencies, that critics have tended to praise Crane's impressionistic style while deploring the novel's lack of a coherent argument or theme (Berthoff 1981).

These problems of interpretation are exacerbated by the fact that Crane's original manuscript was extensively revised by him in response to suggestions by his editors at D. Appleton & Company. The overall effect of the revisions and excisions was to tone down the narrative's satire of Henry's vainglorious posturing, and to add a final sentence that does not appear in any Crane manuscript: "Over the river a golden ray of sun came through the hosts of leaden rain clouds" (Crane 1998: 117). The problem of deciding whether this is to be read as a parody of "feelgood" endings to historical romances, or an earnestly intended symbol of hope is thus compounded and complicated by the disputed character of the text itself (Parker 1986). *The Red Badge of Courage* became one of the bestsellers of the 1890s, achieving average sales of nearly 10,000 copies a year. But Crane was unable to profit from the book's success because he signed a standard contract agreeing to an annual royalty of 10 percent, with no provision for foreign rights, and no payments until

Appleton's costs had been met. Crane's literary labors were poorly rewarded by a mass market in which writing featured as just another commodity (Borus 1989: 41–3).

Edith Wharton

The career of a professional writer in the mass market provided Edith Wharton with an ambiguous means of escaping the role of decorative leisure-class female that, as a member of New York's elite Knickerbocker society, she was born into. Against both a genteel-amateur ethos, in which writing featured as *belles lettres*, and a sentimental-domestic tradition in which women's writing evangelized for the virtues of the domestic sphere, Wharton embraced the role of realist author with specialized, expert knowledge of society, as well as a literary craft that could realize sales. Alone among the authors considered in this chapter, Wharton's commitment to remunerative employment as a novelist could figure as downward mobility: something considered, within her class, as lying "between a black art and a form of manual labor" (Wharton 1993b: 47). But even as Wharton embraces authorship as a form of self-making, her novels reveal a set of fears and anxieties about the personal costs of marketplace exposure, and the ethics of trading personal intimacies in the form of public narratives.

Lily Bart, the heroine of Wharton's bestselling novel, *The House of Mirth* (1905), first appears as seen through the eyes of Lawrence Selden in the afternoon rush at Grand Central Station. Point of view plays a vital role as both a formal feature and a thematic concern of Wharton's narrative. Lily has a "faculty for adapting herself, for entering into other people's feelings" (Wharton 1990: 44). With her talent for immersion in experience, for subjection to impulse, affect, and the gaze of the other, she is a figure for the author as purveyor of sensational, mass-market fictions. Selden, by contrast, preserves "a certain social detachment, a happy air of viewing the show objectively" – the author as professional writer and realist (p. 45). While Selden is able to take refuge outside the "great gilt cage" of society, in which the elite display themselves "for the mob to gape at" (p. 45), Lily is abjectly dependent on the effects she is able to contrive for her audience both inside and outside its confines. Some of the strangest and most subtle effects of the narrative are produced when Lily finds herself "scanning her little world" through Selden's "retina," as though Wharton the popular author is subjecting herself to the interrogation of a better self, an ideal artistic ego (p. 45). Selden's presence has the effect of "cheapening" Lily's aspirations, of "throwing her whole world out of focus" and replacing the "pink lamps" of artifice and performance with the "dusty daylight" of realism (pp. 70, 45).

Spectatorship features in the narrative as both connoisseurship, the trained and discriminating exercise of individual vision, and consumption, the debased and sensationalized habits of the mass audience. Lily first appears before Selden as the epitome of the upper-class lady. "Highly specialized" in her beauty, she dwells in a region "apart from the crowd," so glowing she seems covered by a "fine glaze" (pp. 5, 6, 7). At the same time, Selden has the "confused sense that she must have cost a great deal to make, that a great many dull and ugly people must, in some mysterious way, have been sacrificed to produce her" (p. 7). Lily is both work of art and mass-produced commodity, the result of an obscure, social process of production. These ambiguities cling to her as she attempts to convert her conspicuousness into a society marriage while retaining her romantic ideals: a conflict of motives which results in a relentless downward mobility.

The plot of *The House of Mirth* centers on some love letters written to Selden by the imperious Bertha Dorset, who banishes Lily from society for the imputed crime of seducing her husband. The letters are retrieved from Selden's wastepaper bin by his charwoman, Mrs Haffen, and purchased from her by Lily. Lily is urged by Rosedale to sell them back to Bertha Dorset as the price of her readmission, and to marry him. But she is repelled by the exposure this would involve, the subjection of intimacy to the logic of the market, and so burns them. In doing so, Lily condemns herself to the humiliating experience of manual labor as a milliner, "seeing the fragmentary and distorted image of the world she had lived in reflected in the mirror of the working-girls' minds" (Wharton 1990: 223). Wharton constructs a plot in which she is able vicariously to experience both sides of the "social tapestry" (p. 215): inside, with Selden and the artist's vision; outside, with Lily and the prying, licentious eyes of the public.

Newland Archer, the ambiguous hero of *The Age of Innocence* (1920) also struggles with the problem of intimacy versus publicity. Asked by his legal employer to "run [his] eye" over "certain papers" relating to the divorce of Countess Ellen Olenska, Archer is plunged into "an atmosphere" in which he "choked and spluttered" (Wharton 1993a: 67). He accepts responsibility for keeping the Countess's "secrets" from being "bared to other eyes" (p. 67) – including those of the reader – and persuades her not to seek a divorce. But in doing so Archer condemns his own secret passion for the Countess to perpetual frustration.

Critics have differed on the question of whether *The Age of Innocence* presents a critical portrait (Ammons 1980: 143–52) or a nostalgic one (Wolff 1977: 341) of the Old New York of the upper-middle class, a question that attention to point of view in the text may resolve. The novel is constructed around the tensions and inconsistencies of Archer's perspective: he is at once keenly satirical of the "hieroglyphic world" of New York society in the 1870s, and deeply complicit with its codes for the supervision and control of women (Wharton 1993a: 32). Wharton's fictional achievement is to manipulate our view of Archer and his predicament so that we see him, and the world he inhabits, both critically and sympathetically. We are given first of all, a detached "objective" vision of leisure-class codes and rituals, down to the finest details of manners, costume, cuisine, and decor – in tacit acknowledgment that we, like Ellen Olenska, are outsiders, looking at this world through the wrong end of a telescope (p. 55). So the narrator decodes for us Mrs Archer's remark that the rum punch served at the newly married Archers' first formal dinner made all the difference: "not in itself but by its manifold implications – since it signified either canvas-backs or terrapin, two soups, a hot and a cold sweet, full *décolletage* with short sleeves, and guests of a proportionate importance" (p. 230). This is a kind of hyper-realism, in which realistic details are given to excess, a technique that adumbrates the confined, fetishistic contours of Archer's world. The narrator summarizes Archer's dilemma, his entrapment in the "inexorable conventions," then enters into Archer's point of view, adopting his language – "he was not quite such an ass as Larry Lef-ferts" (p. 31). The subtle modulations of the free indirect style allow Wharton to shift from a detached perspective to a sympathetic one: a movement that mimes Archer's ambivalent posture, his pattern of muted rebellion against society and reab-sorption into it.

Archer is the hyperrealist as fetishist: lacking Ellen's bodily presence, his mind becomes "wholly absorbed" in "delicious details" or tokens of it (1993a: 218). In her apartment, he stoops to kiss her foot; seated next to her in a brougham he unbuttons her "tight brown glove" to kiss her palm (p. 201); finally, in search of her, he kisses the handle of a silk parasol that turns out not to be hers. (Archer's favorite episode in the melodrama *The Shaughraun*, is a "sad, almost monosyllabic, scene of parting," in which the "wooer" pauses "on the threshold," and "steals back" to secretly kiss the "narrow black velvet ribbon" on the woman's dress [p. 80].) "Reality" for Archer comes to mean the secret raptures of an aestheticized passion. He tells Ellen that she gave him "my first glimpse of a real life," but, at the Metropolitan Museum, turns her into an artwork, a "pure harmony of line and colour" that should never have to suffer "the stupid laws of change" (p. 218). Ellen warns him not to look at "visions" but at "realities," meaning that she will have to be his mistress, since she cannot be his wife (p. 204). The novel struggles with the question of what is more "real": the inner life of the emotions or the responsibilities of social existence. While it experi-ments with the possibilities of an expanded consciousness and the depiction of extreme, hazardous emotional states, the novel decides that it is finally society that must be given its due, and that what Archer terms "the most exquisite pleasures" are to be derived from renunciation (p. 170). "The only way I can love you is by giving you up," Ellen tells Archer. In late middle age, after the death of his wife, Archer seems to have accepted this logic. In the novel's final chapter, he refuses the chance of seeing Ellen once more in her Paris apartment, telling his son that it's "more real" to him to remain outside (p. 254).

Wharton's short novel *Ethan Frome* (1911) has long held a canonical place as the most artistically perfect and formally accomplished of her fictions. But the novel also foreshadows *The Age of Innocence* in its exploration of repressed and unlawful passion: with the difference that the characters are drawn from the rural poor of New England rather than the leisure class of Old New York. Many of the features of the later novel are present: the "poignant" contrast between "inner needs" and "outer situation" (Wharton 1987: 17), and the unreality of a life beset by mocking, ritual repetitions – this time, the "consecrated formulas" of Zeena Frome's sickness and the crushing routines of farm and domestic labor (p. 107). Ethan Frome is awakened into a new sense of reality by his love for his wife's cousin, Mattie Silver, and, like Archer, driven to locate his desire in sacramental objects and clandestine signs: the "strip of stuff" Mattie sews serves the same erotic function as Archer's ribbons, shoes, gloves, and parasols. Anxieties about authorship run through the narrative as well. The narrator, a professional man on an engineering job in the district of Starksfield, Massachusetts, hears of Ethan's story "bit by bit, from various people," first of all from the stage driver, Harmon Gow, then from his landlady, Mrs Ned Hale, before finally meeting with Ethan himself (p. 3). He then constructs a "vision" of the story, in a retrospective third-person narrative that adopts Ethan's point of view (p. 25). The narrator tells us that "the deeper meaning" of the story is "in the gaps" between the facts reported to him (p. 7). But this deeper meaning is literally unspeakable, the vision of a living hell in which desire is doomed to be eternally frustrated by social convention, of individuals pressed into a proximity that only mimics real intimacy. It's perhaps unsurprising that Wharton had to tell this story in the guise of a New England tale, with its requisite dialect, local color, and spectral hauntings, before she could relate it closer to home.

Theodore Dreiser

Theodore Dreiser's *Sister Carrie* (1900) reproduces the standard sentimental plot in which a young girl journeys from the rural hinterland to the sinful city. But Dreiser inverts and distorts this convention: here, the maiden's seduction results in her fortunes rising rather than falling. The novel is dominated by commercial imperatives, which mix uneasily with affective, or sentimental ones. Carrie Meeber loses her virginity to a traveling salesman, Drouet, in order to gain food, clothing, and shelter; runs off with a saloon manager, Hurstwood; deserts him when he falls on hard times, and finally succeeds as a showgirl on the Broadway stage. Dreiser quantifies Carrie's success for us in stark, monetary terms. Arriving with "four dollars in money" (Dreiser 1991: 1) she ends with a weekly salary of 150 dollars, "paid to her in greenbacks — three twenties, six tens, and six fives" (p. 334). Critics have been unable to agree on how we should interpret the copresence of "sentimental" and "realistic" perspectives in the novel, although what Kaplan calls its "discordant narrative registers" have been the focus of much attention (Kaplan 1992: 140).

These discords are apparent from the first pages, which are crowded with precise, documentary details. It is, we are told, "August, 1889"; Carrie sports a "cheap imitation alligator-skin satchel" as part of her "total outfit" (Dreiser 1991: 1); Drouet belongs to the "class" of "drummers," but is also a "masher," a "still newer term, which had sprung into general use among Americans in 1880, and which concisely expressed the thought of one whose dress or manners are calculated to elicit the admiration of susceptible young women" (p. 3). This kind of "documentary" notation has made the novel an invaluable resource for social historians, or anyone interested in what urban life was like in the 1890s: *Sister Carrie* provides abundant information on shoe factories, the new department stores, Chicago mansions, the Broadway theatre, streetcar strikes, even the menus of cheap eating-houses. But another kind of narrative discourse jostles for our attention alongside the realistic description. Carrie produces "a gush of tears at her mother's farewell kiss" (p. 1). The narrator tells us: "When a girl leaves her home at eighteen" she either "falls into saving hands" or "assumes the cosmopolitan standard of virtue," and describes Carrie as "a half-equipped little knight" (pp. 1, 2). The glib, the moralizing, the conventional, intrude into what is otherwise colloquial, unvarnished, rigorously up-to-date.

This discrepancy becomes progressively more noticeable as the narrative advances. When he comes to consider Carrie's "mental state" and her relation to a modern standard of morality, the narrator asks us to: "Answer, first, why the heart thrills; explain wherefore some plaintive note goes wandering about the world, undying; make clear the rose's subtle alchemy evolving its ruddy lamp in light and rain. In the essence of these facts lie the first principles of morals" (p. 68). This highfalutin language, with its straining for poetic effect, jars against other, more material "facts" given to us by the narrator, such as the details of Carrie's labor in the shoe factory "punching eye-holes" in leather uppers (p. 27), or the menu she scans offering "Half broiled spring chicken – seventy-five [cents]" (p. 44).

Sprawling and cumbersome in its construction and narrative development, *Sister Carrie* nevertheless represents, in its linguistic self-consciousness, a high point in the development of reflexive realism. Dreiser parodies a series of debased languages – those of sentimental fiction, melodrama, and popular song – in order to show how they mystify the conditions of life in an advanced, capitalist society. These languages are all Carrie has at her disposal. While they allow her to dream of a better life imagined as the possession of consumer trinkets and fulfilled desires, sexual and monetary, they cannot account for waged labor, exploitation, or the violent repression of strikes. The commodified language of sentiment points to a loss of affect in human relationships: Dreiser's characters drift and dream, they respond to the call of the commodity, the sensory intensity of the shop-window, but they rarely *feel*. As a former editor of a promotional magazine for a music-publishing magazine, *Ev'ry Month*, Dreiser had first-hand experience of this language. (His brother, Paul Dresser, was a successful writer of popular songs.) The bitterness of Dreiser's parody comes through most starkly in his chapter titles: "When Waters Engulf Us We Reach for A Star" is comically irrelevant to Hurstwood's desperate theft of 10,000 dollars.

As Amy Kaplan has noted, late realist novels have trouble ending, typically resorting to nostalgia, empty rhetoric, or a puzzling ambiguity (Kaplan 1992). *The Ambassadors* ends with Strether's exclamation "Then there we are!" – but where we are, exactly, remains far from clear (James 1973: 393). Tom Sawyer's protracted escapades constitute one of the most painful and puzzling endings in American fiction, while Huck's "I reckon I got to light out for the Territory" has charmed and perplexed readers as both a bid for freedom and a cry of desperation (Twain 1985: 369). Henry Fleming's new "store of assurance" in his manhood seems as arbitrary and tacked-on as the "golden ray of sun" that appears through "the hosts of leaden rain clouds" (Crane 1998: 117). *Sister Carrie* has, in effect, two endings. In the first, Hurstwood commits suicide in a Bowery flophouse, the narration all grim fact. In the second, Carrie sits by her Waldorf Hotel window in her rocking-chair, yawning over Balzac's *Père Goriot*, and reviewing her success, "her gowns and carriage, her furniture and bank account" (Dreiser 1991: 367–8). She has achieved "applause," "publicity," and "beauty," but these things have become "trivial and indifferent" to her (p. 368). In the "tinsel and shine of her state" she is nevertheless "unhappy" (p. 368). Readers have been perturbed by Dreiser's descent into "bad" writing at the close of the novel: "Oh, Carrie, Carrie! Oh, blind strivings of the human heart! Onward, onward, it saith, and where beauty leads, there it follows. Whether it be the tinkle of a lone sheep bell o'er some quiet landscape, or the glimmer of beauty in sylvan places . . ." (p. 369). Dreiser is parodying the incongruous, pastoral language in which Carrie attempts to make sense of her urban situation: these are Carrie's inchoate thoughts, dreams, and desires, mediated through the conventions of sentimental literature. The sentimental mother is absent, and so are tears: all that remains of this residual structure of feeling are some worn-out platitudes, and a rocking-chair. At the same time, Carrie represents a set of authorial anxieties. The narrator identifies her with "the poets and dreamers," those who "respond to every breath of fancy," "responding with desire to everything most lovely in life," and in doing so, marks Dreiser's identification with his creation (p. 368). Carrie resembles the author who, rather than following the path of "honest labor" takes "the despised path" that leads to dreams "quickly," seeking a quick market-entry and audience approval, rather than following a lengthy period of literary apprenticeship and polishing his craft. "Your happiness is within yourself wholly if you will only believe it," Ames tells Carrie in a passage Dreiser deleted from the published text, "The huzzas of the public don't mean anything" (Dreiser 1991: 383). The problem is that Carrie, like Dreiser, cannot quite believe it.

The late realist novel marks a kind of half-way house in the evolution of the novel towards modernism: unable to proclaim the modernist aesthetic of autonomy outright, it is forced into a series of canny and conflicted engagements with the mass market. The friction generated from these engagements produces a newly reflexive sense of the parameters of the novel form: a declension of omniscience, a blurring or obscuring of the authorial bond with the reader, a deepening of subjectivity, a heightened sense of the constraints and possibilities of point of view. The human subjects whose eyes we learn to look through are typically perplexed, self-divided, unsure of their ground. Vistas open up, only to be abruptly closed down; the experience of looking turns into the experience of being looked at; the bursting of constraints is matched by a confrontation with confining structures. Live all you can, within the extended networks of late capitalism, these novels seem to say to us: even though this form of life may not, finally, be enough.

References and Further Reading

Agnew, Jean-Christophe. (1994). The consuming vision. In Ruth Bernard Yeazell (ed.), *Henry James: A Collection of Critical Essays* (pp. 190–206). Englewood Cliff, NJ: Prentice-Hall.

Ammons, Elizabeth. (1980). *Edith Wharton's Argument With America*. Athens: University of Georgia Press.

Anesko, Michael. (1986). *"Friction With the Market": Henry James and the Profession of Authorship*. New York: Oxford University Press.

Arac, Jonathan. (1997). *"Huckleberry Finn" as Idol and Target: The Functions of Criticism in Our Time*. Madison: University of Wisconsin Press.

Bell, Michael Davitt. (1993). *The Problem of American Realism: Studies in the Cultural History of an Idea*. Chicago: University of Chicago Press.

Bentley, Nancy. (1995). "Hunting for the real": Wharton and the science of manners. In Millicent Bell (ed.), *The Cambridge Companion to Edith Wharton* (pp. 47–67). Cambridge, UK: Cambridge University Press.

Berthoff, Walter. (1981). *The Ferment of Realism: American Literature 1884–1919*. Cambridge, UK: Cambridge University Press.

Borus, Daniel H. (1989). *Writing Realism: Howells, James, and Norris in the Mass Market*. Chapel Hill: North Carolina University Press.

Brooke-Rose, Christine. (1986). Ill logics of irony. In Lee Clark Mitchell (ed.), *New Essays on "The Red Badge of Courage"* (pp. 129–46). Cambridge, UK: Cambridge University Press.

Chatman, Seymour. (1972). *The Later Style of Henry James*. Oxford: Basil Blackwell.

Crane, Stephen. (1979). *Maggie, A Girl of the Streets*, ed. Thomas A. Gullason. New York: W.W. Norton & Co.

Crane, Stephen. (1998). *The Red Badge of Courage and Other Stories*, ed. Anthony Mellors and Fiona Robertson. Oxford: Oxford University Press.

Dreiser, Theodore. (1991). *Sister Carrie*, ed. Donald Pizer. New York: W. W. Norton.

Gray, Richard. (1989). *Writing the South: Ideas of an American Region*. Cambridge, UK: Cambridge University Press.

Hochman, Barbara. (2001). *Getting at the Author: Reimagining Books and Reading in the Age of American Realism*. Amherst: University of Massachusetts Press.

Howells, William Dean. (1971). *A Hazard of New Fortunes. A Selected Edition of William Dean Howells, Vol. 16*, ed. David J. Nordloh et al. Bloomington: Indiana University Press.

Howells, William Dean. (1977). *A Modern Instance. A Selected Edition of William Dean Howells, Vol. 10*, ed. David J. Nordloh and David Kleinman. Bloomington: Indiana University Press.

Howells, William Dean. (1986). *The Rise of Silas Lapham*. Harmondsworth, UK: Penguin Books.

James, Henry. (1873/1971). Review of George Eliot, *Middlemarch*. In David Carroll (ed.), *George Eliot: The Critical Heritage* (pp. 353–59). London: Routledge & Kegan Paul.

James, Henry. (1905/1972). The lesson of Balzac. In *The Question of Our Speech. The Lesson of Balzac: Two Lectures* (pp. 55–116). New York: Haskell House Publishers.

James, Henry. (1965). *The Wings of the Dove*. Harmondsworth, UK: Penguin Books.

James, Henry. (1966a). *The Portrait of a Lady*. Harmondsworth, UK: Penguin Books.

James, Henry. (1966b). *What Maisie Knew*. Harmondsworth, UK: Penguin Books.

James, Henry. (1973). *The Ambassadors*. Harmondsworth, UK: Penguin Books.

James, Henry. (2001). *The Golden Bowl*. Harmondsworth, UK: Penguin Books.

Kaplan, Amy. (1990). Romancing the empire: The embodiment of American masculinity in the popular historical novel of the 1890s. *American Literary History* 2, 4: 659–90.

Kaplan, Amy. (1992). *The Social Construction of American Realism*. Chicago: University of Chicago Press.

Knights, Pamela. (1995). The social subject of *The Age of Innocence*. In Millicent Bell (ed.), *The Cambridge Companion to Edith Wharton* (pp. 20–46). Cambridge, UK: Cambridge University Press.

Lowry, Richard S. (1996). *"Littery Man": Mark Twain and Modern Authorship*. New York: Oxford University Press.

Meisel, Perry. (1987). *The Myth of the Modern: A Study in British Literature and Criticism After 1850*. New Haven, CT: Yale University Press.

Nilon, Charles H. (1992). The ending of *Huckleberry Finn*: "freeing the free Negro." In James S. Leonard, Thomas A. Tenney and Thadious M. Davis (eds), *Satire or Evasion? Black Perspectives on Huckleberry Finn* (pp. 62–76). Durham, NC: Duke University Press.

Parker, Hershel. (1986). Getting used to the "original form" of *The Red Badge of Courage*. In Lee Clark Mitchell (ed.), *New Essays on "The Red Badge of Courage"* (pp. 25–47). Cambridge, UK: Cambridge University Press.

Pearson, Gabriel. (1972). The novel to end all novels. In John Goode (ed.), *The Air of Reality: New Essays on Henry James* (pp. 301–62). London: Methuen & Co.

Petry, Sandy. (1977). The language of realism, the language of false consciousness: A reading of *Sister Carrie*. *Novel* 10, 2: 101–13.

Schmitz, Neil. (1971). Twain, *Huckleberry Finn*, and Reconstruction. *American Studies* 12: 59–67.

Seelye, John. (1991). The hole in Howells/the lapse in Silas Lapham. In Donald E. Pease (ed.), *New Essays on "The Rise of Silas Lapham"* (pp. 47–65). Cambridge, UK: Cambridge University Press.

Seltzer, Mark. (1992). *Bodies and Machines*. New York: Routledge.

Solomon, Eric. (1967). *Stephen Crane: From Parody to Realism*. Cambridge, MA: Harvard University Press.

Twain, Mark. (1985). *The Adventures of Huckleberry Finn*. Harmondsworth, UK: Penguin Books.

Twain, Mark. (1986). *A Connecticut Yankee at King Arthur's Court*. Harmondsworth, UK: Penguin Books.

Wharton, Edith. (1987). *Ethan Frome*. Harmondsworth, UK: Penguin Books.

Wharton, Edith. (1990). *The House of Mirth*, ed. Elizabeth Ammons. New York: W. W. Norton.

Wharton, Edith. (1993a). *The Age of Innocence*. London: J. M. Dent.

Wharton, Edith. (1993b). *A Backward Glance: An Autobiography*. London: J. M. Dent.

Wolff, Cynthia Griffin. (1977). *A Feast of Words: The Triumph of Edith Wharton*. New York: Oxford University Press.

9
Naturalism: Turn-of-the-Century Modernism

Donna Campbell

Writing in *The Wave*, a weekly travel and culture magazine, in June 1896, the young San Francisco writer Frank Norris sought to explain a new form of literature – naturalism – to a well-to-do audience accustomed to lighter fare. "The naturalist takes no note of common people, common in so far as their interests, their lives, and the things that occur in them are common, are ordinary," he writes in "Zola as a Romantic Writer." "Terrible things must happen to the characters of the naturalistic tale. They must be twisted from the ordinary, wrenched out from the quiet, uneventful round of every-day life, and flung into the throes of a vast and terrible drama that works itself out in unleashed passions, in blood, and in sudden death" (Norris 1986e: 1107). "Zola as a Romantic Writer" was not the first of Norris's forays into the subject; he had earlier that month reviewed Zola's novel *Rome*, and the second in his series of generally light courtship sketches called "Man Proposes" portrayed the Zolaesque romance of a coal-heaver and a washerwoman. Accustomed to Norris's usual writing for the magazine, which often ran to accounts of polo matches, interviews with actresses, and light, facetious short stories, readers of *The Wave* may have been less receptive to his earnest exposition of the principles of naturalism and the "vast and terrible drama" it portrayed.[1] Yet the fact that Norris could even write about such a subject for an audience of socialites says something about the place that naturalism occupied at the turn of the century. By announcing in *The Wave* that the literature of Zola and his followers would focus not on ordinary middle-class life, the subject of late nineteenth-century realism, but on the "terrible things" and lives "twisted from the ordinary" that were the subject of naturalism, Norris served notice that this literature was worthy of attention even by the complacent upper-middle class. *The Wave*'s subscribers may not have been adherents of naturalism, and they may not have looked forward to reading sordid descriptions of the lives of the poor, but they were alert to what was fashionably modern, and, in promoting naturalism, Norris strategically positioned naturalism as the literature of the modern age.

Pessimistic in outlook and realistic in observational technique, the naturalism that Norris introduced to his readers portrayed life as reduced to its fundamental elements, the better to understand the underlying motives and physical laws governing human behavior. Following Zola's "The Experimental Novel," which in turn derived its method from Claude Bernard's *Introduction to the Study of Experimental Medicine*, naturalism in its narrowest sense adopted science as its model and empiricism as its method. But American naturalism encompassed a broader range of writing than that suggested by Zola's precepts. Although Norris proclaimed himself a disciple of Zola, other naturalistic writers such as Jack London and Theodore Dreiser credited the evolutionary theories of Darwin and Herbert Spencer with their interest in the biological basis for human behavior, whereas Stephen Crane drew on his own experiences in the Tenderloin district of New York for the depictions of the naturalistic urban jungle. In their attempts to bend the methods of science to fiction, however, these writers shared common cause with Zola, for all were determined to represent the truth about life. Works of naturalism pictured a deterministic universe in which life at the margins of society was reduced to the basic imperatives of food, clothing, and shelter; within this environment, human beings displayed the full panoply of primitive drives and emotions, among them sexual desire, greed, jealousy, and rage. In so doing, naturalism mirrored and unmasked the era's anxieties about the effects of urban life and industrialization, among them the threatened dissolution of the self and the sense of anomie inflicted by the modern city; the precarious physical and social position of those at the bottom of the social scale; the brutish, sometimes violent behavior of people in the grip of elemental emotions; the mingling of blood and ethnic "races" as defined by the philosophically inconsistent yet tendentiously held scientific theories of the day; and the fragility of a sense of personal autonomy, free will, and agency in a world seemingly governed by the forces of heredity and environment. As Frank Norris wrote in one of his last essays, "The Responsibilities of the Novelist," "the novel is the great expression of modern life" (Norris 1986c: 1206), and, as a medium of modernity, "an instrument, a tool, a weapon, a vehicle" (p. 1208), it bore the responsibility for transmitting the truth to his own and future ages. Announcing that the "People have a right to the truth as they have a right to life, liberty, and the pursuit of happiness" (p. 1210), Norris transforms the novel into a kind of public utility for dispensing truth and the novelist as the trustee of this venture. In linking modernity with its expression in the form of the novel, and the novelist's responsibility to tell the truth with the interests of the nation, Norris forges naturalism into a technology for representing modernity.

Naturalism is "turn-of-the-century modernism" in its response to the crisis of modernity, since as Tim Armstrong suggests, the definition of modernism is that it is a "cultural expression of modernity" (Armstrong 2005: 4). It does not, however, resemble the classic modernism of the 1920s as exemplified by James Joyce, T. S. Eliot, Ezra Pound, Gertrude Stein, and Ernest Hemingway, and indeed, naturalism's approach was diametrically opposed to that of classic modernism. First of all, whereas modernists of the 1920s focused on rendering subjective states of consciousness, the naturalists struggled to render objectively the states of being that they observed and tried to do so with scientific objectivity; the works of Theodore Dreiser, Frank Norris, and Jack London are filled with terms borrowed from science. It is this focus on external reality rather than internal states of being that Virginia Woolf critiques in the well-known essay "Mr. Bennett and Mrs. Brown." Famously observing that "on or about December 1910, human character changed" (Woolf 1928/1970: 3), she goes on to castigate the British realist novelist Arnold Bennett and his fellow Edwardians, like John Galsworthy, for their focus on the external appearance and financial condition of her fictional Mrs Brown rather than the rich interior life of emotion that she represents. Woolf's exasperation with the Edwardians' fascination with physical and financial details – "hot-water bottles" and "freehold villas and copyhold estates" (p. 23) in Woolf's terms – echoes the modernists' impatience with realist observation as a methodology. Moreover, the naturalists' insistence on accumulating incidents and details as a key to understanding life was anathema to Woolf and the other modernists. For the modernists, representing the cultural certainties shattered by World War I required an equal fragmentation and dislocation of narrative method, and attempting to represent the totality of an experience, as the naturalists did, was seen as at best naive and at worst presumptuous or dishonest. Naturalism, and its later counterpart the social problem novel of the Progressive Era, were exhibits A and B of the kind of fiction that modernists were determined not to write. The modernists' interests lay in the aesthetic rather than the pragmatic dimensions of life, the stylistically sophisticated rather than the earnestly realistic mode in matters of style, the individual rather than the type in matters of character, and the interior and psychological rather than the externally described and biological basis for human behavior. In short, although both movements respond to a crisis of modernity, classic modernism inverts the principles of classic naturalism.

To understand naturalism as an expression of turn-of-the-century modernity, as Norris did, requires an understanding of the multiple and conflicting visions of the movement both by its practitioners and its critics. Naturalism in the United States had no school, no group of artists formally committed to its principles as was the case with the Pre-Raphaelite Brotherhood or the American transcendentalists of the 1840s and 1850s. Even the term "naturalism" was in dispute, with some critics labeling as realism any fiction not directly identifiable as romantic, from the genteel fiction of W. D. Howells to the sensational and sordid dramas of Zola, whereas others, like Zola himself, called all such works "naturalistic" that aligned themselves along "the positivistic orientation of philosophical naturalism" (Link 2004: 15). Nor did twentieth-century critics have a sharper or more consistent definition of the movement. As Charles Child Walcutt commented in 1956, "Shocking, bestial, scientific, messianic – no sooner does [naturalism's] outline seem to grow clear than, like Proteus, it slips through the fingers and reappears in another shape" (Walcutt 1973: 3). Generally speaking, naturalism meant turn-of-the-century literature that dealt with lower-class urban characters in whom primitive traits roiled beneath a thin veneer of civilization. Pressed by forces of heredity and environment not only beyond their control but beyond their understanding, these characters were pushed to the limits of endurance. They responded to the sordid, frightening, and altogether compelling circumstances in which they found themselves by striking out in desperate ways unacceptable to their middle-class audience: through drinking or taking drugs, resorting to prostitution or theft, or lashing out in violent ways, even committing murder on occasion.

Within these general outlines, however, critical perspectives on naturalism differ. For example, George Becker's definition of naturalism as "pessimistic materialistic determinism" in his introduction to *Documents of Modern Literary Realism* (Becker 1963: 35) summed up naturalism's principal philosophical framework, yet as Donald Pizer points out, naturalism consists of two tensions not accounted for by such a definition: first, despite naturalism's lower-class characters, the naturalist author portrays "those qualities of man usually associated with the heroic or adventurous" (Pizer 1984: 11) and second, naturalists depict a "compensating humanistic value" (p. 12) in their characters, both traits at odds with pessimism and determinism. Nor was there agreement about naturalism's origins: critics such as Richard Lehan have traced its principal ideas to Zola and French writers, whereas Donald Pizer and others have emphasized its roots in American culture. Malcolm Cowley denigrated the naturalists' style, saying that the naturalists have "all used language as a blunt instrument" as if such an observation were a critical commonplace (1947/1998: 238), yet Lee Clark Mitchell (1989) has demonstrated a rhetorical subtlety in such works as Jack London's "To Build a Fire." More recently, Jennifer Fleissner has challenged the conventional reading of the naturalist plot as one of inevitable decline, arguing instead that its true movement is repetition, a focus on "an ongoing, nonlinear, repetitive motion . . . that has the distinctive effect of seeming also like a stuckness in place" (Fleissner 2004: 9). Finally, even the mode of naturalism has caused controversy: for some critics, including early reviewers, naturalism seemed a debased version of realism, a type of hyperrealism that dwells on the unpleasant details of life, while for Norris and Dreiser, its coincidences, improbable happenings, and "twisted from the ordinary" circumstances placed it in the realm of romance.

But these debates are secondary to the more central issues of the writers' relationship to naturalism, to the literary climate of their times, and to contemporary discourses of nationalism and modernity. Although the novels of Norris, Crane, London, and Dreiser share certain naturalistic themes, variations in their approaches to questions of naturalism and modernity become evident when their work is examined more closely. In what ways did the naturalists themselves articulate, directly through their critical statements or indirectly through their work, their relation to naturalistic theory? To what extent did they see themselves as in conversation with contemporaries or predecessors who shared their ideas about evolution, atavism, degeneration, and race? Moreover, how did these writers conceptualize their writings as modern if not "modernist" – in other words, as a response to the crisis of modernity? And finally, to what extent was their writing of naturalism a bracing corrective to a nation envisioning itself as a bastion of material progress and prosperity, rather than as a country in which social, governmental, industrial, scientific, and racial forces conspired to crush the individual? To a certain extent, naturalism emerged from the crisis of modernity to become a literature of paradoxical anxieties that undercut supposedly scientific laws about human nature. Despite the belief in biologically determined gender categories, for example, naturalism expresses anxieties about the survival of masculinity under the twin threats of the New Woman and the feminization engendered by overcivilization. The burgeoning underclass should have posed no threat to the supposedly invincible Anglo-Saxon, according to the era's theories of race, yet naturalism resounds with fears about increasing class mobility and the threat posed by teeming masses of ethnic and racial others. Furthermore, if human beings were already biological machines governed by heredity and environment, increasing mechanization and industrialization should have caused no anxiety, since these would add but one more determinant to humankind's already predestined fate, yet anxiety about this, too, runs like a dark thread through naturalist texts. Exploring the dimensions of naturalism, then, means examining the movement not only in terms of what naturalistic writers believed themselves to be doing but also in terms of the anxieties over modernity that run through their writing. To illustrate turn-of-the-century fiction through these intersections of naturalism and modernity, it is useful to consider the practice of naturalism along four of the dimensions that commonly characterized the movement: its intellectual roots in Zola's naturalism and Howells's realism, as demonstrated in Norris's approach through scientific and literary theories; its focus on women's experiences and its experimental style, as shown in the work of Stephen Crane; its representations of modernity, anomie, and desire in the urban environment, as seen in Dreiser's use of the city as a determining force; and its examination of the forces of poverty and ethnicity in working-class lives, as shown in the work of Jack London. In addition, brief comparisons of these naturalist writers with others less generally recognized as writing naturalism, such as Edith Wharton, Kate Chopin, Paul Laurence Dunbar, and Anzia Yezierska, demonstrate the elasticity and usefulness of naturalism as a strategy for representing modernity.

Frank Norris is the American author most commonly identified as a naturalist writer, and with good reason: from "Zola as a Romantic Writer" through the essays collected and published posthumously as *The Responsibilities of the Novelist*, Norris was the movement's most visible theorist and practitioner. Moreover, Norris, unlike his contemporaries, repeatedly acknowledged his debt to Zola and French naturalism. For example, in addition to his championing of Zola in the pages of *The Wave*, Norris playfully referred to himself as the "boy Zola" (Crisler 1986: 160) in a letter to his friend Isaac Marcosson, an allusion not only to his professed admiration for Zola but also to the critics' consistent comparison of him to the French proponent of naturalism. Norris construed naturalism as a form flexible enough to represent what was most significant about life: the extraordinary events residing even within the realm of the commonplace. He believed that "Naturalism is a form of romanticism, not an inner circle of realism" (Norris 1986f: 1108), and that, like the work of Victor Hugo, Zola's work had "enormous scenic effects, the same love of the extraordinary, the vast, the monstrous, and the tragic" (p. 1108). Zola is not a realist but "the very head of the Romanticists" (1986c: 1166), and, unlike the false and bombastic romancers writing of ages past, he takes as his subject contemporary life or the recent past. Norris was a critic, however, not an unthinking disciple, for when Zola failed to live up to his own principles by indulging in explicit social commentary, as he did in *Fécondité*, Norris was quick to point out the problem: its "sermons on the fruitfulness of women, special pleading, [and] a farrago of dry, dull incidents" show that even Zola nods on occasion (Norris 1986a: 1198). Yet although he chose different features of Zola's novels to praise throughout his career, Norris consistently looked to Zola as a touchstone for his own practice of naturalism.

If Zola represents one pole of Norris's theorizing about naturalism, William Dean Howells represents the other, and Norris consistently compared the two in his reviews. The premier literary critic of his day, Howells championed realism first as editor of *The Atlantic Monthly* and then, from 1886 to 1892, as the serious if avuncular voice of the "Editor's Study" columns for *Harper's New Monthly Magazine*. Several of Howells's words echo in Norris's essays. For example, to a late nineteenth-century reader, the repeated use of "common" in Norris's statement about a literature "twisted from the ordinary" would have gained added resonance from its use in the realism promoted by Howells. Realism, Howells had declared, is "nothing more and nothing less than the truthful treatment of material" taken from life (Howells 1889: 966), a literature that shows "the light of common day" (Howells 1901: 227). It signifies a commitment to representing the real rather than the ideal, a distinction that Howells demonstrates in his allegory of the real and the ideal grasshopper in an "Editor's Study" column from December 1887. To show that artists are discouraged from taking subjects from life and are taught instead to worship an abstract ideal, Howells imagines a conversation in which the art establishment suggests copying a wire-and-cardboard model of a grasshopper rather than a real grasshopper. No one, Howells argues, would give a scientist this model and propose that he study that instead of a real one, yet imitating ideal models is standard advice given to artists and writers. Like the scientist, the artist should instead study from life (a principle of naturalism), and, when told that "The thing that you are proposing to do is commonplace," should persevere because "the simple, natural, and honest" should be the standard for art (Howells 1887: 155). Norris, too, believed that the artist should be like the scientist and look directly at life, but, as with Zola, his discipleship under Howells went only so far. In "Theory and Reality," Norris praised Howells's *A Parting and a Meeting* and *A Modern Instance* for their respective treatment of sexual desire and sexual jealousy – or, as he put it more delicately for the readers of *The Wave*, the "dangerous subject" of "the ultimate physical relation of man and woman" (Norris 1986d: 1103). Yet he chides Howells for limiting his treatment to characters who are "well behaved and ordinary and *bourgeois*" (p. 1106), instead of representing the extraordinary characters and events that constitute naturalism. Even the term "commonplace" undergoes a transformation: Howells implies that it is a term of opprobrium and suggests instead that it be adopted with pride as signifying the real ("the simple, natural, and honest"), but for Norris the Howellsian "commonplace" could be only a point of departure for a naturalistic treatment of material. Norris also parsed Howells's use of the word "truthful," as in "the truthful treatment of material," until it, too, underwent a sea change. He dissects the meaning of "truth" and "accuracy" in his weekly letter for the *Chicago American Literary Review* in 1901, using, like Howells, the example of an animal to illustrate his point. If the novelist faithfully depicts a black sheep as representative of the whole, Norris argues, his picture is accurate, because the animal is indeed a sheep, but such a picture is not true because it leaves the false impression that all sheep are black. In Norris's terms, accuracy is less desirable in literature than truth, which may eschew mere accuracy in its quest to convey a true picture. Adding to the realism/naturalism and realism/romanticism binaries he has already established, Norris proposes that "Accuracy is realism and Truth romanticism," with naturalism at its best encompassing both (Norris 1901/1986: 1142). Versed in the proper relation – Norris's relation – between truth and romanticism, novelists need not "take up that harsh, loveless, colorless, blunt tool called Realism" (Norris 1986b: 1166) but can instead use naturalism as a technology for representing contemporary life.

In his novels, too, Norris was a proponent of naturalism, although his practices changed over the course of his career. The novels considered his best each present a slightly different perspective on naturalism: *McTeague* (1899), *The Octopus* (1901), and *The Pit* (1903). Of these, *McTeague* adheres most closely to the Zola of *L'assommoir*, with its depictions of alcoholism, poverty, and brutality, but the perspective was Norris's own. Inspired by newspaper accounts of an Irish laborer murdering his charwoman wife in a kindergarten, Norris began to write the sketches later incorporated into *McTeague* as a series of daily themes for Lewis Gates's English 22 class at Harvard, earning comments such as "gruesome" from his grader but apparently praise from Gates himself.[2] *McTeague* exemplifies Zola's method of experimenting with characters and their environment as the primary basis for the naturalistic novel; like other such works, it quickly reaches a point of balance and gradually descends into chaos and death. Like *L'assommoir*, *McTeague* features long stretches of equilibrium, usually summed up in a chapter or elided in phrases such as "three years passed" punctuated by abrupt catastrophes and descents into a lower level of existence. McTeague, a dentist in the working-class district of Polk Street in San Francisco, exists in a state of near-somnolent stasis until he is struck by twin calamities masquerading as luck: the first is meeting Trina Sieppe, the woman he will marry; and the second is incurring the enmity of his friend and Trina's former suitor, her cousin Marcus Schouler, when Trina wins $5,000 in a lottery. These two events arouse the elemental emotions of desire – on McTeague's part, for sex and, on Trina's, for money – that tap into a biological heritage of addiction for each. Operating on an anesthetized Trina, McTeague is overcome by the spectacle of her helplessness and by an inner brute, "long dormant" but "now at last alive," that causes him to kiss her "grossly, full on the mouth" (Norris 1899/1997: 22). It is the first but by no means the last appearance of the brute, called to life here by the "foul stream of hereditary evil, like a sewer" (p. 22) that flowed in his veins. The brute emerges again when McTeague abandons beer for whiskey, which "roused the . . . brute in the man and . . . goaded it to evil" (p. 169). For Trina, the tipping point occurs not when she wins the $5,000 but when she marries McTeague and gives herself to him sexually; as Barbara Hochman suggests, she seeks to replace what she has lost by saving "another treasure" (Hochman 1988: 70), her money, replacing the sexuality that she cannot control with the money that she can. Like McTeague's hereditary "foul taint," Trina's German-Swiss ancestry predisposes her to a miserliness that she at first dismisses as a "good fault" (Norris 1899/1997: 141) until she is as addicted to money as McTeague is to alcohol.

Environment as well as heredity plays a role, for what precipitates their decline is living in a modern economy governed by the appearance of things rather than the things themselves. The modern economic system of exchanging pieces of paper, such as diplomas, licenses, certificates, or banknotes, that represent respectively knowledge, power, and money, ruins the McTeagues and becomes increasingly irrelevant to them as they descend the economic ladder. When Marcus Schouler spitefully reports McTeague's lack of a license to practice dentistry to the authorities, all of McTeague's protests – "I've been practicing for ten years" (Norris 1899/1997: 146) – will not allow the substance, his knowledge of dentistry and practical experience in it, to substitute for the piece of paper that certifies the substance. Events in the novel put the lie to one piece of paper after another, from the "Made in France" stickers Trina adds to the Noah's Ark animals she whittles and the "non-poisonous paint" she uses to finish them, to the happy wedding photograph of the McTeagues. The ultimate rejection of the world of representation for the world of things occurs when Trina feels driven to exchange the paper promise of money for the gold it represents: she exchanges a draft drawn on the $5,000 she has deposited for investment with her Uncle Oelbermann for gold, which she hoards. As Walter Benn Michaels notes, McTeague and Trina "are united in their distaste for 'representative' paper" (Michaels 1987: 151), but Trina goes a step further in literally transferring her sexual desire from McTeague to the gold, spreading it in her bed and "taking a strange and ecstatic pleasure in the touch of the smooth flat pieces the length of her entire body" (p. 198). After brutally murdering Trina by beating her to death, McTeague returns to the Western mining country of his youth, a land in which actions and gold, not paper representations of them, hold meaning. Although he is now a natural man in a natural landscape, a site at last suited to his brute strength and instincts, McTeague's determination to carry Trina's gold with him dooms him, for gold is the one signifier that holds its value in wild as well as civilized spaces. Hearing of the murder, Marcus Schouler follows McTeague, although he is driven more by the thought of McTeague's possession of Trina's gold, gold that Marcus believes was his by right, than by a desire for justice. The two men meet in Death

Valley, and, their water gone, fight pointlessly over Trina's gold. After killing Marcus with blows from his "fists, hard as wooden mallets" (p. 243), McTeague discovers that Marcus has handcuffed himself to him. Symbolism in naturalist novels is not always a subtle affair; as reviewers and critics have noted, the gold symbolism in *McTeague* is pervasive, with McTeague's canary, the gold tooth that signifies his profession, and Trina's money all amplifying its significance. Norris's concluding image is equally forceful and symbolic. McTeague is left sitting in the middle of a deadly environment, chained literally as well as figuratively to a body that his limitations have never allowed him to escape.

Norris's last two major novels, *The Octopus* and *The Pit* echo expansive social problem novels such as Zola's *Germinal* and *La Terre* rather than *L'assommoir*. Both *The Octopus* and *The Pit* were part of Norris's plan for a trilogy concerning the production, sale, and distribution of wheat as a "great and resistless force moving from west to east, from producer to consumer" (Crisler 1986: 173), a plan cut short when Norris died in October 1902 before the publication of *The Pit*. In scope and subject matter, *The Octopus* marked a departure from the severe confines of *McTeague*'s classic plot of naturalistic decline, for although, like the murder in *McTeague*, the novel was inspired by an actual event, the Mussel Slough battle between Southern California farmers and railroad operatives in 1880, Norris transforms the event into a commentary on everything from the role of the artist to inevitable triumph of the wheat and the market forces that make its dissemination possible. At the beginning of *The Octopus*, Presley, Norris's artist alter ego, seeks a fit subject for his projected American epic and believes he has found it in his vision of the West and its land as a "colossus, benignant, eternal, strong, the nourisher of nations, the feeder of an entire world" (1986b: 614). As he walks across the land at night, his naive literary longings shatter when he watches as an equally titanic force, a "crack passenger engine" (p. 616), thunders across the land and slaughters a flock of innocent sheep that have wandered onto the track. The episode literally and symbolically shows the modern age murdering the pastoral age of Presley's imaginings, with the train, the novel's symbol of the "monster" of technological modernity, impersonally destroying the natural world. The rest of the novel presses the point home, with its set pieces of physical carnage, such as the organized massacre of jackrabbits caught by an ever-tightening circle of farmers, anticipating the farmers' own extinction when caught in the arms of the octopus, the Southern Pacific railway that feeds on their toil in building up the land. Of all Norris's characters, only Vanamee, the mystic philosopher of *The Octopus*, transcends both time and modernity through a belief in reincarnation that restores to him his lost love, Angele, in the person of her daughter. "Men were naught, death was naught, life was naught; FORCE only existed," Presley thinks in *The Octopus* (Norris 1986b: 1084), and it is the examination of this world of forces, modernity among them, that marks Norris as a classic naturalist.

The same clash of forces animates *The Pit*, which in its equation of business speculation and the marriage market recalls Edith Wharton's *The House of Mirth*. In *The Pit*, the wheat for which the ranchers fought and died in *The Octopus* is traded in the

Pit of the title, the trading floor of the Chicago Board of Trade. Like W. D. Howells's *The Rise of Silas Lapham*, *The Pit* juxtaposes a romance plot, the marriage of its protagonists, Curtis Jadwin and Laura Dearborn, with a business plot, Jadwin's attempts to corner the market in wheat. His attempts to control both Laura and the market illustrate, as does *The Octopus*, the impossibility of controlling one's destiny in the midst of a world ruled by overwhelming forces, in this novel the forces of the marketplace and Jadwin's addiction to trading and speculation. In both novels, Norris's true subject is a naturalistic examination of human desire when confronted with the Frankenstein's monster of outsized forces, whether technological or economic, that humankind has created and set in motion but can no longer control. The unavoidable monster, as Norris saw it, was not time, with its inevitable progress toward death, but modernity, created from the human compulsion to regulate and resist time's dictates, as one more force in the world of forces that govern the lives of human beings. The addiction to speculation and its causes, the underlying attempt to stop time, that Norris gives to Jadwin is also the tragic flaw of Lily Bart, Wharton's protagonist in *The House of Mirth*. Born into a social position that she has the breeding but not the money to maintain, Lily, at age 29, has only one means of livelihood open to her: to marry a wealthy man. Her beauty and charm would seem to render this an easy goal to reach, but Lily, like Jadwin, has a fatal propensity for speculating in the marketplace, in her case the marriage market. Having captured the attention of the rich but dull Percy Gryce, she overplays her hand by ignoring him in favor of flirting with the much poorer lawyer Lawrence Selden, who is repeatedly drawn to Lily but chooses not to marry her. Unable to capitalize on her assets by an innate disdain for the shallow society that constitutes her world, Lily descends the social ladder by making one disastrous choice after another, pressed by social forces that she can set in motion but cannot control. By the end of the novel, Lily, like Crane's Maggie Johnson, has spent time in sewing for a livelihood and later slips into poverty and death. Like Maggie, too, she is better than her surroundings, but her finer sensibilities only demonstrate her failure to adapt and survive, a circumstance that Wharton describes in Darwinian language as Lily recognizes that she is "a mere spindrift of the whirling surface of existence, without anything to which the poor little tentacles of self could cling before the awful flood submerged them" (Wharton 1905/1990: 248).

Stephen Crane, like Kate Chopin, explored the workings of naturalistic determinism through gender, and, like Chopin, showed a sophisticated grasp of style and symbolism. As he explained in an inscription in Hamlin Garland's copy of *Maggie: A Girl of the Streets*, the book "tries to show that environment is a tremendous thing in the world and frequently shapes lives regardless. If one proves that theory, one makes room in Heaven for all sorts of souls (notably an occasional street girl) who are not confidently expected to be there by many excellent people" (Crane 1988: 53). Unlike Norris, however, Crane liked to present himself as *sui generis*, an author who worked primarily without models in the service of truth: "I developed all alone a little creed of art which I thought was a good one. Later I discovered that my creed was identical with the one of Howells and Garland . . ." (p. 63). Despite his friend Joseph Conrad's comment that Crane "knew little of literature, either of his own country or any other" (Sorrentino 2006: 250), according to James Nagel, Crane read "Anatole France, Henry James, George Moore, Mark Rutherford, Bierce, Hardy, Twain, and Kipling" (Nagel 1980: 20), a list that, as Nagel indicates, does not include such contemporaries and friends as Harold Frederic, Joseph Conrad, and Ford Madox Ford. Nor does Crane mention French influences, despite the recollection of his friend and roommate Frederic M. Lawrence that collections of de Maupassant's stories and a book by Zola were among their possessions (Sorrentino 2006: 116).[3] Less extensive and specific than Norris's, Crane's theorizing about naturalism shares one important value with that of Norris: that representing life as it is really lived by prostitutes and others disdained by middle-class society reveals truths about the human condition inaccessible to standard varieties of realism, and that such representation must follow not the middle-class practice of Howells's fiction but the spirit of his realism, with its belief that, as Crane paraphrased it, "we are the most successful in art when we approach the nearest to nature and truth" (Crane 1988: 63). Despite misgivings over dialect and profanity not seen in his own works, Howells hailed Crane's *Maggie: A Girl of the Streets*, calling it "the best thing he did" (Howells 1900/1973: 62) and finding it superior even to the novel usually considered Crane's masterpiece, *The Red Badge of Courage*. *The Red Badge of Courage* has its naturalistic moments, most notably in its ironic description of a peaceful chapel-like forest in which sits a filmy-eyed dead man over whose gray-skinned face "ran little ants" (Crane 1984b: 126). But Crane's slum sketches and tales, particularly *Maggie*, not only reveal his understanding of the deterministic coordinates of gender but also illustrate the ways in which his impressionistic style anticipates those of twentieth-century authors.

First published privately in 1893 at Crane's expense and later reissued in a bowdlerized edition by Appleton in 1896 after the success of *The Red Badge of Courage*, *Maggie: A Girl of the Streets* both derives from and rejects the slum story popular at the time. It is contemporary in its subject matter and, like the rest of Crane's work, distinctly modern in its ironic, impressionistic style. As Keith Gandal (1997) demonstrates in *The Virtues of the Vicious*, unlike slum tales such as Edward Townsend's *A Daughter of the Tenements* or Arthur Morrison's *Tales of Mean Streets*, Crane used the ethnographic perspective of Jacob Riis's *How the Other Half Lives* to critique the conventional nineteenth-century moral tale of reformation. Moreover, *Maggie's* origins, as George Monteiro shows in *Stephen Crane's Blue Badge of Courage*, are set firmly in the temperance tracts and poems of Crane's youth, whose "familiar paradigms" he used "without always seeing how the mediation of those paradigms and that rhetoric also worked to shape (and occasionally limit) his ability to see the reality around him" (Monteiro 2000: 34). In *Maggie*, Crane deflates the conventional elements of slum tales and temperance tracts, such as Maggie Johnson's tenement upbringing, her seduction, her turn to prostitution, and her death. As Alan Trachtenberg succinctly puts it, it is "a complicated piece of parody written with a serious regard for the task of rendering a false tale truly" (Trachtenberg 1982: 145). Crane's emphasis on environment over heredity is apparent in his choice of heroine, for Maggie seems to inherit few characteristics from her monstrously drunken mother and abusive father; instead, she is a genetic anomaly, a pretty girl who "blossomed in a mud puddle" (Crane 1984a: 24) and takes steps to impose order and beauty on her ugly and disorderly world. But biology disguised as romantic desire begins the corrective process of inducting Maggie into the mean streets of her birth when she meets Pete, her brother Jimmie's friend and a bartender whose saloon is the cleanest and most orderly space in the novel. In due course, Pete introduces her to culture, in the form of trips to the Central Park Menagerie, the Museum of Art, and a vaudeville show; seduces her, and leaves her for another, after which she takes to the streets. When she reemerges as "a girl of the painted cohorts" (p. 70) after a period of months, she accosts an increasingly unpleasant series of potential male clients until she stands by the "deathly black hue" of the river with "a huge fat man" whose "whole body gently quivered and shook like that of a dead jelly fish" (p. 72). Unlike the traditional "girl who went wrong," Maggie neither bears an illegitimate child nor succumbs to disease, yet her fate is sealed by her mother's hypocrisy in throwing her out of the house, and, by extension, by the entire hypocritical social system that regards her as unclean, like the "stout gentleman in a silk hat and a chaste black coat" (p. 69) who avoids Maggie. The environmental forces that ruin her are thus as much social as biological, with Crane indicting "the false moral environment" imposed on her life rather than her physical environment for her death (Pizer 1984: 151).

Crane's approach to modernity is evident in his modern use of stylistic impressionism and irony as well as in his subject matter. Commenting on Crane's "carefully-chosen details, his insistence on the main theme, and his avoidance of irrelevance," an anonymous reviewer for *Literature* concludes that "Mr. Crane is an Impressionist, and not a mere descriptive writer" ("Crane's Defective Impressionism" 1898/1973: 218), a judgment echoed by other contemporaries. Crane's almost cinematically objective point of view in some scenes in *Maggie* helps to render her life impressionistically, as does what James Nagel calls the "juxtaposition of two or more narrators describing the same pattern of events" (Nagel 1980: 24), a technique Crane uses when contrasting Pete's seduction of Maggie with her brother Jimmie's avoidance of women he has seduced. Such juxtapositions also contribute to the novel's use of irony, which is evident at the level of theme as well as style. For example, Maggie's innocence ironically leads to her downfall because she is unable to distinguish the romantic from the real. She clothes Pete in the garb of a shining knight and does not understand his shortcomings, just as she is unable to grasp the concept of the ventriloquist's dummies until Pete tells her that they are "some damn fake" (Crane 1984a: 32). More pointedly ironic is her drunken, monstrous mother's hypocritical espousal of middle-class morality, for when "the red, writhing body of her mother" tells Maggie "Go teh hell an' good riddance," the narrator simply reports, "She went" (p. 41). Discarded by Pete some time later with the same instructions – "Go teh hell" – she puts a single question to herself: "Who?" (p. 69). Read both as "Who will take care of me?" and "Who am I?" it is virtually her last word in the novel, except for the inconsequential "Ah, there" with which she accosts potential clients. "Who?" registers her recognition that she has lost both name and self in her struggle for survival. Subsumed by the modern city, which reads her as a series of types, Maggie loses her individuality and eventually her life.

Kate Chopin's *The Awakening* traces the similarly limited choices of its heroine, Edna Pontellier, within a modern deterministic universe. As well-to-do and privileged as Maggie is poor, Edna, too, is something of an outsider in her surroundings: her St Louis roots have not prepared her for the Creole traditions of New Orleans and the summer community at Grand Isle. She cannot read Creole customs accurately and mistakes its culture of courtly flirtation for one of sensuality, a misreading that in part causes her to fall in love with Robert Lebrun. Leaving her husband and children behind during a day trip to the lush, tropical island of Chênière Caminada, Edna falls asleep and wakes up to a renewed sense of herself as an individual. Edna's awakening is intellectual and emotional as well as sexual, for in addition to her infatuation with Robert, she responds to Mademoiselle Reisz's piano playing with "a keen tremor down [her] spinal column" accompanied by "an impress of the abiding truth" (Chopin 2006: 906). Although she is seduced by the practiced roué Alcée Arobin, Edna's true declaration of independence consists in leaving the home of her husband and children for a smaller "pigeon-house" in which she is free to paint and to be herself. But despite her privileged existence, Edna can no more escape the confines of biological forces and social disapprobation than Maggie can. She tells her friend Dr Mandelet that "it is better to wake up after all, even to suffer, rather than to remain a dupe to illusions all one's life" (p. 996), but her awakening leads her only to the recognition that she never can escape, given the culture she inhabits. Reflecting that "To-day it is Arobin; tomorrow it will be someone else" (p. 999), Edna imagines a parade of lovers rather like Maggie's parade of clients, a recognition that leads her, like Maggie, to death by drowning. But Edna chooses her fate, an affirmative act. Having learned to swim after being afraid of the water, Chopin's symbol not only for sexual experience but for the entire experience of life, Edna sheds her clothes as she has shed society's conventions and swims far from shore, becoming one with nature but only achieving this union in death.

Theodore Dreiser and Paul Laurence Dunbar identify the modern city as the intersection of modernity and human experience that comprises the subject matter of naturalism. Although in *Sister Carrie*, Dreiser's first novel, Carrie Meeber finds rather than loses her individuality in the city, Clyde Griffiths of *An American Tragedy* illustrates the integration and disintegration of the self through the forces of American culture. Like Carrie, he is a "waif amid forces," drawn by, and to a large extent shaped by, the trappings of modernity he encounters in the modern city. Drawn, like Norris's *McTeague*, from a murder case, *An American Tragedy* borrows heavily from the 1906 drowning of the pregnant Grace Brown at the hands of Chester Gillette in upstate New York, even using verbatim accounts from the Gillette trial in the novel. The book is an inevitable tragedy of aspiration, arranged in three acts. Book One follows Clyde, the rootless son of itinerant evangelists, as he leaves Kansas City after an automobile accident in which he was implicated. In Book Two, Clyde arrives in Lycurgus, New York, the home of his uncle Samuel Griffiths, a wealthy manufacturer. Finding himself shut out from the social world of the Griffiths, Clyde seduces a factory girl, Roberta Alden; when his American dream seems about to be realized through the love of the upper-class Sondra Finchley, Clyde is dragged back to earth by Roberta's untimely pregnancy. Trapped by biology and by the social opprobrium that would render his eventual marriage to Sondra impossible, he makes plans to take Roberta on a trip to Big Bittern Lake, with the thought of drowning her. As he sits in a canoe with Roberta in a deserted section of the lake, however, Clyde vacillates about his actions, wanting to be rid of Roberta but reluctant to take the necessary steps to murder her. When Roberta leans toward him, he accidentally strikes out at her with the camera in his hand, hitting her in the face and overturning the boat; he then swims to shore as she drowns. Although Clyde believes he has not technically murdered Roberta, he is nonetheless convicted of murder by an ambitious district attorney, sentenced to death, and executed in the electric chair, the legal processes that comprise Book Three.

In adapting the Gillette case, Dreiser emphasized its ambiguities in order to focus attention less on Clyde's guilt than on society's in promoting an impossible ideal and to explore the forces at work upon Clyde's character. In naturalistic terms, Clyde is a reactive rather than an active character, pushed as he is in multiple directions by internal and external forces, including those symbolized by Roberta and Sondra. Yet as Joseph Karaganis points out, in addition to classic determinants such as "instinct, mechanism, the sex drive, [and] survival of the fittest" (Karaganis 2000: 160), Clyde is driven by the peculiarly modern desire for "spectacularity" or celebrity, the pleasure of being seen (p. 165). As Warren Susman (1984) notes in "'Personality' and the Making of Twentieth-Century Culture," the early decades of the twentieth century marked a shift from a culture of character, marked by concepts such as duty, moral order, and responsibility to community, to one of personality, with its overtones of expressive individualism and primacy of the self. Dreiser renders this shift graphically in Book Two when Clyde is buffeted alternately by letters from Sondra and Roberta, the former written in a cloying baby-talk that reeks of personality and modernity, and the latter evocative of old-fashioned sentimental appeals to character and Clyde's duty to her (see Rhodes 1996). Clyde's commitment to personality rather than to character, to Sondra rather than to Roberta, marks him both as modern and as insubstantial. This trait is also emphasized in Clyde's engagement with the visual commercial culture that surrounds him. Before moving to Lycurgus, Clyde works as a bellhop at the Green-Davidson Hotel in Kansas City, and after the visual impoverishment of the drab street corners of his childhood, the sumptuousness and sensuality of the hotel, with its variety of people and its constant movement, enchants him. At the Green-Davidson, his job is to watch doors and the scenes within the rooms, as he will later watch both the home of his relatives, the Griffiths family, and of Sondra, who works hard at being a spectacle worth watching by flourishing props such as her pet dog or her red Spanish shawl. As Tim Armstrong has commented about the city in *Sister Carrie*, the city itself becomes an addiction in Dreiser: "the craving for light, luxury, commodities is a poison; the individual is 'plugged in' to its energies, desires, and rewards" (Armstrong 1998: 29).

Clyde's values are thus shaped wholly by the lives he sees and by the objects he covets. In Lycurgus, he is aware, indeed hypervigilant, about the degree to which he is watched as "a Griffiths," but as in his earlier identity as a bellhop, he does not escape the uniform of identity established by a social institution with which he is associated, whether the institution is the Green-Davidson or the Griffiths factory. He falls in love with Sondra because she, too, presents the spectacle of an identity; she "dressed awfully well, and was very rich and in society and her name and pictures were always in the paper," Clyde testifies at his trial (Dreiser 1925/2000: 721), a celebrity that Clyde shares when Sondra falls in love with him. Later, of course, Clyde works equally hard at not being seen, as when he tries to pretend that Roberta is not traveling with him to Big Bittern Lake or when he escapes from the scene of Roberta's drowning. In fact, he is amazed when a parade of witnesses testifies to his movements when he had "imagined himself unobserved" (p. 685). Even the instrument that the prosecution contends was used to kill Roberta is associated with an instrument of seeing: a camera. Fished up from the depths near Roberta's body, the camera yields evidence both real and manufactured of Clyde's presence: its ghostly images prove his relationship with Roberta, and the hairs planted between the lens and the lid by Burton Burleigh, a backwoodsman who wants to ensure Clyde's conviction, attest falsely to his violence toward her. At Clyde's trial, as at Gillette's trial, all the evidence is circumstantial and suggestive of facts rather than definitive proof of them. Dreiser uses this sense of insubstantiality – of a personality first refracted through the lens of the city and then reconstituted through the recollections, real or imagined, of the witnesses and objects at his trial – to render Clyde as a figure of modern man, driven and defined by others. The best defense that his lawyers Belknap and Jephson can offer for him, in fact, is a variation of this idea: Clyde is, they tell the jury, a "mental as well as a moral coward" (p. 703) – in effect, a man as insubstantial and fictitious as the "Clifford Golden" alias he had used in his trip with Roberta. Clyde cannot "be a man" because the institutions that define him have given him personality but not character. Like that of Crane's Maggie, whose individuality is erased and whose words are silenced by the forces of the city, Clyde's personality, always inchoate and subject to external forces, is gradually erased. From pretending to a sophistication that he does not possess to court Sondra Finchley to adopting the "dummy or substitute for the real" (p. 662) story that his lawyers Belknap and Jephson concoct to defend him, Clyde collaborates in creating his fictitious selves until, progressively dehumanized by the machinery of the law and the prison system, he can only parrot the Reverend McMillan's words about "the joy and pleasure of a Christian life" (p. 850) shortly before his death. As he walks to the electric chair, he hears his "voice sounding so strange and weak, even to himself, so far distant as though it emanated from another being walking alongside of him, and not from himself" (p. 852), but this is just the last in a series of dissociative states that he has experienced throughout his life as a character ruled by naturalistic forces.

Dunbar's *The Sport of the Gods* recounts a similar story of the innocent shaped and cast aside by the city, a familiar plot in naturalist texts. In it, Berry Hamilton, an African-American butler to the white landowner Maurice Oakley, is unjustly accused of a theft actually committed by Oakley's brother-in-law, tried, and imprisoned, after which his family moves to New York and disintegrates into poverty and a rootless existence. Dunbar satirizes the plantation myth in the early pages of the novel as the Oakleys unhesitatingly consign Hamilton to prison despite his years of devoted service, an act that reveals their racism and the false depiction of the white landowner as benevolent paterfamilias. *The Sport of the Gods* follows the lives of Hamilton's two children, Joe and Kitty, as both lose their innocence. Pursued by a married man, Kitty escapes by becoming a musical comedy star, a plot that recalls Theodore Dreiser's *Sister Carrie*, while Joe's lack of will in resisting the city's pleasures recalls Clyde Griffiths's plight. Bereft of his trade as a barber initially because of gossip about his father's imprisonment, Joe takes refuge in the substitute family of the Banner Club saloon where, like Clyde, he is subject to the power of a dominant woman who loves him, the saloon singer Hattie. Settling passively into the life of Hattie's kept man, Joe degenerates until Hattie throws him out, after which Joe murders her in a fit of anger. His rage frees him from years of inaction with a single incident of violent action, yet, like Clyde's, Joe's efforts are not only wrong but wrongly directed. Like Dreiser, Dunbar tries to suggest the dangers of the city, although his description of its pleasures belies his sermonizing about its perils: "the stream of young negro life would continue to flow up from the south, dashing itself against the hard necessities of the city and breaking like waves against a rock . . . until the gods grew tired of their cruel sport," the narrator concludes (Dunbar 1902/2005: 414), yet as both Dreiser's and Dunbar's novels make clear, "the hard necessities of the city" cannot dissuade those like Clyde Griffiths and Joe Hamilton whom the city fascinates with its pleasures. If modernity is spectacle, they wish not only to view it but to be part of it, and this desire leads to a fatal immersion in the city as an organism.

Although many naturalist authors addressed working-class lives, Jack London and Anzia Yezierska infused their writing with a more physical, visceral sense of poverty's effects than most. Both vividly render not only the backbreaking labor of the poor but the hunger, dirt, and despair that separate their characters, who are poverty-stricken outsiders, from the material and intellectual wealth surrounding them. Although he never lost interest in chronicling human nature and its reversion to primitive behavior under the stress of extreme and inhospitable environments, whether that included the frozen Yukon of the Northland stories or the toxic tropics in the South Seas stories, London also published social fiction and nonfiction such as *The People of the Abyss*, an ethnographic study of the slums of east London. He was also deeply influenced by the potential for human betterment implied by the writings of Herbert Spencer, whose *First Principles*, he said, had "done more for man-kind . . . than a thousand books like *Nicholas Nickleby* . . . and *Uncle Tom's Cabin*" (London 1988: 104) and whose ideas are a central theme in *Martin Eden*. London's *Martin Eden*, like Yezierska's *Bread Givers*, is an autobiographical or self-ethnographic piece of fiction that casts a cold eye on the success narrative of working-class upward mobility.

In *Martin Eden*, the roughneck sailor Martin is introduced into a middle-class culture that has as its avatar Ruth Morse, whose angelic blonde looks and university education initially hide her fundamental philistinism. Spurred by his love for Ruth and his determination to work with his brains, not his hands, Martin undertakes a breathtakingly intense self-education program of reading and writing, interrupted only by equally intense intervals of backbreaking labor, such as a stint working in a laundry, sweating through hours of "nerve-racking, body-destroying toil" (London 1993: 195) so that "on the broad verandas of the hotel, men and women, in cool white" could "[sip] iced drinks" to keep "their circulation down" (p. 194). At first humbled by the cultural sophistication of the Morses and their friends, Martin comes to see their perspective as fundamentally shallow, and, worse, dishonest, especially after he discovers the intellectual delights of socialism and Russ Brissen-den, a cynical but honest poet. After years of poverty, Martin gains fame but loses his sense of self. Sickened by the hypocrisy of those who once spurned him but now want to cash in on his fame, including Ruth, Martin returns again and again to two things: desire for a "patriarchal grass house" in Tahiti (p. 420), the quintes-sential escape from civilization; and repulsion at those who praise him for what he repeatedly calls "work performed" (p. 446). Like Clyde Griffiths, he experiences these visions of the future and the past as psychological and visual interruptions, nearly hallucinations, from an intolerable present reality. Separated from those in his own class, like the working girl Lizzie Connolly, and disgusted by the middle-class pseudointellectuals whom he had originally revered, Martin has nowhere to go. In one final act of will, he slips out of a porthole on the steamer carrying him to Tahiti and drowns himself. Like that of Chopin's Edna Pontellier, his drowning is at once an affirmation and a negation: it affirms his will and control over his body, but it derives from a disillusionment with society so complete that death is preferable to living among people.

Yezierska's *Bread-Givers*, like *Martin Eden*, is an autobiographical tale of escaping poverty through hard work. Its protagonist, Sara Smolinsky, fights her way out of the Hester Street ghetto despite being hampered by her domineering father, Reb Smolinsky, whose invocations of Jewish tradition barely conceal his monstrous selfish-ness. Like Ruth Morse, whose idea of improving Martin is to force him into a mundane job so that he will support her, Sara's father wants to make her into an ideal daughter, a docile breadwinner who submits to him in everything and supports him in as much luxury as she can manage. Refusing to be bullied into an unsuitable marriage, as her sisters have been, Sara moves out to attend night school. She accom-plishes this feat, as Martin does, by working in a laundry to fund her intellectual pursuits. Like London, Yezierska uses laundry work to emphasize the gulf between working people and the leisure class: when Sara attends a physical education class at college after working hard all day in the laundry, she finds herself "dripping with sweat worse than Saturday night in the steam laundry" (Yezierska 1925/1999: 216), highlighting the difference between those who build up their bodies for recreation and those who use every scrap of muscle simply to survive a brutal working environment. A characteristically naturalistic environment in its squalor, Sara's room is crowded with dilapidated furniture and the grime of poverty, with the "thick dirt" and "mud of ages" (p. 162) encrusted on the window depriving her of light and air. But for Sara it is, actually and metaphorically, the room of one's own that Virginia Woolf had proposed as necessary to an intellectual life, and Sara sets an ambitious course of study for herself. Like Martin, she feels the pangs of physical as well as intellectual hunger, the former subsiding as the latter is satiated, and, like him, she too falls in love with someone socially and intellectually above her, Hugo Seelig. As Seelig helps Sara to erase her accent, and with it the exterior, audible ties with her ethnicity, Sara returns to her past. She asks her father, now living in poverty since no one will support him, to live with her. In doing so, she discovers that she still bears the burden of "the generations who made my father" (p. 297) and unlike Martin Eden, she is able both to rise from her origins and to embrace them as part of the person she has become.

Within the work of Norris and Wharton, Crane and Chopin, Dreiser and Dunbar, and London and Yezierska, then, naturalism responds to the crisis of modernity in ways that deserve the title of modernism. In addition to exploring the forces of heredity and environment, their transformation of Zola and of Howellsian realism for a modern context, their stylistic experiments and daring treatment of sexuality, their examination of the lure of the city, and their chronicling of poverty and working-class lives help to identify these authors as naturalistic. Moreover, in shedding and remaking class-bound, gendered, and ethnic identities, that rite of self-conscious modernity, their characters negotiate environments that range from bewilderingly hostile to indifferent, often urban spaces in which they are more frequently trapped by the forces of desire or poverty than by the physical boundaries of the place. For Crane, Norris, Wharton, Dunbar, and Chopin, the environment reinforces the divide between natural and unnatural, the supposedly innocent and the dubiously corrupt, as characters follow the naturalistic plot of decline based less on their circumstances alone than upon some way in which they have failed the Darwinian test of evolutionary adaptation. Some, like McTeague, are atavistic remnants of an earlier time whose grasp of modernity is always tenuous; others, like Joe Hamilton and Lily Bart, have been shaped for a different sort of environment and are unable to adapt successfully. In later works, such as those by Dreiser, London, and Yezierska, working-class backgrounds thwart characters who try to infiltrate a class-bound culture marked as modern by its use of language, literacy, and technology. Class mobility in the form of racial, ethnic, or class-based passing is not part of the performative vocabulary of Clyde Griffiths, Martin Eden, or Sara Smolinsky, for despite their efforts, they are marked in a seemingly indelible manner by their early environment, a past that haunts them despite their best efforts to escape it. The naturalistic plots and themes of these novels capture a particular moment in time, one in which the crisis of modernity was represented through radical ideas but a less than radically realist style, despite Crane's impressionism and the experiments of London and Dreiser with representing alternative states of consciousness. Naturalism in the hands of such writers reveals itself as more than the deterministic and materialistic universe implied by simple definitions. Rather, it is a surprisingly flexible and useful means of treating modernity in the turn-of-the-century novel, and is, in fact, a type of modernism *avant la lettre*, one that promotes a realistic immersion in details that Woolf rejected, but in doing so found a way to chronicle the shifting currents of turn-of-the-century life.

NOTES

1 Robert Morace identifies four ways in which Norris connected with his audience at *The Wave*: its status as a magazine, which meant that its value lay not in currency but in "various literary 'tricks'"; the "relationship in time" between Norris's pieces and lectures, concerts, and other events in San Francisco; the geographic specificity of the San Francisco location; and the first-hand knowledge that Norris had of upper-class social life (Morace 1980: 55).

2 For Norris's extant themes and the text of the grader's comments see Hart (1970); for com-

mentary on these see McElrath and Crisler (1974: 153–87).

3 References to Crane's knowledge of Zola appear in the unreliable biography *Stephen Crane* by Thomas Beer but are not substantiated elsewhere except in sources possibly influenced by Beer. See Paul Sorrentino's account of Crane's reading in *Stephen Crane Remembered* (2006: 331). On the unreliability of letters purported by Beer to have been written by Crane, see Stanley Wertheim and Paul Sorrentino's introduction to Crane's letters (Crane 1988).

REFERENCES AND FURTHER READING

Armstrong, Tim. (1998). *Modernism, Technology, and the Body: A Cultural Study*. Cambridge, UK and New York: Cambridge University Press.

Armstrong, Tim. (2005). *Modernism: A Cultural History*. Cambridge, UK: Polity Press.

Becker, George J. (1963). Modern realism as a literary movement. In George J. Becker (ed.), *Documents of Modern Literary Realism* (pp. 3–38). Princeton, NJ: Princeton University Press.

Campbell, Donna. (1997). *Resisting Regionalism: Gender and Naturalism in American Fiction, 1885–1915*. Athens: Ohio University Press.

Chopin, Kate. (2006). *The Complete Works of Kate Chopin*, ed. Per Seyersted. Baton Rouge: Louisiana State University Press.

Cowley, Malcolm. (1947/1998). "Not Men": A natural history of American naturalism. In Donald Pizer (ed.), *Documents of American Realism and Naturalism* (pp. 225–38). Carbondale: Southern Illinois University Press.

Crane's defective impressionism. (1898/1973). In Richard M. Weatherford (ed.), *Stephen Crane: The Critical Heritage* (pp. 218–19). London and Boston: Routledge and Kegan Paul.

Crane, Stephen. (1984a). *Maggie: A Girl of the Streets*. In *Stephen Crane: Prose and Poetry*, ed.

J. C. Levenson (pp. 7–78). New York: Library of America.

Crane, Stephen. (1984b). *The Red Badge of Courage*. In *Stephen Crane: Prose and Poetry*, ed. J. C. Levenson (pp. 79–212). New York: Library of America.

Crane, Stephen. (1988). *The Correspondence of Stephen Crane*, ed. Stanley Wertheim and Paul Sorrentino. New York: Columbia University Press.

Crisler, Jesse (ed.). (1986). *Frank Norris: Collected Letters*. San Francisco: Book Club of California.

Dreiser, Theodore. (1925/2000). *An American Tragedy*. New York: Signet/New American Library.

Dunbar, Paul Laurence. (1902/2005). *The Sport of the Gods: And Other Essential Writings*, ed. Shelley Fisher Fishkin and David Bradley. New York: Modern Library.

Fleissner, Jennifer. (2004). *Women, Compulsion, Modernity: The Moment of American Naturalism*. Chicago: University of Chicago.

Gandal, Keith. (1997). *The Virtues of the Vicious: Jacob Riis, Stephen Crane, and the Spectacle of the Slum*. New York: Oxford University Press.

Graham, Don (ed.). (1980). *Critical Essays on Frank Norris*. Boston: G. K. Hall.

Hart, James D. (ed.). (1970). *A Novelist in the Making; A Collection of Student Themes and the Novels* Blix *and* Vandover *and* The Brute. Cambridge, MA: Belknap Press of Harvard University Press.

Hochman, Barbara. (1988). *The Art of Frank Norris, Storyteller*. Columbia: University of Missouri Press.

Howells, William Dean. (1887). Editor's study. *Harper's New Monthly Magazine* 76, 451: 153–6.

Howells, William Dean. (1889). Editor's study. *Harper's New Monthly Magazine* 79, 474: 962–7.

Howells, William Dean. (1900/1973). Howells on Crane as a slum novelist. In Richard M. Weatherford (ed.), *Stephen Crane: The Critical Heritage* (pp. 59–60). London: Routledge and Kegan Paul.

Howells, William Dean. (1901). *Heroines of Fiction*, 2 vols. New York and London: Harper and Brothers.

Karaganis, Joseph. (2000). Naturalism's nation: Toward *An American Tragedy*. *American Literature* 72, 1: 153–80.

Link, Eric Carl. (2004). *The Vast and Terrible Drama: American Literary Naturalism in the Late Nineteenth Century*. Tuscaloosa: University of Alabama Press.

London, Jack. (1988). *The Letters of Jack London*, ed. Earle Labor, Robert C. Leitz, and I. Milo Shepard. Stanford, CA: Stanford University Press.

London, Jack. (1993). *Martin Eden*. New York: Penguin Books.

McElrath, Joseph, Jr. and Jesse S. Crisler. (1974). *Frank Norris: A Reference Guide*. Boston: G. K. Hall.

Michaels, Walter Benn. (1987). *The Gold Standard and the Logic of Naturalism: American Literature at the Turn of the Century*. Berkeley: University of California Press.

Mitchell, Lee Clark. (1989). *Determined Fictions: American Literary Naturalism*. New York: Columbia University Press.

Monteiro, George. (2000). *Stephen Crane's Blue Badge of Courage*. Baton Rouge: Louisiana State University Press.

Morace, Robert. (1980). The writer and his middle class audience: Frank Norris, a case in point. In Don Graham (ed.), *Critical Essays on Frank Norris* (pp. 53–62). Boston: G. K. Hall.

Nagel, James. (1980). *Stephen Crane and Literary Impressionism*. University Park: Pennsylvania State University Press.

Norris, Frank. (1899/1997). *McTeague: A Story of San Francisco: Authoritative Text, Contexts, Criticism*, ed. Donald Pizer, 2nd edn. New York: W. W. Norton.

Norris, Frank. (1901/1986). Frank Norris's Weekly Letter – August 3, 1901. In *Frank Norris: Novels and Essays*, ed. Donald Pizer (pp. 1139–42). New York: Library of America.

Norris, Frank. (1986a). The novel with a "purpose." In *Frank Norris: Novels and Essays*, ed. Donald Pizer (pp. 1196–1200). New York: Library of America.

Norris, Frank. (1986b). *The Octopus*. In *Frank Norris: Novels and Essays*, ed. Donald Pizer (pp. 573–1098). New York: Library of America.

Norris, Frank. (1986c). A plea for romantic fiction. In *Frank Norris: Novels and Essays*, ed. Donald Pizer (pp. 1165–9). New York: Library of America.

Norris, Frank. (1986d). The responsibilities of the novelist. In *Frank Norris: Novels and Essays*, ed. Donald Pizer (pp. 1206–10). New York: Library of America.

Norris, Frank. (1986e). Theory and reality: An old author and a new writer consider the same problem. In *Frank Norris: Novels and Essays*, ed. Donald Pizer (pp. 1103–5). New York: Library of America.

Norris, Frank. (1986f). Zola as a romantic writer. In *Frank Norris: Novels and Essays*, ed. Donald Pizer (pp. 1106–8). New York: Library of America.

Pizer, Donald. (1984). *Realism and Naturalism in Nineteenth-Century American Literature*, revised edn. Carbondale: Southern Illinois University Press.

Rhodes, Chip. (1996). Twenties fiction, mass culture, and the modern subject. *American Literature* 68, 2: 385–404.

Sorrentino, Paul. (2006). *Stephen Crane Remembered*. Tuscaloosa: University of Alabama Press.

Susman, Warren. (1984). "Personality" and the making of twentieth-century culture. In *Culture as History: The Transformation of American Society in the Twentieth Century* (pp. 271–85). New York: Pantheon Books.

Trachtenberg, Alan. (1982). Experiments in another country: Stephen Crane's city sketches. In Eric Sundquist (ed.), *American Realism: New Essays* (pp. 138–54). Baltimore: Johns Hopkins University Press.

Walcutt, Charles Child. (1973). *American Literary Naturalism, a Divided Stream*. Westport, CT: Greenwood Press.

Wharton, Edith. (1905/1990). *The House of Mirth*, ed. Elizabeth Ammons. New York: Norton.

Woolf, Virginia. (1928/1970). Mr. Bennett and Mrs. Brown. In *The Hogarth Essays*, ed. Leonard Woolf and Virginia Woolf (pp. 3–29). Freeport, NY: Books for Libraries Press.

Yezierska, Anzia. (1925/1999). *Bread Givers: A Novel*, revised edn. New York: Persea Books.

10
Money and Things: Capitalist Realism, Anxiety, and Social Critique in Works by Hemingway, Wharton, and Fitzgerald

Richard Godden

I

Writing in 1931 for the *Saturday Evening Post*, in nostalgic vein, Fitzgerald observed that "the Jazz Age . . . raced along under its own power, served by great filling stations full of money" (Fitzgerald 2005: 134), fueling, presumably, Dos Passos's "billiondollar speedup" (Dos Passos 1937: 526). Whether treating of the opulent, the merely respectable, or the poor, the fiction of the 1920s seems well aware of "The Big Money." It may be Gatsby's enormous liquid assets or Clyde Griffiths's "downpour of small change" (Dreiser 1926: 51), but its influence is felt across the board. On the evidence of a rise in disposable income and an increase in consumer credit, it would be fair to assume that, if not on your street, then on someone else's, "a whole race [was] going hedonistic, deciding on pleasure" (Fitzgerald 2005: 132). The Lynds note dryly of Middletown – their "mid-channel sort of American community" – that "more and more of the activities of living are coming to be strained through the bars of the dollar sign" (Lynd and Lynd 1929: 80–1).

The 1920s were *par excellence* a commercial age. Monopoly capitalism flourished, as corporations, employing criteria of efficiency, standardized production in the pursuit of steadily rising sales – and were successful. After the slump in demand (1920–2) and the labor unrest of the immediate postwar years (1919–21), American capital persuaded its workforce to buy it out of trouble. By learning the equation that Christine Frederick in 1929 expressed as "Pay them more, sell them more, prosper more" (quoted in Ewen 1976: 22), with an emphasis on the last two terms, capital nominally avoided the overproduction latent in its war-prompted technological revolution. "Ten years after the war conspicuous consumption had become a national mania" (Leuchtenburg 1958: 200). Chain stores, car lots, service industries, cinemas, and advertising agencies proliferated. Shop windows were necessarily everywhere.

Window gazing with their average 14 percent wage increase (between 1922 and 1929), the manufacturing workers could not know, but might have suspected, that the prevailing financial growth of corporations, over the same period, was running at 286 percent. A boom in consumer credit was the workers' placebo and the corporations' mainstay. Nonetheless, a reorganization of capital on the scale of the teen years and the 1920s must involve crisis. It is to be remembered that even as the war stimulated the centralization of capital, so, during each year of the USA's participation, over a million workers struck (more than in any single year prior to 1915). Furthermore, between 1915 and 1922, the ratio of striking to employed workers in all industrial and service industries remained constantly on a par with levels reached between 1934 and 1937. The economic historian James O'Connor argues: "Economic recoveries and expansions occur when capital successfully restores its domination of labor by restructuring the directly producing class itself" (O'Connor 1984: 29). Put crudely, postwar capital offered its workforce full Taylorism for a fuller consumption basket, and the offer was accepted, though not without anxiety, since being drawn "through the bars of a dollar sign" must necessarily hurt.

The compensatory consumer dollar may be perceived as inflicting structural pain in two areas – on the laboring and on the purchasing body. Workers received an enlarged share of the consumption basket, but only at the cost of massive workplace innovation: "time and motion," "job segmentation," "speed up," "flow," and the increasingly visible hand of management, silk-gloved in "science," effectively obliterated a class – the craft worker. Iron molders, rollers, and heaters, glass blowers, bricklayers, machinists, jigger-men in potteries, lasters in shoe factories, mulespinners . . . the roll is as long as the replacement list is short: for the most part by the mid-1920s "machine minders" were supervised by "managers." Systematic management grew from systematic deskilling, itself reflecting a clash of class wills during which middle managers (a new salariat) separated labor's head from its hands, and redistributed its working body in search of a maximization of labor time. F. W. Taylor, primary theorist of that dismemberment synonymous with time-and-motion study is plain: as early as 1911 he insists that, "the great mass of traditional knowledge, which in the past has been in the head of the workman" must be transferred to management. Force will be necessary if worker autonomy and codes of ethical work behavior are to be abolished: "it is only through *enforced* standardization of methods, *enforced* adoption of the best implements and working conditions, *enforced* cooperation that this faster work can be assured" (Taylor, quoted in Montgomery 1979: 114, italics in original). The net gain was a 50 percent increase in manufacturing production between 1922 and 1929, prompting wage increases to counter the risk of overproduction. The enlarged wage, like the fast line, was a form of labor control. As part of a history of technological change they, like the history of most things, are elements in a "story of who rides on whom and how" (Genovese and Genovese 1983: 212).

What is disarming about the labor history of the 1920s after 1922 is the ease with which the riders and the ridden appeared to enjoy their "progress." Strikes were rare, union membership fell away steeply from its five million high, and the entire tone of labor's struggle changed. Between 1910 and 1922 it was characterized by a direct, mass-involved challenge to managerial authority, and was explicitly dedicated to "workers' control." The primary demand for the eight-hour day should be read as a demand for the management of "time." Increasingly, post-1922, with the eight-hour day grudgingly won, and wages raised, the employed manufacturing worker was ready to see labor protest less as class antagonism than as a means to the right to be a better consumer, though consumption, like production, carried risk of structural damages associated with shrinkage of the social body. In order to maximize profit, capital must privatize need; there is more money to be made from the gratifications of the *isolato* than from the shared satisfactions of a group. For example, if the home can be privatized and the family individualized, then potential points of sale are multiplied. During the 1920s "professionalized motherhood" and "scientific house-work" were heavily marketed. By subdividing a previously unified activity like housework into various distinct tasks, each of which requires a machine, capital produces a range of separate industries and of separate opportunities for surplus. Throughout the decade new kitchens shrank, since the segmentation and capitalization of home production meant that space was no longer required for canning, sewing, bread baking, cleaning. At the same time the sociability latent in those activities diminished. With fast foods and clothing brands readily purchasable, satisfaction increasingly became a matter between individuals and their dollars. The "individual" is therefore a market target: social indivisibility must give way to "individualism," as selfhood is persuaded to reside in the isolated and full gratification of needs through commodities.

This, of course, is an abstract fantasy: need is never purely a form of capital. To read *Middletown* is to recognize that needs construed as commodities, and often satisfied as such, were experienced as social needs frustrated. Time and again the new means to leisure elicit reference to older pleasures. A voice will celebrate the private home ("I do very little visiting – mostly keep in touch with my friends by telephone") while another recalls the neighborhood ("Neighbors used to be in each other's houses much more than they are now") (Lynd and Lynd 1929: 274). "Radio" recalls "chorus choir," "washing machine" recalls "laundry" (pp. 174–5), and the repeated allusions to cars and movies rarely occur without recognition of their decentralizing effects on the family. The associations are not nostalgic: they are resentful – based on an active experience of the slippage of "use" into "exchange" which attends the historical extensions of abstract labor and of the abstracted individual. The Lynds imply that even at the decade's height consumerism was a troubled comforter.

As the segmentation of markets proliferated and the hard sell hardened, the consumer was more likely to experience the tensions latent within "individualism": free, but at liberty to buy; autonomous, but market-dependent; internally atomized, while addressed as the single focus of knowledge, sensation, and decision; intensely active (whether as a worker or a manager) and yet passively receptive of goods which satisfied while dissatisfying. The contradictions concentrate into a cultural type for whom the

shop window induces anxiety and resentment as a muted underpinning to the pleasures on display.

II

For Hemingway, at least, the great good place did not lie in the shop window. He
offers open spaces, trout streams, mountain slopes and bullrings as venues where "the
real thing" may be experienced directly. Tony Tanner classically typifies a dominant
reading when he assures us that for Hemingway "only concrete things, perceptible
manifestations of nature, have certain value," and that "the prose makes permanent
the attentive wonder of the senses: it mimes out the whole process, impression by
impression" (Tanner 1977: 241, 247). He adds that the liaison between nature's
objects and human senses is most pure when undertaken by one man alone in the
natural world. Little seems more innocent of the big sell than an uncaught trout far
from any town:

> He watched them holding themselves with their noses into the current, many trout in
> deep, fast moving water, slightly distorted as he watched far down through the glassy
> convex surface of the pool, its surface pushing and swelling smooth against the resistance
> of the log-driven piles of the bridge. At the bottom of the pool were the big trout. Nick
> did not see them at first. Then he saw them at the bottom of the pool, big trout looking
> to hold themselves on the gravel bottom in a varying mist of gravel and sand, raised in
> spurts by the current.
>   Nick looked down into the pool from the bridge. It was a hot day. A kingfisher flew
> up the stream. It was a long time since Nick had looked into a stream and seen trout.
> They were very satisfactory. As the shadow of the kingfisher moved up the stream, a
> big trout shot upstream in a long angle, only his shadow marking the angle, then lost
> his shadow as he came through the surface of the water, caught the sun, and then, as
> he went back into the stream under the surface, his shadow seemed to float down the
> stream with the current, unresisting, to his post under the bridge where he tightened
> facing up into the current.
>   Nick's heart tightened as the trout moved. He felt all the old feeling. (Hemingway
> 1954: 187)

In the era of the Model T Ford, of federal highway expansion and a growing
national park system, it must have been increasingly difficult to find a trout stream
which, at least conceptually, was not an extension of the workplace. To be amused,
in a decade noted for the production of amusement goods, is to prolong production; and "'leisure time' . . . quite characteristically in a pecuniary society is
'spent'" (Lynd and Lynd 1929: 225, also see Currell 2005: 12–30). Nick Adams
seeks to forget the larger context, emphatically reassuring himself that, "The river
was there" (Hemingway 1954: 186). Hemingway is compliant, emphatically
burning the township of Seney to establish Nature in contrast to Society – and

yet what Nick watches are effectively cryptograms for the intrusion of industrial production into Nature and into the nature of perception. My phrasing derives from Adorno. Commenting on the ears of corn blowing in the wind at the close of Chaplin's *The Great Dictator* (1940), Adorno notes, "Nature is viewed . . . as a healthy contrast to society, and is therefore denatured. Pictures showing green trees, a blue sky, and moving clouds make these aspects of nature into so many cryptograms for factory chimneys and service stations" (Adorno and Horkheimer 1979: 149).

To make a case for rereading Hemingway's blue skies from within the system of commodity production that was his historical environment, I shall try to relocate his central preoccupation with perception and the perceived object in what for me is its true context – the context of consumption. My main concern is to establish the hegemony of price in Hemingway's fiction, so that the poverty of critical terms like "real," "matter of fact," "objective," "immediate," "concrete," and "experiential" may at least be considered. By drawing analogies between things behind shop windows and Hemingway's "real thing," and between the uniquely seeing, feeling, smelling, hearing Hemingway hero and the individualized consumer, I hope to establish grounds for an alternative way of reading Hemingway.

There is something abstracted about the phenomenological innocence through which Nick Adams views his trout: "the real-thing, the sequence of motion and fact" (Hemingway 1932: 10), arrives in the prose attended by a commercial after-image. The trout would not look out of place behind glass. An object in a shop window is a strange kind of object. If it could speak, and were honestly inclined, it might confess to a double life, both real and abstract. Existing here and now and in immediate fullness, it prompts passers-by to consider not its uses, but the advertising copywriter's promise of its uses. For George F. Babbitt a khaki blanket "bought . . . for a camping trip which had never come off" symbolizes "gorgeous loafing, gorgeous cursing, virile flannel shirts" (Lewis 1965: 14). Babbitt mentally fingers copy, not cloth. Nick Adams succeeds in getting away from it all; however, as he watches the "slightly distorted" trout "far down through the glassy convex surface of the pool," he too sees with an eye conditioned by consumption. He is like any window shopper. Gradually, the onlooker distils an image of the object: but with touch and use denied by the glassy surface, the image may misrepresent. Behind their windows the equivocal promise of objects is most manifest:

> There, in the market place, things stand still. They are under the spell of one activity only; to change owners. They stand there waiting to be sold. While they are there for exchange they are not there for use. A commodity marked out at a definite price, for instance, is looked upon as being frozen to absolute immutability throughout the time during which its price remains unaltered. And the spell does not only bind the doings of man. Even nature herself is supposed to abstain from any ravages in the body of this commodity and to hold her breath, as it were, for the sake of the social business of man. (Sohn-Rethel 1978: 25)

Those with an eye to Nature would challenge my intrusion of the marketplace into Nick's perceptual habits. Tanner emphasizes immediacy and transience: his reading of the story casts Nick as a meticulous observer whose refusal to be distracted from the present pays off – intense moments of experience are achieved, and through them a "rapport," albeit "fading," "with nature." The reading is partial. The gleam of light on the side of the leaping trout is anything but momentary, since it can never re-enter the stream: it is forever a snapshot of immediacy. The trout is timeless, but not with the recurrent and cyclical eternity of the so-called "natural world": it has a history because its "now" contains the "now and forever" promised by the window display. More correctly, the trout's promise is multiple, each stage of its leap being recorded and fixed in immutability. Much of the effect results from the repetition of the possessive "his" in "his shadow": initially the phrase could refer to the kingfisher or to the fish – a trout rising to strike at a bird's shadow as at a fly – the third usage undoes the elision, defining the shadow as the trout's. The pronoun does not shift in pursuit of the exact "facts of the matter" or to recover "the textures and contours of the objective world" (Tanner 1977: 255): "his" is precisely *in*accurate in order to prejudice our eye in favor of a radical segmentation of objects. Delayed, and eventually sorted out, the trout yields several trout, rising, jumping, turning, returning – a photographic sequence worthy of the *National Geographic*.

Nick sees like a good consumer, "successively" (Tanner 1977) in private, and without much thought. To think too much might be to waken numerous anxieties. Consumerism sticks with surface and sensation, the better to ignore "the iron man" and all the complexities of labor, capital, and credit, from which the surfaces take their shine. As Nick fishes the Black River, corporate capital subdivides the senses in order to sell to each and every manufactured modality. Nick's eye is culturally responsive; his sight increases gratification by granting autonomy to each of the trout's several parts.

Nature, Nick, and the reader hold their breath as, via the immutability of time and place that the image guarantees, the trout passes through reverence towards price. Such transitions are delicate: the trout remains a trout, but everything is changed. The objective structures of the animal are no longer simply "natural," rather they express the cultural moment of the perceiver's life. As objects increasingly exist for their price, so their physicality is translated. Instead of money being the temporary realization of the price of commodities, the commodities become temporary realizations of their price. The manner of the trout's abstracted physicality embodies a particular moment in the history of exchange abstraction.

III

Perhaps the trout might best be comprehended as an instance of "capitalist realism" (Marchand 1985: xviii), an item seen from within a cultural habit of perception that accedes reality to the sales imperative: as Wolfgang Haug puts it, in a study of commodity aesthetics, considered from "the viewpoint of exchange" (Haug 1986: 15, also see Haug 1987: 103–20) an object's use amounts to a "transitory phase" or "lure" existing merely to accomplish the vital sale smoothly. For this to happen the use of objects and persons must be subordinated to their appearance, or, in advertising terms, to their capacity to carry an image (see Debord 1973, particularly section 34). It follows that any commodity's function as part of the needs of someone is subordinated to the item's ability to propose a "promise" that will ensure purchase. "Use" takes on a "double reality," with the emphasis on its second or promissory term, since "use," gone to market, atrophies to "appearance of use," "impression of use," or "promise of use." Consequently "[the commodity's] aesthetic promise of use value . . . becomes an instrument in accumulating money. . . . Sensuality in this context becomes the vehicle of an economic function" (Haug 1986: 16).

What happens to bodies, whether of persons or trout, under such conditions? They grow double-bodied, and in the split between the body of use and the body according to exchange, the concreteness of the former recedes. Fredric Jameson notes: "in the commodity age, need as a purely physical and material impulse (as something 'natural'), has given way to a structure of artificial stimuli, artificial longings, such that it is no longer possible to separate the . . . primary from the luxury satisfaction in them" (Jameson 1986: 78). "Capitalist realism" is plainly a realm of artifice, but of *real* artifice, or of artifice made real by the fact that consumers contribute their senses to a promissory illusion. The spectacle of commodity fascinates because its images take their sensualized bodies (in a kind of optic dialogue) from the sensuality of the possible purchaser. In advertisements, people are effectively shown the unfulfilled aspects of their lives by way of commercial images which promise satisfaction – the promissory image works by taking desires from the eyes of its viewer and bringing those desires to the surface of the commodity. Through such borrowings, commodities take on sexuality as an assistant, and any exchange is ghosted by an aura of sexual enjoyment (Haug 1986: 56). Of course, the sex of these circumstances is an illusion, whose real substance is the currency it exists to elicit. Disappointment attends such liaisons, at least at the level of use; so much so that satisfaction remains curiously hooked to the level of exchange itself. The frisson begins to lie in the moment of purchase, which becomes the climax of sexuality as it is practiced within "capitalist reality." If objects and bodies become sensual, in so far as they are excuses for exchange, their true sensuality lies in their ability to elicit purchase. Money becomes the new sensuality, and bodies are sexual in so far as they mirror the process of exchange. Because value resides in image (or appearance) use is *de*sensualized and image is eroticized. Under such circumstances, the body is disembodied as it passes into the "second skin" of commodity, which is itself simply a guise worn by profit. Which amounts to saying that money has become more exciting than the body which is its vehicle, and that, as a result, the body itself is sensualized primarily in and through money.

What I have done by way of Haug, Marchand, and others is to theorize the promoter's wildest hope. I do so in order to characterize a cultural dominant, emergent in the 1920s, from the perspective of those who dominate. From within such a perspective, habitués of commodity tend to partial or fetishized sight: consider how consumers are encouraged to forget production, and how, as a consequence, when looking at things they may well most typically see objects, to the exclusion of the human processes that went into them. Such sight lines are a learned cultural preference, by way of which things seen are only and actually parts of things. But to sense that partiality – experienced as a pain akin to loss – premises the potential of escape from impairment.

Nick Adams's trout and the eroticized "second skin" of aestheticized commodities each, in differing degree, instance reification, or the process whereby human experience takes on the quality of things (on reification see Rose 1978: 27–51, Bewes 2002: 3–90). To recognize reification necessarily involves anxiety over that transmutation whereby the inevitable sentient continuity between subject and object (the "you" and the "not you") tilts in favor of commodified objects. Nick Adams, for example, fishing the Black River, thinks in "things" (Flint 1972, Williams 1950), those things in effect becoming "the objective body of his subjectivity" (Marx 1965: 69). As such, he exemplifies Hemingway's dictat, "You've got to see it, feel it, smell it, hear it" (quoted in Stipes-Watts 1971: 19), but try "not to think about it" (Hemingway 1985: 29); by which means – stylistically transcribed into a prose imagism involving a language of concrete nouns, ambulatory verbs, prepositions, and precious little else – objects, or "what really happened in action" (Hemingway 1932: 10) will stand in for interiority. Writing in 1919, T. S. Eliot proposes that interior states can be externalized as formulaic objects. Eliot's and Hemingway's objectivity is symptomatic of a more general problem:

> The only way of expressing emotion in the form of art is by finding "an objective correlative"; in other words, a set of objects, a situation, a chain of events which shall be the formula of the *particular* emotion; such that when the external facts, which must terminate in sensory experience are given, the emotion is immediately evoked. (Eliot 1932: 145, italics in original)

The claim is preposterous, but partially convincing to a culture whose members are increasingly encouraged to treat themselves as objects and to pleasure themselves through objects. Take,

> Arms that are braceleted and white and bare
> (but, in the lamplight downed with light brown hair!)
> (Eliot 1968: 15)

Depending upon one's cosmetic-politics, the undepilated arm is more or less attractive. Immaculately mimed, its expressive precision is limited. What Eliot has produced is an overpowering object freighted with an aura of unplumbable depths. Hemingway's famed omissions (the icebergs of critical commonplace; see Wilson

1997 for a classic instance) are similarly engineered. But as with the trout (one of the devices through which Nick displaces his anxiety over fishing the swamp), such depths (all on the surface), reflect the structures of the commodity rather than the consciousness of the perceiver. Or, more exactly, they reflect the subject who, in taking a certain kind of "thing" as his expression and extension, subsumes himself within that which (because it is partial) resists knowledge. I would stress that the opacity of the commodity derives neither from itself (as an object), nor from consciousness, but inheres rather in the economic process of commodity production itself (see Rose 1978: 45, 47). Marx notes, in his chapter on "The Commodity" in the first volume of *Capital*:

> The mysterious character of the commodity-form consists therefore simply in the fact that the commodity reflects the social characteristic of men's own labor as objective characteristics of the products of labor themselves. . . . [Furthermore] the commodity form, and the value-relation of the products of labor within which it appears, have absolutely no connection with the physical nature of the commodity and the material relations arising out of this. It is nothing but the definite social relations between men themselves which assumes here, for them, the fantastic form of a relation between things. (Marx 1976: 164–5)

The reason for such a "fantastic" transmutation lies in the owner's need to obscure from the worker the extent to which the value of the product derives from and expresses the worker's labor: or, differently put, from the owner's need "to sever the worker from his own extended body" (Scarry 1985: 251), as substantiated in the product. Hence labor is abstracted into "labor time"; and this "labor time" is abstracted into wage or price, which is, from the viewpoint of exchange, held to be the *modus vivandi* of the product (that without which it cannot go to the store). The appearance of the good in the shop window compounds the owner's abstractions, by abstracting production from the product. Amnesia has always been a staple of a successful commodity culture; however, as the sales pitch broadened during the 1920s, forgetting became imperative. The advertisers' journal, *Printer's Ink*, noted retrospectively in 1938:

> The first advertising sold the name of the product. In the second stage the specifications of the product were outlined. Then came emphasis upon the use of the product. With each step the advertisement moved farther away from the factory viewpoint and edged itself closer to the mental processes of the consumer. (quoted in Ewen 1976: 86)

Much has to be forgotten for the immediate and yet disembodied materiality of the commodity to take its promissory form. Indeed, Adorno might be offering a theoretical annotation of the *Printer's Ink* observation, when, in a letter to Walter Benjamin, commenting on Benjamin's essay, "On Some Motifs in Baudelaire," he notes: "All reification is forgetting: objects become purely thing-like the moment they are retained for us without the continued presence of their other aspects: when something of them has been forgotten." He adds that to formulate "a proper critique of reification" would require an "unfolding [of] the contradictory moments that are involved in such forgetting" (Adorno and Benjamin 1999: 321). Approaching the shop window from the factory floor, workers during the 1920s might be held potentially equipped for critique. They were, after all, the first generation of American labor to benefit from the Fordist premise, "Pay them more, sell them more, prosper more." But experience of the shop floor, in both senses of that phrase, might better be deemed grounds for a double dose of disembodiment – a conclusion ratified by the quietude of organized labor during the decade. Nonetheless, once reification is understood historically as a structural product of Fordist capital's need to impose amnesia and body loss on its workforce and consumer base, reification seems unlikely to appear without an attendant anxiety over the experience of impairment, and this anxiety might in turn operate as a locus for critique (see Bewes 2002: 89, 94).

Nick Adams goes fishing to recuperate from spinal injury and to forget.[1] Though comforted by his dominion over things, he seems unable to resist a certain anxiety resident in those things. So, for example, his trout, transcribed from perception to page, arrives as both "the real thing" and a trophy, seen through a "glassy . . . surface." Symptomatically, many of Hemingway's routes to the real involve sports productive of heads, horns, skins, and mounted fish. Taxidermy is implicit in much of the fiction. The presence of stuffed beasts is awkward for a writer preoccupied with "the real thing." The taxidermist, like the capitalist realist, is engaged in intimate interferences productive of unnatural naturalism. He too produces the real from the real for gain. His product looks like itself, is tagged and very often stands behind glass. Hemingway is aware of his secret-sharer. *The Sun Also Rises* (1926) contains a number of references to taxidermy and features the projected stuffing of several dogs, two racehorses, and a horse-drawn cab, not to mention the more conventional bull's head and fish. The joke is both simple and anxious, expressive of Hemingway's suspicion that the authenticity of his real things tends to stilled life; as such it catches the anxiety without containing its cause – that within a Fordist regime of accumulation concreteness is in laughable retreat from itself.

Read through Marx's work on reification, Hemingway's taxidermic tendency contains a critique of commodity as structurally duplicitous: a thing required simultaneously to function as use ("coarsely sensuous"), and as price ("exhibiting not an atom of matter"), and therefore at once alive (immediate) and dead (an abstracted value) (Marx 1976: 138–9). Since that critique stays latent within the perception of Hemingway's hurt perceivers, he and they remain formalists, at a loss among the things that wound them.

Hemingway's "things" are truly knowable only through the anxiety that attends them, and this anxiety raises a question: how else – and perhaps more fully – might one know "things" as they emerge towards critique in the literature of a commodifying culture? Before attempting an answer I will consider an example of an alternative response to a commodity. Regarding leisured New Yorkers of the 1870s from the perspective of 1920 Edith Wharton is much preoccupied with social transition as registered in mannered artifacts: hence her attention to "Worth dresses" in *The Age of Innocence*. The company gathered at Mrs Archer's Thanksgiving dinner are concerned as to whether it is "vulgar" to wear Parisian fashions bought at Worth in the year of their purchase, or whether custom requires that such garments be "put away" for two years prior to display. One guest, Miss Jackson, blames the banker Beaufort for starting "the new fashion by making his wife clap her new clothes on her back as soon as they arrived: I must say at times it takes all Regina's distinction not to look like . . . like . . ." (Wharton 1974: 216). Beaufort is a banker of uncertain origin and questionable probity, who stabilized his liquidities by marrying Regina Dallas, "a penniless beauty . . . [from] one of America's most honoured families," given " '*droit de cité*' . . . in New York society" (p. 20) by her relation to the Mansons and the Rushworths. Miss Jackson's ellipses contain two options: "like . . ." an advertisement, or "like . . ." a prostitute (ameliorated through such euphemisms as "actress" or "mistress"). The missing word transforms the words that surround it, so that if Regina displays her sensuality too overtly for purposes of profit, her name shifts from the regal towards the vaginal (it should be remembered that Wharton names Beaufort's mistress and second wife, Fanny Ring). "Worth" too is destabilized: even as a reduction in the turnover time of a particular "look" realizes enhanced profits for the fashion house, so retail outlets, like "Worth," will change their emphasis. Plate glass, an invention of the 1870s, allows fashion to be "flaunt[ed]," and mitigates against the laying away of any garment so that it may "mellow under lock and key" (p. 215). Where "Worth" is synonymous with throughput, its value shifts from the register of ethics to that of price.

Miss Jackson's tongue is stopped by a number of awkward conjunctions, spatial, temporal and social. She pauses, perhaps, as the "marble palaces" (or department stores), which proliferated during the decade, come under pressure from the furnishings, "the heavy carpets, the watchful servants, the perpetually reminding tick of disciplined clocks" (Wharton 1974: 183), so characteristic of the interiors of the haute bourgeoisie. Her hiatus may owe something to the retrospection of those New York clocks, which ensure that each social season repeats the timetable of the last, as they confront, in the "perpetually renewed stack of cards and invitations on the hall table" (p. 183) beneath them, a temporal "lock and key" – evidence of the need to monitor the meetings of bourgeois sons and daughters in department store and park, the new social spaces orientated to the futurity of display. That Sillerton Jackson should resolve the lapse occasioned by his sister's lost analogy, with "the air of producing an epigram" (p. 183), marks his attempt tonally to trump the social antagonisms tying his sister's tongue. His solution, "Like her rivals," tacitly reminds Mrs Archer's guests that Regina *has* a rival: the clashing of the spoken and unspoken names is replete with social disparity. That the conversation should pass immediately from the unmentionable mistress to Beaufort's "speculations" indicates how absolutely debates about the proper disposition of a dress displace, and yet reflect, economic tensions between kinds of capital and classes of women. An incomplete analogy has filled the room with different ways of life. The manner in which it is completed, in keeping with the furniture, aestheticizes the irreconcilable, eliciting a murmured "Oh, –" from the ladies present, and allowing the assembled company the comforting thought that form – in this case a form of words – can transform unpalatable social mutation into a repeatable *bon mot*.

My quasi-archeological itinerary for an elliptical moment of social awkwardness is both speculative and far from exhaustive, but should serve to show that an item from a shop window may be replete with divergent social scenes and interested parties, whose interference with one another materializes its meaning. Four years separate the literary creation of Wharton's Worth dress (1920) and Hemingway's trout (1924). Fifty years separate their historical contexts, though their joint inception remains "the viewpoint of exchange." Differences result less from their respective periods than from their divergent moments within the history of exchange abstraction. Wharton, apprenticed to the first hundred families of New York, understood with Thorstein Veblen that "the pervading principle and abiding test of good breeding is the require- ment of a substantial and patent waste of time" (Veblen 1970: 51). The late nine- teenth-century leisure class of her young adulthood enjoyed "conspicuous leisure" allied to "conspicuous consumption" (Veblen 1970: 41–60), but did so from a secure property base which permitted the purchase of time for training in "invidious com- parison" (James 1952: 33). To the leisured went the hard and "useless" work of pro- ducing, refining, reading and rereading distinctions, so as to maintain a grip on the information network invested in taste, and adding up to cultural power. Presumably, it took time to gloss a dress so dense with nuanced practice and contested information.

Pierre Bourdieu, writing of the passing of "manners" from one generation to the next, notes:

> nothing seems more incommunicable, more inimitable, and therefore, more precious, than the values given body, *made* body by the transubstantiation achieved by the hidden pedagogy, capable of instilling a whole cosmology, an ethic, a metaphysic, and political philosophy, through injunctions as insignificant as "stand up straight" or "don't hold your knife in your left hand." (Bourdieu 1977: 94)

Elaine Scarry adds, "What is remembered in the body is well remembered" (Scarry 1985: 109). I would quibble with Bourdieu only to suggest that at times of perceived change the implicit pedagogy of manners, requiring overt defense, slips from hiding towards discussion, as in Mrs Archer's dining room. Those of Beaufort's party, in the matter of female attire, wear their capital on their backs or more properly on the backs of their wives, mistresses, and daughters; in effect, they object that mannered time mitigates against turnover time, the new time necessary to shop-bought fashion.

Hemingway's trout, though differently dense, is equally remembered in the body and by way of a radically transformed shop window whose instructions – circa 1924 – stay secret and not a little anxious. With the turnover time of goods reduced, and the hard sell accordingly broadened, commodities in the 1920s existed in a temporality just as socially synthetic as that which surrounded a Worth dress, but having different imperatives. Goods in the pervasive shop window *must* sell. To do so, according to Sohn-Rethel, they "stand still," temporally speaking, requiring their purchasers to forget not only the past time of production, but also the present time of mutation (the window effect notwithstanding, products *do* change behind glass), in order to exist in a present which absorbs the future insofar as the good inhabits a future made perfect by its implied promise to be always as it *is* at the optimum point of sale. Such goods (after Adorno) are "objects become purely thing-like" because "something of them has been forgotten" – not least that distentive mix of times characteristic of human temporality (see Ricoeur 1990, particularly pp. 5–30).

Wharton's Worth dress, care of leisured pedagogy, retains a "whole cosmology" under dispute (see Lukács 1971: 198). Hemingway's trout, en route to the *National Geographic*, leaps into the enormous (and enormously vacant) present of "capitalist realism," from which, as perfectly disembodied as an advertising image, it "prepare[s] the way for the real distribution of commodit[ies]" (Haug 1986: 50). That distribution would be entirely more problematic if, to adapt Adorno, "the contradictory moments" which underpin a commodity's "thing-like" immediacy were exposed; if, that is, the anxieties and woundings which ground that commodity's commercial viability were part of its perceptual package. To risk further twisting my comparison: to understand Wharton's dress we are required to remember; to appreciate Hemingway's fish we must forget. The meaning of the Worth item is as volatile as the trout is fixed. Consequently, in *The Age of Innocence*, reification yields to a form of realism – antithetical to "capitalist realism" – best summarized by Brecht:

Realistic means: discovering the causal complexes of society/ unmasking the prevailing view of things as the view of those who are in power/ writing from the standpoint of the class which offers the broadest solutions for the pressing difficulties in which human society is caught up/ emphasizing the element of development/ making possible the concrete, and making possible abstraction from it. (Bloch, Lukács, Brecht, Benjamin, and Adorno 1980: 82)

IV

Zelda Fitzgerald's Alabama Knight, heroine of *Save Me the Waltz* (1932), observes, "We grew up founding our dreams on the infinite promise of American advertising" (p. 228). On the face of it, Gatsby complies: his properties – car, voice, smile, shirts, suit, mansions – seem to drift directly from "the nation's advertising showcase" (Marchand 1985: 7). However, to assume that Gatsby "resemble[s] the advertisement of the man" (Fitzgerald 1990: 114), and little else, is to ignore the temporal structure of the novel. Fitzgerald premises *The Great Gatsby* (1925) on an awkward recollection, as Nick Carraway attempts to remember the summer of 1922 from the significant distance of two years. Memory turns a man whose voice sounds like a quick flick "through a dozen magazines" (p. 65) into the son of a dirt-farmer. As Gatsby's ante-cedents emerge and are repressed, "contradictory moments" form within the text, moments that threaten to "unmask" its glamorous surfaces, exposing those "causal complexes" upon whose occlusion the spectral "concreteness" of capitalist reality entirely depends.

Nick's first encounter with his neighbor establishes a pattern for the narrator's habits of recall. Gatsby indulges in a theatrical autobiography, prefaced by the mimed taking of an oath, and ranging from American childhood to Oxford educa-tion. Nick is persuaded, but cannot shake the suspicion that he is being lied to: indeed, an enquiry as to place of birth should have undermined the whole performance:

> "What part of the Middle West?" I enquired casually.
> "San Francisco."
> "I see."
> "My family all died and I came into a good deal of money."
>
> His voice was solemn, as if the memory of that sudden extinction of a clan still haunted him. For a moment I suspected that he was pulling my leg, but a glance at him convinced me otherwise. (Fitzgerald 1990: 64)

Does Gatsby *know* where San Francisco is? If he does, his response is an odd gesture – as Nick would have it, "if personality is an unbroken series of successful gestures, then there was something gorgeous about him" (p. 8). Except that Gatsby's gestures are broken, and by Gatsby himself. To "tell . . . God's truth" he raises his right hand – isn't that taking truth a little too seriously? When speaking of loss he pauses in the right place, indeed, in a place so right that the addendum "all dead now" might just be bad acting, not lying. The creator of a criminal network operating bond fraud on a national scale can surely manage better lies than the one about San Francisco?

If Gatsby is acting, to what end does he perform his *un*successful gestures? "He lifted up the words and nodded at them – with his smile. The smile comprehended Montenegro's troubled history and sympathized with the brave struggles of the Mon-tenegrin people. It appreciated fully the chain of national circumstances which had elicited this tribute from Montenegro's warm little heart" (Fitzgerald 1990: 65). Gatsby performs "sympathetic understanding" in a manner which "submerge[s]" Nick's "incredulity . . . in fascination." Yet elsewhere Carraway will annotate the smile more skeptically:

> He smiled understandingly – much more than understandingly. It was one of those rare smiles with a quality of eternal reassurance in it, that you may come across four or five times in life. It faced – or seemed to face – the whole external world for an instant; and then concentrated on *you* with an irresistible prejudice in your favor. It understood you just as far as you wanted to be understood, believed in you as you would like to believe in yourself, and assured you that it had precisely the impression of you that, at your

best, you hoped to convey. Precisely at that point it vanished – and I was looking at an elegant young roughneck, a year or two over thirty, whose elaborate formality of speech just missed being absurd. Some time before he introduced himself I'd got a strong impression that he was picking his words with care. (Fitzgerald 1990: 48)

The smile is essence of empathy; infinitely renewable and endlessly pleasing. It mirrors the recipient's ideal profiles, beliefs, and hopes. Gatsby markets his face as though he stood in an exclusive window. Like any item of great price, his smile obliterates the actual relations and contexts that produce it, presenting itself as a unique facet of the onlooker's needs. The gesture seals an exchange, granting the beneficiary access to the house, the car, the romance, the class as perfect environments for his or her own best self-image. When the smiling stops, Gatsby displays his own past.

Given that Gatsby decides when and if to stop smiling, we should perhaps remember that "Gat," the root shared by Gatz and Gatsby, in German means "hole" and in Dutch "hole, gap, break."[2] The name announces its bearer's purpose, which is to interrupt the assumptions of others. Even at their first encounter, Nick's memoir indicates that he has a capacity to stumble on the holes that his subject introduces into his text. Take "clan": "His voice was solemn, as if the memory of that sudden extinction of a clan still haunted him" (Fitzgerald 1990: 64). The word is inappropriate, though one can see why Carraway uses it; Gatsby has just spoken of "ancestors" and appealed to "a family tradition." "Clan" is in keeping with the tenor of the dialogue – but was that tenor ever right? Nick knows better; he too has a clan ancestor:

The Carraways are something of a clan, and we have a tradition that we're descended from the Dukes of Buccleuch, but the actual founder of my line was my grandfather's brother, who came here in fifty-one, sent a substitute to the Civil War, and started the wholesale hardware business that my father carries on today. (Fitzgerald 1990: 8)

"Clan" then makes respectable the little murders from which family fortunes rise. Nick is quite capable of interrupting Gatsby's faked and funeral family history. Indeed, Gatsby's "solemnity," so like a leg-pull, prompts him to do so. Perhaps Carraway cannot respond because he has too much to defend. In 1924, living again in the Midwest (from which he had moved "permanently" east in 1922, p. 9), so far back in the bosom of his family that he tends to "snobbishly repeat" what his father "snobbishly suggest[s]" (p. 7), perhaps now working in the wholesale hardware business and married to the woman whose upper lip sweats when she plays tennis, he cannot afford to "lift" the word "clan" and "nod at it with his smile." Instead, across the conspicuous interruption of two years and half a continent, he insists, "Then it was all true" (p. 65), while sensing that it was not.

Before considering why Carraway writes a "life" that Gatsby does not deserve, I must establish the "San Francisco" remark as typical of its perpetrator. Several and crucial are the novel's partially discerned "[un]successful gestures." Although space demands that a listing replace full analysis, I cannot resist a briefly extended gloss on Gatsby's abrupt remark as to the delights of Daisy's voice: " 'Her voice is full of money,' he said suddenly. That was it. I'd never understood before. It was full of money – that was the inexhaustible charm that rose and fell in it, the cymbals' song of it . . . High in a white palace the king's daughter, the golden girl . . ." (Fitzgerald 1990: 15). Nick's punctuation registers shock: two brief sentences and a repetition suggest that he scarcely believes what he has heard, before choosing not to listen. After the dash, his rhythm grows melodious, his phrasing assonant, his reference literary in an orchestration of the cash nexus. As commentary on Gatsby's observation, Nick's whole statement is liable to fall to pieces, with fault lines developing along the ellipses: in the gaps, love meets money and adultery speaks to class – a dialogue in which Nick would rather not participate, but one which Gatsby's remark indicates that he wants articulated. That dialogue, glossed, might be cast as incidents in a class war.

In 1907, James Gatz, son of "shiftless and unsuccessful farm people" (Fitzgerald 1990: 95), encountered the copper baron Dan Cody, whose yacht represented "all the beauty and glamour of the world" (p. 96). Gatz "smiled," and on the basis of that smile, and a "brand new name" (so close to "brand name"), Jay Gatsby became Cody's personal assistant for five years (p. 96). Access to "glamour" required that he suppress his antecedents in agricultural labor. Later (in 1917), and with his "penniless[ness]" masked in "the invisible cloak" of an officer's uniform, he stole the "badge," "token," or "prize" of the leisure class (Veblen 1970: 33–40). The theft of Daisy took time (1917–22); the time it took for Gatsby to amass a "lure" of sufficient "promise" to attract a woman whose "voice is full of money." A déclassé but upwardly mobile Gatsby seeks status via the release and theft of the feminine leisure-class body; adultery allowing "Mr Nobody from Nowhere" (p. 123) to harden his liquid (bootlegged) and speculative (bond fraud) assets. In response Tom Buchanan, having disembodied his own wife for the purposes of display, and achieved temporary satisfaction through the body of the working-class female (Myrtle Wilson), extends the hegemony of his class to the abused industrial male (Mr Wilson). One can only speculate on how it was done, but it would seem likely that appeals to sexual ownership prompt a man with minimal property and resident in an industrial "valley of ashes" (p. 26) to murder Gatsby and destroy himself. The double death secures Buchanan's grip on the leisure-class "token" and releases him from the growing threat of his own uneasy liaison with the industrial class. Along the way, vengeance is enacted by the leisure-class female on the offending body of her working-class counterpart – one of Myrtle's breasts is left flapping, the blood drains away and her vitality is conspicuously evacuated (p. 131).

Nick cannot afford to write this kind of murder story. Social speculation, leading to a fuller sense of class relations, could induce in him a discovery of "casual complexes," from which perspective his own social position among the Carraway accumulations (founded on the sending of a substitute to kill or be killed) might grow uncomfortable. Yet part of Gatsby wants the story told – else why the one about San

Francisco, his line on Daisy's voice, or the broken smile. The list of calculated interruptions is readily extended. In asking Nick to set up a meeting that will preface the
affair with Daisy, and in requesting the use of Nick's bungalow for his purpose,
Gatsby is hiring a pimp to make a "gonnection." There is a payoff: Nick is offered
"confidential" information about bonds in a conversation which he sees as "one of the
crises of my life" (Fitzgerald 1990: 80). However, "because the offer was obviously
and tactlessly for a service to be rendered" (p. 84), Nick changes the subject. Why
then does Gatsby abjure subtlety? With Cody and Daisy he has his subtleties, with
Nick he is obvious, risking "crisis" in order to juxtapose crime and adultery. Jay
Gatsby plays and is the lover: we remember the cut grass, the white flowers, the dripping lilac trees; do we remember that just before the liaison he reads "a copy of Clay's
Economics" (p. 82) – an apt choice, given that Gatsby engages in economic subversion.
Having stolen the "token" that he loves, he stops the promissory parties, turns out
the lights and fires the servants, in a conspicuous interruption of his lifestyle. Gatsby
staffs his house with criminals and sets a villain at the door to play butler. His thin
rationale is that he will prevent gossip over Daisy's afternoon visits (p. 119). He can
hardly hope to protect Daisy's good name by making the house of assignation conspicuous and by advertising its owner as one who consorts with criminals. Domestics,
local tradesmen, particularly when aggrieved or fired, are gossip's very medium: the
grocery boy reports that the kitchen looks "like a pigsty," and the village is of the
opinion that "the new people weren't servants at all" (p. 108). Gatsby does not then
protect Daisy: rather he interrupts his smooth passage from purchaser through adul-
terer to husband. The ploy allows him to witness contradictions within himself. He
who consents to steal the "trophy" of the ruling class recognizes that his chosen course
is neither obligatory nor apt. Daisy's price will be separation from Wolfsheim and his
like. Gatsby, at the very moment of his success, takes the "prize" and sets it within
the criminal milieu that made the theft possible. He makes his self-division apparent:
dramatizing his opposed allegiances, he stands as a parable of the relationships
between leisure-class capital and the industrial base that it criminally exploits and
ignores.

Put another way: as Gatsby assumes those "mysterious . . . commodity form[s]"
that amount to capitalist reality, he displays that reality's repression of his own prior
materiality. In this, the pink suit is a master stroke. On the hot day of revelations,
and having warned Nick that his confession of adultery to Tom will be "harrowing,"
he selects entirely the wrong color for the "scene" (Fitzgerald 1990: 109). That the
garment should meet a complementary carpet is a fortuity engineered by Fitzgerald
to underline his character's disruptive impulse. "Gatsby stood in the centre of a
crimson carpet and gazed around with fascinated eyes. Daisy watched him and
laughed, her sweet exciting laugh; a tiny gust of powder rose from her bosom into
the air" (p. 110). The colors clash in a social collision that casts the garish light of
carnival on the surfaces of the Buchanans' drawing-room. While Tom Buchanan
telephones a working-class mistress, his wife – the very skin of her bourgeois bosom
powdering – is beguiled by an ex-proletarian capitalist of uncertain station.

To Georg Lukács, addressing reification:

> . . . it even appears as if the decisive crisis period of capitalism may be characterized by the tendency to intensify reification, to bring it to its head. . . . [so that] there is an increasing undermining of the forms of reification – one might describe it as a cracking of the crust because of the inner emptiness. (Lukács 1971: 208)

Gatsby's suit, smile, and house extend "the forms of reification" even as he deploys them to display the class contradictions from which they take their "gorgeous[ly]" (p. 8) empty forms. Nick witnesses "the cracking of the crust" only, and with stylish haste, to misrepresent what he has seen. Typically, he assures us that Gatsby reads Clay's *Economics* "with vacant eyes" (p. 82): we should not be reassured.

Nick bears anxious witness, at times reliable and unreliable in the same breath, a mode of narration that yields textual instability. Three usages may serve to indicate the implications of my point. Take "gorgeous," in Nick's early observation concerning Gatsby: "if personality is an unbroken series of successful gestures, then there was something gorgeous about him" (Fitzgerald 1990: 8). The hypothetical allows the negative a certain latitude, particularly since Nick's claim immediately succeeds his assertion of a seemingly contradictory position – "Gatsby . . . represented everything for which I have an unaffected scorn" (p. 8). "Un" released by "if" may yield "broken" and "*un*successful," before retrospectively troubling "unaffected" with the intimation that Nick's "scorn" may prove an "affection." Such semantic sleight of hand, inducing a skid of negatives, would be merely ingenious were it not that Nick goes on to compose a memoir studded with "broken gestures" and scant evidence of "scorn."

Consider also, "nonolfactory" (Fitzgerald 1990: 67). Driving with Gatsby over "the great bridge" into New York, "with the city rising up across the river in white heaps and sugar lumps," Nick describes the skyline as "built with a wish out of nonolfactory money." "Olfactory" ("of, or pertaining to a sense of smell"), as a portmanteau negative proves indigestible: in the previous paragraph, Gatsby has been pulled over for speeding by a "frantic policeman" on a vehicular allusion (p. 66). The motorcycle's "jug-jug-*spat*" recalls "The Waste Land" line, " 'Jug Jug' to dirty ears" (Eliot 1986: 64), though the "*spat*" might be thought further to soil Eliot's soiled sound effect. In "A Game of Chess," Eliot alludes to Philomel, pursued by Tereus and translated into a nightingale, as the source of the "Jug Jug" song. Nick's revision of New York is no less metamorphic, though the odor sticks notwithstanding: "nonolfactory," heard through "dirty ears," contains "factory" (recalling "the valley of ashes," driven through en route), ensuring that Gatsby's car will, for all the "wild promise" of the city seen from the Queensboro bridge, pass a hearse, in whose accompanying carriages, mourners from "south-eastern Europe" represent exactly that influx of cheap immigrant labor into the factories, from whose labor the "nonolfactory" skyline rose. I am reminded that the name "Carraway" refers, like "Daisy" and "Myrtle," to a flower, but to one whose seeds are traditionally thought "to ease the pains of the wind colic," and which have long been used to encourage digestion and evacuate noxious gases (*Culpeper's*).

Arguably, Carraway is a great deodorizer, who, whenever the contradictions within his subject become too disquieting, turns social aspiration into "dream," sexual politics into "romance," and translates class conflict as "tragedy." Carraway oil, in its "nonolfactory" capacity was often taken on "sugar lumps."

Nick attempts further fallible prose herbalism when (in my third example), he imagines Gatsby's body, shot by Wilson, floating on an airbed in a swimming pool: he refers to "its accidental course with its accidental burden" (Fitzgerald 1990: 154), having noted the "poor ghost" of the killer, "drift[ing] fortuitously about . . . like [an] ashen fantastic figure." Nick's emphasis on accident and fortuity should not survive the impact of his ellipsis, there being nothing either "fortuitous" or "accidental" about Mr Wilson's destination. He did not "drift," he was sent. Nick hesitates twice, creating, via reiteration and ellipsis, a gap or break in keeping with his subject, before overwriting the anxieties he senses in his own voice. The murderer emerges as an "ashen and fantastic" figure; "fantastic" because Nick refuses to conceive of Wilson's world and of the world of Gatsby's origins, "ashen" because Nick cannot deny that he has seen the industrial heartland, witnessing in the valley of ashes Adorno's "something . . . forgotten," or the material conditions from which Gatsby's real but immaterial existence has been produced.

Each usage ("gorgeous," "nonolfactory," "accidental") permits meaning to form, prior to prompting (though anxiety), the reversal of that meaning. Consequently, "gorgeous" retains its opposite; "nonolfactory" releases industrial odors, and "accidental" proves determinate. The potential dissolution of one meaning by another ensures that the facts referred to (a gesture, a skyline, a corpse) for all their concreteness, contain the realization that another world is possible; which possibility, available through the edginess of Nick Carraway's voice, amounts (after Adorno), to the imminent formulation of "a proper critique of reification," that is, to the "unfolding of the contradictory moments" that disrupt the given capitalist reality of early Fordism.

NOTES

1 Hemingway's heroes of the 1920s typically return wounded from war: their wounds cluster around the groin. Nick Adams is hit in the spine; Jake Barnes in *The Sun Also Rises* (1926) is sexually but unspecifically damaged; Frederick Henry in *A Farewell to Arms* (1929) is wounded in the leg. Perhaps the extreme type for all three is the unnamed self-castrater in "God rest you merry, gentlemen" (1933); the youth, refused medical assistance, operates on himself and misguidedly removes the member while leaving the means. My account seeks to suggest an alternative, and nonmilitary source, for the preoccupation with wound-

ing. Phallic ambivalence arises, I would argue, from an absolute contradiction between what capitalist production does to the individual, and what bourgeois ideology claims for the maimed and individualized self. Capital wounds what the ideology would heal with its notion of "autonomous individualism." Its destruction of the social will is veiled by the offer of a private and restorative will. Acceptance authenticates the senses as the locus of all satisfaction, while at the same time modifying the body.

2 By the close of the nineteenth century Germans had settled in considerable numbers

throughout the Midwest. During the last decades of the nineteenth century the Dutch, expanding from their earliest centers of settlement in Michigan and Wisconsin, spilled over into south-western Minnesota. By the first decade of the twentieth century Dutch farming communities were well established in Gatz's home state (and in the region of Fitzgerald's birthplace, St Paul).

REFERENCES AND FURTHER READING

Adorno, Theodor and Max Horkheimer. (1979). *Dialectic of Enlightenment*. London: Verso.

Adorno, Theodor W. and Walter Benjamin. (1999). *The Complete Correspondence 1928–1940*, trans. Nicholas Walker. Cambridge, UK: Polity.

Bewes, Timothy. (2002). *Reification or the Anxiety of Late Capitalism*. London: Verso.

Bloch, Ernst, Georg Lukács, Bertolt Brecht, Walter Benjamin, Theodor Adorno. (1980). *Aesthetics and Politics*, trans. R. Taylor. London: Verso.

Bourdieu, Pierre. (1977). *Outline of a Theory of Practice*, trans. Richard Nice. Cambridge, UK: Cambridge University Press.

Culpeper's Complete Herbal. (1653). London: W. Foulsham.

Currell, Susan. (2005). *The March of Spare Time*. Philadelphia: University of Pennsylvania Press.

Debord, Guy. (1973). *Society of the Spectacle*, trans. Fredy Perlman and John Supak. Detroit: Black and Red.

Dos Passos, John. (1937). *The Big Money*. New York: Constable.

Dreiser, Theodore. (1926). *An American Tragedy*. London: Constable.

Eliot, T. S. (1932). "Hamlet." In *Selected Essays, 1917–1932* (pp. 139–47). London: Faber.

Eliot, T. S. (1968). The Love Song of Alfred J. Prufrock. In *Collected Poems: 1909–1962* (pp. 13–17). London: Faber.

Eliot, T. S. (1986). *The Complete Poems and Plays of T. S. Eliot*. London: Guild Publishing.

Ewen, Stuart. (1976). *Captains of Consciousness: Advertising and the Social Roots of the Consumer*. New York: McGraw Hill.

Fitzgerald, F. Scott. (1990). *The Great Gatsby*. Harmondsworth, UK: Penguin.

Fitzgerald, F. Scott. (2005). Echoes of the Jazz Age. In *My Lost City: Personal Essays, 1920–1940*, ed. James L. W. West (pp. 106–15). Cambridge, UK: Cambridge University Press.

Fitzgerald, Zelda. (1982). *Save Me the Waltz*. Harmondsworth, UK: Penguin.

Flint, F. S. (1972). Imagisme. In Peter Jones (ed.), *Imagist Poetry* (p. 129). Harmondsworth, UK: Penguin.

Fox-Genovese, Elizabeth and Eugene Genovese. (1983). The political crisis of social history: A Marxian perspective. In *Fruits of Merchant Capital* (pp. 179–212). Oxford: Oxford University Press.

Haug, Wolfgang Fritz. (1986). *Critique of Commodity Aesthetics*, trans. Robert Bock. Oxford: Polity Press.

Haug, Wolfgang Fritz. (1987). *Commodity Aesthetics, Ideology and Culture*. New York: International General.

Hemingway, Ernest. (1932). *Death in the Afternoon*. London: Jonathan Cape.

Hemingway, Ernest. (1954). Big Two-Hearted River: Part I. In *The First Forty-Nine Stories* (pp. 186–95). London: Cape.

Hemingway, Ernest. (1985). *The Sun Also Rises*. London: Granada Publishing.

James, Henry. (1952). *The Bostonians*. London: John Lehmann.

Jameson, Fredric. (1986). *Marxism and Form*. Princeton, NJ: Princeton University Press.

Leuchtenburg, William. (1958). *The Perils of Prosperity*. Chicago: Chicago University Press.

Lewis, Sinclair. (1965). *Babbitt*. London: Cape.

Lukács, Georg. (1971). Reification and the consciousness of the proletariat. In *History and Class Consciousness: Studies in Marxist Dialectics*, trans. Rodney Livingstone (pp. 83–222). London: Merlin.

Lynd, Robert and Helen Lynd. (1929). *Middletown*. New York: Harcourt and Brace.

Marchand, Roland. (1985). *Advertising the American Dream: Making Way for Modernity, 1920–1940*. Los Angeles: University of California Press.

Marx, Karl. (1965). Grundrisse. Fourth and fifth notebooks. In *Karl Marx: Pre-Capitalist Economic Formations*, trans. Jack Cohen, ed. E. J. Hobsbawm (pp. 67–120). New York: International Publishers.

Marx, Karl. (1976). *Capital: A Critique of Political Economy*, vol. 1, trans. Ben Fowkes. Harmondsworth, UK: Penguin.

Montgomery, D. (1979). *Workers' Control in America: Studies in the History of Work, Technology and Labor Struggles*. Cambridge, UK: Cambridge University Press.

O'Connor, James. (1984). *Accumulation Crisis*. New York: Basil Blackwell.

Ricoeur, Paul. (1990). *Time and Narrative*, vol. 1, trans. Kathleen McLaughlin and David Pellauer. Chicago: University of Chicago Press.

Rose, Gillian. (1978). *The Melancholy Science: An Introduction to the Thought of Theodor W. Adorno*. London: Macmillan.

Scarry, Elaine.(1985). *The Body in Pain: The Making and Unmaking of the World*. Oxford: Oxford University Press.

Sohn-Rethel, Alfred. (1978). *Intellectual and Manual Labor: A Critique of Epistemology*, trans. Martin Sohn Rethel. London: Macmillan.

Stipes-Watts, Emily. (1971). *Ernest Hemingway and the Arts*. London: University of Illinois Press.

Tanner, Tony. (1977). *The Region of Wonder*. Cambridge, UK: Cambridge University Press.

Veblen, Thorstein. (1970). *The Theory of the Leisure Class*. London: Unwin.

Wharton, Edith. (1974). *The Age of Innocence*. Harmondsworth: Penguin.

Williams, William Carlos. (1950). A sort of a song. In *The Collected Later Poems of William Carlos Williams* (p. 7). New York: New Directions.

Wilson, Edmund. (1997). Hemingway's gauge of morale. In *The Wound and the Bow* (pp. 174–97). Athens: Ohio University Press.

11
Chronic Modernism

Leigh Anne Duck

Nor do I know whether accepting the lesson has placed me in the rear or in the avant-garde.
(Ralph Ellison, Invisible Man)

Though the closing date of modernism is difficult to specify – and may not, as many critics argue, have even occurred – Ralph Ellison's opus, published in 1952, includes several stylistic and philosophical traits associated with the transition to postmodernism. Throughout the novel, the protagonist fears that his identity, his senses, or his body itself may be absorbed into an amorphous, technologically mediated array of images and energies amid which he has no agency – "surrounded by mirrors of hard, distorting glass," "driven by a furious bellows," and "pumped between live electrodes like an accordion between a player's hands" (Ellison 1952/1990: 3, 416, 232). He tries to resist this potential disintegration into postmodern system or simulacrum, however, by aligning himself with transformative ideologies and projects of the sort that Marshall Berman has since proclaimed characteristic of modernism. These include the racial uplift propounded at the protagonist's black college, which serves "a young, though a fast-rising people," and the "scientific revolution" promised by the Brotherhood, a loosely Leninist organization that seeks, at "a terminal point in history . . . [to] determine the direction of events" (pp. 133, 307). Because Ellison's unnamed narrator depends on such ideas of history and progress for his senses of ethical and even bodily integrity, he is devastated when he discovers that these organizations are corrupt. Framing the novel by explaining that he has descended into a hidden basement where he seeks to recognize some contingent "pattern to the chaos" or potential "moment for action," the narrator positions himself in what is now recognized as an epochal and epistemological quandary (pp. 580, 13). While the narrator's interest in social change, like his intense desire to construct an autonomous identity, suggests a modernist effort to traverse past and future, his hallucinatory exploration of this isolated space – with its apparent remove from linear time and its enthusiastic theft from Monopolated Light & Power – suggests his containment in a postmodern present, in which alternate futures seem unimaginable and resistance has become so highly localized as to be, at worst, strictly private (Jameson 2003: 695, 710).

But it is not only this tension between his modernist longing to believe in progress and his fascination with a postmodern world "without boundaries" and "outside of history" that leads to the narrator's confusion as to whether he has become a representative for the past or the future (Ellison 1952/1990: 498, 499). Before he can even accept the postmodern idea that a human trajectory need not be linear but might rather be "crabways and crossways and around in a circle," he is troubled by his awareness that whole categories of people are often excluded from accounts of progressive history, such that even within discourses of racial uplift or class revolution, sharecroppers are deemed "primitive" and ex-slaves are consigned to the "dump heaps" (pp. 510, 47, 290). Afraid that he, too, might be labeled a relic, the narrator identifies all the more vigorously with ideas of modernization and success, but this attachment effectively fractures his psyche, leaving him unable to acknowledge attributes or experiences that might identify him with the past. Throughout the novel, his memories seem to exist "around a corner" – not quite accessible to his conscious mind (pp. 273, 508). And to represent this anxiety and cognitive difficulty, the narrative foregrounds its most modernist forms – the combination of folkloric tropes and dadaistic nonsense that characterizes his dialogue with doctors while he is hooked up to an electroshock machine, the "stream-of-consciousness" monologue through which he seeks to remember and analyze his experiences, and the sudden surrealistic emergence of posttraumatic visions. Ultimately, then, while this novel foregrounds a character's effort – through "hibernation" – to withstand an epochal change between a period of rapid modernization and one figured as a chaotic stasis (the postmodern "end of history"), it also insists that, throughout the narrator's life, both his own psyche and his larger society have been fissured by temporal incongruities (Ellison 1952/1990: 6, Felski 2000: 138).

Such skepticism or anxiety concerning linear time – uniform, moment-by-moment chronological progression – appears in many US novels from the first half of the twentieth century and marks, in itself, a somewhat paradoxical historical change. The times announced by global clocks did not begin to be synchronized, after all, until the late nineteenth and early twentieth centuries, when such technological changes as the expansion of rail travel and the invention of the telegraph both called for and facilitated the standardization of time across geographic zones (Kern 1983: 11–15). Calibration of time also intensified during these decades, as managers and engineers sought to increase human and mechanical efficiency (Kern 1983: 110–17). During the early years of this transition, as in the decades immediately prior, most novels written in the United States and Europe followed the formal dictates of literary realism: they followed a generally linear chronology that corresponded to the social time of capitalism and emphasized individual and societal progress (Seltzer 1992: 43). In contrast, modernist writers tended to rebel against this "objectified, socially measurable time . . . (time as a more or less precious commodity, bought and sold on the market)," focusing instead, as Matei Calinescu argues, on "the personal, subjective, imaginative *durée*, the private time created by the unfolding of the self" (Calinescu 1987: 5). And as suggested by Ellison's narrator, their representation of temporal multiplicity was also shaped by the belief – accepted, rejected, or continuously considered – that diverse cultural forms and classes of people might be embedded in distinct types of time.

The term "chronic," then, is used here chiefly to indicate a concern with time: obsolete in current uses of the word, this meaning can nonetheless be derived by shortening the more standard expression in literary criticism – "chronotopic," or having to do with the time and space of a narrative (Bakhtin 1981). I do not mean to dismiss the significance of geographic thought, which provides a fruitful context through which to examine modernist representations of time, which often focus, after all, on such spatial differences as urban versus rural. Modernist fiction also foregrounds an analytic problem central in spatial theory itself: that is, the complex relationships among physical (material), social (encoded/enacted), and mental (psychological) spaces (Soja 1989: 120–1). But while the dimensions of space and time are inextricably related – combining, after all, to constitute a world – novels are typically designated "modernist" because of their experimental efforts to represent the effects of modernization, which was understood among its architects and in the West more generally as a process of historical unfolding. Though modernists varied in their assessments of the technological, economic, and social changes that affected both local cultures and geopolitical relationships in this period, none failed to note the "dogma of progress," or the senses of global teleology (capitalist, communist, imperialist, and/or nationalist), through which these changes were understood (Calinescu 1987: 266). Observing spatial differences in this process of transformation – a "culture of incomplete modernization," as Fredric Jameson (2003: 699) describes it – modernists became particularly concerned with how to situate spaces, bodies, and cultural forms in time. Accordingly, while many commentaries concerning fiction in this period explore the tension between modernists' aesthetic innovation (which could seem to replicate the broader emphasis on economic and social modernization) and their simultaneous skepticism toward such ideas of development (a trait often dubbed their "antimodernist modernism"), I am concerned here with the attribute that unites these two tendencies, which is their effort to understand and represent how modernization might alter human experiences of time.

Struggling with questions concerning whether and how distinct forms of time could be mapped and differentiated geographically, such that residents of different spaces might be said to inhabit "*non-contemporaneous . . .* but *chronologically simultaneous*" times, modernists also asked how such a fragmented social world might affect the less mappable space of the mind – that is, whether individuals could traverse temporal differences as effectively as spatial ones (Osborne 1995: 16, emphasis in original). Further, as ideas of personal and societal progress became increasingly hegemonic, such that backwardness was seen as a kind of deficiency, these writers explored how individuals might respond to their inevitable experiences of psychological idiosyncrasy – those dynamics or desires, so widely cited in this era, that flaunt their disregard for concepts of linear progress. Modernists in the United States were influenced, of course, by a national context deeply concerned with its own uneven and often convulsive process of economic and social change. But given that this process – and the conflicts it highlights and often produces – has not ceased to transform the globe, they were also participating in an aesthetic project that, as many critics now argue, was global in its spatial dimensions and has not reached its chronological end (Williams 2000: 24–35). That commonality between the early twentieth century and our own era suggests a less etymological way in which modernism is "chronic": in seeking literary forms through which to describe and comprehend the effects of rapid and largely capitalistic social change, these writers explored conceptual and experiential problems that continue to reverberate in the US and more broadly (Friedman 2006: 425–35).

Space, Culture, Bodies: Chronic Development

European and US modernisms have long been considered chiefly urban phenomena whose central themes and formal innovations were shaped by artists' experience of "the imperial and capitalist metropolis," characterized by intensified concentration of economic influence, display of commodities, and technological change, as well as by the arrival of immigrants from nonindustrialized and often colonized regions and nations (Williams 1989: 47). Such arguments reflect the perception that modernized urban cultures differ significantly from rural ones, which maintain both a slower pace and a stronger sense of tradition. As Susan Hegeman argues of the United States in the early twentieth century, such spatial divisions between industrial and agrarian regions, or between urban centers and rural provinces, were seen as cultural as well, such that "never before (nor since) were issues of taste and cultural value articulated in such geographic terms" (Hegeman 1999: 23, 20–7). In aesthetic representation, these cultural and geographic differences were often figured as temporal – appreciation for or anxiety regarding the new, as typically located in the city, or of the primitive, as sited within ethnic, racial, or rural enclaves. But in modernists' fiction, as in their often very mobile lives, these purported geographic, temporal, and cultural distinctions could not be strictly maintained. Instead, they perpetually collide, in ways that create both hopes for productive exchange and concern over possibly irreducible or palpably exploitative conflict.

Especially prominent among modernists' representation of rural life was the possibility that indirect or limited contact with urban culture might stimulate desires that could prove destructive in small-town contexts, particularly when these metropolitan excitements clash with conservative gendered and sexual mores. For example, in "Mother," a vignette from Sherwood Anderson's highly unified short story cycle *Winesburg, Ohio*, a teenaged girl becomes fascinated with the "traveling men" who stay at her father's hotel; "urging them to tell her of life in the cities out of which they had come," she experiences "a great restlessness" that leads her to experiment with cross-dressing and sex, the latter accompanied by "strange wild emotions" and "sobbing repentance" (Anderson 1919/1977: 45–6). Though she enjoys these forms of expression, they yield "a somewhat shaky reputation" in her small town, and she is soon ensnared in a miserable marriage, hoping only to facilitate her son's escape to the city, but unsure how to help him (p. 45). Crucially, this narrative conveys not merely spatial enclosure, but also an erratic temporality, as Elizabeth vacillates between her wrenching desire for change and her pained surrender to stasis (p. 45). Similarly, the socialite protagonist of Willa Cather's *A Lost Lady*, when confined by her husband's failed health and fortune to a small prairie town where "nothing ever *does* happen," seems almost continuously to suppress "a quivering passion"; this sense of incongruity between her internal instability and her external consistency – her semblance of "tempered steel" – provides the main fascination of the character and the narrative (Cather 1923/1990: 112, 114, 84).

Female characters were not alone, of course, in serving to demonstrate such collisions between urban and rural rhythms or between the desires and sensations stimulated by modernization. In Nathanael West's *The Day of the Locust* (1939), persons of all types from across North America (but mainly the "Middle-West") arrive in Los Angeles to seek a change of pace after lifetimes of routinized "dull, heavy labor," but their "boredom becomes more and more terrible" (West 1962: 80). Daily consuming movies and newspapers that "fed them on lynchings, murder, sex crimes, explosions, wrecks, love nests, fires, miracles, revolutions, wars," they discover that "nothing can ever be violent enough to make taut their slack minds and bodies" (pp. 177–8). Surrounded by persons seeking to perfect the art of self-commodification as well as by an array of architectural styles and costumes far removed from the historical contexts they are meant to evoke, these new Los Angelenos manifest a "need for beauty and romance" that is "truly monstrous" in its effects (p. 61). Distanced from any local social networks that may have influenced their early life (though such a sense of human connectedness is utterly absent in West's narrative, even in flashback), they seek coherent systems of meaning of the sort provided by religious traditions. In West's excruciatingly modernized metropolis, however, even these desires, so often considered timeless (associated with eternity or at least the unconscious), "have been brought under the sway of the political economy and have solidified into the obsolescent materiality of buildings and commodities": his "worshipers" attend, for example, the "Church of Christ, Physical," where "holiness" is sought through weight-lifting (Barnard 1995: 173, West 1962: 142).

Nor was US fiction unique in suggesting that the speed of cultural change might be exceeding the pace of human adaptability. The popular sociological study *Middletown*, for example, held that residents of this Midwestern locale (Muncie, Indiana) were "learning new ways of behaving towards material things more rapidly than new habits addressed to persons and non-material institutions" (Lynd and Lynd 1929: 499). Such assessments were driven in large part by technological innovation and the increased availability and variety of commodities, but as West suggests, the spread of the culture industry – or the broad dissemination of magazines, "pulp" fiction, film,

and radio – also elicited anxiety. Critics argued that these mass media were dehumanizing, as well as homogenizing – paradoxically flattening time while producing an
impression of ceaseless innovation: on the one hand, entertainments manifest "a constant sameness," and, on the other, "there is never-ending talk of ideas, novelty, and
surprise" (Horkheimer and Adorno 1944/1972: 134). And as these cultural forms
spread throughout the nation, observers wondered whether diverse audiences could
appreciate or even withstand such encounters. Regionalists, in particular, worried
whether Americans could "absorb and adjust" to the changes that were proceeding
"faster, faster, further, further, more, more, new, new, now, now" (Odum and Moore
1938/1966: 629, 624).

Such questions about whether all individuals or groups were prepared to participate
in modernity had long been racialized in US political discourse as a justification for
denying legal rights to Native Americans, African Americans, immigrants, and residents of US colonies. Labeling nonwhite peoples "savage" or "backward," such arguments located them outside the temporality in which individuals exercise the right
of political self-determination, or become, in Berman's terms, "subjects as well as
objects of modernization" (1982/1988: 5). This history fuels the fear of Ellison's narrator, for example, at the thought that he might "plunge outside history": he suspects
that if he is associated with "primitive" persons whom history has "passed . . . by," he
will lose his opportunity to participate in progress, which he associates with full
enfranchisement (Ellison 1952/1990: 377, 291). The theme that "Jim Crow" segregation and other forms of discrimination had placed African Americans in a paradoxical
relationship to political and economic modernity – a conundrum described decades
earlier by W. E. B. Du Bois in *The Souls of Black Folk* as the state of being "swept on
by the currents of the nineteenth while yet struggling in the eddies of the fifteenth
century" – was explored by many African-American modernists, whose work, as Alain
Locke argued, participated in a global reckoning with the legacies of racism and
colonialism (Du Bois 1903/1989: 142, Locke 1925/1992: xxvii). But white US modernists' work also registered awareness – and often alarm – that, as Patricia Chu argues,
"the West's others were not passively modernized but active participants in worldwide
modernization" whose movements and actions were changing both province and
metropolis (Chu 2006: 162).

And while modernists varied in their understanding of race, few corroborated the
hegemonic and celebratory account of political modernity as a "cheerful and uncom-
plicated story of progress, in which ever more groups would come to benefit from the
fruits of Western development" (Felski 2000: 57). In that case, writers seeking greater
social justice would argue that temporal homogeneity has been achieved and enfranchisement should be universal, and others would seek to ascribe minority groups to
an archaic time, preserving modernity for designated groups. Here again, though,
modernist novels maintain an ambivalent or skeptical stance toward purported temporal boundaries: those who seek to represent other races as "primitive" reveal that
temporal interest itself to constitute a characteristically modernist desire, while those
who represent a racially diverse modernity are nonetheless wary of modernization.

Gertrude Stein's 1909 novella "Melanctha," for instance, readily fits the description of racial primitivism: that is, the novel overtly idealizes an instinctive and unsophisticated way of being, which it labels as black – that is, "the warm broad glow of negro sunshine" (Stein 2006: 53). On the other hand, such stable simplicity proves untenable in the narrative, which repeatedly pauses to ponder how this purported racial essence is superseded, often by various forms of interracial interaction. One character, for example, is said to have "the simple, promiscuous unmorality of the black people" but the narrative then qualifies this claim while noting that she was "brought up quite like their own child by white folks"; in a further contradiction, she is the text's strongest proponent of marriage (pp. 53–4). Though the narrative often claims that its mixed-race characters, such as Melanctha, are especially "complex, desiring," other characters are influenced by their relationships with her: thus her father, a "big black virile negro," becomes "brutal and rough" in part because of his frustration with his "disturbing child" (pp. 54, 54, 57).

Ultimately, the work's one character who is said to embody the primitive ideal of "a warm broad glow . . . [with] never . . . anything mysterious" serves as a case study in modernist confusion (p. 86). Alarmed by people who are "always wanting new things and excitements," Jeff Campbell believes in a more modulated linear progress – "I want to see the colored people . . . live regular and work hard and understand things"; in his relationship with Melanctha, however, he, too, experiences a painful incongruity between desire and determination, or between the cycles of his own emotions and the regular pace of work that he so values (pp. 73–4). Stein's primitivism is complicated still further by the fact that "Melanctha" constitutes both her first overtly experimental narrative and a revision of her previously unpublished semi-autobiographical novel *Q.E.D.* Reading these works together reveals the supposedly simple Jeff Campbell to be both a masked modernist – a figure for the author herself – and a product of modernization. Though Stein's narrative insists on its desire for unsophisticated joy and its belief that such qualities must be found among black people, both her prose and her process disrupt these premises, suggesting instead that this desire is produced amid a world of "excitements" and "wanderers" in which black lives, like white ones, are diversely disrupted.

Where Stein creates black characters that suggest the impossibility of a desired racial stasis, Osage writer John Joseph Mathews produces an Indian agent's narrative in order to mock the white paternalism that seeks simultaneously to modernize Indians and to sequester them from modernity. Rarely examined among modernist texts, Mathews's *Wah'Kon-tah: The Osage and the White Man's Road* nonetheless experiments with the telling of history: including excerpts from the journal of Major Laban Miles, the work adds fictional anecdotes and occasional internal monologue in order to narrate the progression of Osage landscape from one of "wild spaciousness" to one characterized by "the coughing of the pumps carried from the oil fields" (Mathews 1932: 19, 342). Upon his arrival at the reservation, Miles – as figured by Mathews – examines his journal notes and doubts whether he can represent the Osage without becoming "sentimental," as he feels that they "had remained a part of nature and had not developed . . . that softness and self-indulgence which was called civilization" (pp. 40–1). From here, the work explores the degree to which Miles can overcome his tendency to romanticize a culture that he views as part of another era; in this, Miles replicates the tendency, common to anthropology in this period, to view native cultures as part of a distinct and unified space-time (Fabian 1983: 47). But Miles's goal is to modernize the Osage: he believes it "a race against time to prepare the younger generation as fast as possible to meet the conditions which the white men were forcing" (Mathews 1932: 258).

Though the novel repeatedly cites Miles's good intentions and his efforts to learn from the Osage, it proves skeptical concerning the ability of individuals raised in Western culture to overcome their perceptions of temporal difference. Miles, for example, is willing to sacrifice the happiness and even mental health of Osage children in order to fortify them for the culture clash he foresees; he concludes, for example, that compulsory boarding schools are necessary even if the children experience them as "prisons" (p. 101). And though they suffer for their knowledge, he refuses to trust the understanding they have gained; he projects that they must experience some version of his difficulty in incorporating understanding of other cultures, which is that "he could not lose himself . . . there had been too many generations of the stern teachings of Right and Wrong, for the Amer-European iron in his soul to have dissolved" (p. 63). Accordingly, when he pronounces judgment on transtribal romances (with an Arapaho, for example, or a white person), he doubts the insight of Osage youth, and his opinions are repeatedly flawed. Finally, as he is confronted with white "barbarism and outlawry," he realizes the destruction he has feared comes not from Indian "shock" at whites' "civilization" but from the latter's predatory behavior (pp. 306–7). But despite this critique, Mathews confirms Miles's perception that modernization would badly damage Osage society, as he closes the narrative by depicting the contempt of a contemporary generation of Osage for tribal elders and culture. His fears of deracination are rendered especially acute in his representation of African Americans, who appear on the reservation from "no-one-knew-where," are "slovenly" in appearance and too enthusiastic in "very disagreeable" – that is, violent – work, and generally support the claim that "conditions" have grown "worse and worse" (pp. 312, 330, 313, 314).

Though many narratives in this period explored how modernization might affect racial minorities, some, of course, reflected the concerns of declining elites. In a society where no space was immune from metropolitan influences and small towns were increasingly integrated into a complex national economy, even the descendants of local leaders lacked the social position that they would have expected, and they experience this change as a sign that they are unsuited to the contemporary era. Accordingly, in William Faulkner's *The Sound and the Fury*, set chiefly in the fictional Jefferson, Mississippi, the oldest son of the Compson family, Quentin, feels an overdetermined sense of inadequacy. Devastated by the combination of decline in his family's landholdings and social status (particularly in contrast with his grandfather, the General, who was "always right"), his continuing virginity, his sister Caddy's promiscuity (which is presented as both a familial shame and a personal reproof against Quentin's lack of sexual adventurousness), and his inability to "look after" his alcoholic father and his incapacitated brother Benjy as Caddy has asked, Quentin describes his sense of futility in explicitly temporal terms, echoing his father's complaints about "the long diminishing parade of time" (Faulkner 1929/1990: 176, 115, 76). Where Quentin mourns a heroic conception of progressive time – one in which he might be able to intervene and effect change (a desire he seems to fulfill, rather morbidly and paradoxically, through suicide), his younger brother Jason bemoans his lack of up-to-dateness, which is both geographical and temporal: because he is not "right up there on the ground" where commodity futures are traded, his delayed knowledge renders him vulnerable, as he feels "they were using the telegraph company to defraud" (p. 227).

The novel recognizes that the very changes that confound the Compson brothers might offer opportunities for those marginalized by the declining social order. Jason projects his frustration onto others in his community – particularly the women, African Americans, and poor whites – who are excited by the advent of the carnival to town: his paternalistic contempt for how they pay for entertainment – providing money to an enterprise that will "pick up Saturday night and carry off at least a thousand dollars out of the county" – masks his feeling that he, too, lacks agency in the modernizing economy (p. 231). But while his critique of economic and cultural change aligns with so many from this period, the novel's representation of this brutal, grasping, and self-deluded patriarch alerts readers to the corruption of the pre-existing social formation, which accords him what power he still retains. Ultimately, what alienates Jason is freeing for his niece: aided by her lover who works for the carnival (and is revealed to be cruel in his treatment of Benjy), young Quentin (Caddy's daughter) reclaims the money Jason has been stealing from her in order to escape the constraints of her life in Jefferson. And though the Compson family members routinely seek to deny it, the novel implicitly recognizes the movement of African Americans from small, segregated southern towns to other regions that promised greater opportunity.

But despite these allusions to the possible opportunities afforded by modernization, Faulkner, like perhaps all of the writers studied here, remained skeptical of its effects. Observing a pattern of social, economic, and cultural change that served to create sharp hierarchies between the new and the old, atomizing and often fetishizing the latter – creating spectacular or stereotypical portraits of the primitive while providing very little sense of how one might maintain a meaningful relationship to cultural traditions while participating in modernization – modernists saw a world in which various bodies "carr[ied] earlier things with them," either as lingering ways of life, belligerent attachments to fading cultural forms, or attributes projected onto them by others who wished to visualize an alternate temporality (Bloch 1977: 22). Observing early fascist Germany in 1932, Ernst Bloch captured the broader reality that many in a modernizing society "stand on a bad footing with Today" because of resentment, material immiseration, or both (p. 27). As writers in the US pondered what such persons might do or suffer, they rarely embraced the optimistic view of modernity, in which it "promises us adventure, power, joy, growth, transformation of ourselves and the world" (Berman 1982/1988: 15). In a later novel, Faulkner abandoned ideas that modernization might increase opportunity and described it instead as cannibalistic, consuming participants and then thrusting them aside: "There was no time; the next act and scene itself clearing its own stage without waiting for property-men . . . commencing the new act and scene right in the midst of the phantoms, the fading wraiths of that old time which had been exhausted, used up" (Faulkner 1951/1975: 191).

Micromapping: Chronic Anxiety

In exploring the temporal relationships among diverse demographic groups, as suggested in the preceding section, modernists reflected prominent trends in US social science and political thought more generally. But while their participation in this project was sufficient, in Walter Benn Michaels's argument, to constitute a "commitment to identity – linguistic, national, cultural, racial" (Michaels 1995: 3), their interest in group identities was undercut by their exploration of individual identity, which was seen in this period as distinctly incoherent. Demonstrating that even the self proves unknowable to the individual in question, they implied the impossibility of delineating a stable and essential identity for any demographic category. This was a period, after all, in which "the irrational became the subject of public debate and even political controversy" (North 1999: 67), a project begun in philosophy and psychology but vigorously fueled by the developing profession of public relations. And in modernist explorations of mental space, as in their approach to social space, temporal multiplicity proves particularly vexing. Novels from this era suggest the disturbing possibility that even as social space might contain nonsynchronous bodies (persons, as we have seen, who appear "economically obsolete" or who long for "transcendence in the past"), the individual psyche might also contain nonsynchronous elements – cognitive habits, emotional attachments, or unconscious fragments that seem not only discordant but even incommensurable with the linear time of modernity (Bloch 1977: 24, 26).

To an extent, modernists' emphasis on the distinct rhythms of the psyche could seem an empowering form of resistance to the constraining conformity often considered characteristic of modernizing societies. Such confrontation, at least, was implied by Henri Bergson's philosophy of mind (which was influenced by Stein's mentor William James), which held that the sense of "homogeneous" or linear time was imposed as "our ego comes in contact with the external world at its surface," distinguishing this artificial perception of inner life from those which arise from more thorough attention to "the deep-seated self which ponders and decides, which heats and blazes up . . . whose states and changes permeate one another" (Bergson 1912: 125). In some fictional works, too, this willingness to acknowledge multiple forms of time – particularly those informed by emotional or spiritual needs and desires, over and against the linear logic of the marketplace – is linked to a more fully realized wisdom. Ellison's narrator, for instance, prefaces his Bildungsroman by describing his perceptions as he smokes a "reefer" and listens to Louis Armstrong, each of which, he explains, alters one's temporal sense: "Instead of the swift and imperceptible flowing of time, you are aware of its nodes, those points where time stands still or from which it leaps ahead" (Ellison 1952/1990: 8). (Because modernism so often foregrounds such chemically enhanced lowering of inhibitions and epistemological insight, we might consider it "chronic" in this meaning as well.) Presenting this experience as an impetus to record his tale "in black and white" and as a catalyst enabling him to comprehend "the incompatible notions that buzzed within [his] brain" (p. 14), he alerts the reader that a flexible, questioning approach to time constitutes a key to his life story.

Of course, as we have seen, the younger self whose experiences he narrates fears such suggestions of temporal multiplicity, not only because he does not want to be cast out of political and economic modernity by powerful and racist observers, but also because his mental life does not consistently accord with his goals of "hard work and progress and action"; rather, it "revolved again and again back" to a confusing experience from his youth (Ellison 1952/1990: 576, 574). He is haunted by the recollection of his grandfather, an ex-slave of whom he is, as a young man, "ashamed," but who repeatedly appears in his dreams – an apparent embodiment of desires the narrator cannot consciously accept (p. 15). On his deathbed, the grandfather told his descendants to use "grins" and "yeses" to doom white people to "death and destruction," but the narrator wants the approval of powerful men, in order to pursue his goal of becoming "influential with wealthy men all over the country, consulted in matters concerning the race" (pp. 16, 101). Doubtful and "guilty" concerning his grandfather's words, when he later serves as chauffeur to a white trustee of his black college, he compulsively does exactly as his grandfather has advised (p. 40). Listening to Mr Norton narrate his life of privilege and his role in helping recently freed slaves "who seemed," as Norton described them, "almost without individuality," the narrator "suddenly decide[s] to turn off the highway, down a road that *seemed* unfamiliar," but which soon serves to reveal the ways in which Norton's college has failed to help the African Americans who live nearby and has instead stimulated class conflict between students and sharecroppers (p. 40, emphasis added). Though the narrator repeatedly states that he is "sorry" to be making such "mistake[s]," his actions could not be better calculated for demonstrating the folly of Norton's concept of "destiny"; he even forces the older man to confront his fascination with incest, a sign of the "degenera[cy]" he condemns (pp. 46, 49, 41, 47). Unable to enjoy this subversion, however, the narrator feels an intense and self-effacing identification with Norton: "I wanted to . . . show him tears . . . like those of a *child before his parent*; . . . to assure him . . . that I believed in his own goodness and kindness in extending the hand of his benevolence to helping us poor, ignorant people out of the mire and darkness" (pp. 15, 99, emphasis added).

In playing the role of trickster simultaneously to Norton and to himself, the narrator illustrates why modernists tended to represent as dangerous those psychological dynamics that diverge from linear time. The era's foremost theorist of individuals' temporal idiosyncrasy was, after all, Sigmund Freud, who argued in "The Unconscious" (1915) that a large portion of mental life is both unorganized (*"timeless"* and inaccessible to negation) and inaccessible to conscious control; further, he held that elements of this chaotic mental content were determined to "discharge" their aims or energy in the conscious mind or even in inadvertent behavior (Freud 1989: 582, 573–4). As if these claims were not disturbing enough, Freud explained elsewhere that the unconscious was the repository for particularly unsettling mental dynamics. In "Repression" (1915), he held that the unconscious contains "instinctual impulses" whose aim is so "irreconcilable with other claims and intentions" that their fulfillment would "cause pleasure in one place and unpleasure in another," and in *Beyond the Pleasure Principle* (1920), he confirmed his earlier suggestion that overwhelming memories – those whose contents are so devastating as to fracture consciousness – are also retained there (1989: 509, 607–11). For Ellison's narrator, such dangerous memories seem to include even those of his attachments to family members in the segregated South: he is so afraid of "los[ing] caste," even when he wants to believe otherwise, that merely to recall his childhood poverty requires the lifting of a psychological repression – "some painful yet precious thing which I could not bear to lose, something confounding, like a rotted tooth that one would rather suffer indefinitely than endure the short violent eruption of pain that would mark its removal" (Ellison 1952/1990: 265, 273). Afraid that his internal divisions may induce social divisions – having recognized that his unconscious may lead him to alert others to precisely the ways in which he diverges from hegemonic norms – he feels as beset from within as he does from without; less afraid of the racism that assaults him regularly than of his own barely repressed identifications and desires.

Invisible Man thus demonstrates a strategy common to many modernist novels, in which exploration of the unconscious enables narrative to illustrate and to question the various forms of repression that enable characters to function, however erratically, in modern society. Here, as in juxtaposing alternate models of social time against each other (urban vs. rural, "primitive" vs. sophisticated), they both highlight the role of time in securing ideological distinctions (the mad degenerate vs. the successful modern) and undercut those distinctions themselves (as the unconscious intrudes upon the plans of even the most linear thinker). They also reveal how characters displace their own fears of psychological distress and its associated temporal disorganization onto marginalized demographic groups. Ellison's narrator, for example, is not only anxious that he might be grouped with sharecroppers or ex-slaves, but also alarmed that his world might be frighteningly feminine. Observing that Rinehart – who achieves success as both pimp and pastor – chooses to be a "man of parts" instead of a single personality, the narrator is "both depressed and fascinated" to consider that the goal that has driven all his actions – the construction of a powerful, internally consistent identity – might be poorly suited to success in his contemporary world

(Ellison 1952/1990: 498). Invoking a trope common among male modernist characters imagining an existence not driven by a clearly individuated ego, he determines that he inhabits "a vast seething, hot world of fluidity" – an engulfing and dangerous womb, which also serves as his figure for what it means to live in "chaos," or "outside history" (p. 498).

Such associations were informed not only by patriarchal narratives and images in which "women are seen to be anchored in an eternal biological cycle of death and birth that transcends the contingencies of historical time," but also by the celebrated Freudian emphasis on early relations in patriarchal families (Felski 2000: 18). Describing the development of identity in "The Ego and the Id" (1923), Freud attributes much of this process – that leading to the "higher, moral, supra-personal side of human nature" – to the child's identification with the father, who intervenes in the earlier sense of connection with the nursing mother: in this model, accordingly, such a sense of connectedness appears a kind of developmental regression (Freud 1989: 642, 640). Freud acknowledged complications in his model, including both the way in which gender expectations differ more for children than do their early experiences and the importance of bisexuality in children's desires and later identifications – each of which suggests that sexed and gendered identities must develop in highly variable ways. Nonetheless, in much modernist fiction, both femininity and homosexuality are represented as threats to the achievement of an active modern self – dangers all the more alarming because they could be pleasurable. Thus, Tod Hackett, in *The Day of the Locust*, describes the "return of the womb" as a form of catatonia and degeneration "better by far than Religion or Art or the South Sea Islands," and Quentin Compson, who is suggested in *The Sound and the Fury* and elsewhere to have erotic feelings for his roommate Shreve, loses consciousness precisely at the moment he hears another man described as an "old maid" (West 1962: 171, Faulkner 1929/1990: 147–8; see also Seitler 2001). Nor are such anxieties restricted to men's writing: in Nella Larsen's *Quicksand* (1928), the modern, cosmopolitan Helga Crane becomes "possessed" by the "weird orgy" she encounters in a church service, "particularly . . . the writhings and weepings of the feminine portion . . . with its mixture of breaths, its contact of bodies, its concerted convulsions"; she ultimately "sink[s] back into the mysterious grandeur and holiness of far-off simpler centuries" (Larsen 1986: 113–14).

In sum, the early decades of the twentieth century in the United States encompassed both an increasing emphasis on progress, modernization, and, as Ellison notes, "conformity" on the one hand, and, on the other, increased awareness of psychological divergence – not only between one individual and another, but more profoundly, between what one knows and does not know about oneself (Ellison 1952/1990: 577). This combination raised the uncomfortable possibility not only that one could be seen as culturally marginal or "backward" in regard to the dominant strain of modernity but also that one could harbor or manifest elements of nonsynchronicity without one's own awareness. In an era when "up-to-dateness" was considered vital to success, these idiosyncratic temporal differences were more often presented, from the characters' perspectives, as sources of anxiety rather than as potentialities to be explored.

(Modernists, as I have suggested, examined such mental faculties quite vigorously.) Some celebrated characters, however, do successfully negotiate multiple temporal forms: the protagonist of Zora Neale Hurston's *The Eyes Were Watching God*, for example, incorporates into her life folkloric play, modern medicine, and the cycles of romantic passion. But even this more optimistic novel ultimately requires a kind of tempered and capacious individualism, as Janie encounters hostility in every community: she ends the novel alone in her bedroom, having "pulled in her horizon like a great fish-net . . . [and] called in her soul to come and see" (Hurston 1937/1978: 286).

Conclusion: Chronic Politics

One of the earliest arguments (first published in 1945) in scholarship concerning modernist fiction was that its "spatial form" – which tended to foreground relationships across synchronic space or to juxtapose fragments from what could otherwise be recognized as distinct eras – effaced linear time and collapsed temporal distinctions between past and present (Frank 1991: 63–4). For critics seeking to promote transformational political or cultural projects, however, this aspect of modernist prose has always been particularly troubling, as it appears to contravene the "purposeful and hopeful relationship toward future time" on which such efforts (which were, after all, important to many modernists themselves) depend (Felski 2000: 22). One difficulty here is that numerous developments in twentieth-century modernity foregrounded the "spatial logic of social differences" – nation and region (particularly as shaped by alternate patterns of economic and political development), culture and class (which can be seen to coalesce and migrate through patterns of association and residence), and psychology (which, even in the individual case, may respond differently to diverse aspects of modernity) – in ways that disrupted the "totalization of historical time," forcing participants to acknowledge that experiences of modernity have differed significantly in ways that cannot be delimited geographically (Osborne 1995: 198, Felski 2000: 61–74).

The effect of this recognition on narrative has been substantial and, from the point of view of those who might wish that one could look to literature for revelation of "the truth of our social life as a whole," severe: as Jameson argued in 1975, "the modern writer" (by which he means contemporary literature, which he here believes to follow patterns established in the early twentieth century) is "imprisoned in those serried ranks of monads that are the ultimate result of the social fragmentation inherent in our system" (1975/1988: 131, 132). Ironically, from the perspective of the twenty-first century – with its networks for instantaneous communication, the "microtemporality" of decision making in finance capital, and the real and metaphorical "circuits of the new transnational cybernetic" – Jameson notes the relative "sensitivity to deep time in the moderns" (2003: 704, 706, 701, 699). This shift suggests the degree to which scholarly understandings of modernism are changing as the continuities and ruptures between the early twentieth century and our own era become clearer, but it also indicates that efforts to think through the particular cultural and economic formations of the twentieth century lead critics back to modernists' experiments in the representation of time. As our understanding of late global modernity evolves, their efforts to comprehend and to figure temporal multiplicity may prove more than entertaining – not as early standard-bearers for a celebratory postmodernism eschewing "any sense of the coherence, linearity, or collective experience of time," but as attempts to imagine a more inclusive and flexible approach to time, which may prove a necessity in recognizing and supporting possibilities for a more inclusive and flexible modernity (Felski 2000: 11).

References and Further Reading

Anderson, Sherwood. (1919/1977). *Winesburg, Ohio*. New York: Penguin.

Bakhtin, M. M. (1981). Forms of time and of the chronotope in the novel. In Michael Holquist (ed.), *The Dialogic Imagination: Four Essays*, trans. Caryl Emerson and Michael Holquist (pp. 84–258). Austin: University of Texas Press.

Barnard, Rita. (1995). *The Great Depression and the Culture of Abundance: Kenneth Fearing, Nathanael West, and Mass Culture in the 1930s*. Cambridge, UK: Cambridge University Press.

Bergson, Henri. (1912). *Time and Free Will: An Essay on the Immediate Data of Consciousness*, trans. F. L. Pogson. New York: Macmillan.

Berman, Marshall. (1982/1988). *All That Is Solid Melts into Air: The Experience of Modernity*. New York: Penguin.

Bloch, Ernst. (1977). Nonsynchronism and the obligation to its dialectics, trans. Mark Ritter. *New German Critique* 11: 22–38.

Calinescu, Matei. (1987). *Five Faces of Modernity: Modernism, Avant-Garde, Decadence, Kitsch, Postmodernism*. Durham, NC: Duke University Press.

Cather, Willa. (1923/1990). *A Lost Lady*. New York: Vintage.

Chu, Patricia E. (2006). *Race, Nationalism and the State in British and American Modernism*. New York: Cambridge University Press.

Du Bois, W. E. B. (1903/1989). *The Souls of Black Folk*. New York: Bantam.

Ellison, Ralph. (1952/1990). *Invisible Man*. New York: Vintage.

Fabian, Johannes. (1983). *Time and the Other: How Anthropology Makes Its Object*. New York: Columbia University Press.

Faulkner, William. (1929/1990). *The Sound and the Fury*. New York: Vintage.

Faulkner, William. (1951/1975). *Requiem for a Nun*. New York: Vintage.

Felski, Rita. (2000). *Doing Time: Feminist Theory and Postmodern Culture*. New York: New York University Press.

Frank, Joseph. (1991). *The Idea of Spatial Form*. New Brunswick, NJ: Rutgers University Press.

Friedman, Susan Stanford. (2006). Periodizing modernism: Postcolonial modernities and the space/time borders of modernist studies. *Modernism/Modernity* 13, 3: 425–43.

Freud, Sigmund. (1989). *The Freud Reader*, ed. Peter Gay. New York: W. W. Norton.

Hegeman, Susan. (1999). *Patterns for America: Modernism and the Concept of Culture*. Princeton, NJ: Princeton University Press.

Horkheimer, Max and Theodor W. Adorno. (1944/1972). *Dialectic of Enlightenment*, trans. John Cumming. New York: Seabury Press.

Hurston, Zora Neale. (1937/1978). *Their Eyes Were Watching God*. Urbana: University of Illinois Press.

Jameson, Fredric. (1975/1988). Beyond the cave: Demystifying the ideology of modernism. In *The Ideologies of Theory: Essays 1971–1986, Volume 2: The Syntax of History* (pp. 115–32). Minneapolis: University of Minnesota Press.

Jameson, Fredric. (2003). The end of temporality. *Critical Inquiry* 29: 695–718.

Kern, Stephen. (1983). *The Culture of Time and Space, 1880–1918*. Cambridge, MA: Harvard University Press.

Larsen, Nella. (1986). *Quicksand and Passing*, ed. Deborah McDowell. New Brunswick, NJ: Rutgers University Press.

Locke, Alain. (1925/1992). Foreword. In Alain Locke (ed.). *The New Negro*. New York: Atheneum/Macmillan.

Lynd, Robert S. and Helen Merrell Lynd. (1929). *Middletown: A Study in American Culture*. New York: Harcourt, Brace and Co.

Mathews, John Joseph. (1932). *Wah'Kon-Tah: The Osage and the White Man's Road*. Norman: University of Oklahoma Press.

Michaels, Walter Benn. (1995). *Our America: Nativism, Modernism, and Pluralism*. Durham, NC: Duke University Press.

North, Michael. (1999). *Reading 1922: A Return to the Scene of the Modern*. New York: Oxford University Press.

Odum, Howard W. and Harry Estill Moore. (1938/1966). *American Regionalism: A Cultural-Historical Approach to National Integration*. Gloucester, MA: Peter Smith.

Osborne, Peter. (1995). *The Politics of Time: Modernity and Avant-Garde*. New York: Verso.

Seitler, Dana. (2001). Down on all fours: Atavistic perversions and the science of desire from Frank Norris to Djuna Barnes. *American Literature* 73, 3: 525–62.

Seltzer, Mark. (1992). *Bodies and Machines*. New York: Routledge.

Soja, Edward W. (1989). *Postmodern Geographies: The Reassertion of Space in Critical Social Theory*. New York: Verso.

Stein, Gertrude. (2006). *Three Lives and Q.E.D.: Authoritative Texts, Contexts, Criticism*, ed. Marianne DeKoven. New York: W. W. Norton.

West, Nathanael. (1962). *Miss Lonelyhearts & The Day of the Locust*. New York: New Directions.

Williams, Patrick. (2000). "Simultaneous uncontemporaneities": Theorizing modernism and empire. In Howard J. Booth and Nigel Rigby (eds), *Modernism and Empire* (pp. 13–38). Manchester: Manchester University Press.

Williams, Raymond. (1989). *Politics of Modernism: Against the New Conformists*. New York: Verso.

12

New Regionalisms: Literature and Uneven Development

Hsuan L. Hsu

The meaning of "regionalism" changed dramatically between its prominence as a picturesque literary genre in the 1880s and 1890s and its rise as a mode of sociological inquiry and political administration in the 1920s and 1930s. In the late nineteenth century, authors like Hamlin Garland, Bret Harte, Sarah Orne Jewett, and Kate Chopin popularized regionalist or "local color" fiction as a form that recorded, preserved, and interrogated the dialects, folk culture, and preindustrial practices of villages and farms far removed from urban industrial centers. Although the popularity of these authors was overshadowed by imperialist historical romances and naturalist novels of the 1890s and the cosmopolitan ethos of postwar modernism, the 1920s saw a regionalist resurgence that would play an important role in US literary history.

As Donna Campbell writes, when it fell out of fashion at the turn of the last century "local color did not disappear; it instead became fragmented, dissolving into a host of new literary trends" (Campbell 1997: 47). While twentieth-century regionalist discourse spans a range of genres and media – including the poetry of Robert Frost and Edgar Lee Masters, the painting of Grant Wood and Thomas Hart Benton, Thornton Wilder's plays, and Rupert Vance's social geography – this chapter will focus on its influence in works of prose fiction. I will consider regionalism not as a genre but as a discourse distinguished by discrepancies in culture, wealth, or power between regional settings and metropolitan centers: the word "region," after all, derives from the Latin *regere* ("to rule"), and denotes a spatial unit of control (Williams 1982: 59). While other factors – such as a narrative focus on setting and character rather than plot, a nostalgic sense of the inevitability of regional change, and an ethnographic interest in the cultural idiosyncrasies of regional "folk" – play roles of varying importance, the description or imagining of a local community that at least appears to be distinct from external forces is definitive of regionalist literature.

This essay will consider how literary regionalism contributed to the production of US regions as sites of commercialized agricultural production. While providing an overview of regionalist texts from the 1880s to the 1940s, I will argue that regionalist literature does not merely represent or record local cultures increasingly threatened by industrialism, but actively participates in the ongoing struggle by which regions are imaginatively and materially reproduced as natural, agricultural, or tourist landscapes. Instead of taking the nostalgia of "local color" at face value, I suggest that fiction can serve diverse interests ranging from national pride to agrarian socialism, from local boosterism to nostalgic antimodernism. I begin with an overview of scholarship that has been influential in contextualizing regionalism's audience, object, and politics, as well as the nineteenth-century regionalist texts that have often anchored these discussions. Next, I show that the shift in regionalism's literary authority evident in the work of Sherwood Anderson, Sinclair Lewis, and John Steinbeck was linked to the rise of regionalist social sciences in the 1920s–30s, and that this "New Regionalism" – as Carey McWilliams called the movement – was more openly engaged with programs of regional planning that linked local and national developments. I conclude by considering a subgenre of ethnic regionalism whose practitioners introduced issues of racialization, diaspora, and border thinking to the project of imagining – and hence reproducing – the nation's diverse regions.

Regionalism and the City, 1891–1914

Critical studies of nineteenth-century regionalism often focus on the genre's expression of resistance to postbellum developments such as national consolidation, urbanization, and industrial capitalism. Amy Kaplan, for example, notes that regions often represented microcosms of Anglo-Saxon racial nationalism: "The decentralization of literature contributes to solidifying national centrality by reimagining a distended industrial nation as an extended clan sharing a 'common inheritance' in its imagined rural origins" (Kaplan 1991: 250–1; see also Robison 2003: 62–3). Richard Brodhead (1993) has tracked the influences of urban, middle-class magazine readers on regionalist conventions, and numerous scholars have pointed out regionalism's ties to international histories of imperialism, commerce, and "development" (Greeson 2006, Joseph 2006, Bramen 2000: 115–55). The motif of a local community characterized by face-to-face interactions, oral or folk culture, and the rhythms of daily life offered urban readers a kind of "imperialist nostalgia" (Rosaldo 1989: 69) in which urban readers mourned, as a thing of the past, the small-scale community that urban modernity was undermining. But despite these external determinants and urban audiences, critics have also demonstrated how individual authors leveraged the cultural power of regionalism to critique tendencies towards uniformity, standardization, and alienation ascribed to modernity and urban life. By drawing attention, even indirectly, to such factors, regionalist authors often managed to incorporate into their works a materialist consideration of the forces that continually circumscribe, reproduce, and redefine unevenly developed regions in the present.

Literary regionalism in this period was perceived as a genre suitable for women writers such as Sarah Orne Jewett, Mary Wilkins Freeman, Kate Chopin, and Celia Thaxter. Whereas supposedly more serious genres like realism and naturalism dealt with overt social and political issues in the public sphere, regionalism often purported to suspend such questions in favor of landscape description, ethnographic detail, and impressionistic character sketches. Indeed, in their introduction to the Norton anthology of *American Women Regionalists 1850–1910*, Judith Fetterley and Marjorie Pryse have drawn an influential distinction between the exoticizing "local color" fiction of white men and the more nuanced and resistant work of women regionalists, arguing that "in practice the regionalists did differentiate themselves from the 'local colorists,' primarily in their desire not to hold up regional characters to potential ridicule by eastern urban readers but rather to present regional experience from within, so as to engage the reader's sympathy and identification" (1992: xii). While Fetterley and Pryse offer a useful overview of the dynamics of place-based identification, relationships between women, and narrative sympathy within the texts they include, their relatively narrow definition of regionalism risks exaggerating the genre's resistance against modernizing tendencies, and also constraining resistance itself to the dynamics of sympathy and readerly identification. Ironically, Hamlin Garland – one of the "local colorists" against whom Fetterley and Pryse position the women regionalists – also made one of the strongest statements for the indigenous nature of local color: "Local color in a novel means that it has such quality of texture and back-ground that it could not have been written in any other place or by any one else than a native. . . . It means a statement of life as indigenous as the plant-growth" (Garland 1894/1952: 64). Having worked on a number of Midwestern farms, however, Garland would have known that even local plant populations, rapidly transformed in the wake of the Homestead Act, could no longer be described as entirely "indigenous."

In most regionalist texts, indigeneity turns out to be a fantasy, and the border between country and city is repeatedly traversed. Regionalist authors may depict isolated places that resist external influences, but their texts are nevertheless addressed to urban readers. Garland's collection of stories, *Main-Travelled Roads* (1891), takes its title not from the Midwestern farms where its plots unfold, but from the roads that connect those farms to the nation's metropolitan centers. "Up the Coulée" presents the book's most poignant exploration of the power differential between regionalism's bourgeois readers and relatively poor, uneducated, and immobile characters. The story begins with Howard McLane, a successful New York actor and dramatist, on his way to visit his family in Wisconsin after a long absence. As he nears his brother's house, the landscape he passes is filtered through his dramaturgical perspective, appearing as "a panorama of delight" and a "majestic amphitheater of green wooded hills"; even a town crony appeals to him on account of "the dramatic power" with which he recites his stories (Garland 1891/1962: 54, 55, 56). Howard is gradually disillusioned, however, in his urbane expectations of a picturesque homecoming, as he finds that his brother Grant is embittered by the monotonous and exploitative nature of commoditized farm labor. The city-dweller's clothing and manner immediately establish a barrier between the brothers, as Grant says he is too dirty from milking the cow to shake his brother's hand. Garland draws out the story to impress upon his readers the dullness of everyday life and labor in the rural home, where "cattle-raisin' and butter-makin' makes a nigger of a man" (p. 85). Howard finally acknowledges that he has neglected his family to indulge in "a horse and a yacht" and go on foreign "expeditions" with his wealthy friends. But even Grant's forgiveness cannot undo the gap in development, culture, language, and physiognomy that this history has created: "The two men stood there, face to face, hands clasped, the one fair-skinned, full-lipped, handsome in his neat suit; the other tragic, somber in his softened mood, his large, long, rugged Scotch face bronzed with sun and scarred with wrinkles that had histories, like saber cuts on a veteran, the record of his battles" (p. 97).

Scholars have linked this developmental gap between country and city with the dynamics of imperialism, particularly in the case of the postbellum South. Even after the end of radical Reconstruction, the South remained a virtual colony in the hands of Northern centers of political and economic influence. The cultural geographer Gail Hollander, for example, writes that "Northern capital, attracted by low wages and natural resources, gravitated toward primary commodity production, thereby limiting industrialization's effect on urbanization and capital accumulation in the region" (Hollander 2006: 272; see also Greeson 2006). Charles Chesnutt's *The Conjure Woman* (1899) explores this relationship in the complex dynamic between its frame narrator – a Northern businessman who moves to North Carolina because "labor was cheap, and land could be bought for a mere song" – and Uncle Julius, the landless black coachman who narrates the vernacular tales (p. 31). If the dialect and colorful plots of Julius's stories satisfy his employers' ethnographic curiosity, they also subtly manipulate the sympathy and actions of the narrator and his sentimental wife. Chesnutt's amicable native informant customizes each of his stories for the occasion, invoking sympathetic or frightening ghosts of slavery in order to dissuade the narrator first from buying the land, and then from encroaching upon the "haunted" spaces that are of use to Julius and the local black community. As Brodhead puts it, "By telling stories of 'slabery days' . . . Julius persuades his hearers to curtail their development plans and so protects his residual uses of their land" (1993: 202).

If Chesnutt's stories demonstrate that regionalist curiosity could never access a purely "indigenous" culture, others proposed that indigeneity could be acquired through everyday practice and sustained inhabitation. In *The Land of Little Rain*, Mary Austin offers ethnographic character sketches not, primarily, of people, but of mice, squirrels, vultures and rabbits – which she refers to as "little people" and "furry folks" (1903/1996: 9, 10) – as well as the Southwestern desert landscape itself. A naturalist in the tradition of Thoreau and Celia Thaxter, Austin presents an intimate map of the desert's vital water trails, its meteorological characteristics, and the inhabitants of this sparsely populated region. Along the way, she presents two character sketches that acknowledge the presence of external market forces even in this arid region: "The Pocket Hunter" depicts an acquisitive gold-seeker hoping to unearth enough ore to fund a comfortable life in London, and "The Basket Maker" features an independent Paiute woman who "made baskets for love and sold them for money" to support herself and her child (p. 47). However, Austin suggests that such commercial incursions are insignificant compared with the experience of dwelling in the land: "But the real heart and core of the country are not to be come at in a month's vacation. One must summer and winter with the land and wait its occasions" (p. 2). In her 1932 essay, "Regionalism in American Fiction," Austin theorizes that "regional environment" shapes every aspect of character and comportment:

> It orders and determines all the direct, practical ways of his getting up and lying down, of staying in and going out, of housing and clothing and food-getting; it arranges by its progressions of seed times and harvest, its rain and wind and burning suns, the rhythms of his work and amusements. It is the thing always before his eye, always at his ear, always underfoot. Slowly or sharply it forces upon him behavior patterns such as earliest become the habit of his blood, the unconscious factor of adjustment in all his mechanisms. (Austin 1903/1996: 97)

Glossing over a range of social hierarchies, Austin wonders, "what is race but a pattern of response common to a group of people who have lived together under a given environment long enough to take a recognizable pattern?" (p. 97).

This notion of the land's influence on individual and social character also informs the prairie novels of Willa Cather and Ole Rolvaag. *O Pioneers!* (1913), the breakthrough novel that Cather dedicated to Jewett, presents a much more positive picture of farming than Garland's *Main-Travelled Roads*. When the engraver Carl Linstrum returns to Nebraska from a long stay in New York as a "trim, self-satisfied city man," it is he and not Alexandra Bergson who feels a failure: "I've been away engraving other men's pictures, and you've stayed at home and made your own" (Cather 1913/1988: 68). Alexandra, the novel's independent, innovative heroine, responds by explaining that she had only to have faith in the land to succeed as a farmer: "The land did it. It had its little joke. It pretended to be poor because nobody knew how to work it right; and then, all at once, it worked itself. It woke up out of its sleep and stretched itself, and it was so big, so rich, that we suddenly found we were rich, just from sitting still" (p. 69). While this passage supports the idea that prolonged intimacy with the region makes a daughter of Swedish immigrants into an ambitious, self-reliant American, Cather's animation of the soil ("It worked itself") suppresses the activities of manual labor and land speculation that have been the true sources of Alexandra's wealth. Rolvaag's *Giants in the Earth* (1924–5) – first published in Norway in the author's native language – presents a similar narrative of environmental determinism by building its plot around the tension between Per Hansa, an optimistic homesteader in the Dakota Territory, and his wife Beret, who pines for the comforts and culture of the city. Although Rolvaag portrays the male homesteaders as folk heroes equal to the challenges of the vast, intractable prairie, he balances this narrative of progress with both Beret's agoraphobic depression and troublesome indications that the land had been previously occupied by Indians and Irish-American soldiers.

But even texts that resist the commodifying influence of a regionalist literary market targeted at armchair tourists tend to assume that regions exist as such – that their local forms of life can be differentiated, isolated, and appreciated as distinct objects, dialects, and "cultures." Raymond Williams has described this tendency as a "fly-in-amber quality" characteristic of much rural fiction: "Its essential strategy is one of showing a warm and charming, or natural and even passionate, life, internally divided by its own rhythms, as if rural Britain, even in its most remote and 'unspoiled' parts, had not been shot through and through by a dominent [*sic*] urban industrial economy" (Williams 1982: 61; see also Dainotto 2000). More recently, cultural geographers have analyzed the material and social processes by which regions are themselves produced as shifting units of agricultural production (Massey 1994, Henderson 1999). Literature contributes to the ongoing imagining of regional communities by representing, and at times repressing, relationships between specific places and larger, translocal flows of labor and commodities. For example, Jewett's *Country of the Pointed Firs* (1896) both describes and performs the reconfiguration of the coastal Maine village of Dunnet Landing: in the course of describing the region's prior cosmopolitanism as a vibrant port whose families sailed all over the world, Jewett actively represents the village as a picturesque vacation destination for city dwellers. Jewett's quiet sketches track her region's transition from a hub of commercial exchange and lumber production to a site of recreation and social reproduction for the urban leisure class.

Attending to the literary dynamics of regional production helps us understand how texts mediate the complex and multidirectional influences among regions, cities, the nation, and the world. The following section focuses on the relation between regions and the nation during a period when regionalism emerged as an influential political and sociological discourse, as well as a literary genre. In "The Cultural Work of American Regionalism," Stephanie Foote has suggested that "Regionalism is the signal genre of the late nineteenth century, not simply because it was the bearer of so much of its culture's otherwise half-expressed anxiety and wonder about the role of the strange and the local in its own self-conception, but because it was itself a genre dedicated to culturalizing all forms of difference" (2003: 28). If reducing difference and resistance to the level of culture characterizes most nineteenth-century regionalism, twentieth-century regionalists wrote in a different atmosphere, where regionalism had become a political tool as well as a cultural discourse.

A Nation of Regions, 1918–1941

The nostalgia that characterized nineteenth-century regionalism – from the vacation destinations described by Jewett and Chopin to Frederick Jackson Turner's closed frontier – could not last forever. In time, regional change would be not only disavowed and mourned, but also acknowledged as an important framework for research and planning. Between the 1902 National Reclamation Act – which funded irrigation projects in the West – and numerous attempts at regional planning initiated under the New Deal, federal agencies became increasingly interested in studying, controlling, and even redefining the nation's regions. This shifted the relation between literary regionalism and power from a stance of marginal resistance, or cultural distinctiveness, to one of heightened participation and interconnectedness: thus Robert Dorman writes that the new regionalists "attempt[ed] to formulate regionalism as a full-fledged national *ideology*, showing the one 'way out' that America must follow if it were to preserve [its tradition of cultural] exceptionalism" (Dorman 1993: 25). At the same time, literary regionalism became more widely recognized (and hence more often practiced by male authors) as regional centers developed their own cultural apparatuses ranging from university presses (such as Chapel Hill and Oklahoma) and "little" magazines (such as *Southwest Review*, *Folk-Say*, and the New Mexico-based *Morada*, which billed itself as "an expression of regional literature in articulation with the new universality") to institutions like the Texas Folk-Lore Society (McWilliams 1930: 8). No longer imagined as cultural remnants superseded by industrialization, regions had become a prominent analytical tool for geographers, social scientists, and political reformers interested in mapping and reshaping the circulation of migrants, agricultural products, and capital investments across the national landscape.

In conjoining regionalist conventions with modernist techniques, Sherwood Anderson's *Winesburg, Ohio* (1919) played a seminal role in the development of the New Regionalism. Anderson's collection of sketches would influence Hemingway, Steinbeck, and Faulkner – the last of whom he famously advised to write about "that little patch up there in Mississippi where you started from" – as well as more marginal figures like Toshio Mori, José Garcia Villa, Jean Toomer, Richard Wright, and even Ray Bradbury (Faulkner 1953/1965: 8). Originally titled *The Book of the Grotesque*, Anderson's book combines the regionalist character sketch perfected by authors like Jewett and Austin with a Gothic interest in the psychological consequences of isolation and sexual repression. Instead of nurturing picturesquely unconventional personalities, idiosyncratic crafts, and local traditions, Winesburg's distance from centers of industry and mass culture leads to the proliferation of sympathetic but malformed personalities, "grotesques" like the nervous and reclusive Wing Biddlebaum, the respectable and violently misogynist Wash Williams, and a number of idiosyncratic philosophers who brood on ideas they are seldom able to communicate. Anderson explains that personalities such as the zealous megalomaniac Jesse Bentley, who imagines that he has been divinely elected to found a dynasty among the "Philistines," were only possible before the "revolution" brought on by industrialism, "interurban car lines," automobiles, and the national mass culture of magazines and newspapers that followed the Civil War: "In our day," by contrast, "a farmer standing by the stove in the store in his village has his mind filled to overflowing with the words of other men" (1919/1960: 71).

But if Anderson ascribes his psychological grotesques to regional isolation in such passages, he also indicates that these men and women have already been touched by industrial and intellectual forces that stretched far beyond Winesburg. Several have worked outside Winesburg: as a schoolmaster, a reporter, a telegraph operator, and a Standard Oil agent for towns situated along the railroad. The sketch entitled "Loneliness" tells of Enoch's years of self-imposed solitude in a New York apartment overlooking Washington Square; and even Jesse Bentley finances his dynasty-building by buying "machines" for farming, reading "newspapers and magazines," and generally capitalizing on "the most materialistic age in the history of the world" (p. 81). George Willard – the young journalist whose sexual and intellectual coming of age unifies the sketches – represents an outlet for expression for Winesburg's residents, a possible means of communicating their histories to the world. Yet, when George finally departs for a writer's life in the city, Anderson momentarily shifts to the perspective of the train conductor, who "had seen a thousand George Willards go out of their towns to the city," in order to point out that even this long-awaited "Departure" is merely one more mundane link between the town and the metropolitan centers whose mass culture and industrialism had already deformed every aspect of Winesburg's daily life (p. 246).

Whereas Anderson's nostalgic sketches prompted several writers to experiment with regionalist conventions, Sinclair Lewis renewed the reading public's interest in regional themes with the bitterly satirical *Main Street* (1920) – a novel whose publication has been called "the most sensational event in twentieth-century American publishing history" (Schorer 1961: 268). It sold over two million copies in two years (compared to *Winesburg*'s initial six thousand copies sold), and readers across the nation saw themselves in its energetic progressive heroine, Carol Kennicott, and her frustrated efforts to reform the village of Gopher Prairie (Schorer 1961: 269–70, Davies 1998: 10). Although some readers initially opposed *Main Street*'s satire of village corruption and mediocrity, even Lewis's hometown of Sauk Center, Minnesota soon forgave and even embraced the novelist (Campion and Fine 1998).

The real target of Lewis's satire, after all, was not Sauk Center but a nationwide streak of complacent conservatism. The novel's prefatory note begins, "This is America – a town of a few thousand, in a region of wheat and corn and dairies and little groves" and then goes on to establish the novel's concern with a particular conjunction of regional towns and national standardization:

> The town is, in our tale, called "Gopher Prairie, Minnesota." But its Main Street is the continuation of Main Streets everywhere. The story would be the same in Ohio or Montana, in Kansas or Kentucky or Illinois, and not very differently would it be told Up York State or in the Carolina hills. (Lewis 1920/2003: 2)

Lewis's references to Ford automobiles, railway stations, the Movie Palace, and the idea of "God's Country" remind us that, like the town of Winesburg, Gopher Prairie

Figure 12.1 George Annand and Carl Van Doren, *A Map of Sinclair Lewis' United States as it Appears in His Novels*. New York: Doubleday, 1934. Image courtesy of Yale Collection of American Literature, Beinecke Rare Book and Manuscript Library.

has largely been rendered grotesque – in this case grotesquely mediocre – by the incursions of national culture; indeed, when Carol briefly leaves her husband to live in Washington, DC, Lewis notes that "Always she was to perceive in Washington . . . a thick streak of Main Street" (pp. 2, 490; see Figure 12.1). On the other hand, the proletarian philosophy voiced by the novel's most colorful character – the outspoken anarchist Miles Bjornstam – represents an alternative regional identity based not in the town's "drab" bourgeois houses, but in "the slum of 'Swede Hollow'" and other communities of impoverished ethnic farmers (p. 132). Gopher Prairie's problem is not only the cultural lassitude that Carol struggles against, but the class stratification that renders the region's farmers and domestic servants socially and politically invisible; this latter problem, Bjornstam explains, is too systematic to be fixed by "dinky reforms" (p. 136). Nevertheless, Carol remains the novel's sympathetic center, and both her attempts to enlighten her neighbors and her own perceptions of Minnesota's towns as utterly "planless" (pp. 24, 45) suggest that more effective regional planning could ameliorate the social and cultural backwardness of America's small towns.

These recurrent references to regional agricultural labor and the need for planning exceed the rebellious or satirical mode attributed to *Main Street* by both its supporters and detractors. In "The Revolt From the Village" (1921), for example, Carl Van Doren cites *Main Street* – along with Edgar Lee Masters's *Spoon River Anthology* (1915) and *Winesburg* – as prominent examples of modern writers who rejected the sentimental "cult of the village" that characterized many earlier regionalist texts (Van Doren 1921: 407). Mary Austin, on the other hand, observed that Lewis's *Main Street* and *Babbitt* present

> just the broad, thin, generalized surface reflection of the American community and American character which the casual observer receives. Babbitt is an American type, the generalized, "footless" type which has arisen out of a rather widespread resistance to regional interests and influences, out of a determined fixation on the most widely shared, instead of the deepest rooted, types of American activity. (Austin 1932: 99)

These accounts, however, overlook Lewis's implicit interest in planning regions along more democratic lines that take into account not only the interests of genteel villagers but the culture and experiences of laborers like the Swedes of Gopher Prairie. To the extent that they involved legal codifications of property, citizenship, and wage labor, these issues indicate a failure of imagination at the national as well as the local scale, as Richard Wright would point out when he recalled, in *Black Boy,* that

> My first serious novel was Sinclair Lewis's *Main Street.* It made me see my boss, Mr. Gerald, and identify him as an American type. I would smile when I saw him lugging his golf bags into the office. I had always felt a vast distance separating me from the boss, and now I felt closer to him, though still distant. I felt now that I knew him, that I could feel the very limits of his narrow life. (Wright 1945/1998: 249)

Reading *Main Street* in the Jim Crow South, Wright saw it not as a satire of a particular town, but as a broader critique of the dehumanizing effects of bourgeois culture, racial hierarchy, and class stratification.

These literary attacks on small-town life may seem diametrically opposed to the agrarianism that emerged in the 1920s and 1930s; however, both the "Revolt from the Village" and the champions of agrarianism originated in a growing frustration with the effects of industrial capitalism. *I'll Take My Stand* (1930), the conservative manifesto published by "Twelve Southerners" and featuring statements from the "Fugitive" poets who had published influential work in Tennessee in 1922–8, does not simply defend the South's tradition of farm labor from the mechanizing and commercializing influences of modernity – it also recommends agrarianism as a way of life that, insofar as it unifies culture and labor, offers the nation an alternative to the dehumanizing influences of "progress": "The theory of agrarianism is that the culture of the soil is the best and most sensitive of vocations, and that therefore it should have the economic preference and enlist the maximum number of workers" (1930/1978: xlvii). Despite their nostalgia for the Old South and their reluctance to address the problem of racial segregation, the Southern Agrarians endorsed agricultural reforms at a national scale: "How may the Southern and the Western agrarians unite for effective action? Should the agrarian forces try to capture the Democratic party[?]" (p. xlvii). In one of the book's most eloquent essays, John Crowe Ransom describes not a conflict between North and South, but a broader struggle between capitalism and humanity:

> A man can contemplate and explore, respect and love, an object as substantial as a farm or a native province. But he cannot contemplate nor explore, respect nor love, a mere turnover, such as an assemblage of "natural resources," a pile of money, a volume or produce, a market, or a credit system. It is into precisely these intangibles that industrialism would translate the farmer's farm. It means the dehumanization of his life. ("Twelve Southerners" 1930/1978: 20)

Ransom goes on to explain that arousing sectional sentiment would be a form of "*Realpolitik*" aimed at influencing the political relation between the region and the federal government (p. 24). Separatism is not the goal, but the emotional means of achieving a greater influence in national politics; instead of restricting agrarianism to the South, Ransom suggests pursuing alliances with "other minority groups in the Union which are circumstanced similarly" – such as Western farmers – and insists that "the rural life of America must be defended, and the world made safe for the farmers" (p. 25).

In addition to bolstering the Southern Renaissance whose authors included Faulkner, Thomas Wolfe, Tennessee Williams, and Katherine Anne Porter (see chapter 14 in this volume), *I'll Take My Stand* also put Southern literature in conversation with the concerns of the emergent regional sociology. Along with the Southern Sociological Society founded in 1935, the "Chapel Hill Regionalists" – a group that included Rupert Vance, Howard Odum, and Arthur Raper, as well as the former "Fugitive" Donald Davidson – published influential work on the social geography, folklore, and culture of the South. Studies such as Vance's *Human Geography of the South* (1932) and Odum's *Southern Regions of the United States* (1936) made profound contributions to the development of human geography, elaborating on connections between social and physical influences in the areal differentiation of the South. The spirit of this research was not merely descriptive, but prescriptive in proposing new strategies for Southern development: Vance notes that his study was deliberately "projected to feature the regional-national as opposed to the local-sectional emphasis. Such a regional premise manifestly would avoid any hypotheses of a self-contained or self-sufficing South and would stimulate a greater degree of federal interest and participation on the part of the South" (Vance 1932: 2–3). Odum, too, argues for the long-term coordination of regional economies, lamenting that "We do not practice regional housekeeping, we have no theory of regionalism; instead we trust to the invisible hand, beloved of Adam Smith, to guide our isolated activities" (Odum 1936: 484). In *The Attack on Leviathan* (1938), Davidson synthesizes the discoveries of the preceding decades in chapters devoted to regionalism in history, the arts, and the social sciences, arguing throughout that regions are compatible with and indeed constitutive of national culture.

During the 1930s, planners and social scientists attempted to bring these insights to bear upon the widespread rural poverty precipitated by the Great Depression. In 1935, Franklin Delano Roosevelt's National Resources Committee proposed dividing the nation into 12 regions in order to facilitate federal administration. The same year, presidential advisor William Yandell Elliott took this idea further, arguing in *The Need for Constitutional Reform* that the Constitution should be amended to supplement inefficient state governments with larger "regional commonwealths" (Elliott 1935: 186). Also in 1935, the National Resources Planning Committee emphasized the regional scale of resource management in an influential study of *Regional Factors in National Planning and Development*. Many social scientists and political commentators agreed with these reports' assumption that states were arbitrary and weak as administrative units, particularly in light of the expanded scale of transportation, communication, migration, and planning brought about by the previous century's technological developments. In *American Regionalism: A Cultural-Historical Approach to National Integration* (1938) – a human geography of the nation divided into six "societal regions" – Odum and Harry Moore go so far as to insist it is "only natural that the proposal should be heard that the feeble state be replaced by a region large enough and representative enough of a characteristic area of the nation to make its voice heard and its influence felt" (quoted in Meinig, vol. 4: 144).

As their titles suggest, these studies share a belief in the region's central role in economic regulation and national governance – a conviction that American regions could be delineated and adjusted through a careful combination of research,

propaganda, and legislation. During the 1930s, the federal government experimented with regional planning in numerous projects, employing regionalists like
Vance, Odum, and Benton MacKaye to work with the National Resources Committee, the Civil Works Administration, and the Tennessee Valley Authority. The
Federal Writers' Project (FWP), established in 1935 to conduct cultural, social,
and ethnographic research in individual states, employed thousands of writers and
fieldworkers with liberal or leftist inclinations – including Arna Bontemps, John
Steinbeck, Studs Terkel, Richard Wright, and Zora Neale Hurston (see Coats and
Farooq 2003, Hirsch 2003). Despite a troubling tendency – often imposed by
national editors despite authors' good intentions – to downplay race and class
hierarchies by marginalizing African-American populations and fetishizing workers
as "folk," the FWP provided impetus for regionally grounded inquiries that would
resonate long after the program was discontinued in 1941 (Coats and Farooq 2003:
87–9).

The left-wing "cultural front" that flourished during the New Deal provided
the momentum for a "proletarian regionalism" whose practitioners (including
Meridel Le Sueur, Benjamin Appel, and John Steinbeck) "wrote of regional transitions from agriculture to industry . . . and emphasized new forms of industrial
folklore" (Denning 1998: 133–4, 219–21). In *The Grapes of Wrath* (1939), Steinbeck dramatizes the national scale of regional transformation by juxtaposing the
experiences of Dust Bowl refugees with the rise of large-scale agribusiness in California. By interspersing narrative chapters on the Joad family's sufferings with
impersonal chapters that offer a broader history of the mass migrations of the
1930s, Steinbeck presents a sentimental commentary on the commercialization of
agriculture:

> . . . crops were reckoned in dollars, and land was valued by principal plus interest, and
> crops were bought and sold before they were planted. Then crop failure, drought, and
> flood were no longer little deaths within life, but simple losses of money. And all their
> love was thinned with money, and all their fierceness dribbled away in interest until
> they were no longer farmers at all, but little shopkeepers of crops, little manufacturers
> who must sell before they can make. (Steinbeck 1939/1992: 315–6)

As farmers inevitably failed to pay off their loans, their lands were purchased by
capitalists whose farms grew larger; the farmers thus became wage laborers "freed"
from the land to fend for themselves in a degraded labor market: "[Industrial
farmers] imported slaves, although they did not call them slaves. Chinese, Japanese,
Mexicans, Filipinos. They live on rice and beans, the business men said . . . And if
they get funny – deport them" (p. 316). While Steinbeck's bestselling novel intensified the nation's outrage concerning the plight of Dust Bowl migrants, it stops
short of exploring the connections between white and racialized workers that Steinbeck gestures towards in designating the migrant farmers "harvest gypsies." The
following section will examine a group of ethnic regionalist texts that deploy

regionalist conventions to analyze the mutually constitutive relations between race and region.

Ethnic Regionalism

As several critics have observed, much of the color in "local color" writing has been supplied by voiceless and marginal racialized characters: Mexican subplots in *The Awakening* and *O, Pioneers!*, Twain's speakers of black dialect, Kate Chopin's eroticized mulattas, Austin's Indians, Bret Harte's Chinese laundrymen, and Jack London's idealized *kanakas* (see Barrish 2000, Birnbaum 1994, Frost 2005: 139–64). Even modernist masterpieces like Faulkner's novels and Hemingway's regional Nick Adams sketches feature "serviceable" black figures that seem to have more to do with setting than with character (Morrison 1993: 32). However, the increasing prominence of regionalist social science, socialist politics, and ethnic literary outlets in this period also enabled the development a tradition of ethnic regionalism whose diverse practitioners shared a critical consciousness of the linkages between uneven geographical development and racialization.

By reducing racialized bodies to figures of *cultural* difference, classic regionalist texts suppress the organization of labor achieved and reproduced by geographically uneven development – by the production of regions that restrict the mobility and life possibilities of nonwhite bodies. Regarding the New South, Hollander writes that "Growers in a variety of settings . . . developed, with a great deal of state support, a highly racialized labour supply as a strategy for controlling farm workers" (2006: 270). This historical pattern challenges us to bring racial analysis together with the study of regional transformation, because, as Hollander explains, "Racialization . . . is an ongoing process that constructs particular meanings of race and racial identity in particular places and historical moments [with] significant implications for the geography of labour markets" (p. 270). Legal discrimination, extralegal violence, and the racist pseudoscience that underlay farm management all contributed to the maintenance of wage differentials and vulnerable, hierarchized workforces throughout America's agricultural regions (see Henderson 1999: 91–3).

Insofar as it gives voice to peripheral locations and incorporates ethnographic techniques, regionalist literature has often been associated with ethnic writing. Philip Fisher, for example, writes of a new twentieth-century regionalism, where "local color was not that of climates and regions, but of hyphenated Americans: Jewish-Americans, Italian-Americans, Irish-Americans, WASPs, Chinese-Americans, Polish-Americans, Swedish-Americans, and Russian-Americans. This was a regionalism of languages, folk customs, humor, music, and beliefs set against the pull of what came to be called Americanization" (Fisher 1999: 174). An understanding of regionalism in terms of cultural hybridity leads Fetterley and Pryse to categorize Sui Sin Far as a writer who applied regionalist techniques to a number of different US Chinatowns, despite her cosmopolitan background and predominantly urban settings (2003: 280–314). Tom

Lutz has recently argued that regionalist writing played a crucial role in the development of an inclusive and implicitly color-blind ethos of "literary cosmopolitanism"
in American literature (2004: 4). Whereas these attempts to link the regional with
the ethnic emphasize the "literary" aspect of the phrase "literary regionalism," this
section will focus on the material dynamics of regional production and the differential
allocations of labor, mobility, and rights that it requires. Regions and races are not
distinct phenomena to be compared with one another; rather, regions have played key
roles in the expropriation, abjection, and exploitation of racialized subjects. Nor does
ethnic regionalism simply instill readers' identification and sympathy with individual
nonwhite characters: it also explores historical processes of racialization in locations
ranging from Indian reservations to the Jim Crow South and the Rio Grande Valley,
and it often imagines collective rather than interpersonal solutions to the inequalities
that it documents.

Unlike Charles Chesnutt and Sui Sin Far, who largely voiced their social criti-
cism through the ethnographic conventions of dialect and local color, Zitkala-Sa
(Gertrude Bonnin) directly protested the regional transformation imposed upon the
Dakotas by federal legislation in a series of articles and stories collected in *American
Indian Stories* (1921). The collection's early sketches – several of which had appeared
in the *Atlantic* and *Harper's* in 1900–2 – present familiar regional themes: the
Indian child's immersion in a rich tradition of oral legends and beadwork, the missionaries who tempt her with marbles and "big red apples" to leave the reservation,
and the "army of white teachers" that was drawing an entire generation of children
into a racially hierarchized national and religious culture while preparing them for
lives of menial labor (Zitkala-Sa 1921/2003: 51, 111). However, Zitkala-Sa makes
it clear that her tribe has only the most tenuous connection to the land they inhabit:
as her mother says in the first section of "Impressions of a Indian Childhood," "the
paleface has stolen our lands and driven us hither" (p. 69). In another sketch, she
responds to the question "Why Am I a Pagan?" (the original title of "The Great
Spirit") by linking spirituality with landscape, reminding us that "pagan" derives
from the Latin word for inhabitants of the countryside: "When the spirit swells my
breast I love to roam leisurely among the green hills; or sometimes, sitting on the
brink of the murmuring Missouri, I marvel at the great blue overhead" (p. 114).
Moreover, *American Indian Stories* concludes with two sketches that add a critique
of "the white man's law" to the preceding narratives of cultural loss. "The Widespread Enigma Concerning Blue-Star Woman" narrates two moments of expropriation: first, the orphan Blue-Star Woman is denied both the share of tribal land
guaranteed by the Dawes Act (1887) and the rights that come with an "individual
name" because her family name had gone "unrecorded in books" (pp. 144–5); sec-
ondly, Chief High Flier must sell half his land to pay for lawyers to defend him
when he is wrongly accused of burning down a government office. The book's final
sketch presents an uncharacteristically direct appeal to Zitkala-Sa's readers – "the
women of America" – detailing the injustices of the "legal disability" imposed upon
Native Americans and explaining that the loss of privatized tribal lands is an

inevitable consequence of the fact that "Wardship is no substitute for American citizenship" (pp. 155–6).

The history of the lower Rio Grande Valley includes similar moments of deracination, where both Mexican landholders and the chaparral itself were removed to make way for Anglo-American farms. In *George Washington Gómez* – a novel drafted in 1936–40 but not published until 1990 – Américo Paredes dramatizes the violence and psychological damage involved in the process of regional transformation during the century that followed the Treaty of Guadalupe-Hidalgo (1848). The novel carefully unfolds the long, international history that informs its setting – a fictionalized version of Brownsville, Texas:

> For more than half a century Jonesville remained a Mexican town, though officially part of the United States. . . . Then came the railroad early in the 20th century, and with it arrived the first real-estate men and the land-and-title companies, and a Chamber of Commerce, of course, which renamed the little town "Jonesville-on-the-Grande" and advertised it to suckers from up north as a paradise on earth: California and Florida rolled up into one. Mexicans labored with axe and spade to clear away the brush where the cattle of their ancestors had roamed. To make room for truck farming and citrus groves. And the settlers poured in from the U.S. heartland, while Mexicans were pushed out of cattle raising into hard manual labor. (Paredes 1990: 36)

The novel's opening chapters draw on the folk culture of *corridos* – border ballads that celebrate demotic heroes who resisted the vigilantism of the Texas Rangers (see Paredes 1958/1970) – to portray a historic moment of regional resistance along the lines of the Plan de San Diego, a short-lived 1915 conspiracy to form a multiracial and transnational alliance of Mexicans, blacks, and Japanese to liberate the Southwest from the racial dictatorship of the United States. However, Guálinto Gómez, the "hero" of Paredes's ethnic *Bildungsroman*, grows up in ignorance of his father's involvement in these struggles, and gradually abandons Jonesville's Mexican-Texan community while pursuing his family's dreams of education and uplift.

Paredes juxtaposes the narrative of Guálinto's disappointing *Bildung* as a *vendido* or race traitor (1990: 296) with brief, sympathetic depictions of minor regional characters: the impoverished but passionate folk musician Antonio; the Mexican day laborers who suffer a particularly violent version of "La Chilla," or the Depression; and Guálinto's uncle Feliciano, who transitions from working as a shopkeeper to support his nephew's education to a more satisfying living as an independent farmer. Despite its assimilated, middle-class protagonist, *George Washington Gómez* is deeply concerned with the minor characters and forms of regional folk culture – songs, ghost stories, dances, and border violence – that Guálinto disavows or represses as he leaves Jonesville for Washington, DC, only to return as a "first lieutenant in counter-intelligence" employed by the US army. Paredes positions Mexican-American folklore in opposition to the racist analysis of white regional experts such as Walter Prescott

Webb – who, as Paredes points out elsewhere, propagated white supremacist myths of the Southwest (1958/1970: 17) – and K. Hank Harvey, the novel's version of the white folklorist J. Frank Dobie. Such experts, Paredes explains, "were needed to point out the local color, and in the process make the general public see that starving Mexicans were not an ugly, pitiful sight but something very picturesque and quaint, something tourists from the North would pay money to come and see" (1990: 271).

If Paredes generally leaves racialized wage laborers in the margins of his narrative, other ethnic regionalists would explore the consequences of commercial agriculture upon local labor markets. Large-scale, monocrop agriculture made it increasingly unrealistic to imagine regions in terms of self-contained, pastoral communities. Vance, for example, observed that

> Cotton, corn, wheat, rye, oats, and fruits are pampered monstrosities created and kept alive by man. This alien complex he has maintained by force of plow, hoe, and fertilization against the encroaching wilderness and the weeds, which themselves have become domesticated outlaws. . . . In our modern workaday world the staple, artificially propagated and guarded from its rivals who would crowd it from the common table of light and soil, offers a key to the region. This complex unity of flora and fauna thus counts more in the world economy than native vegetation and animal life. (Vance 1932: 6)

Noting the particularly "unnatural" demands of cotton upon soil and labor, Vance wrote that "national literature may expect in some near future to be enriched by an epic of cotton comparable to the trilogy planned for wheat by Frank Norris" (p. 16), unaware that W. E. B. Du Bois had already published such an epic in 1911. Although *The Quest of the Silver Fleece* was not widely read, it is significant for having combined the economic and regional issues explored in Norris's wheat novels (*The Octopus* and *The Pit*) with the analysis of racialization Du Bois had presented in *The Souls of Black Folk* (1903). Recounting the political, economic, and racial engineering that underpin a scheme to corner the cotton market, Du Bois's epic of cotton stretches from rural Alabama to Washington, DC and New York. Despite the force with which he lays out the problems and violent contradictions of cotton's production and distribution, Du Bois ultimately relies too much on conventional resolutions like a marriage plot, a deathbed "atonement," and a sublime, transcendent vision of the cotton: "The glimmering sea of delicate leaves whispered and murmured before her, stretching away to the Northward. She remembered that beyond this little world it stretched on and on . . . in a great trembling sea, and the foam of its mighty waters would one time flood the ends of the earth" (Du Bois 1911/2004: 18–19). Richard Wright would provide a bleaker picture of the cotton economy's dominion over Southern blacks in *Twelve Million Black Voices* (1941): "we had to raise cotton to clothe the world; cotton meant money, and money meant power and authority and prestige. To plant vegetables for our tables was often forbidden, for raising a garden narrowed the area to be planted in cotton. . . . Our days are walled with cotton . . ." (Wright 1941/2000: 39, 49).

Although it was less commonly grown than cotton, sugar also played a significant role in the Southern exploitation of black labor. The overwhelmingly sweet scent of a sugar refinery sets the tone for Jean Toomer's collection of stories, poems, and drama, *Cane* (1923), by embodying the combined beauty and oppressiveness of black workers' lives in rural Georgia; likewise, the title of Toomer's book evokes the biblical Cain, associating sweetness with violence and banishment. Toomer's South is both the birthplace of black folk culture and a space of terror imposed by lynching. The book's opening sketches describe sexually liberated women whose lives are constrained by rural codes and customs; "Blood-Burning Moon" concludes this section with a graphic, fictionalized description of one of the widespread lynchings that were motivating factors for the Great Migration (Griffin 1996: 27). *Cane* then shifts its setting north-ward to Washington, DC and Chicago, but Toomer concludes by turning back to Georgia in "Kabnis," a long dramatic narrative whose placement complicates the usual regionalist trajectory from country to city. Influenced by Sherwood Anderson, Toomer begins "Kabnis" with a schoolteacher and aspiring writer from the North wondering whether he "could become the face of the South" (Toomer 1923/1975: 84); unlike George Willard, however, Kabnis's contact with the locals is limited, and he ends up dismissing the utterance of Father John, a prophetic black patriarch described as "the dead blind father of a muted folk" (p. 106).

Toshio Mori's *Yokohama, California* (1949) – which Lawson Fusao Inada calls "the first real Japanese-American book" – leans towards a more cosmopolitan sensibility inspired by *Winesburg, Ohio*, echoing Anderson's interest in the universality of solitude and sympathy (Mori 1949/1985: v). In a sketch titled "The Seventh Street Philoso-pher" Mori portrays a launderer who decides to present a public lecture on "The Apology of Living" at Asahi Auditorium. Although only 11 listeners show up, Motoji Tsunoda impresses the narrator with "the spectacle [of] the individual standing up and expressing himself, the earth, the eternity, and the audience listening and snoring" (p. 32) – a mundane, deflated event perceived by the narrator in sympathetic, even epiphanic terms. Mori's sketches consistently sentimentalize the tension between local and larger worldly concerns, describing, for example, a woman's difficult choice between buying groceries from an incompetent Japanese peddler or from the much cheaper Safeway; Toshio Mori's own visits to San Francisco in search of "the return of undivorced feeling toward the world" (p. 39); and a "plain," unmarried woman's obsession with Clark Gable (p. 162). These subtle attempts to establish that the Japanese are "typical . . . regardless of their nationality" would have a strategic role in the early 1940s, when *Yokohama* was accepted for publication, and when anti-Japanese sentiment was on the rise (p. 155). Ironically, the internment of Japanese Americans – Mori's family among them – postponed the book's release until 1949, when its regionalist descriptions and their strategic rhetoric of cosmopolitan human-ism could only be read in nostalgic terms as documents of a decimated community.

Carlos Bulosan presents a more critical picture of globally induced regional change in *America is in the Heart* (1946). Bulosan's "personal history" of Filipino-American immigrant experiences encompasses the transpacific dynamics of regional formation, quickly moving from pastoral descriptions of farm work in Mangusmana to the rise of large-scale agriculture in the wake of the Philippines' US-sponsored "development," and then documenting his protagonist's encounters with racism and exploitation after migrating to the US. The first section of Bulosan's text, set in the Philippines, situates the gradual expropriation of Allos's family against a broader backdrop of absentee landlords, peasant revolts, and foreclosed mortgages throughout the countryside. Ironically, the promise of a son's education in a US-sponsored school leads Allos's father to sell his family's land, send his children away to hire themselves out, and walk until his feet bleed looking for land to cultivate. Thus the racialized migrant workforce that sustained many farms throughout the American West was formed abroad: when Allos and his brothers migrate to the US in search of work, they have already been expropriated by the Philippines' corrupt colonial government.

The rest of Bulosan's narrative describes the provisional bachelor communities formed by Filipinos following seasonal harvests throughout the US, as well as their frustrated struggles to organize migrant laborers in the face of racist sentiment among both capitalists and the working class. Although the promise of democracy and unalienated labor is never realized in the novel's plot, Allos's account of his own intellectual development provides a hopeful picture of cross-racial solidarity as imagined and disseminated by literary experience. Reading Faulkner, for example, not only teaches Allos about the "decadent institutions" of the Jim Crow South, but also induces involuntary memories that clarify the global dimensions of his own experiences as colonial subject and migrant laborer:

> I returned to some of William Faulkner's books. I wanted to be confirmed. Strange that I remembered many things! I could even remember a cousin who used to scare the girls when they bathed in the creek near our village. He would hide in the bushes and then spring from them with a growl. . . .
>
> When I was in Montana, during the beet season, I met a Jewish girl in a drugstore. I remembered what she had said: "It is hard to be a Jew!"
>
> I also remembered a man in Binalonan who had killed another man when he had tried to steal water from his irrigation ditch. He sent his son to the town police to inform them of his crime. (Bulosan 1981: 242)

Despite the strategic patriotism announced by the book's title, it is regional fiction that instills a sense of interracial solidarity (the difficulty of being Jewish, black, or Filipino), and inspires him to "someday write a book about my town's characters" – a book that would expose the corrupt, internationally conditioned class politics of the Philippines (p. 243). Soon, Allos's reading encompasses the globe without losing sight of capitalism's uneven developments: he recounts how "one writer led to another" as he moved from the Russian vagabond, Gorki, to Jack London, Mark Twain, and William Saroyan, to the peasant folklore of Federico Garcia Lorca and the Filipino

Manuel Arguilla. Although he describes these readings in terms of an experience of literary cosmopolitanism where "place did not matter," Allos remains insistent on each author's ties to the land, the peasantry, and "the social dynamics of their time" (p. 246). The nationalism of the book's title and of its more sentimental passages is thus tempered with an experience of "America" as a nation (indeed, a world) of unevenly developed regions and racialized workers whose class consciousness has been tragically obstructed by racial divisions.

Bulosan's overview of a global process whereby peasants are expropriated into vagabonds and migrants suggests that regionalism should be understood not only in terms of social and economic geography, but also as a means of imposing and exploiting differential relationships to mobility. Whereas regionalist literature has always featured the vicarious mobility of its urban readers and, in many cases, the eventual mobility of its cosmopolitan protagonists, the geographer Doreen Massey explains in "A Global Sense of Place" that "Different social groups have distinct relationships to this anyway differentiated mobility: some people are more in charge of it than others; some initiate flows and movement, others don't; some are more on the receiving-end of it than others; some are effectively imprisoned by it" (Massey 1994: 149). The converse is also true: being rooted in place can be experienced as either privilege or constraint, either a mode of agrarian independence or an inability to change one's circumstances. As both ethnic and mainstream traditions of twentieth-century regionalism demonstrate, regions can function, for some readers and characters, as terrains that embody and expand the scope of American identity, as in the natural rhythms of Austin's desert or the face-to-face community described in *The Country of the Pointed Firs*. They can also, however, serve as sites of captivity or foreclosure – as in *Main Street* or the bleak "Kabnis" section of *Cane* – or as sites where racially differentiated groups are allowed to work but prevented from dwelling, included as bodies but excluded as landowners, citizens, or social equals.

References and Further Reading

Anderson, Sherwood. (1919/1960). *Winesburg, Ohio*. New York: Viking.

Austin, Mary. (1903/1996). *The Land of Little Rain*. New York: Dover.

Austin, Mary. (1932). Regionalism in American fiction. *English Journal* 21: 97–107.

Barrish, Phillip. (2000). *The Awakening*'s signifying "Mexicanist" presence. *Studies in American Fiction* 28: 65–76.

Birnbaum, Michele A. (1994). "Alien hands": Kate Chopin and the colonization of race. *American Literature* 66, 2: 301–23.

Bramen, Carrie Tirado. (2000). *The Uses of Variety: Modern Americanism and the Quest for National Distinctiveness*. Cambridge, MA: Harvard University Press.

Brodhead, Richard H. (1993). *Cultures of Letters: Scenes of Reading and Writing in Nineteenth-Century America*. Chicago: University of Chicago Press.

Bulosan, Carlos. (1981). *America is in the Heart: A Personal History*. Seattle: University of Washington Press.

Campbell, Donna M. (1997). *Resisting Regionalism: Gender and Naturalism in American Fiction, 1885–1915*. Athens, OH: Ohio University Press.

Campion, Amy and Gary Alan Fine. (1998). *Main Street* on Main Street: Community identity and the reputation of Sinclair Lewis. *Sociological Quarterly* 39, 1: 79–99.

Cather, Willa. *O Pioneers!* (1913/1988). Boston: Houghton, Mifflin.

Chesnutt, Charles. (1899/1993). *The Conjure Woman and Other Conjure Tales*, ed. Richard Brodhead. Durham, NC: Duke University Press.

Coats, Lauren and Nihad M. Farooq. (2003). Regionalism in the era of the New Deal. In Charles L. Crow (ed.), *A Companion to the Regional Literatures of America* (pp. 74–91). Oxford: Blackwell.

Crow, Charles L. (ed.). (2003). *A Companion to the Regional Literatures of America*. Oxford: Blackwell.

Dainotto, Roberto. (2000). *Place in Literature: Regions, Cultures, Communities*. Ithaca, NY: Cornell University Press.

Davidson, Donald. (1938). *The Attack on Leviathan: Regionalism and Nationalism in the United States*. Chapel Hill: University of North Carolina Press.

Davies, Richard O. (1998). *Main Street Blues: The Decline of Small-Town America*. Columbus: Ohio State University Press.

Denning, Michael. (1998). *The Cultural Front: The Laboring of American Culture in the Twentieth Century*. London: Verso.

Dorman, Robert L. (1993). *Revolt of the Provinces: The Regionalist Movement in America, 1920–1945*. Chapel Hill: University of North Carolina Press.

Du Bois, W. E. B. (1911/2004). *The Quest of the Silver Fleece*. New York: Random House.

Elliott, William Yandell. (1935). *The Need for Constitutional Reform: A Program for National Security*. New York: McGraw-Hill.

Faulkner, William. (1953/1965). A note on Sherwood Anderson. In *Essays, Speeches, & Public Letters*, ed. James B. Meriwether (pp. 3–10). New York: Modern Library.

Fetterley, Judith and Marjorie Pryse. (1992). *American Women Regionalists 1850–1910: A Norton Anthology*. New York: Norton.

Fetterley, Judith and Marjorie Pryse. (2003). *Writing Out of Place: Regionalism, Women, and American Literary Culture*. Urbana: University of Illinois Press.

Fisher, Philip. (1999.) *Still the New World: American Literature in a Culture of Creative Destruction*. Cambridge, MA: Harvard University Press.

Foote, Stephanie. (2003). The cultural work of American regionalism. In Charles L. Crow (ed.), *A Companion to the Regional Literatures of America* (pp. 25–41). Oxford: Blackwell.

Frost, Linda. (2005). *Never One Nation: Freaks, Savages, and Whiteness in U.S. Popular Culture, 1850–1877*. Minneapolis, University of Minnesota Press.

Garland, Hamlin. (1891/1962). *Main-Travelled Roads*. New York: Signet.

Garland, Hamlin. (1894/1952). *Crumbling Idols: Twelve Essays on Art and Literature*. Ann Arbor, MI: Edwards Brothers, Inc.

Greeson, Jennifer Rae. (2006). Expropriating *The Great South* and exporting "local color": Global and hemispheric imaginaries of the first Reconstruction. *American Literary History* 18, 3: 496–520.

Griffin, Farah Jasmine. (1996.) *"Who Set You Flowin'?": The African-American Migration Narrative*. Oxford: Oxford University Press.

Henderson, George L. (1999). *California and the Fictions of Capital*. New York: Oxford University Press.

Hirsch, Jerrold. (2003). *Portrait of America: A Cultural History of the Federal Writers' Project*. Chapel Hill: University of North Carolina Press.

Hollander, Gail M. (2006). "Subject to control": Shifting geographies of race and labour in US sugar agroindustry, 1930–1950. *Cultural Geographies* 13: 266–92.

Hsu, Hsuan L. (2005). Literature and regional production. *American Literary History* 17, 1: 39–69.

Joseph, Philip. (2006). *American Literary Regionalism in a Global Age*. Baton Rouge: Louisiana State University Press.

Kaplan, Amy. (1991). Nation, region, and empire. In Emory Elliott (ed.), *Columbia History of the American Novel* (pp. 204–66). New York: Columbia University Press.

Lewis, Sinclair. (1920/2003). *Main Street*. New York: Barnes & Noble Classics.

Lutz, Tom. (2004). *Cosmopolitan Vistas: American Regionalism and Literary Value*. Ithaca, NY: Cornell University Press.

Massey, Doreen. (1994). *Space, Place, and Gender*. Cambridge, UK: Polity.

McWilliams, Carey. (1930). *The New Regionalism in American Literature*. Seattle: University of Washington Book Store.

Meinig, D. W. (2004). *The Shaping of America: A Geographical Perspective on 500 Years of History*, 4 vols. New Haven, CT: Yale University Press.

Mori, Toshio. (1949/1985). *Yokohama, California*. Seattle: University of Washington Press.

Morrison, Toni. (1993). *Playing in the Dark: Whiteness and the Literary Imagination*. New York: Vintage.

Odum, Howard W. (1936). *Southern Regions of the United States*. Chapel Hill: University of North Carolina Press.

Paredes, Américo. (1958/1970). *With His Pistol in His Hand: A Border Ballad and Its Hero*. Austin: University of Texas Press.

Paredes, Américo. (1990). *George Washington Gómez*. Houston: Arte Público Press.

Robison, Lori. (2003). Region and race: National identity and the Southern past. In Charles L. Crow (ed.), *A Companion to the Regional Literatures of America* (pp. 57–73). Oxford: Blackwell.

Rosaldo, Renato. (1989). *Culture and Truth: the Remaking of Social Analysis*. Boston: Beacon Press.

Schorer, Mark. (1961). *Sinclair Lewis: An American Life*. New York: McGraw-Hill.

Steinbeck, John. (1939/1992). *The Grapes of Wrath*. New York: Penguin.

Toomer, Jean. (1923/1975). *Cane*. New York: Liveright.

Twelve Southerners. (1930/1978). *I'll Take My Stand: The South and the Agrarian Tradition*. Baton Rouge: Louisiana State University Press.

Vance, Rupert B. (1932). *Human Geography of the South: A Study in Regional Resources and Human Adequacy*. Chapel Hill: University of North Carolina Press.

Van Doren, Carl. (1921). The revolt from the village. *The Nation* 113 (October 12): 407–12.

Williams, Raymond. (1982). Region and class in the novel. In Douglas Jefferson and Graham Martin (eds), *The Uses of Fiction* (pp. 59–68). Milton Keynes, UK: Open University Press.

Wright, Richard. (1941/2000). *Twelve Million Black Voices*. New York: Thunder's Mouth Press.

Wright, Richard. (1945/1998). *Black Boy*. New York: Harper.

Zitkala-Sa (Gertrude Bonnin). (1921/2003). *American Indian Stories, Legends, and Other Writings*, ed. Cathy N. Davidson and Ada Norris. New York: Penguin.

13

"The Possibilities of Hard-Won Land": Midwestern Modernism and the Novel

Edward P. Comentale

Something quite remarkable happens in the middle of Sherwood Anderson's *Winesburg, Ohio* (1919). For a moment, Seth Richmond's life becomes truly extraordinary. Seth, a restless Midwestern teen, believes he is marked as different, but then so do all of the boys in Winesburg. He's a "dreamer," a "deep one," who stands smugly apart from the "chattering crowd," but his sense of distinction is paradoxically common, boring even. Seth's fretting, in fact, masks an even greater sense of his own average-ness: "He, like most boys, was deeper than boys are given credit for being, but he was not what the men of the town, and even his mother, thought him to be. No great underlying purpose lay back of his habitual silence, and he had no definite plan for life." In a seemingly rash moment, inspired by the desire to "become thoroughly stirred by something," he decides to pursue Helen White, the "richest and most attractive girl in town." But, here too, he mimics the desires of a handful of local men, particularly George Willard, who also sees Helen as "something private and personal to himself." Later that night, Seth seeks her out, hoping – somewhat contradictorily – to declare his intentions to leave town and to woo her with his decisive-ness. However, walking along the street with Helen, he abandons his amorous plan and blurts out, "George Willard's in love with you. . . . He's writing a story, and he wants to be in love. He wants to know how it feels." Here, though, at the moment of self-negation, in the resigned aftermath of his rage, he begins to regret his decision to skip town and realizes that "It would be something new and altogether delightful to remain and walk often through the streets with Helen White." At this moment, the Midwestern teen gives in to the Midwest, to middling itself, to a life quite ordi-nary – and this feeling, to him, seems "new and altogether delightful." In the absence of dreams, of plans, of talk itself, his body relaxes and his mind indulges, just briefly, in a Midwestern idyll. He sees a field, a tree, a swarm of bees – he hears a powerful humming and smells the "overpowering fragrance" of the air around him. Helen, too, feels something of this powerful scene. She muses on the "certain vague desires that had been invading her body" and, for an interval, she sees her backyard as "mysterious and vast, a place that with Seth beside her might have become the background for strange and wonderful adventures." In this moment, the ordinary becomes quite extraordinary and dull actuality reveals its glorious potential. Middling life – caught between desire and restraint, home and away, adolescence and maturity – presents itself as a fount of power and affection. And yet the moment exists only as potential, and perhaps willfully so. Even in his fantasy, Seth flinches – "A peculiar reluctance kept him from kissing her lips, but he felt he might have done that if he wished." He stirs uneasily, braces himself, renews his vow to skip town, and so once again the ordinary becomes *merely* ordinary. Helen's garden "now seemed no more than an ordinary Winesburg back yard, quite definite and limited in its outlines." And her "vague adventure" of the night, like the kiss itself, "would now never be realized" (Anderson 2002: 111, 116–25).

This essay considers the Midwest as a real place and as a significantly real place within the modernist imaginary. It declines the smug perspective of a continental flyover for a grounded tour through the main sites of the Midwestern landscape. Dwelling on the prairies, towns, and cities of the Midwest, it seeks to remap the literary terrain of the early twentieth century and restore a sense of the vitality of this often overlooked region of literary production. Of course, a simple tour of literary origins already begins to suggest the flaw in modernism's urban-centered scope: T. S. Eliot and St Louis, Missouri; Ezra Pound and Hailey, Idaho; Ernest Hemingway and Oak Park, Illinois; F. Scott Fitzgerald and St Paul, Minnesota; Willa Cather and Red Cloud, Nebraska; Sherwood Anderson and Camden, Ohio. Undoubtedly, experiences of nonurban America, if not the rural Midwestern terrain itself, lie behind much American literary experimentation: one need only recall Pound's interest in arboreal growth as a model of poetic genesis; Fitzgerald's fretful correlation of pioneering, consumer desire, and narrative form; Hemingway's preoccupation with survivalism, natural resources, and verbal reserve. This essay seeks to define a specifically Midwestern modernism that draws cultural and literary value from the region itself. It hopes to show that a truly experimental tradition took root in the prairie lands and middling towns of the continent and, as a whole, this literature provided a significant response to the logic of modernity at large. In contrast to traditional accounts of modernism that emphasize its cosmopolitan, marginalist ethos, I hope to show that the Midwest – precisely in its middling qualities, in its lack of distinction and its persistent refusal to be written – provided a counternarrative and a counteraesthetic to the logic of progressive modernity at large. First and foremost, this Midwestern turn focuses on potential in an economic sense, drawing sustenance from a long-standing national faith in the untapped economic resources of the region and an early twentieth-century desire – born out of World War I, the Depression, and the New Deal – to redeem the economic promise of American abundance in its local manifestations. Aesthetically, this Midwestern turn reveals – most notably in the work of Willa Cather, Sherwood Anderson, and Theodore Dreiser – alternate modes of literary creation, a sense of material, perspective, and cultivation that served to counter the productivist ethos and machine aesthetics preached from Eastern cities and their European influences. At its most radical, though, Midwestern modernism locates itself within a logic of potential as such. Extending the persistent myth of Midwestern promise, the fiction of the region explores potential in its purest sense, as possibility in reserve, and thus complicates its relation to modernism at large. For many Midwestern moderns, the region is also a significant antiregion, a region that has "not yet been" and only "ought to be," and the desire to produce often gives way to a decision not to produce, to remain silent and thus maintain or extend a state of potential. Indeed, when Fitzgerald's Midwestern narrator, Nick Carraway, declares his belief that "reserving judgments is a matter of infinite hope," he grounds his story in a regional correlation of restraint and possibility, one that radically unsettles modern ideals of America identity and American progress (Fitzgerald 2004: 2).

For the Moderns, then, the Midwest was never simply empty. Rather, many writers turned to the region as the scene of immense change, the spectacle of which was all the more dramatic because of the large canvas upon which it was being written. Heavy industrialization, vast transportation networks, a rapidly expanding immigrant population, the extension of a national marketplace, military drafts, government relief programs: modernity and modernization cut across the terrain in drastic and obvious ways, marking the prairie in each instance with the forms of a seemingly implacable history. Indeed, as in the work of Cather and Anderson, the Midwest was often depicted as more cosmopolitan than the cosmopolis, as a significant site of cultural production where shifting configurations of power, identity, and desire marked the open ground with increasing depth. Paradoxically, in the works discussed below, the center becomes the radical fringe – the scene of radical transformation, of bracing resistance, registering all of the shocks and pangs of modern life without any of the ironic detachment or neurotic defenses of the Big City. By and large, Midwestern literature weighed and measured these changes against the region's slower-paced transitions and its own grounded reserve. The openness of the land and its elemental stubbornness to rapid industrialization allowed writers to register subtle shifts in taste and consciousness that might otherwise go unnoticed among the teeming crowds of New York, London, and Paris, and thus fostered a "climate of innovation and experimentation" in their own expressive fiction (Spears 2005: 210). Modernist interest in the region, however, focused not only on crises of identity and representation, but also on issues of production and, specifically, the logic of potential and actualization. Many explored the possibility of shaping the vast nothing of the Midwest into a vital center of national growth, and their literature proves distinct insofar as it connects material production with the difficulties of meaning-making itself. In other words, in this work, cultivating the land became at once an economic and a cultural proposition – plowing the land was tantamount to writing the land, a singular process in which, given the scale of such an endeavor, the whole nation became witness to its potential fate. What follows, then, involves two radical interventions. First, with Midwestern modernism, regionalism shifts away from issues of representation, and it eschews the expressivist logic of what D. H. Lawrence (1968) once called the "spirit of a place." Rather, here, regionalism is increasingly bound to issues of resources, production, and potential, and the region finds expression only in a tireless activity of cultivation; traditional modes of representation give way to an inscriptive process, a sort of graphic plowing that links material production to the process of meaning-making itself. At the same time, with Midwestern modernism, the region as such, as geographical locale, coincides with its often overlooked potential – the potential to produce and the potential to mean. Indeed, in the most experimental Midwestern literature, the region, as bounded space, as cartographic reality, becomes a radically open proposition; here, narrative gives way to spatialization, representation becomes a matter of cultivation, and a certain stylistic emphasis on gesturalism, verbal reserve, and the subjunctive mood works to expose and extend a sense of regional promise. Ultimately, with Midwestern modernism, there is little distinction between cultivating the landscape and the work of culture itself. The region, with its scrubby fields, neat borders and vast machinery, becomes a living map of itself.

Today, of course, the Midwest struggles to shake off its reputation as an economic failure and a cultural black hole. If anything, its aesthetic is approached with heavy irony – a corrupt ethos is expressed in the ersatz naturalism of plastic deer and tin flowers. And while a certain Midwestern kitschiness has caught the postmodern imagination, the region is received by and large with a wink and a snigger, emptied of true significance. The Midwest, though, has always been a nonplace, an antiregion, one whose boundaries and contents are vague even to those who live within it. Despite Jefferson's best efforts and the Northwest Territories Act of 1787, it has remained somewhat invisible, ambiguous, slippery within the cultural landscape – a place to move through, a place to enter and a place to leave. If at all, the Midwest is defined (like Seth Richmond) through a series of vague distinctions – Ohio is too eastern, Iowa is too western, Michigan too northern. Both geographically and ideologically, it is barely distinct from mainstream America itself, and thus has consistently failed to establish its own definitional narrative. Even those terms used to characterize its people and their habits seem bland, too vaguely universal to be of any use for the rest of us: openness, solidity, reserve, spareness, warmth (see Cayton 2001: 149–50, Martone 2000: 105–6). The following proposes that any hope of challenging this perspective lies not in a simple negation of the region's emptiness, but in seeing middling itself as the very source of renewal. Of course, there are many ways to middle and many kinds of Midwestern fiction. A complete mapping of the literary terrain reveals significant differences between, say, the pioneering literature of the middle country (O. E. Rolvaag's *Giants in the Earth*, Ruth Suckow's *Country People*); the melodramas of small-town middling (Margaret McCarter's *The Peace of the Solomon Valley*, Edgar Howe's *The Story of A Country Town*); the social romances of the middle class (Meredith Nicholson's *The House of a Thousand Candles*, Booth Tarkington's *The Magnificent Ambersons*); the political fiction of the Midwestern proletariat (Josephine Herbst's *The Executioner Waits*, Jack Conroy's *The Disinherited*); the naturalism of the Midwestern city (Theodore Dreiser's *Sister Carrie*, Nelson

Algren's *The Man with the Golden Arm*); and of course the rough satires of the middle class and middle age (Sinclair Lewis's *Babbitt*, Carl Van Vechten's *The Tattooed Countess*). (For a contemporaneous history/catalogue of Midwestern literature, consult Frederick 1931.)

For the most part, the study that follows draws a distinction between middling as it informed the civic boosterism of the modern Midwest and middling as a historical and regional experience of indistinction, of incompletion, and thus as it inspired the more radical forms of Midwest fiction. It distinguishes between popular Midwestern fictions in which middling served as a quaint palliative to the extremes of industry and ethnicity that marked life in the city, and modernist fictions in which middle America was the underdetermined and inchoate ground out of which more radical visions of the nation may be improvised. The first, largely historical, section explores potential as an economic prospect, as it informs both the modern regionalist turn and the modernist interest in the Midwest. The second section, drawing upon Georgio Agamben's theories of potential and modernity, treks through the three most important sites of Midwestern fiction – prairie, town, city – to understand how and why this area of the nation inspired unique experiments in literary style and form. As we will find, this literature draws from the experience of the region in order to develop alternative models of signification in which potential is at once actualized, preserved, and extended. As a form of production in its own right, this literature – freed from any referent upon which standard critical accounts of modernism still rest – renews the modernist project with vigor, at once reclarifying and restoring language in its response to radical historical change.

Modernist Regionalism

Historically, modern regionalism has been linked to the nativist fears and economic panic of the 1920s. For many scholars, the widespread cultural turn to rural values and local traditions was born out of a much greater postwar malaise, one rooted in the tragedies of the Great War, the failures of Wilsonian optimism, the gross xenophobia embodied in the Johnson–Reed Act of 1924, and the stock market crash of 1929. In the work of Grant Wood, Thomas Hart Benton, Edgar Lee Masters, and Sherwood Anderson, we can read a postwar, post-avant-garde withdrawal from international affairs and, particularly in light of the Great Depression, an attempt to restore natural order through the sound moral and fiscal values that seemed to define life in the inner recesses of the nation (see, e.g., Czestochowski 1981). By and large, this return – particularly in its emphasis on middling classes and middling regions – inspired thinkers and writers to turn to the ideological and geographical middle of the nation. Middling, as a lack of distinction, as the bland indifferentiation of person and place, became the formless promise out of which national greatness might be restored, and the Midwest – insofar as it seemed to balance regional excesses of age, class, and politics – figured as the untapped poten-

tial of a nation largely in crisis (see Shortridge 1989: 28–35). Importantly, the ideological history of the Midwest has always depended upon a slightly dubious conflation
of incompletion and promise. Whether in its original mythic form as promised land
of Republican independence, or in its confounded history of middle-class conformity, or even in its current depiction as economic wasteland, the Midwest has
remained only always its own potential – a great American "ought." In fact, while
much of the national rhetoric surrounding the Midwest focuses on progress, development, and resources, it does so always in a subjunctive sense. At the start, with
the signing of the Northwest Ordinance of 1787, the Midwest was "yet to be," and
then, when passed over for the West proper, it became a problematic "could have
been." As Ohio lawyer and future president Rutherford B. Hayes declared, "If we
do but try . . . we *can* be, for all the purposes of everyday happiness, precisely *what
we could wish* to be." A similar note of deferral marks the work of Cincinnati writer
William Davis Gallagher, who once described the Old Northwest as an "Experiment
in Humanity" that points towards "a Day . . . drawing upon this North-Western
region" (Hayes and Davis quoted in Cayton and Gray 2001: 10–11). Even at the
height of Midwestern euphoria, as the first decades of the century saw a rapid uplift
of both Midwestern economy and Midwestern morale, commentators stuck to the
language of potential. Boosters proffered nothing more substantial than the "opportunities of the land," and, by and large, the region was linked to the nation, tenu-
ously, in the future: "The civilization that the middle west creates within the next
fifty years will be the American civilization" (quoted in Shortridge 1989: 31, 40).
Of course, this vague reputation for potential, which consistently fails to perceive
the Midwest as an actuality, tends toward a certain stagnation, allowing visions of
past or future greatness clouding the present reality. The modernist moment,
though, sought to tap into this potential as such, turning inactuality into a value
in its own right. In both popular consciousness and inner avant-garde circles, indistinction became the promise of the nation at large: it was at once a source of stability, a renewable resource, and a phenomenal experience of both spatial and temporal
openness.

For the most part, studies of American regionalism have focused on late nineteenth-
century authors and their efforts to reconfigure the relations between local difference
and the nation at large. In the work of Hamlin Garland or Sarah Orne Jewitt, for
example, the region is presented as the site of an intense struggle for representation,
by turns asserting and resisting the pluralistic premise of nationhood at large. By and
large, this writing and its success depended upon its approach to issues of cultural
and ethnic demography, and its facility with narrative strategies of adulteration,
decentralization, and containment (see Joseph 1998, Foote 2001). While modernist
scholars can trace similar dynamics in the work of regional writers such as Cather
and Toomer, the literature of this later period is not nearly so humanistic, or even
democratic. In fact, modernist regionalism is never simply representational, but
phenomenal and experiential, and its allure is never simply political or moral, but
economic and productive. Susan Hegeman provides some direction as she tracks the

twentieth-century shift in cultural logic from issues of temporality to issues of spatialization. Modern anthropological thinkers, such as Ruth Benedict and Waldo
Frank, tended to eschew models of cultural growth and decline for a sense of regional
mapping in which they could "hypothesiz[e] a diversity of cultures . . . as if arrayed
on a map of cultural possibilities" (Hegeman 1999: 94). Culture, in this regard,
became an experiential domain, with each scene attaining something of its own "personality" and thus its own "potential." For the cultural arbiters of the modern period,
the correlation of culture and region transformed culture into something "usable" in
a substantial sense, as an entity in its own right – a site to visit, explore, cultivate,
and transform (pp. 103, 129–30). Relatedly, in *A Sense of Things*, Bill Brown (2003)
notes a significant transformation in the modernist relation to region and regional
objects. Modernist regionalism, he asserts, confounds the expressive bond between
people, places, and things, representing an epistemological shift away from "objects
as a source of secure meaning" towards "objects as the source of phenomenological
fascination." In modernist writing, radical circulation of people and objects dislodges
the naturalist bent that informed the anthropological thinking of the nineteenth
century and informs a sense of the provisional relations between people and their
environment: "the tragedy of not being artifactually materialized in a proper place,"
Brown writes, "points to the very possibility of being liberated from such propriety:
of expropriations and dislocations that enable new affiliations, not restricted by things
but inspired by them" (pp. 127, 135). Importantly, the equation of culture and cultivation becomes explicit in the regional (and largely rural) writing of the South and
the Midwest, where decisively nonurban landscapes inspired efforts to preserve and
attenuate regional distinctions. The Midwest, though, sharing none of the South's
sense of tragic past or rebel gumption, found itself in a unique position to explore
mainstream modernization as both an economic and a cultural prospect. The region
– as a middling region, caught between cultural moments and cultural spaces, between
modes of production and the cultures they inspired – became the site of an intense
national discussion about not only *what* it means to be an American, but *how* it means
to be an American (Holman (1995: 17) outlines a similar distinction in the temporal
registers of Southern and Midwestern literature).

Thus, in the 1920s and 1930s, many cultural arbiters turned to local systems as a
means of querying the modern world and the productivist ethos that seemed to inform
it. In a 1920 issue of *The Dial*, James Oppenheim called for a turn to American
environments and American speech in order to cultivate a "national art" that is "open,
spacious, free," singling out the prairies for a sense of newness that stood in stark
contrast to the prefabricated poses of the cultivated East. Later that year, in the same
journal, John Dewey declared the need to bring the nation "back to earth" and experience the country as it appears in its smaller regions, "Just local, just human, just at
home, just where they live." Dewey's pragmatism located not just representational
variety, but the actual "making" of the nation in its local instances, "For the country
is a spread of localities, while the nation is something that exists in Washington and
other seats of government" (1920: 684–5). Josiah Royce, in a lecture on "Provincial-

ism" that proved influential for a number of Midwestern writers, explored middling itself as a source of both local and national potential (see Frederick 1931: 3). Royce calls for a delicate balance between local and national registers. While he celebrates regional culture for its mulish opposition to modern excess, he warns against the ways in which provincial logic can become *mere* provincialism – a complacent sense of pride and thus reified habit. For Royce, the region must remain a vital entity, both supple and responsive to the world outside. His argument, though, depends on a telling economic metaphor: the region is compared to a small trader or manufacturer and the nation at large figures as a vast corporate entity, in which "ingenuity and initiative become subordinated to the discipline of an impersonal social order" (Royce 1908: 75). Here, regional wealth becomes an issue of representation and production: the logic of democratic representation coincides with capitalist economy in which "provincial pride helps the individual man to keep his self-respect even when the vast forces that work toward industrial consolidation, and toward the effacement of individual initiative, are besetting his life at every turn" (p. 79). In a final twist that proves typical of modernist writing on region, Royce insists that a healthy region should never lose sight of its potential, its openness in time as well as space. "It is necessary," Royce concludes, "that in our temporal existence what is most worthy should appear to us as an ideal, as an ought, rather than as something that is already in our hands" (p. 100).

Waldo Frank's *Our America* (1919) takes us all the way home. As has been well documented, Frank's starry-eyed populism led him to explore American localisms as far-flung as New York, Hollywood, Kansas, and South America (see Hegeman 1999: 104–13, Michaels 1995: 135–6). *Our America*, his compelling guidebook of American regional difference, details his researches, providing vivid contrasts between a series of regional identities as they point – dialectically – towards a vaguely romantic conception of what the author calls "the Whole." Drawing from a long-established distinction between the aggressive American pioneer and the disciplined puritan, Frank depicts a fractured America scene in which Jews and Pueblos, New Yorkers and Chicagoans play out the national drama according to type. Here, culture is at once spatialized and excessive – the logic of cultural "personality" expresses itself in a certain tautological mode, in which region at once defines and grounds a rigid sense of difference. Throughout, though, Frank's willful lessons in type point towards a possible balance. In fact, the writer puts great stock in the notion that America as a "Whole" exists *in potentia*. As a land of vitality, idealism, and great transformative power, the nation has yet to realize itself: "For us of the younger generation," he writes, "America is a promise and a dream," and, in a constructivist twist, he adds, "In the infancy of our adventure, America is mystic Word. We go forth all to seek America. And in the seeking we create her" (Frank 1919: 8, 10). Most remarkably, between the lines of his regional mapping, Frank points towards the Midwest as a region of organic unity, of a grand middling out of which a truly whole America may arise. Lincoln, in fact, appears as a great middler who was able to unify the destructive excesses of the nation during the Civil War. "His mental average," Frank writes, "kept him close to the crude ore of the American world; kept him faithful to a Dream that seemed absurd enough during that saturnalia of disgusting disillusion; made it possible for him at least to achieve that 'divine average'" (p. 51). Frank's greater example is Whitman, another middling mystic. He praises the Whitmanian vision for encompassing both body and spirit, land and sea, east and west, local and foreign in a romantic dream of American greatness. "*I am large – I contain multitudes,*" the poet declares, and in this Frank finds a region at once local and divine, at once a "particular, actual corner of the earth" and a space of spiritual grandeur in which "all boundaries converge" (pp. 202–3). For Frank, the Midwest is the last fecund, uncultivated region of the Nation, the meeting point of all American contrasts and thus potential reconciliation of American promise. His book culminates with a paean to Chicago and a celebratory list of Midwestern authors: Masters, Dreiser, Sandberg, and Anderson; in this region and its literature we find a "fecund" life and "insatiate desire," unrealized potential and "unuttered life" (pp. 117, 123). The Midwest – at once landed and progressive, rural and urbane – generates a kind of spiritual rapture for Frank, but, importantly, it remains only potential. There is rapture on the streets of Chicago, in the song of Sandburg, but it is the rapture of "tomorrow" – the Midwest and Midwestern literature is "material impregnate," only just about to be (pp. 134, 143).

If Midwestern modernism manifests itself through ideas about landscape, resources, and cultivation, it is not surprising that it has been primarily defined through the work of its visual artists. Art historians have long established the antimodernist edge of regionalist painting in the 1920s and 1930s, and more than a few have noted the ideological contention that pitted Midwestern craftworkers against urban aesthetes (see Kendall 1986, Roberts 1995). However, considering the landscape painting of Grant Wood, one quickly realizes that the modernist turn to the Midwest was anything but a simple celebration of agrarian values and the virtues of craftsmanship. While Wood's work – along with that of Thomas Hart Benton and John Steuart Curry – has been celebrated for its antimodern return to traditional form and its healthy depictions of rural life, his landscapes present the Midwest as a startlingly unsettled proposition, one in which the ground itself – in a state of perpetual construction – confounds any sense of stability. In paintings such as "Young Corn" (1931) and "Fall Plowing" (1931), Wood reveals an intense preoccupation with the material landscape as both economic and painterly resource. The various surfaces here reveal a remarkable fecundity – trees, grass, and dirt are excessively present, offered up in abundance and ready to be sown. And yet, at the same time, Wood's depictions confound any sense of purity, of naturalness. His landscapes are remarkably tidy, constructed, excessively formed – everywhere, human intervention distorts (abstracts, to use a more formal term) the region of plenty. In later, more radical works, such as "Spring Turning" (1936) and "Spring in Town" (1941), the landscape bears strange, geometric configurations, squares, and shapes that reveal as much a cubist sense of form as an agrarian work ethic. Here, cultivation is also culturation, a process at once practical, aesthetic, and social. The surface of the land is an inscriptive surface, ready to be written and rewritten according to the farmer's needs. In "Fall Plowing," the plow literally etches its design into the surface of the field; it perforates the landscape (if not the canvas itself), creating an unsettling play of surface and depth in which plow, pen, and brush coalesce in a single act of inscription. In fact, a careful eye quickly realizes that the seemingly "natural" parts of Wood's landscapes are already artifactual. His fields double as cross-stitched blankets and corduroy denims; his trees sprout buttons, hemlines, and patches; towns are arrayed in gingham patterns. Here, in a set of inversions that would dizzy a Dadaist (not to mention our most radical postmodernists), all nature proves decisively unnatural, while unnatural materials are mistaken for God's own goods (see Marling 2004). Again, though, this constructivist play serves to reveal a sense of potential that is at once real and persistent. The blank potential of the land extends through its own actualization, throbbing beneath all manner of intervention, whether agrarian, industrial, avant-gardist, or New Dealist.

In Wood's work, then, the actuality of the region finds itself decisively troubled by a sense of potential. Each painting exceeds its own "realism" on both sides – as brute potential and pure artifice – and so the viewer fails to find a stable ground on which values (whether moral, economic, or aesthetic) can be realized. But while some critics have noted the exaggerated formalism that sullies Wood's regionalist turn, few have realized the extent to which it radicalizes our sense of region and environment (Dennis 1995 comes closest). Even Wood's copioneers in the regionalist movement – Benton and Curry – tended towards idealized versions of the Midwest. Their work provides largely iconic visions of the rural life, largely allegorical readings of the region which were easily linked (often publicly) with an ugly racism and extreme nativism (for a discussion of this more virulent strain of Midwestern regionalism, see Hegeman 1999: 126ff.). Wood, though, sustained a sense of radical constructivism through his radical belief that "The naked earth in its massive contours, asserts itself through anything that is laid upon it" (quoted in Czestochowski 1981: 14). In fact, in his lively manifesto "Revolt Against the City" (1935), Wood describes his work on decisively nonsymbolic grounds, as a material effort to practice a different sort of cultivation in the Midwest. From the start, Wood's rhetoric, like that of Royce, strikes a register at once economic, moral, and aesthetic: "It is certain that the Depression Era has stimulated us to a re-evaluation of our resources in both art and economics, and that this turning has awakened us to values which were little known before that grand crash of 1929 and which are chiefly non-urban." After this brief salvo, Wood outlines his aesthetic reform effort as it rests upon the logic of cultivation and the use of native materials. The American spirit, he argues, is founded upon "certain true and fundamental things which are distinctively ours to use and exploit" and the new regionalism entails not sentiment, but a "common-sense utilization for art of native materials" (Wood 1935/1981: 130–1). His biases find summation in a turn to the Midwestern scene, which, he claims, has its own "physiography, industry, psychology." Midwestern modernism – as an economic and an aesthetic proposition – provides the key to American modernism at large: "I am willing to go so far as to say that I believe the hope of a native American art lies in the development of regional art centers and the competition between them. It seems the one way of building up of an honestly art-conscious America" (p. 136).

Midwestern Regions

In many ways, Ruth Suckow is *the* quintessential Midwestern writer, and not simply because her prose has failed to distinguish itself for literary historians. Her fiction demands attention for a quiet objectivity and psychological reserve that suggests as much about American modernism as it does the drama of progress that once played out across the Iowan landscape. If anything, her prose is artfully bland and unobtrusive, and this tendency would lead to dullness if it didn't ultimately expose the intense vitality of her native state and its modern inhabitants. Her prose excels at moments of immanence and comes quite close to establishing a Midwestern sublime; at its most engaging, it depicts pioneers as they confront – physically, psychologically, ethically – a landscape at once "silent, significant, motionless, immense" (Suckow 1926: 183). In a short essay on "Middle Western Literature," Suckow suggests something of how this experience shaped the literary forms of the Midwestern movement. The author first defines the recent literary turn to the Midwest as a vital "cause" and a true "awakening" to the local terrain. Arguing for a balanced approach, though, she praises contemporary literature for conveying the land's "richness" as well as its "homogeneity," and even its "barrenness." In the midst of this discussion, though, she hits on a strange tautology, asserting that the Midwest is defined mostly by its "middlewestishness." Not without a certain irony, she claims that this "undistinguishing quality" is "yet exactly what distinguishes" the region. She recognizes that more specific labels might apply ("a certain downright quality, a plainness, a simple freshness"), but she remains committed to the blandness of her approach, affirming, "This section is naturally what it is." Later, in a more forceful effort to define this lack of definition, she outlines the ways in which the Midwest negates other regional qualities. Unlike New England or the Southwest, she claims, the Midwest is decisively unmarked, free of distinguishing qualities, radically central: "it has, in a sense, a great homogeneity, a firmer stamp, than any other section." By stressing the homogeneity of the terrain, though, Suckow avoids any representational valuation of the Midwest and, instead, presents it as a phenomenological paradigm. At once emergent from and set against the open terrain, Midwestern being attains an authenticity and fullness unmatched anywhere else in the Nation: "It is open to the eye – so open, that all too frequently the eye passes over its essential nature. Main Streets are Main Streets, utility is utility, adornment is all too truly adornment, the farms are farms, the houses are just American houses" (Suckow 1932).

Fullness and reserve, indistinction and intense presentism, a perspectival play of object and terrain – these terms define much of the narrative content and stylistic experimentation of the fiction discussed below. The work of Cather, Anderson, and

Dreiser explores the logic of potential and actualization as it informs both economic and cultural production in the Midwest field, town, and city. The following analyses, though, are informed by Giorgio Agamben's attempt to theorize potentiality as a significant feature of both modernist phenomenology and modernist literature. While many theoretical strands weave in and out of Agamben's work, his efforts to think potentiality as it persists through the moment of actualization informs his most radical conceptualizations of modern culture and politics. Drawing upon Aristotle, Agamben eschews a causal definition of potentiality, in which it is revealed only in its loss, as it becomes actual, spent in a finished project, and he rejects specifically productive models, in which potential is linked to ideologies of progress and industry, and thus gives itself up to an instrumental planning. Potentiality, he avers, must be seen in its own right, in its own original openness, before use or application, as "not simply the potential to do this or that thing but potential to not-do, potential not to pass into actuality" (Agamben 1999a: 180). Everywhere, in fact, Agamben celebrates restraint and reserve, if not outright negation, as the basis of a more radical potential: "To be potential means: to be one's own lack, *to be in relation to one's own capacity.* Beings that exist in the mode of potentiality *are capable of their own impotentiality*; and only in this way do they become potential. They *can be* because they are in relation to their own non-Being" (1999a: 182). For Agamben, this model often leads to a certain silence (and the specifically modern silences of Kafka), but it also works to extend potential through actualization, through speech itself, insofar as the moment of actualization entails a whole new set of negations, not least of which is the loss of potential, the impotentiality of impotentiality: "*if a potentiality to not-be originally belongs to all potentiality, then there is truly potentiality only where the potentiality to not-be does not lag behind actuality but passes fully into it as such.* This does not mean that it disappears in actuality; on the contrary, it *preserves itself* as such in actuality" (1999a: 183).

What concerns us here is not just the philosophical maneuvers of Agamben's approach, but also his attempts to locate the ways in which modernity renews this radical form of potential. For Agamben, modernity – in the collapse of sovereign structure and its ethical reference – prepares an open field in which language, and thus being itself, is restored to its original potential. A crisis of legitimation creates a situation in which language (and language as law) begins to operate without structured reference; it constructs provisional relations upon the nonrelational, and, in this, in its tendency towards gesture, becomes indistinguishable from life itself: "For life under a law that is in force without signifying," Agamben claims, "resembles life in the state of exception, in which the most innocent gesture or the smallest forgetfulness can have the most extreme consequences"; the modern subject "moves in an absolute indistinction of fact and law, of life and juridical rule, and of nature and politics," and this state is full of potential for both glory and disgrace (1995: 20–1, 52, 186). For the most part, Agamben struggles to realize potentiality in its positive form. By and large, his work emphasizes the negation of actuality, the derealization or "decreation," that he finds stitched into all production. And like many of the

Midwestern modernists below, he defends an aesthetics of bareness, reserve, and silence, seeking to suspend actualization and thus preserve something like the originary fullness of potential (see Agamben 1999b). And yet, at its most optimistic, Agamben's work also accounts for the widespread aesthetic innovation of the period, and, more generally, a sense of "experimental life" that works the seam of language and matter in new and innovative ways (see Deladurantaye 1990). In the studies that follow, a similar dynamic of potential and actualization marks the origins of Midwestern modernism (the pioneer confrontation with the open field), and it inspires an equally radical sense of both language and literary form. In moving from prairie to town and then to city, we can see how potential as such persists amidst the developing modernist terrain, at once informing, constructing, and haunting its most advanced structures.

Prairie

For Willa Cather, the prairie is at once fertile terrain, inscriptive surface, and the site of unique perspective. In her two novels that focus specifically on the prairie, *O Pioneers!* (1913) and *My Ántonia* (1918), the Midwestern landscape – in its openness, fecundity, and expansive vista – becomes the site for rethinking the relations between cultivation and culturation and thus the logic of novelistic form itself. The earlier novel, in fact, more dramatically depicts the difficult resistance of the material landscape and the slow, piecemeal process whereby it becomes shaped by its inhabitants. The prairie – inchoate, unmarked, unyielding – only occasionally gives itself up to form, and then only provisionally. All human developments on the Divide are precarious, prone to revert at any moment back to formlessness: "Most of them were built of the sod itself, and only the unescapable ground in another form. The roads were but faint tracks in the grass, and the fields were scarcely noticeable" (Cather 1995: 12). *My Ántonia* carefully frames this drama of cultivation as a matter of inscription. The novel opens with Jim Burden's memory of his youthful arrival on the Nebraska plains. He notes that there "seemed to be nothing to see; no fences, no creeks or trees, no hills or fields. There was nothing but land; not a country at all, but the material out of which countries are made." More startlingly, he recalls a feeling of disorientation, a near total loss of selfhood occasioned by the absence of human markers: "I had the feeling that the world was left behind, that we had got over the edge of it, and were outside man's jurisdiction. . . . Between the earth and that sky I felt erased, blotted out. I did not say my prayers that night: here, I felt, what would be would be" (Cather 1994: 11–12). Here, on the open sea of the Midwest, Jim marvels at the region's overwhelming indistinction, a terrestrial sublime that at once confounds the self and its bearings. This place without referent, without law or even plotting, presents itself as fullness and freedom. He describes the vital fecundity of the landscape and, later, entertains a state of bliss, a feeling of "Lightness and content" in which "Nothing happened" and "I did not expect anything to happen" (pp. 18–19). The landscape, though, soon yields up its potential to a kind of human writing and slowly rewards its farmers with "Long, sweeping lines of fertility." Over time, it becomes a palimpsest that changed before the very eye, developing "like watching the growth of a great man or a great idea" (p. 227). Slowly, Jim, a budding lawyer and writer, begins to appreciate the immense symbols and patterns that have been carved into the terrain. He marvels over an Indian circle in the grass, the marks of plough on field, and then a heroic image of a farmer against the sun. The perspective of the prairie is privileged for its scope and scale. Prairie pioneer and prairie writer share a remarkable ability to conceive of things that are "far away," and each is attuned to the ways in which the region's "scarcity of detail" heightens the presence of each of its markings (pp. 17, 28). Jim slowly develops an appreciation of the aesthetic forms and relations on the prairie, which, in a telling phrase, he calls "picture writing" (p. 183). Later, at school, he abandons his lessons in the classics for daydreams about his "own naked landscape and the figures scattered upon it": echoing Virgil's passion to bring the muse to his country, he envisions a truly regional writing in which "the pen was fitted to the matter as the plough is to the furrow" (p. 198).

The work of cultivation informs Cather's sense of meaning-making in a larger sense, as a psychological and a cultural phenomenon. Insofar as the prairie at once inspires and resists structuration, she emphasizes both the necessity and provisionality of human effort to generate significant order. In *O Pioneers!*, as Carl scans Alexandra's cultivated farmlands, he marvels at the process of creating order, its incredible difficulty and its necessary repetition. In this, though, he pushes Cather's idea of "picture writing" towards a more general theory of narrative construction. "Isn't it queer," he remarks, "there are only two or three human stories, and they go on repeating themselves as fiercely as if they had never happened before; like the larks of this country, that have been singing the same five notes over for thousands of years" (1995: 70). For Cather, these repeated stories often concern disaster and survival, migration and return, loss and restitution; in each case, though, personal meaning mimics the logic of cultivation, proving arduous, repetitive, and insistent: for Carl, life on the prairie is always "the old story writing itself over," and Alexandra concurs, adding, "Only it is we who write it, with the best we have" (p. 179). In *My Ántonia*, Cather pursues this line to its more radical (and undeniably modernist) ends. Beginning with her title and its personal possessive form, the novel as a whole reconceives meaning-making as largely gestural and always anxious – a momentary shaping of material without recourse to larger narrative reference. Jim Burden's narrative consists of a series of sketches of snapshots from his past that attain significance only in his willingness to claim them as such. This is decisively *his* Ántonia and her brown eyes bear the full weight of his meaning only because of their complete absence of any prior referent. In fact, all the moments and objects of Jim's reverie – killing the rattlesnake, eating the dried mushroom strip, the Christmas tree with its paper figurines – prove significant only in his isolated memory, a faculty which is celebrated as much for its Proustian sharpness as for its generative power. In this, though, he is no different from a host of other characters – the Russians Pavel and Peter, Jake and Otto, Lena

Lingard – for whom Cather interrupts the narrative to explore their own efforts to create meaningful structures. Perhaps more than anything else, this emphasis on meaning-making determines Cather's interest in decisively foreign, if not fully orphaned characters. The foreigner's disconnection to the land radicalizes the effort to generate meaning and sustain order. Some fail to take to the new environment (Mr Shimerda, Frank Shabata), but others succeed in cultivating lives of great economic and spiritual value (Alexandra, the Harlings); many, though, reinvent themselves continually, living ad hoc lives of multiple distinctions (Ántonia, Jim, and, in the later fiction, Tom Outland and Thea Kronborg). Always, though, Cather's pioneers are at once detached and engaged, estranged and affiliated, and, in this middling state, they negotiate meanings that are both personal and communal, attesting to both the flexibility of human affections and the suppleness of human gestures. (Millington 2005 interprets Cather's emphasis on gestures and provisional meaning-making as the basis of her modernist aesthetics.)

In a brief chronicle written for *The Nation* in 1925, Cather ends her region's history with the year 1910, a decisive marker of modernism proper. By this time, she explains, the Midwest's "largely transatlantic" population had reconfigured the landscape and thus began to impact the region's sense of aesthetic value itself. Norwegians and Swedes, Czechs, French, and Germans had brought not only a range of new "social ideals" and certain diverse "qualities of feeling," but also a more vital sense of artistic form. The Midwest, she proclaims, has become a "great cosmopolitan country" in which we find the "hard molds of American provincialism broken up" (1925: 237–8). Indeed, in Cather's fiction, the Midwest is always also foreign, if not exotic, and its people are "warm, mercurial, impressionable, restless, over-fond of novelty and chance" (1925: 238). One need only recall that Jim Burden shares his train to Nebraska with a Bohemian family; his introduction to the prairie is also an introduction to people and habits from a diverse set of cultures: Arabia, Mexico, Austria, Germany, Russia (1994: 9–15). And like this mottled, uneven, and constantly shifting terrain, Cather's novelistic forms are at once varied, disjointed, and fortuitous. Her narratives are spotty, unevenly developed like the checkerboard patterns of the fields themselves, and the unplowed spaces between stories and voices are at once bare, wild, and alive. Tellingly, Cather's fiction always points towards allegory, but it never sustains this rigid mode to its tidy ends. Fatalistic Bohemians and stoic Norwegians, spirited farmgirls and brittle society ladies – Cather recognizes the types and their archetypal clashing, but she often only raises the possibility of allegory only to draw our attention to its wild, tattered limits. Marie is not simply the wild spirit of the land itself; Emil does not exhibit his family's pioneering drive; Frank's brutal self-pity is not an ethical trait. Plotwise, Ántonia's Bohemian background does not prepare us for her first tragic marriage; Jim Burden's life on the prairie does not quite explain his career as a lawyer or even his ability to write Ántonia's story. Cather works through weak, faulty allegories – they never quite fit, they never quite cover the terrain, and at their broken, scrubby ends we see something of the wild potential of the landscape itself.

These qualities extend to the level of the sentence itself. Cather's prose is notably halted, fragmentary, restrained, and provisional. Each line conveys an awkward brokenness, a clumsy process of signification, but also a refusal to define or delimit, and a sense of radical otherness. In this, she mimics the broken English of the prairie's immigrant population, as their speech withholds completion before the unfinished project of the landscape. If anything, a sense of reserve preserves both the vitality of each utterance as well as that which lies behind it. In *My Ántonia*, Cather describes this as "the gift of moving and simple expression"; in describing Jim's grandfather, she writes, "Because he talked so little, his words had a peculiar force; they were not worn dull from constant use" (1994: 67). Similarly, in *The Professor's House* (1925), she praises Outland's writing for its vital "austerity," a quality in which "one felt the kindling imagination, the ardour and excitement of the boy, like the vibration in a voice when the speaker strives to conceal his emotion by using only conventional phrases" (1990: 238). Cather's own descriptions of the terrain reveal a certain reserve or hesitation that is unsettling in its slightness, a breathy, broken quality through which the fullness of the environment seems to burst:

> The homesteads were few and far apart; here and there a windmill gaunt against the sky, a sod house crouching in the hollow. But the great fact was the land itself, which seemed to overwhelm the little beginnings of human society that struggled in its somber wastes. It was from facing this vast hardness that the boy's mouth had become so bitter; because he felt that men were too weak to make any mark here, that the land wanted to be let alone, to preserve its own fierce strength, its peculiar, savage kind of beauty, its uninterrupted mournfulness. (Cather 1995: 9)

A strange language, this – one that can assert without denying, actualize without losing its original potential. Again, though, its force lies in its radical play of presence and absence, which can be read both in the occasion of each line as well as in the space between each line: "In that singular light every little tree and shock of wheat, every sunflower stalk and clump of snow-on-the-mountain drew itself up high and pointed; the very clods and furrows of the field seemed to stand up sharply" (p. 238).

Ultimately, Cather's Divide is at once a geographic and a phenomenological proposition, a site that both produces and dissolves personal and cultural identities. It is a decisively "neutral world," the open center of the country, and thus a rich terrain for both Slav and Scandinavian, rich and poor, old and young, male and female. It is the place where all stories (personal as well as national) tend to emerge, dissolve, and begin again. In this, the Divide is a site of American potential, and Cather seeks to preserve this openness in her own writing, throughout the process of naming, inscription, actualization. In terms of theme and narrative, this effort finds expression in her fascination with youth and the generational logic of the prairie plot. As is well known, Cather's novels convey a singular fascination with youth as a decisively renewable resource. In *O Pioneers!*, *My Ántonia*, and *The Professor's House*, the rough drama of age and decline finds relief in "warm-hearted and impulsive" romance, a sense of youth as the "acceleration of life," and a vitality that is almost "too delicate, too intangible, to write about" (1995: 173, 178). Tellingly, cultivation of the fields must be matched by a ceaseless human generation, one that resists traditional property lines and the standard discursive framing of the novel itself. The open land develops across generations, passing uneasily from age to youth, demanding, always, "a fresh crop of dreamers," and belonging, decisively, "to the future" (1995: 175, 179).

But, structurally, Cather's work also seems to halt these processes. Indeed, if her novels often end inconclusively, with only vague stirrings of spring and youth, they bury potential and allow it to linger, unrealized. Taken in order, her novels shift focus from nascent to ancient cultures and, by and large, reveal an increasing interest in failed gestures and buried communities. Later plots, in fact, focus on the artifactual remains of dead pioneers and their dead civilizations: broken pots, irrigation ditches, fenceposts, and entire cities. In these, though, Cather suggests something of her reverence for potential as such, as embalmed in the failed gesture, the unrealized life. In *The Professor's House*, for example, the young Tom Outland finds an affective connection and a renewed sense of cultural identity in the preserved remains of an ancient Indian tribe. As he explains, "To people off alone, as we were, there is something stirring about finding evidences of human labour and care in the soil of an empty country. It comes to you as a sort of message, makes you feel differently about the ground you walk over every day" (1990: 173). Increasingly, Cather buries her most vital discoveries and creations. She plants them, literally, in the ground, where they remain preserved, embalmed – their potential never realized and thus extended into the future. Always, though, this preservationist tendency – which is at once philosophical and practical – seems to halt time itself and thus counter insistent narratives of national progress and expansion. Tellingly, in her brief history of Nebraska, Cather's attention ultimately shifts away from the vital terrain and its heroic pioneers towards the region's numerous cemeteries. Discussing the influence of foreigners on the prairie, she muses on the mute grave markers: "I have always the hope," she remarks, "that something went into the ground with those pioneers that will one day come out again" (1925: 237). Oddly, her history ends here, with buried life and a certain silence. And yet it also just begins. With this gesture, narrative becomes pure potential, at once the end and the beginning of all stories.

Town

But we must venture towards the town, where the fields grow into houses, buildings, entire communities and a certain history. In Sherwood Anderson's Winesburg, middling is decisively a psychological condition, at once background and effective cause for all manner of human striving. His Midwest is populated by dreamers, indistinct souls with vague, unexplained longings. Their desire, however, relates to a lack that is external rather than internal – again and again, the inchoate fullness of the Midwestern subject confronts a world that refuses to provide objects of satisfaction. In this, everyone in Winesburg contains the "seeds of something very fine," but they often fall – unrealized – like "twisted little apples" to the ground (Anderson 2002: 16–17). George Willard is not a "dull clod," but his energy is restless, unfocused; it lacks objects, models, references, and so his identity is at once overwhelmingly bland and remarkably vital (p. 25). His mother, too, has a "secret something that is striving to grow." She remains haunted by a "girlhood dream," that only briefly and unsuccessfully clarified itself as a decisive longing for a life on the city stage. It persists unrealized, *in potentia*, as "something unexpressed" and thus grown monstrous with age; she roams the halls of their lodging house, suffocating under the weight of her own unused power, wishing for death as the only form of "release" (pp. 27–8). More often than not, in Winesburg, personal potential is left to rot. Always, though, Anderson foregrounds the tension between this excess of power and the failure of available form, of expression. Enoch Robertson, a quiet, artistic sort, dwells solely within his fluid imagination. His isolation stems from both the fullness of his mental life and his singular inability to communicate any of his vision. The inchoate power of his mind, which Anderson equates with "the child in him," finds him "bumping against things, against actualities like money and sex and opinions" (not to mention a street car). Moreover, Enoch's passion finds only an awkward fit in the words available for expression; he is too intense, too excited to talk – even amidst like-minded artists, he is frustrated by the presence of "something else" that demands and yet destroys all efforts to frame. Trying to describe one of his paintings, he stammers, "There is something else, something you don't see at all, something you aren't intended to see" – tellingly, the picture depicts a Midwestern landscape (pp. 153–4).

At one and the same time, though, these characters are torn between a manic need to actualize this desire and a melancholic desire to preserve it as such. They are by turns lonely, sullen, aggressive, and frantic; they often mutter and shout to themselves, trying to reconcile form with fever and thus passion with purpose. Their stories move in jerky fits and starts, ending abruptly with moments of possession, hallucination, and spasm. Anderson's success with the short story form suggests something of his characters' own fretful relation to form. Writerly passion finds provisional form, but then, dissatisfied, moves on again, rewriting itself over the terrain. Moreover, his voice is at once indistinct and overprecise. In his own struggle to match content to form, he manages to write both the blandness of George Willard and the freakish desperation of Wing Biddlebaum, Joe Welling, and Elmer Cowley. In this, though, his collection begins to capture something of the creative force of Midwestern history at large. For it culminates with one truly decisive act, and this moment finally discloses the full power of the region at large. George Willard is in fact Anderson's most indistinct creation – he suffers assaults, seductions, and betrayals with a bland passivity, and his work for the local newspaper presents him as a neutral scribe for the more colorful personalities around him. If anything, he is a strangely androgynous figure – at once male and female, boy and man, rube and sophisticate – whose middling status allows him to reconcile, much like Tiresias in *The Waste Land*, the competing visions and dreams of his neighbors. And yet his indistinction becomes his uniqueness, as if in Winesburg only the truly bland can provide a sense of difference. More precisely, George manages to turn drab middling into a valid (and sustainable) principle in itself. At the end of Anderson's collection, George does not simply leave Winesburg – rather, he becomes a figure of pure "ambition." His leaving is not a decisive act, but a phenomenal state, one perhaps informed by Anderson's own multiple crossings between Ohio and Chicago (see Spears 2005: 222ff.). Specifically, in the text, George's departure is carefully presented as a moment of maturity. For the first time, he is able to look back on his memories and this makes him feel like an adult. As the narrator explains, he "crosses the line into manhood," and both past and future are splayed before him, reminding him of all that has become and all that has not. In an instant, George also realizes that he is always crossing a line, that the moment of actualization is also a moment of potential – his transition marks transit in general, a ceaseless process in which delimitation also always dissolves all limits. Tellingly, at this moment, Anderson turns to one of his favorite, and most radical, phrases – "something happens." In its Midwestern simplicity, the phrase manages to suggest both the definitive nature and radical openness of the act (not to mention Anderson's prose); "something happens," but without final reference, without established cause or effect. The decisive act does not limit possibility, for it at once attests to the presence of potential and opens up space and time to greater potential. As for George, he moves, in this decisive moment, towards a more radical indecisiveness: "From being quite sure of himself and his future he becomes not at all sure." In the moment of change, at once personal and historical, "a door is torn open and for the first time he looks out upon the world, seeing, as though marched in procession before him, the countless figures of men who before his time have come out of nothingness into the world, lived their lives and again disappeared into nothingness" (2002: 218).

In his next novel, Anderson tried to show how this process drives historical change at large. *Poor White* (1920) has often been read as a national allegory that attempts a Midwestern reconciliation of the competing ideals of the puritan and the pioneer. It has also been seen as a prophetic screed against the rise of heavy industry and corporate business which puts forth a competing romance of the agrarian life (see Hegeman 1999: 120–5, Tichi 1987: 184–94). While these readings capture some of the book's ideological force, they miss its attention to the phenomenology of production and its related interest in the lived experience of historical progress. Anderson certainly presents the Midwest, here represented by the fictional town of Bidwell, as the site of ideological reckoning, but his efforts are rooted in the logic of potential and its transformation into history. McVey, the poor white trash of the title, first appears as a detached, "naturally indolent" boy, whose future as an inventor rests on his ability to shape his capacity for dreaming into purposeful industrial form. Early chapters trace the slow evolution of his indefinite mind and his rough training, at the hands of a puritan foster mother, to "be definite and do definite things" (Anderson 1993: 5). As McVey matures, the unproductive life – of dreaming, drifting, and indistinction – slowly gives way to purposeful self-alienation, an actualization in form that is also always a denial of fullness. The process of matching dream to form proves both wondrous and horrific, at once the promise and the disaster of the nation at large. At one point, in fact, McVey's mind relaxes and he imagines fields and farmers waiting, hushed and silent for an unrealized bounty, but the vision quickly turns into a nightmare, a dark industrial wasteland of deadening labor and violent struggle: "The dreaming man felt himself a part of something significant and terrible that was happening to the earth and to the people of the earth" (pp. 28–9). For Anderson, the marriage of dream and form is a problem of historical actualization, and the nation must figure out how to create itself without violence. As with McVey, the town struggles to harness its potential without destroying it as such; while they find some excitement and relief in the promises of industry and corporatism, the latter prove capable of only cutting and crushing out the spirit of the town; slowly, the call to do "definite things," to actualize the region's potential, sweeps away all "thinking and dreaming" (pp. 60–2).

Anderson struggles to provide a healthy model of Midwestern production. By and large, he tracks McVey's struggle to reconcile desire and form, but again and again the inventor's efforts lead only to greater repression, exploitation, and conformity. However, in the spring of his second year in Bidwell, McVey sneaks onto the French farm to watch the workers setting plants and comes to a startling revelation. Studying the workers as they move across the moonlit field, he is struck by how their labor seems to reconcile motion and form, vitality and a machine-like repetition. McVey, moreover, recognizes that the fruitful processes of the natural world always involve a certain degree of abstraction; the moonlit scene serves to reconcile him to the fact that all human growth depends on the reconciliation of energy and design (1993: 77). Thus, as an inventor, he begins to practice a sort of bodily mimesis, "relating" his own limbs to the mechanical forms he finds at work in the fields (p. 80). In this, though, the process entails not simply the negation of identity, but a new openness to other forms of being. Slowly, McVey's inclination to dreams, "balked by the persistent holding of his mind to definite things," begins to assert itself in a startlingly fluid relation to "steel, wood, and iron" (p. 68). At these moments, McVey loses his bearings, becomes ghostlike, and yet experiences a certain sublimity, a fever both mechanical and animal. The moment of creation – an intercourse at once destructive and creative – involves not merely a loss of self, but an extension of self and thus its potential: "Now there was no defeat, no problem, no victory. Within himself something new had been born or another something that had always loved with him had stirred to life" (pp. 318–19). And the town, too, caught up in the rush of the inventor's "forward-moving impulse," finds a new source of wonder in the "Dumb masses of material taken out of the earth . . . and molded by his mind into fantastic shapes" (pp. 70, 68). In fact, with this increased activity of invention, the town grows to feel a new sense of regional identity, one rooted in the potential of the land itself, the "wonder and mystery of the wide open places" (p. 224).

And yet Anderson remains aware of the ways in which this process can be perverted by external factors. Insofar as abstraction is stitched into all production (even natural production, as Marx argued), both producer and product are left open to a certain appropriation. Tellingly, at almost each moment of human invention, Anderson reverts to his signature formulation, "something happened," and thereby points to the undecidability of events as they occur within the industrial order (1993: 80, 323, 325). More importantly, Anderson also recognizes that the moment of actualization is always also a loss of potential, a delimitation of resources as well as identity. Not surprisingly, with each invention, the economy seems to contract rather than grow: job opportunities decrease, land becomes scarce, and the town's profits fall into just a few (Eastern) pockets. Quickly, in Bidwell, lines are drawn, doctrines are preached, and labels are applied – as a whole, the town finds itself locked within a rigid political grid, a "system" (pp. 327–8). Yet ultimately, confronting this crisis, Anderson finds himself forced to rethink the logic of actualization. His inventor, sickened by the misuses of his creative power, begins to recognize that every act of creation is also a form of decreation, that realization involves a certain derealization, a restoration of nothingness, and thus, in Agamben's terms, a restoration of potential. McVey, in other words, confronted repeatedly with his own derealization, begins to gain a certain respect for nothingness itself and cultivates the latter as a personal credo. Tellingly, towards the end of the novel, he reverts to dreaming and a sense of creative play that exists apart from "definite things." In fact, his dreaming is put forth specifically as a mode of creation in which – in a surprising reversal of Anderson's privileged phrase – "Nothing happened." Abandoning his research one evening, McVey takes a long walk through the developing town; upon returning, and somewhat baffled by his own (lack of) activity, he declares, "The evening has been wasted. I have done nothing" (p. 354). Soon, though, he begins destroying his plans for future inventions, and then, in an aestheticist twist, he begins to play with colored stones. At this moment, McVey seems fully relieved from the burden to create and decreate; if anything, the play of stones restores him to a ceaseless actualization without any diminishing of potential: "The gods have thrown the towns like stones over the flat country," he muses, "but the stones . . . do not burn and change in the light" (p. 358). Granted, at this point, the novel has lost some of its political force. The inward retreat and its newfound aestheticist logic seem to relieve Anderson from the burden of history. At the same time, though, these concluding passages are not merely sentimental – they seem to eschew any easy regional romance as they recognize the need to reconcile, rather than halt, production with play. If anything, the novel reveals a commitment not to a Midwest that never was, but to a Midwest that has never yet been. The struggle has shifted from the issue of production to the issue of potential, and, in this, the Midwestern town reveals its

potential in history – not yet completed, never fully realized, it persists as the inchoate dream of the nation at large.

City

From the opening lines of Theodore Dreiser's *Sister Carrie* (1900), Chicago threatens
to sever all traditional binds of time and space. The city churns up the very ground
of the Midwest and destroys, in its wild sensorium, the stable forms of Midwestern
identity. "Of an intermediate balance," Dreiser's droll narrator explains, "under the
circumstance, there is no possibility"; "Half the undoing," particularly for a sensitive
mind, "is accomplished by forces wholly superhuman. A blare of sound, a roar of
life, a vast array of human hives, appeal to the astonished senses in equivocal terms"
(1999: 4). Dreiser's Chicago, as scene of modernity proper, defines itself only in its
violent turns. The city creates itself anew at each instant, as new inventions, new
identities, and new affections ceaselessly crowd out the old. This very same tumult,
though, frees the mind, allows it to wander, to construct, to generate. As nihilistic
kaleidoscope, as vertiginous "swirl of life," the city inspires – as with Carrie – "vain
imaginings about place and power, about far-off lands and magnificent people"
(1999: 106). Dreiser, like his characters, knows enough about the "city to know
that its mysteries and possibilities of mystification were infinite" (p. 374). Carrie
can rewrite her biography at an instant; Hurstwood can strike it rich or land broke
at any moment's notice; money falls out of the sky, a star is born in a flash, a novel
can simply begin again on a different street with a different set of characters. For
Dreiser though, the city's potential is not universal, but decisively Midwestern. Its
fecundity – its "infinite" potential – emerges from the soil on which it is built and
out of the feverish imagination of its rural inhabitants. At one and the same time,
the empty fields give birth to the city and that city in turn extends "miles and
miles of streets and sewers" across the prairie, a "pioneer of the populous ways to
be" (p. 22). Nothing more radically confounds the relation of country and city, of
rural past and urban future, than the attitudes of Dreiser's displaced Chicagoans.
Simply put, Carrie – his prairie heroine – arrives in the city already charged with
a sense of possibility and an utterly modern craving for newness. She is one of many
characters who seem to embody the spirit of the Midwestern city in essence, thus
defying the deterministic logic normally presumed to be the touchstone of Dreiser's
naturalism. Carrie, in fact, first appears in transit, on the train heading to Chicago,
and her passion quickly outstrips her traveling speed. While machines now bind
prairie and city, her vast imagination arches over both: "She gazed at the green
landscape, now passing in swift review, until her swifter thoughts replaced its
impression with vague conjectures of what Chicago might be" (p. 4). Far from
establishing the city as a site of Carrie's possible corruption, Dreiser presents
Chicago as a natural setting for the exercise of her imaginative openness. The city
merely actualizes her already voracious appetite for novelty and her supple power of
continual self-creation. If anything, through Midwestern eyes, the city becomes a

scene of subjunctive pleasure in which the small-town *should* is swept away by a big-city *could*.

At first glance, Chicago's potential seems to derive from what Georg Simmel famously described as the "indifference" of urban life (1950: 409–24). Dreiser's novel, in fact, often alludes to "indifference" as a general affective stance against the shocks of urban life and as it underlies the immorality of urban economics. As Carrie looks for work she quickly learns the ways in which "indifference" determines "independence": whether in a blank stare, a late night theft, an economic merger – a certain ethical neutrality underlies both the promise and the pain of urban life at its most aggressive (Dreiser 1999: 32). And yet, in this novel, "indifference" does not quite account for the city's positive dynamism. As with Anderson, Dreiser's protagonists are keenly aware of "something happening" or "about to happen"; at all times, urban life roils with the creation of new forms and new sensations, and Carrie, as character and fictive device, exists solely in terms of this fortuity. "A shop girl," the narrator explains, "was the destiny prefigured for the newcomer. She would get in one of the great shops and do well enough until – well, until something happened. . . . Things would go on, though, in a dim kind of way until the better thing would eventuate" (p. 21). For Dreiser, this active potential is explicitly aligned with middling rather than indifference. His characters are actively torn between possibilities, and their fretful desire, balanced precariously between nothing and something, fuels a healthy urban economy. "There is nothing in this world more delightful than the middle state," his narrator explains, "in which we mentally balance at times, possessed of the means, lured by desire, and yet deterred by conscience or want of decision." Such middling, as Carrie reveals in a department store jaunt, remains open to potential on all sides and thus figures as both motive force and source of pleasure itself:

> Now she paused at each individual bit of finery, where before she had hurried on. Her woman's heart was warm with desire for them. How would she look in this, how charming that would make her! . . . All the time she wavered in mind, now persuading herself that she could buy it right away if she chose, now recalling to herself the actual condition. (1999: 92)

As a critical concept, "middling" may lend some weight to Michaels's claim that the novel's preoccupation with desire and disequilibrium affirms the economic terms of modernism at large (1980: 382–4). Middling, though, is not merely a fluke of Carrie's nature or even the consumer economy, but the motive force of modern history itself. As Dreiser's narrator explains, "Our civilization is still in a middle stage, scarcely beast, in that it is no longer wholly guided by instinct; scarcely human, in that is not yet wholly guided by reason." The modern subject lacks all balance, being caught between instinct and free will, past and future, east and west. But in this the subject proves decisively creative: "In this intermediate stage he wavers . . . He is even as a wisp in the wind, moved by every breath of passion, acting now by his will and now by his instincts, erring with one, only to retrieve by the other, falling by one, only to rise by the other – a creature of incalculable variety" (1999: 101–2).

But, ultimately, Dreiser's city remains bound to the Midwest in its peculiar affective register. Chicago's potential is decisively unrealized potential, and it expresses itself in a mood of "mingled expectancy, dissatisfaction, and depression" (1999: 70). Tellingly, Carrie's charming face is melancholic, and its appeal, for Drouet, for Hurstwood, for the teeming crowds at the theatre, derives from a "finer mental strain in her that made possible her depression and loneliness" (p. 95). For Dreiser, possibility flowers precisely in response to this "old, helpful melancholy" (p. 405). Whether perusing shopgoods, hunting for a job, or choosing a lover, Carrie's sense of "dazzling interest" is piqued by the fact that "not any of these things were in the range of her purchase" (p. 31). Even later, after she finds a modicum of success in both love and economics, she cultivates a sense of deep melancholy as a way of augmenting her longing and thus reopening the spaces of potential around her. Hearing a strain of sad music, she turns "as wistful and depressed as the nature which craves variety and life can be under such circumstances"; considering the comparative worth of her rooms, she allows her heart to sink toward a state in which "She was sad beyond measure, and yet uncertain, wishing, fancying" (pp. 140, 156–7). In these moments, Carrie begins to cultivate the affective stance that captivates first the Chicago middle class and then the nation at large. On stage, her wistful expression seems to represent an alluring middle state of thwarted youth, failed effort, and, overall, an untapped potential for happiness. A certain grief commingles with a "freshness of spirit," revealing a checked, but undeniably full spirit. For her largely middle-class audiences, her face becomes the face of every commodity, of modern experience itself, at once expressing and relieving an "old melancholy of desire" (p. 243).

Tellingly, a Midwesterner theorizes the full potential of Carrie's melancholy. Ames, an inventor from Indiana, appears in the second half of the novel as the genial voice of the region that Carrie has left behind. At once industrious and reserved, he is able to translate the latter's melancholic longing into an idealized vision of national culture at large. Contra Walter Benn Michaels, who sees Ames as a failed representative of Midwestern restraint and economic balance, the latter seems to redeem the economics of potential as cultural potential (Michaels 1980: 386). Rejecting the showy, wasteful, and unwholesome atmosphere of the urban scene, Ames promotes an ideal of restraint and remorse, of "sorrows and sacrifices," but only insofar as such tend towards the production of a higher cultural good (1999: 427). Carrie, immediately, recognizes that the inventor was "far ahead of her," and thus she sees him as a new ideal by which to translate her personal, explicitly consumerist, longing into a greater cultural longing (pp. 426, 430). Musing on her own work in the cultural sphere, she thinks, "So, too, the ideal brought into her life by Ames remained. He had gone, but here was his word that riches were not everything; that there was a great deal more in the world than she knew; that the stage was good, and the literature she read poor" (p. 443). Again, though, this potential exists only in a certain "pathetic strain." The dream of culture persists through an active melancholy, a decisive refusal to act. In fact, in a final encounter, Ames urges Carrie to cultivate her melancholy into a true dramatic art. Carrie considers the idea, but her story ends indecisively, with the protagonist rocking in her chair, musing sadly, wondrously, upon all she has not yet done. "Still she did nothing – grieving," the narrator falsely grumbles, "It was a long way to this better thing – or seemed so – and comfort was about her; hence the inactivity and longing" (p. 637). Carrie's rocking, like Ames's message, serves to reconcile several competing tensions in the book. She becomes, in one sense, a perpetual motion machine, propelled forward by her own insatiable desire, and yet the chair itself symbolizes listlessness and a certain domesticity, if not Midwestern blandness itself. Moving – perhaps fretfully – both forward and back, checking progress against restraint, she remains suspended between two ideals, two regions, two moments. And yet, in her middling, her anxious push and pull towards the future, her mind spins out a range of glorious futures, possibilities both personal and cultural. (Spears argues that Carrie's rocking reconciles Dreiser's conflicted feelings of nostalgia and urban-centered progress, 2005: 116.) The novel thus concludes with a Midwestern girl rocking in her chair at the heart of New York City. In this, the "inexplicable longing" of the Midwest extends itself beyond prairie, town, and city itself, transmuted into a "thing the world likes to see, because it is a natural expression of its longing" (1999: 635). The center becomes the margins, middling proves a source of both cultural and historical distinction, and potential is restored to modernity at large.

References and Further Reading

Agamben, Giorgio. (1995). *Homo Sacer: Sovereign Power and Power Life*. Stanford, CA: Stanford University Press.

Agamben, Georgio. (1999a). On potentiality. In *Potentialities: Collected Essays in Philosophy* (pp. 177–84). Stanford, CA: Stanford University Press.

Agamben, Georgio. (1999b). Bartleby, or on contingency. In *Potentialities: Collected Essays in Philosophy* (pp. 243–71). Stanford, CA: Stanford University Press.

Anderson, Sherwood. (1993). *Poor White*. New York: New Directions.

Anderson, Sherwood. (2002). *Winesburg, Ohio*. New York: The Modern Library.

Brown, Bill. (2003). *A Sense of Things: The Object Matter of American Literature*. Chicago: University of Chicago Press.

Cather, Willa. (1925). Nebraska: The end of the first cycle. *The Nation* 117 (September 5): 236–8.

Cather, Willa. (1990). *The Professor's House*. New York: Vintage Books.

Cather, Willa. (1994). *My Ántonia*. New York: Vintage Books.

Cather, Willa. (1995). *O Pioneers!* Boston: Houghton Mifflin Company.

Cayton, Andrew R. L. (2001). The anti-region: Place and identity in the history of the American Midwest. In Andrew R. L. Cayton and Susan E. Gray (eds), *The American Midwest: Essays on Regional History* (pp. 140–59). Bloomington: Indiana University Press.

Cayton, Andrew R. L. and Susan E. Gray. (2001). The story of the Midwest: An introduction. In Andrew R. L. Cayton and Susan E. Gray (eds), *The American Midwest: Essays on Regional History* (pp. 1–26). Bloomington: Indiana University Press.

Czestochowski, Joseph. (1981). *John Steuart Curry and Grant Wood: A Portrait of Rural America*. Columbia: University of Missouri Press.

Deladurantaye, Leland. (1990). Agamben's potential. *diacritics* 30, 2: 3–24.

Dennis, James M. (1995). Grant Wood's native-born modernism. In *Grant Wood: An American*

Master Revealed (pp. 43–63). San Francisco: Pomegranate Artbooks.

Dewey, John. (1920). Americanism and localism. *The Dial* 68, 6: 684–8.

Dreiser, Theodore. (1999). *Sister Carrie.* New York: Modern Library.

Fitzgerald, F. Scott. (2004). *The Great Gatsby.* New York: Scribner.

Foote, Stephanie. (2001). *Regional Fictions: Culture and Identity in Nineteenth-Century American Literature.* Madison: University of Wisconsin Press.

Frank, Waldo. (1919). *Our America.* New York: Boni and Liveright.

Frederick, John T. (1931). Ruth Suckow and the Middle Western literary movement. *The English Journal* 20, 1: 1–8.

Hegeman, Susan. (1999). *Patterns for America: Modernism and the Concept of Culture.* Princeton, NJ: Princeton University Press.

Holman, David Marion. (1995). *A Certain Slant of Light: Regionalism and the Form of Southern and Midwestern Fiction.* Baton Rouge: Louisiana State University Press.

Joseph, Philip. (1998). Landed and literary: Hamlin Garland, Sarah Orne Jewitt, and the production of regional literatures. *Studies in American Fiction,* 26: 147–70.

Kendall, M. Sue. (1986). *Rethinking Regionalism: John Steuart Curry and the Kansas Mural Controversy.* Washington: Smithsonian Institution Press.

Lawrence, D. H. (1968). *Studies in Classic American Literature.* New York: Viking.

Marling, Karal Ann. (2004). Primitive modernism: The Midwestern experience. Transcript of a paper presented at the symposium "Remapping the New: Modernism in the Midwest, 1893–1945," September 2004, Terra Museum of American Art and the Union League Club of Chicago.

Martone, Michael. (2000). *The Flatness and Other Landscapes.* Athens: University of Georgia Press.

Michaels, Walter Benn. (1980). *Sister Carrie*'s popular economy. *Critical Inquiry* 7, 2: 373–90.

Michaels, Walter Benn. (1995). *Our America: Nativism, Modernism, and Pluralism.* Durham, NC: Duke University Press.

Millington, Richard H. (2005). Willa Cather's American modernism. In Marilee Lindemann (ed.), *Cambridge Companion to Willa Cather* (pp. 51–65). Cambridge, UK: Cambridge University Press.

Oppenheim, James. (1920). Poetry – our first national art. *The Dial* 68, 2: 238–42.

Roberts, Brady M. (1995). The European roots of regionalism. In *Grant Wood: An American Master Revealed* (pp. 1–41). San Francisco: Pomegranate Artbooks.

Royce, Josiah. (1908). Provincialism. In *Race Questions: Provincialism and Other American Problems* (pp. 57–108). New York: The Macmillan Company.

Shortridge, James R. (1989). *The Middle West: Its Meaning in American Culture.* Lawrence: University Press of Kansas.

Simmel, Georg. (1950). The metropolis and mental life. In *The Sociology of Georg Simmel,* ed. and trans. Kurt H. Wolff (pp. 409–24). New York: The Free Press.

Spears, Timothy B. (2005). *Chicago Dreaming: Midwesterners and the City: 1871–1919.* Chicago: University of Chicago Press.

Suckow, Ruth. (1926). *Iowa Interiors.* New York: Alfred A. Knopf, Inc.

Suckow, Ruth. (1932). Middle Western literature. *The English Journal* 21, 3: 175–82.

Tichi, Cecelia. (1987). *Shifting Gears: Technology, Literature, Culture in Modernist America.* Chapel Hill: The University of North Carolina Press.

Wood, Grant. (1935/1981). Revolt against the city. In Joseph Czestochowski, *John Steuart Curry and Grant Wood: A Portrait of Rural America* (pp. 128–36). Columbia: University of Missouri Press.

14

Writing the Modern South

Susan V. Donaldson

In the 1920s Virginia Woolf famously observed that human nature seemed to have changed around December 1910 and suggested, half-seriously, that therein lay the beginnings of modernism. Although the celebrated Postimpressionist exhibition shown that year in London partly shaped that extravagant claim, she also had in mind changes in families, marriages, and labor that were leaving their impact on other forms of human activity, from politics to literature. For writers of the US South, though, that sense of a breach in history, dividing the era of modernity from the past, could be traced back to a much more specific date – and one further back in time – January 1, 1863, the day Abraham Lincoln issued the Emancipation Proclamation setting free all slaves in Confederate territory not yet under Federal control. Not until Appomattox would the full impact of emancipation be felt, but by then everyone, slaveholder and freed slave alike, knew that the end of slavery meant a radical break in time with all that had come before – from the economic modes of production to intertwined social definitions of black and white manhood and womanhood.

"All that we were seemed to be passing away," lamented one Georgia planter as quoted by historian James L. Roark in his 1977 study, *Masters without Slaves*, an examination of the disorientation and sense of loss that came to define the slaveholding class at war's end (Roark 1977: 207). Nearly 30 years later, Michael O'Brien largely concurred with that assessment in his magisterial *Conjectures of Order* (2004), in which he concludes that the war's end seemingly propelled Civil War diarist Mary Boykin Chesnut into a confrontation with modernity's upheaval and the necessity of finding new narrative forms to express that breach in history. By contrast, for those who were awarded their freedom by the Proclamation and by the Confederacy's defeat, emancipation suggested a new universe of possibility and an embrace of modernity. Toni Morrison (1992) would not be alone in her assertion that freedom for African Americans forged a lasting alliance with the forces of modernity. African Americans were acutely aware that emancipation had made them symbols and avatars of social and personal transformation, and it was that sense of identification with modernity that came to be seen as the very essence of "the New Negro Movement," as Alain Locke would declare in his celebratory manifesto of the Harlem Renaissance (Locke 1925/1992).

For the US South, then, modernity – with its pronounced sense of change, disruption, upheaval, and fluidity – seemed to arrive with breathtaking suddenness, with much of the sense of dissolution and liquidity that sociologist Zygmunt Bauman sees as a defining feature of modernity – its proclivity for "melting the solids" of an earlier, seemingly more stable world with all its rules, hierarchies, and restrictions (Bauman 2000: 3). It is no wonder that so many white Southern writers with family roots in that pre-emancipation world saw the Civil War itself as the region's defining historical experience, one of defeat, impoverishment, failure, and guilt apart from a larger, more mainstream US culture of success, abundance, and exceptionalism. Indeed, from the perspective of many white Southern writers, it became something of a foregone conclusion to see and describe the Civil War and Confederate defeat as the defining feature of regional memory and history. That particular sense of historical consciousness, C. Vann Woodward argued in his pivotal *The Burden of Southern History* (1960), would continue to set the South off from the rest of the nation even in the midst of the "Bulldozer Revolution" transforming the region's rural landscape in the aftermath of World War II.

Woodward's thesis, indebted in part to Reinhold Niebuhr's *The Irony of American History* (1952) and to the literary scholarship of self-consciously conservative white Southern critics, would help shape the scholarship of the next two generations to come – but as African-American critics and historians have been quick to add, his thesis tells only part of the story of modern Southern literature and historical consciousness – that of white Southerners who had long defined both their sense of region and individual identity through the exclusion, repudiation, and disavowal of those who had once been held in bondage, and through the erasure of slavery itself, for that matter, from the public sphere. To tell the whole story of writing the modern South means to reinstate not just those who were excluded, but the dialogues, debates, and interlocutions crossing lines of race, class, gender, and region that prompted those exclusions in the first place.

From the earliest days of exploration and European conquest, in fact, the region's literary productions have resonated with conflicting and multiple voices about who has the authority to tell Southern stories and who does not, what those stories should look like, how they should define their audiences, and above all, how they should be wielded to shape both individual and communal identity. The slavery/antislavery debate contributed a good deal to the cacophony of those voices, so much so that the slaveholding South went to extraordinary lengths in the antebellum period to silence black voices and to barricade itself against the mounting press campaign for abolition by censoring the US mails and implementing repressive slave codes prohibiting the education of slaves. But the fluidity and uncertainty of the period immediately following the Civil War accelerated and intensified the debate on narrative and cultural authority, as Southerners white and black, confronted with the demise of slavery, pondered new ways of telling stories about the region, its past, its present, and its inhabitants.

The fluidity that historian Edward Ayers (1992) sees as the region's defining feature in the immediate postwar period – and that Zygmunt Bauman associates with the modern condition – raises central questions about when and where modern Southern writing – or the Southern Renaissance, as white Southern new critics Allen Tate, Donald Davidson, Robert Penn Warren, and John Crowe Ransom termed it – actually began. By mid-century Tate was arguing that the flowering of modern Southern letters began after World War I and largely followed the lead that he and his colleagues at Vanderbilt University had established, first with their poetry journal *The Fugitive* (1922–25) and then with their joint publication of *I'll Take My Stand* (1930), a manifesto of 12 essays defending a white Southern agrarian tradition against industrialism and urbanism. Tate and his colleagues, in fact, quite consciously defined the Southern Renaissance in their own image – white conservative men disturbed by the vagaries of modernity and nostalgic, after the fashion of T. S. Eliot, for the traditional, hierarchical society that the antebellum South had come to mean to them. Hence they were quick to dismiss white women writers, whom they tended to associate with literary sentimentalism and bestsellers like *Gone with the Wind*, and to disregard African-American writers altogether – even though both groups achieved considerable public success as early as the 1920s. As Michael Kreyling has persuasively argued in his *Inventing Southern Literature* (1998), the Fugitive-Agrarians, by dint of publications and strategically placed academic and editing positions, did their best to exert something very like ownership over modern Southern letters, but they never quite succeeded even to their own satisfaction.

Their leadership, after all, was by no means uncontested. As soon as *I'll Take My Stand* appeared, the Fugitive-Agrarians drew immediate fire from African-American critics, who pointed out the parallels to be drawn between the Agrarian defense of a rural, hierarchical, traditional society and proslavery arguments made in the antebellum South. White women writers in turn frankly questioned Fugitive-Agrarian custodianship of the past in much the same way that women writers, white and black, had long interrogated and debated assumptions about Southern stories in general and those about women in particular. Carol Manning (1993), for one, makes a good argument for shifting the beginnings of modern Southern writing at least back to the 1890s, when women writers including African-American activists like Frances Ellen Watkins Harper, Anna Julia Cooper, and Ida B. Wells and white writers like Kate Chopin and Ellen Glasgow took it upon themselves to narrate the proliferating new stories that seemed to be available to both black and white women in the aftermath of slavery.

For black women writers, telling new stories meant in part building on the tradition of slave narratives defined by their opposition to proslavery arguments. In *Incidents in the Life of a Slave Girl* (1861), Harriet Jacobs had resolutely declared that Northern visitors who subscribed to white Southern stories of the peculiar institution's "beautiful feature[s]" would have heard "a different story" altogether from the slaves who lived under that institution: "We could have given them a chapter of wrongs and sufferings, that would have touched their hearts, if they *had* any hearts to feel for the colored people" (Jacobs 1861/1987: 146). As her narrative pointed out time and again, her own story of fending off the sexual overtures and traps laid out by her owner belied the stereotype of the black Jezebel working her wiles on white men, and it was precisely that kind of reversal and rebuttal that was needed by black women writers of the New South, as black educator Anna Julia Cooper would declare three decades later in her feminist manifesto *A Voice from the South* (1892). Of Southern literature in general, Cooper declared, "The 'other side' has not been represented by one who 'lives there.' And not many can more sensibly realize and more accurately tell the weight and the fret of the 'long dull pain' than the open-eyed but hitherto voiceless Black woman of America" (Cooper 1892/1988: ii).

It was a declaration of narrative independence with which Cooper's peers, journalist Ida B. Wells and Frances Ellen Watkins Harper, thoroughly concurred. In the pages of her Memphis newspaper and later from Chicago newspapers, Wells pursued her antilynching crusade by frankly questioning the credibility of cultural scripts that argued that white women were vulnerable to the sexual predations of black men – assumptions that had, significantly enough, emerged in the last years of the Civil War and immediately thereafter in response to emancipation and new definitions of black masculinity. Harper for her part took on the motif of the tragic mulatta inherited from the debate on slavery and produced in her bestselling 1892 novel *Iola Leroy* a narrative of the black woman drawing from traditional slave resources of subterfuge, coded language, silence, and self-imposed invisibility to rewrite her sense of self and to consciously choose and redefine her own racial identity.

Across the color line, white Missouri-born Kate Chopin signaled her own break with tradition in short stories like "Desirée's Baby," which subtly but unmistakably countered white patriarchal privilege with the hidden narratives of femininity and blackness that made that privilege possible. But it would be in her 1899 novel *The Awakening* that Chopin would explore the implications of modernist alienation for a white woman deliberately breaking with the tradition of marriage and general expectations of behavior for white middle-class women. Chopin herself fashioned her self-image in the mode of French writer Guy de Maupassant, whom she admired for his rebellion against tradition and authority, and in many respects, like Edna Pontellier, the protagonist of *The Awakening*, Chopin, "apprehended instinctively the dual life – that outward existence which conforms, the inward life which questions" (Chopin 1899/1981: 190).

Chopin would later retreat from public life after the outcry greeting the publication of *The Awakening*. But in a manner of speaking she would be joined in her rebellion against oppressive tradition by Richmond writer Ellen Glasgow, who immersed herself in Darwinian science during her youth, forthrightly argued that what the region needed in its literature was "blood and irony," and announced her intention to produce a multivolume social history in fiction of Virginia that would dare to broach tabooed topics like interracial sex and economic injustice. An avowed feminist, in a series of novels produced in the 1910s and 1920s she skewered the mythology of white Southern womanhood that she saw as crippling and dehumanizing. In her 1913 novel *Virginia*, a portrait of a white Southern lady rendered anachronistic by changing times, she condemned out of hand all the forces that conspired to turn white women into abstract and wispy ideals, including educational expectations and standards most concerned with protecting young women from "the contaminating presence of realism," as the novel's narrator declared (Glasgow 1913/1989: 40). These were early feminist texts that frankly resisted assimilation into the Cult of the Lost Cause commemorating the antebellum South, including its defining institution of slavery, but their resistance to tradition could also be detected in the forms of their novels, which hesitated between naturalist concerns underscoring the diminishment of individuals by large impersonal forces and increasingly modernist inclinations toward fragmentation of narrative viewpoint, character, and plot.

Even more daring interrogations of literary realism and its ability to represent the real — and in particular the aftermath of slavery — would be undertaken by two writers themselves loosely associated with American literary realism — George Washington Cable, a former Confederate soldier turned social critic, and Charles Waddell Chesnutt, an African-American writer who saw as his mission the education of white audiences in the nuances and complexities of race and racism. In his 1880 novel *The Grandissimes*, which is sometimes referred to as the first modern Southern novel, Cable resorted to a historical narrative about New Orleans just after the Louisiana Purchase of 1803 to construct a hard-hitting critique of legalized segregation and heightened racism in the late nineteenth-century South. Chesnutt in turn produced in his path-breaking 1901 novel *The Marrow of Tradition* a thinly disguised account of the 1899 race riot in Wilmington, North Carolina, in order to examine the fictions wielded by whites to define political and racial power and ultimately their own whiteness.

Briefly allied as critics of white racism and the emerging system of segregation, Cable and Chesnutt were also bound by strikingly similar strategies of fictional reflexivity that reveal the "real" as constructed and highly contested, and race and whiteness in particular as mere fictions subject to dismantling. In novels that questioned the relationship between narratives and their referents in "reality," Cable and Chesnutt also oddly anticipated the self-reflexivity and even antirealism of modernism to come. Their most immediate concern, though, was to expose the codes and narrative techniques necessary to create the fictions of whiteness and blackness by which the late nineteenth-century white South had come to define both its nostalgically viewed antebellum past and its racially troubled present. To a startling degree, both novels drew attention to the political and exclusionary uses to which storytelling and memory were being set by segregation-minded white Southerners seeking in memory and the past what historian Grace Elizabeth Hale calls "the legitimizing narrative of origin for the culture of segregation" (Hale 1998: 48).

In *The Grandissimes* Cable's narrator follows the entry of a German immigrant named Joseph Frowenfeld into the closed ranks of early nineteenth-century New Orleans, presided over by a complicated hierarchy of French Creole families resistant to change and in particular any alteration of the racial status quo established by slavery. As Joseph comes to read "the Book of New Orleans," he learns how permeable the line between whiteness and blackness is as he mistakes brothers separated by the color line for each other and discovers the political purposes of stories about the past, particularly those about a rebellious slave, broken by his masters, whose defeat seemingly symbolizes the permanence of slavery and white privilege. It is a story, ultimately, that tells the white families of the proud city who and what they are and as such serves notice of the manifold ways that narratives can serve the purposes of power.

Strongly influenced by Cable, who served as something of a mentor, Chesnutt explores the fabrications concocted by powerful white men in a scarcely veiled Wilmington, North Carolina, to reassert their sense of authority and white privilege and to reimpose subordination upon African Americans who had by then enjoyed more than a generation of freedom. Resorting to charges of rape and murder, the white men set off a firestorm of racial violence and in doing so reveal the violence required to maintain racial fictions and white authority. It is a novel, ultimately, that ponders the ease with which white Southern stories can kill – and yet, like *The Grandissimes*, it also underscores how intertwined white and black stories have always been as it explores the fortunes of two families and their connected fates across the color line.

Both novels presented powerful critiques of white Southern stories and their consequences but also appeared to be profoundly pessimistic about finding alternatives – and by implication alternative realities – to those stories and the Southern communities they upheld. The response of white New Orleans was to upbraid Cable for his critical portrayal of the city's French Creole community, and by the time Cable had published his searing attack on segregation, "The Freedman's Case in Equity," a few years later, local hostility had become so pronounced that Cable found it necessary to decamp for Massachusetts. Chesnutt was similarly attacked outright by white critics who simply could not accept the "reality" portrayed by *The Marrow of Tradition*. No less a figure than William Dean Howells, the dean of American letters and foremost champion of literary realism, simply dismissed the novel as "bitter." Chesnutt himself would turn away from pursuing a career in letters although he would continue to write in the dark years that became known as the "nadir" of African-American history.

By then a good deal of white Southern literature had been, in historian Edward L. Ayers's eloquent phrasing, "reduced to a shrill, virtually hysterical white scream" (1992: 371), captured most fully in Thomas Dixon's wildly popular and rabidly racist novels *The Leopard's Spots* (1902) and *The Clansman* (1905) – and in the film made from those novels, *The Birth of a Nation* (1915). The film in particular, which relied on "historical facsimiles" to capture moments from the Civil War and Reconstruction, was widely hailed by whites for its "realism" about the putative abuses of black freedom during Reconstruction, and its dark picture of emancipation's consequences and the perils of black governance was pronounced "gospel truth" by President Woodrow Wilson himself, a historian as well as a politician. Ending with a "march" of the Ku Klux Klan through a Southern hamlet "liberated" from black rule, the film played out nearly every imaginable white fear of black sexuality and white vulnerability. Perhaps even more to the point, the film presented a final vision of unified whiteness, composed of reunited white Northern and Southern veterans participating in the Klan march; even the audience was manipulated toward racial solidarity, as director D. W. Griffith's clever camera angles situated theatre spectators among the cheering crowd.

Considering the impact of the film – the country's most popular until *Gone with the Wind* – and considering the angry resistance to Chesnutt's and Cable's novels of social protest, one can see why so many African-American novelists in this period, as William Andrews observes in his study of Chesnutt's literary career, found themselves resorting to "the model of the escape narrative, reminiscent of the antebellum slave autobiography, as an appropriate means of dramatizing the southern black man's reversed prospects in his homeland at the turn of the century" (Andrews 1980: 187–8). The alternative, James Weldon Johnson posed in his anonymously published *Autobiography of an Ex-Coloured Man* (1912), was to have to face a controlling white gaze that designated whiteness and blackness, as well as the ever-present specter of violence necessary to enforce those racial distinctions. For Johnson's protagonist, who lives on both sides of the color line, the answer is finally to take refuge in whiteness, but it is a decision that costs him the richness of his black heritage – the music he could have written and the multiple black narratives he could have excavated.

Escape and estrangement, curiously enough, became recurring narrative motifs in the 1920s for aspiring Southern modernists. Many of them, white and black, were as much drawn to the new narrative and poetic experiments of international modernists like Virginia Woolf, T. S. Eliot, and James Joyce as they were horrified by what appeared to be an increasingly benighted regional culture defined by segregation, poverty, racial violence, and sexual repressiveness. That backward South was regularly lampooned by journalist and satirist H. L. Mencken, whose audience seemed to grow with each year. In Nashville the apprentice poets who became known as the Fugitives, after the title given to their poetry journal, announced forthrightly that they fled "from nothing faster than from the high-caste Brahmins of the Old South," and they took quite seriously in their earliest poems references to aliens and Demon Brothers (*Fugitive* 1922/1967: 1). For the first few years of *The Fugitive*'s publication, though, they seemed to have had difficulty finding their own poetic voices or even deciding whether to affiliate themselves with the modernist revolution that T. S. Eliot's 1922 poem *The Waste Land* had ushered in.

Allen Tate, as a brash young Vanderbilt University undergraduate, quickly designated himself a disciple of Eliot, but in the first half of the 1920s he was still looking for an idiom to evoke his sense of estrangement from regional tradition. His search led him, surprisingly, to the 1923 volume *Cane*, a highly adventurous and self-consciously experimental collection of sketches, poems, short stories, and even a concluding play that a young black Washingtonian named Jean Toomer had just published. In an enthusiastic review for a Tennessee newspaper, Tate lavishly praised the book for resisting the caricatures and sentimentality he associated with plantation school writers like Joel Chandler Harris and Thomas Nelson Page and even went to the trouble of twice trying to meet Toomer – without success. What probably attracted Tate initially to *Cane* was its frank affiliation with Cubist collage and the aesthetics of imagist poetry, but what also likely drew the Fugitive poet were Toomer's portraits of troubled, rootless would-be artists who seemed to find fleeting glimpses of wholeness in rural Georgian life and in the sensual, earthy women inhabiting the countryside (such figures dominated the first third of the collection). It was a world, though, on the verge of extinction, one that briefly illuminated the dying legacy of slavery; and its folk spirit, Toomer's artist-figures declared, would disappear into the cities that were drawing more and more African Americans away from the rural South. Roughly a third of the volume, in fact, is set in the urban North – in Washington, DC and in the Midwest – and though the final third of the book posits the possibility of returning to one's roots, a return that the concluding drama's protagonist Kabnis wistfully ponders, his reunion with the past is eventually thwarted by his own sense of estrangement from a rural world deeply foreign to him and by his terror of racial violence.

Tate himself would later explore those motifs of estrangement, escape, and yearning for origins in his most famous poem, "Ode to the Confederate Dead," begun in 1926 and revised for several years thereafter. Chief among its concerns was the elusiveness of the past for the modern poet estranged in the present. It was a theme to which he would return repeatedly in his poetry, his essays, and eventually in his 1938 novel *The Fathers*, where he tried to make sense of the break between the Old South and the New by exploring the conflict between the traditionalism of a white Southern planter and the modernity of his urban son-in-law – and to comprehend something of his own sense of loss that became for him the defining mark of the white Southerner marooned in the twentieth century. In the story that he and Donald Davidson would later tell of the road that led them from their early sense of alienation as Fugitives to their embrace of the antebellum South as an ideal to be expounded in the pages of *I'll Take My Stand*, they would often cite the notorious 1925 Scopes trial in Dayton, Tennessee, which attracted harsh national commentary on the region's generally perceived benightedness. What really engaged their attention, though, in the years immediately thereafter, in book reviews and essays, poems and Confederate biographies, was not the defense of religious fundamentalists or antievolutionists but the urgency they felt in trying to preserve a regional heritage fast disappearing in the bustling decade of the 1920s. In this project they were joined by a host of white and black Southerners across the region whose response to an increasingly urbanized and fast-paced economy and in particular to the increasing political militancy and visibility of African Americans was heightened interest in the regional past and its preservation, from grand Charleston mansions to historical novels to the collection of folklore. Civil War novels, culminating with the 1936 publication of Margaret Mitchell's *Gone with the Wind* and the distribution of the 1939 film version, represented yet another aspect of this new quest for a usable past, but so did the short stories, poems, novels, and plays of the black Southern past that began to appear from writers associated with the Harlem Renaissance like James Weldon Johnson, Langston Hughes, W. E. B. Du Bois, Claude McKay, Nella Larsen, Sterling Brown, Zora Neale Hurston, and Arna Bontemps.

For a white Mississippian writer named William Faulkner, who seemed to find his voice and his subject with the publication of his fourth novel, *The Sound and the Fury* (1929), that project of retrieving and representing the past was both alluring and disquieting. The past haunts all four narrative sections in the novel's Cubist-like collage and even threatens at times to extinguish the present altogether. At the same time, though, the past appears to be as elusive as the novel's central character, Caddy Compson, whose absence forms the heart of the novel and who in a manner of speaking inspires and motivates each of the narratives seeking out her presence. What predominates is the liquidity of the present and its dissolution of tradition, ideals, and customs, whether the idealization of female virginity that Caddy's elder brother Quentin sees as a touchstone for family honor, or hierarchically arranged black–white relations. In the world of Harvard inhabited by Quentin in 1910, neither maintains any sort of solidity, and one of the distinguishing features of the novel's second narrative section is its tour-de-force stream-of-consciousness capturing of Quentin's growing sense of disorientation, caused in no small part by his inability to navigate his way through the seemingly fluid world of early twentieth-century Massachusetts. In the urban North, from Quentin's perspective, African Americans no longer seem to feel any remaining bonds of subordination to whites, and women and girls seemed to be allied with the forces of change redefining womanhood, manhood, and sexuality.

Some of the novel's sense of disquiet over changing notions of women's roles and their sexuality very probably originated in part in the 1920s work of iconoclastic white women writers like Atlanta-born Frances Newman, who openly satirized traditional white Southern expectations about female chastity and purity and explored the confinements that those expectations continued to exert even upon white women who styled themselves as New Women breaking away from the shibboleths of nineteenth-century True Women. In her 1926 novel *The Hard-Boiled Virgin*, the very title of which got it banned in Boston, Newman drew heavily from Virginia Woolf's experiments with stream of consciousness to produce a satirical *Bildungsroman* of a young woman thoroughly defined by her society's expectations about romance and marriage despite her own literary ambitions. In the novel that followed, *Dead Lovers are Faithful Lovers* (1928), Newman experimented with shifts in point of view between a wife and a mistress to evoke something of the daily emotional reality of ordinary women. With a certain amount of glee, Newman claimed to be among the first to relate what women were really feeling and thinking, and more than one review at the time commented on the power of her wit and satire and their consequences for the status quo in Southern culture.

The strident voices of writers like Newman, who did not hesitate to point out the dehumanizing nature of white Southern myths of womanhood, might well have accounted for a good deal of the anxiety about women, their voices, and their changing roles marking the pages of *The Sound and the Fury*. It is, then, one of the great ironies of Faulkner's first great novel, grieving for the past's lost certainties of gender, race, and hierarchy, that it required a woman writer, a self-declared New Woman exemplifying many of those anxieties about change and fluidity voiced by Quentin Compson, to provide an explication of sorts for the difficult novel's popular consumption. As Mary Wheeling White recounts in her study, *Fighting the Current* (1998), Tennessee-born Evelyn Scott had early on rebelled against the strictures of Southern white womanhood by eloping to Brazil in 1913 with a married Tulane University professor and then by writing about the experience in an impressionistic, fragmented memoir titled *Escapade* (1923). The same year that *The Sound and the Fury* was published Scott had created a considerable stir with her Civil War novel called *The Wave*, which resorted to ever-multiplying narratives and characters across society and region to capture the conflict's immensity and complexity. Sharing Faulkner's publishers – Harrison Smith and Jonathan Cape – Scott had already written a short critical essay for the publishers' in-house use on *The Sound and the Fury*, one that impressed Harrison Smith so much that his firm decided to distribute the essay as an explanatory pamphlet accompanying limited numbers of Faulkner's breakthrough novel.

Faulkner would later dismiss Scott's own work with the words, "pretty good . . . for a woman" – thereby revealing some of his own assumptions about the gendered nature of the literary profession and of Southern modernism in particular (quoted in Meriwether and Millgate 1968: 49). He would be almost immediately hailed as the defining figure of the Southern Renascence by Allen Tate, John Crowe Ransom, Robert Penn Warren, and Donald Davidson, who recognized an ally of sorts in Faulkner's portrait of the tortured Quentin Compson longing for past certainties and betrayed by modernity. Faulkner himself, though, tended as a general rule to keep himself apart from literary circles, and one can even make an argument of sorts for his rewriting and perhaps even repudiation of Agrarian sentiments and Old South nostalgia in the novels that followed in the 1930s and early 1940s – *Sanctuary*, *As I Lay Dying*, *Light in August*, *Absalom, Absalom!*, *Pylon*, *The Hamlet*, and *Go Down, Moses*. From *Sanctuary* on, in fact, the Mississippi writer began to address issues of race, racialization, segregation, and eventually slavery on a level that almost immediately set him apart from Agrarian politics, which by the mid-1930s were already beginning to blur into defenses of segregation.

By then Faulkner had a number of allies who also took issue with Agrarian notions of the Southern past, among them writers of the "New Negro Movement" like Arna

Bontemps and Zora Neale Hurston as well as white women writers of rising importance, like Texas-born Katherine Anne Porter and a Mississippi short story writer
named Eudora Welty who would turn to the novel in the early 1940s. Bontemps in
particular took a certain amount of pleasure in excavating black histories unacknowl-
edged by the white plantation tradition and Agrarian nostalgia, like the 1802 slave
conspiracy in Richmond known as Gabriel's Rebellion, the dynamics of which he
explored in his 1936 novel *Black Thunder*. But it would be in his 1939 novel *Drums
at Dusk* that he would probe white anxieties about black freedom that the Agrarians
themselves inadvertently revealed in the pages of *I'll Take My Stand*, which resonated
with nostalgia for the stability of slavery and uneasily acknowledged fears of racial
warfare underlying Agrarian accounts of the Civil War and Reconstruction. The novel
begins with the point of view of a young Frenchman newly arrived in the colony of
Saint-Domingue and sympathetic to the restlessness of slaves and freed men of color,
but with the abrupt appearance of the rebel leader Toussaint Breda the narrative
becomes a commentary of sorts upon the liberation of black stories unshackled from
white confinements.

Bontemps, along with Sterling Brown, a gifted folklorist and poet, was joined in
the task of excavating hidden Southern pasts by Florida-born Zora Neale Hurston.
Trained by Columbia University anthropologist Franz Boas, Hurston energetically set
herself to collecting African-American folklore throughout the Deep South. Her
fieldwork among black storytellers and conjurors along the Gulf Coast resulted in the
1935 volume *Mules and Men*, the first major study of black folklore published by an
African-American scholar – and something of a primer on how to tell and listen to
African-American stories in the South. Two years later her field work was put to good
use in her 1937 novel *Their Eyes Were Watching God*, which abounded in multiple
scenes of storytelling and interpretation punctuating the life of a black woman who
learns from her community's folklore tradition how to tell her own story and how to
define her sense of self on her own terms rather than those of her frightened and cowed
grandmother or her three husbands. The narrative strategies to which Hurston resorted
– double-voiced discourse blending Standard English with folk dialect – underscored
both the novel's modernist orientation toward narrative experiment and its commitment to unearthing multiple black voices.

White women writers like Katherine Anne Porter and Eudora Welty for their
part found themselves scrutinizing the politics of memory and narrative that had
become by the 1930s and 1940s a dominant – and highly contested – theme in
novels by white and black Southern writers alike. In her 1937 novella "Old Mortal-
ity," Porter enters into something like an intertextual exchange with Faulkner's *The
Sound and the Fury* by examining the politics of white women's bodies used as sites
of memory, archives crystallizing moments of memory in an era of diminished
remembering and mass forgetting. For the central character Miranda – who became
something of an alter ego for Porter herself – and for her sister Maria, stories and
photographs of their dead cousin Amy serve simultaneously as an ideal of womanhood and as a cautionary tale on the dangers of rebellion, but by the end of the story

family memories have seemingly become conflicted, with Miranda herself uncertain about which stories of the past to believe. Eudora Welty's second novel *Delta Wedding* (1946) wittily evokes the plantation tradition of the nineteenth-century South in her story of a family planning a wedding on a Mississippi Delta plantation in 1923, and like Faulkner and Porter, for that matter, she examines the politics of inscribing family memories upon the body of a favorite family member – in this case a man doted upon by its predominantly female members who take on the primary responsibility of storytelling. But as a good many critics of Welty's work have pointed out, the sense of good fortune captured in the family name – Fairchild – is illusory at best; the world of the Fairchilds as painted by the novel is one on the brink of change, held off for the time being by the stories the family tells as though to ward off disaster. There is, for one thing, the confusing issue of who owns what among the Fairchilds' several plantations, and there are also the strange black and white women who hover in the shadows of the Fairchilds' world and lend to it a sense of foreboding. It is, in the end, a portrait of a seemingly serene world on the edge of an abyss, and here the novel's actual date, 1946, recalls not just the upheavals of World War II and the abrupt ending posed by Hiroshima and Nagasaki, but the advent, with the return of galvanized African-American military veterans, of the Civil Rights Revolution.

In a similar vein, Richard Wright's best-selling 1940 novel *Native Son* signaled the increasingly untenable nature of mid-twentieth-century race relations by tracing the trajectory of a young black man recently arrived in Chicago from the South who fulfills the worst fears and racial stereotypes of white America by killing a white woman. As Wright noted later in his essay "How Bigger Was Born," his central character was rooted in Wright's Mississippi childhood, in the black boys and men he remembered who rebelled against Jim Crow and defined themselves through violence and as outlaws. From his own perspective Bigger had become "a meaningful and prophetic symbol," an eruption of repressed darkness, and a sign of disruptions and rebellion to come (Wright 1940/1993: 441). Above all, Bigger emerges as a living repudiation of all master narratives – of white denials of his humanity, of the white paternalism defining his employers, and even of his own victimization by an unrelenting hostile world. In the last scene, Bigger even repudiates the narrative of powerlessness and victimhood that his Communist lawyer sketches for him. Startling his lawyer with sudden laughter, Bigger forthrightly denies the historical struggle of capital, labor, and race that his defender briefly summarizes, and takes ownership of the murder he has committed: "What I killed for must've been good!" he insisted. "When a man kills it's for something. . . . I didn't know I was really alive in this world until I felt things hard enough to kill for 'em" (Wright 1940/1993: 429).

In his words one hears not just a repudiation of the white stories that have imprisoned him or the overtly deterministic orientation of his lawyer but something approximating and anticipating a postmodern interrogation of mastery – and even more, an appeal for recognition of who and what he is and a genuine dialogue crossing the boundaries of race and difference. In many respects that appeal for recognition was indeed acknowledged – and even by a few white southern writers, like North Carolina newspaperman Jonathan Daniels, who wrote in his review for the *Saturday Review of Literature* that Bigger Thomas "is the child of our living in this land" (Daniels 1940/1978: 51).

It was an appeal, moreover, that Wright's former disciple, the Oklahoma-born Ralph Ellison, would signify upon in his own novel, the 1952 masterpiece *Invisible Man*, which burlesqued, satirized, and disrupted virtually the country's entire history and narrative archive about race, mastery, slavery, and segregation. Seven years in the making, *Invisible Man* represented Ellison's immense ambition to write, in Arnold Rampersad's words, "the Great American Novel about race" (Rampersad 2007: 249), and considering the novel's historical sweep, from memories of slavery to Harlem political struggles, one would be hard-pressed not to acknowledge the novel's successes in pursuing that ambition. Ellison's nameless narrator, who announces in the first sentence that he is indeed "an invisible man" speaks from nothing so much as the nation's racial unconscious, a chaotic archive of racial stereotypes, music, historical and personal memories, folk tales, anxieties, jokes, violence, and the lasting legacy of slavery. A self-described nightmare and stereotype reduced to invisibility, the narrator explores that archive in a series of picaresque adventures that begin to repeat themselves with unsettling regularity because the narrator keeps plunging into the same set of experiences again and again – which is pursuing the quest for identity and acceptance from a selective and judgmental group, whether it be local white patrons in his hometown, black university officials, New York City capitalists and industrialists, or Communist Party activists.

Along the way the narrator keeps receiving blues-tinged advice counseling the benefits of contradiction, masking, and subterfuge, all echoing his grandfather's inexplicable advice to his family on his deathbed to "overcome 'em with yeses, undermine 'em with grins, agree 'em to death and destruction, let 'em swoller you till they vomit or bust wide open" (Ellison 1952: 16). It is advice that the narrator never quite manages to understand, and therein perhaps from Ellison's perspective lies what he called "the joke at the center of the American identity" – the uneasy, unstable performance of race in modern America that ultimately underscored "the true interrelatedness of blackness and whiteness" (Ellison 1964: 55). It is a performance, Ellison suggests in *Invisible Man*, that dates all the way back to slavery, and thus Americans white and black would be well advised to confront the shifting nature of those performances in the midst of modernity – as well as the legacy of slavery that has been all too often denied in the US South and in the nation's history as a whole.

Ellison's narrator is himself not above trying to deny that legacy from time to time, and hence his periodic confrontations – with his grandfather's "curse," with haunting dreams of weeping slave mothers, and even with emancipation papers that he inadvertently spies in a Harlem eviction – are potent reminders of the country's propensity for erasing part of its history as well as interlocutions across time, race, and region on the perimeters of race, identity, and community. The narrator confronts one of those reminders in the vivid Harlem eviction scene as he surveys the belongings of an elderly couple whose lives bridge the span between slavery and twentieth-century urban life. In those scattered belongings, he glimpses something of the coexistence of past and present, slavery and freedom, tradition and modernity, in ways that anticipate a postmodernist acceptance of plurality, difference, and multiple histories. Ellison himself would call for something like that acceptance at the Southern Historical Association meeting in 1968, where he declared that the Civil Rights Revolution, which his novel had in many respects anticipated, would require the remaking of American histories as well as stories about that remaking.

One of the great achievements of Ellison's *Invisible Man*, then, is its frankly postmodern acceptance of those multiple voices and stories that a good deal of white Southern writing in particular had tried to deny or repudiate since Emancipation. A huge encyclopedia of Southern and American stories about race, identity, and community, *Invisible Man* ultimately celebrates the fluidity and diversity that had unnerved so many earlier writers and calls for the reader to celebrate that fluidity as well. To do so means to acknowledge that "interrelatedness of blackness and whiteness" lying at the heart of American identity as Ellison saw it and to confront as well one's own sense of interdependence and intersubjectivity – lessons that have been hard-won indeed in modern Southern writing. That those lessons continue to be contested is underscored in the novel's parting question of uncertainty: "Who knows but that, on the lower frequencies, I speak for you?" (Ellison 1952: 568).

REFERENCES AND FURTHER READING

Andrews, William L. (1980). *The Literary Career of Charles W. Chesnutt*. Baton Rouge: Louisiana State University Press.

Ayers, Edward L. (1992). *The Promise of the New South: Life After Reconstruction*. New York: Oxford University Press.

Bauman, Zygmunt. (2000). *Liquid Modernity*. Malden, MA: Polity Press.

Brundage, W. Fitzhugh (ed.). (2000). *Where These Memories Grow: History, Memory, and Southern Identity*. Chapel Hill: University of North Carolina Press.

Cartwright, Keith. (2002). *Reading African into American Literature: Epics, Fables, and Gothic Tales*. Lexington: University of Kentucky Press.

Chopin, Kate. (1899/1981). *The Awakening and Selected Stories*. New York: Modern Library.

Cooper, Anna Julia. (1892/1988). *A Voice from the South*, introd. Mary Helen Washington. New York: Oxford University Press.

Daniels, Jonathan. (1940/1978). Review. *Saturday Review of Literature*, March 2, 1940. In John Reilly (ed.), *Richard Wright: The Critical Reception*. (pp. 50–1). New York: Burt Franklin & Co.

Ellison, Ralph. (1952). *Invisible Man*. New York: Random-Vintage.

Ellison, Ralph. (1964). *Shadow and Act*. New York: Random-Vintage.

Fabre, Geneviève and Robert O'Meally (eds). (1994). *History and Memory in African-American Culture*. New York: Oxford University Press.

The Fugitive (1922–5/1967). Introduction by Donald Davidson. Gloucester, MA: Peter Smith.

Gardner, Sarah E. (2004). *Blood and Irony: Southern White Women's Narratives of the Civil War, 1861–1937*. Chapel Hill: University of North Carolina Press.

Glasgow, Ellen. (1913/1989). *Virginia*, introd. Linda Wagner-Martin. New York: Penguin.

Goldfield, David. (2002). *Still Fighting the Civil War: The American South and Southern History*. Baton Rouge: Louisiana State University Press.

Gray, Richard. (1979). *The Literature of Memory: Modern Writers of the American South*. Baltimore: Johns Hopkins University Press.

Gray, Richard. (1986). *Writing the South: Ideas of an American Region*. New York: Cambridge University Press.

Gray, Richard. (2000). *Southern Aberrations: Writers of the American South and the Problem of Regionalism*. Baton Rouge: Louisiana State University Press.

Hale, Grace Elizabeth. (1998). *Making Whiteness: The Culture of Segregation in the South, 1890–1940*. New York: Pantheon.

Handley, George B. (2000). *Postslavery Literatures in the Americas: Family Portraits in Black and White*. Charlottesville: University of Virginia Press.

Jacobs, Harriet. (1861/1987). *Incidents in the Life of a Slave Girl Written by Herself*, ed. and introd. Jean Fagan Yellin. Cambridge, MA: Harvard University Press.

Jones, Anne Goodwyn and Susan V. Donaldson (eds). (1997). *Haunted Bodies: Gender and Southern Texts*. Charlottesville: University Press of Virginia.

Jones, Anne Goodwyn. (1981). *Tomorrow is Another Day: The Woman Writer in the South, 1859–1936*. Baton Rouge: Louisiana State University Press.

Jones, Suzanne and Sharon Monteith (eds). (2002). *South to a New Place: Region, Literature, Culture*. Baton Rouge: Louisiana State University Press.

King, Richard H. (1980). *A Southern Renaissance: The Cultural Awakening of the American South, 1930–1955*. New York: Oxford University Press.

King, Richard H. and Helen Taylor (eds). (1996). *Dixie Debates: Perspectives on Southern Cultures*. New York: New York University Press.

Kreyling, Michael. (1998). *Inventing Southern Literature*. Jackson: University of Mississippi.

Manning, Carol (ed.). (1993). *The Female Tradition in Southern Literature*. Urbana: University of Illinois Press.

Ladd, Barbara. (1996). *Nationalism and the Color Line in George W. Cable, Mark Twain, and William Faulkner*. Baton Rouge: Louisiana State University Press.

Ladd, Barbara. (2007). *Resisting History: Gender, Modernity, and Authorship in William Faulkner, Zora Neale Hurston, and Eudora Welty*. Baton Rouge: Louisiana State University Press.

Locke, Alain. (1925/1992). *The New Negro*, intro. Arnold Rampersad. New York: Simon & Schuster/Touchstone.

McDowell, Deborah E. and Arnold Rampersad (eds). (1989). *Slavery and the Literary Imagination*. Baltimore: Johns Hopkins University Press.

Meriwether, James B. and Michael Millgate (eds). (1968). *Lion in the Garden: Interviews with William Faulkner, 1926–1962*. New York: Random-Vintage.

Morrison, Toni. (1992). *Playing in the Dark: Whiteness and the Literary Imagination*. Cambridge, MA: Harvard University Press.

Niebuhr, Reinhold. (1952). *The Irony of American History*. New York: Scribner's.

O'Brien, Michael. (2004). *Conjectures of Order: Intellectual Life and the American South, 1810–1860*, 2 vols. Chapel Hill: University of North Carolina Press.

Rampersad, Arnold. (2007). *Ralph Ellison: A Biography*. New York: Alfred A. Knopf.

Roark, James L. (1977). *Masters without Slaves: Southern Planters in the Civil War and Reconstruction*. New York, London: W.W. Norton.

Romine, Scott. (1999). *The Narrative Forms of Southern Community*. Baton Rouge: Louisiana State University Press.

Simpson, Lewis P. (1990). *The Brazen Face of History: Studies in the Literary Consciousness of America*. Baton Rouge: Louisiana State University Press.

Sundquist, Eric J. (1993). *To Wake the Nations: Race in the Making of American Literature*. Cambridge, MA: Harvard-Belknap.

Tate, Allen. (1945). *Essays of Four Decades*. Chicago: Swallow Press.

Twelve Southerners. (1930/2006). *I'll Take My Stand: The South and the Agrarian Tradition*, intro. Susan V. Donaldson, 75th Anniversary edn. Baton Rouge: Louisiana State University Press.

White, Mary Wheeling. (1998). *Fighting the Current: The Life and Work of Evelyn Scott*. Baton Rouge: Louisiana State University Press.

Williamson, Joel. (1984). *The Crucible of Race: Black-White Relations in the American South Since Emancipation*. New York: Oxford University Press.

Woodward, C. Vann. (1960). *The Burden of Southern History*. Baton Rouge: Louisiana State University Press.

Wright, Richard. (1940/1993). How Bigger was born. In *Native Son*, introd. Arnold Rampersad (pp. 431–62). New York: Harper/Perennial Classics.

Yaeger, Patricia. (2000). *Dirt and Desire: Reconstructing Southern Women's Writing, 1930–1990*. Chicago: University of Chicago Press.

15

What Was High About Modernism? The American Novel and Modernity

John T. Matthews

By this point in the early twenty-first century, students of culture rarely encounter terms like "modern," "modernist," and "modernity" without a familiar prefix: "*post-modern*," "postmodernist," "postmodernity." We've grown accustomed to thinking of our own era as decidedly postmodernist, regardless of whether we view its principal effects as liberating or licentious, playful or decadent, connective or isolating, empowering or oppressive. The "post" in such characterizations of the present suggests the degree to which they depend on a conceptualization of the period that preceded ours, and it is the case that efforts to come to terms with the forceful emergence of new economic, social, political, and cultural practices in the 1950s and 1960s stimulated investigation into what had made the first half of the century "modern," if the second half was granted to be its "post." For some scholars the line of demarcation showed up most brightly in the cultural sphere. John McGowan observes that the "term 'postmodernism' was used in reference to architecture as early as 1947," and then was taken up by literary critics to distinguish the contemporary fiction of Jorge Luis Borges, John Barth, and Donald Barthelme from their "high modernist" predecessors (leading examples would be James Joyce, Virginia Woolf, and William Faulkner) (McGowan 2005: 1).

Ihab Hassan was among the first literary scholars to attempt a taxonomy of postmodernist features, in an essay entitled "POSTFACE 1982: Toward Postmodernism," the epilogue to his influential study of twentieth-century writers (Hassan 1971/1982). Hassan decides that the way to get at postmodernism is to chart its "schematic differences from modernism" (p. 267). As he considers what more recent American novelists of the 1960s and 1970s like Barth, Thomas Pynchon, and William Burroughs have in common with each other, as well as with writers of their generation from other national traditions like Vladimir Nabokov and Borges, with artists in other media, even with then-emerging "poststructuralist" theorists in various analytical discourses like philosophy, psychoanalysis, and literary criticism, Hassan begins to construct a system of dichotomies. The elements he identifies as defining postmodernism find their opposite numbers in modernism: so if postmodernist artistic works exhibit "open" form, "disjunctive" components, and a sense of "play" and "chance," modernist works are "conjunctive," "closed," and marked by "purpose" and "design." Hassan's usefully suggestive list runs to more than 30 attributes, although the neatness of the oppositions leads him to be as skeptical about their firmness as we should be. Still, even a loose aptness in such differentiating traits not only suggests that the term "postmodernism" does point to a wide-ranging shift in mentality and expressive practices beginning as early as the 1950s, but also demonstrates that it was the manifestation of postmodernism that compelled a more searching investigation into the nature and limits of modernism. We learned more about modernism in the process of defining postmodernism.

Hassan remarks that prominent American champions of modernist literature began lamenting the passing of its classic phase by the 1960s. He mentions Irving Howe and Harry Levin, and we might add Lionel Trilling as perhaps the most influential of such celebrants of modernism. Contemplating the sea-change that would amount to postmodernism, Howe touted the achievement of modernism as he felt it drawing to an end. Like Hassan, Howe largely restricts his analysis to the formal features of the work of art. Modern art, including literature, made its mark by being difficult, by deliberately being hard to understand; its formal inventiveness and inscrutability constituted a revolt against the recipient's familiar expectations, against comfortable habits of art consumption. Modern artists aimed to offend bourgeois society, to strip away habitual beliefs and values, and to demand acts of self-scrutiny and metaphysical exploration. Howe finds an impatience with reason in modern art, and a corresponding abandonment to preconscious, primitive, or other modes of more authentic experience.

Such views also exemplify a common inclination to present the history of artistic periods as a succession of styles, aesthetic convictions, and quests for imaginative originality. There's something like internal cultural history at work in accounts like these, and in studies of modernism and postmodernism, their results reveal a rich tradition of artists speaking to one another through acts of fierce concentration on the work of art itself. Christopher Butler's (1994) study of early modernism in music, painting, and literature, for example, chooses to focus on "the mental world" of the artists he discusses, under the conviction that "philosophical concerns" were the chief stimulants of modernist innovation. From Butler's standpoint, modernism developed as a rebellion against a tradition of realism that more and more failed to maintain the difference between art and other forms of representation like journalism or photography. Similarly, questions of aesthetic language organize Peter Nicholls's (1995) examination of the efforts of various modernists to purify expressive resources sullied by everyday use or outworn literary conventions, and to make new things of and with words. Philip Weinstein (2005) identifies the purposes of modernist fiction as dismantling a long-dominant epistemology associated with Enlightenment rationality; in his view, works of experimental modernism challenged long-standing confidence in empiricism, logic, unified selfhood, a knowable environment, and truth-bearing narrative.

However, as even my sketchy summaries may suggest, such accounts also display some awareness that cultural history is not exclusively a self-enclosed procession of fashions in style and form. Not only must we see the primarily aesthetic projects outlined above as necessarily in tension with social, political, and economic contexts, but a closer look at the project of modernism reveals that the very notion of an "autonomous" work of art, one that holds itself to be above "contamination" by mass culture, pervasive commoditization, monopoly capitalism, political and scientific discourse, technological production of goods and extensions of communication – in a word, all that we associate with the historical event of modernization – derives from a particular solution to the degrading effects of modernity favored by modernist artists. The most trenchant attack on modernism's desire to rise above the reality of modernization came from the Marxist critic Georg Lukács (1963), who complained even in the heyday of modernist writing that the new art was excessively psychological, passively apolitical, and weakly negative. A work like *The Sound and the Fury* (1929), Lukács argued, failed to render the totality of historical circumstances that confined the protagonists to their states of individual confused alienation. Faulkner's stream-of-consciousness technique, however brilliant in rendering subjectivity, amounted only to a reinforcement of the futility of historical knowledge. The novel's immersion in eccentric mentalities contributed to "an attenuation of reality" endemic to other modernist works, most influentially Joyce's *Ulysses* (1922). Modernist texts may carry charges of discomfort with modernity, Lukács acknowledged, but they are feeble and diffuse. Lukács remained an advocate of realism, and, even if his more doctrinal version of socialist realism eventually faltered itself, his criticism of modernism's tendencies to flee historical reality for the indifference of high art set the terms for much subsequent debate.

Theodor Adorno, a member with Walter Benjamin, Max Horkheimer, and other luminaries of the Frankfurt School of critical thought from the 1920s through the late 1930s (until as Jews many of them were driven from Germany by the Nazis), counters Lukács's critique by developing a more sympathetic understanding of art's capacity for negation. For Lukács, as we have seen, modernist works protested too meekly against the realities of exploitation and social injustice produced by modern capitalism, with all its attendant technological, speculative, and administrative incursions into social life and private consciousness. Adorno, on the other hand, saw how the demands of difficult modern art might jam the smooth hum of market exchange and commercial culture-consumption. In their intractabilities, he believed, certain forms of modern art, like certain forms of critical philosophical reflection, might block and reverse the rush toward ever-increasing instrumental rationalism, abstract thinking, and political coercion (eventuating in fascism, Nazism, and finally the unimaginable barbarism of genocide).

Adorno and Horkheimer famously wrote about the degradations of modern commercial culture in their essay "The Culture Industry," and about the violent tendencies intrinsic to Enlightenment rationalism in their piece on anti-Semitism (both reprinted in Horkheimer and Adorno 1994). Andreas Huyssen argues that Adorno conceived of the difference between serious art and debased industrial culture (like Hollywood movies or commercial jazz) as a "Great Divide." Huyssen proposes this term to measure the "categorical distinction between high art and mass culture" in Adorno's thinking (Huyssen 1986: viii). Writing in 1944, after a stint in Hollywood imposed by their flight from Germany during World War II, Adorno and Horkheimer condemn from up close what they call "the culture industry." Formulaic plots, simplistic styles, sappy sentimentality, and overly administered effects of pleasure all contribute to mass culture's disciplinary homogenization of its audiences. According to Huyssen, Adorno's faith in modernism had everything to do with its power to negate the reification of culture (that is, the reduction of culture to objects of mass production and profit): "It indeed never occurred to Adorno to see modernism as anything other than a reaction formation to mass culture and commodification" (p. 24). In this interpretation, modernist art for Adorno *is* high art: "Adorno's modernism theory relies on certain strategies of exclusion which relegate realism, naturalism, reportage literature and political art to an inferior realm" (p. 25).

Yet for all the modernist work's yearning to vault above debased culture, Adorno's model insists on the necessary *contact* between the realms on either side of the Great Divide. Adorno understands that the work's autonomy is achieved only in dialectical struggle with its opposite. His model of the high modernist work's autonomy is dynamic, not static: "Adorno makes the even stronger claim that in capitalist society high art is always already permeated by the textures of that mass culture from which it seeks autonomy" (Huyssen 1986: 35). The recognition of mutual constitution and conflict across the divide distinguishes Adorno's subtle and productive version of modernist autonomy from that of the American New Critics. Reactionary American (and particularly Southern) enthusiasts of modern poetry like John Crowe Ransom and Allen Tate fled to modernist literature as a sanctuary from modernity (they called their short-lived journal of new poetry *The Fugitive*). But that sort of highness – a bastion of disdain and obliviousness – differs from the sort of vital engagement Adorno imagines as the transfigurative potential of modern art, even if he shares their dim view of modern vulgarity. On the other hand, liberal intellectuals like Lionel Trilling advocated modernist literature especially as the bulwark of the sanctity of the individual threatened by homogenized bureaucratic and mass culture, and touted the indispensability of the oppositional imagination for liberal democratic societies.

For the Frankfurt School critics, it is because high modernist art challenges mass culture, with the aim of creating art that functions as *negation* of social and cultural norms, that it reanimates the revolutionary motives of earlier avant-garde movements. Those projects from the first decades of the twentieth century – like Dada, Surrealism, Futurism – assaulted the institutions of artistic legitimation (Burger 1984), with the intent of incorporating exhilarating novelties of modernity like technology into artistic practice. The fading of avant-gardism around World War I (1914–18) opens up social and cultural divides that modernism accepts and tries to negotiate, though certainly with less utopian or progressivist confidence. You can see the persistence of such enthusiasm – however guarded – for the possibilities of modern technology applied to culture in Walter Benjamin's (1969) hugely influential essay, "The Work of Art in the Age of Mechanical Reproduction." The drift of Benjamin's meditation on what it means for cinema to succeed drama, and photography painting, tends toward regret over the loss of uniqueness possessed by any individually crafted piece of art. Yet Benjamin also grasps how cinema allows multiple points of view to be represented simultaneously, creating new kinds of perceptual and conceptual totalities, and how altered filming velocities and camera movement "see" things normally undetectable in social life.

The purported menace of mass culture serves as a front for more widespread and profound changes associated with the onset of modernity. Huyssen expands the significance of mass culture to encompass several sorts of social uprising, all of them represented by the empowerment of women: "In the age of nascent socialism *and* the first major women's movement in Europe, the masses knocking at the gate were also women, knocking at the gate of a male-dominated culture" (Huyssen 1986: 47). Mass culture, Huyssen observes, is "obsessively" gendered female as a result of the host of threats perceived by white male ruling class privilege (p. 47). Modernism, in other words, settles in to adversarial friction with modernization, in a broad spectrum of manifestations. These more concrete or material conditions of modernity anchor David Harvey's (1992) account of what modernism (and postmodernism) does.

Like Hassan (1982), Harvey also employs a comparative strategy of differentiation, but he is interested in the material bases of the transformations that distinguish successive socioeconomic regimes: modernity and postmodernity (not the cultural responses to each that materialized respectively as modernism and postmodernism). For Harvey, modernity centers on new modes of production, particularly of goods, described as Fordism (after the American automobile pioneer Henry Ford). Fordism reorganizes the factory around mass production, the assignment of workers to single tasks, and the more efficient circulation of manufactured objects rather than laborers; it cultivates a better-paid laboring force as a new consuming class; it encourages the growth of urbanization – with its key sensations of the ephemeral and chaotic; it favors discreet state intervention to stabilize market unpredictability; it expands toward international quests for cheap labor and resources, along with new markets for its goods; and it develops sophisticated new techniques of credit, capital investment, and profit-taking.

Harvey sees that modernist art attempted early on to capture and resist the degrading effects of modernity; later in its career, though, modernism became less adversarial, partly as the result of its canonization in the curricula of schools and universities following World War II, where, especially in the US, it was treated apolitically under prevailing New Critical methods of formalist analysis. That's the stage Harvey considers to be "high modernism" – "high" indicating less the autonomy of art above everyday life, as it did for Adorno, and more the official sanctioning of cultural value. It can be compared with "High Church": ceremonial, hierarchical, formally ornate. When the modernist art work reaches this stage of authorization, its features rigidify into formal protocols. Huyssen offers the following list of hallmarks:

- The work is autonomous and totally separate from the realms of mass culture and everyday life.
- It is self-referential, self-conscious, frequently ironic, ambiguous, and rigorously experimental.
- It is the expression of a purely individual consciousness rather than of a Zeitgeist or a collective state of mind.
- Its experimental nature makes it analogous to science, and like science it produces and carries knowledge.
- Modernist literature since Flaubert is a persistent exploration of and encounter with language. Modernist painting since Manet is an equally persistent elaboration of the medium itself: the flatness of the canvas, the structuring of notation, paint and brushwork, the problem of the frame.
- The major premise of the modernist art work is the rejection of all classical systems of representation, the effacement of "content," the erasure of subjectivity and authorial voice, the repudiation of likeness and verisimilitude, the exorcism of any demand for realism of whatever kind.
- Only by fortifying its boundaries, by maintaining its purity and autonomy, and by avoiding any contamination with mass culture and with the signifying systems of everyday life can the art work maintain its adversary stand: adversary to the bourgeois culture of everyday life as well as adversary to mass culture and entertainment which are seen as primary forms of bourgeois cultural articulation. (Huyssen 1986: 53–4)

If these traits represent what the modernist work of art "has become as a result of successive canonizations" (p. 53), not only do they caricature the volatile exchange between cultural realms described by Adorno, they also exclude many other kinds of artistic engagement with the vast enterprises of modernity. By contrast, once we take modernism more broadly as a *set* of imaginative responses to the grounds of modernity, numerous other kinds of modernism, or numerous other modernisms, come to light.

In an important consideration of modernism and imperialism, Fredric Jameson (1990) enumerates some of the central features of modernity that modernist literature may treat. In the following sentences you'll see that the key claim of his argument appears first: Jameson will contend in this piece that works of British modernism (exemplified here by E. M. Forster's 1910 novel *Howards End*) figure out how to evade the reality of modern colonialism (in the instance of Forster's novel by offering distracting visions of a harmonious English countryside), while a work like *Ulysses*, written from the position of colonial subjugation, manifests the bruising reality of exploitation, and forces the issue of coherence by resorting to mythological parallels, which provide only a partial answer. In the latter part of the passage, Jameson identifies several other major elements of the modern:

> I want in fact to suggest that the structure of imperialism also makes its mark on the inner forms and structures of that new mutation in literary and artistic language to which the term modernism is loosely applied. This last has of course multiple social determinants: any general theory of the modern – assuming one to be possible in the first place – would also wish to register the informing presence of a range of other historically novel phenomena: modernization and technology; commodity reification; monetary abstraction and its effects on the sign system; the social dialectic of reading publics; the emergence of mass culture; the embodiment of new forms of the psychic subject on the physical sensorium. (Jameson 1990: 44)

Writing in 1988, Jameson anticipates many of the projects that eventually comprised the so-called New Modernist Studies movement over the next two decades. In a wide range of efforts to look behind (or below) the modernist work's assumed pretense to absolute autonomy, scholars of modernism have investigated almost every conceivable sector of modern life to see how the period's literature responded to its truly seismic upheavals. (See Mao and Walkowitz 2008 for a summary of the movement's defining features.)

The ultimate consequence of such projects has been to challenge earlier views of modernism as oppositional to dominant bourgeois culture. Anthony Appiah maintained that "a rough consensus about the structure of the modern-postmodern dichotomy" had been reached on the basis of the contrasting sociological functions of art in each period (Appiah 1992: 142), a distinction best articulated by Jameson:

> high modernism, whatever its overt political content, was oppositional and marginal within a middle-class Victorian or philistine or gilded age culture. Although postmodernism is equally offensive in all the respects enumerated (think of punk rock or pornography), it is no longer at all "oppositional" in that sense; indeed, it constitutes the very dominant or hegemonic aesthetic of consumer society itself. (Jameson 1988: 196, quoted in Appiah 1992: 142)

Postmodernism emerges within this "waning" of the "dialectical opposition" between high modernism and mass culture. Jameson sees the sociological distinction as a solution to the problem that modernist and postmodernist works of art cannot in fact be distinguished formally, on the basis of their aesthetic techniques or style, or even their subjects.

But the careful study of modernism's engagement with social, economic, and cultural discourses it presumably opposed, ends up suggesting that modernist works reproduced as much as resisted the features of their habitat. Perhaps the most influential assault on the oppositional status of modern American fiction has been Walter Benn Michaels' *Our America* (1995), a book arguing that principal novelists of the period like Hemingway, Fitzgerald, Wharton, and Faulkner accepted assumptions of white racial purity and the ideology of blood even as they refined or ignored the more vulgar varieties of such thought. Investigations of modernist texts' saturation with other contemporary ideas and language has cast doubts on the more heroic versions of modernism espoused by Adorno or Trilling. Newer studies of modernism suggest how it *absorbed* modernity rather than uniformly negating it.

Jameson's first category – modernization and technology – reflects a common view that unprecedented mechanical innovations in communication, manufacture, and transportation from the 1870s through the 1910s (the telephone, phonograph, conveyer belt, automobile, airplane, etc.) constituted the leading edge of revolutionary modernity. Raymond Williams (1989) cautioned some time ago that technology on its own never determined social change, since any invention gets adapted and creates effects as the result of its interface with established social and economic institutions and practices. Still, the modern age was presented with numerous novelties – many of them with profound implications for conceptualizations of space and time, the human body, labor, creative media, and so on. Studies by Tichi (1987), Steinman (1987), and Knapp (1988), for example, took up the effects of modern technology on literary themes and even style. (Knapp, for instance, argues that some modernist poets incorporated a taste for efficiency and streamlining into their minimalist verse.) This line of inquiry does have a precedent in Hugh Kenner's (1975) musings on how literature was affected by the new sensations of air flight, or the effects of composition at the typewriter to the poetic line, but Kenner's interests are exclusively formal, as opposed to thematic or political. Taussig (1993) explores the consequences of prosthetic extensions of the body (including those of the mechanically reproduced and transmitted voice); Armstrong (1998) looks at a variety of modern semiscientific discourses designed to improve the body and their reflection in modern American fiction around the turn of the twentieth century.

We might consider more sophisticated systems of production and administration as modern technological apparatuses too. Institutions of capitalism grew stronger and more complex beginning with the era of incorporation following the Civil War. Studies like two by Richard Godden (1990, 1997) examine how modernist writers such as Fitzgerald, Allen Tate, and Faulkner, among others, reflect critically on modernity as shaped by late capitalism: the universalizing commodification of goods; the establishment of an exclusive money economy; the rise of a culture of consumption; and the transformation of laborers into a waged class. Walter Benn Michaels' book on literary engagements with the controversy over the gold standard (1988) suggests how debates about the modern economy found their way into turn-of-the-century naturalist writing, where they produced parallel anxieties about the grounds of truthful depiction versus the proliferation of mere representation.

The modern American state bulked up to perform duties required to ease injuries inflicted by the roaring engines of capitalism: to suppress labor insurgency, and to supplement the social wage when companies failed to cover it (most conspicuously in the New Deal's springing up to save capitalism from its inherent contradictions by devising props for weakened businesses, payments for unemployed workers, new social services for longer-term casualties, etc.). Patricia Chu (2007) has written recently about the various imaginative modes resorted to by early twentieth-century novelists and filmmakers as they sought to imagine the individual's refashioned relations to the augmented modern state. She argues that modernism ought to include a raft of creative subgenres, used in certain ways, once excluded by the restrictive criteria of "high" modernism: the sentimental, melodrama, the Gothic (in this case *White Zombies*, a movie set in Haiti that probes the costs of citizens' voluntary affiliation to the modern state). Pericles Lewis (2000) conducts a similar study of Anglo-European modernists, arguing that a writer like Joyce, for example, detects the failure of the English Victorian state to ensure the rights of colonial subjects under the sanction of progressive liberalism, and instead imagines another kind of security for individual self-realization in mythical ethnic solidarities like Irishness. Chu makes a similar claim about Griffith's displacement of state authority by racial brotherhood in *The Birth of a Nation*. Michael Szalay (2000) suggests how the emergence of the modern welfare state insinuated itself into national mentalities, showing up, say, as attitudes toward risk and chance even in the remote corners of poetry by Wallace Stevens or William Carlos Williams.

When Jameson speaks of "the social dialectic of reading publics" above, he may be thinking of sociological accounts of modernism like those of Pierre Bourdieu. In his influential book *Distinction*, Bourdieu (1984) describes how modernist writers and publishers evolved a strategy to deal with the rise of mass commercial literature. By crafting intellectually demanding and formally challenging works for a small appreciative coterie, such producers deliberately renounced popularity. They gambled instead that discerning readers in the present, as well as in the future, would pick their work out of the dross surrounding it, and that they, and their publishers, eventually would win (permanent canonized reputation) by losing (immediate mass sales). The dialectic involved in such high modernist strategies can be illustrated by Michael North's paradigm-shifting work on the relations between folk and popular culture, on one side of the divide, and "serious" writers, on the other. In *Dialect of Modernism*, for example, North (1994) demonstrates how poets like Ezra Pound and T. S. Eliot mined (and mimed) African-American folk culture and other forms of contemporary popular culture in order to absorb it into an art that simultaneously incorporated allusions to high traditions of art, religion, mythology, philosophy – globally. The result was what North considers a special, exclusive language of modernism: a kind of dialect. North emphasizes the rejuvenating effects of such "lower" forms, though he also allows that such material was handled carefully by its purveyors lest the significance of, say, African-American folk culture as a repository of slave experience blow up in their faces.

Bourdieu also speculates that because high modernist writing occupies a position of subordination to popular works, it has a tendency to sympathize with those in positions of social subordination. Leftist inclinations among serious writers may have been more typical of the French cultural scene, with its long-standing commitment to Marxist socialism, but in the US, the possibility may be illustrated by the example of James Agee, a Harvard-educated Tennessean, an enormously talented journalist and film critic for *Fortune* and *Time Magazine*, and a stylist beyond compare, whose assignment to report on the lives of several Alabama tenant farm families in 1934 spun out into a vast reverie upon impoverishment, in super-Faulknerian prose, published as *Let Us Now Praise Famous Men* (1941). Studies such as Ann Douglas's (1995) and Michael Denning's (1996) expand the category of modernist art to include a wide array of takes on the social ills of modernization, particularly as they affect dominated classes, races, and sexual minorities. Douglas surveys a vibrantly heterogeneous cultural scene in Manhattan – one that ranged from Edith Wharton to the Cotton Club in Harlem. Denning argues that the leftist tradition in modern American culture has to include more than just doctrinal communist proletarian writers of the sort Foley (1993) writes about; for him, many artists qualify as members of the so-called cultural front that emerged in the 1930s. Seminal works by Houston Baker (e.g., Baker 1987) insisted that a black modernism had to be acknowledged as well, and Baker makes the case for seeing even a relatively conservative thinker like Booker T. Washington as devising a distinct version of modernist style to engage what W. E. B. Du Bois had defined as *the* problem of the twentieth century: the national color line dividing black from white under both lawful Southern and practical Northern forms of segregation. More recently, Paul Gilroy (1993) has challenged the national boundaries of modernist practices, suggesting that the art of modern diasporic Africans must be understand as a function of the century's waves of anticolonialism. Brent Edwards (2003) zeroes in yet more specifically on the connections between worldwide anticolonial activism in the 1920s and the modernist sensibilities of the Harlem Renaissance, recast by Edwards as an international phenomenon.

A number of recent books have taken up the question of how late nineteenth- and early twentieth-century American literature engages more broadly with the rise of US imperialism. Amy Kaplan (2002) finds anarchy as the desired condition for the exercise of authority both abroad and in the private domestic sphere in the 1890s. John Carlos Rowe (2000) examines the interplay between foreign and domestic domination at selected historical moments from Poe to Hurston. Du Bois's own vehement opposition to the acquisition of foreign territories in the so-called Spanish–American War (1898), which brought the Philippines and Cuba under US control, stemmed from what he had learned about racism and colonialism in his study of the African slave trade (the subject of his doctoral dissertation in history); from his experience of state racism in the South under Jim Crow law; from his theoretical grasp of labor exploitation and racism in his reading of Marx. The essays published in *Darkwater* (1920) leave no doubt that Du Bois takes the central task of modern culture to be the acknowledgment and rectification of American racism (with its history in the nation's origins as plantation colonies, especially, but not exclusively, in the Southern regions). That American fruit and coffee companies were busy establishing Southern-style plantations throughout Latin America, or that the US sent troops to Haiti and the Dominican Republic in the interwar years and modeled its occupation on lessons learned during federal reconstruction of the US South after the Civil War, exemplify the contact points between the South's plantation past and the nation's imperial future.

It's at this juncture that I'd like to return to Jameson's interest in the relation between modernism and colonialism. Jameson contends that modern writers' explicit consideration of British imperialism (as in Conrad) itself finesses or hides the more brutal practices of outright colonialism that underwrite the mission of enlightenment, Christianization, and civilization attributed to the ideal of imperialism. But Jameson is also sensitive to the formal devices by which the refusal to represent England's material relations to its enriching colonies is smoothed over rather than allowed to create puzzling gaps or effects of incoherence. In the second section of my essay I want to demonstrate how a number of modern American novels confront the tradition of silence about the national history of plantation colonialism and racism at the very point the US is emerging as a neo-imperial power, poised to create the so-called American Century. My idea is that a surprising number of modern novels bring the problem of racial colonialism into problematic visibility. They present isolated images or fragmentary narratives that identify the problem without being able to integrate it entirely into a new narrative of national confession and restitution. Rather, we might say, following Malcolm Bull (2000), that the issue of racial colonialism is brought *into* hiding – from the status of being entirely out of mind to one in which it is registered as an absence, felt as hidden.

There aren't many novels published before the first part of the twentieth century that look closely and critically at the way the historical project of plantation colonialism was the foundation of US prosperity. There were, of course, plenty of well-known works that entered the fray over the related questions of abolition, slaveholding, and Southern secession that led up to the Civil War. It could be that the most famous of all American novels is *Uncle Tom's Cabin* (1852), but its portrait of plantation life understands it as a sectional anomaly and a national offense, not as the culmination of hemispheric Anglo-European plantation colonialism descending from the sixteenth century. Almost from the beginning of the early republic's determination to define its political essence in terms of Enlightenment ideals centered in personal liberty, the contradictions of a democracy practicing racial chattel slavery had to be solved. As Jennifer Rae Greeson (1999) demonstrates, strategies of disassociation began to take the form of pretending that such unenlightened ways of life were peculiar to the region of "the South," a place unlike the rest of the nation: feudal, decadent, racist, and violent. One could argue that there's been an exceptional capacity for denial in the North about its dependency on slaveholding and slave-trading economies – the commerce in black bodies and plantation staples that enriched those in the New England sea trade, for example, or the northern textile industry that drew its raw materials from southern producers.

As Susan Donaldson proposes in her essay in this volume, we may be able to trace the origins of what came to be understood as experimental modernist narrative in the US at least in part to the revolutionary (and ultimately modern) transformations overtaking the South following the end of Reconstruction in the mid-1870s. Perhaps one phase of the struggle with modernity that provokes modernist reaction in the US has to do with the painful acknowledgment of guilt at the moment a traditional way of life – and the technologies of disavowal upholding it – are passing from the scene. David Harvey thinks such a situation endemic to modernism generally, and speculates that the US failed to develop much of an avant-garde movement because "the very lack of 'traditionalist' (feudal and aristocratic) resistance, and the parallel popular acceptance of broadly modernist sentiments . . . made the works of artists and intellectuals rather less important as the avant-garde cutting edge of social change" (Harvey 1992: 27). Harvey means the United States as a whole, but as is typical, he is thinking of the North; he knows Chicago ought to have been the "catalyst for modernism after 1870 or so" (p. 27), for example, but was not; hence the hypothesis about a lack of traditionalist resistance.

Had Harvey looked south, though, he might have noticed the very feudal and aristocratic elite missing elsewhere in the modernizing nation. Catalysts for modernism do turn up in places like Virginia and Mississippi. It is not a coincidence that the dynamic of resistance to modernity and the rebelliousness of modernism plays out most prominently in the South, and that the nation's pre-eminent modernists are almost all Southerners or at least have significant Southern ties: Faulkner, most obviously, but also T. S. Eliot, Willa Cather, Sherwood Anderson, Jean Toomer, Eudora Welty, Thomas Wolfe, Erskine Caldwell, F. Scott Fitzgerald, Zora Neale Hurston, Katherine Anne Porter, Richard Wright, Flannery O'Connor, Ralph Ellison, and so on. That American modernism was Southern modernism may be the result of the region's more intense and violent experience of modernization. And if we grant that the emergence of US neo-imperialism was a pivotal component of such modernization – as numerous historians of the American century have established, and as we have seen Jameson assume more broadly in taking British imperialism as a key to Anglo-modernity – then the matter of plantation colonialism becomes central rather than incidental to the modern American novel. It becomes a force precisely because it threatens to break through the systems of disavowal that kept it at bay for so long.

Let me illustrate how the colonial plantation South's problematic status may spur the emergence of modern American fiction by turning to Willa Cather's *My Ántonia* (1918), a work that bids to locate the origins of national greatness in the plains of the Midwest. In *My Ántonia*, Cather acknowledges the plantation South only as an apparent anomaly of national history, dealt with by being both written into and written out of her reverential epic. The novel's vision of national destiny rests on the confidence that the sacrifice of past generations is justified by the country's modern ascendancy. The narrator, Jim Burden, a legal representative for one of the railways spanning the continent, surveys the improvements that have transformed the Nebraska of his youth: "The changes seemed beautiful and harmonious to me; it was like watching the growth of a great man or of a great idea . . . all the human effort that had gone into it was coming back in long, sweeping lines of fertility" (Cather 1918/1995: 197). Jim takes as exemplary the fate of his childhood immigrant friend Ántonia; he wants to believe that the future redeems the damage her Bohemian family has sustained by uprooting from Europe and resettling in frontier America, and projects the heartland's "vitality" onto her. Ántonia embodies the ideological fantasy warranting Jim's epic of national development.

The euphemistic phrase "human effort," though, hardly covers the millions of obscure lives that have been hurled into the machinery of American progress (like that of a tramp who kills himself by jumping into a thresher, or of Ántonia's father, who commits suicide out of homesickness, or even of Ántonia herself, who joins the novel's numerous women in sacrificing their interests for what Jim considers the land's "fortunate issue"). Jim's fantastic accounting lets him act as if he does not know otherwise. He never wonders that he alone is destined to rise, having "forgotten" that his grandparents arrived in Nebraska from Virginia already advantaged with social capital unavailable to foreign immigrants.

In a generally episodic narrative – Jim insists "it has n't any form" (p. 244) – one seemingly anomalous incident underscores the story's tendency to conceal unwanted knowledge in plain view. Jim recalls an evening from his youth during which a touring black piano player performs "barbarously" wonderful music. This sightless prodigy, known as Blind d'Arnault, immediately makes Jim think of his native South, but in a register of surprising racial stereotype:

> It was the soft, amiable Negro voice, like those I remembered from early childhood, with the note of docile subservience in it. He had the Negro head, too; almost no head at all; nothing behind the ears but folds of neck under close-clipped wool. He would have been repulsive if his face had not been so kindly and happy. It was the happiest face I had seen since I left Virginia. (Cather 1918/1995: 118)

What's hard to account for here is the eruption of disgust. Jim's recourse to harsh stereotype betrays anxious ambivalence: the comfortable New Yorker is both attracted to and repulsed by this shade of the past. On the one hand, as d'Arnault plays, he becomes a "glistening African god of pleasure, full of strong, savage blood" (p. 123). He embodies all that Jim Burden lacks, the prosperous capitalist having fulfilled his ambitions via an ethic of Protestant self-denial. On the other, Jim resists this historical revenant of Africans in Virginia who toiled on the farms of the nation's first frontier. The novel gapes open here briefly to record d'Arnault's history as the product of slaveholder miscegenation and racial abuse – a history implicit in the plantation songs he circulates on the plains.

The magisterial equanimity of Jim's national mythmaking is nearly blindsided by this challenge to his faith that the American epic redeems "all the human effort" that has gone into it. The American slave is given no place in Jim's story. It is one thing to fuse the stories of European immigrants, another to integrate the barbarity of plantation slavery. D'Arnault may be "an African god of pleasure," but Jim will not follow the implications of this episode either to the African origins of the South, or to the Southern origins of national greatness. For him plantation Virginia will always be what he calls, with the force of denial, the "Far South" (p. 119). Jim confines d'Arnault's visitation to an isolated episode never welcomed into the novel's plot. By cauterizing the memory of commandeered land and coerced labor, Jim is free to fetishize the later-arriving European immigrant as the figure of national destiny, harmony, and productivity.

Jean Toomer wants to explore Southern origins that Cather barely makes room for. Toomer's *Cane* (1922) reflects the effort by a black artist from the urban North to discover his Southern roots. Toomer himself left Washington DC, where he had been raised by his mother and her parents, to investigate the place in Georgia where his father, a descendant of slaves, had been rumored to return when he abandoned his family. Toomer's extraordinary book comes out of that stay, and another in South Carolina, during which he reimagined rural black folk culture and its relations to modern black metropolitan life in the 1920s. Toomer's portraits of modern Southern life are moved by his sense that forms of expression descending from slave culture were dying out. *Cane* captures the bruised beauty of folk ways – the crude eloquence of its work songs, the powerful prophetic visions of racial emancipation – but it also acknowledges the fruits held out by modernization: education, economic opportunity, a better chance to define your own racial identity and escape the terror of Jim Crow segregation. The deeper anxiety of *Cane* stems from Toomer's suspicion that the modern age has prepared forms of neo-slavery for black people in the Americas, that the color line represents the modernized future of racism. In a way, then, *Cane* may be understood as an antiplantation novel, a kind of Cubist, collage-like, multigeneric challenge to popular fantasies of white mastery.

Cane's South, though, is not just the Georgia of its ostensible setting (however deeply Toomer drew on local history for inspiration). I want to suggest that it is also a kind of floating island of plantation history. Benitez-Rojo speaks of the New World colonial plantation system as essentially a floating island – machines of production that replicate themselves throughout the hemisphere, oblivious to local communities, customs, and values. The indistinctness of Toomer's South creates the impression that *Cane*'s could be scenes from plantation life anywhere: the hallucinatory repetitiveness of racial violence and slave labor suggests how the modern South has reimposed the assumptions of a plantation regime throughout the post-Civil War South, and has also reinspired racial discrimination in the North. But Toomer also suggests that the "Dixie Pike has grown from a goat path in Africa" (1922/1988: 12), and one character enters a trance that creates a "visioned African" who suggests the immediacy in the South of a long history of Western slave trade: "An while he was agazin at th heavens, heart filled up with th Lord, some little white-ant biddies came an tied his feet to chains. They led him t th coast, they led him t th sea, they led him across th ocean an they didn't set him free" (pp. 22–3). The stories of cane/ *Cane* oscillate between rural Souths, Chicago, and Washington DC, as if to suggest a modern national network of peripheral production, Northern industry, and state administration. At one point, a young son of the South looks out over Chicago's South Side:

> Paul follows the sun, over the stock-yards where a fresh stench is just arising, across wheat lands that are still waving above their stubble, into the sun. Paul follows the sun to a pine-matted hillock in Georgia. He sees the slanting roofs of gray unpainted cabins tinted lavender. A Negress chants a lullaby beneath the mate-eyes of a Southern planter. (Toomer 1922/1988: 73)

This subvision of Toomer's modernist novel culminates in a figure even more enigmatic than Cather's Blind d'Arnault. In the last section of *Cane*, a drama called "Kabnis," members of a black community struggle with their obligations to racial uplift. The work's conclusion pictures a blind black elder known as Father John, long silent, who finally delivers himself of an oracular truth. The lesson of his experience, Father John reveals, is that white people have perverted the Bible to authorize racial crime. The pronouncement feels anticlimactic given the absence of much attention to matters of traditional religious life in the South, and hardly news at that. But the iconography of the scene points to a highly relevant embedded history. Father John has been sleeping in a cellar known as "The Hole" below a wheelwright's shop; the space evokes the tight quarters and nether regions of the middle passage. The old man is lifted from this pit to issue his pronouncement, and Kabnis makes its import explicit as he addresses John: "An do y think you'll ever see th light of day again, even if you wasn't blind? Do y think youre out of slavery? Huh? Youre where they used t throw th worked-out, no-count slaves" (p. 115). Toomer bears witness to the persistence of American plantations and neo-plantations, not to mention the modern nation-state rising above them.

Suppose, then, that another sense of "high" – in addition to referring to the modernist work's desired autonomy, and to its eventual canonization – might be "above," in a geopolitical and economic sense. In an influential analysis of what he called "the southern question" in Italian politics, Antonio Gramsci (1926/1978) showed how the country's southern agricultural region had been treated like a colony by its northern industrial part, leading to a geopolitics of territorial and intellectual domination. Taking up this suggestive formulation, I wonder if we might think of high modernism as related to imaginative work typically consumed within the controlling spheres or regions of modernity (the global North), but engaging a new mindfulness of the global colonial South. From this perspective, we might notice how a number of other novels associated with high modernism represent, as do Cather and Toomer, the colonialist foundation of the nation in the figures of black male bodies that abrupt anomalously on stories that (cannot quite) contain them.

Such a character appears in E. E. Cummings's novel about his detention in France during World War I, *The Enormous Room* (1922). The aim of this lightly fictionalized account is to mock the idiocies of war conduct, particularly the hypocrisies and contradictions that make a shambles of life on the home front. Cummings treats the reader to a series of portraits that savor the vivid characters he encounters in prison. One of the most arresting arrivals is a gigantic black man Cummings calls "Jean Le Nègre." Jean is first of all a living stereotype: the "divine laugh of a negro" precedes his appearance at the door of the enormous room, and he enters as "a beautiful pillar of black strutting muscle topped with a tremendous display of the whitest teeth on earth" (1922/1999: 204). Cummings and the others first spy this "NIGGER" through a "peep-hole" (p. 204), and Jean gets elaborated in something of a peep-hole narrative: a single chapter, devoted exclusively to him, the fetishized object of Euro-American colonialism, bearing on his very body the traces of a global history of enslavement. Jean speaks French – he *is* French, but problematically, since he is from the colonies – so his blackness imports the reality of far-flung colonized subjects making their way to the "homeland" and claiming French justice in the national tongue, a regular pattern for 1920s anticolonialists.

Like Aimé Cesaire or Frantz Fanon, who insisted on being subjects of France after starting out subjugated by the French, Jean Le Nègre embodies the contradictions of colonialism come home. He shows up wearing an English officer's uniform, which he has bought on a whim in a French shop, and is fully bedecked – "not forgetting the Colonial, nor yet the Belgian Cross," having earlier "sallied importantly forth to capture Paris" (p. 208). As "Le Nègre" Jean bears a derogatory term equivalent to "nigger," rather than the more polite "le noir" (for "black"). Here is another reversal of colonial fiction; since Jean is called "le noir" only by his enemies, we're told, he presumably prefers "le nègre" as the more truthful designation of his status as a denigrated colonial subject. Jean gets connected to other points on the colonial map too – jangling the nerves of a fellow prisoner "known as the West Indian Negro" (p. 210) when he mentions the word "Liberté"; being associated in playful doggerel "avec des pickaninee" (p. 209); prompting the indignant "Cummings" once to defend him in explicitly American terms to the authorities: "There are a lot of Jeans where I come from. You heard what he said? He is black, is he not, and gets no justice from you" (p. 216).

Jean Le Nègre functions like the other characters in the novel, as an isolated study; in fact, *The Enormous Room* is hardly a novel at all, more a collection of character sketches, satirical set pieces, homely fables. Like Blind d'Arnault, then

(Jean too is once called "a Samson," p. 216), Le Nègre serves as a picture of colonial dependency and abuse that never gets attached to a coherent narrative about the making of present-day Europe. Colonial questions were matters of explicit concern in these decades, since the Great War was commonly understood as a conflict of rival imperialist powers over holdings in Africa, South America, and Southeast Asia. Yet imperialism appears only marginally in *The Enormous Room*. One way Jean functions as an object of disguised visibility (or felt hiddenness) may be seen in the figurative language used to describe his appearance. Repeatedly we have "Jean's chocolate-coloured nakedness" (p. 220), Jean as "a chocolate-coloured thing" (p. 221), "the wonderful chocolate carpet of his skin, [as] his whole body glistened with sweat" (p. 215). Here the image of delectable chocolate offers to transfigure toiling black bodies on cocoa and sugar plantations into the very products of their labor ("café sucré" is also mentioned earlier in the chapter), a form of forgetfulness indispensable for metropolitan consumers of colonial spoil. Jean Le Nègre speaks only French, and such restricted intelligibility echoes the expressive blocks on a number of tantalizingly divulgent characters (one named Zulu manages nothing but gibberish). These figures function as the colonial uncanny – familiar but not quite recognized.

The most spectacular example of William Faulkner's imagining of the plantation South – and also a signature work of high modernism – is *Absalom, Absalom!* (1936). Faulkner's novel is a culmination of a slow recognition in his early writing of the colonial residues of New World slavery especially legible in the New Orleans he knew so well, portal to the deep South's overlooked affiliations with Caribbean slave culture and commerce. The most accomplished of modern American novelists, Faulkner assays Southern history in a series of boldly experimental novels as he edges toward a full-scale retelling of the region's plantation origins. *The Sound and the Fury* (1929) represents in a fragmentary narrative the splintering of the Compson family, members of the declined plantation elite – the helter-skelter story reflecting the break-up of master narratives, the commitment to stream-of-consciousness technique indicating Faulkner's sympathy for the raw incoherence of broken mentalities. *As I Lay Dying* (1930) extends Faulkner's modernist phase by counterpointing the South's subjugation as a kind of colony to the North with domestic permutations of male domination over women's lives, another kind of colonization the novel registers. Perhaps the most distinctive element in Faulkner's telling of the story of the South by the time he is ready to tell it whole in *Absalom* involves its colonial New World bearings. Though it takes a long while for the storytellers to get to that inaugural phase of Thomas Sutpen's career, we do eventually learn how Sutpen's rise to the planter elite of the Mississippi frontier first takes him to Haiti in the 1820s.

Native of Appalachian western Virginia, born about 1807, the dirt-poor teenager Sutpen heads toward the coast and sets his sights on the West Indies, to which a schoolteacher has told him white men go to get rich. He lands in the country of Haiti, already by the 1820s a place soaked in centuries of racial bloodshed, the whole island a theatre of past rebellions and massacres, with the stage now set for another imminent insurrection. Yet Thomas Sutpen in his ignorance of New World history remains oblivious to the very ground beneath his feet, "not knowing that what he rode upon was a volcano" (Faulkner 1936/1990: 202). One narrator reminds us of what the novice plantation overseer who was there never fathoms: that the fields of sugar cane rise from "soil manured with black blood from two hundred years of oppression and exploitation" (p. 202), soil compacted of "the planting of men too: the yet intact bones and brains in which the old unsleeping blood that had vanished into the earth they trod still cried out for vengeance" (p. 202). And not only "the torn limbs and outraged hearts" of African slaves are to be recounted, but also the corpses of French plantation masters executed during Haiti's slave revolution two decades earlier, the island still "breathed over by the winds in which the doomed ships had fled in vain, out of which the last tatter of sail had sunk into the blue sea, along which the last vain despairing cry of woman or child had blown away" (p. 202).

The ruinous social and moral consequences of much New World colonial history are evoked by these images: its very cradle, on an island named Hispaniola by Christopher Columbus, where the native Arawak people became the first victims of New World enslavement; the acts of revolt by the island's next enslaved population, the Africans first imported in the early seventeenth century when the Indians had died out, and their establishment of the New World's first black republic in 1804 (promising to end those "two hundred years" of exploitation); the tremors of slave rebellion felt in the antebellum US plantation South for half a century; and, during the time Faulkner was writing the novel, the just-ended US military occupation of both states on the island, Haiti and Santo Domingo, the troops deployed to provide security for American investors (much of it still in sugar agriculture). After witnessing the misery caused by the plantation system – for everyone it touched – one of its participants concludes that in the Civil War "the South would realize that it was now paying the price for having erected its economic edifice not on the rock of stern morality but on the shifting sands of opportunism and moral brigandage" (p. 209). In *Absalom, Absalom!* Faulkner imagines how the initial insult of reducing human beings to instruments of labor and commodities of exchange dooms a society to concussions of brutality, domination, and revenge. Those offenses coalesce in another enigmatic figure of plantation racial bondage: Charles Bon, the mixed-race Haitian son whom Sutpen repudiates. Bon is called the "curious one" (p. 74), and his status, origins, ancestry, and purposes never really do get resolved. He is an even more insistent version of the anomalous black body that is refused a place in the narrative of region and nation.

In her novel *Nightwood* (1937) Djuna Barnes imagines a yet more advanced historical stage of the metropolitan black body as the marker of modern imperialism. Barnes's book is a brilliant meditation on the ruined state of European culture between the world wars; it is a pageant of grotesques living out stories of raging desire, morbid decline, and sardonic disillusionment. The principal voice of the novel belongs to an expatriate Irish American who pontificates ceaselessly about the vanity of life. In an early scene Dr Matthew O'Connor finds himself at a party presided over by a number of men "looking as if they were deciding the fate of a nation" (Barnes 1937/1961: 14). With their "parliamentary attitudes," the group keys us to Barnes's intense conviction that political urgencies in postwar Europe penetrate the most private of spaces. *Nightwood* is a stunningly perceptive study of the increasingly violent enforcement of bourgeois discipline in 1930s Germany and Austria. Barnes connects the psychic contortions and injuries caused by the extreme rigidity of heterosexual "norms," ethnic "purity," and cultural "superiority." Women fall in love with each but cannot shed their senses of guilt or restlessness; European Jews struggle desperately to invent ancestries and "intermarry" so as to assimilate; the nations defeated in the Great War share their conquerors' suspicion that the European hostilities have been nothing but a catastrophic invalidation of the entire course of Western progress. Barnes – or more exactly O'Connor – comes up with a flamboyant character who epitomizes the desecration perpetrated in the name of European civilization.

O'Connor begins a riff that conjures up the recollection of "Nikka, the nigger who used to fight the bear in the *Cirque de Paris*" (p. 16). Nikka performs "crouching all over the arena without a stitch on, except an ill-concealed loin cloth all abulge," so he enters the imaginative register of the novel like Blind d'Arnault and Jean Le Nègre, in the trappings of stereotype: bestial, primitive, sexually rampant. Tellingly, though, Nikka functions less as a reminder of premodern naturalness, and more as the text of modernity itself: his entire body is covered with elaborate tattoos that become legible as the record of imperial domination. One faded inscription is rumored to spell out "Desdemona," a name that not only denotes the tragic racialization of love, but also evokes the crucible of European colonial trade in Venice. Among the extensive intricacies of Nikka's inscriptions appear on his chest "beneath a beautiful caravel in full sail, two clasped hands, the wrist bones fretted with point lace" (p. 16). So implausible a tribute to Elizabethan seafaring gets doubled by a single infamous word – a profanity – uttered once by a member of English Tudor royalty that was "so wholly epigrammatic and in no way befitting the great and noble British Empire that [O'Connor] was brought up with a start" (p. 16). Nikka winds vine work about his legs, "topped by the swart ramble rose copied from the coping of the Hamburg house of Rothschild" (p. 17), while – as the pièce de resistance – he has incised "Garde tout!" ['Look out!'] over his anus. O'Connor admits to curiosity about "why all this barbarity," and Nikka answers perversely that he "loved beauty and would have it about him" (p. 17).

Nikka inscribes the marks of European imperialist fancy on his very body, in mute acknowledgment of but also protest against the barbarity forced on people like him. He converts the maiming brought by such uses of his body – trained to perform in the rings set up in metropolitan capitals – into a form of beauty, but also a warning: Garde tout! Treated like shit, eliminated as the waste of imperial modes of production, the colonial subject wants the scandal of his status (like the anus, something "you mustn't mention," p. 17) plainly visible. Barnes's prescience deepens Nikka's significance, moreover; he's not just the representative of far-flung dark-skinned peoples subject to foreign imperialism, he's also a version of domestic aggression against hated internal minorities. O'Connor thinks of Nikka just after an exchange about Jews; the Irish-American doctor considers them "a lost nation" because they know how "to keep humor in the family," and an Austrian Duchess immediately shouts her assent in German. There's doubtless something anti-Semitic in the idea of Jews directing humor at themselves, to begin with, but Barnes goes far beyond such a minor observation and develops a grasp of European hatred toward assimilated Jews that corresponds to the nearly contemporary speculations of Adorno and Horkheimer on the inherence of anti-Semitism to Enlightenment modernity. Their argument is that anti-Semitism flourished in ruined postwar societies like Germany's and Austria's because Jews became objects of resentment and envy to the suffering working classes. While international captains of finance and industry reaped profits from the war and even its aftermath, the condition of workers worsened. But rather than see through to the structural exploitation of labor by capitalism, the working class had Jews dangled before them by elites as substitute figures of resentment. Traditionally confined to occupations like money-changing, but also prominent in intellectual circles, Jews appeared as infuriating objects of working-class envy: prosperous to the point of luxury, yet content in their powerlessness. Adorno and Horkheimer contend that European Jews became the scapegoats of modern capitalism – the economic development of which was everywhere intertwined with colonialism. With anti-Semitism as the touchstone, *Nightwood* elaborates an intricate web of violent domination in numerous spheres of private life. Barnes's text proves modernist in the sense I'm suggesting by bringing the historical residue and imminent consequences of imperialism into hiding. Nikka's tattoos inscribe his history as a colonial subject even as they obscure and morselize it. It's all as plain as the skin on your . . . whatever, though no one's translating.

In F. Scott Fitzgerald's *Tender is the Night* (1934), a new kind of empire comes into view, one we might associate with postmodernity. A Hollywood movie starlet vacationing on the Riviera, and enjoying her first serious crush on a married man, encounters a blot on her bliss: she returns to her hotel room one afternoon to discover a strange black man in her bed, dead. The dazzling Dr Dick Diver with whom she's enamored comes to the panicked teenager's rescue, saving Rosemary's innocence – the ingenue's most valuable commodity – from the taint of scandal. Fitzgerald's sprawlingly ambitious novel attempts nothing less than a survey of brand new cultural technologies reorganizing modern postwar life. *Tender is the Night* explores the popular spread of psychoanalysis, the onset of a culture of consumption, the birth of a nation of moviegoers, and the formation of an international (or perhaps transnational) plutocracy. Wealth rules in Fitzgerald's world, and the power accruing to owners of real estate, resources, and inventions extends to those possessing ideas, systems of production, and means of publicity. American expatriates discovering how much they can buy in postwar France and Italy signal what the century of American hegemony will look like. Rosemary's brush with an out-of-place black casualty, however, suggests the presence of hidden stories troubling the otherwise oblivious beneficiaries of US prosperity in the 1920s. The Divers, riding high on Nicole Warren Diver's family money (a Chicago meat-packing fortune), construct their magnificent Villa Diana on a hillside above Cannes, the novel barely pausing to note that "peasant dwellings" had been combined to create the house, and others destroyed to make the gardens (p. 26). The villa sits near the "ancient hill village of Tarmes," a repressed reminder of Roman empire that returns in the form of the last film project we see Rosemary involved with, a movie entitled *The Grandeur that was Rome*. The Divers know that the magical effects conjured by their wealth depend on keeping the taint of labor out of mind: servants must be as unnoticed as those former peasants have become, and the Divers spend a good deal of time congratulating themselves and their kind on their "essential" difference from those who lack taste (which really means money plus the discretion not to flaunt it).

That distinction takes an ethnic form, to be sure, with cuddly Jews like Abe North tolerated (though eventually sacrificed, a suicide to dissoluteness and lost confidence), but Aryan blondes like Rosemary (who's once cautioned by her new friends to be careful about sunburn in the bright heat of the Riviera: you've got "important skin," they insist) are the ones who matter. Such class narcissism eventuates – given Fitzgerald's withering mockery of it – in the act of literal incest at the heart of the book – the capitalist magnate Devereux Warren taking his daughter Nicole to bed when the child's mother, his wife, dies. Such self-love knows no bounds, seems Fitzgerald's point, but the idea that money is the basis for a new *kind* is also augured by so monstrous an act. The Divers once arrive at the beach, "her white suit and his white trunks very white against the color of their bodies" (p. 280). Late in the novel Nicole leaves Dick, to take up with a swarthy Frenchman named Tommy Barban. His name and dusky complexion notwithstanding, he's enchanted with Nicole's nearly inhuman whiteness: she even has "new white eyes" (p. 294), though she insists they are her grandfather's crook's eyes. Whiteness isn't what you are, it's what you wear, how you see – with willful innocence and a limitless capacity for desire.

That realization is one Dick Diver fails to grasp. His father born and buried in Virginia, Dick unwittingly carries forward old-fashioned racial prejudices, recoiling from dark-skinned people as if they were all Southern Negroes. He dismisses the corpse in Rosemary's bed as "only some nigger scrap" (p. 110), and erupts jealously over one of Rosemary's movie lovers, Nicotera – "He's a spic!" (p. 218). Diver's most damning error of this sort shadows his whole slow collapse into self-embarrassment: visiting an old friend who has recently remarried a native of India, Dick mistakes his host Hosain's sisters for domestic servants, precipitating a drunken confrontation in which he refers to Mary's husband too as a "spic," then "a smoke." The novel has already noticed that Hosain would be "not quite light enough to travel in a Pullman south of the Mason-Dixon" (p. 258), and that his union with Mary North (the Jewish Abe North's widow) makes her the stepmother of "two very tan children" (p. 259). Such racial hypersensitivity arises I believe precisely as the meaning of race begins to fade on the stage of global capital. Hosain is an avatar of a transnational elite; he's functionally white because he owns untold mineral resources and has been made a count by the government of Italy in recognition of his wealth. Out of a command of the science of consciousness, entertainment media, technologies of production and consumption, and the wealth consequent to them, a new elite forms. The irony for Dick is that the Negro in Rosemary's bed isn't at all what the Southerner takes him to be; Jules Peterson is a Scandinavian business-man who actually gets murdered as the result of his effort to stand up for Abe North, who has been victimized by a "Negro" thief. According to the narrator, Peterson is "a small respectable Negro, on the suave model that heels the Republican party in the border States" (p. 106). If he's offensive to Dick in this additional way, it's because he represents the fading of color before the power of money. *Tender is the Night* anxiously feels its way toward a nearly unimaginable state of affairs – the very substance of postmodern reality, under which everything is commodified – in which the significance of racial difference has yielded to the question of financial means. Wealth is the new white.

REFERENCES AND FURTHER READING

Agee, James. (1941/2005). *Let Us Now Praise Famous Men; A Death in the Family; and Shorter Fiction*. New York: Library of America.

Appiah, Kwame Anthony. (1992). *In My Father's House: Africa in the Philosophy of Culture*. New York: Oxford University Press.

Armstrong, Tim. (1998). *Modernism, Technology, and the Body: A Cultural Study*. New York: Cambridge University Press.

Baker, Houston, Jr. (1987). *Modernism and the Harlem Renaissance*. Chicago: University of Chicago Press.

Barnes, Djuna. (1937/1961). *Nightwood*. New York: New Directions.

Benjamin, Walter. (1969). The work of art in the age of mechanical reproduction. In *Illuminations*, ed. and intro. Hannah Arendt, trans Harry Zohn (pp. 257–51). New York: Schocken Books.

Bourdieu, Pierre. (1984). *Distinction: A Social Critique of the Judgement of Taste*, trans. Richard Nice. Cambridge, MA: Harvard University Press.

Bull, Malcolm. (2000). *Seeing Things Hidden: Apocalypse, Vision and Totality*. London: Verso.

Burger, Peter. (1984). *Theory of the Avant-Garde*, trans. Michael Shaw, foreword Jochen Schulte-Sasse. Minneapolis: University of Minnesota Press.

Butler, Christopher. (1994). *Early Modernism: Literature, Music, and Painting in Europe, 1900–1916*. Oxford: Clarendon Press.

Cather, Willa. (1918/1995). *My Ántonia*. Boston: Houghton Mifflin.

Chu, Patricia. (2007). *Race, Nationalism and the State in British and American Modernism*. Cambridge, UK: Cambridge University Press.

Cummings, E. E. (1922/1999). *The Enormous Room*. New York: Penguin.

Denning, Michael. (1996). *The Cultural Front: The Laboring of American Culture in the Twentieth-Century*. New York: Verso.

Douglas, Ann. (1995). *Terrible Honesty: Mongrel Manhattan in the 1920s*. New York: Farrar, Straus, and Giroux.

Du Bois, W. E. B. (1920). *Darkwater, Voices from within the Veil*. New York: Harcourt, Brace and Howe.

Edwards, Brent Hayes. (2003). *The Practice of Diaspora: Literature, Translation, and the Rise of Black Internationalism*. Cambridge, MA: Harvard University Press.

Faulkner, William. (1929/1990). *The Sound and the Fury*. Vintage International edn. New York: Random.

Faulkner, William. (1930/1990). *As I Lay Dying*. Vintage International edn. New York: Random.

Faulkner, William. (1936/1990). *Absalom, Absalom!* Vintage International edn. New York: Random.

Fitzgerald, F. Scott. (1934). *Tender is the Night*. New York: Scribner's.

Foley, Barbara. (1993). *Radical Representations: Politics and Form in U. S. Proletarian Fiction, 1929–1941*. Durham, NC: Duke University Press.

Gilroy, Paul. (1993). *The Black Atlantic: Modernity and Double Consciousness*. Cambridge, MA: Harvard University Press.

Godden, Richard. (1990). *Fictions of Capital: Essays on the American Novel from James to Mailer*. Cambridge, UK: Cambridge University Press.

Godden, Richard. (1997). *Fictions of Labor: William Faulkner and the South's Long Revolution*. Cambridge, UK: Cambridge University Press.

Gramsci, Antonio. (1926/1978). Some aspects of the southern question. In *Selections from Political Writings (1921–1926)*, trans. and ed. Quintin Hoare. London: Lawrence and Wishart.

Greeson, Jennifer Rae. (1999). The figure of the South and the nationalizing imperatives of early United States literature. *Yale Journal of Criticism* 12, 2: 209–48.

Harvey, David. (1992). *The Condition of Postmodernity: An Enquiry in the Origins of Cultural Change*. Oxford: Blackwell.

Hassan, Ihab. (1971/1982). *The Dismemberment of Orpheus: Toward a Postmodern Literature*, 2nd edn. Madison, WI: University of Wisconsin Press.

Horkheimer, Max and Theodor W. Adorno. (1994). *Dialectic of Enlightenment*, trans. John Cumming. New York: Continuum.

Howe, Irving. (1967). The idea of the modern. Introduction to Irving Howe (ed.), *The Idea of the Modern in Literature and the Arts* (pp. 11–40). New York: Horizon Press.

Huyssen, Andreas. (1986). *After the Great Divide: Modernism, Mass Culture, Postmodernism*. Bloomington: Indiana University Press.

Jameson, Fredric. (1988). *The Ideologies of Theory: Essays 1971–1986. Volume 2: The Syntax of History*. Minneapolis: University of Minnesota Press.

Jameson, Fredric. (1990). Modernism and imperialism. In Terry Eagleton, Fredric Jameson, and Edward W. Said, *Nationalism, Colonialism, and Literature* (pp. 43–66). Minneapolis: University of Minnesota Press.

Kaplan, Amy. (2002). *The Anarchy of Empire in the Making of U.S. Culture*. Cambridge, MA: Harvard University Press.

Kenner, Hugh. (1975). *A Homemade World*. New York: Knopf.

Knapp, James F. (1988). *Literary Modernism and the Transformation of Work*. Evanston, IL: Northwestern University Press.

Lewis, Pericles. (2000). *Modernism, Nationalism, and the Novel*. Cambridge, UK: Cambridge University Press.

Lukács, Georg. (1963). The ideology of modernism. In *The Meaning of Contemporary Realism*, trans. John and Necke Mander (pp. 17–46). London: Merlin Press.

Mao, Douglas and Rebecca L. Walkowitz (2008). The new modernist studies. *PMLA* 123, 3: 737–48.

McGowan, John. (2005). Postmodernism, 2nd edn. The Johns Hopkins Guide to Literary Theory and Criticism. <http://litguide.press.jhu.edu/cgi-bin/view.cgi?eid=212&query=postmodernism>.

Michaels, Walter Benn. (1987). *The Gold Standard and the Logic of Naturalism: American Literature at the Turn of the Century*. Berkeley: University of California Press.

Michaels, Walter Benn. (1995). *Our America: Nativism, Modernism, and Pluralism*. Durham, NC: Duke University Press.

Nicholls, Peter. (1995). *Modernisms: A Literary Guide*. Berkeley: University of California Press.

North, Michael. (1994). *The Dialect of Modernism: Race, Language, and Twentieth-Century Literature*. New York: Oxford University Press.

Rowe, John Carlos. (2000). *Literary Culture and U.S. Imperialism: from the Revolution to World War II*. New York: Oxford University Press.

Steinman, Lisa. (1987). *Made in America: Science, Technology, and American Modernist Poets*. New Haven, CT: Yale University Press.

Szalay, Michael. (2000). *New Deal Modernism: American Literature and the Invention of the Welfare State*. Durham, NC: Duke University Press.

Taussig, Michael T. (1993). *Mimesis and Alterity: A Particular History of the Senses*. New York: Routledge.

Tichi, Cecilia. (1987). *Shifting Gears: Technology, Literature, Culture in Modernist America*. Chapel Hill: University of North Carolina Press.

Toomer, Jean. (1922/1988). *Cane*, ed. Darwin T. Turner. New York: Norton.

Trilling, Lionel. (1955). *The Opposing Self*. New York: Viking Press.

Weinstein, Philip. (2005). *Unknowing: The Work of Modernist Fiction*. Ithaca, NY: Cornell University Press.

Williams, Raymond. (1989). *The Politics of Modernism: Against the New Conformists*. London: Verso.

16

African-American Modernisms

Michelle Stephens

In the spring of 1926, the editors of the NAACP magazine, *The Crisis*, published a symposium entitled "The Negro in Art – How Shall He Be Portrayed?" The symposium began with a survey, sent to many leading black writers and intellectuals of the period, that posed the following questions:

1 When the artist, black or white, portrays Negro characters is he under any obligations or limitations as to the sort of character he will portray?
2 Can any author be criticized for painting the worst or the best characters of a group?
3 Can publishers be criticized for refusing to handle novels that portray Negroes of education and accomplishment, on the ground that these characters are no different from white folk and therefore not interesting?
4 What are Negroes to do when they are continually painted at their worst and judged by the public as they are painted?
5 Does the situation of the educated Negro in America with its pathos, humiliation and tragedy call for artistic treatment [that is] sincere and sympathetic . . . ?
6 Is not the continual portrayal of the sordid, foolish and criminal among Negroes convincing the world that this and this alone is really and essentially Negroid, and preventing white artists from knowing any other types and preventing black artists from daring to paint them?
7 Is there not a real danger that young colored writers will be tempted to follow the popular trend in portraying Negro character in the underworld rather than seeking to paint the truth about themselves and their own social class?

With this set of questions, the editors of the *Crisis* magazine initiated a discussion that would come to characterize, even dominate, African-American creative expression during the modernist period and on throughout the twentieth century. For black artists, questions of identity – what does it mean to be black? – often turned on issues of representation – how does one portray blackness and how is blackness seen?

African-American modernisms represent some of the very moments when black artists in the Americas began to define answers to questions concerning the meaning of blackness for themselves.

A distinctive feature of the various forms of black artistic production that occurred in Harlem and beyond throughout the 1920s and 1930s is their inherently performative dimensions, the products of an artistic movement forced to be ever aware of its social audience. At the very beginnings of the modern era, Virginia Woolf defined twentieth-century modernity as entailing a shift in human relations beginning approximately in 1910. African-American modernisms reflect the impact of that shift on black–white relations, the intercultural relationships blacks and whites in the Americas shared as they reinterpreted their pasts and present together at the turn of a new century.

For a canonical black modernist such as Alain Locke, the art of the "New Negro" blended the "motive" of "being racial" with the modernist imperative "to be so purely for the sake of art," producing a uniquely black "idiom of style" that combined urban sophistication with "the instinctive gift of the folk-spirit" (Locke 1992: 51). Locke was one of the primary figures spearheading the New Negro movement of the early twentieth century, which by 1925 had consolidated enough to produce an anthology of the same name. What both the *Crisis* survey, edited by W. E. B. Du Bois, and *The New Negro* anthology edited by Locke, reveal was that embedded in the African-American modernisms of the early twentieth century was an often unwilling awareness of the text and the art work as inextricably intertwined within, and in dialogue with, a modern racialized social reality. David Krasner distinguishes between black artistic production and other forms of modernism by saying: "many Europeans sought autonomy through art for art's sake (*l'art pour l'art*). They wanted to remove art from social reality. African American modernists were trapped in a defensive position and were continually made aware of their 'place' in society. Hence, rather than eschew social realism, their art was informed by it" (Krasner 2002: 10). Consequently, in the inescapable racial context of the United States in the early twentieth century, black art would have as much to say and reveal about blackness and black performers as about the whiteness of the American audience.

The New Negro movement emerged in the late nineteenth century and continued on into the twentieth to become the most powerful ideology of blackness of the Harlem Renaissance. In the trope of the New Negro a racial politics was bound within gendered prescriptions in the service of a project to reconstruct the "image of the black." This New Negro, representative of the new possibilities available in the urban North, possessed a "spontaneously generated black and self-sufficient self" (Gates 1988: 129). As one author would describe this figure physically at the very beginning of the century in 1904, "Here is the real new Negro man. Tall, erect, commanding, with a face as strong as Angelo's Moses . . . every whit as pleasing and handsome" (Gates 1988: 142). This most representative modern black self was primarily male, although his masculinity would also be paired with certain prescriptions concerning the respectability of the New Negro woman during this period (Gates 1988).

The class dimensions of New Negro ideology were also revealed in the *Crisis* survey's concern that black artists and authors feel free to represent their "social class," "Negroes of education and accomplishment," the presumably more respectable members of the race, rather than "the sordid, foolish and criminal." The New Negro movement, as both a cultural and political formation of African-American modernism, represented the consolidation of a black bourgeoisie, the New Negro men and women who were populating and setting up residence in Harlem, block by block, throughout the 1920s. These were the members of a rising black middle class often imaged in the photographs of famous Harlem photographer James Van Der Zee: Du Bois's imagined "talented tenth" of the black elite, often formally posed in bourgeois domestic settings and apparel. In the absence of any real political power, art became the preferred venue for black middle-class intellectuals and elites to achieve a form of cultural recognition that would ultimately lay the groundwork for political recognition in the civil rights era to follow.

However, there is another backdrop against which to view the dialogue initiated in the pages of the *Crisis* concerning the cultural politics of blackness. As the last question of the survey reveals, by 1926 the New Negro "popular trend" had achieved a certain degree of cultural legitimacy and an audience in white circles, as evidenced by the success of the 1921 all-black musical *Shuffle Along*. Yet, alongside the hegemony of an older generation of black intellectuals and cultural critics, there were other, parallel, forces at work in black modernity that would assert themselves in the artistic concerns of a younger generation of black artists. They too were finding their voices in 1926 and their work would carry on into the 1930s. Exploring some of the forces this younger group represented, as they intersected with an African-American modernism often seen as "the by-product of an emergent black American urban identity rooted in Harlem" (Coyle 2001: 247), reveals the intersecting class divisions and sexual tensions that also shaped the various forms black modernisms would take in the early years of the twentieth century.

Black Faces: Racial Masquerade and Early African-American Modernism

In the *Crisis* survey, the comparison between literary portrayal and painting was not accidental, for much of the cultural politics of blackness in the modernist period revolved around the visual dimensions of blackness. A constitutive feature of modern black art was its focus on visuality, as Henry Louis Gates, Jr. puts it: "Black Americans sought to re-present their public selves in order to reconstruct their public, reproducible images" (Gates 1988: 129). At the turn of the century, caricatured, racist portrayals of black people dominated the American popular media in the form of newspaper cartoons and graphics, and in items of material culture such as Sambo, Uncle Tom, and Mammy black statuettes and dolls. These cultural representations not only demeaned black people, but also exaggerated color and physiognomy as the essence of what it meant to be black at the start of a new century.

In their search for more appropriate portrayals of the modern Negro, black artists developed a profound awareness of the specular dimensions of their art. As they attempted to provide new meanings for the color and the face of the race, they also engaged in a much more visual semiotics, where the politics of race relations also became a cultural politics of the image. If some saw the potential for real economic and social integration in the smaller, cosmopolitan world of Harlem, this possibility also revealed the need for a new black cultural and political identity, a vision of blackness that could erase from American cultural memory the figure of the "darky" or the plantation slave. Many shared Alain Locke's conviction that the "Negro physiognomy must be freshly and objectively conceived on its own patterns if it is ever to be seriously and importantly interpreted. Art must discover and reveal the beauty which prejudice and caricature have overlaid" (Locke 1992: 264). Locke pitted "the conventional blindness of the Caucasian eye with respect to the racial material at their disposal" against an Africanist artistic spirit and tradition that was "at its best in abstract decorative forms. Design, and to a lesser degree, color, are its original *fortes*" (p. 267).

In the more traditional performative arenas of the theatre and the concert stage, the minstrel form also defined popular black drama at the turn of the century as primarily comic, vaudevillian burlesques with stereotyped black characters. By the mid-1920s, African-American cultural critics called for a more serious, and more modern treatment of urban black life. In his essay on "The Negro in American Literature," also included in Locke's defining 1925 anthology, William Stanley Braithwaite lamented that the writers of more popular forms of entertainment "refused to see the tragedy of the Negro and capitalized [on] his comedy" (Locke 1992: 31). In the debate over the status of the serious and the comic in the theatrical productions of the New Negro, the politics of representation were elaborated onstage. While the goal of African-American theatre was ostensibly to re-present black life and history authentically, many critics of the Harlem Renaissance argued for a Negro theatre that could also function as a form of Americanization, using the demonstration of African Americans' cultural heritage as a way to legitimate their claims to citizenship in America. African-American cultural forms could "work as passports proclaiming a slave worthy of citizenship," and art itself could become a "universalizing, humanizing passport" to African-American freedom (Fraden 1996: 50, 64).

Different critics imagined their cultural "passports" of blackness working in radically different ways. Early in his career W. E. B. Du Bois used the dramatic form of the pageant to chronicle a separate black history that not so much blended with American history as ran alongside it. Despite his strong criticisms of Marcus Garvey several years later, in his 1913 pageant, "Star of Ethiopia," Du Bois attempted to use the popular form of the mass spectacle in very similar ways to his Jamaican contemporary – to empower and inspire in African Americans a sense of their entitlement to citizenship through a glorious display of their imperial past.

Earlier, at the very turn of the century and with slavery still a haunting presence, Du Bois chose to foreground another performative black art in his account of Southern black life, *The Souls of Black Folk*. In the soulful refrains of the spirituals, later popularized for a national audience by Paul Robeson in his first concert on April 19, 1925, Du Bois heard in musical form "the very means for imagining black people as integral to the national political community and for imagining black culture as a form of national culture" (Carby 1998: 89, 91). By the mid-1920s however, members of the black cultural elite described this form of identifiably black music as still too close to "'the slave people' among whom the songs had originated" (Duberman 1989: 33).

Another challenge black performance artists faced in the early years of the century was the prevailing presumption in theatrical circles that black actors were naturally emotive and dramatic, a guiding assumption of earlier, late nineteenth-century constructions of blackness on the minstrel stage (Fraden 1996). The "naturally dramatic" elements of African-American modernisms, however, were less the features of an art instinctively geared toward entertainment than the products of a black artistic sensibility uniquely cognizant of the reality of a social audience. In their everyday experiences, black artists were profoundly aware that they lived in a racial modernity in which literally "all the world was a stage." For artists working in visual mediums – the photographer Van Der Zee and painters such as Aaron Douglas and Archibald Motley – and in the work of the early black filmmaker Oscar Micheaux, who combined in his films both visual and dramatic elements of a new and modern black aesthetic, "color consciousness" represented a positive awareness of the visual politics of race and the potentialities inherent within blackness as an object or image to be manipulated by black and white artists alike.

The *Crisis* symposium gave a substantial number of writers the opportunity to weigh in on the debate, many of them the key literary figures of the movement that would also come to be known as the Harlem Renaissance. The range of responses anticipated many of the issues central to black cultural politics throughout the twentieth century and beyond, a sense of the black art work as an inherently intercultural object, produced with an ever constant awareness of its racial audience and that audience's limited understanding of African-American identity as concentrated in the color of the skin. In "The Paradox of Color," an essay by Walter White also written for *The New Negro*, "color consciousness" was contrasted with race consciousness as a more negative form of experiencing one's race. Race consciousness involved a certain historical awareness of the condition of blacks in the Americas and the relevance of that history for their modern status. Color consciousness reflected attitudes of mind that fixated on the color of one's skin, attitudes that characterized *both* racism from without and insidious forms of internal prejudice located within the African-American community (Locke 1992: 366). Passing was a symptomatic form of color consciousness for it was based on the negative experience of one's racial identity through the color, or in this case, lack of color, in one's complexion and appearance.

The blackface minstrel, played (in)famously throughout the 1910s by the comedian Bert Williams, a West Indian immigrant to the United States, was a vilified figure throughout the African-American intellectual community. Both onstage and onscreen, Williams "blacked up" for a predominantly white American audience in comic song and dance routines, using burnt cork as a cosmetic agent to darken his complexion for the caricatured roles he played on stage. In his performances, Williams embodied visually the plantation types that had carried over from the late nineteenth century, caricatured and stereotyped images of African Americans as Aunt Jemimas, Sambos, or Coons, that dominated both visual and dramatic representations of black people at the turn of the nineteenth and beginning of the twentieth centuries (Krasner 2002: 12). Given the prominence of these racist images and portrayals, it was a matter of extreme urgency to black social and political leaders that writers and artists create new images that reflected black people's changing lifestyles.

However, Bert Williams also represented a less visible form of racial masquerade, one rarely noted in discussions of African-American modernisms. In a recent assessment of the significance of Williams's West Indian background, Louis Chude-Sokei argues that the performer represented and embodied ethnic forms of blackness that were literally unrecognizable, and therefore unmarketable, to American audiences. If the early years of the twentieth century saw West Indians migrating to the United States, and Harlem specifically, in record numbers, it was also true that to an outside white world these Caribbean immigrants "passed" in Harlem as African Americans (Allen 1991, Watkins-Owen 1996, Kasinitz 1992). Culturally, West Indians in Harlem during the 1920s were forced to perform African-American racial identities as the only recognizable way of being black. Chude-Sokei identifies this as another, unremarked upon, form of racial masquerade, as a "particularly black West Indian process and strategy of passing as an African American through the mastery of black vernacular speech and symbolic/cultural codes" (Chude-Sokei 2005: 104). Throughout the New World more broadly, blacks appropriated the minstrel mask and other sanctioned performances of black masculinity, "in order to construct a face" that could be recognized according to dominant constructions of blackness shaped by American racial concerns (Chude-Sokei 2005: 14).

In the early years of the twentieth century, West Indians' assimilation into American society was represented precisely by their willingness to become not so much Americans as African Americans, to substitute African-American racial identities for their Afro-Caribbean ethnicities. Bert Williams epitomized a certain dynamic amongst the members of black New World cultures, namely, their constant performance and self-creation of black identity in each other's presence as the inhabitants of a circum-atlantic New World (Roach 1996). British Caribbean author Caryl Phillips sets his biographical novel on Bert Williams (*Dancing in the Dark*, 2005) in a Harlem populated by newly arrived black migrants from the Caribbean and the US south. Here the blackface minstrel performance is observed and adapted by various other modern black subjects, diverse in their ethnic, class, and gendered makeup. From this

perspective, the Harlem Renaissance as a modern, African-American cultural formation becomes "a complex metaphor for an extended cultural moment that cut across
geographic boundaries both within the United States and the black diaspora" (Coyle
2001: 247).

These were the widened geographic boundaries that characterized the fiction of one
less well-known West Indian artist of the Harlem Renaissance, the writer Eric
Walrond, whose collection of short stories, *Tropic Death*, was also published in 1926.
In his fiction Walrond answered the call of the writers of the *Crisis* survey in new and
unexpected ways, offering a different type of class narrative of modernist black art
than the editors may have intended.

New World Negroes: Modernism, Modernity
and the Black Diaspora

As the world experienced the upheaval and aftermath of World War I, black migrants
from both the American South and the Caribbean were traveling to northern cities
such as Harlem in unprecedented numbers. They came to escape poverty and racial
discrimination in the South and in the colonies, and to benefit from wartime economic
prosperity in the North. Known as the Great Migration, this mass movement of black
migrants also represented the integration of black peasants from the rural Caribbean
and American South into the modern industrial economies of the northern United
States. The poetry and fiction of Walrond's more famous West Indian contemporary,
Claude McKay, traced precisely this trajectory from the dialect poems of the Jamaican
peasantry in *Constab Ballads* (1912) to the modern vernacular of black urban America
in the picaresque novel *Home to Harlem* (1928), which followed an African-American
and Haitian character through the streets of American cities such as Philadelphia and
New York. Differentiating his work from that of white modernists of the lost generation writing after World War I – from "[their] confusion – all the ferment and
torment and turmoil, the hesitation and hate and alarm, the sexual inquietude and
the incertitude of this age, and the psychic and romantic groping for a way out" –
McKay used the documentary tools of social realism to capture and express his fascination with the modern rhythms of American commerce and industry (McKay 1970:
247).

With tales set in both the Caribbean and the United States, Walrond's fiction
described the New World Negro's transition from rural to industrial economies, a
transition experienced by West Indian peasants both in their movements within the
Caribbean and from the Caribbean to the United States. Yet in contrast to McKay,
Walrond's writings did contain elements and themes that more closely resembled
those found in the literature of white American modernists. Formally, his literary
style reflected many of the tricks in the high modernist repertoire – "fragmentation,
the primacy of form, the integration of non-poetic material, and the sense of a
culture in crisis" (Coyle 2001: 86). As has been said of other interracial pairs of

poets and writers working in the modernist period, such as Langston Hughes and Ezra Pound, if we compare the formal elements of the work of a T. S. Eliot with that of a writer such as Walrond, "in every way that counts – the mask, the fragment, the vernacular, the myth, the reworking of genealogies – the literary movements [they represented] are truly distinguishable only in terms of race" (Coyle 2001: 86–7).

Whereas many modernists would turn to the Caribbean and Africa for fetishes of the primitive that they hoped would help animate their own creative work, Walrond attempted to counter these exoticized images of New World blackness with the much grimmer realities captured in the title of his collection, *Tropic Death*. Though the book is not a novel *per se*, the stories in *Tropic Death* do thread together to constitute a narrative; as fictional fragments they capture in snapshots an inter-American space consisting of the United States, the Caribbean, and Latin America, with movement between these places also serving as the strands connecting each story. Both in structure and in tone, Walrond's collection resembled that of his African-American contemporary Jean Toomer, whose novel *Cane* tells a story of the American South in a similarly fragmented form, with a first section composed of short vignettes, and the second a short novella. Toomer's *Cane*, however, for all of its similar borrowing from literary styles available to high modernists, retains a nostalgia and lyricism about the South that is not Walrond's focus in turning to the Caribbean. Instead, Walrond contrasted the romantic discourse of tropical "islands in the sun" with images of that which was dying in the Caribbean as rural black subjects entered the modern economies of a new twentieth-century world. His migratory, black laborers lived in the space where the modern tempo of life and the lifeworld of the peasant collided. One could say that a black modernist such as Walrond transferred the site of the modern wasteland from Europe to the Americas, from the "First World" to the "New World."

Tropic Death consisted of 10 short pieces set mostly in Barbados and Panama. The stories were linked, on the one hand, by the "grisly deaths" that occurred in each of them and, on the other, by their celebration of "the resilience of Caribbean people in the face of the harshness of the environment and the pervasive legacy of colonialism" (Parascandola 1998: 12). In his use of dialect and his employment of tropes of folk culture, Walrond highlighted elements that were also predominant in black American approaches to literature during this period – a focus on the folk as central protagonists of black narratives, and on black dialect as a form of expression particular to their lifeworld and experience (Parascandola 1998: 13).

The subjects of Walrond's vignettes were not the beleaguered aristocracy of Europe's Victorian age nor were they yet the members of the black bourgeoisie or the urban proletariat in the United States. Rather, they were West Indian peasants uprooted from their island homes and employed by the United States, often as workers constructing the Panama Canal. Here they received their first introduction to American ways and racial codes. If, for white modernists after World War I, modern Europe had become a wasteland ravaged by war and nationalism, in *Tropic Death* the persistent

backdrop is a Caribbean landscape transformed by modernization and industrialization. Furthermore, in the work of black modernist writers of the Americas such as
Walrond, we find a perspective that identifies colonialism as the historical force
behind both modernism and the World War.

Walrond's New World writings expanded the worlds of both black and white
modernists alike. In his hands and literary imagination, the Harlem Renaissance
becomes less "a cultural phenomenon located specifically in New York during the
1920s" and more the product of a black geography that stretched from "Sepia,
Georgia [to] a backwoods village in Barbadoes" (Coyle 2001: 247, Parascandola
1998: 23). Mary Ann Calo observes that if we follow African-American modernisms
beyond Harlem and beyond the national borders of the United States, we discover
"a good deal of creative activity taking place in Paris, London, and the Caribbean
during the inter-war decades" (quoted in Coyle 2001: 247). This broader landscape
of black creative expression provides a perspective particularly relevant for the visual
artists of the period who worked both outside of Harlem and also outside of the
timelines usually associated with the literary Renaissance. Her observation applies
equally well to Eric Walrond's writings, as he attempted to portray a Caribbean
version of blackness that lay both adjacent to and underneath the mask of assumed
African-American racial identity in the North. During the 1920s, both in his prose
essays on black art and magazine stories of modern black life, Walrond revealed
how the focus on blackness as a primarily visual, epidermal phenomenon had
expanded outward from the United States to further define blackness in the New
World.

The meeting of African Americans and Caribbeans in the early years of the twentieth century represented a unique moment of black intercultural encounter, when
intellectuals and artists from different locations in the New World engaged back and
forth in a conversation about the nature of black identity, its relationship to stories
of the racial past, the cultural and entertainment technologies of the present, and the
politics of black liberation in the future. Eric Walrond's black transnational perspective contributed to this discussion by locating "color consciousness" – the visual politics of blackness, race, and race relations within the United States – within broader
hemispheric and colonial genealogies that shaped diasporic race consciousnesses.
Alongside transatlantic, Anglo-American modernisms he traced a diasporic, black
Atlantic modernity, one that expanded in the 1920s to include the Martinican René
Maran, the first black colonial author awarded the French literary prize, the Prix
Goncourt, for his novel *Batoula* (1921) (Walrond 1998: 53).

Walrond's essays also reveal his sense that there were two kinds of black art representing two very different visions of the race. In one form the ground of racial identity
was a historical consciousness of racial oppression. As Walter White observed: "The
constant hammering of three hundred years of oppression has resulted in a race consciousness among the Negroes of the United States which is amazing to those who
know how powerful it is" (Locke 1992: 366). This historical consciousness of race,
whose dimensions included "that deep spirituality, that gift of song and art, that

indefinable thing which perhaps can best be termed the over-soul of the Negro" also drove the narrative in Du Bois's turn-of-the-century classic, *The Souls of Black Folk* (Locke 1992: 364). Du Bois's work was another early attempt to locate this "indefinable thing," this race essence generated out of a particular New World history, by studying and describing the conditions of the once enslaved black populations of the rural South. However, by the 1920s the visual politics of the New Negro revealed black artists' engagements with a different notion of racial identity, one less invested in a narrative history of the race's progress "up from slavery."

This other notion of black art was driven by color consciousness and a cultural politics of the skin. Walrond's essays during this period reveal his deep concerns about the conversion of racial history into epidermal performance, the visual "fact of blackness" becoming the dominant trope guiding the political vision of African Americans and maybe even their sense of self. Describing the melancholic Bert Williams as possessing a "nostalgia of the soul," Walrond imagined the comedian asking himself, "Is it really worth it – lynching one's soul in blackface twaddle" (Walrond 1998: 65). In the 1922 story "On Being Black," visuality becomes central to the plot and the main character's "color ordeal," setting up a clear tension between narrative and visual forms of apprehending race and racial meanings.

The story begins with the main protagonist's visit to an optician to be fitted for glasses, and his subsequent misidentification as a "colored chauffeur." The false identification is in terms of class, but the scene nevertheless becomes a racialized encounter, followed by equally excruciating scenes of interracial interaction in which the visual continues to play a key role. At employment agencies the narrator is self-consciously aware that he is "black, foreign-looking and a curio" (Walrond 1998: 77). As he determinedly eradicates his "sensitivity" to being seen, he is suddenly no longer seen – "they do not see me. I am just one of the crowd." When he tries to escape "to the tropics," described in a "sheaf of booklets telling me all about the blueness of the Caribbean, the beauty of Montega Bay," he still has to pass through the gateway of the travel agent's question, "White or colored?" and when he enters the booking agency "a dozen pairs of eyes are fastened upon me. Murmuring. Only a nigger" (p. 79).

The ending of "On Being Black" reveals a plot strategy Walrond continued to employ, one of relocating his black characters to the Caribbean. Walrond's African-American characters move away from the United States and escape to New World spaces where the black American subjects are no longer the only sign of blackness, neither to themselves nor, as importantly, to Walrond's white and black American readership. In this small way, Walrond attempted to denaturalize American forms of "color consciousness," where black skin becomes the only and absolute signifier for what it means to be black and what it means, more broadly, to be raced. In Walrond's fiction, the world of color, composed of a variety of "darker" races speaking many languages, is fragmented into so many shades and cultures that American and African-American understandings of blackness do not disappear, but are reframed within different geohistorical contexts.

Techniques of "linguistic imitation and racial masquerade" are often described in the works of white modernists when race is seen as central to the project of transatlantic modernism (Coyle 2001: 258). In Walrond's black New World sensibility and geography, such techniques also became applicable for the analysis of black, cross-cultural relations and circumatlantic cultural production in the period. These formal, black cross-cultural connections were undergirded by deeply historical concerns shaped by the political economies of the New World emerging in the early twentieth century. They continued to shape African-American modernisms from the years following the Harlem Renaissance and on into the mid-twentieth century. In 1954, at the very end of what would be described as the modern period, African-American modernist Richard Wright drew a connective line between his own Southern black past, as described in his autobiography *Black Boy* (1945), and the Caribbean world of his contemporary, George Lamming, as described in the latter's first, semiautobiographical novel, *In the Castle of My Skin* (1970). Wright's autobiography told a classically black American story, one of his migration North from brutal and racist conditions in the South, and the continued shaping influence of those conditions on his own character development and sense of self. Lamming's novel, on the other hand, is a coming-of-age story of the boy narrator and his troupe of friends, all the children of rural folk on the island of Barbados. Their story becomes an analogy for the Caribbean transition into economic modernization and political modernity. In his preface to the American edition of the novel, Richard Wright saw deep connections between his life story and the autobiographical resonances of Lamming's modern Caribbean fiction.

Like Walrond 30 years before, Wright described at mid-century the forces of modernity and industrialization shaping diasporic black identities at this meeting-point of Southern and Caribbean lifeworlds. "What, then, is this story that Lamming tells?" Wright asked, and answered by defining the Caribbean novel as "a symbolic repetition of the story of millions of simple folk who, sprawled over half of the world's surface and involving more than half of the human race, are today being catapulted out of their peaceful, indigenously earthy lives and into the turbulences and anxiety of the twentieth century" (Wright 1953: vi). For Wright, the historical forces that had created these conditions placed black subjects in modernity in a unique way:

> The Negro of the Western world lives, in *one* life, *many* lifetimes. . . . His is the story of *two* cultures: the dying culture in which he happens to be born, and the culture into which he is trying to enter. . . . Such a story is, above all, a record of shifting, troubled feelings groping their way toward a future that frightens as much as it beckons. (Wright 1953: vi)

For other black writers throughout the twentieth century, such as the Francophone Edouard Glissant and the African-American Ralph Ellison, this was the definitive condition of American modernity that shaped "the novel of the Americas" regardless of writers' different literary and racial genealogies.

Edouard Glissant extends this "shifting, troubled" sensibility to the writers of the Americas as a whole, describing them as sharing a common condition, "the irruption into modernity, the violent departure from tradition, from literary 'continuity'" (Glissant 1989: 144). He goes on to say that the "American novelist, whatever the cultural zone he belongs to, is not at all in search of a lost time, but finds himself struggling in the confusion of time" (p. 144). During the first half of the twentieth century, such confusion often produced the desire to draw clearer boundaries rather than affording the American writer a new sense of freedom. Hence Ralph Ellison's sense that color consciousness was the very outcome of a violent modernity in the Americas, both its product and its mirror image or reflective sign, and that black stereotypes represented an America in which "humanity masked its face with blackness" (Ellison 1994: 44). Both Ellison and Glissant concerned themselves with describing in their fiction this "mask of blackness," Glissant in his focus on creolized African/ European/ New World languages of expression, and Ellison in his groundbreaking novel, *Invisible Man* (1952). In the latter work, the unnamed protagonist is so overwhelmed by the contradictions between his own hypervisibility in American culture and invisibility in the social sphere, that a dark, underground basement becomes the only place from which he can find the clarity to narrate the events of the novel.

Ellison was even more explicit in his prose writings where he reframed the black "darky" stereotype not just as the phantasm of a racist white American consciousness, but also as indicative of a deeper level of confusion and unrest that could be said to characterize New World modernity as a whole. In "Twentieth-Century Fiction and the Black Mask of Humanity," he argued that the point of the Negro stereotype as myth was to impose a type of order onto the social chaos of a racialized America. As he put it:

> The Negro stereotype is really an image of the unorganized, irrational forces of American life, forces through which, by projecting them in forms of images of an easily dominated minority, the white individual seems to be at home in the vast unknown world of America. Perhaps the object of the stereotype is not so much to crush the Negro as to console the white man. (Ellison 1994: 41)

The attempt by black artists to reinterpret that stereotype would produce a shaking up of white assumptions concerning blackness, and by extension, white racial identity. In African-American modernisms we find the actual world of American racial modernity, what Toni Morrison describes as "a fabricated brew of darkness, otherness, alarm and desire that is uniquely American" (Coyle 2001: 128).

Whether borrowing "American Africanisms" or ignoring black art altogether, high modernists translated color consciousness into literature by creating modernist forms whose racial politics were shaped as much by their disavowed absences as their dark presences (Krasner 2002, Morrison 1993, Coyle 2001). Into the breach left by white modernism would step black artists, on the one hand bearing their color consciousness as an imprint and mark on their very bodies – on the other, resituating the racist gaze of white modernists as a performance of spectatorship that reflected back on themselves. It has been said that the awkward dialogues that occurred between black and white poets such as Ezra Pound and Langston Hughes represented in American cultural terms "not the putting on, but the taking off of a mask" (Coyle 2001: 80). Similarly, in black American modernisms as a whole, the performance of blackness for a white audience, whatever form it took, represented neither the act of "blacking up" nor the disavowal or effacement of the meaning of race. Rather, it was in the intercultural space between the black actor and the white audience that the meaning of race in the Americas was most often on display.

Bert Williams chose to negotiate his cultural invisibility as a West Indian by literalizing in blackface the visual politics that shaped perceptions of blackness and understandings of race in US society. As a writer, Eric Walrond opted instead to situate his fictional narratives in a black New World space of difference, an archipelagic Americas in which black modernity could be perceived and performed in multiple modes, genres, and registers. Walrond was unique in his attempts to extract African Americans, with their narratives of racial history intact, from the United States context, relocating them in a New World of color that made visible the hemispheric and colonial genealogies within which various racial stories were first created. Yet as much as African-American modernisms reflected certain forms of black mobility within the Americas at large, and domestically within the United States, in the 1920s there were other voices articulating the needs and desires of the peoples and cultures "left behind." These writers, often prominent black female artists, articulated new meanings for folk culture and the relationship between different black classes in their reproduction of those relations in different classes and "colors" of women. In their sense of an Americas that was modern and African, women of color staged a different kind of intrablack dialogue during this period, one shaped by the realities of performing their black sexual and gendered identities in the presence of white audiences and in the face of the male gaze.

Black Looks: Women of Color Facing White Modernism and Black Modernity

New Negro African-American modernisms represented a certain racial attitude, one that was very much an assertion of black cultural and class power. What is often less marked is that this was also a male speech act, exemplified by figures such as Du Bois in his role as the editor of *The Crisis*, and Locke in his role as the editor of *The New Negro* anthology. The masculinism of the New Negro movement represented not only a gendered, but also a sexual politics, with many of the Renaissance's leading male figures involved in intimate relationships with each other (Hull 1987). Rare were the appearances, however, of the sexual politics of the New Negro, for the politics of respectability required a policing of black sexuality on the part of both men and women, and its relegation to, at best, a black private sphere.

As generative as the prescribed image of the New Negro was for some forms of black art and literature, questions of black male sexuality and intrablack sexual relations remained a muted force, a subtext or tertiary storyline in a dominant narrative of black entertainment and white spectatorship. In the early years of the twentieth century, Aida Walker, the wife of Bert Williams's partner George Walker and female star of his shows, described the taboo nature of representations of black couples and black romantic storylines on the American stage (Krasner 2002, Philips 2005). The emergence of a new generation of black modernists in 1926 represented not only a new set of options for portraying racial identity, but also new parameters for staging those identities in performances of black gender and sexual identity before white audiences, on and off the stage. Just as an older version of the New Negro movement was inscribing itself on the national American cultural consciousness, a new and younger group of black artists emerged — fleetingly — to celebrate the messier, less regulated elements of black identity. Edited by Wallace Thurman, and featuring plays, short stories, and poetry by Langston Hughes, Zora Neale Hurston, and Richard Bruce Nugent, the first and only issue of *Fire!!*, "a quarterly devoted to the younger Negro artists," appeared in 1926. *Fire!!* sought to provide a literary venue where aspects of blackness not prescribed by the rigid gender contours of the New Negro as a social role — those typically relegated to the margins of New Negro discourses of blackness — could be taken up.

Many of the artists involved in the creation of *Fire!!* called on other artists to imagine more options for their work than simply catering to white interests. In his 1926 essay, "The Negro Artist and the Racial Mountain," Langston Hughes described this new imperative by stating: "We younger Negro artists who create now intend to express our individual dark-skinned selves without fear or shame. If white people are pleased we are glad. If they are not, it doesn't matter. . . . If colored people are pleased we are glad. If they are not, their displeasure doesn't matter either" (Hughes 1975: 476). In this black "left-wing literary modernism" as Alain Locke described the writers of *Fire!!*, blackness meant the assertion of a different black aesthetic in the presence and in the face of a white audience, a different form of speaking back to the power of the racialized and racializing gaze. The broader context for the *Crisis* survey could be seen as its simultaneous publication in 1926 with *Fire!!*, a magazine that ran for only one issue and yet reflected something fundamentally different about a new, black modernist aesthetic than that represented by the male generation of Locke and Du Bois.

Fire!! represented less the articulation of new racial concerns than new options for exploring those concerns in differently gendered idioms of style and in new expressions of black sexuality. Zora Neale Hurston was an exemplary figure of this younger black modernist aesthetic. Herself one of the bright, new, young and jazzy females of a stylish, urban black Harlem, she chose to reframe the black modernist experience through the eyes of the very people watching the future from a disintegrating black past. These were the peasants Eric Walrond had spoken for before her, looking back from that past to a modern space of disorientation and confusion, both in the

Caribbean and in the United States. As a woman Hurston performed her own unique form of urban female blackness, very different from the prescribed roles of respectability for New Negro women at the time. But she also spoke for a group who had received little attention in the intercultural dialogue about black identity that was being shaped by masculine concerns. Hurston spoke for the poor Southern black woman left behind in the South, and concomitantly, for a Caribbean folk culture left behind on the islands.

In addition to Jean Toomer's 1923 novel *Cane*, which represented the Southern woman as an object of the black male gaze, the West Indian author Claude McKay also made the switch to portraying a folk female protagonist in his 1933 novel *Banana Bottom*, the story of a young Caribbean girl of peasant background returning to the island of her birth. Wallace Thurman, the editor of *Fire!!* and a contemporary of Hurston's, was another male author who focused on marginalized black women as central subjects and characters. Both Thurman's and Hurston's pieces in *Fire!!* (respectively, "Cordelia the Crude" and "Color Struck") were dramas that emphasized the color ordeals of a dark-skinned black woman. As such, they revealed the forms of gender performativity such women 'lived and enacted throughout diasporic black cultures, their particular sexualized experience of blackness as color. *Fire!!* also included Richard Bruce Nugent's "Smoke, Lilies and Jade," a fragmented, color-infused story of male homosexuality, where the imaging of black love becomes also an expression of loving blackness, and of seeing black masculinity from a perspective other than that of a desiring white audience.

Not unaware of the color politics of the New Negro men and women who were her cohort, in her drama and fiction Hurston reframed the issue of color and the epidermal as a constraint on black female sexuality specifically, and black sexual mores and lifestyles more broadly. Her novel *Their Eyes Were Watching God* is now seen as a classic in black women's fiction, shining a very different and less romanticized light on the female protagonist of an all-black Southern town, Eatonville, Florida. The novel traces the character Janie's increasing self-growth as she moves through a number of marriages, sexual awakenings, and loves. In her own autobiographical writings and self-presentation, Hurston modeled alternative and more confident ways of experiencing her color, her sexuality, and her relation to her black and white audiences.

In her 1928 essay, "How It Feels to Be Colored Me," Hurston described how black and white relations of mutual spectatorship became reified in her own color consciousness in adolescence, constituting her sense of self: "In my heart as well as in the mirror, I became a fast brown — warranted not to rub nor run." "But I am not tragically colored," Hurston continued, and proceeded to elaborate the white racial imagination also articulated in the phantasm of black and brown skin: "The position of my white neighbor is much more difficult. No brown specter pulls up a chair beside me when I sit down to eat. No dark ghost thrusts its leg against mine in bed." Hurston articulated an understanding of her own race as a cultural product of white and black social interaction: "I feel most colored when I am thrown against a sharp white background. . . . When I sit . . . with a white person, my color comes." An anthropologist by training, Hurston wrestled with the variety of locations from which blackness could be understood, both that of the observer and the observed, facing both the white and black male modernists of her generation with an alternative language and performance of black female sassiness: "When I set my hat at a certain angle and saunter down Seventh Avenue, Harlem City . . . in a most aristocratic manner . . . The cosmic Zora emerges. I belong to no race or time. I am the eternal feminine with its string of beads."

White Masks: Performing Modern Blackness

The key issue at stake for understanding the import of African-American modernisms lies in differentiating between a notion of race and blackness as expressed in discrete cultural and ethnic forms, and an understanding of racial discourse as a form of politics that generates cultural texts and artifacts. In both of these understandings of race the visual plays a key role, but in the latter, the active relationship between audience and artist, spectator and performer, is understood as the site from which meaning is generated. Race understood as an ethnic and cultural discourse presumes that meanings are generated from within the body and bodies of a people. Race as a politics of intercultural interaction implies that collective identities – national, religious, racial, classed, gendered – are assigned meanings generated out of peoples' interactive histories.

Since the publication of key works by Ann Douglas and George Hutchinson, it is no longer a novel idea to suggest that the Harlem Renaissance be seen in black and white as a multiracial artistic formation. Similarly, in modernist studies some have argued, "any critical account of modernism that ignores the impact of black culture fails to grasp the complexity of modernity . . . as chiaroscuro," as from its inception the site of "intercultural and interracial collaboration" (Coyle 2001: 250). In the more positive forms of this discussion, artists engage in mutual acts of racial masquerade and cultural borrowing; in the more negative, racial performativity becomes the site where the white gaze positions black artists as others.

African-American modernisms also inhabit a different social space, however, for it is here that we see black subjects not only as actors and roles, but also as social audiences for white America. African-American modernisms reveal the active presence of a black audience for white racial attitudes and cultural artifacts, despite the evidence of their invisibility to white modernists. Intercultural interactions, the idea that cultures perform in each other's presence, implies not just a vision of artists working together in interracial collaboration. Less often explored, the intercultural can also be defined through the self-conscious awareness of one group of artists that the racial other is also a member of their audience, resituating and redefining their acts of performed racial spectatorship. To describe black culture in Harlem during the modernist period as specular is precisely to evoke the double meanings of the term, as captured in the images of the glass mirror or the white mask. Blackness becomes a metaphor for something you can see yourself through, an image of yourself as an audience reflected back to you. Few white artists dared to cross the threshold of imagining a black audience, or incorporating the notion of a black audience, into their work, whether through fear or simply the socially prescribed belief that no such threshold existed to be crossed and no such black audience existed.

If this essay began with the question "What was blackness in the early twentieth century?" it ends by asking: what then is African-American modernism as scholars look back at the beginning of the twenty-first? How are we to understand the modern American novel in light of the concerns first raised by the editors of the *Crisis* survey? How do those concerns look when placed side by side with other intrablack tensions, and ethnic and sexual tendencies, traveling at the margins of a modern urban discourse of blackness and shaping the art of the period? The black artist in the social world is shaped by a limited number of choices, a type of constrained mobility that reveals itself both in the tropes and formal features of a given text or literary work, and in the artist's gendered performance as its own black "idiom of style." Whether the maligned minstrel "darky," the urban, self-determined New Negro, the migratory, laboring peasant, or the dark woman of color, the modes of black art and identity available to African-American modernisms resulted not from a new freedom of black expression, but from an ever-evolving set of cultural constraints.

Interacting with the constraints on black expression imposed from without – the hegemonic gaze of a white subject – were the constraints produced from within – the black artist's effort to create ever more options for the performance of gendered, sexed, raced, and classed identities in a shifting new world of the twentieth century. As Toni Morrison observed in *Playing in the Dark*, the question of how we see blackness, artistically, culturally, visually, socially, politically, economically, is often the shadowy underside of an experience of whiteness, a shadow haunting our willingness to interrogate the racial underpinnings of how we see ourselves. African-American modernisms represent those moments when black artists in the Americas wrestled, and encouraged their white modernist counterparts to wrestle, with the meaning of their own racial identity – and with the way languages and images of race had trapped them in prescribed ways of answering the question: "How shall the Negro be portrayed?"

REFERENCES AND FURTHER READING

Allen, Ernest, Jr. (1991). The New Negro: Explorations in identity and social consciousness, 1910–1922. In Adele Heller and Lois Rudnick (eds), *1915, The Cultural Moment: The New Politics, the New Woman, the New Psychology, the New Art and the New Theatre in America* (pp. 48–68). New Brunswick, NJ: Rutgers University Press.

Carby, Hazel V. (1998). *Race Men*. Cambridge, MA: Harvard University Press.

Chude-Sokei, Louis. (2005). *The Last "Darky": Bert Williams, Black-on-Black Minstrelsy, and the African Diaspora*. Durham, NC: Duke University Press.

Coyle, Michael (ed.). (2001). *Ezra Pound and African American Modernism*. Orono, ME: The National Poetry Foundation.

The Crisis. (1926). The Negro in art: How shall he be portrayed? March: 219–20, November: 28–9.

Douglas, Ann. (1996). *Terrible Honesty: Mongrel Manhattan in the 1920s.* New York: Farrar, Straus and Giroux.

Du Bois, W. E. B. (1969). *The Souls of Black Folk.* New York: Penguin Books.

Duberman, Martin B. (1989). *Paul Robeson: A Biography.* New York: Knopf.

Ellison, Ralph. (1994). Twentieth-century fiction and the black mask of humanity. In *Shadow and Act* (pp. 24–44). New York: Quality Paperback Book Club and Random House, Inc.

Fraden, Rena. (1996). *Blueprints for a Black Federal Theatre, 1935–1939.* New York: Cambridge University Press.

Gates, Henry Louis Jr. (1988). The trope of a New Negro and the reconstruction of the image of the black. *Representations* 24: 129–55.

Glissant, Edouard. (1989). *Caribbean Discourse: Selected Essays.* Charlottesville: University Press of Virginia.

Hughes, Langston. (1975). The Negro artist and the racial mountain. In Arthur P. Davis and Michael W. Peplow (eds), *The New Negro Renaissance: An Anthology* (pp. 471–6). New York: Holt, Rinehart and Winston.

Hull, Gloria T. (1987). *Color, Sex, and Poetry: Three Women Writers of the Harlem Renaissance.* Bloomington & Indianapolis: Indiana University Press.

Hurston, Zora Neale. (1928). How it feels to be colored me. *The World Tomorrow* 11: 215–16.

Hutchinson, George. (1997). *The Harlem Renaissance in Black and White.* Cambridge, MA: The Belknap Press of Harvard University Press.

Kasinitz, Philip. (1992). *Caribbean New York: Black Immigrants and the Politics of Race.* Ithaca, NY: Cornell University Press.

Krasner, David. (2002). *A Beautiful Pageant: African American Theatre, Drama and Performance in the Harlem Renaissance, 1910–1927.* New York: Palgrave Macmillan.

Locke, Alain (ed.). (1992). *The New Negro: Voices of the Harlem Renaissance.* New York: Atheneum.

McKay, Claude. (1970). *A Long Way from Home.* New York: Harcourt, Brace & Company.

Morrison, Toni. (1993). *Playing in the Dark: Whiteness and the Literary Imagination.* New York: Vintage.

Nugent, Richard Bruce. (2002). *Gay Rebel of the Harlem Renaissance: Selections from the Work of Richard Bruce Nugent.* Durham, NC: Duke University Press.

Parascandola, Louis J. (ed.). (1998). Introduction. In *Winds Can Wake Up the Dead: An Eric Walrond Reader* (pp. 11–42). Detroit, MI: Wayne State University Press.

Phillips, Caryl. (2005). *Dancing in the Dark.* New York: Knopf.

Roach, Joseph. (1996). *Cities of the Dead: Circum-Atlantic Performance.* New York: Columbia University Press.

Walrond, Eric. (1998). *Winds Can Wake Up the Dead: An Eric Walrond Reader*, ed. Louis J. Parascandola. Detroit, MI: Wayne State University Press.

Watkins-Owens, Irma. (1996). *Blood Relations: Caribbean Immigrants and the Harlem Community, 1900–1930.* Bloomington: Indiana University Press.

Wright, Richard. (1953). Introduction. George Lamming, *In the Castle of My Skin* (pp. v–viii). New York: McGraw Hill.

17
Ethnic Modernism

Rita Keresztesi

Why did God make me an outcast and a stranger in mine own house? (W. E. B. Du Bois,
The Souls of Black Folk*)*

*"Civilization's going to pieces," broke out Tom violently. "I've gotten to be a terrible pessimist
about things. Have you read 'The Rise of the Colored Empires' by this man Goddard?"*

"Why, no," I answered, rather surprised by his tone.

*"Well, it's a fine book, and everybody ought to read it. The idea is if we don't look out the
white race will be – will be utterly submerged. It's all scientific stuff; it's been proved."
(F. Scott Fitzgerald,* The Great Gatsby*)*

*Strangely, the foreigner lives within us: he is the hidden force of our identity, the space
that wrecks our abode, the time in which understanding and affinity founder. By recognizing him within ourselves, we are spared detesting him in himself. A symptom that precisely
turns "we" into a problem, perhaps makes it impossible. The foreigner comes in when the
consciousness of my differences arises, and he disappears when we all acknowledge ourselves
as foreigners, unamenable to bonds and communities. (Julia Kristeva,* Strangers to
Ourselves*)*

Tom Buchanan's view of the nation's changing racial makeup in Fitzgerald's *The Great
Gatsby* expresses the anxiety many felt during the early 1920s over the white race
being overrun by the "colored" and immigrant masses. Similarly, advocates of literary
high modernism have been unable and sometimes unwilling to account for ethnic and
minority texts as modern. Du Bois's lament about the status of African Americans at
the turn of the twentieth century and Kristeva's later recognition of the "stranger
within" are vivid and accurate depictions of the position ethnic and minority others
have occupied within the nation-state in general, and within American modernist
literary discourse in particular.

The term "ethnic modernism" attempts to reframe the way we conceive of modernist literature of this period and, at the same time, challenge conventional images of America and American literary history. By engaging with modernist literary studies from the perspective of minority discourse, we may achieve two main goals. First, we rethink modernism with the help of critical tools that postmodernism and ethnic and postcolonial studies have introduced and, consequently, we question the validity of modernism's claim to the neutrality of culture, the leftover cosmopolitanism from the Enlightenment project. Second, we re-evaluate American literary high modernism as a product of a racially biased and often xenophobic historical environment that therefore necessitated a politically conservative and often prejudiced definition of modernism in America (for a fuller version of the argument in this essay see Keresztesi 2005).

American ethnic modernism embraces texts written by African-American, Native American, and immigrant writers during the era of cultural modernism. In the first half of the twentieth century new groups of American authors entered the literary scene with an unprecedented force and called into question the aesthetics and politics of high modernism. Up to the 1970s, critics once focused their analyses of high modernism, both in Europe and the United States, on middle-class male white writers, who were often sympathetic to racism, anti-Semitism, misogyny, and authoritarian politics, even while being radical in the formal and thematic aspects of their art. But several ethnic groups wrote alongside and sometimes in direct response to high modernism's discriminatory politics and to its restless impulse to formal innovation.

Many ethnic modernist texts exhibit aspects of language use, literary form, and address to their public closely analogous to canonical modernist works. Yet, because their writers were addressing specific ethnic communities, often outside of the metropolitan centers of modernism, and because they were drawing upon the idiolects and narrative resources of these communities, they have been inappropriately considered regionalist or otherwise marginal to the modernist project. Considering them in light of modernism not only broadens the canon of works but also more adequately reveals the defining characteristics of modernist writing, which occurred in a variety of cultural settings, not just in literary London, Paris, Vienna, and New York.

For our argument I appropriate Werner Sollors's term of "ethnic modernism" because it best describes the historically, spatially, and culturally specific approach concerning the literary movement of high modernism, most often described as a cosmopolitan artistic phenomenon that took place in Europe and North America between 1890 and 1939. Ethnic modernism implies the converging of two literary traditions usually considered separate: the peripheral field of ethnic literatures and the literary canon of American high modernism. Ethnic modernism points to congruencies between the modernist project and ethnic writing between the two World Wars. Sollors suggests that "if ethnicity and modernity go well together, there are also important modernist writers who challenge all the clichés of ethnic discourse, if not ethnicity itself" (Sollors 1986: 255). However, our focus is aimed at how ethnic discourse poses a challenge to the critical construct of American high modernism. In the

US the condition of modernity was closely connected to the emergence of an imperialistic and at the same time multicultural political economy, a factor that should be considered when defining and drawing up the literary canon of this particular brand of modernism. Because of the varied racial and ethnic makeup of the American nation and its efforts for imperialistic expansion and world dominance, American literary modernism must be judged on different terms from those of its European counterpart.

The purpose of developing the term "ethnic modernism" is to democratize the urban, Anglocentric, Eurocentric, and often elitist definition of high modernism. Traditionally, the study of modernism excludes the texts of ethnic others from the American literary canon and confines them to the peripheries of nonliterary studies such as history, ethnic studies, or American studies. For example, the novels of Countee Cullen, Nella Larsen, or Zora Neale Hurston are almost exclusively discussed within the Harlem Renaissance movement but are hardly ever included in discussions about modernism. Similarly, the works of Anzia Yezierska and Henry Roth are addressed in the context of the Jewish-American literary experience, as if they were outside of or irrelevant to the canon of American high modernism. Josephina Niggli is mentioned in American literary history only as a marginal figure of an emergent Mexican-American literature. The novels of Mourning Dove, D'Arcy McNickle, and John Joseph Mathews are regarded as precursors to the American-Indian literary renaissance of the late 1960s but not worthy of being included in discussions of early twentieth-century American national literature. The presence and contributions of these authors necessitate the need to rethink the canon and scope of American modernism in ethnic and racial terms.

Ethnic modernism also refers to a particular period that marks a transitional stage between high modernism during the first two decades of the twentieth century and postmodernism emerging after World War II.[1] But most importantly, we use the term as a localized and culturally particular category that had to adapt to the cultural diversity and specific characteristics of American modernization. The term "ethnic modernism" reflects a discourse that is produced by writers living in an American landscape that was increasingly and visibly multicultural and multiethnic during the interwar era. As such, it is a particular version of literary modernism in America that defines both a literary-historical period and a more "localized" culture concept. Therefore, we would suggest that literary modernist studies should take into consideration different ethnic, racial, and cultural groups that engage with the "modern condition" in its specific American locales in unique ways.

Postmodernism and the academic disciplines of ethnic studies, American studies, and cultural studies have mostly focused on the production of culture from particular subject positions determined by situated gender, race, and class distinctions. Ethnic modernism can be viewed as a transitional period between high modernism and postmodernism that brought visibility to the writings and concerns of non-Anglo ethnic and racial groups – the literary precursors to the civil rights era and to the ethnic renaissance of the 1960s and 1970s.

From the early 1910s on, modernism in the United States was situated within an expanding imperialistic nation-state that became increasingly culturally diverse. Alienation and reification (as Georg Lukács uses the term) were not merely the generalized conditions of monopoly capitalism and modernization in the United States; they specifically involved selves and communities "other" than those that were Anglo-Saxon, Protestant, white, male, heterosexual, or middle class, whose members found their anxiety and bewilderment about the rapid changes in contemporary life expressed in the experimental literary forms and genres of high modernism. Ethnic modernist writers, however, were more concerned with specifically American social, political, and economic conditions that were unique to a spatial and culturally situated version of modernism.

Ethnic modernism could be defined based on the presence of one or more of the following four features: (1) the effects of specific historical and political events, such as the influx of a large number of immigrants from Europe, Asia, Africa, the Caribbean, and Central and South America during the first two decades of the twentieth century, and the migration of southern and rural blacks to the urban northeastern centers of the country – as opposed to a purely period concept of literary history in which modernism is usually defined as the decades between 1890 and 1939; (2) the importance of space or location – as opposed to high modernism's emphasis on periodization, time, and chronology; (3) the culturally specific recycling of genres from previous eras, such as the romance narrative or the *Bildungsroman* – as opposed to the narrow focus on formalist innovations of high modernism; and finally, (4) the emphasis on the cultural specificity and cohesion of an ethnic or racial group – as opposed to the universalistic cosmopolitanism of Euro-Anglo high modernism.

The category of ethnic modernism forces us to rethink the project of American literary modernism from the perspectives and peripheral locales of ethnic writers. Looking at modernism from its perceived margins allows us to reconsider a number of its aspects. In particular, reading ethnic modernist fiction against and in dialogue with high modernist literary productions challenges the traditionally accepted notions of center and periphery in modernism, not only geographically but also aesthetically. Moreover, ethnic modernist authors often freely recycle previously popular genres and modes of representation to "make it new" (in a manner not quite the same as Ezra Pound's). A focus on the ethnic peripheries exposes the ideological investments and interests served in the traditional definitions of modernism while it also widens its cultural import. The recovery of a more or less coherent ethnic modernist production that paralleled its high modernist "other" demystifies and brings to the surface the definitional processes and received ideas of high modernism.

The term "ethnic modernism" best describes a critique of the narrow focus of Anglo high modernism. Ethnic modernism implies the converging of two literary traditions usually considered separate: the peripheral field of ethnic literatures and the "centrally" positioned literary works of high modernist American writers. Ethnic modernism signals a congruence between the modernist literary project and the writings of ethnic authors – who often represented the avant-garde of modernity and progressivism – and texts written between the two World Wars. By turning the focus on modernism's ethnic other, we aim to question the critical constructs of high modernism.[2]

The general concept of modernism and its companion terms, modernity and the modern, used across the disciplines, have stirred much debate and confusion (see Wohl 2002 for an overview of the use of modernism and modernity in the field of history and Friedman 2001 on the confusing usages of the modern, modernity, and modernism in the field of literary studies). It is not our goal here to settle those debates. Rather, our purpose is to explain the need for distinguishing between high or Anglo modernism and ethnic modernism. Raymond Williams defines the terms "modern," "modernism," and "modernist" in the twentieth century as the equivalents of "improved," as opposed to a previous nineteenth-century sense and its associates (where "modern" was – unfavorably – compared to "ancient" or "medieval"): "**Modernism** and **modernist** have become more specialized, to particular tendencies, notably to the experimental art and writing of c.1890–c.1940, which allows a subsequent distinction between the modernist and the (newly) modern" (Williams 1983: 208). Williams situates the concept of the "modern" within a historical continuum: he not only defines it as a period concept but also as an ideological construct that is itself subject to historicization. The need to rethink modernism's scope and place in history is even more urgent now, at the beginning of the twenty-first century, because of the insights the postmodern debates have shed on modernism in literary and cultural studies, and also because our notions of "majority" or "minority" populations in political and social discourses have become problematic if not obsolete.[3] Since literary modernism is often associated with the twentieth century itself, the beginning of the twenty-first may allow for a much-needed distance from and perspective upon the critical construct of "modernism."

Lately, discussions on postmodernism have yielded to a productive re-examination of modernism itself. For example, when trying to define the "condition of postmodernity" David Harvey poses the problem through a set of questions and through various narratives about both modernism and postmodern culture (Harvey 1989: 42). Harvey points out that "somewhere between 1962 and 1972 . . . we see postmodernism emerge as a full-blown though still incoherent movement out of the chrysalis of the anti-modern movement of the 1960s" (Harvey 1989: 38). He then cites Ihab Hassan's widely used chart to point out the polarities and continuities between the modernist and postmodernist phenomena in the forms of contingent dichotomies (Harvey 1989: 43, Hassan 1985: 123–4). More recently, Hassan has been much less systematic about his definition of postmodernity. He says:

> Like a ghost, it eludes definition. Certainly, I know less about postmodernism today than I did thirty years ago, when I began to write about it. This may be because postmodernism has changed, I have changed, the world has changed . . . The term, let alone the concept, may thus belong to what philosophers call an essentially contested category. (Hassan 2001: 1)

Hassan gives a working definition in order to distinguish postmodernism from post-modernity: "For the moment, let me simply say that I mean postmodernism to refer to the cultural sphere, especially literature, philosophy, and the various arts, including architecture, while postmodernity refers to the geopolitical scheme, less order than disorder, which has emerged in the last decades. The latter, sometimes called postco-lonialism, features globalization *and* localization, conjoined in erratic, often lethal, ways" (p. 3).

Fredric Jameson views modernism and the history of modernist literary criticism as products of the "paradigm or epistémé" of "late monopoly capitalism" – or as pris-oners of such ideology (Jameson 1988, vol. 2: 117, 132). In his analysis, which relies heavily on Georg Lukács's theories of ideology and realism and on Deleuze and Guattari's *Anti-Oedipus* for a critique of capitalism, Jameson sees realism and modern-ism as flipsides of each other in their responses to the advance of capitalist production and its impact on everyday life. According to such a paradigm the meaning-producing "machines" of both realism and modernism exclude and reject modes of expressions "such as mass or media culture, lower-class or working-class culture, but also those few surviving remnants of genuine popular or peasant culture from the precapitalist period and in particular of course the oral storytelling of tribal or primitive societies" (Jameson 1988, vol. 2: 117). He defines such "repressions" of cultural expressions from the realist and modernist canons as "the ultimate structural limits of that outlook" or as a "painful realization of the ethnocentrism in which we are all, in one way or another, caught" (Jameson 1988, vol. 2: 117). Besides his acknowledgment of the "ethnocentrism" of most definitions and critique, Jameson leaves out the elements of culture and ethnic alterity from his analysis of the ideology of modernist literary criticism, and instead he focuses on the culturally unspecific and ubiquitous notion of "history": according to the "cultural logic of late capitalism" – an argument Jameson furthers in his later work on postmodernism – both realists and modernists "leave out history itself" and "both positions are completely ahistorical" (Jameson 1988, vol. 2: 122). Based on this logic, modernism is not a break with the older Vic-torian bourgeois realism, instead "it simply reinforces all the latter's basic presuppo-sitions, only in a world so thoroughly subjectivized that they have been driven underground beneath the surface of the work, forcing us to reconfirm the concept of a secular reality at the very moment when we imagine ourselves to be demolishing it" (Jameson 1988, vol. 2: 130–1). Since reality – Jameson's "history" or the condition of "late monopoly capitalism" – has become impossible to be told or narrated accord-ing to the generic attributes of realist expression, modernist writers took over "this wholly subjectivized untruth" and wrote it out in fragmented images and in forms of privatized speech (Jameson 1988, vol. 2: 131). In that sense, modernism is just a more appropriate twentieth-century expression of the "truth" or mimetic principle of an outmoded nineteenth-century realist narrative mode. The form of the content has changed but the plot is still that of life under the exploitative but also liberating forces of an ever-expanding market economy. Even though Jameson recognizes the "ethnocentrism" in the ideology of modernism, he does not develop this line of argument further. Jameson's latest book on the subject, *A Singular Modernity*, comes to a conclusion about postmodernism's persistent dependence on "what remain essentially modernist categories of the new" (Jameson 2002: 5) and about the unshakable hold of modernism (and for that matter, capitalism) as an ideology upon our present.

Recently Ronald Schleifer has defined "cultural Modernism" through its most problematic, symptomatic, and inextricably intertwined attributes: abundance and time. According to Schleifer's definition, "twentieth-century Modernism responds to the second Industrial Revolution" that took place between the late nineteenth century and World War I (Schleifer 2000: 4). During that time an "enormous multiplication of commodities" took place, fundamentally altering various disciplinary practices, such as "production," "wealth," and "use," ultimately altering the conceptions of temporality in the early part of the twentieth century (p. 4). With the transition into an economy of abundance, a profound sense of crisis became normalized, disrupting previously and seemingly secure Enlightenment notions of subjectivity, agency, action, ethics, production, consumption, reason, narrative, and time (p. 232). The material abundance, which upset the previous balance between production and consumption, subject and action, and between reason and contingency, made its most visible and palpable mark on our sense of time and temporality. Accordingly, "Modernism" has come to figure as art's "answerability" to the changes that took place in the social and technical discourses after the second Industrial Revolution (pp. 21–2). Post-Enlightenment thought and culture "replace[d] (but not altogether) the principle of contradiction with temporal alternations, the economics of sufficient reason with overdeterminations, and the aesthetics of given moments with repeated, momentary comprehensions of time" (pp. 230–1). Schleifer's argument follows these phenomena through the various disciplines and through selected readings of British modernist fiction. While he pays attention to issues of social stratification such as class and gender, there is a noticeable lack of mention of time's "other" dimensions, such as space and cultural difference. Thus, through his equation of modernity with temporality and abundance, he generalizes the experience of time as universal and not culturally or geographically specific.

While it is important to combine social and economic concerns with those of aesthetics and to point out temporality and abundance as the determining factors to the discussion on modernism, I find it necessary to also add the dimensions of cultural specificity and geographical location to the debate. As a result of a similar concern, Susan Hegeman incorporates spatiality and culture into her argument on modernism. She starts out by suggesting that modernism is "characterized by a nexus of related historical, intellectual, technological, and aesthetic developments," as opposed to a more narrowly defined "set of formal traits or styles" (Hegeman 1999: 19). Hegeman then describes the devastating effects of World War I, the "scientific concepts of relativity and uncertainty," "Freud's theory of the unconscious and infantile sexuality," the effects and consequences of living in a "consumer culture" and in mass societies, various technological inventions and innovations, the consolidation of "global-spanning European empires," the emergence of the United States as an empire, the eruption of "social revolutions," awareness of the "rapidity of change" and of a violent rupture with the past, among other developments (Hegeman 1999: 20). Ultimately, the project of modernism, according to Hegeman, is to break with previous models of "teleological progress," linear development, and "superficial notions of evolution" in favor of "re-articulating historicity itself" (Hegeman 1999: 35). She identifies as key to the rearticulation of historical time the concept of "culture," more specifically a spatial rethinking of modernity in relation to culture and difference.

The need for such an inclusion of a "spatial culture concept" in discussions about American modernism is substantiated by several events and trends that took place in the early decades of the twentieth century. After World War I notions of American identity, previously thought stable, became increasingly problematic: the seemingly secure hold of white supremacy was perceived to be under attack by the newly arrived "hordes" of immigrants and by the massive restructuring of the political and racial landscape of American society through internal migrations. Hegeman herself argues for a revision of the accepted terms that signify the modernist critical canon: that is, that it is international, cosmopolitan, a product of modern rootlessness, and that it "belongs to the avant-gardes of a few European capitals" (Hegeman 1999: 20). Hegeman's work is a direct critique of Hugh Kenner's (1975) definition of American modernism as a "homemade world." She suggests that, instead of the clichés of apolitical cosmopolitanism, alienation, and formal experimentation, we must also pay attention to the culturally specific contents of American writing between the World Wars. She goes on to say that the "supposed opposition between formal experimentation and political activism" must be revisited and the "intercultural and interracial quality of aesthetic experimentation" be revealed and addressed, as has been done by critics, such as Ann Douglas, Houston A. Baker, Jr., Cary Nelson, Walter Kalaidjian, and others (see Hegeman 1999: 21, 220). But as Hegeman astutely points out, it is not enough to just recover a new canon, which in turn would only produce "counter-canons" (Hegeman 1999: 21). Instead, she calls for the need to historicize modernism – both as the practice and the experience of modernity (Hegeman 1999: 22). Our challenge in defining ethnic modernism is to provide more than just adding more marginalized texts and writers to the list of canonical greats already promoted by Kenner and others. Therefore we need to rethink modernism as a complex set of concerns that do take into consideration particular cultures and subjectivities previously deemed marginal to the modernist project. Besides the temporal and universalizing dimensions of modernism, we must also take into consideration its spatial, cultural, or particular racial and ethnic aspects, and its specific locations.

The ethnic – spatial and cultural – dimension of modernism became a dominant feature of American literature after the Great Depression. Much as Susan Hegeman places modernism and modernity into the paradigm of the spatial rearticulation of culture, Thomas J. Ferraro also focuses on the chronological aspect of the concept that he identifies as the decade of the 1930s when the "ethnic passage" occurred in

American culture (Ferraro 1990: 2). Thus he distinguishes the decade of the 1920s – which gave rise to high modernist experimentation and voice to immigrants still speaking in realist tones and through autobiographical genres – from the decade of the 1930s, which saw a peculiar convergence between modernism and ethnicity (p. 16). As Ferraro explains:

> ethnic voices seem absent from the "forefront" of American literature in the crucial years, 1912–1930, because we have now accepted those years as the birth of modernism. During 1912 to 1930, the children of the immigrants shaped their literary ambitions in reference to the experimentation of the expatriates in Europe, continuing and indeed promoting the realist and naturalist techniques in self-conscious, if not always fully articulated opposition to high modernism. (Ferraro 1990: 2)

In his argument, Ferraro reiterates the age-old debate about modernism: could formal experimentation and aesthetic mastery be reconciled with the social and political commitments of ethnic writings that traditionally have demanded older realist forms?[4] Or, to put it more bluntly: could the modernists' message of "universalistic high art" be combined with "parochial ethnicity" (Ferraro 1990: 9)? The ethnic experience "mandated the sociological treatment that only realism could provide," and "the literary experiments of London and Paris were regarded as threats to ethnic consciousness" during the 1910s and 1920s for writers in the ethnic and immigrant ghettos (p. 3). For several of the new writers of the 1930s, however, the experimentations of high modernism became the vehicles for the ethnic experience: "Entrance into the *avant-garde* was now conceivable without abandoning the problems experienced during one's ghetto past and raised by leaving the ethnic community. The politicization of American letters and the ethnicization of the *avant-garde* went hand in hand, feeding off one another" (pp. 4–5). Thus for Ferraro the period of the 1930s was that peculiar era when there was a democratic streak to modernism, a possibility for the "interpenetration between ethnicity and modernism" (p. 16). Ferraro's main concern is to reconcile aesthetic value with social commitment, modernism with ethnic consciousness in the literatures of the 1930s.

Walter Kalaidjian picks up the project of "revisioning modernism" where Thomas J. Ferraro leaves it off: Kalaidjian gives voice to the century's "contentious social context" silenced by the postwar's academic scholarship on high modernism (Kalaidjian 1993: 2). His goal is to redirect the modernist "canon's narrow focus on a select group of seminal careers" (p. 2) to a more varied chorus of voices, concerns, and genres. He seeks to recover the buried plurality of the modernist project within the paradigms of "transnational, racial, sexual, and class representation" and within the scope of a larger set of cultural texts that do not only involve aesthetic and formalist concerns within a limited circle of literary texts by a handful of canonized authors. Rather, he is concerned with a more interdisciplinary approach to literary modernism: that is, he places the issues of politics and social order, which are usually considered to be representatives of nonliterary genres and more symptomatic of popular or low culture,

besides and against the elitist aesthetic of literary high modernism. He also foregrounds the concern with "global multiculturalism," which postmodern cultural
critical practices have introjected into the rethinking of the modernist project (p. 2).
By employing the critical tools of a postmodern socioaesthetics, he is hoping for a
needed "spread of a more democratic field of cultural representation" (p. 3). In defense
of his "postmodern reading of American high modernism," Kalaidjian argues that
reading modernism from our own postmodernist moment would be beneficial for the
following reasons:

> Such an exchange would negotiate between, on the one hand, the kind of populist aes-
> thetics that reached fruition during the Great Depression and, on the other hand, a
> poststructuralist understanding of language, subjectivity, and the latter's ideological
> investments in discursive form. What emerges from this crossing of the historical avant-
> gardes and postmodernism is something that has long eluded the postwar academic
> canon: a post-individualistic solidarity among sexual, racial, class, and ethnic subject
> positions, at once formally sophisticated and critically responsive to America's cultural
> diversity. (Kalaidjian 1993: 5)

Kalaidjian's "revisionary modernism" pays needed attention to cultural diversity and
to the contestations of "nationality and aesthetic formalism. Moreover, this new map
of modernity would shift the boundaries of critical reception that have segregated the
interbellum avant-gardes in the United States from contemporaneous transnational,
African-American, feminist, and proletarian traditions of cultural critique"
(Kalaidjian 1993: 5). Kalaidjian's "revisionary modernism" promises to take on a
spatial remapping of the field, very much like modernist anthropology's understanding of the culture concept as practiced by Franz Boas and his students at Columbia
University during the early decades of the twentieth century. But instead of the
narrow ethnographic meaning of culture the author adds the multigenred and multi-
faceted notion of culture that Raymond Williams defined as "a particular way of life"
(Williams 1983: 80, quoted in Kalaidjian 1993: 4). Indeed, Kalaidjian's book is an
exciting resource that relies not only on textual but also visual icons of contemporary American as well as international popular culture. While the author aims to
mend high modernism's elitism, his book mainly focuses on the issues of nationalism,
class, and gender, excluding the equally important issues of race and ethnicity.

Following but also revising Hegeman's, Ferraro's, and Kalaidjian's examples, we
suggest the rethinking of American modernism not just at the level of canon formation but also on a larger theoretical and critical scale. Therefore we must look at
modernism in specific spatial and cultural locales that harbor just as many differences
as similarities. When modernism is examined as an ideologically laden critical tool
for understanding diversity during the interwar era, the critical concept itself becomes
a historically and socially constructed entity which is also subject to historicization,
just like its subject matter. In trying to establish a genealogy of modernism it is useful
to imagine its concept in several, sometimes coexisting, stages which function as

"emergent," "dominant," and "residual" stages of modernism (Williams 1980: 40–1). Ethnic modernism was in its "emergent" stage in the second half of the nineteenth century, and after World War II a new set of concerns emerged, making it a "localized period" in its "residual" stage.

Besides viewing modernism, both high and ethnic modernism, as a literary-historical period concept that is also spatially located and culturally situated, we draw connections between texts that are thematically, geographically, and culturally connected and produced by historical and social forces that can be loosely collected under the label of "the condition of modernity."[5] Ethnic modernism does not refer to a unified movement of writers with set aesthetic or political agendas. Rather, ethnic modernism is itself a self-conscious procedure of bringing into dialogue authors who are usually categorized as belonging to separate traditions – African-American and Native American literary traditions and the immigrant experience.[6] This is not to make them members of a movement, but to highlight their "family resemblances" so that historically and aesthetically significant connections become visible that had been hidden in the high modernist attempt to "ghettoize" ethnic texts. Modernism thus becomes a category with nuance in its politics of aesthetics. By reimagining high modernism from its ethnic "other's" perspective, this conflict-ridden and exclusionary construct may become more self-aware of its artifice and less fixed in its boundaries.

The condition of "modernity" in America refers to a broad range of interrelated historical forces including, though not limited to, the following list of characteristics: economic relations of production, distribution and consumption; the new technologies of mechanical reproduction; the effects of neocolonialism, imperialism, and the black migration from the South to Northern urban centers; the new waves of immigration from Europe, Asia, and the Americas; urbanization and democratization; and the rearticulation of normative systems based on race, class, nationality, sex, and sexuality. "Modernism," in its broadest sense, refers to the cultural forms, practices, and relations – elite and popular, commercial urban and rural folk – through which people attempted to make sense of and represent modernity. The "modern" implies alienation from and nostalgia for an imaginary past (see Felski 1995: 60 on nostalgia). This temporal and spatial displacement is projected as a standard of "culture" (see Williams 1980) against the modern.

"Ethnic modernism" is a useful term only as long as it makes the critic aware of the pre-existing theoretical and critical biases in "modernism." By redirecting our attention to modernism's culturally and historically specific literary productions, we can tame the elitist streak in high modernist criticism. Following Marjorie Perloff's suggestion, we may even "forget about centering modernism to begin with" (Perloff 1992: 171). Modernism then becomes a masquerade of different disguises in which ethnic modernism becomes one mode of self-creation among others. The monolith of modernism fractures into cultural particulars and localized productions, and "ethnic modernism" emerges as just another mask of the modernist project.

To demonstrate how to implement and use the category of ethnic modernism, we discuss a few select texts with regard to their place within the history of modern

American literature. The US became an emerging multicultural state even before the modernist era, as captured in Herman Melville's last published novel in his lifetime, *The Confidence-Man: His Masquerade* (1857). Melville – only known as an obscure writer of sea romances before the 1920s – became a canonical figure of American literature after the posthumous publication of his short novel, *Billy Budd, Sailor* (1924). Melville's canonization constituted an effort by American modernists to solidify the status of American literature as a separate field of study. Melville's novel also suggests an alternative conception of literary modernism that includes the questions of race and ethnicity. In *The Confidence-Man* Melville allegorizes the nation as a "ship of fools" and represents participation in the national project as a confidence game. Melville addresses the issue of an emerging multicultural America in his novel. Modernists found a model in his writings for addressing their own issues in the 1920s.

Besides questions concerning periodization and canon formation, our historical and political reassessment of American modernism needs to reread other literary traditions that were contemporaneous with high modernism, such as the Harlem Renaissance, writings by immigrant authors, and the emerging voices of Native American writers. Rather than merely defining modernism according to formalistic literary criteria, I would suggest that we pay particular attention to the enormous historical, political, and cultural impact caused by the sudden jump in the numbers of immigrants and internal migrants that changed the ethnic and racial makeup of the United States in the first few decades of the twentieth century. Modernism's preoccupation with alienation, modernization, and industrialization took on a different emphasis when examined in the immigrant, African-American, and Native American literary contexts. In those communities bourgeois values of education, material prosperity, and urban living were considered positive goals.

The importance of space and locale and their close conceptual connection to ethnic and racial identity becomes even more prominent within the context of early twentieth-century Native American writing. In their novels Mourning Dove, D'Arcy McNickle, John Joseph Mathews, and others grapple with the devastating impacts of changing federal policies concerning American Indian tribes between the 1880s and 1930s. Each of these authors responds to the political climate of the so-called "assimilation period," when the US government systematically opened up reservation lands for white settlement. Thus modernization affected Native Americans quite differently from those, mostly of Anglo-Saxon origin, who enjoyed the benefits of membership within the nation. Native Americans did not become citizens of the United States until 1924. Because of their peculiar situation, Native Americans – considered all but extinct while romanticized as the "ideal American" in popular culture – had to battle projected stereotypes in their writings. Native authors were keenly aware that Native American identity had been extensively appropriated, narrativized, and colonized.

In line with the issue of periodization within modernist studies, we would posit Ralph Ellison's *Invisible Man* (1952) as a border text between ethnic modernism and postmodernism. While it was necessary to create a term for ethnic modernism within modernist studies because of the formalism, cultural elitism, and the seemingly culturally neutral cosmopolitanism of Anglocentric and Eurocentric high modernism, with the postmodern cultural turn diversity and pluralism came to the forefront of debates in American literary and cultural studies. The two novels, *The Confidence-Man* and *Invisible Man*, may be viewed as representatives of the "emergent" and "residual" stages of ethnic modernism. Moreover, Ralph Ellison's novel explicitly addresses the masked-ball atmosphere of American race relations. For Ellison the duplicitous political rhetoric of the nation that preaches unity at the expense of racial, ethnic, or cultural difference – the confidence game of America – reaches an extreme. Stripped of all options for resistance, Ellison's nameless "hero" goes underground and accepts invisibility. A consummate confidence man, he is also the ultimate American "stranger."

One of the most common themes ethnic modernist texts share with high modernist narratives is what I call, using Georg Simmel's term, the "discourse of the stranger." The figure of the stranger appears in both high modernist and ethnic modernist novels. High modernists cast the stranger in the role of the alienated figure of the artist, whereas ethnic modernist texts appropriate the figure of the stranger as the figure of the "other": the petty con man or woman, the trickster, or the outcast. The outcast has been a recurring figure of American literature, but in ethnic writing his or her character gains a special significance. The figure of the stranger in ethnic modernist texts exposes what Fredric Jameson calls the "political unconscious" of an increasingly multiethnic America.

Melville's *The Confidence-Man* did not receive a favorable critique until the modernist Melville revival in the 1920s and 1930s when a renewed interest was sparked in Herman Melville by both readers and academics in search of an "authentic" American literature. As a result, Melville's works became the center of literary interest and the symbol of a new confident voice of "home-grown" literature. Carl Van Vechten, a patron and friend to Gertrude Stein and Nella Larsen, was one of the first admirers of *The Confidence-Man*. In Vechten's interpretation Melville was satirizing Emersonian Transcendentalism as a philosophical confidence game. During the 1920s, however, there were only a few commentaries, most often by nonacademic literary people who were puzzled by its enigmatic structure and lack of plot. In the 1940s the academic study of Melville burgeoned, and Elizabeth Foster's Yale dissertation (1942) was the first sustained interpretation of *The Confidence-Man*.

The coincidence of the modernist literary movement and the recovery of Melville as a major American author is of interest to the argument on ethnic modernism, since Melville's modernity found a new audience at a time when American modernism was trying to find its own roots on the American continent. For example, *Billy Budd*, a short novel written in Melville's last years, was not published till 1924. Melville achieved canonical status at the height of the modernist movement and was read increasingly as a forebear of twentieth-century sensibilities. The modernist affinity towards Melville may be explained by Melville's foresight of what would become the dominant factor in the American Union: not its revolutionary heroic beginning and religious tolerance, but its ambiguity toward racial, ethnic, religious, and cultural alterity. *The Confidence-Man* conveys an apocalyptic vision of the Union and is sometimes compared to another twentieth-century apocalyptic text, Ellison's *Invisible Man*. In terms of literary periodization, they are both "border" texts: Melville's novel forecasts a new multicultural and modernist paradigm, while Ellison's points forward to a new postmodern approach to shifting subject positionalities. They both critique American nationalism, and they both argue, indirectly, for a more inclusive and tolerant – that is, a truly democratic – multicultural state. According to such a rereading of Melville's novel, *The Confidence-Man* could be viewed as an "emergent" modernist text that critiques the homogenizing tendencies of the expanding nation-state, a critique it shares with ethnic modernist texts. The novel's interpolated tales and metanarrative chapters function as counterdiscourses and alternative critical voices to an "emergent" American modernity. By keeping the confidence man's identity ambiguous, Melville puts on a minstrel show of the nation.

Writing against the tradition of minstrel shows, popular with white audiences at the turn of the twentieth century, was on the cultural agenda of the Harlem Renaissance movement. For example, Countee Cullen's only novel, *One Way To Heaven* (1932), makes its protagonist a lower-class one-armed con man. While African-American authors attempted to discredit the racist stereotypes rampant in American culture, some also fought against the middle-class confine of promoting W. E. B. Du Bois's "talented tenth." While American high modernists saw themselves as iconoclasts who broke with petit bourgeois values, African Americans sought middle-class respectability against the legacy of slavery. The novel's competing storylines function as counterdiscourses to the Harlem Renaissance's bourgeois ideology of the "New Negro." The question of middle-class respectability is even more acute in the case of African-American women who for centuries were viewed as either sexually available to or as caretakers of their white masters. While the white "New Woman" sought liberation from the confines of bourgeois marriage and social values, black women walked a narrow path of respectability – defined not only by whites but also by the mostly male leadership of the New Negro movement, the political precursor to the cultural renaissance that was mostly based in Harlem.

Nella Larsen's novels *Quicksand* (1928) and *Passing* (1929) are symptomatic of the estrangement some of the women writers of the Harlem Renaissance experienced at the time of conspicuous consumption before the Crash of 1929. Larsen's characters are strangers exiled from the imagined homeland of Africa, what Countee Cullen calls in his poem "Heritage" a place "three centuries removed." In her novels the nineteenth-century genre of "race melodrama" is transfigured into the modernist story of loss of traditional communities. Both Countee Cullen and Nella Larsen question the feasibility of defining race in nationalistic terms, or recreating an imagined community through literary narratives and political slogans. Instead of reconciling race with unity in nationalistic terms, they both point to disunity within the urban black community based on class and gender differences. Their characters do not find salvation or community within the confines of the nation, church, or marriage. Cullen's *One Way to Heaven* and Larsen's *Quicksand* and *Passing* challenge the patriarchal middle-class and nationalistic tone and agenda of the Harlem Renaissance movement. Larsen's characters suffer physically and mentally under the stress of ambiguous identities: in *Quicksand* the biracial Helga Crane feels suffocated by both groups and listlessly moves between communities and continents. Furthermore, Irene Redfield's mounting hostility for Clare Kendry's passing leads to an aggressive and fatal resolution to racial and gender ambiguity at the end of *Passing*. Larsen grapples with the issue of respectability, but it is specifically connected to issues of race, class, sexuality, and political and national belonging. Helga Crane of *Quicksand* is dangerously close to losing respectability because she is single and does not have the support of her birth family. Moreover, she is constantly ambivalent about affiliating with and committing to the black community or the philosophy of racial uplift. In *Passing*, Clare passes for white and marries a racist wealthy white man in order to escape poverty. In the marketplace of women, marriage – either in the context of a religious community, such as the Reverend Green's congregation in Alabama in *Quicksand*, or in the context of the middle-class milieu and social program of racial uplift in *Passing* – seems to be the only solution for status and respectability. But in each case, the institution of marriage fails to fulfill its promise to provide black women with lasting financial and emotional security or with a nurturing and culturally supportive community. Larsen's two novels, when read together and against each other, exhaust all easy political solutions. The forced middle-class patriarchal and racial unity of Harlem Renaissance ideology proved to be confining for many African-American women writers.

Zora Neale Hurston is one of the first writers to question the masculine, urban, and middle-class message of the Harlem Renaissance that confined black women to respectability exclusively through marriage. Hurston, herself a sharp critic of patriarchy and the institution of marriage, suggested that solidarity between black women was key to the agenda and success of racial uplift for African-American women. While Nella Larsen's characters grapple with the legacy of slavery for black women, trying to find respectability through education, financial independence, marriage, and/or even passing for white, all within the middle-class values of the "talented tenth," others, such as African-American female blues singers and performers or writers like Zora Neale Hurston critique those values and institutions altogether. Hurston's novel, *Their Eyes Were Watching God* (1937), projects an imaginary all-black national utopia upon the "nativist," racially segregated, and white-dominated reality of early twentieth-century America. Her points of reference are African-American folk culture and rural southern communities, which serve as alternatives to the fragmentation, modernization, urbanization, and alienation of Anglo-American culture. Before her rediscovery, Hurston's novel, *Their Eyes Were Watching God*, was an underground phenomenon. In a personal essay, "In Search of Zora Neale Hurston," written for *Ms.* magazine (March 1975), Alice Walker describes going to Florida, where wading through weeds she found Hurston's unmarked grave. She placed on it a marker inscribed: "Zora Neale Hurston / 'A Genius of the South'/ Novelist / Folklorist / Anthropologist / 1901–1960."[7] Walker's marking of Hurston's grave and the publication of the personal essay launched the Hurston revival, which in turn reignited a new renaissance of black woman writers. In addition to four novels, three nonfiction works, and numerous short stories, plays, and essays, Zora Neale Hurston is acknowledged as the first black American to collect and publish African-American folklore. She studied anthropology at Barnard College and Columbia University with Franz Boas, an experience that profoundly influenced her work. During this period, Hurston began publishing short stories and establishing friendships with many important black writers.

Hurston's writings fit uneasily into the constricting, patriarchal and urban, discourse of the "New Negro." She was criticized on all sides: for not writing detached and disinterested academic narratives of ethnography, or for not writing proper "New Negro" fiction that would help the agenda of racial uplift. Instead, she wrote stories about the "low-down" folks in black dialect. Hurston's best-known and most successful novel, *Their Eyes Were Watching God*, focuses on Janie's journey to self-affirmation and freedom after two previous unhappy relationships and a third brief marriage to a fun-loving petty con man and gambler, Tea Cake. The novel is set in an all-black community where Janie returns after a long absence. This time, her return is not initiated by another romance. By not attaching herself to yet another man, she can be independent, somewhat of a stranger, and still belong to the community. She kills the man she loves in order to protect herself: Tea Cake attacks her in a delirious rage caused by rabies he contracted while saving her from the attack of a mad dog during the floods. By not ending the story in the "muck" of the Florida swamps, with Janie and Tea Cake living happily ever after, Hurston favors individuality within community over the claustrophobia of marital bliss. By not staying with the marriage plot, and by making it clear that the all-black community is constantly threatened by its surroundings, by impending natural and social disasters, Hurston subverts the literary cliché of the "tragic mulatto/a." She rewrites the genre as a mixture of the oral and the written, of folklore and fiction, and of autobiography and modernist novel. The novel's narrative structure is circular, the "ending" of the story is connected to the first chapter where Janie starts telling the tale of her adventures to her friend, Pheoby. Rhetorically the ending image of the horizon that Janie pulls in like a fishnet is also part of the opening image. The novel not only questions the logic of linear narrative structure, but it also asserts the "truth" of dreams and personal memories over the logic of facts and reason. Most of the narrative consists of Janie telling her story to Pheoby and, indirectly, to the larger female community of Eatonville. Hurston blends the black oral folk narrative tradition and the dialect of the South with the stylized and ritualized structure of written forms. She also blends ethnography with fiction. By centering the plot on dreams, memories, myths, and oral folk culture written in the first person, Hurston transgresses the horizon of male discourse ("ships at a distance") and brings her memories close by, making them tangible and practical ("draped it over her shoulder"). Hurston's thematic and narrative formal modernity justifies her place within the modernist canon. Because of her use of black dialect, borrowing from oral tradition, blending of genres and disciplines, and her experimentations with form, Hurston is more akin to the modernists than to her "New Negro" cohort or to the protest literatures of the 1940s and 1950s. She was an outsider and a stranger in the circles of the Harlem literati, because she was from the rural South and proud of it, an academic who wrote fiction, and because she held some surprisingly idiosyncratic political views.

Simultaneous with the Southern black migration to the North, millions of immigrants entered the United States between 1890 and 1924. Millions of others were barred from entry by racial exclusion laws and quotas that provided the model for the infamous immigration restriction laws of the 1920s. The successful drive against immigration tapped into the white majority's fears over the growing numbers of Southern and Eastern European immigrants in the United States. Native-born white Americans doubted the nation's ability to absorb the newcomers who brought different values and customs with them. Many of the new immigrants were Catholics or Jews, whose religion clashed with the country's dominant Protestant tone. Moreover, large numbers came from peasant rural backgrounds to the urban areas. Decades earlier, prejudices against Asians had already closed off immigration from Japan and China.

In 1917 the newly established literacy test for all immigrants deterred only a few. In 1921, Congress passed a bill limiting the number of immigrants to 3 percent of each national group, based on the 1910 census. The new law produced results that same year. The National Origins Act of 1924 limited immigration further, to 2 percent of each nationality as reflected in the 1890 census (at that time there were still very few from the "undesirable" areas of South-Eastern Europe and Russia). The 1924 quotas cut the total annual immigration to 164,000 (mainly from Great Britain, Ireland, and Germany). The law admitted only 4,000 Italians, and it excluded Japanese and Chinese immigrants entirely (for historical information concerning immigration laws see Henretta et al. 1987). A more restrictive system took force in 1929, and President Herbert Hoover lowered the quota even further in 1931. During the Depression years more foreigners left than entered. In contrast, 1,285,000 immigrants had entered the country in 1907, the peak year of immigration – the year the first chapter of Henry Roth's novel *Call It Sleep* (1934) is set. With the gates of immigration closing tight in the 1920s, the sole loophole that permitted unrestricted immigration from countries in the Western hemisphere let in only Canadians and Central and Latin Americans who crossed the border in increasing numbers, filling the places vacated by Asians and Eastern and Southern Europeans.

The National Origins Act was just one example of the rise of nativist prejudices during the 1920s. Colleges instituted quotas to limit the enrollment of Jewish students, and many law firms refused to hire Jewish lawyers at all. Henry Ford's anti-Semitism, his warning against the menace of the "International Jew," was well known. The term "cosmopolitan" became an anti-Semitic slur (Suleiman 1988: 1) and nationalism was equated with "American" self-assuring nativism. The most extreme example of nativism of the 1920s was the revival of the Ku Klux Klan at the end of 1916. The new Klan not only attacked blacks, but also Catholics, Jews, and immigrants. Confirming the power of modern media, the Klan found encouragement in D. W. Griffith's epic film The *Birth of a Nation* (1915), a glorification of white Southerners fighting to overturn the social and political changes introduced by the Civil War and Reconstruction. The fear of miscegenation is encoded in the film's melodramatic plot in which the Klan becomes the rescuer of endangered white Southern womanhood and of "native" Protestant white supremacy. Although the revived Klan was mostly a hate organization, Klan members saw themselves as the defenders of an older American order threatened by foreigners, foreign cultures and religions, and by modernity itself. Thus, indirectly and surprisingly, the ethnic threat was entangled with the threat of the modern and of the "new."

Stopping the flow of immigration with quotas also had the unexpected consequence of prompting migratory streams of Mexicans and African Americans into regions vacated by Eastern and Southern Europeans. The result was an intense period of immigration, migration, and remigration that set into motion two seemingly contradictory movements: the racist and xenophobic sympathies of American nativism and hyperassimilationism and the creation of a multiethnic United States. In the climate of nativist hostility issues of immigration, ethnicity, and race became indivisible. In narratives written by immigrants, cultural clash is often represented as a conflict between the old and the new and in economic and political terms. Anzia Yezierska's story of "A Struggle between a Father of the Old World and a Daughter of the New" in *Bread Givers* (1925) familiarizes and psychologizes (or rather "Oedipalizes") the large-scale trends of modernization. But to identify such trends only within high modernist texts, as Kenner does, reveals an elitist bias. Cosmopolitanism in the twentieth century gains a more definite and pejorative meaning. Instead of the elusive foreboding of Melville's stranger, the empty signifier of the "cosmopolitan" is filled with antiforeigner, antistranger, anti-immigrant, and ultimately anti-Semitic significations. Novels such as Roth's *Call It Sleep*, Yezierska's *Bread Givers*, Pietro di Donato's *Christ in Concrete* (1939), or Josephina Niggli's *Mexican Village* (1945) all react to the modern condition of cosmopolitanism and "strangerness" in one way or another. Their narratives encode their "strangerness" or being "exiles in the American grain" in realistic, naturalistic, fairy tale-like, stream–of–consciousness first person, magical realist, autobiographical, novelistic, or in fragmented intertwining narratives. As there is no monolithic and all-inclusive "modernism," immigrant writers also tell their stories in pluralistic plots and forms and in multiple, not easily catalogued, stories.

The early twentieth-century Native American authors, Mourning Dove, D'Arcy McNickle, and John Joseph Mathews were keenly aware that Indian identity has been extensively and historically appropriated and narrativized. Native Americans experienced a particular kind of alienation within the urbanizing, modernizing, and expanding US empire during the 1920s and 1930s. The "stranger" of Native American fiction is usually a mixed blood character who is rejected by the national discourse and often by Native tribal communities. Native American authors often address and narrativize the issue of what Lois Owens calls "contextual identity" through low-brow genres and traditional narratives that are focused on issues of race and ethnicity within a modernist context and philosophical and social framework (see Owens 1992: 5). In response to the long history of narrative appropriations of Indians within American literature, what Owens describes as "literary colonization" (1992: 23), each of these authors utilizes traditional mimetic narratives in order to subvert the very genres that have historically denied them realistic and authentic subjectivity and self-representation in fiction. Thus they purposely avoid employing the formal experimentations of Anglo high modernism. They reuse and subvert the narrative clichés used by mainstream white authors for ideological purposes which are external to Native American identity, and they write in traditional genres, such as realist or naturalist fiction or romance. Instead of representing Indians either as barbarians or as the model but absent original population of the nation (as opposed to the very visible and present growing immigrant and African-American populations in the cities), early Native American authors describe their life and culture from within. Even though they do not make use of the formal mastery and experimentation of Anglo high modernism during the height of Western literary modernism, nonetheless they still develop a poignant critique of the modern condition in the United States that is inseparable from issues of race, ethnicity, and culture. Dove, McNickle, and Mathews write in the old-fashioned nineteenth-century genres of the romance and Western dime novel, or in realist and naturalistic narratives in order to expose the destruction of indigenous cultures and the degradation of the physical environment. They explore the modernist issues of alienation, being strangers in their own lands, and the environmental degradation that were the by-products of industrialization and modernization. Thus the issues of ethnicity and modernity are intimately linked in novels such as Mourning Dove's *Cogewea, The Half-Blood* (1927), McNickle's *The Surrounded* (1936), or Mathews's *Sundown* (1934).

Early twentieth-century Native American authors responded to the political climate of the so-called "assimilation period" (from the 1880s through 1934), when the US government forced "Indians into a cash nexus while systematically opening up reservation lands for white settlement" (Brown 1993: 274). Brown refers to the 1887 General Allotment (or Dawes) Act, which led to the loss of two-thirds of the original treaty lands by 1934. According to the Dawes Act tribal lands were individualized and "surplus" land could be appropriated by white settlers (Owens 1992: 30). During the assimilation period mission schools and boarding schools operated by the Bureau of Indian Affairs (BIA) violently propagated white cultural values to "eradicate Native tribal identities": children were "removed from their homes" and "punished for speaking indigenous languages" (Brown 1993: 274). Native Americans did not gain American citizenship until 1924, when it was finally granted as a direct response to Indians' growing enlistment in the military.

The Indian Reorganization Act of 1934 (also called the Indian New Deal) was meant to reverse the Dawes Severalty Act of 1887 by promoting more extensive self-government through tribal councils and constitutions. With the appointment of John Collier to direct the BIA in 1934 more humane federal Indian policies were enacted.

Early Native American authors aimed to counter the literary and cultural stereotypes piled upon Native Americans since first contacts. Mourning Dove directly addresses and critiques an early twentieth-century ethnographic novel through her own version of the genre of the Western romance. D'Arcy McNickle writes in a realistic and often naturalistic style in order to give an accurate insider's picture of the dilemmas and the fate of contemporary Indians. And finally, John Joseph Mathews gives an unflinching account of the consequences of urbanization, modernization, and industrialization on a rural Indian community through the narrative of a young Osage man. Mathews's story is a contemporary rewriting of the *Bildungsroman* and an exposure of its failure as a genre for properly depicting the coming of age and maturing of Native American men during the modernist era.

Mourning Dove's *Cogewea, The Half-Blood: A Depiction of the Great Montana Cattle Range* is the story of Cogewea, an educated young mixed blood (Okanogan and white) woman, who returns to her home after being sent away to Carlisle, the flagship east coast boarding school for Native American youth. She tries to readjust to life on a cattle ranch that is surrounded by tribal allotments and by the lands of white settlers on the Flathead reservation in Montana. She reconnects with her traditional grandmother, the Stemteemä, but also tries to fit into the world of the surrounding white settlers. Her dilemma is that she is between two worlds, caught between the desire to be like her traditional grandmother and younger sister and the desire to fit into a modernizing and encroaching white society with whose ways she is also familiar. Her dilemma is allegorized in the central scene of the novel, the two "races" (using both meanings of the word) in both of which she participates and wins: the horse race set up by the white settlers (the "Ladies" race) and the other for full-blood Indians of the Kootenai and Pend d'Oreille tribes (the "Squaw" race), during the Fourth of July celebrations. Even though Cogewea wins both, she cannot claim her victory and prize in either, because she is of mixed blood origin. But most of the story is taken up with the melodrama of Cogewea being courted, simultaneously, by a white stranger – the Easterner Alfred Densmore, who later turns out to be a ruthless confidence man who masquerades as Cogewea's suitor but in reality is only interested in her assumed riches in land allotments – and by the mixed blood Jim LaGrinder, the ranch's foreman, who not only ends up marrying her, but unexpectedly comes into a large sum of money that Cogewea inherits from her white father who searched for gold in Alaska. The novel ends with the marriage between the two mixed blood characters who are "corralled" not only in marriage but also by the United States government in reservations. Written during the heyday of high modernism, Mourning Dove recycled the traditional genre of the Western romance and used it to rephrase the narrative of historical "tragedy" as a melodramatic "farce" and to reimagine modernist urban centers in the peripheries of the cattle ranches in Montana. She also argues against the sentimental and biased depictions of Native Americans by white ethnographers whose narratives proliferated during the first few decades of the twentieth century. She ironically rewrites an earlier text, Therese Broderick's *The Brand, a Tale of the Flathead Reservation* (1909), which one-sidedly dramatized the early twentieth-century literary and popular cliché of the "Vanishing American." Mourning Dove revises this cliché through the trope of the legendary rounding-up and corralling of the last free-ranging Michel Pablo buffalo herd in 1908. While Broderick's text reiterates the notion that Native Americans are a "vanishing race," Mourning Dove's novel rejects the white ethnographer's melodramatic reading of Native American culture. Mourning Dove's novel celebrates tolerance, hybridity, as well as racial ambiguity, even though the text commits itself clearly to the cause of the Indian as opposed to the white community culturally. In *Cogewea* Mourning Dove suggests that we should rethink our monologic notions of racial identity and cultural authenticity – through the hybrid and modern genre of ethnographic fiction.

The Surrounded (1936) is D'Arcy McNickle's first novel. The novel centers on a two-year period in the life of Archilde Leon, whose mother is a full-blood Salish Indian, and whose father is a white rancher of Spanish descent. The story opens with Archilde's return to his father's ranch in Montana after being away for nearly a year in Portland, Oregon, where – in Archilde's description: "I played my fiddle in a show house" (McNickle 1964: 2). His parents are estranged, even though they have been married for 40 years and had 11 children: his mother, Catharine Le Loup (Chief Running Wolf's daughter) lives with her people in a small hut, while his father, Max Leon, lives in the big house on his ranch. Upon his return, Archilde learns that his brother stole some horses and is now hiding in the mountains. Life in the Salish community of Sniél-emen (Mountains of the Surrounded) has gradually gotten worse: "The fur trade was gone when he [the merchant George Moser] arrived and the Salish Indians were a starving lot, once their game was killed off. The only money they had was what the Government advanced them, and somebody else got that" (p. 29). Things got even worse with the Dawes Act when the government was "throwing open the Reservation to white settlement" (p. 30). For the assimilated Archilde, returning home to his reservation is an unreal, almost surreal, experience – stripped from any kind of auric significance. McNickle's central allegory of being "surrounded" – geographically and politically – is told in a claustrophobic narrative. His story carries a sense of predetermination and inevitability, a sense of doom and unavoidable failure, similar to the generic conventions of the naturalist novel. McNickle's use of naturalist narrative conventions is an acknowledgment of his academic distance from the subject matter. But his compassionate and intimate knowledge of the inhabitants of the Sniél-emen valley redefine and redirect the voyeurism and alienated stance of the naturalist novel.

Native American novelists in the 1920s and 1930s contributed to the modernist discourse concerning issues of ethnicity and authenticity in representation through the "low" genre of the Western romance or the naturalist novel. Both D'Arcy McNickle and Mourning Dove comment on the specific conditions Indians faced at the beginning of the century. Their accounts add historical dimensions and competing perspectives missing from texts about Native Americans written from a dominant narrative position. Their novels locate the modern experience of alienation within the

colonial condition of reservation Indians. Modernists fought the phantoms of romanticism and realism as well as naturalism aesthetically and the rationalization and
bureaucratization of the world politically. In addition, Native American "ethnic
modernist" novelists responded to a long tradition of textual abuse and stereotyping
of Indians.

High modernists aimed to subvert the romantic or mimetic representations of
previous generations through restless innovation of form and expression. Native
American authors often reached back to anachronistic forms, such as the dime novel
romance or the naturalist novel – which may be viewed as a form of hyperrealism – in
order to reuse and subvert the very genres that have historically cast Indians in
stereotypical roles and images. McNickle and Mourning Dove use those genres to
critique both their form and message. By reappropriating previously popular genres,
they are able to create a dialogue with the very texts they critique. Their novels seem
formally conservative and out of place in the modernist literary scene of compulsive
innovation. By not just reusing earlier and popular genres in the context of a sometimes esoteric and elitist modernist milieu but also filling those forms with new
content, the two authors challenge assumptions about the anachronistic genres and
about modernism itself. They reappropriate the romance, to critique the institutions
of patriarchy and white anthropological authority, and the naturalist novel, in order
to subvert the genre's voyeuristic and outsider's perspective directed at Native
others.

John Joseph Mathews's *Sundown* (1934) – like the novels of Mourning Dove and
D'Arcy McNickle – is concerned with the particularly American modernist themes
of authenticity and ethnic identity, but within the cultural context of the Osage tribe
in eastern Oklahoma. Mathews became an instant success when his *Wah'Kon-Tah:
The Osage and the White Man's Road* was selected for the Book-of-the-Month Club in
1932. It was the first university press book chosen for popular distribution, selling
close to 50 thousand copies in its first year of publication during a period of general
economic collapse. *Sundown* also became an aesthetic and cultural model for the
modern American Indian novel. *Sundown* is a complex mixture of traditional Euro-
American literary genres and their innovative rewriting within the ethnic modernist
context of the Osage in the 1920s. The plot follows the life of Chal or Challenge
Windzer from birth to young adulthood, from naive innocence to his possible integration into Osage and Anglo cultures, quite similar to the generic traditions of the
Bildungsroman. But instead of the simple dichotomies of innocence versus knowledge,
the "idiocy" of the countryside versus the sophistication of the city, or the final integration of a young man into the status quo of bourgeois society, Mathews's main
character must also find his place not only within mainstream Anglo-American values
and hierarchies but also within a changing traditional Osage culture. The text deals
with the related issues of colonization, industrialization, and forced acculturation.
Sundown is set within the "postcolonial scenario" of dislocation, cultural denigration,
and the erosion of the self. The novel opens with Chal's birth and the legacy of his
naming by his mixed blood father, John Windzer, in the Osage Reservation of the

1890s: "He shall be a challenge to the disinheritors of his people. We'll call him Challenge" (Mathews 1987: 4). Chal's childhood and young adulthood are influenced by several events: his education at the University of Oklahoma, serving as a pilot during World War I, and the white fortune seekers' invasion of Osage lands. By the time Chal returns home the Osage Reservation has been thrown open to white settlers and entrepreneurs by the General Allotment (or Dawes Severalty) Act of 1887. What made the Osage a unique case study of forced modernization and industrialization is that their land had enormous underground resources of oil and natural gases that the tribe was able to hold on to after the allotment in 1906. Chal's maturation coincides with the communal history of the Osage being gradually overtaken by white fortune seekers. Often, these men attempted to gain Osage headrights to the underground resources and to the oil money through marriage, miscegenation, and even murder. Mathews resets his plot of violence, corruption, and cultural bankruptcy in Osage Country during the modernist Jazz Age.

Ralph Ellison's *Invisible Man* (1952), a late ethnic modernist novel, self-consciously draws on the literary traditions of Melville and T. S. Eliot, both of whom he quotes in his epigraph. As the invisible man crosses over from a specific historical situation to an absurd existence that seems to be outside of historical linearity and of social hierarchy or spatial congruity, he literally enters a no man's land. The vision of history as a "boomerang" (Ellison 1995: 6) that threatens with injury confirms the violent implications of history in Ellison's novel. In the "Introduction" (written in 1981) the author takes on the critic's role and comments on the meanings and sources of invisibility that inspired the text. According to Ellison, *Invisible Man* "erupted out of what had been conceived as a war novel" (Ellison 1995: vii). Its inspiration was the fresh memory of World War II, and Ellison intended to write a novel that:

> focused upon the experiences of a captured American pilot who found himself in a Nazi prisoner-of-war camp in which he was the officer of highest rank and thus by a convention of war the designated spokesman for his fellow prisoners. Predictably, the dramatic conflict arose from the fact that he was the only Negro among the Americans, and the resulting racial tension was exploited by the German camp commander for his own amusement. Having to choose between his passionate rejection of both native and foreign racisms while upholding those democratic values which he held in common with his white countrymen, my pilot was forced to find support for his morale in his sense of individual dignity and his newly awakened awareness of human loneliness. (Ellison 1995: xi–xii)

The modern stranger finds himself outside of the support of democratic ideals where cosmopolitan agency and equality cease to exist once they are tainted by racial conflict. In the novel, Ellison's existentialist stance of "human loneliness" becomes racially specific. The protagonist steps outside of the historical specifics of wartime black experience. Even the nostalgic backward look to the Harlem Renaissance becomes distanced as his identity fades into whitewashed invisibility. His surroundings turn foreign, more fitting for the apocalyptic visions of the postmodern genre of science or speculative fiction (as Samuel R. Delany uses the term). The invisible man steps out of historical time and space and, thus freed, he taps into the "political unconscious" of American race relations and exposes democracy to be a hoax of color-coded confidence games.

Ellison's novel is a border text, not only politically and linguistically like Josephina Niggli's *Mexican Village*, but also aesthetically. If we think of modernism as a period concept, then *Invisible Man* is a "residual" text in the modernist literary production, already carrying the "emergent" characteristics of a new postmodern era. The invisible man is the modern stranger on his way to a postmodern hyperreality – underground and invisible, possibly dangerous and bordering the inhuman – the cyborg, as Donna Haraway defines it. Commenting on the existential impasse of his original war story's pilot protagonist, Ellison himself writes:

> But while Hemingway's hero managed to put the war behind him and opt for love, for my pilot there was neither escape nor a loved one waiting. Therefore he had either to affirm the transcendent ideals of democracy and his own dignity by aiding those who despised him, or accept his situation as hopelessly devoid of meaning; a choice tanta-mount to rejecting his own humanity. (Ellison 1995: xii)

Here Ellison expresses a break with the romanticism of Hemingway's modernity that leads to escapism in the forms of love and aestheticism. His narrative world is the stark alternative for the subject of postmodern radical alterity. Since romantic heroism is not a feasible political possibility for the African-American protagonist, he rejects the white bourgeois individualism of the "hero" and, instead, chooses invisibility and an apocalyptic loneliness that would permeate speculative film and fiction in the coming decades.

Ethnic modernist authors write their own counterdiscourses to the ideology of modernism and of the nation and empire, carving out new definitions for each. Ethnic modernism addresses the condition of modernity from a particularly American and peripheral subject position. Both Melville's *Confidence-Man* and Ellison's novel are "border" texts between literary eras and expressions of the shifts in discourse and consciousness. The invisible man's response to the ghastly existence forced upon him is to tap into the power grid itself and exploit the system through the 1,369 light bulbs he burns in his underground hole of hibernation, ironically literalizing the underworld of American race relations and turning the system of "Monopolated Light & Power" against itself.

While high modernists experimented with narrative form out of a historical fatigue that required new aesthetic articulations, Ellison originates his fatigue and disillusion-ment from the emptied-out category of democracy that did not offer the double promise of freedom and equality to those not white. Therefore, while high modernism responded to a generalized condition of disillusionment, ethnic modernism addressed a culturally and racially specific political situation by borrowing and subverting previous forms and genres to the end of instigating radical social change: an end to racism and discrimination and a call for affirming and legitimizing diversity in both the base and the superstructure. Ellison adapts his novel's narrative form in order to match the absurdity of reality. But he does not stop at a mimetic gesture, he also affirms his commitment to and his demand for a true democracy, one that can account for and embrace diversity. Thereby, his art becomes the means for political change. His invisible protagonist stays underground to learn the workings of an unfair society, but this artistic and contemplative distance is only temporary, only a preparation for pending political action:

> And, as I said before, a decision has been made. I'm shaking off the old skin and I'll leave it here in the hole. I'm coming out, no less invisible without it, but coming out nevertheless. And I suppose it's damn well time. Even hibernations can be overdone, come to think of it. Perhaps that is my greatest social crime, I've overstayed my hibernation, since there's a possibility that even an invisible man has a socially responsible role to play. (Ellison 1995: 581)

With Ellison's novel the hibernation of ethnic modernism has given way to the more overt political commitments of the civil rights era and to a new literary era of postwar and postmodern fiction that reflects a much more diverse chorus of voices and a contested literary canon dominated by writers of color.

NOTES

This chapter was previously published in different form in *Stranger at Home: American Ethnic Modernism between the World Wars* by the University of Nebraska Press.

1 Werner Sollors suggests that we use the conceptual tool of "ethnic modernism" as a period concept as well. He marks the temporal boundaries as between 1910 and 1950 (see Sollors 2003: 70–7). Thomas J. Ferraro also quotes Sollors, though somewhat differently, when explaining his inspiration for exploring the connections "between ethnicity and modernism" (Ferraro 1990: 1).

2 When I use the term "ethnic," I mean non-Anglo-Saxon and non-Anglocentric texts and identities. I am aware of the slippage between the categories of "race" and "ethnicity," but my primary goal is to make visible the pseudoscience of early twentieth-century theories of race. By using the terms of race, culture, and ethnicity interchangeably, I wish to retain the

signification of "otherness" or "difference" involved in all three terms.

3 According to the Census Bureau's "Census 2000" survey, California, Hawaii, and New Mexico have no racial majorities, thus making the demographic, as well as economic, political, and/or social terms of racial "majority" or "minority" highly problematic (see Ritter 2001).

4 In another article, Marjorie Perloff voices a similar concern in her response to Walter Benn Michaels's *Our America*. When discussing Michaels's choice of "modernists" she faults him for the nonliterary criteria directing his agenda to equate modernism with racist home-grown "nativism": "No matter that no one outside the American Studies classroom would so much as read the many minor ethnic novels that provide Michaels with his exempla" (Perloff 1996: 102). She then goes on to call Michaels an "antiaestheticist" (Perloff 1996: 103), and argues that:

Michaels's brand of cultural studies would like to save literature, to preserve it as a field of study. But it will not do. For why do we need to study literature in order to learn about the identity politics of the 1920s? Surely there are more informative and efficient ways than to read dozens of what are largely undistinguished novels. What, in other words, can "literature" teach us that the study of American history, culture, and politics can't? Indeed, I would posit that if literature has no other function than to be the privileged "carrier of cultural heritage," its study will soon be anachronism. If we can offer our students nothing better than the moral imperative to read the novels of Nella Larsen and Jean Toomer and Willa Cather because they will teach us about the "cultural heritage" that they "carry," the response is likely to be a collective and extended yawn. What nineteen-year-old will be impelled to read lesser novels written seventy years ago on that argument? (Perloff 1996: 104)

I have quoted Perloff's argument extensively in order to demonstrate the kind of elitism and aesthetic bias that has been long part of the modernist canon formation. Besides her obvious discontent with a cultural studies or American studies approach to literary texts, it is also clear that the institution of the university – in this case Stanford University – is committed to the reproduction of the critical discourse of high modernism.

5   Cyraina Johnson-Roullier uses the term "spatiotemporal perspective" when offering her revision of "Euro-American modernism" from a comparative literary and culture studies perspective (see Johnson-Roullier 2000: 47). She uses the trope of "exile" in order to bring issues of modernism and racial as well as sexual differences together in her critique of traditional Euro-American modernism. Her goal is to give voice to previously silenced subject positions of "hybridity, heterogeneity, and multiplicity" (Johnson-Roullier 2000: 39).

6   When defining ethnic modernism, I mostly discuss African-American, Native American, and Jewish or Mexican immigrant writers. Asian-American immigrants faced somewhat different circumstances once in the United States. The Chinese-American, Japanese-American, and Korean-American writers of the early twentieth century – such as Pearl Buck, Sui Sin Far, Jade Snow Wong, Louis Chu (of Chinese descent); Toshio Mori, John Okada, Mine Okubo, Hisaye Yamamoto (of Japanese descent); Younghill Kang (of Korean descent); and Carlos Bulosan (of Filipino descent), among others – produced a body of work that deserves a much more extensive study within ethnic modernism, even though we can make useful comparisons between the experiences and writings of European and Asian immigrants. For an overview of and introduction to Asian American Literature see Baker (1982).

7   Alice Walker marked Hurston's own fabrication of her birth year as 1901 on the grave, instead of the actual year of 1891 used by her biographers.

REFERENCES AND FURTHER READING

Baker, Houston A., Jr. (ed.). (1982) *Three American Literatures*. New York: Modern Language Association.

Baker, Houston A., Jr. (1987). *Modernism and the Harlem Renaissance*. Chicago: University of Chicago Press.

Baker, Houston A., Jr. (1988). *Afro-American Poetics: Revisions of Harlem and the Black Aesthetic*. Madison: University of Wisconsin Press.

Baker, Houston A., Jr. (1990). Archaeology, ideology, and African American discourse. In A. Lavonne Brown Ruoff and Jerry W. Ward, Jr. (eds), *Redefining American Literary History* (pp. 157–95). New York: Modern Language Association.

Boelhower, William. (1987). *Through a Glass Darkly: Ethnic Semiosis in American Literature*. New York: Oxford University Press.

Boelhower, William (ed.). (1990). *The Future of American Modernism: Ethnic Writing Between the Wars*. Amsterdam: VU University Press.

Brown, Alanna Kathleen. (1993). Looking through the glass darkly: The editorialized Mourning Dove. In A. Krupat (ed.), *New Voices in Native American Literary Criticism* (pp. 274–90). Washington: Smithsonian.

Calderón, Héctor and José David Saldívar (eds). (1991). *Criticism in the Borderlands: Studies in Chicano Literature, Culture, and Ideology*. Durham, NC: Duke University Press.

Cullen, Countee. (1991). *My Soul's High Song: The Collected Writings of Countee Cullen, Voice of the Harlem Renaissance*, ed. Gerald Early. New York: Doubleday.

Dearborn, Mary V. (1986). *Pocahontas's Daughters: Gender and Ethnicity in American Culture*. New York: Oxford University Press.

Deleuze, Gilles and Félix Guattari. (1983). *Anti-Oedipus: Capitalism and Schizophrenia*. Minneapolis: University of Minnesota Press.

Di Donato, Pietro. (2004). *Christ in Concrete*. New York: New American Library.

Di Pietro, Robert J. and Edward Ifkovic (eds). (1983). *Ethnic Perspectives in American Literature: Selected Essays on the European Contribution*. New York: Modern Language Association.

Douglas, Ann. (1995). *Terrible Honesty: Mongrel Manhattan in the 1920s*. New York: Farrar, Strauss, and Giroux.

Doyle, Laura. (1994). *Bordering on the Body: The Racial Matrix of Modern Fiction and Culture*. New York: Oxford University Press.

Du Bois, W. E. B. (1989). *The Souls of Black Folk*. New York: Bantam Books.

Ellison, Ralph. (1995). *Invisible Man*. New York: Vintage.

Felski, Rita. (1995). *The Gender of Modernity*. Cambridge, MA: Harvard University Press.

Ferraro, Thomas J. (1990). Avant-garde ethnics. In William Boelhower (ed.), *The Future of American Modernism: Ethnic Writing Between the Wars* (pp. 1–31). Amsterdam: VU University Press.

Ferraro, Thomas J. (1993). *Ethnic Passages: Literary Immigrants in Twentieth-Century America*. Chicago: University of Chicago Press.

Ferraro, Thomas J. (2003). "At long last love": Or, literary history in the key of difference. *American Literary History* 15, 1: 78–86.

Friedman, Susan Stanford. (2001). Definitional excursions: The meanings of modern/modernity/modernism. *Modernism/Modernity* 8, 3: 493–513.

Gilroy, Paul. (1993). *The Black Atlantic: Modernity and Double Consciousness*. Cambridge, MA: Harvard University Press.

Gosselin, Adrienne Johnson. (1996). Beyond the Harlem Renaissance: The case for black modernist writers. *Modern Language Studies* 26, 4: 37–46.

Greenblatt, Stephen and Giles Gunn (eds). (1992). *Redrawing the Boundaries: The Transformation of English and American Literary Studies*. New York: Modern Language Association.

Harvey, David. (1989). *The Condition of Postmodernity: An Inquiry into the Origins of Cultural Change*. Oxford: Basil Blackwell.

Hassan, Ihab. (1985). The culture of postmodernism. *Theory, Culture and Society* 2, 3: 119–32.

Hassan, Ihab. (2001). From postmodernism to postmodernity: The local/global context. *Philosophy and Literature* 25: 1–13.

Hegeman, Susan. (1999). *Patterns for America: Modernism and the Concept of Culture*. Princeton, NJ: Princeton University Press.

Henretta, James A. et al. (eds). (1987). *America's History*. Chicago: The Dorsey Press.

Hoesterey, Ingeborg (ed.). (1991). *Zeitgeist in Babel: The Post-Modernist Controversy*. Bloomington: Indiana University Press.

Hurston, Zora Neale. (1981). *The Sanctified Church*. New York: Marlow & Co.

Hurston, Zora Neale. (1990). *Their Eyes Were Watching God*. New York: Perennial Library.

Jameson, Fredric. (1988). *The Ideologies of Theory: Essays 1971–1986, Volumes: 1 & 2*. Minneapolis: University of Minnesota Press.

Jameson, Fredric. (1981). *The Political Unconscious: Narrative as a Socially Symbolic Act*. Ithaca, NY: Cornell University Press.

Jameson, Fredric. (1986). Third-world literature in the era of multinational capitalism. *Social Text* 15: 65–88.

Jameson, Fredric. (1990). Modernism and imperialism. In Fredric Jameson, Terry Eagleton, and Edward W. Said, *Nationalism, Colonialism, and Literature* (pp. 43–66). Minneapolis: University of Minnesota Press.

Jameson, Fredric. (1991). *Postmodernism; or, the Cultural Logic of Late Capitalism*. Durham, NC: Duke University Press.

Jameson, Fredric. (2002). *A Singular Modernity: Essay on the Ontology of the Present*. London: Verso.

Jameson, Fredric, Terry Eagleton, and Edward W. Said. (1990). *Nationalism, Colonialism, and Literature*. Minneapolis: University of Minnesota Press.

Johnson-Roullier, Cyraina. (2000). *Reading on the Edge: Exiles, Modernities, and Cultural Transformation in Proust, Joyce, and Baldwin*. Albany: State University of New York Press.

Kalaidjian, Walter. (1993). *American Culture Between the Wars: Revisionary Modernism and Postmodern Critique*. New York: Columbia University Press.

Kenner, Hugh. (1971). *The Pound Era*. Berkeley: University of California Press.

Kenner, Hugh. (1975). *A Homemade World: The American Modernist Writers*. New York: Alfred A. Knopf.

Keresztesi, Rita. (2005). *Strangers at Home: American Ethnic Modernism Between the World Wars*. Lincoln: University of Nebraska Press.

Klein, Marcus. (1981). *Foreigners: The Making of American Literature, 1900–1940*. Chicago: University of Chicago Press.

Kristeva, Julia. (1991). *Strangers to Ourselves*, trans. Leon S. Roudiez. New York: Columbia University Press.

Kronfeld, Chana. (1996). *On the Margins of Modernism: Decentering Literary Dynamics*. Berkeley: University of California Press.

Krupat, Arnold. (1989). *The Voice in the Margin: Native American Literature and the Canon*. Berkeley: University of California Press.

Krupat, Arnold. (1992). *Ethnocriticism: Ethnography, History, Literature*. Berkeley: University of California Press.

Krupat, Arnold (ed.). (1993). *New Voices in Native American Literary Criticism*. Washington: Smithsonian.

Larsen, Nella. (1989). *Quicksand and Passing*. New Brunswick, NJ: Rutgers University Press.

Mathews, John Joseph (1987). *Sundown*. Norman: University of Oklahoma Press.

McNickle, D'Arcy. (1964). *The Surrounded*. Albuquerque: University of New Mexico Press.

Melville, Herman. (1971). *The Confidence-Man: His Masquerade*. New York: Norton.

Michaels, Walter Benn. (1993). American modernism and the poetics of identity. *Modernism/Modernity* 1, 1: 38–56.

Michaels, Walter Benn. (1995). *Our America: Nativism, Modernism, and Pluralism*. Durham, NC: Duke University Press.

Michaels, Walter Benn. (1996). Response to "*Our America* and nativist modernism: A panel." *Modernism/Modernity* 3, 3: 121–6.

Mizruchi, Susan. (2003). Becoming multicultural. *American Literary History* 15, 1: 39–60.

Mourning Dove (Hum-ishu-ma). (1981). *Cogewea: The Half-Blood*. Lincoln: University of Nebraska Press.

Nelson, Cary. (1989). *Repression and Recovery: Modern American Poetry and the Politics of Cultural Memory, 1910–1945*. Madison: University of Wisconsin Press.

Niggli, Josephina. (1994). *Mexican Village*. Albuquerque: University of New Mexico Press.

North, Michael. (1994). *The Dialect of Modernism: Race, Language, and Twentieth-Century Literature*. New York: Oxford University Press.

Owens, Louis. (1998). *Mixedblood Messages: Literature, Film, Family, Place*. Norman: University of Oklahoma Press.

Owens, Louis. (1992). *Other Destinies: Understanding the American Indian Novel*. Norman: University of Oklahoma Press.

Patell, Cyrus R. K. (2003). Representing emergent literatures. *American Literary History* 15, 1: 61–8.

Perloff, Marjorie. (1996). Modernism without the modernists: A response to Walter Benn Michaels. *Modernism/Modernity* 3, 3: 99–105.

Perloff, Marjorie. (1992). Modernist studies. In Stephen Greenblatt and Giles Gunn (eds), *Redrawing the Boundaries* (pp. 154–78). New York: Modern Language Association.

Podesta, Guido A. (1991). An ethnographic reproach to the theory of the avant-garde: Modernity and modernism in Latin-America and the Harlem Renaissance. *MLN* 106, 2: 395–422.

Powell, Richard J. (1989). *The Blues Aesthetic: Black Culture and Modernism*. Washington: Washington Project for the Arts.

Ritter, John. (2001). California racial data shifts. *U.S.A. TODAY* (March 30): 1A.

Roth, H. (1934). *Call It Sleep*. New York: Robert O. Ballou.

Ruoff, A. Lavonne Brown and Jerry W. Ward, Jr. (eds). (1990). *Redefining American Literary History*. New York: Modern Language Association.

Saldívar, José David. (1997). *Border Matters: Remapping American Cultural Studies*. Berkeley: University of California Press.

Saldívar, José David. (1991). *The Dialectics of Our America: Genealogy, Cultural Critique and Literary History*. Durham, NC: Duke University Press.

Schedler, Christopher. (2002). *Border Modernism: Intercultural Readings in American Literary Modernism*. New York: Routledge.

Schleifer, Ronald. (2000). *Modernism and Time: The Logic of Abundance in Literature, Science, and Culture, 1880–1930*. Cambridge, UK: Cambridge University Press.

Simmel, Georg. (1950). *The Sociology of Georg Simmel*, trans. Kurt H. Wolff. New York: Free Press.

Simmel, Georg. (1971). *On Individuality and Social Forms: Selected Writings*. Chicago: University of Chicago Press.

Sollors, Werner. (1986). *Beyond Ethnicity: Consent and Descent in American Culture*. New York: Oxford University Press.

Sollors, Werner (ed.). (1989). *The Invention of Ethnicity*. New York: Oxford University Press.

Sollors, Werner (ed.). (1998). *Multi-lingual America: Transnationalism, Ethnicity, and the Languages of American Literature*. New York: New York University Press.

Sollors, Werner. (2003). Ethnic modernism, 1910–1950. *American Literary History* 15, 1: 70–7.

Suleiman, Susan R. (ed.). (1998). *Exile and Creativity: Signposts, Travelers, Outsiders, Backward Glances*. Durham, NC: Duke University Press.

Williams, Raymond. (1980). *Problems in Materialism and Culture: Selected Essays*. London: Verso.

Williams, Raymond. (1981). *Culture*. London: Fontana.

Williams, Raymond. (1983). *Keywords*. New York: Oxford University Press.

Williams, Raymond. (1989). *The Politics of Modernism: Against the New Conformists*. London: Verso.

Wohl, Robert. (2002). Heart of darkness: Modernism and its historians. *The Journal of Modern History* 74: 573–621.

Yezierska, Anzia. (1975). *Bread Givers*. New York: Persea Books.

Yezierska, Anzia. (1991). *How I Found America: Collected Stories of Anzia Yezierska*. New York: Persea Books.

18

The Proletarian Novel

Barbara Foley

In the context of US literary history, the term "proletarian novel" is most applicable to a grouping of approximately one hundred novels that were produced during the years 1929–1941. During the Cold War, and for several decades beyond, the proletarian novel was derogated as aesthetically bankrupt and relegated to the dustbin of literary history. The poststructuralist-based antipathy to totalizing narratives, as well as the identity-based model of "intersectionality" guiding much more recent "gender, race and class" scholarship (based on the premise that an individual's identity is produced as the intersection of class, race, and gender affiliations), have continued to marginalize these leftist texts. Scholars participating in the current resurgence of interest in the proletarian novel – and proletarian literature more generally – are thus called upon first to engage in considerable ground-clearing and stage-setting, both literary-historical and theoretical.

The emergence of the proletarian novel is inseparable from its historical context, which was characterized by three interrelated extraliterary developments: the political and economic crisis of the Depression; the emergence of Soviet socialism and its far-flung challenge to capitalism; and the growth of the American Communist Party (CPUSA), which exercised widespread influence upon writers, first through the John Reed Clubs and subsequently through the League of American Writers and its large American Writers Congress gatherings. It is important to be aware, however, of predecessor literary texts and schools – sometimes explicitly invoked by proletarian novelists – that enabled this literary genre to emerge. Slave narratives, which exhibit similar concerns with oppression and resistance, characteristically featured first-person narrators whose emotional and political development anticipates the class-conscious maturation of proletarian protagonists. Many texts routinely grouped under the rubric of "naturalism" – such as Stephen Crane's *Maggie: A Girl of the Streets* (1893), Hamlin Garland's *Main-Travelled Roads* (1891), and Frank Norris's *McTeague* (1899) – grounded much of their pessimistic determinism in an analysis of the roots of poverty in the class system. Political utopias and dystopias – presented most famously in Edward

Bellamy's *Looking Backward, 2001–1887* (1888) and Jack London's *The Iron Heel* (1907) – raised the mirage of a socialist future – as well as of the tragic cost of its nonrealization – well before the 1930s. Early twentieth-century socialist novels – Ernest Poole's *The Harbor* (1915) and, most famously, Upton Sinclair's *The Jungle* (1906) – placed the class struggle front and center in their treatments of urban industrialism. The *International Socialist Review* and then the *Masses* provided a forum for class-conscious literature and anticapitalist cultural critique.

The radical upsurge of 1919, while rapidly quelled, quickened the political consciousness of many 1920s writers. Journals such as the *Liberator* and its successor, the *Workers Monthly*, continued the work of the *Masses*. The principal organs of African-American radicalism, the *Messenger* and the *Crusader*, defined the postwar New Negro as both cultural radical and social revolutionary. Such novels as Sinclair Lewis's *Babbitt* (1922) and Theodore Dreiser's *An American Tragedy* (1925), while focused more on satire and psychology than class struggle, stressed capitalist commodification as the root cause of their protagonists' alienation. Novels about immigrant experience – Samuel Ornitz's *Haunch, Paunch, and Jowl* (1923), Anzia Yezierska's *Bread Givers* (1925) – injected a searing skepticism into their tales of the pursuit of the pseudo-democratic American Dream. Many novels routinely discussed in the context of a 1920s-bounded and culturally focused Harlem Renaissance – Langston Hughes's *Not Without Laughter* (1930), Claude McKay's *Banjo* (1929), and even Jean Toomer's highly experimental *Cane* (1923), often seen as the Renaissance's founding text – contain hard-hitting indictments of racial violence and class hierarchy. As the decade progressed, moreover, writers and intellectuals became increasingly aware of the harsh conditions experienced by the working class, for whom there had been no Roaring Twenties. The execution of the Italian anarchists Nicola Sacco and Bartolomeo Vanzetti in 1927 galvanized the radicalism of many writers, not least among these John Dos Passos, who would emerge as, arguably, the most important practitioner of the proletarian novel.

To point up such continuities with past texts and traditions is not to engage in an obligatory nod to literary history; nor is it to query the usefulness of viewing the proletarian novel as a distinct genre that came to fruition in a distinct period. It is simply to remind us that the proletarian novel cannot be placed in a temporal ghetto. Categories such as "naturalism" and "Harlem Renaissance," while useful for some purposes, displace economic and political concerns and set arbitrary temporal boundaries, thereby obscuring the "red thread" running through much US literary history – a point that would be stressed by proletarian literary theorist Granville Hicks in his 1933 revisionary literary history, *The Great Tradition*. It is evident, moreover, that some proletarian novelists saw their projects as explicitly aligned with these precedent texts and traditions. Arna Bontemps's *Black Thunder* (1936) is based upon the slave narrative archive at Fisk University; Richard Wright's *Native Son* (1940) is modeled upon Dreiser's tale of crime and punishment in *An American Tragedy*; Mike Gold's *Jews Without Money* (1930) invokes both *The Jungle* and *Haunch, Paunch, and Jowl*.

While in retrospect the proletarian novel constitutes a genre possessing substantive and temporal coherence, its key concerns were subjected to debate and underwent development even during the decade of its heyday. Starting in the late 1920s and gathering momentum by 1932, discussions in the principal leftist cultural organ, the *New Masses*, queried the parameters of the genre. What was the difference between a proletarian novel, a radical novel, and a revolutionary novel? Did the term "proletarian novel" signify authorship, readership, subject matter, or political perspective? Although the quintessential proletarian novel was envisioned as embodying all four of these criteria of differentiation, the operational definition generally settled upon by the mid-1930s was that the proletarian novel described the lives of working-class people from an anticapitalist perspective, one that was intended to arouse militant — at times revolutionary — class consciousness in the text's readers. After 1936, when antifascism superseded revolutionary class struggle among the Communists' strategic priorities, the term "proletarian novel" virtually disappeared from the *New Masses*, the *Partisan Review*, and other journals of the left. It was during the latter half of the decade, however, that the most complex and accomplished proletarian novels emerged, indicating that the challenge of creating effective class-conscious fictional narratives continued to inspire writers throughout the decade.

From the outset the proletarian novel was significantly influenced by international cultural developments, particularly in the Soviet Union. Gold's 1921 *Liberator* essay, "Toward Proletarian Art," called upon American artists and writers to produce their own version of the *Proletkult* movement emerging in the young Soviet Union. Discussions among the theorists in RAPP, a late-1920s Soviet writers' group — particularly with regard to encouraging working-class authorship and documentary writing — were reproduced in the pages of the *New Masses*. Walt Carmon and later Joshua Kunitz were commissioned with the task of keeping US literary radicals abreast of Soviet developments. A number of US writers contributed to *International Literature*, the journal of the Comintern-sponsored International Union of Revolutionary Writers. But US proletarian writers have been unjustly lambasted for subservience to "directives" issued from the USSR. The recommendations of the 1930s Kharkov conference were duly noted and largely ignored. "Socialist realism," which in the early 1930s supplanted the call for proletarian literature in the USSR, never caught on among the Americans. Articles by such luminaries as Anatoli Lunacharsky, Maxim Gorky, and Georg Lukács appeared in US left journals throughout the 1930s, but evidently carried less weight than statements by such prominent Americans as Gold, Hicks, and Joseph Freeman. The program outlined in the 1936 anthology *Proletarian Literature in the United States* was a pure product of America.

Although the standard Cold War account of 1930s literary radicalism would dismiss proletarian novelists as practitioners of a plodding realism, impervious to the subtleties of modernism, in fact the 1930s writers evinced a high regard for literary experimentation. Even those proletarian novelists who opted for conventionally realistic narrative modes were often compelled to draw upon a range of new literary devices to expand their texts' rhetorical range. When they failed to embody left politics in familiar narrative conventions, their critics were often exacting. Many on the literary left, critics and novelists alike, exhibited great interest in utilizing highly experimental novelistic forms to articulate a leftist politics; Clara Weatherwax's *Marching! Marching!* (1935), a novel making use of multiple points of view and a collective stream of consciousness, was the winner of the 1935 *New Masses* contest for the best proletarian novel of the year. Writers and critics on the left may not have generally admired T. S. Eliot, whom they dismissed as a reactionary aesthete. But they had a complex relationship to such writers as Marcel Proust and James Joyce, and they often spoke of their own project as "modern" in terms comparable to Ezra Pound's formulation of "making it new." The post-World War II equation of modernism with a politically quietistic high modernism, itself a product of the Cold War consensus, was alien to the proletarian literary radicals.

If US proletarian writers were neither taking orders from Moscow nor handing over modernism to advocates of art-for-art's-sake, neither were they, as a group, as "left" as has often been supposed. Most of the literary proletarians repudiated the view that art should be propaganda. Although there was a certain amount of talk about literature as a weapon in the class struggle, a close scrutiny of debates over literature and politics carried on the pages of *New Masses*, *Partisan Review*, and the organs of John Reed Clubs reveals that, if anything, many on the US literary left endorsed a cognitivist as opposed to an agitational aesthetic. Many left-wing writers and critics felt uneasy with didacticism and preferred literary strategies that seamlessly conjoined politics with narrative; a discourse involving terms like "weaving," "blending," and "merging" dominated in discussions of novelistic aesthetics. To a degree, of course, such complaints were directed at plain old clumsy writing. But they also evinced a widespread and for the most part uninterrogated acceptance of the bourgeois aesthetic premise that a text should show, not tell.

Although aesthetic principles cannot be traced back to political programs without going through multiple mediations, the literary left's embrace of a largely bourgeois aesthetic program is provocatively linked with various reformist tendencies in the broad political program and outlook of the CPUSA. Even at the height of its radicalism – expressed in such a document as William Z. Foster's 1932 *Toward Soviet America* – the CPUSA sent out contradictory signals about the relationship of reform to revolution, of electoral politics and American "democratic" traditions to revolutionary proletarian internationalism. While these tendencies increasingly prevailed during the Popular Front era, they had been present from the forming of the CPUSA in 1919. One can speculatively connect premises about politics with premises about form: just as leftist organizers should not talk too insistently about revolution, bringing in Communist ideas "from the outside" in the Leninist sense, so should literary texts not too insistently jar their readers with political analyses – conveyed through speeches, mentor characters, or even narratorial voice – coming "from outside" the experiences of literary characters. Even though the literary radicals – like 1930s Marxists generally – called for the "better world" of classless egalitarianism, at times they were hesitant about how best to do so in practice.

Two other features of contemporaneous leftist doctrine and practice are relevant to a consideration of proletarian fiction. Critics of the left, then and now, frequently charge that Marxism – in both theory and practice – precludes appreciation of the special oppression of women and people of color. The record of the 1930s left with regard to both issues – the "Woman Question" and the "Negro Question," in the terms of the day – is somewhat mixed. Left-wing iconography often gendered the proletariat as muscularly masculine; Communist doctrine inadequately theorized the unpaid labor of women in the home. There was a "women's page" in the *New Masses* that featured recipes, along with discussions of child-rearing and husband-handling. Yet in both the *New Masses* and party organs specifically directed to women, such as *Working Woman*, women's participation in the class struggle was emphasized; birth control and abortion rights were promoted; and the altered gender relations in the USSR – complete with the abolition of formal marriage – was often highly praised.

With regard to antiracist struggle, the CPUSA's record is less ambiguous; without doubt the party was the leading antiracist force in the US during the 1930s. The vigorous campaigns against lynching and Jim Crow and supporting sharecropper unions were widely publicized, as was the struggle against "white chauvinism" in the ranks of the party itself, epitomized in the 1931 intraparty "trial" of Harlem janitor August Yokinen. In the early 1930s, Communist-led protests against evictions – such as the one described in Ralph Ellison's *Invisible Man* (1952) – established the party's urban antiracist credentials. The largely party-led National Negro Congress addressed issues ranging from industrial organizing to police brutality to demands for relief; the Congress of Industrial Organizations (CIO) put multiracial unionism on the map. Yet the call for class-based multiracial unity – "Black and white unite and fight" – existed for many years in contradictory coexistence with the call for Negro self-determination in the South's Black Belt. Although the CPUSA continually reviled what it called "narrow nationalism," it advocated the fostering of "the national consciousness of the Negro people" and acknowledged that the future "Soviet America" in the Black Belt, however transitional, would be not socialist, but "democratic." The ambiguous relationship between Negro nationalism and proletarian interracialism in Communist theory and practice would at once spur activism and sow confusion, both in political organizing and in the proletarian literary texts representing the imbrication of race in US class struggles.

Scholarly discussions of proletarian fiction have frequently deployed a taxonomy based upon the range of subject matters covered in the genre. Proletarian novels generally fall into five thematic categories; needless to say, any given text can straddle several categories.

Strike novels. This grouping includes Weatherwax's *Marching! Marching!*; Robert Cantwell's *The Land of Plenty* (1934), another novel set among lumber workers; and Leane Zugsmith's *A Time to Remember* (1936), which treats job actions among workers in a New York department store closely resembling Ohrbach's. John Steinbeck's *In Dubious Battle* (1936) and *The Grapes of Wrath* (1939) both portray the violence accompanying strikes in the California fields. In addition, a number of pioneering proletarian novels address the 1929 textile strike in Gastonia, North Carolina, where the CPUSA first attempted labor organizing in the South. Among the Gastonia novels are Mary Heaton Vorse's *Strike!* (1930), Grace Lumpkin's *To Make My Bread* (1932), William Rollins's *The Shadow Before* (1934), Fielding Burke's *Call Home the Heart* (1932), and Myra Page's *The Gathering Storm* (1932). The high percentage of women novelists treating this strike may be attributable to the legendary role played by the singer and union leader Ella May Wiggins, who was killed by the police.

Novels centering on race and antiracism. Overlapping significantly with the Gastonia novels – where white–black unity emerged as a key issue – this grouping includes such Gastonia sequels as Lumpkin's *A Sign for Cain* (1935) and Burke's *A Stone Came Rolling* (1935), as well as the stories about Southern racial violence and left organizing gathered in Richard Wright's *Uncle Tom's Children* (1940; not strictly a novel, but a unified work of fiction). William Attaway's *Blood on the Forge* (1941) treats the use of African Americans as scabs during the massive 1919 steel strike, the defeat of which was the single most drastic loss for organized labor in the first third of the twentieth century. Three historical novels figure significantly in this category, for they relate past struggles against racism to the 1930s: Guy Endore's *Babouk* (1934) and Arna Bontemps's *Drums at Dusk* (1939), both of which treat the Haitian Revolution; and Bontemps's *Black Thunder* (1936), a fictional recapitulation of the aborted slave revolt in Richmond, Virginia, led by Gabriel Prosser in 1800. It bears noting that many novels included in other categories had subplots relating to fighting racism, which was recognized as a central concern by many proletarian writers.

"Bottom Dogs" novels about nonclass-conscious workers. Taking its name from Edward Dahlberg's 1930 novel about a worker who falls into the lumpenproletariat, this category includes a number of works dealing with hobos and migrants, such as Nelson Algren's *Somebody in Boots* (1935) and Tom Kromer's *Waiting for Nothing* (1935). B. Traven's novels about rootless sailors and would-be miners (*The Death Ship*, 1926, translated 1934, and *Treasure of the Sierra Madre*, 1928) are pre-1930 texts nonetheless belonging within this subgenre of the proletarian novel. Other texts portray workers who react to their exploitation by scabbing (Louis Colman's *Lumber*, 1931, and James Steele's *Conveyer*, 1935) or displacing their alienation into sexual or racial aggression (James T. Farrell's *Studs Lonigan* trilogy, 1934, 1935, 1936, and Wright's *Native Son* and *Lawd Today*, written in the late 1930s, published in 1963). Many other types of proletarian novels, it should be noted, bring in nonclass-conscious workers as part of their structuring character systems.

Novels featuring the development of class-conscious, sometimes Communist, protagonists. These texts feature a range of protagonists and situations. Jack Conroy's *The Disinherited* (1933), an early instance of this subgenre, features the gradual radicalization of a young mineworker turned leftist organizer; Myra Page's *Moscow Yankee* (1935), more dramatically, portrays the changing consciousness of Andy, an unemployed Detroit autoworker who goes to work in a Moscow tractor factory during the USSR's First Five-Year Plan and decides to stay. Agnes Smedley's largely autobiographical *Daughter of Earth* (1929, 1934) depicts the painful maturation, political and emotional, of a young woman resisting both class and gender oppression. Isidor Schneider's *From the Kingdom of Necessity* (1935), also based on the writer's own life, examines the radicalization of a gentle poet; Edward Newhouse's *You Can't Sleep Here* (1934) treats the political maturation of a young journalist living in a Hooverville in New York's Central Park. Albert Maltz's *The Underground Stream* (1940) offers a sophisticated representation of a Communist union organizer who is kidnapped and murdered by homegrown US fascists. Stretched a bit, this category can also accommodate Ernest Hemingway's account of a protagonist achieving full life in the shadow of death in his famous antifascist novel set in the Spanish Civil War, *For Whom the Bell Tolls* (1940).

Novels featuring everyday working-class life. This grouping, often focusing on the effects of capitalism upon families, contains a significant number of texts authored by women. Meridel Le Sueur's *The Girl* (1978) and Tillie Olsen's *Yonnondio: From the Thirties* (1978) (both written in the 1930s) examine working-class women's lives – not avoiding such issues as abortion and marital rape – in the context of class exploitation. Mike Gold's *Jews Without Money* and Thomas Bell's *All Brides Are Beautiful* (1936) treat families for whom what Marx called the "dull compulsion of economics" is an ever-present reality. Conroy's *A World to Win* (1935) contrasts the lives of two brothers following different ideological routes but rediscovering their closeness in the midst of class struggle. Josephine Herbst's *Rope of Gold trilogy* (1933, 1934, 1939) traces multiple generations of a middle-class family, exploring the complex connections between status pressures and political choices on the one hand and the emotional dynamics between husbands and wives, parents and children, on the other. John Dos Passos's *USA* trilogy (1930, 1932, 1936) – examined below in some detail – covers the gamut of subgenres, but for purposes of classification fits perhaps better here than anywhere else, since it offers an exhaustive portrayal of the varieties of false consciousness afflicting the denizens of capitalist society in the opening decades of the century.

While a taxonomy based upon subject matter enables us to map out the thematic concerns embedded in proletarian novels, our understanding of the ways in which radical writers met the challenge of working left-wing politics into fictional form is better enhanced if we consider subgenres based not upon topic but instead upon narrative strategy. Granville Hicks, in an influential 1934 *New Masses* series titled "Revolution and the Novel," proposed a formally based taxonomy that provides the scaffolding for such an investigation. Somewhat revising Hicks's categories, we can think of proletarian novels as clustering into four general types: fictional autobiographies, *Bildungsromans*, multiprotagonist social novels, and collective novels. The fictional autobiography features a first-person working-class narrator-hero who, in the course of the tale, comes to a class-conscious understanding of the forces that have shaped his or her life. Thus Mike Gold's *Jews Without Money* – which consists of about 85 percent autobiography, according to its author – depicts the coming of age of a young Jewish-American Communist on New York's Lower East Side. The closing epiphany – only on the text's somewhat notorious last page does Gold's Mikey hear the revolutionary soapbox speech that changes his life – is largely validated by the reader's awareness of the close convergence of experiencing character with narrating author. In *Daughter of Earth*, Agnes Smedley's portrayal of the internal struggles experienced by her protagonist "Marie Rogers" – combining Marxist social analysis with psychoanalytic probing of subjectivity – is reinforced by the text's felt autobiographical presence. In Jack Conroy's *The Disinherited*, "Larry Donovan"'s decision to abandon the route of petit bourgeois escapism and accept his place in the muck and mire of proletarian life is buttressed by the experientially based realism with which his work experiences are described. In all these fictional autobiographies, the gaining of mature selfhood is portrayed as inseparable from the acquisition of class consciousness. And while the genre's stress upon authenticity runs the risk of a certain economistic workerism, these texts' representations of proletarian self-actualization provide compelling reading.

The proletarian *Bildungsroman* (the novel of individual development) also focuses on a single protagonist, but in a patently fictional way: this is the most conventionally novelistic of the modes of the proletarian novel. Often depicting the transformation of false consciousness into class consciousness, this genre ordinarily deploys omniscient narration and an array of minor characters representing a range of political potentialities and stances. Thus Myra Page's account of Andy's politicization in *Moscow Yankee* – his gradual alignment with a new social order struggling to come into being – is linked with his growing love for an emancipated "new Soviet woman." A production plot, focused on the effort to maximize output while democratizing the division of labor, parallels the love plot. Grace Lumpkin's Gastonia strike novel *To Make My Bread*, which is loosely based on the life of the martyred Wiggins, depicts the emergence of proletarian consciousness in Bonnie McClure, a woman descending from the mountains to the factory: in microcosm, the novel represents the birth of a class. Meridel Le Sueur's *The Girl* portrays an anonymous young Minnesotan waitress whose preparations for out-of-wedlock motherhood are simultaneously preparations for class warfare. Guy Endore's *Babouk* relates the dialectical transformation of African tribal collectivity into a steely resolve to murder the oppressor: Babouk's own internal contradictions mirror the course of historical necessity.

These and other proletarian *Bildungsromans* vary in the degree to which they restrict the reader to the parameters of the protagonist's awareness. Page's novel, as it approaches closure, relies excessively upon its conventional love story to paper over contradictions in its treatment of politics and economics. Lumpkin's novel rarely exposes the reader to any knowledge or voices to which Bonnie is not privy; anticapitalism is implied on every page, but revolutionary politics are virtually absent, except through a vaguely leftist mentor character appearing briefly at the end. Le Sueur's text, with its nearly inarticulate protagonist and its conjoining of child-bearing with changing the world, runs the risk of biologizing – and restricting to women – the development of class consciousness. Endore's novel, by contrast, continually inserts historical information about the twentieth century into his narrative of the Haitian revolution, thus hectoring the reader into seeing the present-day implications of

Babouk's story. *Moscow Yankee*'s reliance upon romantic conventions lessens but by no means effaces the impact of its hero's development into a communist. Despite their differing narratorial voices, however, all these texts attach the reader's growth in political awareness primarily to the main character's development. In the proletarian *Bildungsroman*, the reader's identification with a class-conscious protagonist can serve to challenge the legitimacy of the capitalist social order that validates the possessive individualism upon which the genre was originally based.

Wright's *Native Son* – not routinely read as a proletarian novel, but in fact a key text of the genre – exhibits some of the inventive techniques that could be deployed by a writer using a conventional novelistic single-protagonist form to project a radical political understanding. In this novel Wright was faced with a near-insuperable challenge: how to depict the grounding of Bigger Thomas's consciousness and actions in an analysis of capitalist social relations while keeping the reader centered in Bigger's thoughts, even as Bigger is shown to have only the most limited understanding of the forces that have shaped him. This challenge is compounded by the felt necessity – central to the CPUSA's line on the "Negro Question," and elaborated by Wright in his 1937 *New Challenge* essay, "A Blueprint for Negro Writing" – for African-American writers to "accept the nationalist implications of their lives, not in order to encourage them, but in order to transcend them" (Wright 1978: 40). This feat is achieved, first, by Wright's presentation of contradictions within Bigger's crude black nationalism, which runs from approval of Hitler to an inchoate desire for oneness with other denizens of the urban Black Belt. The material basis of Bigger's limited conceptual range is supplied by such devices as newspaper headlines describing Bigger in bestial terms and overheard conversations revealing the similarly restricted consciousness of other Negroes of the South Side. The long speech by the CP lawyer Boris Max – much more analytical than its structural counterpart in the trial scene in *An American Tragedy* – clarifies the thesis that Bigger is part of a "nation within a nation." In his Jamesian prefatory essay "How Bigger Was Born," Wright notes the many models for Bigger in the Jim Crow South but then – comparing Bigger's alienation with that of Lenin and Gorky observing the Houses of Parliament – observes that there are "millions" of Bigger Thomases, and that many of them are white. The effect of this multilayered mode of representation is to limn the logic whereby black nationalism is to be accepted and then transcended. Bigger does not need to be portrayed as grasping Marxist politics ("What I killed for, I am," he famously insists at his end) in order for the reader to trace the dots connecting race with class.

Intuiting the potential pitfalls accompanying the reliance upon single protagonists to bear the burden of political education, many proletarian writers opted to abandon altogether the single-protagonist format and to explore the possibilities of the multiprotagonist social novel, that is, a conventionally realistic text in which a large cast of characters embody multiple class and ideological positions. In Arna Bontemps's *Black Thunder*, a range of characters, black and white, not only display varying degrees of courage and fear but also expose the reader to a philosophical debate about the "Rights of Man" beyond the range of Gabriel Prosser himself. The continuing relevance of this debate to mid-1930s antiracist movements is subtly implied. Robert Cantwell's *The Land of Plenty* uses the occasion of the lumber mill strike to explore the potentiality for self-rule in the group of workers who make the mill function. It is thus also a novel about the possible seeds of socialism in the capitalist present. William Attaway's *Blood on the Forge* treats the Moss brothers as a tripartite protagonist whose conflicts, among themselves and with their environment, embody the principal contradictions within the emerging black proletariat. While Attaway's novel can still be faulted for restricting the reader to the confines of the characters' awareness – a flaw that Ralph Ellison in his 1941 *New Masses* critique attributed to Attaway's incomplete grasp of Marxist dialectics – as a multiprotagonist social novel it bypasses many of the individualistic limitations of the *Bildungsroman* and proves a useful vehicle for representing the tragic outcome of the 1919 steel strike.

Perhaps the most successful – certainly the most inventive – mode of 1930s proletarian fiction is the collective novel. Similar to the social novel in its portrayal of a broad range of social types, the collective novel goes further by unabashedly taking a whole society as its protagonist. In creating this expanded sense of collectivity, sometimes the text breaks down the notion of "character" as such, creating a group-consciousness in which individual voices become indistinguishable. In Clara Weatherwax's prize-winning novel about striking lumber workers, the workers' meditations about how to respond to a fellow-worker's on-the-job death are rendered as a kind of collective murmur. At times the collective novel features fictional characters who never meet: in Josephine Herbst's *Rope of Gold*, the left-wing journalist Victoria Chance and the union organizer Steve Carson never cross paths. Clearly readers must figure out for themselves why these characters inhabit the same volume: active engagement of the reader in the process of comprehending – and hence shaping – the total social structure is a vital component of many collective novels. Sometimes the text abruptly shifts registers, moving from the fictional lives of individuals to narratorial proclamations about politics and history: the famous interchapters in Steinbeck's *The Grapes of Wrath*, which eloquently announce the movement from "I" to "we," constitute a formal culmination of earlier experiments with the collective novel. Still another technique used by collective novelists is the introduction of documentary materials – headlines, leaflets, songs – requiring the reader to separate the wheat from the chaff and to contemplate the construction of historical discourse itself as arena of class struggle. Although this device is also used in the proletarian *Bildungsroman* – as in *Native Son* – its deployment in the collective novel often plays a more significant role, for it figures centrally in the text's interrogation of the relationship between language and ideology. And where the multiprotagonist social novel routinely relies upon conventions of narrative transparency to project its conception of the social order, the collective novel frequently engages in what might be called "critical totalization." Even as they are invited to connect the dots that limn the social totality, readers are made aware that the nature of that totality is itself a matter of political contestation.

The writer who most fully explored the potentialities of the collective novel – indeed, whose name is often associated with its origination and development – is John Dos Passos, whose *USA* trilogy represents the culmination of attempts to fuse novelistic experimentation with anticapitalist critique. Drawing upon an ecumenical political leftism and written in a kaleidoscopic style drawing upon futurism, cubism, and cinematic montage, the novels of the trilogy provide a trenchant account of politics, economics, and daily life in the first two decades of the twentieth century. *The Forty-Second Parallel* covers approximately 1900–16; *Nineteen Nineteen* focuses on the war years, 1917–19; *The Big Money* covers 1920–28, with provocative nods toward the 1929 stock market crash and the Depression. Overlaid upon the different political movements occurring in these periods are significant shifts within Dos Passos's own political outlook. *The Forty-Second Parallel* portrays the nation's emergence as a global capitalist power and the prewar activities of the Socialist Party and the Industrial Workers of the World (IWW) from the standpoint of the free-wheeling, somewhat bohemian radicalism characteristic of the author throughout most of the 1920s. *Nineteen Nineteen* depicts the carnage of the Great War, the imperialist power grab of the Versailles Peace Conference, and the revolutionary upsurge of 1919 from the closest approach to Marxism in the author's dramatic political orbit. *The Big Money* narrates its history of labor repression and growing consumerism from a stance more technocratic than Marxist, invoking the sardonic spirit of Thorstein Veblen.

Each novel consists of four types of interspersed materials: fictional narratives, biographies, Newsreels, and Camera Eyes. The fictional narratives treat a range of characters – from blue-collar workers to media moguls, left-wing organizers to Hollywood starlets – whose lives embody in microcosm the effects of ideological obfuscation, sexual commodification, the lure of the "big money," and, occasionally, radical politics upon a range of representative Americans. Some characters appear in only one volume, others in all three; some lives intersect frequently, while others remain solitary and marginalized. Although Dos Passos's distanced and ironic approach to his characters has been criticized as mechanical and behaviorist, his array of imagined types is intended to convey a far-reaching critique of the ways in which capitalism dulls human capacities for understanding and love.

The biographies are prose poem jeremiads, alternately ironic and eloquent, depicting men (and one woman, Isadora Duncan) who, for better or worse, shaped culture, technology, and politics in the early twentieth century. Dos Passos's heroes – while rarely portrayed without a trace of irony – include Eugene Debs, Luther Burbank, Wesley Everest, Joe Hill, Big Bill Haywood, John Reed, Randolph Bourne, "Fighting Bob" La Follette, the Wright Brothers, Frank Lloyd Wright, Isadora Duncan, and Thorstein Veblen. His villains – or at least objects of contempt – include Theodore Roosevelt, Minor C. Keith, the House of Morgan, Woodrow Wilson, William Randolph Hearst, Samuel Insull, Henry Ford, and Rudolph Valentino. Two of the most gripping biographies are of anonymous figures: the "Body of an American" buried in the Tomb of the Unknown Soldier (to whom the hypocritical top-hatted Wilson "brought a bouquet of poppies") and "Vag," the unemployed Depression-era hitchhiker, failed by the American Dream, whose anti-Whitmanian portrait closes *The Big Money*. At once challenging the mythology of the "great man" view of history and exploring the role of the individual in history from a class-conscious standpoint, the biographies link the lives of the fictional characters to larger historical forces of which they are largely unaware.

The Newsreels consist of one- to three-page clumps of newspaper headlines, advertising slogans, fragments of speeches, and snatches of popular songs. Principally the newsreels satirize the capitalist mass media's promulgation of jingoism, antiworking-class propaganda ("Jobless riot at agency"), voyeuristic identification with the lives of the rich and famous, consumerist values, and plain old lies ("Lenin Dead"). Occasionally, however, they include snatches from the left press ("Workers March on Reichstag"; "Ex-Servicemen Demand Jobs"). The effect of this ideological montage is at once to reveal the dominant discourses by which consent is manufactured and to highlight the importance of forging, and publicizing, an alternative language through which to comprehend the class struggle.

The Camera Eye passages, written in a stream-of-consciousness style reminiscent of James Joyce, are musings, often verging on incoherence, representing Dos Passos's own gradual growth into the author of the text. The passages in *The Forty-Second Parallel* cover the author's childhood, privileged but sad and sequestered. *Nineteen Nineteen* reveals the authorial self coming of age as a wartime ambulance driver, would-be soldier, and witness to the fizzling of the 1919 upsurge. In *The Big Money*, the Camera Eye explores his mission as a writer of wavering leftist partisanship who reaches clarity as he participates in the movement to save Sacco and Vanzetti. In the famous climactic words of the trilogy, he denounces those who have "taken the clean words our fathers spoke and made them slimy and foul" and declares, "all right we are two nations." Although we as readers are invited to identify with this moment of clarity, we can do so only if we have done the work Dos Passos has set before us in the preceding 1,500 pages. For there is labor involved in penetrating through reification; to grasp what has produced the riven totality that is the USA entails a multi-leveled understanding of the dialectics of history.

Dos Passos always maintained some distance from the left – even when writing *Nineteen Nineteen* – and the doctrinal politics guiding much of *USA* invite leftist critique. His "representative" range of characters contains not one nonwhite, and those African-American, Asian, and Hispanic characters making brief appearances conform to denigrating racial stereotypes; Dos Passos lagged considerably behind other white leftist writers who were attempting to grapple with the realities of race in the United States. Although he ably targets the capitalist social relations that warp gender identities, most of Dos Passos's female characters evince even less agency than the males. Dos Passos's portraits of leftist organizers and activists are often cynical and, especially in *The Big Money*, express his growing affinity for caricaturing Communists as "Stalinist" hatchetmen. Even at his most impassioned, moreover, Dos Passos voices disappointment that the nation has been taken over and betrayed, more than commitment to abolishing the class system he has so brilliantly anatomized. The political assumptions and assertions embedded in *USA* hardly represent the most radical think-ing among proletarian novelists. Nonetheless, in its dialectical and totalizing grasp of American history, as well as its acute awareness of the hegemonic and counterhe-gemonic roles language necessarily plays in narrating that history, the *USA* trilogy represents one of the high marks of US literary radicalism and supplies the basis for Jean Paul Sartre's judgment that Dos Passos was the greatest writer of his time.

While clearly not all fiction writers of the 1930s participated in the project of the proletarian novel, it is a testament to the influence of the genre that various authors not aligned with literary radicalism can be read as reacting to its themes and conven-tions. Nathanael West's *A Cool Million* (1934), primarily a parody of Horatio Alger narratives, treats its hapless hero, Lemuel Pitkin, as a quintessential nonclass-conscious protagonist. His literal dismemberment – he gradually loses various limbs and organs in the course of the narrative – is a surreal play upon the conventions of the "bottom dogs" proletarian novel. Zora Neale Hurston's *Their Eyes Were Watching God* (1937) contains, among other things, a folkish challenge to proletarianism. The sequence in which Janie and Tea Cake enjoy their labor "on the muck," reveling in the music of their Bahamian fellow-laborers, contains an implicit refutation of the emphasis upon exploitation and suffering in contemporaneous proletarian fiction. William Faulkner's *Light in August* (1932) can be read as a non- (or even anti-) Marxist reworking of proletarian themes: the Depression-linked peripatetic existences of both Joe Christmas and Lena Grove are recast in archetypal terms, even as the abolitionist-descended Joanna Burden is suggestively linked with Scottsboro's outside agitators. The chapters in *Absalom, Absalom!* (1936) portraying Thomas Sutpen's descent from the hills into the slave-based plantation economy of the plain, while resonant of classical tragedy, acknowledge the power of a Marxist modes-of-production narrative. Even writers who stayed away from the American Writers Congresses were affected by the radicalism of the decade and, in particular, the model of the proletarian novel, which they might reject but found difficult to ignore.

Finally, it bears noting that the genre of the proletarian novel did not simply dis-appear in the years following World War II. Early novels of the Cold War, such as Chester Himes's *Lonely Crusade* (1947) and Ellison's *Invisible Man*, bear many embed-ded traces of the Marxism – and Communist experience – which they repudiate, while Alexander Saxton's *The Great Midland* (1948) goes against the flow with its abidingly sympathetic portrait of a Communist union organizer. Howard Fast emerged in the postwar years as the source of a steady stream of novels examining the red line of history in a wide range of historical contexts; Truman Nelson, Lloyd Brown, and Harriet Arnow published left-wing novels during the height of McCarthyism. Pres-sures of the Cold War led many left-wing novelists to turn to science fiction; Frederik Pohl and Cyril Kornbluth, in *The Space Merchants* (1952), were early practitioners of a radical futurism continuing to this day in the work of such writers as Kim Stanley Robinson. Novels by Margaret Walker (*Jubilee*, 1966) and John Oliver Killens (*Young-blood*, 1982) examined African-American experience from a highly class-conscious perspective. Novels focusing on labor conflicts and strikes (John Nichols's *The Milagro*

Beanfield War, 1976, Denise Giardina's *Storming Heaven*, 1987) continued to feature the class struggle. Such contemporary writers as E. L. Doctorow, Dorothy Allison, Barbara Kingsolver, Russell Banks, Marge Piercy, and Octavia Butler have devised a range of imaginative means for exploring concerns resembling those that animated proletarian writers of the Depression decade, even as the discourse of "postindustrialism" predominates among pundits and sociologists alike. We can anticipate that, as long as the capitalist system generates contradiction and conflict, novelists will continue to produce texts that can – through a continual reconfiguring and updating of the category – be termed "proletarian."

References and Further Reading

Bloom, James D. (1992). *Left Letters: The Culture Wars of Mike Gold and Joseph Freeman*. New York: Columbia University Press.

Booker, M. Keith. (1999). *The Modern American Novel of the Left: A Research Guide*. Westport, CT: Greenwood Press.

Casey, Janet Galligani (ed.). (2004). *The Novel and the American Left: Critical Essays on Depression-Era Literature*. Iowa City: University of Iowa Press.

Coiner, Constance. (1995). *Better Red: The Writing and Resistance of Tillie Olsen and Meridel Le Sueur*. New York: Oxford University Press.

Dawahare, Anthony. (2003). *Nationalism, Marxism, and American Literature Between the Wars: A New Pandora's Box*. Jackson: University Press of Mississippi.

Foley, Barbara. (1993). *Radical Representations: Politics and Form in U. S. Proletarian Fiction, 1929–1941*. Durham, NC: Duke University Press.

Georgakas, Dan and Ernie Brill. (1998). Proletarian and radical writers. In Mari Jo Buhle, Paul Buhle, and Dan Georgakas (eds), *Encyclopedia of the American Left*, 2nd edn. (pp. 673–41). New York: Oxford University Press.

Hapke, Laura. (2001). *Labor's Text: The Worker in American Fiction*. New Brunswick, NJ: Rutgers University Press.

Mullen, Bill and Sherry Linkon (eds). (1996). *Radical Revisions: Rereading 1930s Culture*. Urbana: University of Illinois Press.

Murphy, James. F. (1991). *The Proletarian Moment: The Controversy over Leftism in Literature*. Urbana: University Of Illinois Press

Rabinowitz, Paula. (1992). *Labor and Desire: Women's Revolutionary Fiction in Depression America*. Chapel Hill: University of North Carolina Press.

Rideout, Walter. (1956). *The Radical Novel in the United States, 1900–1954: Some Interrelations of Literature and Society*. Cambridge, MA: Harvard University Press.

Shulman, Robert. (2000). *The Power of Political Art: The 1930s Literary Left Reconsidered*. Chapel Hill: University of North Carolina Press.

Staub, Michael E. (1994). *Voices of Persuasion: Politics of Representation in 1930s America*. Cambridge, UK: Cambridge University Press.

Suggs, Jon Christian (ed.). (1993). Historical overview. *American Proletarian Culture: The Twenties and the Thirties. Dictionary of Literary Biography Documentary Series: An Illustrated Chronicle* (vol. 11, pp. 1–16). Detroit: Gale.

Wald, Alan M. (1992). *Exiles from a Future Time: The Forging of the Mid-Twentieth-Century Literary Left*. Chapel Hill: University of North Carolina Press.

Wright, Richard. (1978). A blueprint for Negro writing. In Michael Fabre and Ellen Wright (eds), *The Richard Wright Reader* (pp. 36–49). New York: Harper.

19

Revolutionary Sentiments: Modern American Domestic Fiction and the Rise of the Welfare State

Susan Edmunds

In 1919, Arthur W. Calhoun published his massive study, *A Social History of the American Family from Colonial Times to the Present*. His title is not entirely accurate: instead of taking his readers up to the present, Calhoun closes his study with a forecast of the future. His final chapter, "The Family and the Social Revolution," roundly dismisses "sentimental campaigns for rehabilitation or conservation of old values" (Calhoun 1919: 322), and instead endorses "indications" that US "society is working toward Socialism" (p. 326). In earlier chapters, Calhoun had identified the Industrial Revolution and "the revolution in woman's world" (p. 85) as interlocking forces of domestic upheaval. These forces were now strong enough to make a "new family life . . . inevitable" (p. 332). Struggling to keep the joy out of his bleached academic prose, Calhoun conjures up a future likely to startle and bemuse readers of today. His coming socialist American family will rest on a foundation of: "absolute sex equality," "scientific pedagogy of sex relations," "full economic opportunity for all young people so that marriage shall not be influenced by mercenary considerations," and "home ownership" on demand (pp. 326, 327). Prostitution, poverty, and venereal disease will be eliminated. More ominously, "a thoroughgoing eugenics," backed by the state, will emphasize the "significance of the marital relation as the key to race improvement and race perpetuation" (p. 326). But with the emphasis on race improvement will come: "provision of ideal conditions for pregnant women and nursing mothers," voluntary birth control and divorce, "the continual education of young and old," and "equality of opportunity for every child born in so far as social control, and subsidy where necessary, can secure such equality" (p. 327).

Calhoun's history stands out today for the wrongheadedness of its predictions: the "new family life" it describes has long since slipped into the pile of discarded futures we encounter whenever we inquire into the US's past. But for all its misplaced certainty, Calhoun's work captures a vital aspect of the public conversation held on home and family in the early decades of the twentieth century. And it does so precisely because it celebrates radical trends that time would not confirm. In locating the modern American family on the cresting wave of revolution, Calhoun articulates a sense of domestic flux, threat, and possibility widely shared by his contemporaries. This sense had been growing from the 1890s onward, when many of the historical developments Calhoun rehearses became subjects of widespread public discussion and concern. Rapid industrialization and urbanization, coupled with heavy Southern and Eastern European immigration, brought new kinds of families and new kinds of family life into the nation's growing cities. As desperate economic need pulled working-class women and children into factories and sweatshops alongside their husbands and fathers, middle-class observers, shocked as much by capitalist exploitation as by labor militancy, bemoaned deteriorating domestic conditions among the poor. African Americans, widely vilified as a population incapable of sustaining or respecting family life, saw the promises of Reconstruction give way to new forms of economic servitude, disenfranchisement, and racial terrorism, and reacted with renewed campaigns for self-emancipation. Meanwhile, increased agricultural and industrial production, combined with improved transportation and communication systems, made a burgeoning world of advertised consumer goods available to a growing white middle class no longer able or willing to produce at home. Liberalizing trends in marriage, divorce, and property law improved white women's legal status. More white women gained access to higher education and the professions, and the fight for women's suffrage, finally won in 1920, secured their place in the formal political process. For social conservatives, all this spelled doom for the family, and many wondered whether it would even survive.

By the late 1910s, the tendency to associate modern domestic life with the hope or threat of revolution had become commonplace. Only a minority of Calhoun's contemporaries shared his conviction that a coming revolution in the family would be socialist in nature. Many more identified the family with "the revolution in manners and morals," a term devised by Frederick Lewis Allen in 1931 to name the new patterns of mass consumption and liberalized sexual conduct transforming the white middle class. Novelists working in the established genres of the sentimental, realist, and naturalist domestic novel, as well as those exploring new forms of modernist experimentation, gave both revolutionary trends ample representation in their fiction. In addition, modernist writers embraced the "revolution of the word" famously identified with avant-garde activity in the June 1929 issue of the little magazine *transition*. Attacks on middle-class domestic culture formed an important part of the wider avant-garde assault on bourgeois institutions and ideologies in Europe. Novelists in the US incorporated those attacks in their own, increasingly antisentimental depictions of home and family life.

In today's climate, it is tempting to conclude that novelists were as misguided as Calhoun himself when they depicted modern American domestic experience in revolutionary terms. Overshadowed on one side by the nineteenth-century cult of sentimental domesticity and on the other by cozy images of postwar suburban consumerism, the early twentieth-century domestic sphere has been lost in popular reconstructions of US personal and national family histories. But writers of the period were correct when they portrayed the domestic sphere as a primary site and source of modern social transformation. During the Progressive Era, domestic discourse provided the terms for a series of public debates and reform initiatives crucial to the formation of the US welfare state. White women reformers, in particular, played a leading role in charging the state with a moral duty to protect and provide for needy families. Through their activism, they created unprecedented applications for an earlier discourse of sentimental domesticity and successfully used that discourse to reconstitute both the family and the state. Despite Calhoun and other commentators' dismissive evaluation of "sentimental campaigns for rehabilitation or conservation of old values," white women reformers forged a distinctly modern legacy, grounded in a new imbrication of domestic and state agendas, that continues to inform how we fight and what we fight about when we engage in national political struggle today.

The role played by sentimental activism in the creation and ongoing administration of the US welfare state forms an important, if heretofore neglected, context for understanding modern American domestic fiction. Critics have long argued that a revolt against sentimental culture stood at the center of realist, naturalist, and modernist literary production in the US and Europe. Our current critical paradigms continue to interpret this revolt in terms of a generational divide, one which pits energetic and rebellious young Moderns against the formidable, but fading, representatives of a bygone era. In contrast, I would argue that modern American writers struggled so deeply with sentimental culture in their domestic fiction because they recognized that culture as the site of large-scale – and fully contemporary – social contest and change. Novelists sometimes represented sentimental culture as the source of radical transformations underway and sometimes as a repressive and oppressive legacy to be overthrown. Several novelists developed seemingly outlandish possibilities within sentimental discourse in order to affirm liberating domestic outcomes not pursued by sentimental activists themselves. In the end, it may be too much to say that the social changes associated with modern sentimental discourse in the US were revolutionary in nature. But we cannot understand modern American domestic fiction unless we keep the revolutionary tenor of early twentieth-century struggles over home and family life in mind. In the next part of this essay, I'd like to sketch out the ways in which sentimental activists mobilized domestic discourse to build the foundations of a family-centered welfare state, before turning to a discussion of how domestic fiction writers engaged the myriad social struggles associated with this historical trajectory.

Sentimental Activism and Welfare Reform

Most of us associate the origins of the US welfare state with Roosevelt's New Deal and with the 1935 Social Security Act in particular. This Act, which created the nation's first federal and federally regulated social insurance programs, finally brought the United States into line with European states, which had established national social insurance programs as early as the 1880s. But historians actually locate the roots of the US welfare state much earlier than the New Deal, in federal pension programs for Civil War veterans and state mothers' pension programs for white widows with children. The focus of these latter programs reflected the priorities of a Progressive reform philosophy that historians have defined as "maternalist" in nature. Maternalist reformers developed an enlarged view of their own power and responsibility as mothers in order to create new forms of social protection and social provision at the local, state, and federal level. Both white and black women embraced the maternalist reform philosophy. But racial privilege and racial complicity gave white women access to mainstream political institutions from which African Americans were excluded. Thus, during the same years in which black women activists oversaw the creation of schools, hospitals, and old-age homes which state and local governments provided to white people as a matter of course, white women activists trained their eye on shaping state and federal welfare policy.

Theodore Roosevelt spoke to the heart of white women's maternalist philosophy in his presidential address at the watershed 1909 White House Conference on the Care of Dependent Children. There, he prophetically insisted: "Surely . . . the goal toward which we should strive is to help the mother, so that she can keep her own home and keep the child in it" (Michel 1993: 294). With the President's backing, maternalist reformers spearheaded a national drive to set up mothers' pension programs, which passed in 40 states by 1920. During the same years, white women in the National Consumers' League and the General Federation of Women's Clubs joined forces with the male-dominated National Child Labor Committee to protect women and children in the paid labor force. Between 1908, when the Supreme Court upheld hours limits for working women, and the late 1910s and early 1920s, when the Supreme Court invalidated child labor and minimum wage laws, these groups scored multiple victories. White maternalists opened both a Children's Bureau and a Women's Bureau in the US Department of Labor, in 1912 and 1918 respectively. They used these federal offices to craft state-level protective labor laws for women and children that would constitute the major legal precedent for the 1938 Fair Labor Standards Act of the New Deal. But their biggest victory was the Sheppard-Towner Maternity and Infancy Protection Act of 1921. This Act inaugurated the nation's first federal social welfare program. Between 1922 and 1929, when the last federal funds dried up, the Act provided federal grants to states to set up free public health clinics for mothers with infants, regardless of their race, class, or moral status. A strong emphasis on "Americanization" pervaded the clinics, where a wide spectrum of immigrant and African-American cultural practices were defined as inimical to infants' health. Characterizing the Sheppard-Towner Act as "the first national policy to tie cultural and gender-role conformity to the social welfare," historian Gwendolyn Mink notes that its programs, which did save many children's lives, also "made the imitation of a middle-class, Anglo American maternal ideal the price of women's citizenship" (Mink 1995: 71, 73).

Maternalist reformers combined explicit welfare initiatives with a number of other efforts designed to promote the well-being of the nation's families and particularly its children. In some of the ugliest political maneuvering of the period, white clubwomen joined male academics in calling for government involvement in eugenics. The discourse of eugenics, a pseudoscience that declared African Americans and Southern and Eastern European immigrants to be genetically inferior, offered new ways of justifying and extending legal bans on interracial marriage widely introduced at the state level after the Civil War. Thirty states passed laws between 1896 and 1914 that prohibited unions between various categories of the "unfit." Between 1907 and 1930, 24 states passed sterilization laws aimed at the same dubiously defined population; in 1927, the Supreme Court upheld the constitutionality of these laws. Most of the people sterilized by the state were immigrants or the children of immigrants, and most were poor. The 1924 Immigration Restriction Act, which universalized the ban on Asian immigration and sharply curtailed immigration from Southern and Eastern Europe, invested the federal government with still more power to determine the genetic makeup of the nation's future generations.

Anti-immigrant feeling and a sentimental concern for the distressed child jointly informed white clubwomen's drive to set up a second legal system for the young. Between 1899 and 1917 all but three states set up juvenile courts, designed to serve a largely poor, urban, and immigrant clientele, and many also created domestic or family courts, geared toward the growing number of middle-class couples seeking divorce. By the 1920s, a sentimental bias toward the mother's irreplaceable role as caretaker – recast in the new language of psychotherapy – came to dominate the new court system. This court bias helped to block the widespread establishment of nursery schools, desperately needed by working parents, even as it encouraged the proliferation of family-centered therapeutic services: drawing social workers into the legal system as court investigators and probation officers, judges also mandated clients' referral to marriage counseling, child study and child guidance centers, detention centers, and reform schools.

In the area of education, Progressive reformers' efforts to strengthen compulsory education laws worked in tandem with child labor legislation and tougher enforcement policies to put and keep record numbers of children in school. Several federal acts had a broad impact on public education in this period. The vocational training initiative, funded by the Smith-Hughes Act of 1917, made educational tracking a common practice in US schools. In the same year, the major federal study *Negro Education* endorsed the racist practice of routing all black students in the South into segregated vocational education programs. For girls, vocational education meant training in domestic science, later called home economics. Introduced in the land-grant colleges in the 1870s, domestic science departments were installed in 30 colleges and universities by 1900 and 195 by 1916. A series of acts stretching from the Hatch Act of 1887 to the Capper-Ketchum Act of 1928 allotted additional federal funding to afterschool and continuing education initiatives designed to teach girls and women how to be better wives and mothers. African-American and many immigrant girls and women usually got a different lesson: how to be better domestic servants. State-backed domestic instruction provided employment for a growing number of home economists. It also secured the federal government's intimate involvement in the movement to improve and standardize white family life nationwide.

Home economists initially felt only poor people needed instruction in childcare, but by the mid-1920s the profession endorsed parent education for all classes. This shift coincided with a renewed emphasis on individual and family casework among social workers, whose own profession sprang from middle-class women's "friendly visits" to poor families at the turn of the century. The catastrophic upheavals of the Great Depression led a number of social workers, associated with the Communist-backed rank-and-file movement, to question their profession's focus on individual adjustment, to protest the systemic effects of racism and to revive an earlier emphasis on modern poverty as an unjustifiable by-product of capitalism. But by the end of the decade, radical dissent gave way to widespread support for a New Deal which was making trained social workers a pervasive and integral part of the government's address to its citizens. New Deal public assistance programs, combined with increased demand in the public schools and the private sector, opened large new markets for psychologically oriented social casework. Dovetailing with a host of other social initiatives aimed at shoring up the home, the casework model modernized nineteenth-century templates of sentimental domesticity that emphasized the mother's crucial role in determining her children's moral, social, and economic fate.

The Great Depression posed challenges to the nation's fragile welfare network that exceeded maternalist reformers' powers of response: systemic economic breakdown and rising popular unrest made both a new scale and a new kind of social welfare legislation necessary. Franklin Roosevelt had begun creating programs to deal with the crisis as soon as he took office in 1933. But his administration's most ambitious and enduring intervention came with passage of the Social Security Act in 1935. The social insurance programs introduced by this Act offered unprecedented federal protection against losses associated with sickness, unemployment, old age, and death. The very idea of social insurance, implemented in several European nations before World War I, developed outside the tradition of maternalist reform. But the "American" family model to which these social insurance programs were tied had everything to do with that tradition. This model featured a steadily employed and socially insured white male wage-earner, a stay-at-home wife and mother, and their children. Government wage laws secured most white men's right to a "family wage"; white women could choose to work for less and their pay rarely met the costs of childcare. Jobs in agriculture and domestic service – which employed most workers of color – paid so little that mothers had to work, and they were not insured. As a result, all citizens who lacked or lost access to a white man's wage risked falling into a second track of state and federal support, one that quickly accrued the negative connotations we now associate with the word "welfare." Second-track programs like Aid to Dependent Children (later reformulated as Aid to Families with Dependent Children) preserved the maternalist legacy of direct state oversight in the domestic sphere, and helped to keep alive the thoroughly sentimental idea that poor people are poor because their homes are bad.

In 1909, when Teddy Roosevelt vowed "to help the mother, so that she can keep her own home and keep the child in it," he signaled the welfare priorities of a vanguard elite. By the time Franklin Roosevelt presided over the making of the New Deal, the government's hand in helping mothers had lodged itself at the core of a welfare paradigm that standardized domestic norms for white people across the nation, severely compromised the domestic lives of people of color, and transformed the nature of government itself. Writers of domestic fiction engaged this history from the start. In the modern American domestic novel, family members learn to negotiate the terms of their domestic destinies with charity workers, social workers, home economics teachers, nutrition experts, juvenile and family court judges, detention center and reform school officials, public health workers, and welfare agents. In the process, the genre's traditional emphasis on domestic and psychic interiority is supplemented, and in some cases replaced, by a rival focus on the domestic sphere's lateral extension outward in new cooperation or contest with the state. At the level of form, sentimental conventions that had long dominated the narration of American domestic life become a target of politically charged ambivalence, revision, and revolt. Modern writers frequently invoke the discourses of socialist, consumer, and avant-garde revolution in their fraught encounter with the domestic sphere. Most pose antithetical relationships between these revolutionary discourses and maternalist templates of sentimental domesticity. But the maternalist tradition actually bore a complex and ambiguous relationship to the goals of revolutionary socialism and to the consumer revolution in manners and morals. And it became an important conduit for incorporating elements of both revolutionary paradigms into the welfare state the US now possesses.

After the 1917 revolution in Russia, socialist ideas about revolutionizing family life ceased to be merely speculative. In 1918, Soviet lawmakers passed a new Family Code, which granted greater autonomy to women, liberalized divorce and alimony laws, and abolished adoption and the category of illegitimacy. A 1920 law made the Soviet Union the first country in the world to offer women unrestricted legal access to abortion, and the establishment of public day care centers and collective kitchens in major cities by the early 1920s partially fulfilled the state's promise to socialize women's traditional household duties. In the Red scares near the end of World War I, conservative groups in the US made the Soviet "nationalisation of women" a standard feature of anti-Red propaganda (Calverton 1931: 214), and identified maternalist reform networks as living proof of socialist infiltration in the highest ranks of government. Though maternalists themselves routinely denied such accusations, their opponents' arguments proved to be quite powerful. Anticommunist groups won the 1929 repeal of the Sheppard-Towner Act, scuttled early efforts to pass federal child labor legislation, and doused maternalists' hopes to make universal health coverage part of the New Deal. As we will see, proletarian fiction of the 1930s identified the maternalist reform legacy as a pivotal site for asking just how socialist government intervention in the family really was. In a decade when Soviet family policy was itself shifting sharply to the right, leftist writers in the US held up the domestic lives of both black and white working-class families as a key measure for assessing the quality and reach of social justice in the New Deal.

The maternalist reform tradition also drew the state into early and lasting engagement with the revolution in manners and morals. In his 1931 discussion on the topic, Frederick Lewis Allen identifies women's suffrage and professional gains, the flapper look, and the popularization of Freud as forces of a moral revolution which found its "principal remaining forces" in "prohibition, the automobile, the confession and sex magazines, and the movies" (Allen 1931/1986: 99). But subsequent historians have traced the roots of this revolution to much earlier campaigns of the 1890s to liberalize divorce laws (Halem 1980: 42, 47–8) and to the related ideal of "companionate marriage," a childless form of trial marriage grounded in legal access to birth control and no-alimony divorce. First promoted by Judge Ben Lindsey of the Denver Juvenile and Family Court, the ideal of companionate marriage emerged directly from maternalist reform initiatives among the urban immigrant poor. The larger arc of maternalist reform helped to reconcile this liberal ideal of trial marriage with a more permanent model of marriage and family life centered on consumption. Home economics courses in the public schools infused young women's understanding of marriage and motherhood with a set of liberalized consumer expectations characterized by a uniform preference for store-bought over homegrown and homemade goods, a new faith in brand names and the endorsements of experts, and a heightened regard for fashion, efficiency, convenience, and cleanliness. In the 1920s, as home economists branched out to jobs in the corporate sector, state- and market-based promotions of domestic consumption became increasingly hard to distinguish from one another.

Carried into the New Deal, state-backed consumer pedagogies – still directed largely at whites – helped to lay the groundwork for the Keynesian turn in New Deal economic policy. With this turn, the federal government began to understand its own spending programs, geared at increasing aggregate consumer demand, as the necessary engine of national economic growth. The fact that postwar consumer spending centered on the nuclear family was not inevitable. Decades of coordinated instruction – state and market – went into that development. Federal involvement in the housing market, greatly augmented by the terms of the 1944 GI Bill, cast it in stone. The government's two-track housing policy heightened the "stimulus to inequality" which historian Linda Gordon associates with New Deal social legislation as a whole (Gordon 1994: 302). This policy, which endorsed and intensified existing patterns of residential segregation, facilitated white veterans' path to suburban home ownership while confining large numbers of African Americans to underfunded public housing projects and substandard rentals in decaying city neighborhoods. Here as elsewhere, the New

Deal welfare state translated collective demands for social security into an overtly racialized order of selective and detached domestic security. Its programs stigmatized and sidelined the socialist vision that had formed one important strand of the maternalist legacy. At the same time, New Deal programs fully endorsed a second, pro-market vision of liberalized home consumption that marked maternalists' successful reconciliation of the revolution in manners and morals with an older paradigm of sentimental domesticity.

Literary Responses

At the beginning of this historical trajectory, in the early days of the maternalist reform movement, political and literary vanguards within the white middle class located themselves on either side of a cultural divide that would strongly affect the subsequent development of modern American literature. As historian Theda Skocpol has argued, maternalists called on well-known conventions of sentimental and sensationalist fiction to frame their demands for new forms of social provision and protection. Denied access to the formal political process, they turned to media campaigns, directed largely at women readers, to create popular support for their demands; in these campaigns, the figure of the poor but virtuous mother, unable to care for her own children, became a catalyst of social change. But before these campaigns got underway, members of the literary elite launched their own campaign to discredit the literary conventions that maternalists would soon deploy to modernize the state. Historians point to W. D. Howells's role in lodging a critique of sentimental domesticity at the core of the realist novel's development in the US. Howells used his influential editorial positions at the *Atlantic Monthly* and *Harper's Magazine* in the 1870s and 1880s to argue that the sentimental novel offered "a distorted and misleading likeness" of white middle-class experience and had dared to "lie about life" (Howells 1891/1993: 327, 328). The task of the realist novelist, he declared, was to eschew false and dangerous forms of idealism and "portray men and women as they are" (p. 328). Howells's literary and critical practice, faulted in time for its own evasive gentility, institutionalized a dynamic through which successively severe refusals of the sentimental became the badge of the serious writer's resolve to tell the truth about modern society.

In two realist novels of the early twentieth century, Edith Wharton combines the antisentimental stance of the serious writer with strategic glances at the sentimental activism of Progressive reformers. In the collision that results, she forges a new kind of domestic fiction, one attuned to the heightened contradictions of an elite domestic culture in transition. Both *The House of Mirth* (1905) and *The Age of Innocence* (1920) offer chilling portraits of the marriage game in a period when, as one character puts it, "our legislation favours divorce [and] our social customs don't" (Wharton 1993: 110). Wharton's privileged heroines move in a world of exquisite leisure and consumption lightly stirred by talk of women's freedom and the plight of the poor. And yet their own lives remain sharply confined and radically insecure. In *The House of Mirth*, the beautiful, cultured, and moneyless Lily Bart tries to survive in wealthy circles long enough to marry a rich man. Her truest allies turn out to be two other women: Carry Fisher, a two-time divorcée drawn to "municipal reform" and "socialism" (Wharton 1980: 50, 51); and Gerty Farish, a nascent old maid who devotes herself to bettering the lives of poor working women. When unethical opponents falsely accuse Lily of sexual impropriety, she falls into the ranks of the working class upon whom she once idly bestowed her charity. Wharton's plot pairs Lily's fall and eventual suicide with a working-class woman's successful passage into marriage and motherhood, despite a disastrous sexual liaison in her youth. In the contrast between their fates, Wharton questions maternalist reformers' conviction that respectable society's superior moral code protects women in its fold and provides the necessary templates for redeeming an immoral culture of poverty.

In *The Age of Innocence*, Wharton sustains her critique of bourgeois sexual and social mores. The lovely Ellen Olenska cultivates bohemian connections with the likes of "Dr. Agathon Carver, founder of the Valley of Love Community" and visionary proponent of "the Direct Contact" (1993: 157, 158). She also wants to divorce an abusive husband. Ellen's rebellious desire, wrapped up in women's larger demands for "the same freedom of experience" (p. 46) routinely granted to white men, both attracts and repulses Newland Archer, engaged to her placid cousin. In the end, Newland plays it safe. He counsels Ellen to forgo divorce for the sake of the family, and becomes an impeccable family man himself. He also becomes a minor figure in the Progressive reform movement, devoting himself to such projects as "starting the first school for crippled children [and] reorganising the Museum of Art" (pp. 346–7). Newland Archer deflects the moral courage required to challenge his circle's own domestic norms into perfectly respectable efforts to lift up other people's lives, and hence becomes a witness, rather than a participant, in the struggle to create a more liberalized, middle-class, culture of heterosexual intimacy and desire. In this novel, as in *The House of Mirth*, Wharton uses Progressive reform initiatives as an ironic backdrop to highlight inequities and injustices within an elite domestic culture ill-suited to serve as a model of ideal community for the nation as a whole.

In *Quicksand* (1928) and *Passing* (1929), Wharton's younger contemporary Nella Larsen develops a similar set of themes on the other side of the color line. Like Lily and Ellen, Larsen's heroines Helga Crane and Clare Bellew are beautiful, cultured, and disposable; they, too, fall against ironic backdrops of welfare reform. In the black community, largely denied access to early government welfare programs, women played a leading role in setting up private welfare networks and institutions, and they figured prominently in the related work of racial uplift. In *Quicksand*, Helga works in a variety of uplift occupations, from her early job as a teacher to her later job as an employee for "a new Negro insurance company" started with private funds (Larsen 1986: 41). The man she loves, Dr Anderson, starts out the novel as principal at the segregated Southern school where Helga works as a teacher, but later moves to New

York to become "a welfare worker" at a "big manufacturing concern, which gave employment to hundreds of Negro men" (p. 52). Similarly, the plot of *Passing* turns on the disastrous consequences of Clare Bellew's appearance at a charity dance for "the Negro Welfare League" organized by her friend Irene Redfield (Larsen 1986: 197): as Irene busies herself with her responsibilities, her husband falls in love with Clare. In both novels, the sharpened sexual and consumer yearnings of Helga Crane and Clare Bellow clash with the maternalist paradigm central to the project of racial uplift. For Helga, this clash leads to frustration, anger, and flight. Following an impulsive marriage to a Southern preacher, she passes into the fold of rural black Southerners whose lives she had once tried to ameliorate. There, the grinding conditions of poverty and repeated pregnancy mock the maternal ideal. In contrast, Irene Redfield gladly organizes her whole life around the idea that "we mothers are all responsible for the security and happiness of our children" (p. 197). But her concern for the security of her children – and her race – serves as a cover for a desire to control other people and deny them their freedom. Clare explodes this cover at the charity dance, and Irene eventually kills her friend in order to keep what she has. In Larsen's work, which portrays a world where "everything must be paid for" (p. 169), the price of domestic security runs high.

For Wharton and Larsen, the new landscape of welfare reform throws fundamental social contradictions into bold relief: class privilege does not bring women security, and the domestic ideal, far from constituting a superior model of human relation, serves as a front for boundless self-interest, moral cowardice, and material complacency. Other domestic novels from the 1920s give welfare reform a still more central place in the plot. In her 1921 novel *The Girls*, the popular writer Edna Ferber weaves together the stories of three single women, born to successive generations of the same Chicago family. The middle woman, Lottie Payson, begins working as a volunteer with the first woman judge of "the new girls' court" (Ferber 1921: 86). There, she rescues Jennie Kromek, the sister of her own sister's maid, from "a detention home or a Girls' Refuge" (p. 200) by becoming her guardian. Lottie's association with the sexually rebellious daughter of immigrant parents ends up serving as the vehicle of her own transformation. Through contact with Jennie, Lottie gains the courage to defy her own mother and goes to France as a war nurse. She has an affair with a soldier, and returns home to raise her baby out of wedlock. Ferber here inverts the standard story of the middle-class woman who rescues the wayward girl about to be lost to the darker side of the revolution in manners and morals. In *The Girls*, the wayward girl simultaneously rescues and "revolutionizes" Lottie, reshaping her notion of the maternal ideal until it is roomy enough to affirm women's economic and sexual autonomy, freedom of movement, and taste for foreign adventure.

In telling Lottie's story, Ferber deploys overtly sentimental conventions to rewrite the sentimental rescue plots of maternalist reformers. A similar – and similarly unorthodox – investment in the sentimental characterizes the domestic fiction of Anzia Yezierska. In *Salome of the Tenements* (1923) and *Arrogant Beggar* (1927),

Yezierska blasts reform efforts aimed at turning immigrant women into better home-makers and domestic servants. In *Salome of the Tenements*, Sonya Vrunsky condemns the settlement house movement for teaching malnourished people to make cake "without milk, without butter, without eggs" (Yezierska 1995: 135). She'd prefer to turn settlement houses into "marriage centers . . . where live East Side girls like me can catch on to men higher up" (p. 83). In contrast, Adele Lindner, the orphaned heroine of *Arrogant Beggar*, initially embraces the prospect of her own reform when she's given the chance to live in a home for working girls like the one Gerty Farish supports in *The House of Mirth*. Ecstatic that she has finally found "a *real home*" (Yezierska 1996: 34) and "*an understanding* friend, with the power to help me" (p. 35), Adele learns otherwise when her benefactors enroll her in a domestic science program designed to train her as a servant. Not only are her new "friends" prepared to restrict her freedom and reject her love; they also cheat her of her wages. Even the highborn male reformers who fall for Sonya and Adele are only "playing with poverty" (1995: 139). To find true love and true generosity these women must return to the Jewish ghetto. Sonya leaves an uptown marriage for an immigrant fashion designer and a dress shop for working girls dedicated to "beauty that is not for profit": "In the midst of the ready-mades of Grand Street, a shop of the beautiful – that's to be my settlement!" (p. 178). Adele achieves "that home feeling in the heart" (p. 117) when she starts a bohemian coffee shop dedicated to the memory of the impoverished old woman who took her in when she fled more powerful friends. The coffee house introduces Adele to her husband, a brilliant composer, and supplies the money to bring the old woman's granddaughter to America. Like Ferber, Yezierska folds ideals associated with the revolution in manners and morals into the maternalist project of immigrant uplift. Rejecting domestic pedagogies that teach working-class women to know their place, she instead makes new – and newly egalitarian – possibilities of consumption, business initiative, and sexual pleasure integral to the working girl's sentimental rehabilitation.

Ferber and Yezierska's novels suggest the ways in which sentimental domestic fiction continued to provide an important forum for social engagement, protest, and visionary prognosis even after the Eastern literary establishment discredited its con-ventions. Claudia Tate (1992) has argued that African-American writers were among those who embraced sentimental domestic fiction as a valid literary and political medium in the late nineteenth and early twentieth century. As the new century wore on, middle-class activists made sentimental domestic fiction a crucial part of nation-wide campaigns to pass a federal antilynching bill. These campaigns, which came to a head in the early 1920s and again during the New Deal, constituted the major effort on the part of national black organizations to win a role in shaping federal welfare policy. Ultimately unsuccessful, they help to measure just how fully African Ameri-cans were excluded from state-building efforts committed to securing the home lives of whites. Angelina Weld Grimké and Walter F. White both stress the horrific ironies of this exclusion in their fiction. Where Yezierska protests an immigrant woman's vocational tracking into domestic science, Grimké creates African-American heroines who embrace domestic science but cannot practice it. In the unpublished story "The Handicapped," Jocelyn Jessups fails to get a domestic science job in the North "although there was plenty of demand for teachers in that line" (Grimké 1996: 430). Forced South in her search for work, she waits under "a Jim Crow tree" (p. 428) at the train station only to discover that the tree has been used to lynch a woman who accused a white man of sexual assault. In the 1916 play *Rachel*, the heroine, also trained but not employable in domestic science, learns that her own father and older brother were lynched; shattered by the discovery, she decides that the only way she can protect her children in America is not to have them. Grimké uses her heroines' deep investment in domesticity to explode the standard account of lynching. Where many whites accepted the idea that lynchings were a justifiable response to black men's assaults on white women and white homes, Grimké identifies the white male rapist and lyncher as the real destroyer of homes, and questions the justice of a social order that would train African-American women to prepare for domestic lives they will never be safe to enjoy.

Walter White takes a similar approach in his 1924 novel, *The Fire in the Flint*. In this novel, three siblings – a doctor, a lawyer, and a teacher – work to ameliorate the lives of black people in their small Georgian community. At the urging of his fiancée, the doctor decides to start a share-croppers' co-operative society like the ones that served as "the backbone of the movement to get rid of the Czar in Russia": "If the Russian peasants, who certainly weren't as educated as the Negro in America, had made a success of the idea, the Negro in the South ought to do it. By Jove, they could do it!" (White 1969: 144). But local whites put down their revolutionary efforts, raping the doctor's sister and then lynching both brothers with impunity. White investigated lynchings for the National Association for the Advancement of Colored People (NAACP) in the late 1910s and early 1920s. Executive secretary of the organization by the early 1930s, he spearheaded the failed effort to make a federal antilynching bill part of Roosevelt's New Deal. The plot of his novel echoes the findings of his investigative reporting, which identified lynching as a weapon of economic and political domination. In *The Fire in the Flint*, white people's sexual and murderous aggression destroys a black family whose commitment to radical paradigms of African-American self-help constitutes the true offense against white rule. Like Grimké, White uses sentimental conventions to underline the ways in which a selective order of domestic security, actively and passively backed by the state, aggravated the oppression and terrorization of black families denied access to the fold.

With the onset of the Great Depression, the Communist Party joined established reform organizations like the NAACP in the fight against lynching and the struggle for racial justice. Massive unemployment, frequent evictions, hunger and male desertion also shifted Party members' attention to aspects of the class struggle occurring outside the workplace and helped to identify the domestic sphere as a necessary site of radical political intervention. One strand of the proletarian fiction movement, which gained strength in the early 1930s, reflected this new focus. Paula Rabinowitz has identified numerous writers of the 1930s and 1940s who wrote domestic novels that explore the impact of maternalist and New Deal social welfare programs on the lives of poor Americans. An early contributor to this genre, Fielding Burke compares various models of social welfare in her novel *Call Home the Heart* (1932), based on the Gastonia mill strike of 1929. In the first part of the novel, Burke's heroine, Ishma, runs up against the pious moralizing of "county relief," the false benevolence of a privately funded hospital, and the removal tactics of "the welfare department" of the local mill (Burke 1983: 217, 240, 320). When the mill workers strike, the strike committee gives Ishma the job of organizing the distribution of food to the workers' children. Empowered by her success in this work, she goes on to execute the daring rescue of the black union leader, Butch Wells, from the hands of a lynch mob. The vision animating Ishma's struggles – a multiracial workers' society that will "provide for old age, and . . . give our children a chance" (p. 346) – is explicitly socialist in nature. In Burke's portrayal, as in White's depiction of a sharecroppers' co-operative society, the workers themselves organize to enact this vision. But as the 1930s proceeded, the focus on poor people's ability to repossess the means to feed and protect themselves gave way to a focus on the ways in which government relief programs were enacting new forms of dispossession among communities already stripped to the bone.

Caroline Slade called on her own experience as a social worker connected with a New York Children's Court to write a series of novels indicting New Deal social services to the poor. As Paula Rabinowitz (1999) has argued, these novels portray the "corrosive effect" of welfare "on the family, its band-aid solutions to structural unemployment, and its nightmarish bureaucracy" (p. 117). In *Sterile Sun* (1936), Slade faults social workers and the juvenile court system for pushing poor women into prostitution rather than providing viable alternatives to it. Two of Slade's characters have lost their mothers and one loses her children through court judgments that declare their homes unfit. But the alternatives to these unfit homes – foster care, orphan asylums, homes for the feeble-minded, and juvenile and adult reformatories – subject the women to forms of labor exploitation, sexual attack, and psychological abuse that amply prepare them for the sex trade. Only one character blames her own mother for her troubles; alienated from the other women and eager to gain admittance to the respectable society that condemns her, this character provides an ironic measure of just how misleading and destructive modern explanations of social deviance had become. In her 1940 novel *The Triumph of Willie Pond*, Slade uses the theme of female prostitution as the opening wedge to a wider critique of the New Deal. The adolescent daughter, Mary Pond, starts earning money for sex in a defiant attempt to save her family from the pinched and humiliating provisions of the local welfare agencies. After her disappearance, the Pond family struggles to survive the contradictions of a multilayered – local, state, and federal – welfare system committed by turns to breaking up their "unfit home" (Slade 1940: 185) and to helping them back on their feet. Government funds bring the tubercular father, Willie Pond, back to health. But when he discovers that his wife and children will receive better benefits without him, he decides to end his life. Willie's suicide gives a twist to the New Deal assumption that the father should serve as his family's sole provider: for the Ponds, the state ethos that promotes a sentimental model of family life also destroys it.

Meridel Le Sueur's novel *The Girl*, completed in 1939 and revised for publication in 1978, offers a particularly stinging indictment of the welfare state's role in the lives of poor white women. In this novel, New Deal relief agencies jeopardize rather than protect the maternal power of the women they serve. Welfare agents relegate Le Sueur's unnamed heroine and her older female friends to a condemned apartment building, vilify their sexual conduct, and prescribe nutritious foods they can't afford to buy. In a reference to state involvement in eugenics, the girl's social worker covertly recommends "sterilization after her baby is born" (1990: 114), and her friend Clara, a prostitute, receives state-ordered "electric shock treatments" (p. 119). A Communist organizer secures the two women's release from state institutions, but fails to secure the "milk and iron pills" (p. 130) that would save Clara's life and nourish the girl's unborn child. In the novel's conclusion, sharpened by Le Sueur's feminist revisions in the 1970s, the women on relief conduct a public march to protest Clara's unnecessary death and then deliver the girl's first child, another girl, in an act of maternal solidarity directed against the state.

Two powerful naturalist novels of the 1940s examine the New Deal's impact on poor black families. In Richard Wright's *Native Son* (1940), Bigger Thomas feels "in his heart some obscure need to be at home with people" (1966: 255), but he can never "achieve that feeling of at-home-ness" (p. 365) in a world where the state supports two different domestic agendas for poor and rich, black and white. The structure of Wright's story reflects this social structure: Bigger inhabits a domestic novel split between two domestic spaces that never meet – except through him. The mass media and the state govern the terms through which Bigger experiences this division. At the beginning of the novel, Bigger watches a movie before reporting for a new job. In the movie, a "Communist" revolutionary throws a bomb into a nightclub where a married white socialite dances to "a swing band" with her lover (pp. 33, 35). In the job, set up through a Chicago relief agency, Bigger agrees to work as a chauffeur for the wealthy Dalton family. Taking this domestic service job will potentially allow Bigger's family to escape the wretched segregated housing they rent from Mr Dalton's real estate company, while refusing it will cut off their government food stipend (p. 16). As the novel's lynching plot unfolds in the post-Depression urban North, Wright exposes the larger structures of violence that lie behind Mr Dalton's state-mediated philanthropy. But he also exposes the inadequacy of existing paradigms of consumer and socialist revolution, aired in the movie, through which Mr Dalton's daughter and her boyfriend experience their own love of black people. When Bigger kills Mary Dalton and his girlfriend, Bessie Mears, city and state authorities use a language of home to justify aggression against the entire black community. For "the protection of our society, our homes and our loved ones" (p. 372), they conduct "blanket" searches of "every Negro home," round up "several hundred negroes resembling Bigger Thomas," and incite the dismissal of "several hundred" black workers (p. 229). In this raw exposure of state racism, Wright indicts a New Deal administration that supported red-lining and racial covenants in the housing market, upheld gender and racial hierarchies in the labor market, failed to insure the domestic service jobs that African Americans were routinely forced to take, and refused to support the passage of a federal antilynching bill.

In *Native Son*, Wright makes a young black man's experience paradigmatic for African Americans as a whole. In her own naturalist domestic novel, *The Street* (1946), Ann Petry extends Wright's critique of the welfare state while challenging his gender bias. Like Bigger Thomas, Lutie Johnson views racial oppression in domestic terms. In her world, discriminatory housing and labor markets crowd people together in segregated neighborhoods where women never stop working, men stand idle, and children must fend for themselves: like clockwork, these markets break up marriages and destroy families while exploiting black women's power to mother. In the course of the novel, Lutie performs exceptional work as a mother raising foster children for the state and raising a child for a wealthy white couple in Connecticut. But such work jeopardizes rather than secures her ability to sustain her marriage, pay a mortgage, and care for her own child at home. When Lutie and her son, Bub, move to Harlem, the combined struggle to fight her way up the occupation ladder and to avoid the predatory advances of both white and black men ends in defeat. In a rewriting of Bigger's rape and murder of Bessie Mears, Lutie kills a man who tries to rape her when she seeks his help in getting her son out of juvenile detention. The novel ends as Lutie flees to Chicago and Bub awaits transport to a "reform school" (Petry 1985: 430) like the one from which Bigger has emerged in *Native Son*. For Lutie, mean urban streets are both "the North's lynch mobs" – "the method the big cities used to keep Negroes in their place" (p. 323) – and the "mother and father [who] trained your kid for you" (p. 407). As the space between those two social institutions disappears, Lutie and her son are lost.

In the first half of the twentieth century, writers moved between – and often wove together – sentimental, realist, and naturalist strategies of representation in creating their domestic fiction. They also forged vivid accounts of modern American domestic experience using the more opaque strategies of stream of consciousness, narrative discontinuity, and verbal complexity associated with literary modernism. Early critical accounts of modernism stressed the movement's rejection of sentimental literary conventions along with many of the forms of bourgeois realism. These accounts also claimed that the modernist writer's preoccupation with formal experiment eclipsed an engagement with history central to other genres of the novel. More recent approaches allow us to see how a refusal of sentimental culture necessarily drew the modernist writer into a deep engagement with history, one that left its traces on even the most formally innovative texts. A fascination with family history and the domestic sphere pervades the work of one of modernism's most eminent writers, William Faulkner. While he makes only scattered references to the new agents and institutions of welfare reform, the larger political discourse of maternalism shapes core features of his narratives. Faulkner has been widely praised for his antisentimental portrayals of family life, but in truth his plots closely conform to the sentimental patterns of moral and civic judgment currently being taken up by the state. The idea that faulty or absent mothering lies behind all forms of social deviancy animates the storylines of *Sanctuary* (1931) and *Light in August* (1932). In the first novel, Popeye, a rapist and murderer eventually executed for a crime he did not commit, was "already a kind of day pupil at an institution" (1958: 243) by the time he was five, and was soon thereafter "arrested and sent to a home for incorrigible children" because he liked to slaughter pets (p. 244). Diagnosed as feeble-minded and sexually abnormal, he was nevertheless released after five years as "cured" (p. 244). Here, Faulkner mocks modern institutions of social rehabilitation for their hubris, but he also confirms the sentimental notion that criminal natures spring from unfit homes: Popeye's father, "a professional strikebreaker" (p. 239), is long gone; his mother is a syphilitic "invalid" (p. 244); and "his grandmother burned the house down" (p. 244). In *Light in August* Joe Christmas spends his childhood in an orphan asylum and foster care. When he is five, a toothpaste-wielding dietitian, trained in the latest teachings of domestic science, labels him as black to protect the secret of her own sexual adventuring. This labeling inserts him into the lynching script that eventually kills him.

If Faulkner's criminals go wrong because they lack adequate maternal care, so does just about everyone else. Bad mothers stand at the center of two of his most formally innovative works, both of which are domestic novels: *As I Lay Dying* (1930) and *The Sound and the Fury* (1929). In these novels, state institutions await two honest sons, Darl Bundren and Benjy Compson. Darl burns down the barn sheltering his mother's coffin so he won't have to listen to her rotting body betray the "secret" of her infidelity "in little trickling bursts [and] murmurous bubbling" (1990a: 212); he gets committed for insanity. Benjy, a mentally retarded child already sterilized by the state, will be put in an institution for the feeble-minded when his wayward sister, Caddy, and the aging family servant, Dilsey Gibson, can no longer protect him. Caddy herself is an aristocratic version of the juvenile delinquent: "beautiful" (1956: 413) and "doomed" (p. 412), she tries to be the mother she never had, but loses claim to that status when a hasty marriage and divorce publicize her own sexual misdeeds. Faulkner complicates the social message of his novel when he assigns Caddy a nobility of spirit that makes her morally superior to her judges. The respectable but decidedly ignoble Mrs Compson passes judgment on her daughter's unfitness as a mother but refuses to condemn herself on the same charge: as a result, Caddy's daughter, Quentin, grows up even more motherless than Caddy herself. Here, as elsewhere, Faulkner manages to have it both ways: disdaining maternalist paradigms of domestic rectitude as crass and hypocritical, he nevertheless retains the emphasis on the all-determining quality of a mother's care that gave these paradigms their distinctive political and historical force.

A number of other modernist writers in the US joined Faulkner in making the domestic sphere a locus of major aesthetic experiment. Like Faulkner himself, these writers were drawn to avant-garde movements in Europe that had identified home and family life as a privileged site of aesthetic contest, transgression, and upheaval. A manifesto in the June 1929 issue of *transition* formally announced the "Revolution of the Word" that had been transforming literary practice on two continents since World War I. Signers of the manifesto declared a "revolution in the English language," and argued that "we are not concerned with the propagation of sociological ideas, except to emancipate the creative elements from the present ideology" (Boyle et al. 1929: 11, 13). In doing so, they called attention to the role of language in shoring up – or tearing down – the belief and power structures of a given society. This urge to revolutionize language grew out of the larger avant-garde project to use art to transform everyday life. Avant-garde groups shared with proponents of socialist revolution and the revolution in manners and morals a conviction that the leading institutions of bourgeois society needed to be dismantled. Sentimental definitions of women's roles had made the home, and particularly the wife and mother, primary guardians of bourgeois morality, culture and the arts. Consequently, attacks on the home, and on sentimental culture more generally, became integral parts of a campaign to create a new ethos of living.

Avant-garde groups called on one of the oldest revolutionary discourses in Europe – the medieval peasant discourse of carnival – to stage their assault on the status quo. The discourse of carnival features a grotesque aesthetic that mocks and degrades ideal forms, bringing what is high low and placing the low on high. The Italian Futurists signaled their attachment to this aesthetic when they called the bourgeois family, commonly considered a fount of virtue and good taste, a "grotesque squeeze of souls and nerves" composed of "One victim, two victims, three martyrs, one slaughter, one total madness, a tyrant who is losing his power" (Marinetti 1972: 76, 77). For the Dadaists, good taste itself was the enemy; they declared that "Every product of disgust capable of becoming a negation of the family is Dada" (Tzara 1988: 81). The French Surrealists viewed the bourgeois family, newly embraced by the state, as an enemy of "love and true emotions" (Breton et al. 1927: 160). In a manifesto entitled "Hands Off Love" which appeared in English translation in the September 1927 issue of *transition*, they protested the state's involvement in the marital affairs of their beloved Charlie Chaplin, dragged into a US divorce court on charges of immorality by a "housewife with her brats backed up by the figure of the constable, the savings-bank" (p. 163). Buoyed by the revolutionary Family Code of 1918, avant-garde groups in Russia worked to create a *novyi byt* or new everyday life in which the bourgeois family would have no part. Innovators in theatre and film reached back to the old peasant discourse of carnival to generate the terms of the first entirely proletarian national culture. Even dress design, household furniture, and body language had to change if workers were to free themselves of the debilitating attitudes of the past.

US modernists, who kept abreast of these developments in the numerous little magazines of the period, created a new genre of grotesque domestic fiction to stage their own unruly encounters with contemporary home and family life. In working with the grotesque aesthetic, these writers continued to privilege the vertical upheavals of bottom over top traditionally associated with carnival and revolution. But they also chose to activate a second, horizontal, axis of grotesque inversion in order to make a new transfusion or confusion between inside and outside central to their representations of the domestic sphere. This move allowed writers to engage maternalist reformers' own extension of women's domestic roles into public life and the subsequent reintroduction of new, state- and market-sponsored, domestic pedagogies into the private sphere. As they shifted attention away from domestic and psychic interiors to battles being waged on the border between the home, the market, and the state, modernists registered contemporary struggles over domesticity in the form of the novel itself. Faulkner may offer an oblique registration of this shift in *As I Lay Dying*, where the maternal secrets of Addie Bundren gain scandalous exposure as her rotting corpse parades through public streets (Faulkner 1990a: 212). Other writers working in the genre of grotesque domestic fiction engaged the mother's new career in public life more directly.

In two modernist works of the 1920s, *Cane* (1923) and *Ryder* (1928), Jean Toomer and Djuna Barnes turn to the topics of lynching and patriarchal tyranny to question the efficacy of maternalist campaigns to reform the domestic sphere. In her autobiographical novel, set three decades in the past, Barnes narrates the story of the Ryder family, committed to the maverick domestic principles of polygamy, promiscuity, idleness, and freethinking. Throughout the novel, Wendell Ryder and his elderly mother, Sophia, must beat modern-day reformers at their own game if they are to preserve a space for practicing Wendell's "noble philosophy in the home" (1990: 168). Because Wendell does not want to work, Sophia poses as a sweet old widow in order to collect a mother's pension from various wealthy businessmen and politicians. Because Wendell wants to educate his children at home, school authorities bring him up on charges of truancy, but he successfully avoids prosecution by calling attention to hidden pockets of corruption on school property. Yet the freedom Wendell wins does not extend to his wives or children, more dominated than liberated by his heady vision of himself. By the end of the novel, Wendell and Sophia conspire with welfare officials to sacrifice the weakest members of the family to federal law. When a social worker arrives at the doorstep complaining about Wendell's two wives, he decides to save himself by throwing the legitimate wife, Amelia, and her five children onto the street. Adequately protected neither within their home nor beyond it, Amelia and her children become the victims of all domestic reform programs implemented on their behalf.

In the fiction and poetry that make up his experimental collection, *Cane*, Jean Toomer rejects sentimental activism as an adequate strategy for combating modern rituals of white supremacy. He follows other black middle-class writers of the 1920s in equating the practice of lynching with a systemic assault on African-American families and homes. But where Angelina Grimké and Walter White rest their appeals for federal intervention on storylines that feature African-American characters committed to upholding sentimental domestic standards violated by white attackers, Toomer disputes the maternalist paradigms on which such storylines depend. For

Toomer, sexual repression and racist oppression are twin by-products of a dominant culture of domestic rectitude that must itself be overturned. In surrealist adaptations of the lynching plot, he transforms the rising bodies of the raped black woman and the lynched black man into symbols of aesthetic and cultural revolution. And he turns to the new music and dance forms of the urban black working class, central to the contemporary revolution in manners and morals, to stage African Americans' triumph over their oppressors. The dangling bodies of the dead – "dark purple ripened plums, / Squeezed, and bursting in the pine-wood air" – contain the "seed" of "a singing tree" (1975: 12) whose roots and branches spread through the streets, alleyways, and theatre aisles of the urban North. Outside the home on dance floors, stage sets, and chorus lines, Toomer locates the means both to remember and to overcome the nation's long history of racist terrorism and the domestic ideologies that keep that history in place.

In her unfinished novel *Yonnondio* (1974), Tillie Olsen joins Jean Toomer in breaking with domestic ideologies embraced by fellow activists on the Left. Olsen originally wrote the novel between 1932 and 1936 when she was an active member of the Communist Party. Like other proletarian novels of the period, *Yonnondio* sharply criticizes the welfare state's domestic programs for the poor. But its criticisms are more far-reaching. A novel like *The Triumph of Willie Pond* faults government programs for ultimately betraying clients' desire to break out of the cycle of poverty. But Slade's novel does nothing to contest the deeper maternalist premise that only a "nice family" (1940: 257) like Willie Pond's deserves state support in the first place. Social workers employed by "the Board of Child Welfare" (p. 269) initially justify a higher stipend for the Ponds because they know that Willie Pond is at heart "a quiet, gentle little man" who "doesn't ask for much" (p. 262). His older children are "wonderful" and the babies are "just darling" (pp. 262, 263); even "dirty, shiftless" Mrs Pond, if "given a chance, . . . would do very well" (pp. 261, 262). In contrast, Olsen tackles taboo subjects of domestic abuse, marital rape and mental illness, experienced across the class hierarchy, in her grotesque account of white working-class domesticity. And she suggests that existing welfare policies heighten rather than alleviate the violence that haunts her characters' lives. In one scene, Anna Holbrook visits a public health clinic on the advice of a doctor who thinks "they ought to sterilize the whole lot of them after the second kid" (Olsen 1989: 77). There, she picks up the subliminal government message "You Make Your Children Sick" (p. 88). Anna understands that the state will blame her – and take away her power to mother – if her children ever fail or falter. But her desperate efforts to mother her children the government way drive her to abuse. She threatens to beat her children "to a pulp" (p. 67) if they do badly in school, and berates her six-year-old daughter with the icy aphorisms of a social worker: "Dont you know if you cant keep your own things out of a mess, you'll never keep your life out of one?" (pp. 86–7). In Olsen's novel, state-backed paradigms of sentimental domesticity become grotesque when they are imposed on poor families who lack the material resources and real social chances that make such paradigms work for other classes. At a time when many Communists embraced a Popular Front ideology that championed the deep-hearted mothers of the working class, Olsen presents the care work of that same population as an acutely alienated site of class and gender oppression.

In Nathanael West's New Deal Hollywood novel, *The Day of the Locust* (1939), consumer revolution replaces the socialist revolution that Olsen had originally planned to stage among California's farm workers in the unwritten conclusion of *Yonnondio*. West uses his novel to imagine the explosive collision of two forces of consumer demand that rocked California in the 1930s. The first grew out of the revolution in manners and morals long associated with the Hollywood lifestyle. The second grew out of the popular movement led by a since-forgotten Los Angeles visionary, Francis Townsend, who demanded that the government pay retired people monthly checks in order to jump-start the national economy (Martin 1984: 307–8). Townsend's movement pressured Franklin Roosevelt to expand significantly the old-age insurance programs we now identify with the success of the New Deal. But in West's novel, Homer Simpson, a retired Midwestern bookkeeper living on his savings, falls victim to a manipulative young woman, Faye Greener, who spends his money on her own dreams of becoming a Hollywood star. When Faye moves in with Homer, he agrees to play the role of the chaste and self-sacrificing wife and mother so that she can devote all her time to reckless consumption. This grotesque inversion of sentimental gender roles spells the end of society as we know it. A life of enforced domestic leisure, impulse buying, and continually deferred sexual gratification does not bring happiness to either men or women; instead, it generates a "boredom [that] becomes more and more terrible" (West 1983: 192) in both Homer and Faye. After she ransacks the house and runs away, he joins a crowd of rioting consumers at the novel's end; their pent-up rage promises to touch off "civil war" (p. 107). Like Faulkner, West cultivates a rigorously antisentimental style that masks his sustained investment in women's traditional domestic roles. In the very years that the Roosevelt administration embraced a Keynesian model of national recovery tied to liberalized norms of domestic consumption, West portrays the white female consumer as an agent of social dissolution whose powers of upheaval overwhelm even the best-laid plans of domestic containment.

The last grotesque domestic novel I will consider, Flannery O'Connor's *Wise Blood* (1952), follows the Keynesian turn in New Deal policy into the postwar period. Like West, O'Connor questions how well a new paradigm of government-backed domestic consumption satisfies calls for a better society. And she foregrounds the fact that many citizens of the welfare state never get to experience domestic affluence and security at all. In her novel, Hazel Motes, freshly released from the army, journeys to the Southern city of Taulkinham after discovering that his home town in rural Tennessee no longer exists. His fate inscribes the effects of New Deal spending projects in the South, which consolidated land in the hands of agribusiness and pushed many of the rural poor into the cities. Unlike the other displaced rural whites he meets in Taulkinham, Haze has some money: shrapnel wounds entitle him to lifelong support under the 1944 Servicemen's Readjustment Act, better known as the GI Bill.

Haunted by "a longing for home" (1994: 24), Haze enters the postwar city looking for "a private place to go to" (p. 30). Eventually, his government checks allow him to buy the woman, the car, the solitude, and the leisure associated with this ideal. Two teenagers long to join Haze in his good fortune. Enoch Emery, separated from his father by a "Welfare woman" (p. 46) when he was a child, and Sabbath Hawks, sent to "a detention home" after Haze's landlady kicks her out (p. 216), experience only the downside of the welfare state. But Haze is not about to repair their luck. For him, the promise of home coincides with lapsed responsibility for his fellow humans. As he says about his car, what really matters is having "a place to be that I can always get away in" (p. 115). Only when he loses his car on the outskirts of the city and returns to its center does he accept a superior, Christian, meaning of home both large and just enough to embrace even the most unfit family members on equal terms.

In *Wise Blood*, O'Connor condemns a sentimental tradition of welfare reform for breaking with the vision of charity out of which it originally sprang: charity, understood by Christians to be a form of communal participation in God's universal love for humankind, had become its own opposite – a selective guarantee of isolated and detached security. Other novelists were more sympathetic to the secularizing tendencies in US society that so appalled O'Connor. But many shared her conviction that a modern sentimental discourse of social amelioration, rooted in maternalist campaigns to protect the home, had failed the very people its proponents initially aimed to help. Whether they located themselves within the sentimental tradition or against it, modern American domestic fiction writers engaged a fully contemporary process of social transformation that went far beyond the home. At the same time, they recognized a social and political valence to aesthetic form that gave literary writers an important role to play in the fight for a just, equitable, and secure society. As I've sought to demonstrate throughout this essay, contests waged within the modern domestic novel over the form and reach of sentimental culture were inseparable from larger struggles of the period to imagine and attain a better way of life for all Americans.

In his 1940 essay "How Bigger Was Born," Richard Wright famously rejects the sentimental strategies that inform his 1938 story collection, *Uncle Tom's Children*. Glowing reviews of that collection revealed to him "that I had written a book which even bankers' daughters could read and weep over and feel good about. I swore to myself that if I ever wrote another book, no one would weep over it; that it would be so hard and deep that they would have to face it without the consolation of tears" (Wright 1966: xxvii). When we read his remarks in their restored historical context, it becomes clear that Wright is so keen to separate himself from sentimental strategies of social activism not because they're no longer effective by the early 1940s – giving rise to little more than tears – but because they authorize forms of social change that he opposes: the aesthetic refusal of the sentimental in *Native Son* goes hand in hand with Wright's account of the New Deal's devastating impact on black families and black homes. Today, the political leaders of the US have given a new twist to the sentimental history of the country's welfare state. Members of both major parties are prepared to cut back social spending on the poor and some wish to dismantle social insurance programs for the middle class as well. The state's investment in "family values" has never been stronger; but now politicians claim that liberal government intervention threatens the family values that it in fact disseminated, and that state downsizing will give the nation back the strong and happy families that flourished unsupported in olden times. Modern works of domestic fiction tell a different story. This fiction teaches us to ask where our "family values" really come from and how long we've had them. And it pushes us to consider how well such values have served the diverse and often divided populations of the US. If we take these questions seriously, we might find that "even bankers' daughters" have a word to add.

References and Further Reading

Allen, Frederick Lewis. (1931/1986). *Only Yesterday and Since Yesterday: A Popular History of the 20's and 30's.* New York: Bonanza Books.

Barnes, Djuna. (1990) *Ryder*, afterword Paul West. Elmwood Park, IL: Dalkey Archive Press.

Berlage, Nancy K. (1998). The establishment of an applied science: Home economists, science, and reform at Cornell University, 1870–1930. In Helene Silverberg (ed.), *Gender and American Social Science: The Formative Years* (pp. 185–231). Princeton, NJ: Princeton University Press.

Boyle, Kay et al. (1929). Revolution of the word. *transition: An International Quarterly for Creative Experiment* 16–17: 11, 13.

Breton, André et al. (1927). Hands off love. *transition: An International Quarterly for Creative Experiment* 6: 155–65.

Burke, Fielding. (1983). *Call Home the Heart: A Novel of the Thirties*, intro. Alice Kessler-Harris and Paul Lauter. Old Westbury, NY: The Feminist Press.

Calhoun, Arthur W. (1919). *Since the Civil War. A Social History of the American Family from Colonial Times to the Present*, vol. 3. Cleveland, OH: Arthur H. Clark.

Calverton, V. F. (1931). *The Bankruptcy of Marriage.* London: John Hamilton, Ltd.

Cott, Nancy F. (1995). Giving character to our whole civil polity: Marriage and the public order in the late nineteenth century. In Linda K. Kerber, Alice Kessler-Harris, and Kathryn Kish Sklar (eds), *U.S. History as Women's History:* *New Feminist Essays* (pp. 107–21). Chapel Hill: University of North Carolina Press.

Donzelot, Jacques. (1997). *The Policing of Families*, trans. Robert Hurley, foreword Gilles Deleuze. Baltimore: Johns Hopkins University Press.

Ehrenreich, John H. (1985). *The Altruistic Imagination: A History of Social Work and Social Policy in the United States.* Ithaca, NY: Cornell University Press.

Faulkner, William. (1956). *The Sound and the Fury.* New York: Modern Library.

Faulkner, William. (1958). *Sanctuary.* New York: Random House.

Faulkner, William. (1990a). *As I Lay Dying.* New York: Vintage International.

Faulkner, William. (1990b). *Light in August.* New York: Vintage International.

Ferber, Edna. (1921). *The Girls.* Garden City, NY: Doubleday, Page.

Francis, Elizabeth. (2002). *The Secret Treachery of Words: Feminism and Modernism in America.* Minneapolis: University of Minnesota Press.

Goldman, Wendy Z. (1993). *Women, the State and Revolution: Soviet Family Policy and Social Life, 1917–1936.* New York: Cambridge University Press.

Gordon, Linda. (1994). *Pitied But Not Entitled: Single Mothers and the History of Welfare, 1890–1935.* New York: The Free Press.

Gosse, Van. (1991). "To organize in every neighborhood": The gender politics of American communists between the wars. *Radical History Review* 50: 109–41.

Grant, Julia. (1997). Modernizing mothers: Home economics and the parent education movement, 1920–1945. In Sarah Stage and Virginia B. Vincenti (eds), *Rethinking Home Economics: Women and the History of a Profession* (pp. 55–74). Ithaca, NY: Cornell University Press.

Grimké, Angelina Weld. (1996). The handicapped. In Lorraine Elena Roses and Ruth Elizabeth Randolph (eds), *Harlem's Glory: Black Women Writing, 1900–1950* (pp. 423–34). Cambridge, MA: Harvard University Press.

Grimké, Angelina Weld. (1998). *Rachel.* In Kathy A. Perkins and Judith L. Stephens (eds), *Strange Fruit: Plays on Lynching by American Women* (pp. 27–78). Bloomington: Indiana University Press.

Halem, Lynne Carol. (1980). *Divorce Reform: Changing Legal and Social Perspectives.* New York: The Free Press.

Howells, W. D. (1891/1993). *Criticism and Fiction.* In *Selected Literary Criticism: 1886–1897*, Vol. 2, ed. Donald Pizer. Bloomington: Indiana University Press.

King, Desmond. (1995). *Separate and Unequal: Black Americans and the US Federal Government.* Oxford: Clarendon Press.

Kline, Wendy. (2001). *Building a Better Race: Gender, Sexuality, and Eugenics from the Turn of the Century to the Baby Boom.* Berkeley: University of California Press.

Larsen, Nella. (1986). *Quicksand and Passing*, ed. Deborah E. McDowell. American Women Writers Series. New Brunswick, NJ: Rutgers University Press.

Lemons, J. Stanley. (1973). *The Woman Citizen: Social Feminism in the 1920s.* Urbana: University of Illinois Press.

Le Sueur, Meridel. (1990). *The Girl*, revised edn. Albuquerque, NM: West End Press.

Lindsey, Judge Ben B. and Wainwright Evans. (1927/1972). *The Companionate Marriage*, intro. Charles Larsen. New York: Arno Press.

Marinetti, F. T. (1972). Marriage and the family. In *Selected Writings*, ed. R. W. Flint (pp. 76–9). London: Secker and Warburg.

Martin, Jay. (1984). *Nathanael West: The Art of His Life.* New York: Carroll and Graf.

McCann, Sean. (2000). *Gumshoe America: Hard-Boiled Crime Fiction and the Rise and Fall of New Deal Liberalism.* Durham, NC: Duke University Press.

Michel, Sonya. (1993). The limits of maternalism: Policies toward American wage-earning mothers during the progressive era. In Seth Koven and Sonya Michel (eds), *Mothers of a New World: Maternalist Politics and the Origins of Welfare States* (pp. 277–320). New York: Routledge.

Mink, Gwendolyn. (1995). *The Wages of Motherhood: Inequality in the Welfare State, 1917–1942.* Ithaca, NY: Cornell University Press.

O'Connor, Flannery. (1994). *Wise Blood.* New York: Noonday.

Olsen, Tillie. (1989). *Yonnondio: From the Thirties.* New York: Dell Publishing.

Petry, Ann. (1985). *The Street.* Boston: Beacon Press.

Platt, Anthony M. (1977). *The Child Savers: The Invention of Delinquency*, 2nd edn. Chicago: University of Chicago Press.

Rabinowitz, Paula. (1991). *Labor and Desire: Women's Revolutionary Fiction in Depression America.* Chapel Hill: The University of North Carolina Press.

Rabinowitz, Paula. (1999). "Not just the facts, ma'am": Detectives, social workers, and child prostitution in Caroline Slade's novels. *LEGACY* 16, 1: 106–19.

Rabinowitz, Paula. (2001). Domestic labor: Film noir, proletarian literature, and black women's fiction. *Modern Fiction Studies* 47, 1: 229–54.

Salem, Dorothy. (1990). *To Better Our World: Black Women in Organized Reform, 1890–1920.* Brooklyn, NY: Carlson Publishing.

Skocpol, Theda and John Ikenberry. (1983). The political formation of the American welfare state in historical and comparative perspective. In Richard F. Tomasson (ed.), *The Welfare State: 1883–1983* (pp. 87–148). Greenwich, CT: JAI Press.

Skocpol, Theda. (1992). *Protecting Soldiers and Mothers: The Political Origins of Social Policy in the United States.* Cambridge, MA: The Belknap Press.

Slade, Caroline. (1936). *Sterile Sun.* New York: Macaulay.

Slade, Caroline. (1940). *The Triumph of Willie Pond.* New York: The Vanguard Press.

Szalay, Michael. (2000). *New Deal Modernism: American Literature and the Invention of the Welfare State.* Durham, NC: Duke University Press.

Tate, Claudia. (1992). *Domestic Allegories of Political Desire: The Black Heroine's Text at the Turn of the Century.* New York: Oxford University Press.

Toomer, Jean. (1975). *Cane*, intro. Darwin T. Turner. New York: Liveright.

Tzara, Tristan. (1988). Dada manifesto, 1918. In Robert Motherwell (ed.), *The Dada Painters and Poets: An Anthology*, 2nd edn. (pp. 76–82). Cambridge, MA: The Belknap Press.

Weiss, Nancy J. (1983). *Farewell to the Party of Lincoln: Black Politics in the Age of FDR.* Princeton, NJ: Princeton University Press.

Wenocur, Stanley and Michael Reisch. (1989). *From Charity to Enterprise: The Development of American Social Work in a Market Economy.* Urbana: University of Illinois Press.

West, Nathanael. (1983). *The Day of the Locust*, intro. Alfred Kazin. New York: Signet.

Wharton, Edith. (1980). *The House of Mirth*, afterword Louis Auchincloss. New York: Signet.

Wharton, Edith. (1993). *The Age of Innocence*, intro. R. W. B. Lewis. New York: Collier.

White, Walter F. (1969). *The Fire in the Flint.* New York: Negro Universities Press.

Wright, Richard. (1966). *Native Son*, afterword John Reilly. New York: Perennial.

Yezierska, Anzia. (1995). *Salome of the Tenements*, intro. Gay Wilentz. Urbana: University of Illinois Press.

Yezierska, Anzia. (1996). *Arrogant Beggar*, intro. Katherine Stubbs. Durham, NC: Duke University Press.

Zangrando, Robert L. (1980). *The NAACP Crusade Against Lynching, 1909–1950.* Philadelphia: Temple University Press.

20
Lesbian Fiction 1900–1950

Heather Love

The concept of lesbian fiction is shadowed by a persistent cultural understanding of lesbianism itself as fictional – as secondary, derivative, or "hard to believe." In contrast to male same-sex relations, generally understood as unlawful or morally outrageous, female same-sex relations have tended to pass under the radar, beneath the notice of the law and off the grid of cultural intelligibility. Because of women's lack of social and economic power, and because there have been few frameworks for imagining active female sexual desire, the idea of two women together was, for most of the history of Western representation, unthinkable. The ignorance surrounding female same-sex relations has sometimes meant that women's desires for each other were protected from criminalization and stigma. At the same time, the "impossibility" of female same-sex desire has made it difficult to forge a lesbian literary tradition: one confronts not only the problem of the "empty archive" (so characterized by Duberman, Vicinus, and Chauncy 1989), but also the lingering notion that there is something fictitious or improbable about women's relations with each other. This sense of impossibility has persisted long past the moment of the emergence of a public and visible lesbian community in the United States. Modern public homosexual identity emerged in the US at the end of the nineteenth century and developed quickly in the first few decades of the twentieth century. But it is not until after the Stonewall Riots of 1969 that one can point to a self-conscious tradition of writing that is by, for, and about self-identified lesbians (see Zimmerman 1990, Faderman 1981, 1991).

The other significant framework for understanding women's intimacies before the twentieth century is the tradition of romantic friendship. This culturally accepted form of intense female bonds was dominant in the eighteenth and particularly in the nineteenth century; for middle-class women in a world defined by the separation of the sexes, female friendship was a mode of affective, romantic, and sometimes erotic intimacy that characterized life before and sometimes during marriage. While often marked by intense attachment, these relations were not understood as sexual or, except on rare occasions, as a threat to the social order, and they were generally accepted as a natural part of women's emotional lives (see Smith-Rosenberg 1975, Faderman 1981, Brooten 1996, Vicinus 2004, Kent 2003, Marcus 2007).

The modern notion of a political, public identity emerged in the late nineteenth century out of medical and scientific discourses. In the period that Michel Foucault has described as the moment of the invention of homosexuality, sexual and gender outsiders were categorized as deviant in relation to a newly idealized norm of white European heterosexuality. Out of this "specification of individuals" the homosexual, or the sexual invert, emerged as a recognizable social type. Homosexuality emerged in the work of doctors and sexologists including Karl Ulrichs, Richard Krafft-Ebing, Havelock Ellis, and Edward Carpenter as an illness: no longer understood primarily as a sin or a crime, homosexuality in this literature is a medical condition that is racialized and linked with other forms of deviance including criminality and mental illness. While the bulk of sexological research and publication in the period was conducted in Europe, new medical knowledge about homosexuality did circulate in the US soon after, where it was taken up in the context of the sexual and racial anxieties of Jim Crow (see Somerville 2000: 19. For other work on the intersection of racial discourse and the sexological discourse of inversion at the turn of the century see Duggan 2000, Stokes 2001, Carter 2007).

Out of this discourse emerged the figure of the female "invert", a cross-gendered being whose mannish desires drew her to sexual experiences with other women. The social danger of this figure was amplified by the increasing economic and social power of American women at the turn of the century. Intimate friendships between women were no longer understood merely as a way-station on an inevitable path toward marriage; in the increasingly common form of the "Boston marriage," women shared resources and domestic life, choosing to forsake heterosexual married life altogether. Though few women in such arrangements were understood as sexual inverts specifically before the turn of the twentieth century, the influence of legal and medical discourses made such partnerships increasingly suspect. While these late nineteenth- and early twentieth-century discourses of female homosexuality were stigmatizing, they constituted the lesbian as a figure with social presence and reality. Over the next several decades, as the visibility of this figure increased, so did the costs of social exposure: lesbians began to suffer the legal sanction and social violence that had been the portion of male homosexuality.

The early twentieth century also witnessed the beginning of a tradition of lesbian literature. Until that point, representations of lesbianism were rare. One can point to a few key moments: the lyrics of Sappho, Renaissance friendship, decadent and aestheticist writing on the cruel antics of *les femmes damnées*, and a long and fairly robust tradition of pornography (on Sappho's reception and her place in a history of lesbian representation, see DeJean 1987; on representations of female homoeroticism in the Renaissance, see Traub 2002; for an account of male-authored lesbian representation in nineteenth- and early twentieth-century France, see Ladenson 1999). Despite their importance to twentieth-century lesbians in search of ancestors, these scattered moments of lesbian representation did not add up to a lesbian literary tradition or to a social or sexual identity. Terry Castle remarks on the difficulty of identifying lesbian literature before the emergence of a self-conscious lesbian identity in the introduction to her encyclopedic anthology *The Literature of Lesbianism*. She notes "the aggravating ambiguities of the term *lesbian* itself: its psychic and behavioral imprecision, its obscure historical reach, its annoying failure to refer unequivocally, precisely at those moments when one wants most that it should" (Castle 2003: 5). What are we looking for when we look for lesbian literature? Should we look for representations of female eroticism, or intimacy, or love? Or rather to evidence of the kind of social exclusion that has been so important in the making of modern homosexual identity? Does it matter if a representation is authored by a man or a woman, or if the representation is positive or negative? If we are not interested in lesbian representation but in lesbian authorship, then who would count as a lesbian author?

While the increasingly public presence of homosexuality in the early twentieth century makes the identification of lesbian literature somewhat less bewildering, it is hardly straightforward. The term lesbian or female invert was taken up very unevenly in the period. The claiming of Willa Cather as a lesbian author has been extremely contentious, for instance. In her youth, Cather dressed in boys' clothes and signed her name "William Cather, M.D."; she developed passionate attachments to female friends in high school and college and, in her letters, showed an awareness of the stigmatization of such relationships (see O'Brien 1984, Lindemann 1999). But Cather was extremely ambivalent about public expressions of homosexual feeling or identity as is clear from her comments on Oscar Wilde after his 1895 trial (Cather 1966: 390–3). Though she never married and her primary relationships were with women, she rejected modern homosexuality and modeled her relationships on the female friendships of the nineteenth century. We cannot look to Cather's fiction for representations of lesbianism either. With the exception of her early story "Tommy the Unsentimental" about the heroics of a small-town tomboy, Cather's fiction is relatively unconcerned with relations between women and turns its attention to the intensities of male–female and male–male relations (see Sedgwick 1993, Butler 1993, Goldberg 2001, Lindemann 1999, Herring 2004). Even Djuna Barnes, who was involved in the lesbian subculture of 1920s Paris and whose 1936 experimental novel *Nightwood* is central to the canon of lesbian modernism, cannot be unequivocally identified as a lesbian novelist. Regarding her decade-long relationship with Thelma Wood, Barnes famously remarked, "I am not a lesbian. I just loved Thelma." Does that mean that *Nightwood* is not a lesbian novel?

Such examples only begin to suggest the difficulty of pinning down the term "lesbian" in tracing the tradition of the modern lesbian novel. The term "novel" itself presents no small difficulty in this context. During the period, explicitly lesbian literature was only beginning to take shape, and very rarely did it take the shape of a straightforward realist novel. We can point to a range of different kinds of narratives of female same-sex desire: challenging works of modernist experimentation (*Nightwood*, H.D.'s *HERmione*, Jane Bowles's *Two Serious Ladies*), psychological novels (Gertrude Stein's *Q.E.D.*, Nella Larsen's *Passing*), as well as proto-pulp treatments of lesbian subculture (*Diana: A Strange Autobiography*, Dorothy Baker's *Trio*). However, it is really only with the influence of Radclyffe Hall's 1928 novel *The Well of Loneliness* – banned first in England and soon after in the United States – that a recognizable template for the lesbian novel emerges. Hall's novel is framed by an introductory note from the sexologist Havelock Ellis, and her mannish heroine Stephen Gordon considers herself a congenital invert. The novel's plot of social rejection, exile, triangulation and jealousy, romantic suffering, and the ultimate sacrifice of a heterosexual love object by the inverted protagonist sets the terms for decades of novels to come. Through the 1930s and 1940s and beyond, this novel circulated illicitly among women as a sign of lesbianism; iconic fragments of its plot reappear in the novels of the period (for an important challenge to the view that *The Well of Loneliness* is *the* prototypical lesbian novel, see Prosser 1998).

In her influential 1981 article, "Zero Degree Deviancy," Catharine Stimpson discusses the ways that all lesbian novels have had to respond to the "violent yoking of homosexuality and deviancy" in the modern period. She identifies two main responses: "the dying fall, a narrative of damnation, of the lesbian's suffering as a lonely outcast attracted to a psychological lower caste; and the enabling escape, a narrative of the reversal of such descending trajectories, of the lesbian's rebellion against social stigma and contempt" (Stimpson 1981: 364). For Stimpson, as for many other critics, narratives of lesbian damnation are more closely linked with realist psychological and social novels like *The Well of Loneliness*, whereas narratives of escape more often take the form of modernist experiments with the form of the novel.

Implicit in such an argument is not only the idea that sexual and gender marginality is linked to linguistic and formal experimentation, but also the suggestion that traditional narrative form is so closely identified with heterosexuality as to make the lesbian novel something of an oxymoron. In *Are Girls Necessary?*, Julie Abraham (1996) argues that lesbianism cannot be represented within the form of the realist novel. She reads the specific generic features of the twentieth-century lesbian novel – "tortuous romances of fragile female couples" (p. 1), the prevalence of erotic triangles (p. 5), and the prevalence of female characters who identify as men in their desires – as signs that lesbian desire cannot be signified in the novel without reference to heterosexuality. In this context, Abraham writes, a lesbian union "must be represented . . . as the rejection of heterosexuality, if it is to have either social meaning or literary form" (p. 11). In a reading of the lesbian in the American novel tradition, Valerie Rohy cites Judith Roof's argument that lesbianism is a "representational impossibility: it can be there, but it cannot be seen in its own terms because such terms do not exist" (Rohy 2000: 3). Rohy goes on to argue that lesbianism constitutes an epistemological problem within the American novel, and that its appearance inevitably disrupts the closure of narrative realism.

The emergence of lesbianism as a social identity and of a tradition of lesbian fiction in the early twentieth century did not entirely dispel the sense of unreality associated with this form of desire. Instead, the confluence of French decadent representations of the lesbian, the legacy of the female friendship tradition, and new medical and psychoanalytic discourses led to an image of the lesbian as a strangely composite creature: part woman, part man; part reality, part fantasy; part cipher, part "case history"; part idealized friend, part femme fatale; a haunting fiction and a social fact. Even as the lesbian emerges in the early twentieth century as a new social actor, lesbianism itself remains elusive, bound up with traditions that mark it as fantastic or impossible. The modern American lesbian novel bears the traces both of the real and the chimerical in its attempt to come to terms with this hybrid figure.

The turn from the nineteenth century to the twentieth century has often been understood as a turn from a pastoral model of female friendship to a modern, public, and stigmatized version of female homosexuality. While the invention of homosexuality and the increasing popularity of Freud's writing cast suspicion on relations that had, until that point, been seen as socially unthreatening or, in some instances, complementary to heterosexual marriage and family, this historical narrative overlooks the tension, difficulty, and ambivalence that characterize many representations of female friendship (see Marcus's 1991 rereading of female friendship as playing a crucial role in the reproduction of social relations and particularly marriage). Friendship, while generally understood as nonsexual, could nonetheless pose a problem when it was intense or exclusive; strong and enduring attachments between women not only posed a challenge to the primacy of heterosexual bonds but also were marked by the kinds of jealousy and ambivalence generally associated with erotic relationships. In her article "Romantic Friends or 'A Different Race of Creatures'?" Marylynne Diggs (1995) has traced the medical pathologization back to the mid and even the early nineteenth century. She argues that the explosion of sexological discourse in the 1890s intensified but did not invent the view of female same-sex desire as pathological, freakish, and a threat to normal married life. The turn of the century saw the collision of several contradictory frameworks for making sense of female intimacy: the romantic friendship tradition; the decadent, highly sexualized image of the lesbian imported from France; sexological discourses of gender inversion; contradictory understandings of the New Woman as at once sexless and hypersexual; and lesbianism as an emergent US subculture.

A key text for seeing the confluence of many of these different discourses is Henry James's *The Bostonians* (1886). In his notebooks from 1883, James expressed his intention to write a novel concerning "one of those friendships between women which are so common in New England" (James 1947: 47). However, James's novel does not confine itself to a representation of female friendship; rather, it draws on competing discourses including French literature and early sexological discourse to offer a mixed representation that anticipates the modern American lesbian novel (see Castle 1993). The book is set in the abolitionist community of Boston in the 1870s and it concerns the contest between Olive Chancellor, an idealistic, stubborn New England heiress, and Basil Ransom, her distant relation, a deeply conservative and down-at-the-heels Southern journalist, over the affections of the young and impressionable Verena Tarrant. Basil wants Verena for marriage; Olive wants to form a partnership with her to fight for the cause of women, although readers since Edmund Wilson have seen more to Olive's desire for friendship with Verena than devotion to the cause (see Wilson 1969, Jagose 2002).

James incorporates a number of understandings of female intimacy by representing each character's perspective on each other. For Olive, Verena appears to fulfill her deepest desire, which she frames in the language of romantic friendship: "she found here what she had been looking for so long – a friend of her own sex with whom she might have a union of soul" (James 2000: 63). Basil's perspective on Olive is informed not only by his misogyny and his passionate resentment toward the North, but also by new medical discourses on the single woman. For Basil, his relation is a "signal old maid": "There are women who are unmarried by accident, and others who are unmarried by option; but Olive Chancellor was unmarried by every implication of her being. She was a spinster as Shelley was a lyric poet, or as the month of August is sultry" (p. 16). In this framing of Olive as unmarriageable in her being, James offers a representation that draws on medical understandings of female same-sex desire as an ontological condition, a character trait that is graven on the mind and the body. Though we have less access to Verena's consciousness, we are privy to the final agonies of her decision between Olive and Basil. Verena reflects on her relationship with Olive – "a very peculiar thing, their friendship; it has elements which made it probably as complete as any (between women) that had ever existed" (p. 310) – and decides that it would be unbearable to sacrifice it.

While Verena invokes the limiting framework of female friendship, the stark choice that she faces between Olive and Basil raises the relation with Olive to the level of an exclusive marriage: the qualifying phrase "between women" in this moment subtracts very little from the vision of a complete (if peculiar) union between them. While Olive's love can be absorbed within the form of the Boston marriage – which remains a culturally legible and even valorized form of intimacy – Verena realizes the danger that a separation poses to Olive:

> The scene, at the end, would be something that she couldn't face; . . . she had not the right to blast the poor creature's whole future. She had a vision of these dreadful years; she knew that Olive would never get over the disappointment. It would touch her in the point where she felt everything most keenly; she would be incurably lonely and eternally humiliated. (James 2000: 301)

Before her final elopement with Basil, Verena imagines Olive's fate as an abandoned woman. She might also be telling the fate of the lesbian in the modern novel: a poor creature, cast out from the shelter of female friendship, her loneliness the sign both of her romantic exclusion and of the social exile that follows from the exposure of her impossible desire. This ending prefigures a plot that will be common in the modern lesbian novel: a woman torn in her love for a man and a woman ends up choosing to be with the man, leaving the committed lesbian alone, beyond the reach of heterosexuality and narrative itself (see Jagose 2002, particularly p. 59).

While no novel until Hall's *The Well of Loneliness* would offer such a full-blown plot of triangulation and sacrifice, *The Bostonians* is typical of late nineteenth-century fictions that represent female friendship traversed by disturbing currents of desire. Although the stories of regionalist author Mary E. Wilkins Freeman are often understood as classic representations of female romantic friendship, they offer evidence of awareness in the 1880s and 1890s of the dangers lurking in female friendship (see Diggs 1995). In Pauline E. Hopkins's romance of African-American uplift, *Contending Forces* (1900), her mixed-race heroine Sappho Clark is associated with female homosexuality through the connotations of her name and by her excessively close friendships with other women in the book. As Siobhan Somerville notes in her reading of the novel, Hopkins's depiction of these relations "oscillates between models of romantic friendship and lesbian pathology" (2000: 88). Kate Chopin's *The Awakening* (1899) offers another example of a book that explores female friendship and its attendant dangers, although Chopin's novel draws more on the French tradition of decadence to underline the questionable nature of Edna Pontellier's relation to the spinster pianist Mademoiselle Reisz.

The work of Sarah Orne Jewett has been understood, as has Freeman's, as a key site for the representation of female friendship. Jewett, who lived her later life with her companion Annie Fields, offers depictions of female friendship that are not marked by a sense of erotic danger or medical pathology. In Jewett's first novel, *A Country Doctor* (1884), the decision of a young woman to refuse marriage in order to pursue her career as a physician is treated with remarkable equanimity. Late in life, Jewett befriended Cather, and advised her to openly represent affection between women in her work, in a letter that has become famous for its apparent distance from the paranoia and suspicion surrounding female intimacy in the twentieth century. Despite her lack of engagement with the medical and psychological discourses that mark modern representations of female intimacy, Jewett's representations of female romantic friendship are notable for the sense of melancholy that infuses them – a melancholy that is hardly explained by a pastoral account of female friendship as a socially accepted and equitable form of intimacy.

In *Deephaven* (1877), Jewett treats the friendship between two women who spend a summer together in a small Maine coastal town. The intimacy between the narrator Helen and her friend Kate Lancaster is accepted and encouraged by both family and the inhabitants of Deephaven, but the relationship is still marked by doubt and a sense of vulnerability. Helen is intermittently anxious about Kate's attachment to her and the future of their friendship. The end of the summer looms over the summer idyll, and with it the possibility of marriage that will put an end to the kind of intimacy – the unscripted time – that they share.

Jewett treats the fragility of friendship most extensively in a scene early in the novel. The two girls are staying in the home of Kate's deceased maiden aunt, Miss Brandon; looking one day in a drawer in her bedroom, the two girls find a packet of letters tied with a ribbon and next to it a miniature with a lock of brown hair. Seeing that many of these are ship letters, Kate reflects that "she had often heard her mother wonder why her aunt had never cared to marry, for she had chances enough doubt-less . . . So there was a sailor lover after all, and perhaps he had been lost at sea and she faithfully kept the secret, never mourning outwardly" (Jewett 1994: 19). Leaving this packet of letters unread, the girls turn to examine the other contents of the desk and find

> letters from her girl friends written in the boarding-school vacations, and just after she finished school. Those in one of the smaller packages were charming; it must have been such a bright, nice girl who wrote them! They were very few, and were tied with black ribbon, and marked on the outside in girlish writing: "My dearest friend, Dolly McAllister, died September 3, 1809, aged eighteen." The ribbon had evidently been untied and the letters read many times . . . Poor Miss Katharine! it made us sad to look over these treasures of her girlhood. (1994: 19)

The juxtaposition of these two sets of letters, one imagined to be from a dead sailor and the other from a dead schoolfriend, draw a link between heterosexual romance and the same-sex affections of girlhood. Furthermore, these records of intimacy are marked both by secrecy and by a sense of loss. Refusing to draw a strict distinction between heterosexual and homosexual attachment, Jewett recasts spinsterhood as a form of intimacy constituted by mourning and unspoken attachment.

In her masterpiece *Country of the Pointed Firs* (1898), Jewett also considers a number of relations that are constituted by loss or absence, ultimately imagining a community of outsiders living at a distance from the linear temporality of the courtship plot. Narrated, like *Deephaven*, by a summer visitor, the novel offers a number of vignettes about the isolates – widows and widowers, spinsters, bachelors, foreigners, and the chronically heartbroken – who live in the coastal town of Dunnet Landing and its environs. The narrator's closest relation is with Mrs Todd, a widow whose nearest tie is with her elderly mother and her bachelor brother who live off the mainland on Green Island. The narrator is drawn particularly to islanders whose geographic isola-tion makes concrete the loneliness that is the subject of the novel. Particularly striking in this regard is the story of "poor Joanna" who died alone on Shell Heap Island. Like Miss Brandon, Joanna suffered an early heartbreak; as a result, she spends her entire life as a voluntary exile. Throughout the novel, the narrator meditates on her example: "There is something in the fact of a hermitage that cannot fail to touch the imagina-tion; the recluses are a sad kindred, but they are never commonplace. Mrs. Todd had truly said that Joanna was like one of the saints in the desert; the loneliness of sorrow will forever keep alive their sad succession" (Jewett 1995: 84). In this portrait of shared isolation, Jewett indicates the fragility of friendship in a world that does not recognize same-sex bonds as deep or lasting at the same time that she gestures toward a queer community of those who fall outside traditional narratives of marriage and biological reproduction (see Boone 1988).

In her brief novel *Q.E.D.*, Gertrude Stein offers a view of a world relatively untouched by the imperative to marriage and reproduction. Originally written in

1903, the novel was not published until after Stein's death, under the title *Things As They Are*. Like *The Bostonians*, it is structured by an erotic triangle, although it is remarkable for being almost without male characters. Realist in its form, the novel recasts a painful affair that began when Stein was studying medicine at Johns Hopkins. The story is narrated from the perspective of Adele, the character most closely linked to Stein, who is characterized by her attachment to everyday middle-class life. Desire emerges in the story as a problem that Adele has no idea how to solve. The novel opens on shipboard as Adele is making an Atlantic crossing with Sophie Neathe (based on Mabel Haynes) – whose thin, angular body betrays her New England origin – and the passionate and beautiful Helen Thomas (based on May Bookstaver). Stein's training in the field of psychology is evident in her presentation of these psychological types, whose characters are legible off their bodies, gestures, and faces; her familiarity with French literature emerges in her treatment of desire as an indulgence that is particularly available to women together. In the end, the conflicts between different characters or "types" results in a painful narrative stalemate.

Adele, who is initially determined in her cool rationality and announces herself glad that she was not born a woman (1990: 208), is drawn into sexual intrigue against her better judgment. In an argument with Helen over the value of passion, Adele takes on an avuncular, distant, and somewhat cranky tone:

> "Experience for the paltry purpose of having had it is to me both trivial and immoral. As for passion . . . you see I don't understand much about that. It has no reality for me except as two varieties, affectionate comradeship on the one hand and physical passion in greater or lesser complexity on the other and against the cultivation of that latter I have an almost puritanic horror and that includes an objection to the cultivation of it in any of its many disguised forms. I have a sort of notion that to be capable of anything more worth while one must have the power of idealising another and I don't seem to have any of that." (Stein 1990: 209)

In this juxtaposition of "affectionate comradeship" with physical passion, Adele pits a peculiarly American form of intimacy with a cultivation of the erotic that is marked as European. Torn between friendship and an eroticism characterized by secrecy and met with moral revulsion, lesbianism's only chance for redemption is through an idealization that Adele is far too puritanical and rational to indulge.

Still, Adele's attitude gradually changes once Helen gives her a taste – or what she calls a glimpse – of passion itself. While in Tangier and Granada, Adele slowly comes around to the idea that there may be some value in opening herself to this experience. As Jaime Hovey (1996) has argued, the setting of this transformation is important as Stein associates sexual passion with a racially marked otherness and with the seductive but vaguely sinister possibilities available to Americans abroad. While Adele is more and more drawn to Helen, the outburst of real passion between them ("a kiss that seemed to scale the very walls of chastity," p. 240) draws from her a reaction of disgust and effectively ends their intimacy. As Helen is more securely tied to Sophie, Adele withdraws into a frustrated depression, holding only on to her hope that she might some day "find a morality that can stand the wear and tear of real desire" (p. 236).

Stein transformed many elements of this novel for "Melanctha," one of the three narrative portraits in her more formally experimental 1908 book *Three Lives*. Like *Q.E.D.*, the novel begins with female friendship and moves to an account of an erotic triangle. Stein describes the relations between two African-American women, Melanctha Herbert and Rose Johnson, noting that they "like many of the twos with women were a curious pair to be such friends" (Stein 1990: 60). In this story, Adele's moral uprightness and calm steadiness are attributed to Doctor Jeff Campbell, whom the passionate Melanctha loves but with whom she cannot reach an accord. As Melanctha begins to "wander," seeking erotic experience, she draws apart from Jeff, and in the end even Rose – whom she had wanted "more than she had ever wanted all the others" (p. 166) – casts her off. Stein extends the associations of racially marked Europeans with excessive or aberrant sexuality in this tale of deviant African-American sexuality. Still, Stein seems to imagine a parallel between the complexity of female same-sex relations in *Q.E.D.* and the complexity of African-American sexuality in "Melanctha." Melanctha herself is represented throughout the novel as depressed and restless; the causes of her inner torment, though obscure, are located in areas that are both personal and social. Stein writes: "Sometimes the thought of how all her world was made, filled the complex, desiring Melanctha with despair. She wondered, often, how she could go on living when she was so blue" (p. 60).

What makes desire so complex in both accounts is, at least in part, the social conditions that surround it: the moral stigma on female homosexuality, the hypersexualization of black women, and the economic insecurity of the black family. But this link is also clearly internal and psychological for Stein. Turn-of-the-century understanding of both lesbian and African-American desire came out of a common intellectual heritage: the forging of a presumptively heterosexual, presumptively white, moderate and normal sexual identity out of the identification and medicalization of marginal sexualities. There is something inexplicable and excessive about the passion to which Helen introduces Adele; Melanctha too is tormented by desires that she cannot control or name. While both narratives offer generally sympathetic accounts of such inexplicable desires, they persist in the diagnostic mode and do not offer a way out. *Q.E.D.* ends with Adele sinking her head in her arms and declaring the situation a "dead-lock" (p. 262); "Melanctha" ends with its heroine's final isolation and death in "a home for poor consumptives" (p. 167).

The complexity and confusion of desire are emphasized in the series of unpublished experimental autobiographical novels that the imagist poet Hilda Doolittle (H. D.) wrote during the 1920s. While Stein was influenced by medical accounts of sexuality, H. D. was drawn to Freudian theories of desire and the unconscious (she later published an account of her analysis with Freud himself, *Tribute to Freud*, 1956). In the Madrigal cycle of novels – *HERmione, Bid Me to Live, Paint it Today*, and *Asphodel*, H. D. offers a fictionalized account of many of her early romantic entanglements: her brief engagement to Ezra Pound, her relationship with Frances Gregg, her move to Europe, her marriage to Richard Aldington, and the beginning of her lifelong relationship with the poet and heiress Bryher (born Annie Winifred Ellerman). *HERmione* focuses on an early moment in H. D.'s life just after she dropped out of Bryn Mawr and when she is living with her parents in the suburbs of Philadelphia. The central character Hermione Gart is drawn to the bohemian, aloof poet George Lowndes (Pound), but soon she breaks off her engagement, becomes involved with Rabb (Gregg), and leaves for Europe with her and her mother. The other novels take up the complexities of her affairs with men and women once she arrives.

While H. D.'s treatment of identity and desire is generally lyrical and opaque, her discussion of female same-sex relations is marked by a particularly tortuous rendering of reality. A typical passage leaves one in doubt of what, exactly, is the relation between Her and Fayne:

> Her face bent forward, face bent toward Her. A face bends towards me and a curtain opens. There is swish and swirl as of heavy parting curtains. Almost along the floor with its strip of carpet, almost across me I feel the fringe of some fantastic wine-coloured parting curtains. Curtains part as I look into the eyes of Fayne Rabb. "And I – I'll make you breathe my breathless statue." "Statue? You – you are the statue." Curtains fell, curtains parted, curtains filled the air with heavy swooping purple. Lips long since half kissed away. Curled lips long since half kissed away. In Roman gold. Long ere they coined in Roman gold your face – your face – your face – your face – your face – Faustine. (H. D. 1981: 163–4)

H. D.'s description offers an image of erotic doubling and subjective erasure that recalls decadent associations of lesbianism with narcissism and death. H. D. repeatedly invokes a line – "Curled lips, long since half kissed away" – taken from Algernon Charles Swinburne's poem "Faustine" that casts Fayne as a femme fatale while linking her to the classical world and to perverse desire ("Stray breaths of Sapphic song that blew / Through Mitylene / Shook the fierce quivering blood in you / By night, Faustine," pp. 117–20). Decadent imagery ("wine-coloured parting curtains") is invoked to describe an encounter with a female beloved as a ravishment of the senses. Yet there is a sense in which the appearance of Fayne presents an erotic mystery that cannot be named or solved. The ambiguity and the insistence of the prose ("your face – your face – your face") suggest that lesbian desire generates an opacity that challenges the order of realist representation.

In the case of Stein's *Q.E.D.* or H. D.'s Madrigal novels, the opacity of lesbian desire cannot be understood as an effect of censorship, for none of these texts were published while their authors were alive. Still, there has been a tendency in criticism of lesbian novels to read highly charged, ambiguous representations such as these as instances of "coded" desire. There is no doubt that the explicit depiction of lesbianism was excluded from early twentieth-century American literature both because of censorship and more diffuse social threats. Yet Julie Abraham criticizes the "repression hypothesis" because it "implies that there were other, more direct ways for saying what was being said, of writing 'about lesbianism,' that the writer avoided because of social pressure. It implies, moreover, that we know the forms lesbian writing would take were it not for social hostility" (Abraham 1996: 25). In arguing that there is not a stable, explicit lesbian meaning that can be accessed behind the screen of repression, Abraham points to the indeterminacy both of the category of the lesbian and of the literary. The ineffability of the lesbian topic is an effect of a relative paucity of representations of female same-sex relations, but also of a long tradition of understanding such relations as impossible or fantastic.

One of the most significant representations of female same-sex desire from the early twentieth century is not explicitly marked as lesbian at all. Nella Larsen's 1928 novel *Passing* takes place against the background of Harlem in the 1920s and is primarily concerned with the politics of passing and respectability. The novel was published the same year as Hall's hugely influential *The Well of Loneliness* and it is set in a moment of much greater explicitness about same-sex sexuality. In the wake of World War I, changing gender codes and new freedoms for women resulted in the burgeoning of lesbian subcultures in the US as well as in Britain, France, and Germany. Urban centers became a site for new freedoms and possibility. For black Americans, the massive migration to Northern cities opened the possibility for new social worlds and new forms of gender and sexual expression. Harlem in the 1920s was the site of social and artistic transformations and of a greater acceptance of nonnormative gender and sexual expression. In her 1994 biography, Thadious Davis documents Larsen's social connections to many gay and lesbian figures involved in the Harlem Renaissance. Still, desire remains thoroughly opaque in the novel. It was not until Deborah McDowell's 1986 essay on *Passing* in which she argued that it was a novel of same-sex desire passing as a novel of racial passing that scholars began to attend to the lesbian erotics of the text.

Though it traces a friendship between two women, the representation has little to do with the romantic friendship tradition since the relations between the protagonist Irene Redfield and Clare Kendry are so furtive and ambivalent from the start. Clare is a childhood friend of Irene's who has fallen out of touch, married a white man, and is passing for white. Irene sees Clare again for the first time while she is having tea on the rooftop of the Drayton Hotel in Chicago, but she does not recognize her. Irene, generally an upstanding and socially involved member of the black middle class, is temporarily passing in this scene in order to escape the heat of the summer streets. Irene's encounter with Clare is marked by mixed feelings of paranoia and desire, interest and fear.

Did that woman, could that woman, somehow know that here before her very eyes on the roof of the Drayton sat a Negro?

Absurd! Impossible! White people were so stupid about such things for all that they usually asserted that they were able to tell; and by the most ridiculous means, fingernails, palms of hands, shapes of ears, teeth, and other equally silly rot. They always took her for an Italian, a Spaniard, a Mexican, or a gipsy. Never, when she was alone, had they remotely seemed to suspect that she was a Negro. No, the woman sitting there staring at her couldn't possibly know.

Nevertheless, Irene felt, in turn, anger, scorn, and fear slide over her. It wasn't that she was ashamed of being a Negro, or even of having it declared. It was the idea of being ejected from any place, even in the polite and tactful way in which the Drayton would probably do it, that disturbed her.

But she looked, boldly this time, back into the eyes still frankly intent upon her. They did not seem to her hostile or resentful. Rather, Irene had the feeling that they were ready to smile if she would. Nonsense, of course. The feeling passed, and she turned away with the firm intention of keeping her gaze on the lake, the roofs of the buildings across the way, the sky, anywhere but on that annoying woman. Almost immediately, however, her eyes were back again. In the midst of her fog of uneasiness she had been seized by a desire to outstare the rude observer. Suppose the woman did know or suspect her race. She couldn't prove it. (Larsen 1986: 150)

In this bourgeois, segregated space above the city, Irene fears that she will be recognized as black, and the thought sends her mind reeling through a checklist of traits used for racial classification and identification. As she runs through the list, worrying over the gaze that the unknown woman turns on her, Irene stares back, bringing a similar scrutiny to bear on Clare's body. The gaze that passes between the two women is somewhere between a medical examination and an erotic blazon; Larsen explores the "takes one to know one" logic that structures the "closeted" experience of both homosexuals and blacks passing for white in the 1920s (Sedgwick 1990). The erotics of her description of racial characteristics also recalls the historical intertwining of sexological and racialist discourses at the turn of the century, as well as the scrutiny that black women, hypersexualized and objectified in the public eye, must bring to bear on both their racial and their gender and sexual self-presentation.

The rest of the novel narrates Irene's attempts to disentangle herself from Clare's dangerous double life; each time she turns away from her, however, she inevitably finds herself drawn back. This structure of repetition demonstrates Larsen's interest in Freudian psychology, particularly the concept of the "return of the repressed": the more Irene tries to deny her fascination with Clare, the stronger that fascination becomes. Larsen involves her reader in the dynamics of repression, focalizing the narrative through Irene, whose ambivalence and denial make her a classic example of an unreliable narrator. The dialectic of dismissal and return culminates in a final act of violence; Clare falls to her death out of an open window, and though it appears that Irene has pushed her, it is not clear because we only have Irene's account and Irene "never afterwards allowed herself to remember" (1986: 239).

Although the erotics of the relation between Irene and Clare are never made explicit in *Passing* – Irene ultimately persuades herself that Clare is having an affair with her husband Brian, and so routes her desire through a "safer" plot of female rivalry – the novel describes a moment of relative sexual freedom in the US. After the Depression, many of the liberties cultivated in the previous decade collapsed, and the possibilities for gay and lesbian community declined in the 1930s. Lesbian representation during the period bears the imprint of this constraint. Increasing popular knowledge about sexology and psychoanalysis meant that female same-sex desire was no longer as unknown or unmentionable as it had been in the past. However, the dominant mode of representing such relations was in novels of lesbian damnation, and many books from the period show the influence of that classic of damnation, *The Well of Loneliness*.[1]

The pseudonymous text *Diana: A Strange Autobiography* (1939) shows the influence of Hall's novel, even repeating key scenes from that novel.[2] Like *The Well*, *Diana* is prefaced by a statement from a man of science, the doctor and writer Victor Robinson (some have attributed the novel itself to Robinson, while others believe it was written by a woman under the pen name Diana Frederics). Robinson makes a claim for the scientific value of the novel in his preface ("I welcome any book which adds to the understanding of the lesbians in our midst," p. ix), and goes on to present lesbianism as a medical pathology: "That charming women should be lesbians is not a crime, it is simply a pity. It is not a question of ethics, but of endocrines" (p. ix). Diana Frederics offers a foreword to the memoir that casts herself not as an individual, but as a representative of her class: "I must write this book as if I were a person of importance. And, indeed, I can do that if I think of myself as a type rather than as an individual. As an individual I am quite without importance except to myself; as a type I am quite important, for I belong to the third sex."

Gale Wilhelm's 1935 novel *We Too Are Drifting* concerns the love between a committed lesbian and a "normal" woman. Unlike Wilhelm's later novel, *Torchlight to Valhalla* (1938), in which the main character rejects a marriage proposal from an eligible young man to find happiness with a beautiful young neighbor, the earlier novel repeats the tragic plot of lesbian exclusion from the heterosexual couple. The tone of this short novel is spare and melancholic; its title is taken from a 12-word poem that one of the main characters recites: "Poor little leaves, we too are drifting, someday it will be autumn." The haiku implicitly compares the female characters of the story to autumn leaves – haplessly blown by the wind and fated to fall. The main character Jan Morale is an artist haunted by a difficult past. She is involved in a messy and unhappy affair with Madeline when she meets and falls in love with the younger Victoria, who is engaged to be married. Jan is reluctant to take things any further with the naive Victoria, and once she does, she insists that it can be nothing more than a clandestine affair. Torn between her love for Jan and the expectations of her family and her fiancé, Victoria asks Jan, "What can we do about it?" " 'Do?' " Jan replies, "What's to be done about a fact like that? Nothing. We couldn't possibly do a thing to it, my dear. It's a Gibraltar" (Wilhelm 1984: 108). The idea of a sustainable, exclusive lesbian relationship is foreclosed here, so that one cannot grieve for it – one can only regret it.

The "Gibraltar" of heterosexual and familial demands not only means the ruin of the relationship between Jan and Victoria, but also results in Jan's exclusion from the "real" world: identified with the seductive but impossible realm of lesbian desire, she is cast out from the world of kinship, marriage, and public intimacy. In the final scene of the novel, Jan arrives at the San Francisco train station just in time to watch Victoria pull away in the train with her fiancé and her family.

> Jan saw Victoria in a crowd and stopped. It seemed strange that Victoria should have so many friends. Jan looked at them curiously. Looking at them she felt the taste of damp earth in her mouth and she didn't know why. The man and the boy beside Victoria were of course her father and Dan. She looked at Victoria's father and he was smiling and saying amusing things to a lot of young people. She didn't look at Dan. Dan and Jan. She hadn't thought of that before. It would be a simple thing to confuse the names on the tip of your tongue and say one when you meant the other. Victoria was smiling and looking very beautiful and looking at all the faces and beyond them, but she didn't see Jan.
>   At the last moment the men stood back and the girls swarmed around Victoria and kissed her carefully because of their mouths and hers and said, Good-bye, good-bye, good-bye! and Victoria smiled at them and at the porter and stepped up and waved and her eyes were looking everywhere. The train was moving. Jan stood with her hands in the pockets of her trench-coat and her fists pressed into her groins. The train was moving and Dan was with Victoria on the steps and their hands were waving and Victoria's eyes were looking everywhere, the train was moving and the shed was echoing with the sound of the train moving the voices of the girls saying, Good-bye, good-bye! (Wilhelm 1984: 116–17)

The scene offers a classic moment of the exclusion and abjection of the committed lesbian, who stands looking on at a joyful public ritual of heterosexual and familial intimacy. Jan is not only replaced by Dan in this scene, but her very existence is blotted out. Though she is looking everywhere, Victoria cannot see Jan, who is stranded in a sexual isolation so deep that it is compared to death ("she felt the taste of damp earth in her mouth"). Wilhelm underlines the distance between female friendship and lesbian intimacy: Jan is specifically alienated from a heterosexual community of women whose attachments are both general (they approach Victoria in a swarm) and dispassionate (their kisses are careful). The breezy good-byes of Victoria's female friends serve to underline the finality – the almost metaphysical quality – of Jan's separation from her lover and from this social world.

At the same time that so many novels were exploring the bleak isolation of lesbian existence, a handful of authors in the 1930s and 1940s explored the aesthetic and social possibilities of exile in an experimental mode. Djuna Barnes's *Nightwood* is a key text exploring alienation and dispossession among gender, sexual, and racial others in the modernist city. In his account of modernist narrative erotics, *Libidinal Currents*, Joseph Allen Boone writes of "*Nightwood*'s deliberately perverse depiction of an entire universe of outcasts banded in solidarity under the sign of inversion" (1998: 235). Boone sees in this community of exiles an early version of queer collectivity, of outcasts who "revel in their outlaw and pariah status, embracing their supposed 'damnation' and parading their abjection as a sign of divine election" (pp. 234–5). Barnes does not attempt to offer an affirmative portrait of same-sex desire to counter received notions of homosexual abjection or sin. Rather, she describes a disconcerting eroticism as the hallmark of same-sex desire, activating the dark energies of this impossible form of existence for aesthetic renewal.

Barnes's account of a doomed love affair between Nora Flood and the tormented Robin Vote invokes a whole history of decadent representations of homosexuality as well as the sexological concept of inversion and psychoanalytic accounts of unconscious desire. The wandering, somnambulist Robin is a point of convergence for these various discourses; as Barnes shows, her desirability is linked not only to her passivity and her fugitive status, but also to her embodiment of degraded but highly charged images of sexual and gender deviance. Seeking solace from the queer, alcoholic "amateur gynecologist" Dr Matthew O'Connor about her doomed love for Robin, the "girl who resembles a boy," Nora becomes the audience for his tribute to the invert.

> "Exactly," said the doctor. "You never loved anyone before, and you'll never love anyone again, as you love Robin. Very well – what is this love we have for the invert, boy or girl? It was they who were spoken of in every romance that we ever read. The girl lost, what is she but the Prince found? . . . We were impaled in our childhood upon them as they rode through our primers . . . They go far back in our lost distance where what we never had stands waiting; it was inevitable that we should have come upon them, for our miscalculated longing has created them. They are our answer to what our grandmothers were told love was, and what it never came to be; they, the living lie of our centuries." (Barnes 1937: 136–7)

Named by the doctor as the "living lie of our centuries," the sexual invert is a focal point for desires that are pervasive but also disavowed in the culture. Robin carries the unrealized dreams of the past in her body: she is an "impossible person" because she embodies the impossibility of desire in the culture as a whole. In this passage, O'Connor swerves between different registers: sexological, moral, literary critical, psychoanalytic, erotic, historical. The invert emerges at the crux of these different discourses, an object produced by unconscious longing and disappointment – the scapegoat for desires that can never be satisfied. (Rather than seeing such representations of lesbian damnation as mere reflections of negative stereotypes, several critics have understood the figure of the lesbian as a scapegoat for more general cultural negativity: see Rohy 2000, Jagose 2002, Edelman 2004.) Other novelists in the 1930s and 1940s joined Barnes in exploring the alienation of sexual and gender outsiders and in gesturing toward the possibility of a community of outsiders. While Carson McCullers' novels of loneliness and freakery rarely deal directly with female same-sex desire, she links desires for different forms of erotic and affective relations to a much broader range of social exile. (See especially *The Member of the Wedding*, 1946, in which McCullers describes the inchoate and doomed longings of the 12-year-old tomboy Frankie to be included in the marriage of her older brother and his fiancé.) Jane Bowles also identified imaginatively with a community of outsiders broadly defined, as is evident in the nickname she chose for herself: "Crippie, the kike dyke." As in

Nightwood, gender and sexual deviance are tied in Bowles's writing to exile, stigma, erotic suffering, wandering, and abjection; like Barnes, Bowles does not try to shake off these painful associations with female same-sex desire but rather embraces them in an aesthetic of negativity.

Bowles's 1943 novel *Two Serious Ladies* follows the fate of two women, Christina Goering, who begins as a wealthy woman who takes in a female companion but ends by pursuing her own abjection as a kept woman with a series of men, and Mrs Copperfield, whose lesbian desires cause her to wander from her husband. On a trip together in Panama, Mrs Copperfield is drawn to the prostitute Pacifica, and as a result she wanders further and further away from her husband. His letter asking her to return to him moves into a psychological register and warns against the danger of repetitious desire:

> I do not mean to be cruel but I shall write to you exactly what I consider to be your faults and I hope sincerely that what I have written will influence you. Like most people, you are not able to face more than one fear during your lifetime. You also spend your life fleeing from your first fear towards your first hope. Be careful that you do not, through your own wiliness, end up always in the same position in which you began. I do not advise you to spend your life surrounding yourself with those things which you term necessary to your existence, regardless of whether or not they are objectively interesting in themselves or even to your own particular intellect. I believe sincerely that only those men who reach the stage where it is possible for them to combat a second tragedy within themselves, and not the first over again, are worthy of being called mature. When you think someone is going ahead, make sure that he is not really standing still. In order to go ahead, you must leave things behind which most people are unwilling to do. Your first pain, you carry it with you through your whole life but you must not circle around it. You must give up the search for those symbols which only serve to hide its face from you. You will have the illusion that they are disparate and manifold but they are always the same. If you are only interested in a bearable life, perhaps this letter does not concern you. For God's sake, a ship leaving port is still a wonderful thing to see. (Bowles 1984: 110–11)

In her characteristically spare, ironic style, Bowles interweaves Mr Copperfield's plea to his wife to stay with him with a meditation on desire and loss. Desire in the novel acts as a force of personal disintegration: at the heart of the haunted repetition that is her topic is a doomed attempt to realize one's "first hope." While it is not only lesbian desire but all forms of desire that are associated with perversity and stasis in *Two Serious Ladies*, lesbianism is not merely one example among others. With his invocation of the beauty of a ship leaving port and his warning to his wife not to get stuck in the red light district of Colon, Mr Copperfield recalls a narrative of arrested development that is particularly associated with female same-sex desire. In the end, Mrs Copperfield's love for Pacifica can bring her no peace, which is confirmed at the end of the novel, when Pacifica, having become engaged, herself confides to Miss Goering: "What a baby your friend is! What can I do with her? She is like a little

baby. I tried to explain it to my young man, but I can't really explain it to anyone"
(p. 200).

By the end of the 1940s, the powerful social transformations of World War II had
begun to make the lesbian topic less inexplicable. Patricia Highsmith's 1952 novel,
The Price of Salt, rejected by her publisher and eventually released under the pseudonym Claire Morgan, offers an image of lesbian desire that looks forward toward the
more explicit representations of the second half of the twentieth century. The story
concerns a lonely young woman named Therese who meets a beautiful and mysterious
woman named Carol while she is working at a department store. Therese feels a
nagging discontent in her life and in her relations with her boyfriend Richard and
she is drawn to Carol, an older, sardonic woman who is in the midst of a messy divorce.
The two women take a cross-country trip together and become romantically involved;
while they are traveling they realize that Carol's ex-husband has hired a private investigator to follow them in order to gain an advantage in the divorce proceedings. Afraid
of losing custody of her young daughter, Carol cuts off all relations with Therese,
plunging her into profound despair and loneliness.

While in these general outlines and in its hard-boiled realist style the novel
resembles many of the lesbian pulps published around the same time, *The Price of Salt*
holds some powerful surprises in store. The novel is striking in its knowing revision
of several key aspects of the traditional narrative of lesbian triangulation and damnation. In a particularly striking scene, Therese informs Carol that she has broken off
relations with Richard, and she reports his comment that "he couldn't compete" with
Carol. Carol is angry that Therese has mentioned her at all, and withdraws, leaving
Therese in suspense that, in breaking with Richard, she has exposed herself to complete abandonment. Carol's response, when it comes, is surprising; distancing herself
from the dramatic aspects of the triangle, Carol instead comments on the situation
itself as a piece of stock theatre.

> "Lines," Carol said. "I can't compete. People talk of classics. These lines are classic. A
> hundred different people will say the same words. There are lines for the mother, lines
> for the daughter, for the husband and the lover. I'd rather see you dead at my feet. It's
> the same play repeated with different casts. What do they say makes a play a classic,
> Therese?"
>
> "A classic – " Her voice sounded tight and stifled. "A classic is something with a
> basic human situation." (Highsmith 1984: 140–1)

The basic human situation in which Carol and Therese find themselves is more like
a cliché than a classic, so overwritten is it by expectations about the inevitable bad
ending of all same-sex relations. Highsmith underlines the clichéd nature of this literary tradition with the additional line of dialogue that Carol provides. "I would rather
see you dead at my feet" is a direct quotation from a classic scene in Hall's *The Well
of Loneliness*: when Stephen Gordon's mother discovers that she is having an affair with
a local married woman, she says to her, "I would rather see you dead at my feet than

standing before me with this thing upon you – this unspeakable outrage you call love" (Hall 1990: 200). Rather than citing this scene "straight" as many novels from the period did, though, Highsmith cites it in order to point out the limiting clichés of such standard bits of plot, and to gesture toward the possibility of another kind of classic, a more human situation.

The biggest surprise of *The Price of Salt*, though, is the ending, which turns back suddenly from the fate of abandonment, betrayal, and loneliness toward which the narrative seems to tend. After losing in court, Carol finds Therese in New York again and asks her to live with her; at first Therese refuses, but the novel ends as she runs to find Carol:

> She stood in the doorway, looking over the people at the tables in the room where a piano played. The lights were not bright, and she did not see her at first, half hidden in the shadow against the far wall, facing her. Nor did Carol see her. A man sat opposite her, Therese did not know who. Carol raised her hand slowly and brushed her hair back, once on either side, and Therese smiled because the gesture was Carol, and it was Carol she loved and would always love. Oh, in a different way now, because she was a different person, and it was like meeting Carol all over again, but it was still Carol and no one else. It would be Carol, in a thousand cities, a thousand houses, in foreign lands where they would go together, in heaven and in hell. Therese waited. Then as she was about to go to her, Carol saw her, seemed to stare at her incredulously a moment while Therese watched the slow smile growing, before her arm lifted suddenly, her hand waved a quick, eager greeting that Therese had never seen before. Therese walked toward her. (Highsmith 1984: 256–7)

The dynamic suspense of this final passage not only follows the rhythms of a desired reunion with the beloved, but also seems to register a breathless anticipation of a different kind of narrative of lesbian desire. Highsmith includes many elements in this passage of a longer tradition of lesbian narrative: shadowy concealment, the presence of another man, the quick allusion to heaven and hell. But she also insistently signals the difference of this moment: Therese is no longer the prototype of the lonely young woman sure to be abandoned and betrayed by an older, more experienced woman: she is a different person. Carol, too, is changed: she is willing to risk her social position in order to make a life with Therese. That small unfamiliar wave seems directed, as do Therese's fantasies of thousands of different cities and houses, toward a future of queer possibility that will include these women and many others.

We might also read that gesture as one toward a different literary tradition, for the more explicit and positive representations to come in the late twentieth century. Across the first part of the century in both realist and experimental novels, there is something inexplicable, excessive, and opaque about female same-sex desire. That sense of impossibility persists even in the 1920s, 1930s, and 1940s, as the lesbian becomes more visible as a real social actor. While the association of female same-sex desire with perversity and loss persists across the twentieth century and even into the present, moments like the ending of *The Price of Salt* open the way to a new social possibility for lesbianism: still marked by its association with the extremes of heaven and hell, it starts to look less like a cliché and more like a classic – a basic human situation.

NOTES

1 Books such as Dorothy Baker's *Trio* were read in the 1930s and 1940s by somewhat limited audiences; in the 1950s and 1960s many of these titles were reissued as pulp novels and reached a wider audience.

2 *Diana* features a scene that is almost identical to a dramatic moment in *The Well of Loneliness*. In a moment of intense isolation and pain, having been abandoned and betrayed by both her mother and her lover, Stephen Gordon enters the study of her dead father. Looking in his locked bookcase, Stephen finds a cache of sexological textbooks annotated in her father's handwriting and realizes that he had kept from her the secret that she is a sexual invert. In a chapter of *Diana* entitled "Am I a Lesbian?" the young protagonist also finds sexological books in her father's study and it is through this moment that she discovers her identity.

REFERENCES AND FURTHER READING

Abraham, Julie. (1996). *Are Girls Necessary? Lesbian Writing and Modern Histories*. New York and London: Routledge.

Adams, Rachel. (1999). "A mixture of delicious and freak": The queer fiction of Carson McCullers. *American Literature* 71, 3: 551–83.

Allen, Carolyn. (1996). *Following Djuna: Women Lovers and the Erotics of Loss*. Bloomington and Indianapolis: Indiana University Press.

Anders, John P. (1999). *Willa Cather's Sexual Aesthetics and the Male Homosexual Literary Tradition*. Lincoln: University of Nebraska Press.

Barnes, Djuna. (1937). *Nightwood*. New York: New Directions.

Boone, Joseph Allen. (1988). *Tradition Counter Tradition: Love and the Form of Fiction*. Chicago and London: University of Chicago Press.

Boone, Joseph Allen. (1998). *Libidinal Currents: Sexuality and the Shaping of Modernism*. Chicago and London: University of Chicago Press.

Bowles, Jane. (1984). *Two Serious Ladies*. New York: E. P. Dutton.

Brooten, Bernadette J. (1996). *Love Between Women: Early Christian Responses to Female Homoeroticism*. Chicago and London: University of Chicago Press.

Butler, Judith. (1993). "Dangerous names": Willa Cather's masculine names. In *Bodies that Matter: On the Discursive Limits of "Sex"* (pp. 143–66). New York: Routledge.

Carter, Julian. (2007). *The Heart of Whiteness: Normal Sexuality and Race in America, 1880–1940*. Durham, NC and London: Duke University Press.

Castle, Terry. (1993). *The Apparitional Lesbian: Female Homosexuality and Modern Culture*. New York: Columbia University Press.

Castle, Terry (ed.). (2003). *The Literature of Lesbianism: A Historical Anthology from Ariosto to Stonewall*. New York: Columbia University Press.

Cather, Willa. (1966). *The Kingdom of Art: Willa Cather's First Principles and Critical Statements 1893–1896*, ed. Bernice Slote. Lincoln: University of Nebraska Press.

Cather, Willa. (1970). *The World and the Parish: Willa Cather's Articles and Reviews, 1893–1902*, vols. I and II, ed. William M. Curtin. Lincoln: University of Nebraska Press.

Chisolm, Dianne. (1997). Obscene modernism: Eros noir and the profane illumination of Djuna Barnes. *American Literature* 69, 1: 167–206.

Chopin, Kate. (1976). *The Awakening and Selected Stories*, ed. Barbara H. Solomon. New York: Signet.

Davis, Thadious. (1994). *Nella Larsen, Novelist of the Harlem Renaissance: A Woman's Life Unveiled*. Baton Rouge and London: Louisiana State University Press.

DeJean, Joan. (1987). *Fictions of Sappho, 1546–1937*. Chicago: University of Chicago Press.

Diggs, Marylynne. (1995). Romantic friends or a "different race of creatures"? The representation of lesbian pathology in nineteenth-century America. *Feminist Studies* 21, 2: 317–40.

Doan, Laura and Jay Prosser (eds). (2001). *Palatable Poison: Critical Perspectives on* The Well of Loneliness. New York: Columbia University Press.

Duberman, Martin, Martha Vicinus, and George Chauncey, Jr. (eds). (1989). *Hidden From History: Reclaiming the Gay and Lesbian Past*. New York: NAL Books.

Duggan, Lisa. (2000). *Sapphic Slashers: Sex, Violence, and American Modernity*. Durham, NC and London: Duke University Press.

Edelman, Lee. (2004). *No Future: Queer Theory and the Death Drive*. Durham, NC and London: Duke University Press.

Faderman, Lillian. (1981). *Surpassing the Love of Men: Romantic Friendship and Love Between Women from the Renaissance to the Present*. New York: William Morrow and Company.

Faderman, Lillian. (1991). *Odd Girls and Twilight Lovers: A History of Lesbian Life in Twentieth-Century America*. New York: Columbia University Press.

Frederics, Diana. (1939). *Diana: A Strange Autobiography*. New York: The Citadel Press.

Freeman, Elizabeth (2002). "The we of me": *The Member of the Wedding*'s novel alliances. In *The Wedding Complex: Forms of Belonging in Modern American Culture* (pp. 45–69). Durham, NC and London: Duke University Press.

Goldberg, Jonathan. (2001). *Willa Cather and Others*. Durham, NC and London: Duke University Press.

H. D. (1981). *HERmione*. New York: New Directions.

Hall, Radclyffe. (1990). *The Well of Loneliness*. New York: Anchor.

Herring, Scott. (2004). Willa Cather's lost boy: "Paul's case" and bohemian tramping. *Arizona Quarterly* 60, 2: 87–116.

Highsmith, Patricia. (1984). *The Price of Salt*. New York and London: Norton.

Hopkins, Pauline E. (1988). *Contending Forces: A Romance Illustrative of Negro Life North and South*. New York and Oxford: Oxford University Press.

Hovey, Jaime. (1996). Sapphic primitivism in Gertrude Stein's *Q.E.D. Modern Fiction Studies* 42, 3: 547–68.

Kent, Kathryn R. (2003). *Making Girls into Women: American Women's Writing and the Rise of Lesbian Identity*. Durham, NC and London: Duke University Press.

Jagose, Annamarie. (2002). *Inconsequence: Lesbian Representation and the Logic of Sexual Sequence*. Ithaca, NY: Cornell University Press.

James, Henry. (1947). *The Notebooks of Henry James*, ed. F. O. Matthiessen and Kenneth R. Murdock. New York: Oxford University Press.

James, Henry. (2000). *The Bostonians*. New York: Penguin.

Jewett, Sarah Orne. (1911). *Letters of Sarah Orne Jewett*, ed. Annie Fields. Boston and New York: Houghton Mifflin.

Jewett, Sarah Orne. (1994). *Deephaven*. In *Novels and Stories*. New York: Library of America.

Jewett, Sarah Orne. (1995). *The Country of the Pointed Firs and Other Stories*, ed. Suzannah Lessard. New York: Modern Library.

Ladenson, Elisabeth. (1999). *Proust's Lesbianism*. Ithaca, NY: Cornell University Press.

Larsen, Nella. (1986). *Quicksand* and *Passing*. New Brunswick, NJ: Rutgers University Press.

Lindemann, Marilee. (1999). *Willa Cather: Queering America*. New York: Columbia University Press.

Marcus, Jane (1991). Laughing at Leviticus: Nightwood as woman's circus epic. In Mary Lynn Broe (ed.), *Silence and Power: A Reevaluation of Djuna Barnes* (pp. 221–50). Carbondale and Edwardsville: Southern Illinois University Press.

Marcus, Sharon. (2007). *Between Women: Friendship, Desire, and Marriage in Victorian England*. Princeton, NJ: Princeton University Press.

McDowell, Deborah. (1986). Introduction to Nella Larsen, *Quicksand* and *Passing*. New Brunswick, NJ: Rutgers University Press.

O'Brien, Sharon. (1984). "The thing not named": Willa Cather as a lesbian writer. *Signs* 9, 4: 576–99.

Prosser, Jay. (1998). *Second Skins: On the Body – Narratives of Transsexuality*. New York: Columbia University Press.

Rohy, Valerie. (2000). *Impossible Women: Lesbian Figures and American Literature*. Ithaca, NY: Cornell University Press.

Sedgwick, Eve Kosofsky. (1990). *Epistemology of the Closet*. Berkeley, CA: University of California Press.

Sedgwick, Eve Kosofsky. (1993). Willa Cather and others. In *Tendencies* (pp. 167–76). Durham, NC and London: Duke University Press.

Smith-Rosenberg, Carroll. (1975). The female world of love and ritual. *Signs* 1, 1: 1–29.

Somerville, Siobhan. (2000). *Queering the Color Line: Race and the Invention of Homosexuality in American Culture*. Durham, NC and London: Duke University Press.

Stein, Gertrude. (1990). *Three Lives* and *Q.E.D.* New York: Penguin.

Stimpson, Catharine R. (1981). Zero degree deviancy: The lesbian novel in English. *Critical Inquiry* 8, 1: 363–79.

Stokes, Mason. (2001). *The Color of Sex: Whiteness, Heterosexuality, and the Fictions of White Supremacy*. Durham, NC and London: Duke University Press.

Traub, Valerie. (2002). *The Renaissance of Lesbianism in Early Modern England*. Cambridge, UK: Cambridge University Press.

Vicinus, Martha. (2004). *Intimate Friends: Women Who Loved Women, 1778–1928*. Chicago and London: University of Chicago Press.

Wilhelm, Gale. (1984). *We Too Are Drifting*. Tallahassee, FL: Naiad Press.

Wilson, Edmund. (1969). The ambiguity of Henry James. In Gerard Willen (ed.), *A Casebook on Henry James's* The Turn of the Screw (pp. 115–53). New York: Thomas Y. Cromwell.

Zimmerman, Bonnie. (1990). *The Safe Sea of Women, Lesbian Fiction 1969–1989*. Boston: Beacon Press.

21
The Gay Novel in the United States 1900–1950

Christopher Looby

Is the novel fundamentally inimical to queer sexuality? Charles Warren Stoddard was the first American novelist to wonder if this might be the case. Could the fit be so tight between, on the one hand, a literary genre (and its formal conventions) and, on the other hand, the normative organization of sexuality in a given society, so tight that the genre was itself impossible to claim for dissident sexual representation? Stoddard's 1903 novel *For the Pleasure of His Company: A Tale of the Misty City, Thrice Told*, confronts this question both implicitly (in its own formal experimentation) and explicitly (in a conversation two characters have about the writing of novels). In the present essay I will return repeatedly to the stakes of the discussion Stoddard stages between his two aspiring novelists (his protagonist, Paul Clitheroe, and Paul's friend Miss Juno, aka Jack), who articulate contending visions of what a novel must be. Later American novelists who, in one way or another, tried to fit the novel out for queer purposes also confronted the vexing question of the genre's queer potentiality, and arrived at a variety of general answers and formal experiments.

From one general perspective, the novel might seem well suited to queer sexuality. The novel has a long history of discreditation as a low genre, both on the basis of its ostensible formal appeal to dangerous readerly absorption and emotional vagrancy and because of its frequent attention to sexual intrigue, disgrace, deviancy, and so forth. Why, then, shouldn't the novel be a perfectly apt genre for exploring the newly organized field of erotic deviancy described by the rubric of the "homosexual" around the turn of the century? If the novel could do well by countless adulterers, courtesans, seducers and other sexual reprobates, why wouldn't it be perfectly capable of accommodating stories of pansies, dykes, and the like? From another perspective, however, the novel's long affiliation with conventions of romance – and especially its deep investment in narratives of courtship, marriage, and reproduction – might tend to render it recalcitrant when faced with erotic scripts that ran counter to the novel's historically heteronormative bias. The novel had been very good at representing threats to marriage, sexual fidelity, and social reproduction, but it had done so (one could argue) in an essentially disciplinary way. The norms were articulated and reinforced precisely by virtue of the novel's dramatization of what threatened them. Could the novel really do anything with queer sexuality other than add it to the list of disgraceful threats to heterosexual propriety? Could the novel actually defamiliarize received categories of sexual experience, and thus serve the interest of sexual redescription and the remaking of experience? The *question* of the queer novel, the question of its very possibility, had to be confronted by writers who, whether themselves queer (under some description) or not, meant to bring novelistic art to bear upon historically emergent queer sexual experience.

This is the quandary faced by Charles Warren Stoddard. He thought about and struggled with his only novel over many decades, according to his biographer Roger Austen. As early as 1874 he wrote to a friend that he had an idea for a "San Francisco Novel" (Austen 1995: 71), but it was not until the summer of 1883 that he began writing it (p. 100); in the summer of 1888 he was getting William Dean Howells's advice on it, although he did not share the manuscript with Howells until 1896 (p. 116). Austen reports that Stoddard wrote most of it during the summer of 1892 in Hawaii. In 1895 he apparently showed it to Rudyard Kipling, who offered constructive criticism (p. 138). Because it is largely autobiographical, and incorporated material from Stoddard's own life during the decades of its composition, it "thoroughly jumbled up people and events from the late 1860s, 1870s, and early 1880s," that is, from all the periods during which it was underway in one fashion or another. This protracted process of composition resulted in various literary effects that might be criticized as confusing but that are also an index, so to speak, to the history of homosexuality across those crucial decades. To put it most starkly, Stoddard started writing *For the Pleasure of His Company* in the nineteenth-century heyday of "romantic friendship" and published it in a new and different century, after the Wilde trial, after the rise of sexology and the other professional discourses that defined and framed queer sexuality. Its constitutive anachronism is its most remarkable quality. And the style of the novel's prose is genteel, oblique, and more than a bit precious; especially in its highly wrought opening pages, it seems dramatically anachronistic for a novel published in 1903. "She was a smallish moon, looking very chaste and chilly and she peered vaguely through folds of scurrying fog" sounds rather quaint and fussy for a turn-of-the-century novel's first line.

For the Pleasure of His Company has had the reputation, for the few critics who have scrutinized it, and even for Roger Austen, Stoddard's biographical advocate, of being "strange," an "antinovel," and "a failure, mainly because of its obliquity" (Austen 1995: 146). Before any such aesthetic evaluations are made, however, the powerful generic self-consciousness of Stoddard's text deserves to be recognized. Its most striking formal feature is advertised by its second subtitle: it is "thrice told." The book is in three parts, each of which features Paul Clitheroe as protagonist, and describes events in his life over the same period of time; but the plots run on entirely separate, if parallel trajectories. Paul has a fragmented social life, spending time alternately with three different social groups, none of which has any real connection with the others. In Book First, we learn of Paul and his friends and acquaintances among the aspiring young writers and editors of the San Francisco area, chiefly a group of self-styled bohemians who congregate at an inn across the bay in Oakland; in Book Second, we meet Paul in the company of some theatre people who introduce him to an enchanting young woman named Miss Juno, with whom Paul forms a sudden and intense friendship and with whom he later discusses the art of the novel; in Book Third we encounter Paul in the company of yet another discrete group of characters, comprising an eccentric older woman called Little Mama and the various artists and attractive young men whom she collects around herself.

At the same time that the action of the novel is nearly completely divided among these noncontiguous social groups (with Paul the weak link between them), the time of the novel is disjointed. Ostensibly Paul is circulating among these different social groups, shuttling between them, and the time frame of the novel is consistent with this, but of course we read the parts in sequence and do not know, at first, that the action in the three parts overlaps. In addition, as we have seen, Stoddard wrote the novel by fits and starts over the course of several decades, freely incorporating his experiences as he went along, and thus made it impossible to assign the time of the diegesis very confidently to any specific historical moment. Is it all taking place in the 1870s, or 1880s, or 1890s? We cannot say – and this matters, for one reason, because those are exactly the decades when homosexuality was being invented (Foucault 1986). None of the characters in *For the Pleasure of His Company* seems yet to have heard of this invention, however; there are plenty of same-sex (and gender-bending) erotic attachments being formed and re-formed, but no labels seem to attach to those relationships or to their participants in the world of Stoddard's novel. Soon enough, by contrast, in Edward Prime-Stevenson's *Imre: A Memorandum* (1906), the characters will all have read Krafft-Ebing and other professional analysts of homosexuality, and will knowingly inhabit the scientific descriptions and social categories that had been proliferating over the decades of Stoddard's writing; but in Stoddard's novel, the characters have not yet heard of homosexuality as a diagnosis, self-description, or identity. Was Stoddard entering an implicit protest against the onset of sexual categorization, sensing that there might be something pernicious about this new technology of the self? Or was he merely registering – both in the formal manipulation of narrative time in his novel, and in his promiscuous borrowing of experience from three decades of sexual history – the actual unevenness of that history, its complicated interplay of emergent, dominant, and residual sexual formations? (The categories of residual, dominant, and emergent cultural formations are borrowed from Raymond Williams, 1977.) On the one hand, the novel reads as if it belonged to the era of Bayard Taylor's *Joseph and His Friend* (1870), an earlier quasi- or proto-homosexual novel, or the period of the countless tales of "romantic friendship" that Axel Nissen (2003) has collected and discussed.

And yet Stoddard's novel seems preternaturally modern, too, in its vision of a postheterosexual dispensation, a time when rigid sexual identities will have begun to lose their grip on us.

Paul Clitheroe seems, in fact, to lack a sexual identity, or a very strong identity of any kind. He is an aspiring and modestly successful poet, reviewer, and local literary celebrity; he is personally attractive and socially agreeable, and manages to survive his penury by dint of frequent dinner invitations. But even his friends find him curiously elusive and somewhat frustrating. He appears to find physical intimacy only with other men, but enjoys the social company of women and forms his most intense bond with Miss Juno in Book Second, a bond that involves their mutual disregard of gender norms:

> If Paul and Miss Juno had been formed for one another and were now, at the right moment and under the most favorable auspices, brought together for the first time, they could not have mated more naturally. If Miss Juno had been a young man, instead of a very charming woman, she would of course have been Paul's chum. If Paul had been a young woman – some of his friends thought he had narrowly escaped it and did not hesitate to say so – he would instinctively have become her confidante. (Stoddard 1903/1987: 88)

Miss Juno is the only daughter of her mother's loveless first marriage, a regrettable marriage of convenience; she now lives in a bucolic valley outside San Francisco with her mother and her mother's lover, Eugene, a painter. They form a happy family amid their unconventional domestic arrangements, and Paul envies their freedom, mutual affection, and casual disregard for social propriety. When Paul and Miss Juno share confidences about their romantic lives, he learns that she had a brush with trite romantic conventionality once; she was engaged to a young army officer, with whom she exchanged many florid letters while he was stationed far away: "it was rather like a seaside novelette, our love affair," she now admits (p. 94). But her mother and Eugene put an end to the engagement, and, despite her misery at the time of the breakup, Miss Juno now realizes it was for the best. Paul reciprocates her tender confidence with one of his own:

> There was a time when I felt that marriage was the inevitable fate of all respectable people. Some one wanted me to marry a certain some one else. I didn't seem to care much about it; but my friend was one of those natural-born match-makers; she talked the young lady up to me in such a shape that I almost fancied myself in love and actually began to feel that I'd be doing her an injustice if I permitted her to go on loving and longing for the rest of her days. (Stoddard 1903/1987: 94)

This conversation about their futile, abortive heteronormative pasts allows them to dispose of the looming question of marriage between the two of them; henceforth they will be "chums" only (p. 99), and like Miss Juno's best friend at boarding school, Paul will now be allowed to call her by her fond masculine nickname, "Jack." They henceforth spend as much time together as they can, enjoying their shared unconventionality and conversational and behavioral freedom.

Jack intuits that Paul is writing a novel; he in turn asks whether she has ever written a story. She hasn't, and initially dismisses the notion; but he encourages her to try it, because she is a naturally gifted story-teller, and he is sure she can just put down with her pen the stories she tells so fluently and artlessly in ordinary conversation. Jack resists Paul's advice, arguing that a writer must inevitably work within established narrative conventions; ordinary conversation would seem commonplace and unformed, and would not command attention if merely transcribed. Paul grows impatient with her insistence, and thus begins the deterioration of their friendship over a matter of literary technique. Here Stoddard draws attention to his own novelistic practice, by having Jack call attention to their present colloquy – "Our conversation is growing a little thin, Paul, don't you think so? We couldn't put all this into a book" (p. 103) – whereas Paul feels their conversation *could* very well take its place in a novel (and Stoddard, of course, as we can't help noticing, has done exactly that right here in *his* novel).

Finally Paul and Jack agree that each of them shall write a novel, but they will do so on very different plans. "If we are to write a novel apiece," Jack avers, "we shall be obliged to put love into it; love with a very large L" (p. 104). Paul disagrees vehemently – "I'm dead sure we wouldn't; and to prove it some day I'll write a story without its pair of lovers; everybody shall be more or less spoony – but nobody shall be really in love" (p. 104). To Jack, it seems obvious that such a story wouldn't pass muster: "It wouldn't be a story, Paul," she states categorically (p. 104). For her part, she decisively proclaims, "I shall have love in my story" (p. 105). But Paul is determined to resist the generic requirement that there be "love," and a "pair of lovers," in his novel. When he describes his idea for a different kind of novel, he is basically describing the unusual novel of Stoddard's that we are here, in fact, reading:

> It would be a history, or a fragment of a history, a glimpse of life at any rate, and that
> is as much as we ever get of the lives of those around us. Why can't I tell you the story
> of one fellow – of myself for example; how one day I met this person, and the next day
> I met that person, and next week some one else comes on to the stage, and struts his
> little hour and departs. (1903/1987: 104)

Growing rather heated in the face of what he eventually implies is Jack's literary obtuseness, he concedes rather tartly that she "may have all the love you like, and appeal to the same old novel reader who has been reading the same sort of love-story for the last hundred years" (p. 105). On the contrary, he says, "My novel shall be full of love, but you won't know that it is love – I mean the every-day love of the every-day people. In my book everybody is going to love everybody else – or almost everybody else . . ." (p. 106). It seems wrong, given this dramatic discussion of the novel and its generic requirements, and its critical recognition of the erotic norms that are embedded in novelistic form, to judge *For the Pleasure of His Company* to be a "failed" novel; perhaps it is fair to call it an "antinovel," given its strident contestation of novelistic conventions. But it is most important to notice that Stoddard, like Paul, sought a way to turn his literary performance into an instrument of resistance to what (to be anachronistic myself) has been called compulsory heterosexuality (Rich 1994). The "same old novel-reader" has been reading "the same old love-story" for a long time; Stoddard, like Paul, aimed to produce a *different* sort of love story, one not centered on the usual pair of gender-opposite lovers; one bearing little or no resemblance to the trite "seaside novelette" whose script Miss Juno had enacted in her youth. Stoddard's novel aimed to surprise and disorient the "same old reader" and perhaps, in turn, provide that reader with a different erotic script, or with a different sort of imaginative space in which erotic possibilities were relatively open-ended and undetermined rather than one option — heterosexual marriage — being "the inevitable fate of all respectable people."

Imre: A Memorandum by Edward Prime-Stevenson (1906) is a story that emphatically has "love with a very large L in it" (as Miss Juno would say approvingly), and even strikingly resembles the "seaside novelette" on which her first quashed romance with the young soldier was patterned. Miss Juno fell in love with a handsome young military officer; the narrator of *Imre*, an expatriate American named Oswald, falls for a young Hungarian lieutenant, Imre von. N., whom he chances to meet at a café-garden alongside the Danube River in Budapest on a pleasant summer afternoon. Oswald and Imre quickly establish an intimate friendship and become virtually inseparable; more slowly, they acknowledge their homosexuality to themselves and to each other; soon enough they are convinced of their perfect mutual love and their ideal lifelong compatibility. While this story might gratify Miss Juno, fulfilling her essential criterion for a successful novel, it would certainly disappoint Paul Clitheroe. His favored narrative model, as we have seen, would involve a protagonist who "met one person and then another," and so forth — a narrative of social and perhaps sexual multiplicity experimentation, and waywardness, not coupledom and fidelity. And Charles Warren Stoddard, whose novel adhered to the Clitheroe model of aimless narrative and emotional promiscuity, might be expected to have disdained *Imre* as resorting too readily to tired narrative conventions — "the same old story." But contrary to expectation, his biographer reports that Stoddard copied a line from *Imre* into his journal, which would seem to imply a positive interest in his successor's novel, if not approval. "The silences of intimacy stand for the most perfect mutuality," Stoddard transcribed (Austen 1995: 167).[1] Perhaps Stoddard recognized that, for the sake of granting dignity to homosexual love, it was also important to bestow upon it all of the usual romantic conventions, to stake a queer claim to the culturally ingrained patterns of romantic narrative. And perhaps we can recognize that, in 1906, for homosexually inclined readers whose subjectivity had been formed (however uncomfortably) within the regime of those same conventions, a queer love story that in every other respect conformed to mainstream expectations would provide a powerful consolation to other isolated gay men, and perhaps an avenue to understanding for straight readers. Prime-Stevenson implied as much when he had his narrator, Oswald, write in his Prefatory remarks that he hoped it would comfort "any other human heart" or "solitary soul" that was in pain similar to his own (1906/2003: 32).

If the basic plot of *Imre* is stunningly conventional (true love leads to permanent happy coupledom), and its central narrative structure is fundamentally normative, Prime-Stevenson nevertheless surrounds his standard romance plot with intriguing formal delinquencies of various kinds. It may be that while this novel aspires to quasi-normality within the diegesis, its erratic or rebellious energies are embodied at the level of form. And on this level it is, indeed, somewhat eccentric. We might even say that it disclaims the status of novel altogether. Ostensibly the narrative originates in a partial autobiography written by Oswald and sent privately to his friend "Mayne" (Prime-Stevenson himself had published popular boys' books under the pseudonym "Xavier Mayne," so the author is here coyly outing himself). Oswald authorizes Mayne to do with the manuscript as he pleases, and even to publish it after he applies his "editorial hand" to its pages (p. 32). Mayne, we are to infer, has now presumably done the necessary editing, having agreed with Oswald that this narrative is "something for other men than for you and me only" (p. 32), and has consequently published it in a limited fashion. *Imre* was first issued in a private printing of only 500 copies from an English language press in Naples, and it no doubt found its discreet way to at least some of those imagined "other men" – among them, as we have seen, Charles Warren Stoddard – and helped them to feel "a little less alone" (p. 32) as Oswald and his surrogate Mayne intended. But if it is important to note that this "memorandum" (as *Imre*'s subtitle calls it – another marked departure from novelistic convention, calling attention to its intellectual purpose) is expected to circulate among an extended, albeit confined, group of readers whose "hearts" will be linked by it, the diegesis itself projects no homosexual social world beyond the twosome of Oswald and Imre. In this way it is very different from Stoddard's novel, which imagined a postheteronormative world and various complex and oddly sorted networks of friends; Oswald and Imre imagine only their own sanctuary within an unendingly hostile world. They find each other, and find invaluable consolation in their secret love; but they do not expect their private romance to have any public consequences. Rather than hide singly, they will now hide their love together; and their relations with other gay men will consist exclusively of the virtual ones mediated by the discreet circulation of their story in a limited private edition.

But this distinction between the two novels can be framed in another way, too: in *For the Pleasure of His Company* we are told that Paul Clitheroe's private letters, if we could read them, would have been scandalous (pp. 125–6); we never have the opportunity to read them, however, but are left only with the public narrative of the omniscient unnamed narrator relating Paul's outward life. Presumably Paul's private letters are more emotionally and sexually explicit; Stoddard thus gestures toward a form of writing that is less veiled than his own novel. With *Imre* on the other hand, in a sense we *are* reading Oswald's private letter to his friend Mayne, in which he has disclosed the truth of his powerful but outlawed same-sex desires. While it is true that this private communication is made public in a discreet fashion (small private printing abroad), the formal frame of *Imre* breaches the privacy and violates the taboo on public expression that Oswald and Imre preserve vigilantly within the diegesis.

Just as *Imre* is formally unlike *For the Pleasure of His Company*, its conceptualization and representation of same-sex sexuality is utterly different. Oswald's narration is replete with the terminology of late nineteenth-century sexological science: homosexual, homosexualism, Urning, Uranian, uranistic, similisexual, queer, secondary sex, intersex, the sex within a sex, man-loving man, and so forth. The constant churning of this "juggling terminology," as Oswald impatiently terms it (p. 68), testifies to the "incitement to discourse" that sexuality famously became in this era, according to Foucault (Foucault 1986: 17 ff.). Oswald has an extensive familiarity with such vocabularies because, he reports, he read a book: "a serious work, on abnormalisms in mankind: a book partly psychologic, partly medico-psychiatric, of the newest 'school'" (1906/2003: 90–1). The author of this book was a famous physician, an American, and Oswald was led to consult him personally when the doctor was in London; the man was sympathetic, and relatively nonjudgmental, which was valuable in its way for Oswald's self-acceptance, but he did treat Oswald's queerness as a disease to be cured – by prompt marriage. Oswald initially heeded this advice, and became dutifully engaged; but at the last minute a powerful attraction to a new male friend led him to conclude that he in fact "had no disease" (p. 95), but "was simply what I was born" (pp. 95–6). This conviction of a natural, inborn homosexuality as "the secret of my individuality" (p. 64), the deep truth of "myself, my secret, unrestful self" (p. 91), is a classic expression of an essentialist point of view. It leads Oswald to embark upon a course of additional reading: "I met with a mass of serious studies, German, Italian, French, English, from the chief European specialists and theorists on the similisexual topic: many of them with quite other views than those of my well-meaning but far too conclusive Yankee doctor" (p. 96). Oswald's research eventually brings him to the conviction that, while his same-sex erotic orientation is a natural aberration, it is not morally blameworthy and should not be socially punished. He shares this account of his researches and this line of reasoning in the course of revealing himself and his attraction to Imre. Imre, in turn, makes his confession to Oswald: "I am a Uranian, as thou art. From my birth I have been one. Wholly, wholly homosexual, Oswald!" (p. 117).[2] And it turns out that Imre, too, already "had some knowledge of such literature," and, Oswald relates, had "formally consulted one eminent Viennese specialist who certainly was much wiser, far less positive, and not less calming than my American theorist" (p. 118). Theirs is thus a relationship for which the most recent type of socially progressive sexology provides the essential imprimatur.

Plainly Prime-Stevenson's novel aims to provide for its readers the same psychological comforting and moral strengthening that Imre's "Viennese psychiater" (p. 118) provided for him; it could even serve as a guide, for less well-educated readers, toward the burgeoning archive of sexually progressive literature.[3] This therapeutic and pedagogical purpose can only be recognized for the humane program it represents, even as it may give us pause, at our historical distance, because it so completely and avidly adopts the taxonomic apparatus of the sexological field of inquiry. Indeed, an essential aspect of what underwrites the perfect compatibility of Oswald and Imre is that the former is a self-avowed "type," a super-masculine man ("too much man," p. 125), whereas Imre is another type, a man who bears "the psychic trace of the woman" inside him (p. 125); the novel thus fully accedes to an ideology of desire grounded in essential gender difference that is very much of its historical moment.

The contrast I have described between Stoddard's novel and Prime-Stevenson's (involving overt formal experimentation for Stoddard and a comparatively conventional romantic plot for Prime-Stevenson; involving also Stoddard's eschewal of sexual identity categories and Prime-Stevenson's enthusiastic embrace of them) is a contrast that can be located within the recently rediscovered *Bertram Cope's Year* (1919) by Henry Blake Fuller. Written toward the end of his career by this once-celebrated author, self-published in Chicago at the age of 62 when New York publishers all rejected it, the novel features a young protagonist who bears a striking resemblance to Paul Clitheroe. Bertram Cope is a graduate student and instructor in English literature living in Churchton (a thinly disguised Evanston, Illinois), whose handsome appearance and social grace attract the attention of a local matron named Medora Phillips as well as an older bachelor called Basil Randolph. Medora wants Bertram's company, and perhaps wishes to marry him off to one of the young female boarders in her house; Basil wants Bertram as a social companion, traveling partner, and overnight guest. Bertram is generally compliant – he likes people to be pleased with him – but he also passively resists Medora's and Basil's designs, while enjoying the advantages of their friendship and social connections. Bertram does become inadvertently engaged to one young woman (almost exactly as unwittingly as Paul Clitheroe did, and with as little enthusiasm as Oswald did), but he is helped out of that unwanted commitment by the arrival in Churchton of his intimate friend Arthur Lemoyne – someone recognizable as fulfilling the stereotype of the effeminate homosexual (whether or not he recognizes himself in this way). When *Bertram Cope's Year* was reprinted in 1998, the author of its afterword, Andrew Solomon, wrote confidently of its central male characters (Bertram, Basil, and Arthur) as "homosexual," and stressed the nonchalance with which Fuller depicted them as such. This ascription is, of course, entirely unobjectionable, and an argument to the contrary would be plainly absurd. But it also evident that Fuller wrote the novel in such a manner as to make such an easy ascription inadequate, and possibly misleading.

Solomon draws attention to the fact that Basil and Arthur both sense that they are rivals for Bertram's affection, and he argues that this "moment of recognition" between the two entails their mutual membership in "a community within which each can be seen as a threat to the other" (Solomon in Fuller 1919/1998: 290). Fair enough, but what this analysis misses is that Basil and Arthur palpably loathe one another, actively disidentify with one another; their mutual visceral aversion is grounded in their respective adherence to very different canons of sexual personhood. To put it another way, it is not clear that either one of them actively owns up to a particular sexuality, but each of them ascribes to the other a distasteful style of sexual subjectivity – Arthur thinks Basil is a fussy old bachelor whose interest in younger men like Bertram is unseemly, and Basil thinks Arthur is an effeminate twit and a bad influence on Bertram. They are thrown into communication with one another by dint of their mutual interest in Bertram, but they belong to different economies of sexual subjectivity altogether; we might also say that they belong to different eras of sexual history. Bertram is suspended uncomfortably between the two men and the two eras they embody.

Basil is a discreet bachelor, a 40-something man of comfortable means and genteel tastes, always available to complete the guest list at a dinner party; he makes a specialty of befriending attractive young men for whom he provides (he believes) valuable mentorship as well as social introductions. Basil passes muster in the broader Churchton social sphere without any trouble. Does he want physical intimacy of some kind with Bertram or with any other young man? On this point Fuller divulges nothing. Arthur, on the other hand, already enjoys some form or fashion of physical intimacy with Bertram – they share a bed when Arthur visits Bertram at his family's home over Christmas break, they live together in a flat that pointedly is described as having just "the bed" (p. 198) after Arthur arrives in Churchton, they circulate socially as a pair, and carry on an intense and often jealous correspondence when separated (more on their correspondence below) – but his style of sexual being is very different from Bertram's. His theatrical and effeminate mannerisms are repellent to others, a harsh reaction to which Bertram is sensitive. Even the narrator seems to find Arthur unappealing:

> Lemoyne presented himself . . . as a young man of twenty-seven or so, with dark, limpid eyes, a good deal of dark, wavy hair, and limbs almost too plumply well-turned. In his hands the flesh minimized the prominence of joints and knuckles, and the fingers (especially the little fingers) displayed certain graceful, slightly affected movements of the kind which may cause a person to be credited – or taxed – with possessing the "artistic temperament." To end with, he carried two inches of short black stubble under his nose. He was a type which one may admire – or not. (Fuller 1919/1998: 183)

Arthur is more devoted to Bertram than the reverse, and Bertram comes to feel that Arthur is a psychic burden and a social liability. When Arthur undertakes to perform in female drag in a play, and does the feminine not with evident reluctance and comical incompetence (as he would apparently be expected to do), but with great relish and enthusiastic precision – and gets so carried away with his enactment that he makes an inappropriate approach to a fellow actor, who takes severe and violent umbrage at Arthur's pass (pp. 270–1) – he is finally rendered decisively detrimental to Bertram's social standing, and leaves Churchton in disgrace.

Basil and Arthur belong to different gay worlds, we might say; their rivalry over Bertram is waged from positions in those different worlds. Basil would like Bertram to join him in a life of decorous bachelor leisure and social respectability, on a residual model that would have been normative in the nineteenth century. Arthur seems to be itching to have Bertram join him in an emerging world of newly licensed sexual and gender deviation. Bertram does not appear to know what he wants, except, perhaps, that he is not interested in signing on for either of these options – at least not yet. *Bertram Cope's Year* stages the historical transition from one economy of sexual subjectivity to another, and poises Bertram on the cusp of change.

Bertram Cope is fundamentally elusive, indecisive, and opportunistic. The year he spends in Churchton is also a year in which he struggles fitfully with his literary vocation. The novel in which he appears is itself fairly conventional, a campus novel (or a novel of manners), full of muted social comedy, told in the third person, mixing narration and dialogue fairly freely. There is only one place where the extradiegetic narrator explicitly betrays a certain knowingness about Bertram and Arthur, and that moment comes just when Bertram has been relieved in the nick of time (with Arthur's help) of his unwanted fiancée, Amy Leffingwell (who soon marries a young business-man whose occupation makes him the very "type" we had earlier been informed "constituted, ipso facto, a kind of norm by which other young men in other fields of endeavor were to be gauged: the farther they deviated from the standard he automati-cally set up, the more lamentable their deficiencies," p. 82). Once Amy has been dis-posed of, and Bertram and Arthur during a winter walk are both relieved to have that mess behind them,

> They spent ten minutes in the clear winter air. As Cope, on their return, stooped to put his latch-key to use, Lemoyne impulsively threw an arm around his shoulder. "Every-thing is all right, now," he said, in a tone of high gratification; and Urania, through the whole width of her starry firmament, looked down kindly upon a happier household. (p. 211)

"Uranian" was a coded term for homosexual, as we saw in *Imre: A Memorandum*, and this seems to be the narrator's broad hint that Bertram was not just not interested in marrying this girl, and not only emphatically not the marrying kind at all (we already know that Bertram felt a "fundamental repugnance," even an "essential repugnance" toward matrimony, pp. 171, 176), but against marriage *because* his desires are oriented in a different direction, and because he is a different "type" himself, whether he knows it or not. Cope's relief, though – he plainly doesn't share the narrator's knowing view of the matter – has mainly to do with his ability now to concentrate on his research, so that he can complete a master's thesis and receive his degree in the coming June. Throughout the novel he has been unable to settle on a topic: he is tempted by the question of the authorship of Shakespeare's plays (pp. 59–60), and by "Paradise Lost" (p. 60), among other topics, but he is also drawn to a contemporary field – "I think I shall end by digging something out of Here and Now. 'Our Middle-West School of Fiction,' – what would you think of that?," he asks Basil (p. 100). This is one of Fuller's many somewhat oblique ways of linking the question of the literary with the matter of sexuality.[4] Naturally we are not told what he finally decides to write about (p. 221), only that "It was a relief to have come to a final decision" (p. 230). Likewise, at the end of the novel, once Bertram has graduated, we learn that he has "obtained a post in an important university in the East, at a satisfactory stipend" (p. 282), but readers are left to make their own decisions as to whether Bertram is likely to do what Medora predicts – resume his relationship with another of her female boarders, Carolyn Thorpe, propose marriage to her once he feels professionally secure, and send for her to join him in the East – or what Basil anticipates: resume "keeping house together" with Arthur Lemoyne (p. 287), who will have rejoined Bertram once again and begun his own graduate studies in psychology. Ending on this note of uncertainty – with two characters, Medora and Basil, composing for the amenable protagonist of *this* fiction alternate fictions of their own involving divergent emotional and sexual paths for him – ratchets up the analogy between literature and sexuality once again, and leaves readers, along with Medora and Basil, in the position of attributing romantic and erotic choices, and narrative trajectories, to a young man who feels in no hurry to commit himself to any of them.

The obliquity of Fuller's representation of sexuality in *Bertram Cope's Year* is undoubtedly calculated. Stoddard, I speculated earlier, may have been eschewing sexual identity labels in *For the Pleasure of His Company* on purpose. Fuller was certainly doing so. But more to the point, he depicted a range of characters who were all maneuvering – awkwardly sometimes, adroitly on occasion – amid the categories. Among the most telling formal devices in *Bertram Cope's Year* is its presentation of the private correspondence of Bertram and Arthur; the irony is that the candid revelations we might expect (remember Stoddard's insinuation that Paul Clitheroe's private letters would shock our sensibilities and cause scandal) are missing from Bertram's and Arthur's missives. Even in the privacy of his letters to Arthur, when Bertram is complaining that he does not really relish social dancing between the sexes, he will say with seeming innocence, "I like to see soldiers or sailors dance in pairs, as a straightforward outlet for superfluous physical energy" (p. 51). Who is he kidding? Himself? (Surely not Arthur.) Or is he really not kidding at all? The nearest approach to explicit disclosure comes in Arthur's exasperated reply to Bertram's sheepish letter admitting to his inadvertent betrothal to Amy Leffingwell. "The thing can't go on," Arthur remonstrates, "and you know it as well as I do. Nip it. Nip it now. Don't think that our intimacy is to end in any such fashion as this, for it isn't" (pp. 178–9). In Arthur's petulant tone, and in his "you know it as well as I do," one hears him impatiently summoning Bertram into a settled sexual personhood. But in that unfixable word "intimacy," hovering between avowal and euphemism, we can also sense him allowing for Bertram's reluctance, his difference. Bertram, and maybe Arthur too, we might say, would understand Stoddard's prizing of Prime-Stevenson's judgment that the silences in (or of) intimacy could be the ground of perfect mutuality.

There was a spate of gay novels published between 1931 and 1934, according to historian George Chauncey in his authoritative *Gay New York* (1995), an indispensable guide to the historical and cultural context in which the early twentieth-century gay novel appeared. Chauncey lists Blair Niles's *Strange Brother* (1931), *Twilight Men* by André Tellier (1931), *A Scarlet Pansy* by Robert Scully (1932), Kenilworth Bruce's *Goldie* (1933), Richard Meeker's *Better Angel* (1933), and *Butterfly Man* by Lew Levenson (1934) (Chauncey 1995: 324). The list could be extended, either by widening the temporal parameters or loosening the definition of what constitutes a "gay novel." Elsewhere in his study Chauncey also mentions Wallace Thurman's *The Blacker the Berry* (1929) and *Infants of the Spring* (1932), novels of the Harlem Renaissance that feature gay and lesbian characters, as well as *The Young and Evil* (1933), coauthored by Charles Henri Ford and Parker Tyler, and Bruce Nugent's celebrated prose poem "Smoke, Lilies, and Jade" (1926). Very recently a previously unpublished novel by Nugent, *Gentleman Jigger*, has belatedly come to light; its editor, Thomas Wirth, reports that it was written "for the most part between 1928 and 1933," and it is a *roman à clef* featuring fictionalized versions of the same cast of characters that appeared in Thurman's *Infants of the Spring*, the self-named "Niggerati" or younger members of the New Negro movement. It would also be an egregious error to omit mention of Djuna Barnes' *Nightwood* (1936), but the essential point remains: the late 1920s and the 1930s – the years of the Great Depression and its social upheavals – saw an unusual concentration of novelistic depictions of, explorations of, and literary reconfigurations of sexual cultures. Some of these novels are committed to what Scott Herring in a recent book calls "sexual intelligibility," the public definition of sexual types and the clarification of sexual experience that we have seen most clearly in *Imre: A Memorandum*, while others resist the incipient codification of sexuality, as Stoddard's and Fuller's novels arguably do (Herring 2007). For the purposes of this essay I will focus on two of the novels Chauncey mentions (*Strange Brother* and *The Young and Evil*) and a third novel he does not talk about, Dawn Powell's *Come Back to Sorrento* (first published in 1932 as *The Tenth Moon*, but rediscovered and reprinted in 1997 under Powell's intended title). Published in quick succession between 1931 and 1933, these three novels together epitomize the concurrent widely varied possibilities for representing same-sex desire, and the equally various ways in which sexual politics was embedded within formal novelistic choices.

Although at least one recent critic has bestowed upon *Strange Brother* the honorific "queer," crediting it with depicting in the currently approved fashion "multiple identifications across categories of race, sex, and gender" (Boone 1998: 266), this novel is unambiguously devoted to the parsing of categories of sexual identity, even as it liberally allows for the possibility of social mixing between and among those categories. "Blair Niles" was the pseudonym of a popular travel writer, journalist, and novelist, a white woman originally named Mary Blair Rice, who first wrote under the name Mary Blair Beebe when she was married to the scientist C. William Beebe. Together the Beebes published *Our Search for a Wilderness: An Account of Two Ornithological Expeditions to Venezuela and to British Guiana* (1910), which details their efforts to observe, classify, and collect birds, mammals, and reptiles for the New York Zoological Park. After her divorce from Beebe she married Robert Niles, and adopted the pen name that combined her middle and his last name, and most of her writing appeared thereafter as the work of Blair Niles. The classificatory frame of mind evident in her early account of the ornithological expedition, however, can be seen to persist long afterwards in her fiction, explicitly (as in the character of Philip Crane, a manly naturalist whose entomological expedition to the tropics the novel's gay protagonist, Mark Thornton, dreams of joining as a scientific illustrator; and as in the expert opinions of the sexological theorist Irwin Hesse, who generously extrapolates from the large "number of sex forms existing among the social insects" that there must be "more than two hard and fast sex forms in man" as well, p. 173), and implicitly, too, in the pervasive will to know the truth of sex that propels June Westbrook's sympathetic curiosity about Mark's deviant erotic nature.[5] *Strange Brother* is a novel of progressive social purpose, dedicated to elucidating the problem of sexual classification, and wishing to increase moral tolerance of sexual diversity. And it is incidentally highly informative about the morphology of sexual self-understanding, self-representation, and public ascription that obtained in the late 1920s.

Mark Thornton is a poor orphan from the Middle West, living in a settlement house in New York City and teaching art to children while he cherishes ambitions of a career as an illustrator and holds on to hopes of a satisfying emotional and erotic life with another man. June Westbrook is a divorced society woman, a sometime journalist, who meets Mark in a speakeasy in Harlem, where she is slumming with some of her white friends and he is socializing with some of his gay black friends. Mark and June strike up a close friendship of their own, which provides him with solace as well as social connection, and which satisfies her desire to expand her emotional range and social purview. Mark lives a double life, acknowledging his sexual tastes to himself and to a few trusted confidantes, but masquerading in public as straight; he is familiar enough with the discourses of sexual description current in his day to have internalized a sense of himself as a homosexual, although it pains him to be subject to scorn, blackmail, and ostracism, and he cannot shake his own shame. He adheres to a conventional model of masculine gender behavior, and is repulsed by the flamboyant styles of queer effeminacy he sees around him in the city (although he sympathizes with the plight of these fairies). He is altogether miserable, in short, and we as readers can see fairly early on that this story will not end happily.

Like Stoddard and the others before her, Niles gives the literary as such a prominent role in the diegesis, and connects it intimately with sex. Mark sometimes writes his own poetry, and throughout the story he is engaged in the compilation of "an anthology of what poets and philosophers and scientists had written on the subject of man's love for man" (Niles 1931: 230). An important mentor from his youth, Tom Burden – a gay man who carefully and chastely introduced Mark to the idea of his being homosexual, and helpfully called it "our handicap" (p. 141) – sent him a copy of Whitman's *Leaves of Grass*, and Mark had found a copy of Edward Carpenter's *Love's Coming of Age* in a used book store (p. 78). Eventually it occurs to him that he might find moral legitimation for his present sexuality in esteemed literature from the past, and he hopes that after selecting and compiling his anthology he might publish it in an effort to ameliorate the prejudicial sexual standards with which he is often confronted.

The earnest purpose of *Strange Brother* is typically on display in one of the great set pieces of the novel, when June and Mark go together to one of the famous drag balls in Harlem. June wants to go because she is attracted to what she feels to be the bodily freedom and experiential daring of the Harlem social scene. Mark wants to go because it is a vivid exhibition of sexual energy and some of his queer friends will be there. The scene devolves into a weird kind of pathos when June, sitting in the stands with Mark (they are both rapt spectators, but certainly not participants), notices a man in elaborate (masculine) drag in the adjacent box – he is wearing "the old-time dress of a Venetian gondolier," and shares the box with another man wearing "the dress of a woman of the Turkish harem" – and realizes the gondolier is her ex-husband, Palmer Fleming. "Palmer Fleming at a Drag Ball in Harlem!" (p. 218). She is glad, when she moments later watches him enter the dance floor and select a feather-bedecked young fairy for a partner, that she had restrained herself from greeting him: "for the first time, June saw him for what he was" (p. 219). Here, we might say, Niles has reached a limit of her empathetic ethnography, retreating from curiosity about the culture of the drag ball to focus on the chagrin of the shocked heterosexual.

Dawn Powell's *Come Back to Sorrento* resembles *For the Pleasure of His Company* as well as *Strange Brother* in that it features an unusual central friendship between a man and a woman, a friendship that finds no ready-made social sanction, fits no available description. Connie Benjamin has fallen from prosperity and social position by running off as a young woman with a handsome circus performer; she now scrapes by as the wife of the village shoemaker, a simple and devoted man named Gus who was willing to overlook her disreputable erotic past, and she feasts on memories of the brilliant career as an opera singer she fancies she might have had.[6] She is delighted when she meets the new music teacher in town, Blaine Decker, who has recently spent time in Europe in the company of his intimate friend, a novelist named Starr Donnell. Connie and Blaine become closely attached to one another, feeling that they are the only two literate, sensitive, and truly artistically cultivated people in town, and there is some sharp but rueful comedy in the novel about their enablement of each other's delusions; but their mutual dedication to music, their identification with it, and their investment in its sustaining role in their lives is genuine and moving. The jacket copy of the 1997 reprint of *Come Back to Sorrento* has it that Blaine "is a homosexual in a closeted era," and while that categorical assignment certainly doesn't seem wrong, it also seems flat and reductive. We might recall here the challenging argument made by Tim Dean (2000) that sexuality in the twentieth century is misconstrued if we understand it to be only about what people prefer to do with their genitalia. Sexual identity is built as well from broad cultural tastes and activities, Dean argues; plenty of people are less interested in what we would call sex *per se* than in artistic endeavors and cultural undertakings, styles and forms that are associated contingently with particular sexual cultures.[7] That is why someone can be gay and celibate; that is why someone can be straight in bed but "culturally gay" (or nongay-identified, a fan of professional sports, but incidentally into sex with other men). It would have been simple for Dawn Powell to make it explicit that Blaine Decker was a closeted homosexual, but she did not; in her notebooks she recorded observations of identifiable homosexual types she encountered in her New York social life. On February 14, 1934, for instance, Powell recorded some flaming repartee between "two young colored fairies" (Powell 1995: 84). Powell did make it clear in *Come Back to Sorrento* that Connie Benjamin went rather avidly with men, but she showed as well that Connie (like June Westbrook) chafes under the restrictions placed upon a straight married woman, and is strongly drawn to an unconventional intimacy with Blaine that is grounded in something other than a narrowly construed "sexuality." Although Connie is at one point puzzled by Blaine's obvious lack of physical desire for her, and although she notices that other "men look at him a little oddly" because of his affected mannerisms (Powell 1932/1997: 33), she finally thinks "contentedly" that "To Decker she was without gender" (p. 96). For his part Blaine is distinctly averse to the very thought of physical intimacy with Connie or with any woman, but he plainly finds it refreshing and consoling to happen upon a friendship with a woman who is oblivious to the protocols of gender and sexual conformity that elsewhere in his life hold sway.

When the novel ends Decker is on a ship crossing the Atlantic, returning apprehensively to Paris, there to seek out Starr Donnell and resume the role of "Blaine Decker, cosmopolite" rather than "the village music teacher" (p. 184). He has been generously staked to this European sojourn by a wealthy woman in Dell River, Laurie Neville, who also fashioned herself one of the sophisticates of the little town; in his cabin on the steamer he has some books sent along by another of the misfits of the village, a spinster schoolteacher: "On the washstand lay the books from Miss Manning. He picked them up and examined the titles. Novels. He'd never liked novels but probably Starr's crowd would talk about them so he'd better read them" (pp. 184–5). It is a curious note on which to end a novel – this evocation of Decker's dislike of novels on account of their association with a pretentious crowd of Parisian sophisticates in whose company he will feel, he expects, naive and unaccomplished. This correlation of the novel as genre with a brittle scene of cultural aggression is the obverse of Blaine's and Connie's creation of a singular relationship grounded in sentimental musical expression.

It is not literally possible that Miss Manning could have sent *Strange Brother* along with Blaine, but as a thought experiment we might try to imagine what Blaine would have thought of the tortured Mark Thornton. Would he have recognized himself in Mark's sad "type"? Identified with Mark's misery? Been appalled by the conscious sophistication of Mark's New York City crowd? Found the whole matter merely mystifying? It *is* quite possible that Dawn Powell read *Strange Brother* then played its story backwards in her novel of one year later. Mark flees the small-town Midwest where his sexual nature finds no room for expression and no social welcome, and comes to a big city where educated, well-meaning people take a kindly if condescending interest in his plight. But this fate is not satisfying, for in the world of this novel he is condemned to be a "type" and his type is understood to be defined by a "handicap." Blaine Decker, on the contrary, finds it possible to improvise a life of some meager satisfaction for himself, involving an unconventional emotional attachment, in a provincial Midwest town not unlike the one Mark Thornton (and, for that matter, Bertram Cope) eagerly fled. *Come Back to Sorrento* satirizes sentimentality (but it also sentimentalizes small-town life), and it casts a critical glance at the violent fate that, in Niles's novel, awaits Mark with grim inevitability.

Coauthored by Charles Henri Ford and Parker Tyler, *The Young and Evil* (1933) is one of the truly remarkable novels of the twentieth century. First printed in Paris by the Obelisk Press in a limited edition (which customs authorities in England and in the United States blocked on the grounds of obscenity), it had been rejected by commercial publishers at the time and has rarely been readily accessible to readers in the time since then.[8] Among those who initially declined to publish it was Horace Liveright, who had recently issued Niles's *Strange Brother*. Liveright returned the manuscript to its authors accompanied by this charming expression of regret: "I read with infinite pleasure your brilliant novel, but I could not think of publishing it as a book – life is too short and the jails are unsatisfactory" (quoted in Steven Watson's introduction to the 1998 reprint, p. xxiv). Ford and Tyler shared the ambition of some of their predecessors to experiment in novelistic form as a means of exploring erotic freedom and dissolving fast-hardening sexual identity categories. Curiously, Djuna Barnes provided a blurb for the book that emphasized the exactitude of its representation of a congealed homosexual personality: "Never, to my knowledge, has a certain type of homosexual been so 'fixed' on paper," she claimed. And the critic Louis Kronenberger, who published its only American review, said it was "the first candid, gloves-off account of more or less professional young homosexuals" (Watson in Ford and Tyler 1933/1998: xxv). The tension between these claims is revealing: Barnes implies that the homosexual is a pre-existing natural type awaiting candid and accurate literary reproduction. Kronenberger, alternately, picks up on the fact that these characters are, in effect, expertly schooled and skilled in their chosen profession of homosexuality – they have made an art of it, we might say. In Ford and Tyler's novel, the artful inhabitation of a certain style of homosexual existence is itself a literary project.

The Young and Evil makes an instructive contrast with *Strange Brother*: it covers much of the same topical ground (penurious writers and artists with punishable sexual tastes living in New York City in the late 1920s), but its approach could hardly be more different. Several scenes in *The Young and Evil* might even be construed as pointed revisionary responses to scenes in *Strange Brother*, and for the sake of focusing this brief discussion of a complex and challenging novel I will concentrate on two such telling comparisons. One such scene in *Strange Brother* involves a stark encounter between sexual aberrance and the law. A "poor simpering boy" called Nelly is entrapped and arrested by a plainclothes detective in Harlem, and his case engages Mark's interest: "The whole thing sickened him," but "Nelly sickened him too" (p. 66). Mark goes to the court house to see what happens when Nelly is brought before a judge the next day, and is sorry that Nelly doesn't have the sense to modify his effeminate mannerisms in court; Nelly is sentenced to six months in prison, and Mark is led to visit the public library to read about the penal laws respecting "Crimes against Nature" (pp. 122–5), and leaves the library demoralized and scared. Certainly Niles wants her readers to agree with her that such laws are absurd and unjust, but the drama of her story involves only Mark's futile intellectual skepticism toward such laws and his despairing abjection in the face of their power. The comparable scene in *The Young and Evil* is framed and rendered very differently. There, two of the main characters, Karel and Frederick, are cruised (and then gay-bashed) by some sailors in Riverside Park, and when the sailors turn on them two policemen intervene to protect the young men. They are, of course, taken in to the police station (together with one of the sailors), and spend an uncomfortable night in custody, then face a judge the next morning. Frederick kindly advises the rather hapless sailor on courtroom strategy, and inquires with genuine curiosity as to why the sailor tried to hurt them, but the policeman prompts the sailor to lie and say that Karel and Frederick had offered to pay him for sex. The judge, however, is no fool; he meets Karel's eyes, sizes up the situation accurately, perceives immediately that the charges are implausible, and winks at Karel and Frederick to intimate that he knows the score. He discharges them summarily. "Then the magistrate leaned over and said sweetly but be more careful next time!" (p. 191).

The comparison I am making between these analogous scenes is not meant to be merely invidious, although it is hard not to prefer the way Ford and Tyler hilariously and aggressively expose the hypocrisy of law enforcement and imagine a queer-sympathetic judge whose wink allies his authority with their erotic adventuring, while Niles can only stage a scene of pity and abjection. More interesting here and throughout *The Young and Evil* is the way modernist textual techniques and what we might call coercive narrative focalization recruit the reader as a sympathetic and situated participant in the scene rather than a cowering spectator of it. Because the style of the narrative is by turns elliptical, compressed, campy, allusive, and ironic, and shifts quickly and unpredictably between various uncoordinated registers, a reader must work hard to fill in the gaps and connect the dots – read closely, provide a good deal of supplemental information (which implicates him or her as an insider already), follow the allusions, attend to the shifts, veer compliantly between campy gay argot and high intellectual discussion, and so forth. In other words, the various formal devices and extravagances and difficulties of the narrative *induct* readers, willy-nilly, into a very specific gay milieu, and even coerce readers into sympathetic identification with the renegade sexual culture of the protagonists.

The most brilliant scene in the novel, and the most formally inventive – the section that most stridently performs this queer initiation of the reader – also bears comparison with a scene in *Strange Brother*, the Harlem drag ball scene mentioned above. It is Julian and Frederick who go to the drag ball – who knows, maybe the very same ball that Mark and June observed from the sidelines. Whereas Mark and June were detached spectators (and the novel's readers were interpolated as curious onlookers alongside them), *The Young and Evil* does not allow such distance. The characters are "swallowed" by the ball (p. 152), and so are we. Neither Julian nor Frederick is in full drag, but they are wearing enough makeup "to be considered in costume and so get in for a dollar less" (p. 151). They don't sit at tables in the boxes alongside the dance floor (as Mark and June did), but join the boisterous crowd on the floor, as we in effect do too. "Dancing drew the blood faster through their bodies. Drink drusic drowned them. A lush annamaywong lavender-skinned negro gazed at him" (p. 154). That sentence, picked almost at random, gives a taste of the text's experimental modernist strategies. One fairly commonplace sentence of readily intelligible third-person narration (which prepares us for the textual effects of physical stimulation and sensory disorientation to follow). Then an ostentatiously alliterative sentence that rehearses the phonetic transition in the previous sentence from the hard *d* of "dancing" to the compound *dr* of "drew," but tripled in "drink drusic drowned," which evokes the kind of slurry mispronunciation of "music" drunkenness might produce. Then a glancing allusion to Anna May Wong, a Chinese-American movie star of the day, whose characteristic style the oddly hued ("lavender-skinned") dancer is presumably copying, while "lush" semantically recalls the drunkenness of the scene, and the object of the pronoun "him" is not at all clear. They are all moving around a wild dance floor, where people's costumes play wantonly with racial as well as gender identities, and interested glances are skipping promiscuously from person to person. Soon enough the rapidity and fragmentation of the prose, reproducing shards of bright conversation, campy commentary, and obscene innuendo, creates the sensory effect of immersion in the excitement of the dance floor – we seem to be circulating there drunkenly along with Karel and Frederick:

> shut your hole watching
>   them for a moment but when she opened her upstairs cunt and started to belch the greetings of the season I retired in a flurry her boyfriend with the imperfect lacework in the front of his mouth

was a thunderclap could indeed would have been

gentler Fairydale Bedagrace a prize bull in the 2000 pound class and his proud owner
is Harry A.

Koch there's my uncle looking for

me Beulah calm your bowels two o'clock

and not a towel wet that

would be both justice and

amusement Jim! I told you to stay home and mind the babies wished for nothing
better well who could? than a man lover and a woman lover in the same. (Ford and
Tyler 1933/1998: 155)

This careful effect of sensory immersion – even reproducing through its enjambments
(I would argue) the acoustic effect of turning abruptly in relation to another moving
dancer's utterance and hearing it first in one ear and then in the other – leaves the
reader, struggling to find some coherence or continuity among such fragments, no
allowance for distant spectatorship.

The Young and Evil has attracted remarkably little acute critical attention, and
deserves a closer and more extended analysis than can be provided here. Ford and
Tyler were both wont to minimize their technical artistic achievement, preferring to
treat the novel as a near-transcription of their own lives as bohemians and sexual ren-
egades in New York in the late 1920s. It is obviously not (merely) that. It is tempting
to treat it as a knowledgeable revisionary response to the erratic history of the gay
novel as practiced in the United States in the period since Stoddard's *For the Pleasure
of His Company* first imagined that innovation in novelistic form could disturb the
historical emergence and limiting consolidation of types of sexual personhood. Ford
and Tyler's diegesis involves a set of writers and artists and the sexual freedom that
often seems to have obtained in such circles; in this sense it recalls not only Stoddard's
novel but, in various ways and degrees, Prime-Stevenson's, Fuller's, Niles's, and
Powell's novels too (as well as several other gay novels mentioned in passing above –
Thurman's *Infants of the Spring*, Nugent's *Gentleman Jigger*). Parker Tyler is on record
as having claimed that *The Young and Evil* was stitched together by Ford largely from
private letters written to him by Tyler (Watson in Ford and Tyler 1933/1998: xx).
Whatever the literal truth of this claim, it links their text broadly to the history of
the novel as genre, with its long involvement with epistolarity, and more particularly
to the novels that have been discussed here, most of which insistently invoke and cite
and sometimes include the private letters that ostensibly allowed the sexually dissident characters to express themselves more candidly and to position the novel's discourse in relation to protocols of publicity and decency.

Novels that might be construed as gay in the period after *The Young and Evil* tended
to resemble *Imre: A Memorandum* and *Strange Brother*: they took the homosexual category of person for granted, were not particularly sensitive to the historicity of sexuality
as such, and usually constructed melodramas of shame framed as progressive social
critique. They ought not to be dismissed as summarily as this, but the arc of development traced here from *For the Pleasure of His Company* to *The Young and Evil* – in which

the generic form of the novel was both exploited for its received properties and inventively deformed in the interest of literary remaking of the social organization of sexuality – this conjunction of ambitions seems to have lapsed in the 1930s and 1940s. There are noteworthy partial exceptions, Carson McCullers' *The Member of the Wedding* (1946), for instance. In this gorgeous composition the protagonist, Frankie, persistently feels "the need to be known for her true self and recognized" (McCullers 1946/2004: 62), but that true self is difficult if not impossible to name under the regimes of sexual subjectivity available to her. Maybe her small friend and neighbor John Henry, a sissyish six-year-old, is somewhat more intelligible within the system of sexual recognizability that obtained in the late 1940s; he likes to wear the housekeeper Berenice's clothes, and takes a special interest in her mentioning a man by the name of Lily Mae Jenkins who "prisses around with a pink satin blouse and one arm akimbo," fell in love with another man, and "changed his nature and his sex and turned into a girl" (p. 81). The narrative tempts us to pigeonhole Frankie as a tomboy tending toward lesbianism, but also frustrates our inclination to do so. It places its faith in the power of imaginative fiction to complicate such reductive assignments: this is represented by a game Frankie and John Henry and Berenice play after dinner in which they "criticize the Creator." Essentially, they redesign the universe to suit themselves better. Frankie has a long list of improvements to the world she would make, which notably includes the provision that "people could instantly change back and forth from boys to girls, which ever way they felt like and wanted" (p. 97). Berenice says "that the law of human sex was exactly right just as it was and could no way be improved" (p. 97), but John Henry too thinks gender and sexual categories ought not to be fixed. His reconfigured world "was a mixture of delicious and freak," and would bestow on people a "sudden long arm that could stretch from here to California," and would add to the world "chocolate dirt and rains of lemonade, the extra eye seeing a thousand miles, a hinged tail that could be let down as a kind of prop to sit on when you wished to rest, [and] candy flowers" (p. 96), but his most important improvement would be the provision that "people ought to be half boy and half girl" (p. 98). By 1946 when *The Member of the Wedding* offered such "delicious and freak" fantasies, their utopian ambition was decidedly backward.

NOTES

1   Prime-Stevenson's text actually reads "The silences in intimacy stand for the most perfect mutuality" (pp. 46–7). One is tempted to believe that Stoddard approved of this gesture toward the unsaid – toward discretion and obliquity – in a novel that was, by comparison to his own, generally more direct and outspoken.

2   Imre's rather stilted and old-fashioned style of speaking is meant to stand in, it seems, for his actual Hungarian tongue, or to indicate that he learned to speak a rather old-fashioned formal English. But it does have the curious campy effect of placing him in a different literary register – the "seaside novelette" register, perhaps – from Oswald, who speaks a more idiomatic English.

3   James Gifford uses a 1913 short story by Prime-Stevenson, "Under the Sun," in which the con-

tents of a private library owned by a homosexual named Dayneford are listed, to indicate the way in which one text can be a guide to a larger archive of homosexual writing.

4 The novel does this in countless ways, but most incisively in its depiction of the ongoing relationship between Basil and another bachelor, Medora's crippled brother-in-law Joseph Foster, who occupies a wheelchair in the attic of her house and has a visual deficiency that makes it difficult for him to read. Basil visits Foster regularly, to read to him from histories and newspapers and the like, and to engage in guarded speculation about Bertram and Arthur. It is on a day when Foster is feeling particular "blue" and bitchy that Basil wishes he "had brought a novelette" (p. 42).

5 There is an uncanny resonance between *Strange Brother*'s staging of this analogy between human sexual classification and insect taxonomy, on the one hand, and the curious scene staged in *For the Pleasure of His Company* when Paul and Jack first meet in a special room in the theatre director Harry English's house, a "chamber of entomology" crowded with "cases of brilliantly tinted butterflies" that Harry and a friend collect, preserve, and display (pp. 85–6). For Stoddard, this orderly exhibition of an entomological collection serves to set off, by ironic contrast, the natural unclassifiability of Paul and Jack. Mark Thornton, however, does not defy classification at all; he merely awaits his proper description and emplacement within a natural schema ordered according to morally neutral scientific principles rather than punitive heteronormative principles.

6 The intricate relationship between vocal music performance and sexual dissidence – in Powell's novel, in *Bertram Cope's Year* (Bertram

is a talented singer and his performative animation in song grows in Arthur's presence), and elsewhere – would, like the relationship between literariness and sexuality I am tracing here, reward examination.

7 Dean contends, revising a Freudian psychoanalytic concept of sublimation, "that we can have intensely pleasurable experiences and intimate relationships with verbal and visual forms even when those forms aren't ostensibly erotic at all. Such relationships should not be considered secondary to or necessarily less intense than interpersonal sexual relationships, because they draw on the same libidinal sources and fantasies" (p. 277). He is perhaps being hyperbolic when he says soon after that "some people 'love literature' *in exactly the same way* as others love sex" (p. 277), but his theoretical stringency is useful. Another way to put this would be to revise Foucault's (1986: 157) admonition that we cease to speak of "sexuality" and instead speak of "bodies and pleasures," and extend the list: bodies, pleasures, novels, music, food, gardening, etc.

8 The out-of-print 1988 edition published by Gay Presses of New York, with an indispensable introduction by Steven Watson, is the only starting point for informed discussion of the novel. It reprints in facsimile the Obelisk Press edition, adds an informative introduction and notes, and supplements the text with color reproductions of watercolor illustrations from the novel by Pavel Tchelichew, Ford's lover. There is a cheap edition from Olympia Press available, but it is riddled with textual errors and unsuitable for reading, let alone scholarship. I have been unable to obtain a copy of a recent reprint edition from Metronome Press in Paris.

References and Further Reading

Austen, Roger. (1995). *Genteel Pagan: The Double Life of Charles Warren Stoddard*, ed. John W. Crowley. Amherst: University of Massachusetts Press.

Boone, Joseph Allen. (1998). *Libidinal Currents: Sexuality and the Shaping of Modernism*. Chicago: University of Chicago Press.

Chauncey, George. (1995). *Gay New York: Gender, Urban Culture, and the Making of the Gay Male World 1890–1940*. New York: Basic Books.

Dean, Tim. (2000). *Beyond Sexuality*. Chicago: University of Chicago Press.

Ford, Charles Henri and Parker Tyler. (1933/1998). *The Young and the Evil*. New York: Gay Presses of New York.

Foucault, Michel. (1986). *The History of Sexuality Vol. 1: An Introduction*, trans. Robert Hurley. New York: Vintage Books.

Fuller, Henry Blake. (1919/1998). *Bertram Cope's Year: A Novel*. New York: Turtle Point Press.

Gifford, James. (1995). *Dayneford's Library: American Homosexual Writing 1900–1913*. Amherst: University of Massachusetts Press.

Herring, Scott. (2007). *Queering the Underworld: Slumming, Literature, and the Undoing of Lesbian and Gay History*. Chicago: University of Chicago Press.

McCullers, Carson. (1946/2004). *The Member of the Wedding*. New York: Mariner Books.

Niles, Blair. (1931). *Strange Brother*. New York: Horace Liveright.

Nissen, Axel (ed.). (2003). *The Romantic Friendship Reader: Love Stories Between Men in Victorian America*. Boston, MA: Northeastern University Press.

Nugent, Richard Bruce. (2008). *Gentleman Jigger*, ed. and intro. Thomas H. Wirth, foreword Arnold Rampersad. New York: Da Capo Press.

Powell, Dawn. (1932/1997). *Come Back to Sorrento* [*The Tenth Moon*]. South Royalton, VT: Steerforth Press.

Powell, Dawn. (1995). *The Diaries of Dawn Powell 1931–1965*, ed. Tim Page. South Royalton, VT: Steerforth Press.

Prime-Stevenson, Edward. (1906/2003). *Imre: A Memorandum*. Peterborough, ON: Broadview Press.

Rich, Adrienne. (1994). Compulsory heterosexuality and lesbian existence. In *Blood, Bread, and Poetry* (pp. 23–75). New York: Norton.

Stoddard, Charles Warren. (1903/1987). *For the Pleasure of His Company: A Tale of the Misty City, Thrice Told*. New York: Prentice-Hall.

Williams, Raymond. (1977). *Marxism and Literature*. Oxford: Oxford University Press.

22

The Popular Western

William R. Handley

Echoing how the proverbial Western sheriff – and a recent American president – ambivalently wants his villain in territory beyond clear boundaries of law or nation, the slogan "Dead or Alive" can also be taken as a question that literary, film, and cultural critics and marketers have asked about the popular Western genre, even before the 1960s. No sooner has the Western's demise seemed evident than it has suddenly revived, especially in film. Three decades ago, the spectacular failure of the film *Heaven's Gate* (1980) – which gave a staple event of the genre, Wyoming's Johnson County War of 1892 between cattlemen and homesteaders, its most profound treatment ever – suggested the genre's pulse was nearly undetectable. But then the "Best Picture" Oscar-winning films *Dances with Wolves* (1990) and *Unforgiven* (1992) suggested the genre had only been in hiding. When moviegoers responded enthusiastically to the gender-bending controversies of *Thelma and Louise* (1991) and *Brokeback Mountain* (2005), earlier proclamations about the death of the genre seemed, to borrow Mark Twain's response to rumors of his death, highly exaggerated.

For more than a century, writers and filmmakers have revisited the genre, setting it in a past, vanished West and "timeless" geography, yet making it resonate with changing contemporary issues often, but not always, dramatized as a matter of life and death. In the first half of the twentieth century, Westerns written by more than a hundred authors, both men and women, and sold to tens of millions of readers from different economic classes, enacted dramas about gender and power, sexuality and marriage, American democracy and inequality, labor and capital, Native American absence and presence, and both domestic and imperial affairs. Collectively, and often in the same novel, the Western dramatizes the difference between expressing with words and silencing with a gun, as it enacts a cultural drama about whether white Americans have a distinctive cultural idiom and identity or can only borrow or absorb them from others who predate them, both culturally and in their claims to contested lands (whether Indians, Mexican *vaqueros*, British writers, or former makers of Westerns). Often in the same book or film, the Western goes against itself in several respects, undermining the very values it seems to affirm, as if in imitation of the formulaic convention that while the hero must triumph against his enemies or at least achieve the audience's undying sympathy, he, or his values, must also be under threat in order for this to happen – and something must be sacrificed to defend them or give them meaning. Even when a Western hero or actor brings a demonstrated track record to a novel or a film, fully reassuring the audience at the story's start that he is up to whatever challenge will confront him, something always seems to be in question – whether because of the protagonist's reticence and seeming lack of emotion, or his social isolation, or the harsh natural environment, or the news of a crime that cannot be undone. An almost melancholy, even existentialist quality is palpable in many Westerns – which is why Jean-Paul Sartre and Simone de Beauvoir were fans of several Westerns, including John Ford's *The Searchers* (1956). Whoever wins or loses at its end, something has already been lost before a Western begins that can never be recovered. The genre survives as the search continues for both the searchers and the sought, whether the object of the search is dead or alive.

The figure wanted dead or alive in Westerns is often a lone, historically noncontextualized bad white man, but he is also often a representative Indian, Mexican, Mormon polygamist, federal bureaucrat, or capitalist whose context is more historically specific. If nothing else, the Western villain is the enemy of individualism and the equally ambiguous ancillary values it stands in for, liberty and property; the hero embodies this individualism and its related values in his own historically noncontextualized way, especially in Westerns written by men. Demonstrating relational values is the explicit goal of many Westerns written by women in the first half of the twentieth century, some of whom put their men in ranch communities with each other – in B. M. Bower's "Flying U" stories, for example, or Cherry Wilson's "Triangle Z Ranch" stories, one of which even depicts women taking over a town's public offices and outlawing certain male vices. Whereas many Westerns by women in the first half of the twentieth century suggest how communities might survive, male writers of Westerns created, and capitalized upon, the individual cowboy at a time when the historical cowboy figure did not survive the rise of corporate cattle interests.

Despite an increase in their populations, Native Americans continued, in the early twentieth century, to be referred to as "the vanishing American," an ideological phrase that would have had more historical accuracy if applied to the individualistic cowboy, at a time when both of these "vanishing Americans" proliferated in representations of the West in fiction and in film. While they share both an imaginary and real screen for the projection of contradictory kinds of national nostalgia in this period, however, "cowboys and Indians" do not share the literary stage in many Westerns from 1900 to 1950, including the most influential ones.

The novel most often cited as the origin of the modern Western, Owen Wister's *The Virginian* (1902), has only virtual, off-stage Indians, and it begins with a preface by the author that is a historical epitaph for the horseman of the plains: "he will never come again." Yet the novel became nothing like a cultural epitaph for its Western hero. Wister did not write another Western, but he helped *The Virginian* get produced on Broadway and thus gave it, as his huge readership did, added life. *The Virginian* would become in name, if not in exact content, the subject of dozens of plays, films, and television shows up until 2000 (and the subject of an academic volume in 2003). Most Westerns written after Wister's bear little resemblance to it, which makes it as curious an "origin" of a genre as the fact that it begins with an epitaph. The cowboy most certainly *would* come again – at least on the screen – but unlike the Virginian who gets married, has children, and becomes a manager of a corporate cattle operation, he would also leave again, like Jack Schaefer's titular hero in *Shane* (1949), who rides away from the family at the end, as the boy on the homestead famously calls out in the 1953 film version, "Come back, Shane, come back!"

In 1900, the dime novel, first published in 1860, was fading from the literary marketplace. In these adventure stories, the usually white male hero blended savagery and civilization in a manner that warded civilization against lawless white men or Indians even as the hero protected himself from too much civilization (especially women and marriage), remaining an outsider, as Bill Brown has observed, to the society he acts upon and within. Describing Max Brand's 1923 novel *Hired Guns*, Brown writes:

> Just as the novel's isolated community stands outside time, so the hero stands outside the community, resolving its conflicts only to flee. The narrative syntax – the outsider establishes social justice, then returns to the outside – remains the staple of the adventure formula, which depicts a need for social change, but a change that must come from without, and from an individual's changeless heroism. (Brown 1991: 366)

As in James Fenimore Cooper's Leatherstocking tales, the Western adventure hero's blending of savagery and civilization was the sign of cultural negotiation surrounding the significance of frontier settlement for American national identity and history. From the 1890s to the early twentieth century, the historian Frederick Jackson Turner touted the significance to the nation's development of the "frontier" as the meeting point between wilderness (read savagery) and civilization, arguing that without that transformative encounter, Americans would not have become American: self-reliant, egalitarian, individualistic. The meaning of American history and identity were, according to Turner, Theodore Roosevelt, and a number of other myth-makers of the West from the Eastern establishment at the turn of the century, indebted to conditions that the settlement of the West rendered no longer available to Americans after the end of the "frontier phase" of US history. At such a moment, Americans may have been hungry for representations of the process that had purportedly made America what it was; the cowboy became their "changeless" representative who could continually negotiate crises of cultural and national identity, as well as contemporaneous questions about social and economic values, even though the cowboy remained historically and socially outside twentieth-century American readers' actual experience.

The decline of the dime novel, the cowboy's move to center stage in the modern Western, and nostalgia for an older, unchanged West are some of the factors that contributed to the Western's popularity. To these, one should add a general literary shift in popular Western writing from an older economy, often understood as or represented through racial conflict, to a late industrial national economy whose conflicts, transposed onto an older West, were more often understood as or read through gendered rather than racialized difference, by both male and female writers of Westerns in the early twentieth century. In 1904, the *Bookman* proclaimed that the Indian had largely disappeared from print media – at a time when the Indian was appearing (often in order ideologically to continue to "vanish") in early cinema. Yet there is little question that the Western novel usually retained its racial (and frequently racist) dimensions even when there were no nonwhite characters whose roles had been changed or written out. The shift in fictional Westerns from racialized economic tensions and themes to gendered ones had to do chiefly with two historical conditions: the end of wars against Indians that coincided with the consolidation of "frontier" areas into federal lands; and the economic crises of the 1890s that pitted corporate or capitalist interests against laboring masses and individual ranchers and homesteaders. The latter served as emblems of Thomas Jefferson's dream of an agrarian America of yeoman farmers, an ideal that retained a nostalgic pull at the birth of the Cold War and the military-industrial complex, when audience sympathies sided with heroic white settlers and against villainous corporate cattlemen. The individualistic hero of the 1950s had, ironically, started out in *The Virginian* (1902) as a figure of social menace, one who in the end had to be punished by death (an execution that Wister insisted, against producers' wishes, remain in the Broadway production). The Virginian's moral compass aligns with the interests of corporate ownership, which is why he will become ranch manager. His enforcement of extralegal justice for cattle-thieving against his best friend Steve, whose death will later make the Virginian sob as he recalls his friend's bravery before being hanged, is essential to his heroism; by it he proves himself unswayable by any sentimentality, including the moral objections of his fiancée.

The Progressive Era's sense of conflict between the newer, more urban and industrialized America in need of reform and the preindustrial, agrarian past so easily transposed on to an older, frontier West was ineluctably tied to the modern question of women's civil rights and cultural role. The gendered component of this Progressive debate is almost everywhere evident in the modern Western. Theodore Roosevelt, who wanted to "hold on to the fruits of industrialism without losing, at the same time, individual freedom" (Etulain 1971/1980: 58), espoused the masculine "strenuous life" as a curative for modern ills; he drew on a Western mythos indebted to his ranching experience in Dakota and transported to San Juan Hill with his Rough Riders in Cuba. In this, his friend Owen Wister, who dedicated *The Virginian* to Roosevelt, followed suit, imbuing the question of late industrial corporate America's relationship to democracy and individual freedom with an anxiously masculine ethos that was intent on mocking the role of women (and feminized figures like Woodrow Wilson) in the age of Progressive reform. For new nationalists like Roosevelt and Wister, "the American West was the last frontier of freedom and individualism and it had to be preserved as a sacred bulwark against profane industrialism" (Etulain 1971/1980: 58), as well as against emasculating reformers. To lose the older West was to lose one's manhood. In this strain of the modern Western, strenuous masculinity is a form of antimodernism, and the historical fracture is conceived as a gendered one.

The Progressive Era did not, however, invent nostalgia for the American West. The ravenous conquest of Western lands and indigenous peoples in the nineteenth century created a nostalgia even from early on in the nineteenth century for what Americans were changing and claiming – and culturally representing and marketing while doing so. It is no accident that after Frederick Jackson Turner announced his thesis about the significance of the frontier in American history in 1893, he repeated it for 30 years thereafter, and that the cowboy would take center stage in the Western, after having been a bit player in the dime novel, at the same historical moment when, as Wister's novel affirmingly records, corporations and their managers supplanted individual cattle ranchers and homesteaders in a postfrontier economy. Such paradoxical beginnings and endings – in literature and in history – surround the Western at the beginning of the twentieth century, when women fiction writers' authorial perspectives on the same historical circumstances and literary types were published, as they were at the birth of the dime novel, only to disappear for several decades from literary history.

If the nineteenth century, from James Fenimore Cooper to the dime novel, is when the Western developed its features, and the second half of the twentieth century is when "it grew up and gained respect" (Alter 1997: 896), then the first half of the twentieth century would seem a perplexing developmental stage – as if a teenager both found a higher purpose and sloughed it off, only to wake up in middle age a suddenly wiser, more self-aware person who recognized not only that those youthful fantasies were just that, but also that they had been the contradictory cause, all along, of a prolonged midlife crisis of disillusionment, self-deception, and bad faith.

Despite the importance many Westerns attach to life and death struggles, the figuration of a literary genre as having a life span, developmental stages, or periods of vitality or decline is of course not unique to the Western (the novel itself is often so figured). Yet the diagnosis and prognosis of the life of the Western is especially burdened with a host of social, political, and national questions that express anxieties – or wishes – about more than just the survival of a genre. Questions about its rebirth or senescence, as if the Western were reducible to one kind of hero, one historical moment, or one national idea, are always in part ideological questions about the meaning of American pasts and presents, a contest of politics and history in which the contradictions of American experience, at home and abroad, have a showdown in which none of them is easily resolved, and in which all of them can potentially return to fight another day. To read or revisit certain examples of the genre at any given moment in its literary history is to see how historical contradictions are enacted in literary form, particularly the historically distorting American ideology derived from the frontier myth that Americans are continually starting over in some past or future frontier, as if innocence or moral clarity could be continually lost and adolescence could perpetually follow moral reckoning.

With its authors' extensive output, its influence both on other media (especially film) and on "high" art and literature, its political reverberations from the nineteenth to the twenty-first centuries (when Hillary Clinton, the only presidential candidate in 2008 not to have donned any cowboy couture in the campaign, spoke derisively of "cowboy diplomacy"), and in its reach beyond the national culture that originated it, the popular Western has challenged scholars of the American novel to place it within several historical contexts, literary histories, critical methodologies, and theoretical paradigms in order to grasp what made the genre, and made it so powerful and durable. This is especially challenging with regard to the popular Western in the first half of the twentieth century, when it acquired a generic formula and almost at the same time began to reimagine and grow beyond it, in ways that reverberate in American culture and in Western literary scholarship today. Quite a feat, one might say, for a genre whose dime store elements seem so rudimentary, ideologically so schematic and narrow, so indebted to the nineteenth century that it should have died an early death when the dime novel faded at the beginning of the twentieth. But the Western has never been so ideologically clear-cut. It has seemed so, in part, because certain accounts gained ascendancy up through the 1970s that iterated a particular canon (always beginning with Wister) and neglected other writers, especially women.

With a vast readership from 1860 to the turn of the century, the dime novel shaped the modern formula, but it also has shaped, even up to the 1990s, many critical assumptions about what the Western represents. In his study of popular fiction, Ken Gelder calls the Western "the most ideologically focused" of the eight popular genres, which, in addition to the Western, comprise romance, crime fiction, science fiction, fantasy, horror, historical popular novels, and adventure novels (Gelder 2004: 80). Yet, or perhaps as a result of the genre's assumed ideological focus, Gelder's study does not examine Westerns. And perhaps Richard Slotkin's voluminous scholarship on the ideology of the frontier myth across American history suggests it need not be rehashed, especially given Slotkin's sustained Marxist critique. (For the present purposes I have listed only his third volume, from 1992, in the list of references below.) Whether examined thoroughly or not at all, the presumption that the popular Western has a clear national or ideological focus has at times limited scholarship on the genre. In describing one such limiting tendency, Christine Bold argues that of all the popular genres, the Western "has been the most resistant to theorized interrogations, presumably because the genre is so enmeshed in nationalist mythology and so equipped – by setting, plot, and politics – to naturalize its own ideologies and commodification" (Bold 1997: 868–9). Of the resulting critical lacuna, Bold notes that "it is astonishing that a narrative so manifestly preoccupied with the wielding of power has not attracted sustained Foucaultian analysis" (1997: 869). Such common presumptions about the Western – that it is the most enmeshed of popular genres in American nationalist mythology, that it is the most ideologically "focused" – have their undeniable merit, which is perhaps why they are so often rehearsed rather than examined. As other critics have shown, however, the ideology of individual Westerns and of the genre generally is often far more complex and contradictory than is commonly assumed (Tompkins 1992, Robinson 1993, Mitchell 1996, Tatum 1997, Handley 2002).

Seen less as an ideological straight shooter or mass-produced formula than as a cultural clearinghouse of diverse interests and readerships, the popular Western is instructive not just about the market for popular genres but also about the much larger field of Western American literature, particularly in the period 1900–50, when the modern popular genre took shape and some of Western American literature's finest novels began to be published. This fiction absorbed and shaped other literary currents and cultural media (especially film) in a manner that would make the popular genre's conventions, characters, and iconography after the 1960s of interest as much to "high" cinematic art and literature as to advertisers of cars and advisors to presidential campaigns down to the present.

Recent scholarship has complicated the ideological import of Westerns in three main ways: by opening up the canon, by revealing the internal ideological contradictions within and between canonical Westerns, and by showing the extent of the genre's contested ideological terrain in other literary genres and cultural media that both influenced and were influenced by it.

One critical (and often marketing) misconception about the Western that reigned for decades, and that recent scholarship has corrected, is that "only men read Westerns and, by extension, only men write them" (Alter 1997: 893); that the genre is written "by men, for men, about men" (Piekarski 1997: 898) – even that its main readers were predominantly adolescent boys. This was not entirely accurate even at the beginning of the dime novel in 1860; it was much less the case at the beginning of the twentieth century: women writers made a considerable contribution to the genre, although their accomplishments long went unrecognized once a more masculine-centered formula dominated the marketplace during the first half of the twentieth century.

One reason that women writers' contributions went unnoticed for so long is related to conditions of the predominant market for Western fiction in the first half of the twentieth century, the magazine market. Both men and women wrote for "pulp" magazines (and, later, for "slicks"); and some women wrote for the highest paying of the Western pulps, *Western Story Magazine*. Both men and women often wrote under

pseudonyms or with gender-neutral initials for their first names; Frederick Faust –
now known chiefly as Max Brand – employed a whole fraternity of pseudonyms.
Although men and women who wrote Westerns had some similar reasons for pseud-
onymity, namely sales – since the practice multiplied opportunities for publication –
it was only women authors' gender identity that went into hiding for the sake of
profitability. For some women, only British publishers provided a book market for
their longer fiction; in the case of Elsa Barker, who published over 200 Western stories
in the magazine market, her seven Western novels appeared only in Britain, and under
the name "E. M. Barker." The list of women writers of Westerns in the first half of
the twentieth century includes Florence Finch Kelly, Honoré Willsie Morrow, Cherry
Wilson, Eli (Eliza) Coulter, C. K. (Chloe Kathleen) Shaw, Caroline Lockhart, Frances
McElrath, and perhaps the best known – and sometimes the only woman writer named
in earlier scholarship or included in anthologies – B. M. (Bertha Muzzy) Bower, a
contemporary of Owen Wister. (Against Wister's single Western, however, Bower
weighed in with an astonishing 70 titles.)

These writers are significant not simply because they were women or were left out
of literary history until recently, but because their work offers fascinating alternatives
to, parodies of, and critical commentaries on the plots and concerns of male Western
writers, even though it is exceedingly rare to find a female heroine as the protagonist
in any Western novel. Although male Western writers rarely violated the gendered
decorum about violence in their work (only men kill, and they shoot only men),
occasionally a woman writer would have a female character kill or be shot. (A woman
in a Zane Grey novel is shot only because the shooter mistakes her for a man, and she
recovers.) Most often, women writers were distinguished from their male counterparts
through their de-emphasizing of violence and gunplay, and their stressing instead
interpersonal relationships, as well as drawing more from domestic, sentimental, and
romance genres than from the adventure formula. Even with an all-male cast of characters, Westerns by E. M. Bower and Cherry Wilson, for example, did not portray
male characters engaging in violence, but did show them satisfying the need for
familial relationships amongst themselves, often by taking collective care of
orphans.

Male writers of popular Westerns had the most publishing success: when Zane
Grey died in 1939, 27 million copies of his books had been sold; many of his books
are still in print today, selling about a half a million copies each year, and now total-
ing 70 million. Such immense sales and the concomitant success among male authors
in having their novels made into films – no other writer has had more of his books
brought to screen during his lifetime than Zane Grey – helped to reinforce the misconception that the Western was an essentially male genre, based on a narrow sense
of the possibilities of the "formula" that male writers shaped and promoted. By any
standard, the two million copies of her novels that E. M. Bower sold and the seven
films made from Cherry Wilson's novels make them popular writers of Westerns.
Because of their freedom to reimagine and combine generic and plot formulas, women
writers of Westerns had a large readership.

Despite their greater success in the popular Western, male writers cannot even be said to have originated the genre. While the roots of the Western are not singular, and its many sources are not easily identifiable, a few facts surrounding its origins refute the misconception that the Western is by men, for men, and about men, and indicate how literary canons, like the critical assumptions that shape them, both promote and disguise what were in fact possible alternative paths in literary history. To begin with, a woman wrote the first dime novel in 1860. Ann Sophia Stephens's *Malaeska: The Indian Wife of the White Hunter* was the first Beadle and Adams dime novel, having been reprinted from an 1839 story paper. Christine Bold argues that "its claims to occupy a central position in the story of the popular West are considerable" (1997: 864) and has demonstrated how its understanding of American history is a significant departure from the work of James Fenimore Cooper, with whom it shares certain elements. Cooper's plots resolve the wilderness/civilization divide through aristocratic marriage, which Bold argues marks the triumph of Euro-American settlement. But Stephens's novel marks the failure, not the triumph, of that settlement, the end of an aristocratic line, and the failure of Indian integration into American civilization. Although *Malaeska* sold well, it was a subsequent dime novel published that same year, Edward S. Ellis's *Seth Jones; or, The Captives of the Frontier*, that became the dime novel's formulaic template, the result of an editor's preference for its imitation of Cooper over Stephens's variation. In 1950, Henry Nash Smith argued in his seminal study *Virgin Land* that dime novels "lead almost in a straight line from the Beadle publications to the Westerns of the present day." The case of Ann S. Stephens, like that of other women writers, indicates that this line appears "straight" only because of the simplifying effect of retrospection that ignores specific choices writers, editors, and marketers made from among several options. Smith confidently but mistakenly claimed about the Western's history before and after 1900: "Devoid of social and ethical meaning, the Western story could develop in no direction save that of a straining and exaggeration of its formulas," abandoning "all effort to be serious" and sinking "to the near-juvenile level it was to occupy with virtually no change down to our own day" (1950: 119–20).

It is also true that a woman wrote the first cowboy or formula Western novel: whether Emma Ghent Curtis's *The Administratrix* (1889) or Mary Hallock Foote's *The Led-Horse Claim* (1883), which Norris Yates claims with "some justice . . . could be labeled the first formula Western," noting that her later fiction included themes, characters, and action sequences that became staples of the genre (Yates 1995: 11). Owen Wister cited Mary Hallock Foote's work as one of the sources of inspiration in writing *The Virginian*. (Hallock Foote's letters would become both inspiration and literal source for Wallace Stegner's 1971 Pulitzer Prize-winning novel *Angle of Repose*.) The year Wister's novel appeared, so did another Western that dealt with the Johnson County War of 1892 between cattlemen and rustlers: Frances McElrath's *The Rustler: A Tale of Love and War in Wyoming*, which reads as if it were intended as an account of that conflict's significance specifically in opposition to the one Wister's novel would make famous. Victoria Lamont has explored in detail these differences and what they tell us about this important transitional period in the gendered economics and politics of both the West and the Western's marketplace. "Perhaps," writes Lamont, "the genre that we now recognize as the Western became insistently masculine precisely because it, like so many other traditionally masculine spheres in turn-of-the-century American culture and society, had become subject to feminist occupation" (Lamont 2003: 150). The conflict between cattlemen and homesteaders marked a shift in frontier and postfrontier economies, between individual labor and corporate interests, a battle McElrath's novel takes a woman-centered, even proto-feminist position on, showing how it is women's work – traditionally seen as applicable only to the domestic sphere – that will help manage the transition between frontier and postfrontier economies. In Wister's account, it is the Virginian's extraordinary and extralegal defense of corporate interests that is the sign of "good" management and heroic character – as is his ability to put his reform-minded New Woman fiancée, Molly Stark Wood, in her gendered place by novel's end. What Lamont and other scholars have shown is that, contrary to the Western's hypermasculine ethos, in which women seem to have been incidental, it is precisely debates about women's power and place that dramatically shaped the genre in the early twentieth century by authorizing both male and female writers' voices and their competing claims on questions of the politics, economics, and gendered heroics of Western mythologizing.

That this more complicated literary history – quite often by women, for women, or about women – was until recently forgotten or unrecorded in literary histories and anthologies reveals the self-reinforcing nature of the critical assumptions behind the canons that critics shape. The gendered dichotomy that begins with Cooper and that Wallace Stegner and other writers of "serious" Western literature would invoke throughout the twentieth century – women seen as Eastern civilizers, men as Western and wild – has without question an extensive literary pedigree, but when it is taken as axiomatic, this dichotomy reproduces a certain standard but incomplete canon of the popular Western. Jane Tompkins's argument (1992) that what the Western represents is men's desire to escape everything women stand for in the sentimental tradition, such as religion, civilization, and domesticity, may explain why the novels she writes about are all by men. Analyzing works by both men and women together might render a similar argument, but with a rich difference. That difference promises not only to open up the canon of the popular Western but also to allow one to see how certain novels by Grey and Wister and their heroes are indebted to and quite ambivalent about the very things women are seen (in this argument) to represent, among others: religion, communication, female autonomy, and the family.

Indeed, one of the hallmarks of many early twentieth-century Westerns is their "having it both ways" (Robinson 1993) with regard to their ideological contradictions, gender roles, and the deadly serious yet male adolescent impulses that often animate the dialogue and plots. (Perhaps the cowpuncher hero's most famous retort among all Westerns is the Virginian's to a low-life who has cursed him: "When you call me that, *smile*.") After the groundbreaking work in the study of popular culture by Marshall McLuhan, Roland Barthes, Stuart Hall, and others, popular cultural forms are no longer considered by most scholars as "opiates for unthinking consumers but as sites of ongoing struggle for meaning, as fictionalizations of issues that remain highly contested and always partial," according to the Western scholar Lee Clark Mitchell, who goes on to argue that:

> Such resonant self-contradiction is actually the source of popular appeal, with a text not simply offering escapist entertainment but serving as both justification and critique of the very issues from which readers think they are escaping. Mass dreams, like individual dreams, always trace a return of the repressed, but in them as well repressed material is neither obvious nor unambiguous. . . . Like other forms of popular culture, the most successful Westerns covertly question the values they proclaim, allowing diverse audiences different levels of recognition and resistance. . . . Like other popular texts, they only seem at first glance to resolve the issues they engage. Looked at methodically, they achieve something more complex: negotiating a constantly threatened middle terrain, offering narrative forms that disguise contradictions in the ideological premises they celebrate. (Mitchell 1997: 890)

Mitchell demonstrates the subtler purposes of classic Westerns in his 1996 study *Westerns*, arguing that readers responded to novels by Owen Wister and Zane Grey in part because the novels resonated with contemporary questions like the New Woman and white slavery. As with its immediate readers, so with literary and cultural critics: the Western lends itself "to no single or straightforward reading" and attracts different readerly and critical constituencies (Mitchell 1997: 890).

For all of its divergences from the formula it is often seen to have launched, Owen Wister's *The Virginian* is paradigmatic in regard to the Western's internal contradictions and multivalences. Although early in the novel the hero asks, "What's the use o' being married?", the sign of his apparent maturation is that he does get married at the end of the novel. Yet on his honeymoon he wants to regress to some kind of primal boyhood as he imagines that an otter might say to him, "What's the gain in being a man? Come roll on the sand with me." For, after all, a man's responsibilities can be deadly serious: a hero might have to hang his best friend for stealing cattle. In doing so the Virginian kills off something adolescent and possibly forbidden in him, argues Jane Tompkins, even as the honeymoon scene states "openly the counterargument to its own point of view" in the Virginian's questioning of the purpose of masculinity (Tompkins 1992: 155). Perhaps the oddest contradiction in the novel is that while Wister puts his hero through these tests and charts his maturation, he arrives at the beginning of the novel with his virile heroism seductively beyond question, even inborn, living proof that as Wister would have it in the novel's most overt and polemical contradiction, "It was through the Declaration of Independence that we Americans acknowledged the *eternal inequality* of man." Not everyone is born a self-sufficient hero like the Virginian, yet to demonstrate that self-sufficiency, to grant his heroism, Wister must contradictorily depend upon the consent of others – reformist women, unscrupulous cattle thieves, the effete Eastern tenderfoot narrator, and even the implicitly feminized reader, whom the author interrupts the narrative to argue with for siding, Wister assumes, with Molly in her disagreement with her fiancé about the morality of his executing Steve. The Western hero may be an outsider (from Virginia) who has his own moral compass in the world, but the world that makes him matter is the one he is outside of.

Even though Wister's "foundational" Western little resembles what came before and what followed in the genre's history, it remains a continuing index of scholars' explorations of the genre's ideological tensions and of the historical contexts they share. Alan Trachtenberg (1982) argues that the Virginian's final assumption of his role as corporate manager is part of the "incorporation of America," the country's transition from a market to a corporate economy. Despite *The Virginian*'s success, early twentieth-century readers of the Western were more likely to find in the genre an escape from that incorporation, even to find it "as a lesson in escapism: a study in the need for the individual to get beyond society" (Brown 1991: 368). In the immensely popular work of Zane Grey, perhaps the genre's most influential writer, it is precisely the looming threat of incorporating powers – Mormon polygamists, governmental bureaucrats, Christian missionaries, stultifying Eastern culture – that the hero fights against. In Zane Grey's most successful and influential Western, *Riders of the Purple Sage* (which sold a million copies in its first year), the evil Mormon patriarchy, with its powerful designs on the novel's unmarried heroine Jane Withersteen, owner of land and cattle, allegorizes fears of the modern corporation and its powerful "invisible hand," according to Stephen Tatum (1997). The novel's ending, in which the non-Mormon hero rescues Jane and escapes with her into a canyon valley by rolling a large rock down on the Mormon villain, sealing them there without marriage, "dramatizes the survival of the residual values associated with the individualist phases of the market economy from an earlier moment in the nineteenth century" and a resistance to a "modern corporate era in which fluctuating market values, mysterious market forces, and the commodification of desire threaten personal autonomy" (Tatum 1997: 178). Whether this and other novels' historically animating concerns are about immigration, Mormon polygamy, the modern corporation, "white slavery," or altogether a vague anxiety about modernity itself, Westerns are too easily, as Tatum puts it, reduced to "plotted endings or static iconic images" in a search for their politics. Whether that search begins with a presumption that popular genres are all myth and symbol or that the Western reinforces dominant ideology, popular Westerns are profoundly ambiguous facts of history that are in no way divorced from it.

One of the greatest ironies in the popular Western's history is that Wister's Virginian, despite his influence, in the end represents the kind of "evil" man that other, later Westerns demonize in the same historical situation (Francis McElrath's 1902 *The Rustler*, Jack Schaefer's 1949 *Shane*, the 1980 film *Heaven's Gate*, all drawing on the Johnson County War). Marx argued that capitalism produces contradiction; it may be that Westerns are among the most sensitive, if sometimes unwitting literary recorders of such contradictions, feeding on Western history and the literary marketplace that authors, marketers, and readers meet in. Useful as they are, the standard dichotomies that critics long described in the Western – between savagery and civilization, masculine adventure and female domesticity, American national destiny and its racialized others – need to be qualified, for they do not tell the whole story, then or now. The one constant about the Western "formula" is that it has a surprising number of variations; often the formula is there only to be written against. It should not be surprising that a genre that invokes a vast historical landscape of such complexity should, despite some of its simplifications, prove to be so contested and negotiated an imaginative territory.

Among popular genres, the Western is not alone in having had assumptions made too easily about it, though the tendency is exacerbated under the Western's national weight, especially in retrospect. Popular novels, whatever their subgenre, had their own conditions of production and consumption, a specific marketplace, even if their readerships are not easily identified today. Much of the important scholarship on the genre has given attention to this important fact; Christine Bold's *Selling the Wild West* (1987) argues that the conditions of authorship in this marketplace often shaped the formal and aesthetic choices by which some writers would work within the genre's market conventions while simultaneously making an individual imprint upon it. Yet the popular Western is dogged by an assumption that is often twin to the idea that it has a clear, ideologically nationalistic focus: that it is "lowbrow," culturally and academically. These assumptions derive in part from the same fact: writing and selling Westerns have long been immensely lucrative. Money soils art, the logic goes; Westerns make money: ergo Westerns are not art but represent capitalist interests.

The category of "the popular" in the first half of the twentieth century, before the advent of cultural studies in the 1960s brought it serious critical attention, suggested to most critics simultaneously what it is not: "high" art, serious "literature." But many modern American writers, like their expatriate, British, and Irish counterparts, often self-consciously wove popular culture into the fabric of their high artistic intent: Joyce and even Woolf, but also Gertrude Stein, T. S. Eliot, and F. Scott Fitzgerald. Fitzgerald's Jay Gatsby grew up reading *Hopalong Cassidy* stories in the early stages of his self-fashioning, and Fitzgerald's narrator summarily suggests at the novel's end that "this is a story of the West, after all," leaving the reader to untangle its complex geographical, historical, and cultural registers, but leaving no doubt about the serious ramifications of juvenile reading and popularly embraced Western and national myths. Relationships between popular or mass culture and "high" literature, between American literary modernism and film, between regional and national Wests are central to the critical background of many Western American novelists who published between 1900 and 1950: Willa Cather, John Steinbeck, Wright Morris, Wallace Stegner, Frank Waters, Walter van Tilburg Clark, among them.

Willa Cather is perhaps the least transparent among those writers in her debts to popular culture. Her novel about a faded frontier economy, life, and the woman who came to embody such disappointment, *A Lost Lady*, is the book, Fitzgerald confessed to Cather, that had put a spell on him while writing *The Great Gatsby*. The prominence of Virgil in the text speaks for the classical influence on Cather's Western novel *My Ántonia* (1918), but there is also evidence of the popular Western that was selling so well in the literary and magazine marketplace in New York that she worked in and for as an editor at *McClure's* magazine: Jim Burden reads a "Life of Jesse James" as a boy and recalls it, tellingly, as "one of the most satisfactory books I have ever read," and Otto Fuchs, he tells the reader, had been "a cowboy, a stage-drive, a bar-tender, a miner," as if playing various stock Western roles. Owing as much to popular Westerns as to classical literature, Cather's work fashions its own literary idiom not only in Western American fiction but in the modern American novel. Her early Nebraska novels, *O Pioneers!* (1913) and *My Ántonia*, seem, especially in relation to her earlier romantic but fractured writing about Western subjects and her comments about women's writing, around the turn of the century, an awakening to her ideological middle ground about the West and her surpassing artistry about that real and imagined place.

Cather's heroines in these novels – Alexandra Bergson and Ántonia Shimerda – can be read as her response to the popular Western, wrestling as these novels all do with the question of a woman's independence from or dependence on men as they work on the land. Cather's work is original in the sense that she channeled romanticism away from relationships between women and men and toward a woman's relationship with land, in the process regendering the conventional relationship of masculinity and geography. Her heroines' independence – regardless of the men in their lives or their cultural origin – stems from Cather's rewriting of the popular Western's reliance upon national symbolism to make independence and stewardship matter. Whatever the differences in her artistic talent and writing conditions from that of women magazine writers, Cather inscribed herself, as they did, against the grain of the market Western's formula.

Cather was adamantly opposed to having her novels turned into films; only *A Lost Lady* was. Her contemporary Zane Grey, a less talented, more prolific, and vastly more profitable author, was more than happy to have his novels made into films and to participate in their production. The contrast of their literary careers with regard to their participation in other media and the influence of other media on their work illustrates both the perils and profits of the Western's popularity for successful novelists writing about this increasingly iconographic cultural landscape. Grey's 1925 novel *The Vanishing American* was expressly written in order to be made into a film after he showed the producer Jesse Lasky (later to found Paramount studios) the Navajo lands of northern Arizona that the producer had been hoping to use as a setting. (Cather had also found literary inspiration while visiting these landscapes.) Grey first serialized his novel in the middlebrow *Ladies' Home Journal* in 1922, but its conclusion, in which the Indian marries a white woman and implicitly assimilates into American culture by having racially mixed children, shocked the journal's readers. When *Harper's* agreed to publish the novel in 1925 to coincide with the film's release, its editors demanded another ending, and so the Indian hero dies of the flu in Grey's 1925 novel. Even this did not satisfy the filmmakers, however; in the silent film, the Indian hero is shot by another Indian, by accident, during an insurrection by his people against government officials.

When the Western travels to other cultures and nations, as in the hugely popular German Western writer Karl May, it usually retains an American stamp in its settings, character types, and scenarios. Those elements have influenced numerous non-American writers as well as a host of other popular genres. Arthur Conan Doyle drew upon the figure of the Mormon polygamist over a decade before Grey made that figure the villain of his most popular Western, and Edgar Rice Burroughs served in the Seventh Cavalry and herded cows in the American West before he became the writer of *Tarzan*, also published in 1912. "And so," wrote John R. Milton in 1964, "in 1912 the American subliterary scene was blessed with a pair of heroes from whom it has not yet recovered: the ape-man swinging through the trees, and the cowman galloping over the plains" (Milton 1964/1980: 8).

As with relations between popular genres, the interchange between popular and "high" literary forms during the birth of the cinema and the thriving of the pulp Western in the magazine market is an essential context for understanding the development of the modern popular genre. Silent film and early sound pictures fed upon and in turn influenced Western fiction. One of the most prolific categories of early silent film was "Indian and Western subjects," before the film genre of "the Western" had solidified but while the literary Western continued to grow in popularity. Modern cinematic art tied images of the West to modern Americans' understanding of what was, at least visually, significant and distinctive about American culture. The 1920s marked a crisis in culture that was a "crisis *of* culture," as Walter Benn Michaels puts it in his 1995 study of American modernism and its brew of nativism and pluralism. While they were often ascribed vastly different intimacies with "authentic" American culture, Indians, Jews, blacks, and other nonwhites were all representative pawns, and political victims, in white Americans' construction of "their" national culture and identity.

By the end of the half-century, works by major Western writers who wrote against the grain of the popular Western continued to be published, including three novels by Walter Van Tilburg Clark in the 1940s (one of them *The Ox-Bow Incident* of 1940), first novels by Wallace Stegner and Wright Morris – *The Big Rock Candy Mountain* (1943) and *My Uncle Dudley* (1942), respectively – and A. B. Guthrie's *The Way West* (1949), which won the Pulitzer Prize the year that Jack Schaefer's *Shane* was published. In 1950, Frank Waters published his fifth Western novel in a decade, and Henry Nash Smith published his study of Western myth and symbol through materials that were then traditionally "low" cultural forms. Scholarship on Western American literature has put the popular genre in the background, until recently, while justly emphasizing the extraordinary body of literature of the American West that makes the Western – despite its popularity – seem almost incidental. Integrating its cultural centrality is, ironically enough, both the achievement of Smith's *Virgin Land* in 1950 and the achievement of the most recent scholarship that was itself born of a reaction to what was perceived as Smith's "myth and symbol" emphasis. The ironies of Western beginnings and endings continue.

As a popular genre freighted with national and international significance, the Western's history delimits, but also empowers, the terms of creative or ideological consensus or resistance for any writer or filmmaker who engages it, and this is para-doxically why practitioners of the genre as ideologically and aesthetically far apart as, say, Louis l'Amour (who has sold close to half a billion Westerns) and Ang Lee (who directed *Brokeback Mountain*) find its territory so fecund. If one could imagine *Thelma and Louise* without its dramatic Western landscapes and the conventions of the buddy road narrative and the sympathetic outlaw, it would still be possible to imagine its feminist meaning, but impossible to imagine the film's central characters landing on the cover of *Time* magazine. Take away the mountains, the horses, and the cowboy boots, and it is hard to imagine *Brokeback Mountain* becoming the highest-grossing gay-themed film of all time. Western signs and conventions – men and violence, the rugged landscape, masculine reticence and feminine domesticity, work and play – are integral to the meaning of and response to these films and to countless Westerns: the scaffolding *is* essential, whatever thematic formula a book or film follows or writes against, whether or not it is aesthetically complex, whether mascu-line or feminine values prevail or whether they conjoin, whether America is the fulcrum of meaning or merely a sideshow. That scaffolding was largely built in the first half of the twentieth century. Yet it is the sheer breadth, depth, and surprising complexity of the popular Western's emotional and ideological stores, not its shared scaffolding, that has kept the genre alive, well past the historical experiences that gave rise to it.

References and Further Reading

Alter, Judy. (1997). The market for popular western fiction. In Thomas J. Lyon (ed.), *Updating the Literary West* (pp. 893–7). Fort Worth: Texas Christian University Press.

Bold, Christine. (1987). *Selling the Wild West: Popular Western Fiction, 1860 to 1960*. Bloomington: Indiana University Press.

Bold, Christine. (1991). Popular forms, I. In Emory Elliott et al. (eds), *The Columbia History of the American Novel* (pp. 285–308). New York: Columbia University Press.

Bold, Christine. (1997). The popular west. In Thomas J. Lyon (ed.), *Updating the Literary West* (pp. 863–72). Fort Worth: Texas Christian University Press.

Brown, Bill. (1991). Popular forms, II. In Emory Elliott et al. (eds), *The Columbia History of the American Novel* (pp. 357–79). New York: Columbia University Press.

Cawelti, John G. (1976). *Adventure, Mystery, and Romance: Formula Stories as Art and Popular Culture*. Chicago: The University of Chicago Press.

Emmet, Scott. (1996). *Loaded Fictions: Social Critique in the Twentieth-Century Western*. Moscow: University of Idaho Press.

Etulain, Richard. (1971/1980). Origins of the western. In William T. Pilkington (ed.), *Critical Essays on the Western American Novel* (pp. 56–60). Boston: G. K. Hall.

Gelder, Ken. (2004). *Popular Fiction: The Logics and Practices of a Literary Field.* London: Routledge.

Hamilton, Cynthia S. (1987). *Western Hard-Boiled Detective Fiction: From High Noon to Midnight.* Iowa City: University of Iowa Press.

Handley, William R. (2002). *Marriage, Violence, and the Nation in the American Literary West.* Cambridge, UK: Cambridge University Press.

Lamont, Victoria. (2003). History, gender, and the origins of the "classic" western. In Melody Graulich and Stephen Tatum (eds), *Reading The Virginian in the New West* (pp. 148–74). Lincoln: University of Nebraska Press.

Michaels, Walter Benn. (1995). *Our America: Nativism, Modernism, and Pluralism.* Durham, NC: Duke University Press.

Milton, John R. (1964/1980). Overview of the western novel. In William T. Pilkington (ed.), *Critical Essays on the Western American Novel* (pp. 3–19). Boston: G. K. Hall.

Mitchell, Lee Clark. (1996). *Westerns: Making the Man in Fiction and Film.* Chicago: The University of Chicago Press.

Mitchell, Lee Clark. (1997). Critical theory, heading west. In Thomas J. Lyon (ed.), *Updating the Literary West* (pp. 888–92). Fort Worth: Texas Christian University Press.

Piekarski, Vicki. (1997). Women writers of popular westerns. In Thomas J. Lyon (ed.), *Updating the Literary West* (pp. 863–72). Fort Worth: Texas Christian University Press.

Robinson, Forrest G. (1993). *Having It Both Ways: Self-Subversion in Western Popular Classics.* Albuquerque: University of New Mexico Press.

Slotkin, Richard. (1992). *Gunfighter Nation: The Myth of the Frontier in Twentieth-Century America.* New York: Atheneum.

Smith, Henry Nash. (1950). *Virgin Land: The American West as Symbol and Myth.* Cambridge, MA: Harvard University Press.

Sonnichsen, C. L. (1978). *From Hopalong to Hud: Thoughts on Western Fiction.* College Station: Texas A&M University Press.

Tatum, Stephen. (1997). The problem of the "popular" in the new western history. In Forrest G. Robinson (ed.), *The New Western History: The Territory Ahead* (pp. 153–90). Tucson: University of Arizona Press.

Taylor, J. Golden et al. (eds). (1987). *A Literary History of the American West.* Fort Worth: Texas Christian University Press.

Tompkins, Jane. (1992). *West of Everything: The Inner Life of Westerns.* New York: Oxford University Press.

Trachtenberg, Alan. (1982). *The Incorporation of America: Culture and Society in the Gilded Age.* New York: Hill and Wang.

Yates, Norris. (1995). *Gender and Genre: An Introduction to Women Writers of Formula Westerns, 1900–1950.* Albuquerque: University of New Mexico Press.

23
Twentieth-Century American Crime and Detective Fiction

Charles J. Rzepka

In the genre of crime fiction, twentieth-century America is famous the world over for its "hard-boiled" private eyes – tough sleuths like Sam Spade, Philip Marlowe, and Mike Hammer. The roots of hard-boiled detective and crime fiction, however, clutch firmly at the soil of the nineteenth-century. From the antebellum frontier tales of James Fenimore Cooper (1789–1851) and the Western adventure and action stories of the late nineteenth-century dime novel evolved the figure of the lone enforcer. Emotionally undemonstrative, energetic, relentless, and averse to female companion-ship, this action hero typically pursued a higher form of justice outside the restraints of the legal establishment, straddling the line between wilderness and settlement, savagery and civilization.

From the British detective tradition hard-boiled writers borrowed, and extensively modified, the so-called "puzzle element," by which the reader was implicitly invited to compete with the fictional detective as he or she (usually he) searched for a solution to the crime (or crimes) and an answer to the question, "Whodunit?" As epitomized by Arthur Conan Doyle (1859–1930) in the person of his eccentric "calculating machine," Sherlock Holmes, the hero of this "classical" brand of puzzle-oriented detec-tion often worked, like his action hero counterpart, at or just beyond the limits of the law. Doyle's twentieth-century British heirs, including R. Austin Freeman (1862–1943), G. K. Chesterton (1874–1936), Agatha Christie (1890–1976), and Dorothy Sayers (1893–1957), generally created detectives that were, like Holmes, cerebral in method and averse to firearms and fisticuffs, as opposed to the American descendants of Cooper's Natty Bumppo.

This is, of course, a historical simplification. The United States had its own vigor-ous Golden Age of puzzle-oriented detection to rival that of the Mother Country, beginning in 1925 with the first Charlie Chan novel of Earl Derr Biggers (1884–1933), *The House without a Key*, and continuing with the highly intellectual Philo Vance adventures of Willard Huntington Wright (aka "S. S. van Dine," 1887–1939), the many cases of "Ellery Queen" (pseudonym of Frederic Dannay, 1905–82, and

Manfred B. Lee, 1905–71), and stories featuring the corpulent and irascible private eye Nero Wolfe, the creation of Rex Stout (1886–1975). This efflorescence of classical detection in America had barely opened its buds before tough-guy detectives began stomping through the flowerbeds.

The Interwar Years

Hard-boiled crime fiction of the interwar period was conceived in part as a direct challenge to the Anglo-American classical tradition inspired by Holmes. Rejecting the polite manners and diction of Wright, Sayers, and Christie, the tough-guy writers embraced a pared-down vernacular style. In the name of realism, they ridiculed the formal puzzle element, along with the cardboard characters, exotic weaponry, and implausible coincidences that it seemed to demand. Nonetheless, the two giants of hard-boiled detection, Dashiell Hammett (1894–1961) and Raymond Chandler (1888–1959), Hammett's most important protégé, retained the inductive challenge of classical detection under a garish surface of fast-paced events, colorful personalities, and wise-cracking rejoinders, ultimately enabling this new subgenre to prevail among the middlebrow readers who comprised classical detection's principal market.

America's hard-boiled adaptation of the classical puzzle element began just after the end of World War I, between the covers of a working-class, action-adventure pulp magazine called *Black Mask*. Under the leadership of retired army Captain Joseph T. Shaw, who took over as editor in 1926, *Black Mask* began to attract talented young writers like Carroll John Daly (1889–1958), Raoul Whitfield (1898–1945), Erle Stanley Gardner (1889–1970), Cornell Woolrich (1903–68), and Horace McCoy (1897–1955). Along with Hammett, they went on to transform detective and crime fiction in America and throughout the world.

Not all the writers for *Black Mask* wrote detective fiction. Woolrich and McCoy, for example, along with novelist James M. Cain (1892–1977), helped to popularize the seedy, low-life thriller that would later, under the label of *noir*, come to dominate American crime fiction. Erle Stanley Gardner made the cunning criminal defense lawyer, Perry Mason, a household name among mystery fans. All of them, however, conveyed the frenetic, cynical tone of America's Jazz Age. During the Roaring Twenties, widespread stock fraud, price manipulation, and corruption at the highest levels of government flourished, while violent strike-breaking activities were tolerated by law-enforcement officials alarmed by the world-revolutionary ambitions of the Russian Bolsheviks. The economic boom revealed its rotten foundations with the Crash of 1929, followed by the Great Depression. Meanwhile, changes in the role of women and the legal status of alcohol contributed to the postwar turmoil.

While male sleuths dominated the genre then as now, the "New Woman" of the late nineteenth century had already begun to hang out her shingle on detection's

Mean Streets in both Britain and America. The challenge she posed to patriarchal stereotypes of her "place" in society was reinforced by the brief incursion of working women into America's wartime economy in 1917–18, and the passage of the nineteenth amendment in 1920 granting women the right to vote. Some female sleuths, like Violet McDade, the creation of Clive F. Adams (1895–1949), worked as independent investigators, while female "operatives" or "secretaries" often appeared in stories featuring male detectives. Female criminals became commonplace, sometimes as gun molls or outright crooks, sometimes in the role of the femme fatale, a siren figure animated by postwar male insecurity in the face of changing attitudes toward gender.

More important than the nineteenth amendment in its contribution to public disorder and cynicism was the passage of the eighteenth amendment prohibiting the sale of alcoholic beverages in 1919. Enacted in response to agitation by temperance societies, Prohibition encouraged a sharp rise in organized crime and public mayhem as rival gangs competed for market share in the booming bootleg industry. Massive profits made it easy to bribe authorities to ignore a "crime" that few considered wrong. The result was public cynicism toward the law and suspicion of those sworn to uphold it, while the spread of an illegal underground economy fed other forms of criminal activity, such as loan-sharking, prostitution, gambling, and protection rackets.

Clearly, despite America's postwar economic gains, new insecurities were undermining public confidence in the promise of the American Dream. Writers for the pulps responded by portraying an America in which no one could be trusted, least of all wealthy society types and official law enforcers, and where society itself, especially in the big bad city, seemed to be so thoroughly steeped in graft, vice, blackmail, and extortion that it was hardly worth rescuing. The most one could expect was that a few innocent lives might be saved from the wreckage and that a tough detective with "moxie" might save them.

There is certainly material in the writings of both Hammett and Chandler to suggest that the success of hard-boiled writing depended on a complete rejection of the classical British model. "So that's the way you scientific detectives work," says Dinah Brand when the anonymous narrator of Hammett's *Red Harvest* admits that his methods have been largely haphazard. "Plans are all right sometimes," replies the detective, "And sometimes just stirring things up is all right – if you're tough enough to survive, and keep your eyes open so you'll see what you want when it comes to the top" (Hammett 1999: 75). As for Chandler, he once wrote, "When in doubt have a man come through a door with a gun in his hand" (Chandler 1995b: 1017).

It is important, however, to balance such statements against others, and against practice as well. *Red Harvest*, for example, capped a series of short stories featuring its anonymous private-eye narrator, an "operative" employed by the Continental Detective Agency. The Continental Op began literary life as anything but a generic dime-weekly action detective. In fact, he is meant to contrast specifically with the unthinking, trigger-happy vigilante figure popularized by Carroll John Daly in the character of Race Williams, whose debut preceded the Op's in *Black Mask* by just four months in 1923.

Often cited as the world's first hard-boiled fictional detective, Williams was exactly the sort of private investigator (PI) a writer could depend on to come bursting through the door with a gun in his hand when imagination took the day off. By contrast, the Op is short, fat, middle-aged, and easily winded. He is also a cool, wise-cracking, and self-deprecating professional, much like Hammett himself, who had worked for Pinkerton's Detective Agency and knew private investigation inside-out. The Op knows how to use his fists and his gun, but unlike Williams, he is slow to anger. "The proper place for guns is after talk has failed," he says in "Corkscrew" (Hammett 1972: 292). Besides restricting his violence largely to self-defense, the Op is also perceptive and inductively shrewd, and nearly all of the Op stories make a point of displaying, even telegraphing, his mystery-solving abilities.

Red Harvest is a parodic exception to the previous Op tales not because it rejects the puzzle element, but because Hammett's usually self-contained protagonist here finds himself going "blood simple" (1999: 138) and reverting to type in his violent attempts to clean up the town of Personville (pronounced "Poisonville"). In general, however, when the Op "stir[s] things up" he does so in order to test hypotheses based on his current state of knowledge, just like his classical counterparts. In *The Maltese Falcon* (1930) the Op's most famous successor, Sam Spade, employs the same methods of investigation.

Chandler's pronouncements are similarly belied by his practice. His first book, *The Big Sleep* (1939), makes sophisticated use of what Chandler himself considered the height of "literary legerdemain," concealing "a simple mystery . . . behind another mystery" and "making [the reader] solve the wrong problem" (Chandler 1995c: 1007). Chandler's statement on "literary legerdemain" appears in an unpublished essay called "Twelve Notes on the Mystery Story," each numbered entry beginning, "It must." For a hard-boiled writer notoriously critical of Golden Age rule-mongering, Chandler's "notes" are sometimes hard to distinguish from the generic dos and don'ts published by inveterate classicists like Willard Huntington Wright. Among the most important is that mystery writers must avoid "unfairness" to their readers and make sure that, when the "inevitable" solution is revealed, "the fooling was honorable" (pp. 1006–7). But then Chandler himself, though born in Chicago, was raised in England and learned the meaning of "honor" and "fairness" at Dulwich College, an English public school (i.e., preparatory school).

Chandler's nostalgia for a vanished, chivalric code of honor is evident throughout *The Big Sleep* (1939). In the opening scene, Philip Marlowe, Chandler's gumshoe, enters the mansion of his new client, the sordid and cynical General Sternwood, and is immediately confronted by an enormous stained-glass window depicting a knight untying a damsel in distress who "didn't have any clothes on but some very long and convenient hair" (Chandler 1988: 1–2). "If I lived in the house," reflects Marlowe, "I would sooner or later have to climb up there and help him." In short order, Marlowe meets the General's younger daughter, Carmen, a homicidal nymphomaniac whom he later "rescues" from a pornographic photo session in which she is a willing participant. Marlowe's chivalrous rejection of Carmen's sexual advances in subsequent encounters incites her to attempt to murder him. At one point, after finding the moronic young woman lying nude in his bed and tossing her out, Marlowe's eyes alight on his chessboard, forcing him to admit, "Knights had no meaning in this game. It wasn't a game for knights" (p. 156). Later, he is forced to kill gangster Lash Canino while remaining hidden in the dark, something, he reflects, that "a gentleman of the old school" should never do (p. 202).

Despite his chastity (he never sleeps with a woman in *The Big Sleep*), his fealty (he remains loyal to his client despite the General's sinister motives), and his nostalgia for "the old school" of chivalric *noblesse oblige*, Marlowe finds his idealism repeatedly compromised by the "nastiness" (p. 230) of twentieth-century life, where beauty is reduced to "second-hand sex jags" (p. 18), combat to cold-blooded murder, and other human beings in general to "slab[s] of cold meat" (p. 186). Nonetheless, this "shop-soiled Galahad" (Chandler 1995a: 1136) persisted in his quest for self-respect through six more adventures and well into the Cold War era, even as Chandler's sunny Southern California milieu became ever nastier. That milieu became the special province of what came to be known as "*noir*."

Hearts of Darkness

The French term *noir*, or "dark," was used by French critic Nino Frank in 1946 to describe the crepuscular look of postwar Hollywood crime films. Other critics soon extended it to literary as well as cinematic examples. *Noir* is based on the premise that, far from being confined to a "shadowy" criminal underclass, corruption is everywhere – in your neighborhood, your family, and even in you! In this wider sense, *noir* reached back to the 1930s American underworld of *Little Caesar* (1930) and *Scarface* (1932), both written by W. R. Burnett (1899–1982), in which dispossessed immigrants seek to achieve the otherwise respectable American dream of financial success by stepping outside the law. It also overlapped with the rise of a proletarian ethos in popular fiction. Horace McCoy set the *noir* standard for social protest with *They Shoot Horses, Don't They?* (1935), in which the mercy killing of a professional marathon dancer allegorizes working-class hopelessness in Depression-era America.

James M. Cain, however, consolidated the modern version of literary *noir*. In *The Postman Always Rings Twice* (1934) and *Double Indemnity* (1936), Cain gave his readers a good, long look beneath the surface of America's fatuous pursuit of happiness and boosterish faith in self-reinvention. In each book, ordinary people going about their business – slinging hash or selling insurance – are drawn into a whirlpool of violent crime by the allure of sex and easy money. Cain's supreme achievement was to place readers so thoroughly within the mind of the criminal protagonist that their moral repugnance at what he or she was doing never undermined their empathy with his or her reasons for doing it. The result was a recognizably modern shift of focus, not only to the viewpoint of the criminal, but also to the specific contours of his or her astonishing incapacity for moral reflection. Frank Chambers, the rootless road bum who narrates *Postman*, for instance, impresses us as an ordinary guy despite his sadistically predatory sexual appetite and instinct for duplicity and violence, primarily because he is sociopathically obtuse to his own monstrosity. Thus his profession of grief at the funeral of the Greek American whom he has first cuckolded and then brutally murdered comes across as both sincere and grotesquely incongruous.

Cain's unique representation of a banal psychopathy became the stock-in-trade of postwar *noir* writers like Jim Thompson (1906–77) and Patricia Highsmith (1921–95). Thompson's *The Killer Inside Me* (1952) conveys by its title alone the outlook its author adopted throughout his work, while Highsmith's most famous series of novels features the pleasant, polite, and morally vacuous young murderer and confidence man Tom Ripley, a college-educated version of Cain's Frank Chambers, but with societal ambitions and better taste.

Noir and related genres, such as crime suspense and "caper" stories told from the point of view of the criminal, have flourished in the second half of the twentieth century. Serial killers like Patrick Bateman, the protagonist of *American Psycho* (1991), by Bret Easton Ellis have captured the public imagination, along with more creatively inclined psychopaths such as Hannibal "the Cannibal" Lector, mind-game master of *Silence of the Lambs* (1989), by Thomas Harris. Meanwhile, gangster and mob stories received a boost in 1969 from the publication by Mario Puzo (1920–99) of *The Godfather*, as well as from its movie spin-offs, directed by Francis Ford Coppola.

Among the "caper" novelists, George V. Higgins (1939–99) made his impressive debut in 1972 with *The Friends of Eddie Coyle*, a book comprising what is essentially a long-running monologue by the title character. Higgins's experience as a public prosecutor familiarized him with the gritty street-speech of Boston's low life, which he expertly wove into a compelling narrative of desperation and dead ends. Elmore Leonard, who learned a great deal from Higgins about the handling of voice, tone, and diction, remains one of the most artful masters of free indirect discourse in the genre. Leonard started out writing Westerns in the 1950s and switched to crime writing when the market for the Old West declined in the 1960s. One of his latest books, *The Hot Kid* (2005), employs a Wild West plot line and familiar character types, with a young, cocky US marshal hunting down famous outlaws to bolster his reputation in the gangland milieu of 1930s Oklahoma, the scene of Leonard's early boyhood.

Cold War Developments

Both hard-boiled and classical detection declined in sales relative to crime suspense and thrillers immediately after World War II, although all categories of popular crime were buoyed by the paperback revolution that began in the mid-1930s and dominated sales of popular fiction throughout the early Cold War period. Among hard-boiled writers, Mickey Spillane (b. Frank Morrison, 1918–2006) and Ross Macdonald (b. Kenneth Millar, 1915–83) topped the detective best-seller lists at this time, but for almost diametrically opposite reasons.

As the title of Spillane's first detective book, *I, the Jury*, implies, Mike Hammer is a vengeful incarnation of Chandler's Marlowe, with a vigilante ethos harkening back to Race Williams. Spillane, however, concentrated his hero's fury on brainy women, shadowy Communists, and homosexuals, instead of the traditional thugs and grifters. In Hammer, the self-righteous prurience of American Puritanism and the crude misogyny of populist masculinism found their perfect comic book expression. His right-wing violence is the reverse mirror image of Ross Macdonald's liberal-leaning, college-educated hero, Lew Archer, who played the knightly role bequeathed by Chandler as something of a family therapist.

Nearly all of Archer's cases involve crimes that arise from the misdeeds of a previous generation and threaten to pollute the lives of the next. With his "talkable-attable face" (Macdonald 1996: 94), Archer is adept at getting both suspects and witnesses not only to confess, but also to tell their life stories. In the process, they come to understand and forgive both others and themselves. Macdonald's own troubled history as an abandoned child shaped his Lew Archer stories into a series of parables on the need for reconciliation between parents and their children. If Spillane appealed to the Cold War, working-class paranoia of the ordinary GI, Macdonald's popularity soared on the frustrations of a new postwar middle-class struggling to understand and, ultimately, reconcile with their rebellious offspring, who were, by the 1960s, protesting racism, censorship, sexism, the Vietnam War, and all the other sins of their fathers and mothers in ever-increasing numbers.

Despite competition from other crime-related genres, the hard-boiled, male, professional PI has never gone out of fashion. Among his major competitors are the official police detectives who once served as foils to his rugged individualism and quasi-legal methods. Although its origins lie in the French *roman policier* of the nineteenth century, the modern American police procedural did not make its debut until 1945 with the publication of *V as in Victim*, by Lawrence V. Treat (1903–98). Treat introduced many of what were to become the standard features of the genre, including family troubles, career anxieties, and conflicts with peers. In 1956, Ed McBain (b. Salvatore Lombino, 1926–2005) kicked off his long-running 87th Precinct series with *Cop-Hater*, eventually perfecting the multiple-plot form that later became a standard feature of hit TV shows like *Hill Street Blues* and, more recently, *NYPD Blue*. Today, the *noir*-ish, epic-length LA police procedurals of James Ellroy unfold in a 1950s Southern California more violent, chaotic, and corrupt than Philip Marlowe could have imagined. In some ways, Ellroy's LA can be said to have been anticipated, as early as 1957, by the nightmarish New York City of Chester Himes (1909–84), whose Harlem police procedurals featured black police detectives Coffin Ed Johnson and Grave Digger Jones.

Himes did not achieve widespread recognition as a writer until after he emigrated to France in 1953, where the tradition of the *roman policier* had originated. Enlisted to contribute to Editions Galliard's *Série noire* ("Dark Series") of translated American crime writing, Himes wrote his first police novel, *For Love of Immabelle* (1957), in English, translating it into French the following year. It won Himes the distinguished *Grand prix de la littérature policière*, a first for a non-French author. While Himes had never lived in Harlem, the black ghetto depicted in his pages spoke directly, despite its aura of surrealism, to issues being raised by a new generation of angry black protest writers and activists. Unlike many in his African-American cohort, however, Himes reserved his most biting sarcasm for the charlatans, drug-dealers, and religious con-men of his own race who infest the community that Johnson and Jones, working-class cops at heart, attempt to keep within the bounds of law and order. As the Civil Rights Movement gave way to black militancy, however, Himes became more overtly critical of systemic white racism.

Despite the postwar shift of public interest to official police detection, the puzzle-focused or "cozy" detective story featuring an amateur investigator has survived on both sides of the Atlantic, if with a smaller readership than in its heyday. Such tales still adhere to the norms of Golden Age detection, including restricting the story to a relatively small, well-defined community of suspects. Two of the most popular American writers of detection from the 1930s who continued to do well after VJ Day were John Dickson Carr (1906–77) and Mignon G. Eberhart (1899–1996). New writers reviving the tradition of classical detection after the war include Harry Kemelman (1908–96), whose amateur detective Rabbi David Small began his investigative career helping the members of his synagogue in *Friday the Rabbi Slept Late* (1964); Amanda Cross (b. Carolyn G. Heilbrun, 1926–2003), who set her Professor Kate Fansler novels at a New York college suspiciously resembling Columbia University; and Jane Langton, whose stories, often corresponding in part to the structure of crime thrillers, feature Homer Kelley, a former Boston police detective and sometime Harvard academic.

"Alternative" Subgenres and Postmodern Detection

Two important challenges to traditional crime fiction, one cultural, the other formal, arose during the postwar period. What has been termed "alternative" detection (Rzepka 2005: 235) began to interrogate the traditional reliance of fictional detection, particularly in the hard-boiled tradition, on white, male protagonists. Postmodern detection explores the typically unrealized possibilities of the form, such as the use of an open-ended plot, irresolvable conflicts in testimony, indecipherable clues, and impenetrable motives – in short, all the untoward contingencies of real life deliberately excluded from the rational, causally coherent universe of the traditional detective story.

Alternative detective writers seek to challenge traditional assumptions about the nationality, race, or gender of the detective by placing a nonconforming protagonist in the position of primary investigator. Typically, this person will bring to the task of investigation skills and abilities not ordinarily attributed to Western, white, male detectives, and face obstacles that his or her traditional counterparts need never face. These obstacles arise mainly from the prejudices of the dominant culture.

Some alternative detection writers identify the basic inductive methods of the genre itself with Western patriarchal oppression, based as these methods are on modes of investigation originating with the male-dominated sciences of the European Enlightenment. However, there is a limit to how much of the genre's traditional methodology alternative writers can discard without falling outside the generic boundaries altogether. According to Gina and Andrew Macdonald, a perfect balance between alternative cultural practices and scientific investigative methods appears in the Navajo police duo featured in the novels of Tony Hillerman. Joe Leaphorn and Jim Chee represent what the Macdonalds call true "crossroads heroes" who must "pick and choose among the best of each culture" – Native American and Euro-American – into which birth and profession, respectively, have thrust them (Macdonald and Macdonald 1999: 74–6).

African-American detection constitutes a special alternative category. For one thing, African-American detectives, whether male or female, must work through the pervasive and lingering impact of institutionalized antebellum black slavery. Accordingly, writes Stephen Soitos, fictional black investigators are forced by their history and upbringing to see themselves as second-class citizens in the eyes of the dominant white culture before they can see themselves as citizens of the "America" defined by that culture (Soitos 1996: 35). The "Blues Detective" as Soitos calls this protagonist, must struggle against this white-mediated mirror-relationship with respect to his or her own subjectivity in order to achieve the dignity and sense of self-worth that have naturally been accorded white male detectives.

The impact of this complex dynamic of racial self-consciousness, writes Soitos, appears in black detective literature going back to 1901. In that year, Pauline Hopkins (1859–1930) first began serial publication of *Hagar's Daughter: A Story of Southern Caste Prejudice*, in which a character named Venus Johnson takes a momentary turn as a detective. In the first complete African-American detective novel, *The Conjure-Man Dies* (1932), Rudolph Fisher (1897–1934) represents the split consciousness of black detection by splitting the role of amateur investigator between a scientifically trained African-American doctor and an African sorcerer-king, who has emigrated to Harlem to make a living as a soothsayer and, apparently, arisen from the dead to solve his own murder. While Fisher's influence did not extend far, Chester Himes's Harlem police procedurals, a watershed in the tradition of black detection, had a major impact on Walter Mosley, whose Easy Rawlins series of detective novels engage directly with the contradictions imposed on black self-awareness by white cultural mediation.

Inaugurating Mosley's Los Angeles saga, *Devil in a Blue Dress* (1990) relates how World War II veteran Ezekiel "Easy" Rawlins is transformed from a factory worker in an aircraft plant into an unlicensed detective – or more accurately, spy – in the black neighborhoods of South Central Los Angeles. Sometimes he is hired by his neighbors, and sometimes by the Los Angeles police department, which has few contacts in the black community.

Easy begins his underground career by agreeing to find a young white jazz singer named Daphne Monet, the "Devil in a Blue Dress" of the title, who likes the "company of Negroes" (Mosley 1990: 18). Easy not only finds Daphne but falls in love with her, coming face to face with his unexamined feelings about white women. These feelings were exacerbated by his sexual experiences with Frenchwomen in the liberation of Paris during World War II. The ambiguities and ironies of Easy's love for Daphne, and what that love says about his own "uneasy" sense of racial identity in a white-dominated society, are intensified by a secret revealed only near the end of the novel. They are made more complex throughout by Mosley's sophisticated juxtaposition of one "white man's war" (p. 193), the one against Nazism, with another, the war against crime, in both of which black men like Easy are fooled or forced into participating.

The fastest growing category of alternative detection today is feminist and gay/lesbian, especially of the hard-boiled variety. American feminist detection can be said to have begun with *Edwin of the Iron Shoes* (1977), by Marica Muller, which introduced private detective Sharon McCone. Muller's hard-boiled successors include Katherine V. Forrest, creator of lesbian Los Angeles cop Kate Delafield, and forensic pathologist Patricia Cornwell, who packs lots of grisly detail into the adventures of State Medical Examiner Kate Scarpetta.

Two of the most durable exponents of American feminism over the last two decades have been Sara Paretsky and Sue Grafton, both of whom made their debut in 1982. Paretsky's Polish-Italian-American private eye V. I Warshawski is probably the toughest of the feminist hard-boiled sleuths. Daughter of a Chicago cop, she is little given to sentiment as she hunts down the masculinist stooges of the patriarchal system and their shadowy bosses. Paretsky focuses on institutionalized forms of oppression and corruption, and her PhD in history has provided her with the necessary tools for solid research into the massive machinery of day-to-day exploitation.

Given her tomboy appearance and taste for guns and weight-lifting, Sue Grafton's Kinsey Millhone might at first be mistaken for a more "butch" version of Warshawski. But there are important differences between the two. While Grafton appears to be as indebted to generic convention as Paretsky, she takes better advantage of the opportunities for ambiguity afforded her by the male hard-boiled tradition. Raised by her pragmatic spinster aunt, Kinsey has been spared the cultural indoctrination in femininity to which her peers have been subjected, but her overt contempt for the stereotypical female accoutrements of gender, which Warshawski has no trouble embracing, often comes across as a defensive form of acting out, betraying an existential vulnerability true to the basic spirit of Hammett and Chandler.

Postmodern detective fiction, a worldwide phenomenon, can be said to have begun with the publication in 1942 of "The Garden of Forking Paths," by the Argentine fabulist, Jorge Luis Borges (1899–1986). The "Garden" of Borges's title is an imaginary one, wherein a labyrinthine path corresponding to every possible future development of every passing moment of time "forks" into an infinite number of parallel and intersecting future universes. Here Borges made evident one of postmodern detection's most important themes: the way in which material objects, events, and actions in the world, which we take to have an existence preceding and apart from the words we use to describe them, are assigned their meanings by the very narratives within which they are made to appear as "facts." From the viewpoint of postmodernism, there is no definitive chronology of the crime, no single "solution" awaiting us at the end of the narrative of detection; all imaginable chronologies, all of the "forking paths" in the "garden" of the text, have an equal claim to finality.

American writers of postmodern detection have similarly multiplied or suspended narratives of causality, calling into question the reliability of memory and the attribution of motive. The *New York Trilogy* (1985–6) of Paul Auster, like Borges's "Garden of Forking Paths," plays variations on this theme while paying homage to the self-reflexive Gothic tales of Edgar Allan Poe (1809–49), especially those "tales of ratiocination," featuring amateur Parisian investigator C. Auguste Dupin, which inaugurated the modern detective story.

As Auster's trilogy suggests, crime and detective fiction has enjoyed a mutually productive conversation with more "serious" American writing. Ernest Hemingway's laconic, telegraphic style helped to shape the dispassionate, objective aesthetic of Hammett's later novels, while Hemingway's short story "The Killers" exploits the overlapping terrain of gang violence and ordinary life first mapped out by the likes of Hammett. In *The Great Gatsby* (1925), F. Scott Fitzgerald anatomized the desire for self-reinvention animating the grandiose dreams of a highly successful but unhappy Minnesota bootlegger, and in turn provided the armature for Ross Macdonald's tale of another Midwestern boy's ascent from the slums of Windsor, Ontario, to the mansions and country clubs of Los Angeles in *The Galton Case* (1959). Popular crime and detection were clearly on the mind of William Faulkner (1897–1962) when he wrote *Knight's Gambit* (1939), featuring Mississippi county attorney Gavin Stevens in a series of homely whodunits dependent as much on psychological acuity as forensics and testimony. Faulkner had already stepped into the *noir* half-light in 1931 with *Sanctuary*, a perverse tale of kidnapping and rape set among the bootlegging underclasses of the Deep South.

More recently, the distinguished Russian émigré writer Vladimir Nabokov (1899–1977) parodied the American crime thriller in *Lolita* (1955) before turning his attention to plots of detection in *Pale Fire* (1962), a tale of envy, murder, and unreliable narration set in a small college town. In a similar postmodern vein, *The Crying of Lot 49* (1966), the second novel of Thomas Pynchon, incorporates elements of both traditional California *noir*, in its paranoid visions of conspiracy lurking beneath the quotidian glare of modern life, and classical detection of the Gothic variety in Pynchon's choice of a naive young woman, Oedipa Mass, as amateur investigator.

As these works suggest, the popularity, vigor, and influence of American crime and detective fiction show little sign of abating as the nation turns the corner into the twenty-first century.

REFERENCES AND FURTHER READING

Cawelti, John G. (1976). *Adventure, Mystery, and Romance: Formula Stories as Art and Popular Culture*. Chicago: University of Chicago Press.

Chandler, Raymond. (1988). *The Big Sleep*. New York: Vintage.

Chandler, Raymond. (1995a). *The High Window*. In *Raymond Chandler. Stories and Early Novels* (pp. 985–1177). New York: Library of America.

Chandler, Raymond. (1995b). Introduction to "The simple art of murder." In *Later Novels and Other Writings* (pp. 1016–19). New York: Library of America.

Chandler, Raymond. (1995c). Twelve notes on the mystery story. In *Later Novels and Other Writings* (pp. 1004–11). New York: Library of America.

Drew, Bernard A. (1986). *Hard-Boiled Dames: Stories Featuring Women Detectives, Reporters, Adventurers, and Criminals from the Pulp Fiction Magazines of the 1930s*. New York: St. Martin's Press.

Durham, Philip. (1968). The *Black Mask* school. In David Madden (ed.), *Tough Guy Writers of the Thirties* (pp. 51–79). Carbondale: Southern Illinois University Press.

Goulart, Ron. (1972). *Cheap Thrills: An Informal History of the Pulp Magazines*. New Rochelle, NY: Arlington House.

Hammett, Dashiell. (1972). Corkscrew. In *The Big Knockover* (pp. 250–304). New York: Vintage.

Hammett, Dashiell. (1999). *Red Harvest*. In *Complete Novels* (pp. 1–167). New York: Library of America.

Haut, Woody. (1995). *Pulp Culture: Hardboiled Fiction and the Cold War*. London: Serpent's Tail.

Horsley, Lee. (2001). *The Noir Thriller*. Basingstoke, UK: Palgrave.

Macdonald, Gina, and Andrew Macdonald. (1999). Ethnic detectives in popular fiction: New directions for an American genre. In Kathleen Gregory Klein (ed.), *Diversity and Detective Fiction* (pp. 60–113). Bowling Green, OH: Bowling Green State University Popular Press.

Macdonald, Ross. (1996). *The Galton Case*. New York: Vintage.

McCann, Sean. (2000). *Gumshoe America: Hard-Boiled Crime Fiction and the Rise and Fall of New Deal Liberalism*. Durham, NC: Duke University Press.

Mosley, Walter. (1990). *Devil in a Blue Dress*. New York, Norton.

Rzepka, Charles. (2005). *Detective Fiction*. Cambridge, UK: Polity Press.

Soitos, Stephen F. (1996). *The Blues Detective: A Study of African American Detective Fiction*. Amherst: University of Massachusetts Press.

Symons, Julian. (1992). *Bloody Murder: From the Detective Story to the Crime Novel*, 3rd edn. New York: The Mysterious Press.

24

What Price Hollywood? Modern American Writers and the Movies

Mark Eaton

Edmund Wilson once declared that prose fiction was influenced by Hollywood in one of two ways: first, "there are the serious novelists who do not write for the films but are influenced by them in their novels"; and second, there are "actual writers for the pictures like Mr. West and Mr. Cain who produce sour novels about Hollywood" (Wilson 1950: 49). Whether or not they worked for the studios, in other words, writers were inevitably influenced by what rather quickly emerged in the early twentieth century as America's dominant entertainment form. For Wilson, Hollywood's influence on American prose fiction was mostly negative, and all too many writers had succumbed to the temptation of screenwriting contracts. Even sour novels about Hollywood offered little consolation to Wilson, who believed that writers must not compromise their artistic integrity by working in the studios. "Why don't you get out of that ghastly place?" Wilson urged Nathanael West. "You're an artist and really have no business there" (Martin 1970: 338).

But business is precisely what West did have there, because his novels failed to earn enough money to live on. His first three novels made him less than $800 combined, and even his greatest last novel *The Day of the Locust* (1939) sold fewer than 1,500 copies the first year and brought him a paltry $300 in royalties (Martin 1970: 341). "Outlook is pretty hopeless" read a terse telegram about sales of *The Day of the Locust* from his editor at Random House, Bennett Cerf. In contrast, when Darryl Zanuck of Twentieth-Century Fox bought the film rights to *Miss Lonelyhearts* (1933) for $4,000, it must have been readily apparent to West that Hollywood was his best option under the circumstances, given what he viewed as a decline in the demand for serious fiction. "Why make the continuous sacrifice necessary to produce novels for a non-existent market?" West inquired of Malcolm Cowley (Martin 1970: 335). With the rise of movies and other forms of mass entertainment, the prestige value attached to high culture – what John Guillory (1993) has called its cultural capital – was apparently on the decline. "Thank God for the movies," West himself said. "I once tried to work seriously at my craft but was absolutely unable to make even the beginning of a living. . . . So it wasn't a matter of making a sacrifice, . . . but just a clear cut impossibility" (Hamilton 1990: 165). Far from "selling out" to the market, then, West went to Hollywood simply to make his living as a writer.

Edmund Wilson was unmoved by such financial considerations and continued to feel the same about Hollywood. When F. Scott Fitzgerald and West died one day apart in 1940, Wilson again bemoaned the fact that they had squandered their "natural gifts" by writing for hire under the studio system: "their failure to get the best out of their best years may certainly be laid partly to Hollywood, with its already appalling record of talent depraved and wasted" (Wilson 1950: 56). The record was so appalling, in fact, that Wilson dubbed it the "Hollywood Dance of Death" (Chipman 1999: 206). This may be rhetorical hyperbole, yet Wilson expresses the consensus about Hollywood among the literati of his time: that it ruined a lot of talented American writers. When Harold Ross of *The New Yorker* chastised another novelist-turned-screenwriter, Nunally Johnson, for "sucking around the diamond merchants of Hollywood," he too was expressing the typical view of the New York intellectuals. Fitzgerald similarly told Johnson: "Listen, Nunally, get out of Hollywood. It will ruin you. You have a talent – you'll kill it there" (Hamilton 1990: 188–9). Wedded as they were to the ideology that art is incompatible with commerce, even those writers who acknowledged the economic necessity of writing for the studios frequently adopted the view that film art was an oxymoron: "this is no art," Fitzgerald declared elsewhere, "this is an industry" (Phillips 2000: xviii). Since Hollywood was utterly inimical to art, according to the prevailing view, writers must resist the temptation of studio contracts at all costs.

Yet many writers were willing to make the Faustian bargain of fettering themselves to the studio system. "If I do sell my soul to the cinema," novelist Robert Sherwood assured his mother, "it will be for a tidy sum" (R. Fine 1993: 100). Those who sold out often justified their decision in explicitly economic terms, as when Ben Hecht acerbically remarked that "art was a synonym for bankruptcy," or when Sidney Howard, another playwright turned screenwriter who would become the first person to win both a Pulitzer Prize and an Academy Award, insisted that "so long as writers earn their living by writing they are economic nitwits not to earn at least some of it where the pay is both high and certain" (R. Fine 1993: 67, 155). James M. Cain spelled out the economic realities in similarly candid if self-pitying terms in a letter to Edmund Wilson:

> A writer is human, and that $1000 a week, or $1,750, or $2,500, or whatever it is, has its effect. . . . after being paid such sums his own work no longer excites him. With luck, his novel may pay him $10,000, $25,000 if it sells to the pictures. But it will take him six months, perhaps a year, to write, and what are such buttons to a shot who could make $50,000 in the same space of time, working for pictures? His own work ceases to seem real. (R. Fine 1992: 42)

This letter captures the cynicism with which many writers implied that they might as well take the money and run. Adopting a similarly defensive tone, Cain wrote in the *New Yorker*: "I work a few weeks a year [in California], and collect the main part of my living expenses, which leaves me free to do my other work without having to worry about the rent. I don't go nuts" (R. Fine 1993: 156). This from a man who once declared about Hollywood, with the absolutism of youth: "Imagination is free or it is not free. And here it is not free" (Minter 2002: 220). Once resigned to the division of labor between fiction and screenwriting that kept him both solvent and sane, Cain became much less adamant about any fundamental distinction between art and commerce. Although it was pretty clear that screenwriting was "not art, but . . . money," Cain later admitted, "the older I get the more I wonder whether the two are not the same thing" (McCann 2000: 22).

The temptation of writing for the film studios proved to be irresistible for many writers; indeed, nearly every major American writer of the modern period either sold work to the studios or actually worked in them. Even a partial listing of those who wrote for the studios includes not only Cain, Fitzgerald, and West, but also Maxwell Anderson, Stephen Vincent Benet, Raymond Chandler, John Dos Passos, Theodore Dreiser, William Faulkner, Dashiell Hammett, Horace McCoy, Frank O'Hara, Dorothy Parker, Robert Sherwood, and Thornton Wilder, as well as British writers like Aldous Huxley, Christopher Isherwood, and Evelyn Waugh. The fact that so many prominent writers migrated to Hollywood was certainly obvious to many observers at the time. In 1932, *Fortune* magazine claimed, "more members of the literati work under [Irving] Thalberg [at MGM] than it took to produce the King James Bible" (R. Fine 1992: 40). If Hollywood was the mecca of the movies, as French critic Blaise Cendrars described it in 1945, then many writers made the pilgrimage to pay their respects – and to get paid in the process.

Hollywood had a voracious appetite for source material, purchasing film rights to novels almost as soon as they were written and frequently extending invitations to the authors as well. Budd Schulberg recounts that his first job in Hollywood working for producer David Selznick was to read at least one novel a day and write a 20-page synopsis (R. Fine 1993: 110). In the wake of Lew Wallace's $50,000 judgment against Kalem Studios for filming *Ben Hur* without his permission, the studios stopped ripping off writers and started courting them (R. Fine 1993: 46). In 1919, Samuel Goldwyn created Eminent Authors, Inc. to ensure that "all Goldwyn pictures are built upon a strong foundation of intelligence and refinement." In a series of full-page advertisements in the *Saturday Evening Post*, he boasted that his movies would "now rank with the drama and the novel in importance" (R. Fine 1993: 49). If Goldwyn was clearly trying to elevate the cultural capital of moving pictures, the writers for their part proved willing to help. Eminent authors were promised a "$10,000 advance against one third of the film's earnings," an amount that reflects Goldwyn's "surprising confidence in the usefulness of literary talent" (Hamilton 1990: 18). Yet Goldwyn apparently found writers not so useful, after all. Explaining his reasons for disbanding Eminent Authors not long after it was launched, Goldwyn declared:

The great trouble with the usual author is that he approaches the camera with some fixed literary ideal and he cannot compromise with the motion-picture viewpoint. He does not realize that a page of Henry James prose, leading through the finest shades of human consciousness, is absolutely lost on the screen. (R. Fine 1993: 52)

Goldwyn puts his finger on some very real differences between prose fiction and film scripts, which writers ignored at their peril. They are, after all, fundamentally different kinds of writing intended for two different media – the page and the screen, respectively.

Considering the extraordinary pull exerted by Hollywood on writers throughout the early twentieth century, we still need to develop a fuller account of what exactly its influence on modern fiction entailed. Certainly some writers chafed at the financial necessity of screenwriting, which they regarded as siphoning off their energies from the literary fiction they wanted to write. William Faulkner, for instance, viewed screenwriting chiefly as a second source of income, an alternative to the short story market when he needed money. "The way I see it," Faulkner quipped, "it's like chopping cotton or picking potato bugs off plants; you know damn well it's not painting the Sistine Chapel or winning the Kentucky Derby. But a man likes the feel of some money in his pocket" (R. Fine 1993: 155–6). Faulkner's career in Hollywood amounted to brief screenwriting stints so that he could devote his energies to his novels. After returning to Oxford, Mississippi from his first trip to Hollywood in 1933, he was relieved to discover that he still knew how to write: "I have turned out three short stories since I quit the movies, so I have not forgotten how to write during my sojourn downriver." However facetious his comparison of the studio system to a slave plantation may be, it offers a hint of the sense of constraint he felt in Hollywood. The key was to "go there and resist the money without becoming a slave to it," and after a similar sojourn downriver a decade later, he wrote: "It took me about a week to get Hollywood out of my lungs, but I am still writing all right, I believe." Although he found it "difficult to go completely against the grain or current of a culture," Faulkner soon discovered that "you can compromise without selling your individuality completely to it. You've got to compromise because it makes things easier" (R. Fine 1993: 157).

Faulkner struck a compromise with Hollywood in part because of "his own frustrated effort to find a broad audience for his books"; he never wrote a bestselling novel, even when he tried to reach a broader audience, as he did in *Sanctuary* (1929), which was, in his own words, "deliberately conceived to make money" (Lurie 2004: 11, 27). Like other writers, then, Faulkner went to Hollywood to make a living: "My books have never sold, are out of print: the labor (the creation of my apocryphal county) of my life, even if I have a few things yet to add to it, will never make a living for me. I don't have enough sure judgement about trash to be able to write it with 50% success" (R. Fine 1993: 126). By the late 1930s, Faulkner found in Hollywood a fairly reliable source of income to support his other projects. Yet if he was able to segregate screenwriting from novel writing in his mind, they were never altogether distinct in practice. As John T. Matthews contends, "surely the story writing, like his later work on filmscripts, both diverts and informs his novel writing" (Matthews 1992b: 5). Faulkner's novels belie the notion that his time in Hollywood had no discernible affect on his writing, for many of them are shot through with filmic metaphors, references, and techniques (Godden 1997, Lurie 2004).

While some writers managed to keep screenwriting largely separate from their literary endeavors, the juggling act required to keep doing several types of writing simultaneously – novels, short stories, and screenplays – made many writers feel that they were pulled in too many directions at once, resulting in what Richard Fine has called "a crisis of professional identity" among American writers at the time (R. Fine 1992: 243). That crisis was a symptom of the changing conditions for literary and other forms of writing in the 1920s and 1930s, changes which ultimately redrew the map of American writing. The writer Orion Cheney coined the term "novelist's nystagmus" for a new disease caused by "keeping one eye on the typewriter and the other on Hollywood," while the literary critic Richard Fine claims that the writers who went to Hollywood became what he calls "literary schizophrenics" (R. Fine 1993: 74–5, 156). Faulkner appeared to suffer from some such a condition, as for instance when he told his agent Harold Ober: "I have had about all of Hollywood I can stand. I feel bad, depressed, dreadful sense of wasting time, I imagine most of the symptoms of some kind of blow-up or collapse" (R. Fine 1993: 126).

The Coen brothers' film *Barton Fink* (1991) illustrates the lure of Hollywood for East Coast writers when the film's eponymous playwright Barton Fink, flush from the success of his most recent play, is offered a lucrative screenwriting contract by the aptly named Capital Pictures. Overcoming his ambivalence about giving up the stage and his disdain for Hollywood's crass commercialism, Barton accepts the offer to cash in on his Broadway success, and the Coen brothers signal his fateful decision by cutting from a golden cash register in the background of a New York bar to a California beach, the "ka-ching" of the cash register overlapping with waves crashing against a rock a split second before we actually see the change of scenery. This brilliant cut serves as a kind of shorthand way of alluding to the exotic allure of "the coast" for New York writers, and *Barton Fink* goes on to show "the destructive force of Hollywood on serious writers who sought to make fortunes there while preserving their artistic integrity" (Matthews 1996: 51–2). Once in Hollywood, studio boss Jack Lipnick (modeled on Jack Warner of Warner Brothers) assigns Barton to a Wallace Berry wrestling picture, which was also William Faulkner's first Hollywood assignment. In fact, Faulkner makes an appearance in *Barton Fink* as the washed-up alcoholic novelist Bill Mayhew – "America's greatest living novelist," according to Barton. Like Faulkner himself, the Coen brothers envision the writer's relationship to the studios as a kind of indentured servitude. The funniest scene of the film captures the studio boss's simultaneous admiration and contempt for writers when Lipnick first meets Barton Fink in his lavish office and launches into a monologue instructing the writer how to conform to the generic and plot conventions of movies. "Look at me," he declares in mock humility. "A writer in the room and I'm telling him what the story is." Yet Barton does need instruction in how to write to the requirements of Hollywood, and after suffering a week of agonizing writer's block he enlists the help of Bill Mayhew's mistress Audrey, who becomes his muse. He then descends into a sort of Dantean Inferno that echoes and literalizes Wilson's characterization of Hollywood as the Dance of Death. After Lipnick rejects his first screenplay for being, as he puts it, "fruity," Barton is kept on retainer by the studio but not allowed to write. As Lipnick's obsequious assistant tells him, "Right now the contents of your head is the property of Capital Pictures." By the end of the film, his career ruined, Barton sits down on the beach in a three-piece wool suit. Beside him is a box entrusted to him by Charlie Meadows, aka "Madman" Mundt, which may or may not contain Audrey's severed head. Indeed the Coen brothers imply that the box may contain Barton's head, for the price he has paid in coming to Hollywood is nothing less than his creative imagination.

For many American writers, Hollywood represented the last gasp and final stop of their fading careers. Fitzgerald immediately comes to mind as a writer who clung to his image as a once-great writer even as he sank into despair and dissipation. Perhaps this sense of impending doom helps explain why Hollywood inspired a great deal of vitriol among American writers. "Isn't Hollywood a dump – in the human sense of the word?" Fitzgerald once complained. "A hideous town, full of the human spirit at a new low of debasement" (Phillips 2000: xviii). In his "Note on Fitzgerald," which he wrote for Edmund Wilson's posthumous edition of *The Crack-Up* (1945), John Dos Passos agreed: "Whether we like it or not it is in that great bargain sale of five and ten cent lusts and dreams that the new bottom level of our culture is being created" (Dos Passos 1945: 343). One begins to wonder whether such disparagement was in part an affectation – the expected posture of the beleaguered American writer in Hollywood. Recent critics have exposed the disingenuousness of this posture, disclosing how modernist writers assimilated mass cultural images and motifs into their work even as they critiqued it as a debased form of culture. Andreas Huyssen, most prominently, points out that "major American writers since Henry James, such as T. S. Eliot, Faulkner, and Hemingway, Pound and Stevens, felt drawn to the constructive sensibility of modernism, which insisted on the dignity and autonomy of literature." Yet the putative "autonomy of the modernist art work, after all, is always the result of a resistance . . . to the seductive lure of mass culture," Huyssen argues further, and in this sense literary modernism "constituted itself through a conscious strategy of exclusion" (Huyssen 1985: 167, 55, vii).

Across the so-called Great Divide, popular writers complained about being excluded by high literary figures like T. S. Eliot and the critics who championed him. Raymond Chandler, a writer who in many ways bridged the division between serious and popular fiction, lashed out at Edmund Wilson for presuming the authority to make these kinds of invidious distinctions in the first place: "The problem of what is significant literature I leave to fat bores like Edmund Wilson – a man of many distinctions" (Chandler 1995a: 1042). Chandler proposed instead that we do away with such distinctions altogether. "My argument is and has always been merely that there is no such thing as serious literature" (Chandler 1981: 159). To be sure Chandler made this comment in 1950, by which time he was more or less resigned to his fate as far as literary reputation was concerned, and moreover the hard-boiled detective tradition he was associated with had long since been elevated to the status of serious literature if not high art. Yet Chandler's comment about Wilson's "many distinctions" nonetheless prompts us to reconsider the divisions and separations of various forms of writing between roughly 1900 and 1950, specifically the relations between hard-boiled detective fiction, the Hollywood novel, and screenwriting itself. The thread connecting all three modes of writing, of course, is Hollywood.

What Price Hollywood?, the title of George Cukor's popular 1933 film about the national obsession with celebrities, is a question that could well be asked of US literature during a time in which the cinema emerged as arguably the country's dominant form of cultural entertainment. In this time of cinema, what price did American writers pay for attaching themselves to the film studios, and what did they gain in return? Or to put it a bit differently, what price did Hollywood exact from modern American fiction? By posing the question in this way, I do not wish to perpetuate the notion that writers were "selling out"; rather I want to suggest, iconoclastically, that writers ultimately gained more than they lost in Hollywood. Indeed, it is no exaggeration to say that Hollywood was in an important sense the *underwriter* of serious literature. For although writers often – and understandably – disparaged the movies as an inferior art form, Hollywood fascinated even as it disgusted these writers, and its influence was by no means entirely negative. Often it served as an impetus for their fiction. The Hollywood novel and hard-boiled detective fiction, after all, were a direct result of American writers' close affiliation with the film studios. Taking a cue from Edmund Wilson, then, we might envision Hollywood's influence on modern American fiction as occurring in one of three ways: as a conscious or unconscious pressure on literary form; as an influence on literary content; and as a major source of income for writers through selling screen rights to novels and stories as well as through screenwriting contracts.

Hollywood has long held a central place in the US national imaginary – the image America projects to itself and to the world. Yet the various meanings that accrue to Hollywood are multivalent, even contradictory. The very term is a symbolic site where a number of myths are played out: dream factory or dream dump, paradise or dystopia, the apotheosis or nadir of American culture (Springer 2000: 3). "If there was no Hollywood," Anita Loos once remarked, "no doubt we'd have to invent it, a place to project our fantasies and reflect our dreams, no matter how outlandish" (Loos 1984: 161). For Nathanael West, Hollywood was nothing so much as a "dream dump" (West 1962: 123). American writers have by and large tended to be highly critical of Hollywood, exposing its facile promulgation of the American Dream, satirizing its fatuousness, critiquing its industrialization of art under the factory-like studio system. In the best writing about Hollywood, however, cultural critique derives not from the perspective of a detached observer but from a decidedly more implicated one – namely that of the studio insider. As a relatively underappreciated subgenre of American fiction, the Hollywood novel contradicts Wilson's rule of thumb "about Hollywood as a subject of fiction, that those who write about it are not authentic insiders and that those who know about it don't write" (Wilson 1950: 49). On the contrary, Hollywood novels promised readers an unflinching expose of the dream factory, written for curmudgeons and star-struck fans alike by those who had experienced it firsthand.

Touted by *Photoplay* magazine where it appeared as "the first great novel written around the motion picture capital of the World – Los Angeles," Francis William Sullivan's *The Glory Road* (1916) chronicles the experiences of aspiring young actress June Magregor, who comes to Hollywood to work for the Graphic Film Company, falls in love with the handsome movie star Paul Temple, fends off the sexual advances of powerful studio boss Stephen Holt, and devotes herself to the ambitious young director Tom Briscoe. Which is to say that Sullivan's novel already features many of the recurrent character types, settings, and themes that would come to dominate the genre, such as the avaricious producer, the vulnerable female star, the ambitious direc-tor, the disillusioned writer, the down-and-out extra, the Hollywood party, the studio back lot, and the movie premiere. *The Glory Road* also sounds the note of critique that became a defining feature of Hollywood fictions after it, as the publicity blurb in *Photoplay* attests: "Its chapters exude the living atmosphere of the studios, reflect their romantic glamour – and reveal at times the brassiness of the glitter." Even as the blurb appeals to a growing public fascination with the dream factory, it also purports to burrow down "beneath the colorful, gay surface" to reveal that, in fact, "there were dark and hidden things" underneath (Springer 2000: 12–13, 18).

Samuel Merwin's *Hattie of Hollywood* (1922) similarly warns of the supposed dangers for young women lured to Hollywood by promises of stardom. No sooner does naive young Hattie agree to a screen test for the suave European director Armand de Brissac than he proceeds to give her an unsentimental education in the nefarious ways of Hollywood:

> "Now, my dear," he said, taking her hand and playing with her soft little fingers as he spoke, "you and I had better understand each other right at the start. If you'll do exactly as I say – place yourself unquestioningly in my hands – I will make you. If you won't, I can't help you." (Springer 2000: 112)

Hattie's education continues at the hands of a more sympathetic writer named Julian Dempster, a "highbrow" literary type who likes to think of Hattie in poetic terms as "a fragrant wild rose here in this big hothouse called Hollywood." Hattie's initiation is not complete until she becomes a full-fledged movie star named Harriet John. Like *The Glory Road* before it, *Hattie of Hollywood* delves into the sordid realities "of mystery, of whispered romance and scandal, of (recent) murders and underworld con-spiracies" beneath its glamorous surface (Springer 2000: 113–14).

Both these early Hollywood novels establish the clichés of what John Springer has called star fictions, which typically fall into one of two groups: novels in which the heroine experiences sudden fame and then disillusionment only to achieve happiness in the end; and novels in which the heroine either fails miserably or simply throws away her success. Adele Rogers St. Johns' *The Skyrocket* (1925), Anne Gardner's *Reputation* (1929), Jack Preston's *Screen Star* (1932), and Maysie Greig's *Romance for Sale* (1934) belong to the first group, in which the heroine is saved from the perils of movie-star disillusionment, often by marriage and a "soft-focus happy ending" (Springer 2000: 125). Edgar Rice Burroughs's *The Girl from Hollywood* (1924), Frances Marion's *Minnie Flynn* (1925), Keane McGrath's *Hollywood Siren* (1932), Haynes Lubou's *Reckless Hollywood* (1932), and Vicky Baum's *Falling Star* (1934) belong to the second group, in which the heroines are portrayed as "tragic figures" or "sacrificial lambs" who fall prey to sexual predators and compromise themselves for the sake of stardom, or succumb to dissipation of one sort or another, only to lose everything in the end (Springer 2000: 125–6).

Written by the author of *Tarzan of the Apes* (1914), *The Girl from Hollywood* reads like a morality tale played out in the jungles of Hollywood. Gaza de Lure hails from "a little town in the Middle West" and, "burning with lofty ambition," she arrives in Hollywood eager for fame (Burroughs 1924: 43). She gets derailed from the path to stardom by a series of unfortunate events: one unscrupulous director offers a leading role to someone else after Gaza snubs his sexual advances by saying "she would rather have caressed a rattlesnake as willingly as she would have permitted a married man to make love to her" (pp. 48–9). It turns out that sexual predators are not the only danger lurking in Hollywood. Another director introduces her to drugs, and before long she finds herself addicted to morphine and destitute (pp. 50–3). *The Girl from Hollywood* offers a glimpse of the dark underside of Hollywood success stories, even if it does so in obviously moralistic terms. "The story of success is always the same," wrote Adele Rogers St. Johns in *Photoplay* magazine. "But the story of every failure is different. . . . What becomes of the rest of the ten thousand?" (Springer 2000: 142). Novels about star-crossed heroines offered one answer to that question, and it must be said that these parables may well reflect real-life tales of heartbreak and tragedy, for instance that of Peg Entwistle, an actress who committed suicide in 1932 by jumping off the Hollywood sign (Springer 2000: 133).

The epitome of this doom-and-gloom school of Hollywood fiction is Rupert Hughes's *Souls for Sale* (1922), with its prudish protagonist Reverend Dr Steddon, for whom Hollywood is a "new Babylon," "the corrupter of our young men and women – the school of crime" (Hughes 1922: 1). For Dr Steddon's daughter Mem, however, Hollywood represents not hell but "the Eden of the movies," and she ventures out West to become its Eve (Hughes 1922: 65). After apparently eating from the orange groves of knowledge, Mem is astonished to discover that her beauty is a valuable commodity, "for which the grateful public would pay with gratitude and fame and much money." She soon finds that she "could take care of herself better than men had ever taken care of her" (pp. 185, 379). If *Souls for Sale* sets out to provide a prurient inside look at Hollywood debauchery – as if looking over the shoulder of Dr Steddon as he "gazed aghast at the appalling posters with their revolting blazon of the new word 'Sex'" (p. 5) – the novel ends up heralding the age of the New Woman. *Souls for Sale* was so successful that Samuel Goldwyn asked Hughes to adapt his novel for the screen and even allowed him to direct the film version.

The most important early novel about the dream factory for sheer narrative ingenuity is Harry Leon Wilson's *Merton of the Movies* (1922). A former editor of the journal *Punch* and a frequent contributor to the *Saturday Evening Post*, where *Merton* was first serialized, Wilson spent only a few months in Hollywood, but from his brief stay he wrote one of the funniest, if not the most plausible, novels about the place (D. Fine 2000: 64–5). *Merton of the Movies* opens with a narrative sleight of hand: for five pages we read about how the beautiful Estelle St. Clair has been abducted by the villain Snake le Vasquez. Just as she is about to be rescued by Buck Benson, a "strong, silent" type of the American West, this rapturous dime-Western narrative is suddenly interrupted by the voice of Amos Gashwiler, who admonishes his employee Merton Gill for holding a mannequin of Snake le Vasquez over his head while enacting the adventure we have just read: "Have you gone plumb crazy, or what? Put that thing down!" (Wilson 1922: 1–5). After this rude interruption of "the vivid tale" going on inside Merton's head, we return not to the mundane reality of the store in Simsbury, Illinois, but to another daydream: Merton's fantasy of becoming the dashing Clifford Armytage, once a "humble clerk" in the "so-called emporium of Amos G. Gashwiler," now a "sterling star" of the silver screen (p. 6). The passage introduces us to Merton's most persistent fantasy of all: his dream of becoming a movie star.

Merton's penchant for fantasy ironically becomes an asset as well as a liability. Inside the gates of the fictional Holden Studios, Merton realizes that the "fragile contrivances of button-lath and thin plaster" that make up the sets are part of what he calls the "real falseness" of movie magic (Wilson 1922: 74). What he once thought of as "the fine and beautiful art of moving pictures" now appears to him a "thing of shame, of machinery, of subterfuge" (pp. 20, 166). He discovers furthermore that his childhood idol Beulah Baxter, "the slim little girl with a wistful smile" (p. 32), is married (for the third time) to her director Sig Rosenblatt, which brings about "the swift and utter destruction of his loftiest ideal" (p. 175). But Merton's idealism is then restored by well-known actress Sarah Montague – "the Montague girl" (p. 330) – who takes pity on him and introduces him to Jeff Baird, a Mack Sennett-like director of so-called "Buckeye Comedies" designed to appeal to "the coarser element among screen patrons" (p. 90). By assuring him that they are serious dramatic films, Sarah and Jeff trick Merton into appearing in them, and Merton, like Truman in *The Truman Show*, becomes the butt of an elaborate joke. Needless to say, the films themselves are a hit, and Merton's fortunes take a dramatic turn when he marries Sarah Montague at the end. Concluding "with a magazine article that focuses on his domestic life," the novel evinces ambivalence about celebrity and cinema, which mirrors Merton's confused attitude shifts (Rhodes 1998: 129). One reviewer worried that "there are millions who might read this story and see nothing in it to laugh at" (Springer 2000: 77). Yet the story clearly made audiences laugh in numerous stage and movie incarnations, first as a hit on Broadway in 1922, as a silent film in 1924, then as sound films in 1932 (Paramount) and again in 1947 (MGM). Surprisingly, Gertrude Stein considered it "the best book about twentieth-century American youth that has yet been done" and asked for an introduction to Wilson on a visit to California (Rhodes 1998: 123).

Another novel admired by the highbrows that has only recently received the critical attention it deserves is Anita Loos's *Gentlemen Prefer Blondes* (1925), written in the form of a diary by the hilariously brash and unself-conscious narrator, Lorelei Lee, who negotiates an upwardly mobile path from small-town debutante to society lady to authoress to movie star. William Faulkner for one, who met Loos through Sherwood Anderson, admired Lorelei's witty companion Dorothy. "Please accept my envious congratulations on Dorothy," he wrote, adding, "I wish I had thought of Dorothy first." Edith Wharton told a close friend in January 1926, "I was just reading the Great American novel (*at last!*) 'Gentlemen Prefer Blondes,' & I want to know if there are – or will be – others, & if you know the funny woman, who must be a genius" (Matthews 1992a: 207–8). And when philosopher George Santayana was asked, "what was the best book of philosophy written by an American?" he answered drolly, *Gentlemen Prefer Blondes* (Loos 1925/1927/1998: xli). These positive responses, albeit with mixed envy and condescension, suggest less stable boundaries between high and popular literature than are generally assumed. How else can we account for Wharton's obviously tongue-in-cheek but still quite startling tribute in calling *Gentlemen Prefer Blondes* the Great American novel at last?

Whereas many novelists felt the pull of planet Hollywood, Loos gravitated towards the literary establishment, turning an already successful screenwriting career into an unlikely second act as a bestselling novelist: "She proved to be one of the few writers in the world who moved successfully from a career in script writing to other mediums" (Acker 1991: 178). Loos expertly negotiated her place in the literary field, facilitated by newly forged connections between the fiction market and the Hollywood studios. *Gentlemen Prefer Blondes* mediates the issues of gender, authorship, and cultural value that Loos was facing herself. Lorelei muses at one point, "It would be strange if I turn out to be an authoress. I mean the only career I would like to be besides an authoress is a cinema star and I was doing quite well in the cinema when Mr. Eisman made me give it all up" (Loos 1925/1998: 4, 6). Lorelei Lee's success in *Gentlemen Prefer Blondes*, moreover, is not unlike the success of the novel itself, as Loos inadvertently suggests when she later conflated the protagonist with the actual novel in her autobiography: "From the beginning, my tough little blonde proved to be a healthy financial enterprise" (Loos 1974: 12). When *Blondes* first appeared in *Harper's Bazaar*, newsstand sales nearly tripled; the novel then sold out the first printing overnight and went through 19 printings within three years, making Loos a millionaire by the end of the decade (Loos 1925/1927/1998: xli, Matthews 1992a: 207).

The extraordinary success of *Gentlemen Prefer Blondes* can be attributed, in part, to fluctuating valuations of cultural capital within the literary field as a whole. Loos brings her considerable satirical gifts to bear on those very fluctuations in a sequel to *Blondes*, cleverly titled *But Gentlemen Marry Brunettes* (1927). In the sequel, Lorelei undertakes a program of cultural refinement by subscribing to the Book of the Month Club, which as she puts it, "tells you the book you have to read every month to make your individuality stand out" (Loos 1927/1998: 135). Joan Shelley Rubin's work on the Book-of-the-Month-Club's middlebrow pedagogy helps illuminate Lorelei's assumption that it will improve her cultural taste; the Club's advertising in the mid-1920s promised to keep subscribers abreast of "*all the important new books*" so that they can "know about them and talk about them" and "become 'cultured' before anyone else" (Rubin 1992: 104). Going well beyond book clubs in her pursuit of cultural refinement, Lorelei seeks out the authors themselves and somehow gets herself invited to a luncheon with all the "High Brows" who meet regularly at the Algonquin Hotel: "H.L. Mencken, Theadore [sic] Dreiser, Sherwood Anderson, Sinclare [sic] Lewis" (Loos 1927/1998: 138). By the end of the novel, however, Lorelei is back in Hollywood, where she finds herself "to [sic] busy going over my scenarios with Mr. Montrose, to keep up any other kind of literary work" (Loos 1927/1998: 123). The end point of her climb up the ladder of success, in other words, is not high society but Hollywood. Loos once opined that any reputable "movie writer wouldn't have dreamed that my heroine had any place on celluloid" (Loos 1925/1998: xl). Marilyn Monroe proved her wrong, of course, and today *Gentlemen Prefer Blondes* is remembered primarily for Howard Hawks's very successful 1953 musical, with a "corresponding devaluation in its literary prestige" (Hegeman 1995: 546).

The comic potential of young heroines overcoming all obstacles on their path to stardom was mined by another popular writer, Elinor Glyn, who came to Hollywood from her native Britain on a contract with Famous Players-Lasky and became, like Loos, a well-known early female screenwriter who wrote more than a dozen screenplays for the studio. Glyn's novel *It* (1927) featured a modern flapper protagonist in the mold of Lorelei Lee, and together with the subsequent film adaptation starring Clara Bow, *It* sparked the "It Girl" craze of the late 1920s. Glyn herself defined "It" as a "strange magnetism" possessed by certain women – and men – which makes them irresistible to others. According to Joseph Roach, the term derived in part from Glyn's frank "assessment of the liberated sex lives of actresses," and the author, herself notorious for sexual escapades recounted in an earlier succès de scandale *Three Weeks* (1907), almost certainly meant the term "It" as a euphemism for sexual intercourse, more freely indulged in by young women reacting against the strictures of an earlier era (Roach 2007: 4, 21, 24–5).

J. P. McEvoy's wise-cracking Dixie Dugan, the heroine of his comic Hollywood novels *Showgirl* (1928) and *Hollywood Girl* (1929), both of which were made into movies by Warner Brothers as *Showgirl* and *Showgirl in Hollywood* (1930), uses her sexual allure to advance her career, but without losing her self-respect. "To hell with love anyway," Dixie Dugan exclaims. "I'm going in for a career" (McEvoy 1929: 43). Written in "hallucinatory first person" much like Loos's *Gentlemen Prefer Blondes*, *Hollywood Girl* exposes the false pretenses under which men attempted to seduce a "blonde goddess" like Dixie Dugan: "my God do I have to be mauled and muzzled over by every man I go out with . . . [by] the bear who comes along and says hello baby how would you like to go into movies . . . wouldn't you love to be a star" (McEvoy 1929: 83–8). *Hollywood Girl* takes the form of letters and telegrams to her friends and family back home: "I could tell you stories that would curl your hair," she says. Dixie herself manages to beat the odds through sheer ingenuity and boundless wit, metaphorically rising from "the sub-basement next to the boilers" all the way "up to the roof garden where the stars . . . munch caviar and flip cigarette butts down on an adoring world." "I've been tossing my share over the rail this last few weeks," Dixie announces triumphantly, "and boy how I love it. This is la vie" (McEvoy 1929: 222–4).

Carl Van Vechten came to Hollywood on assignment from *Vanity Fair* in late 1926, just after *Nigger Heaven* (1926) was published, and he translated his experiences into a Hollywood novel titled *Spider Boy* (1928), about a short story writer and playwright, Ambrose Deacon, who, flush from his successful play on Broadway, is offered the chance to write Imperia Starling's next film. "Call it an industry, call it an art," explains her director Herbert Ringrose, sensing Deacon's reluctance. "Why quibble? The writer is perhaps the most essential single factor – saving always the director – in Hollywood" (Van Vechten 1926: 41). The director adds that Deacon can have more cultural influence as a screenwriter: "How many people see one of your plays? A few paltry thousands every week, while *millions* look at my pictures" (p. 49). "Think what would happen if you wrote for the films," she continues. "There it would be always gleaming on silver screens all over the globe" (p. 49). Seduced by this logic, Deacon signs a contract for "a sum of money which seemed fantastic" (p. 132), and Imperia puts him up in her 27-room Beverly Hills "bungalow," where he is less a guest than a prisoner. Almost immediately Ambrose has second thoughts, and Hollywood begins to seem like a "place where playwrights were seduced to become prostitutes for the motion pictures" (p. 164).

"The linkage of studio and whorehouse," as David Fine puts it, is also "a recurring motif" in Carroll and Garrett Graham's darkly satirical novel *Queer People* (D. Fine 2000: 68). Here the protagonist Theodore Anthony "Whitey" White is, much like Van Vechten, a journalist who comes up with an elaborate ploy to masquerade as a gossip columnist for the *Examiner* and do an exposé on what he calls "the three Hollywood G's – girls, gin, and gynecology" (Graham and Graham 1930/1976: 225). To get in on "the real money," however, he decides to become a writer. "You don't have to be good," one veteran screenwriter tells him. "It doesn't make any difference what you do, the director will hash it up anyway" (p. 149). Neither talent nor experience is required, but this doesn't prevent some writers from harboring rather lofty goals about their work. Take Rethea Clore, for instance, a recently hired writer with only one novel to her credit. "Although she had never attempted motion pictures before," Whitey muses, "she was about to demonstrate her all embracing genius by making *The Tigress* the most artistically and commercially successful film production in history" (pp. 93–4). Another writer sets out to write "the great American novel," only to wind up "rehashing the worst American gags" for inane comedies (p. 46). Screenwriting is "no profession for a grown man," one established Hollywood insider tells Whitey, adding, "But, what the hell! There's money in it" (p. 146).

John Dos Passos also compared his predicament as a writer in Hollywood to a form of prostitution, complaining to his publisher: "If you people sold more books you wouldn't have me out in the red-light district like this" (Dos Passos 1973: 442). The author projected an image of being above Hollywood even as he took advantage of the opportunity to earn a studio paycheck. Thus when Paramount hired him in the summer of 1934, he wrote his friend Ernest Hemingway, "I've just signed up to serve a term of five weeks in Hollywood. I was in a sort of a gap in my work and thought I might as well take a stab at it, restoring my finances and taking a look at the world's great bullshit center" (Dos Passos 1973: 437). His tone is as self-pitying as it is pungent, yet I believe there was an ulterior motive for Dos Passos to get "a short glimpse of Hollywood" (p. 442), for he had not yet finished *The Big Money* (1936), the final volume of his *USA* trilogy (1930–6). Michael Denning provocatively calls *The Big Money* Dos Passos's Hollywood novel, one so good it takes "its place next to the Hollywood dystopias written by the studio radicals like Nathanael West and Horace McCoy" (Denning 1997: 191). This categorization is supported by the title itself, as Dos Passos often referred to Hollywood by that phrase. "Having been for a few weeks in the big money makes us feel strangely broke," he related to one friend with bitter irony. "I don't think the big money is what it's cracked up to be" (Dos Passos 1973: 444).

Dos Passos's experience in Hollywood was finally an unhappy one – for one thing, he contracted rheumatic fever shortly after arriving in California; for another, he learned that a younger writer was "ghosting" the screenplay he was working on (Dos Passos 1973: 443). He often bemoaned the formulaic nature of movies and worried that serious fiction was threatened by a lack of public interest and professional viability. All the rewards went to hack writers like Fitzgerald's fictional Pat Hobby who churned out pulp fiction for magazines. Dos Passos was convinced he must leave Hollywood to preserve his integrity. "I've said goodbye to Paramount," he told Malcolm Cowley, "so I feel very much better. . . . It's like endorsing absorbine junior or Beauty mattresses" (Dos Passos 1973: 445). Yet as Dos Passos once confessed to Fitzgerald, "Hollywood has been enormously instructive" (Dos Passos 1973: 446). Hollywood taught him, among other things, that there is finally no necessary distinction between the aesthetic and the commercial. It obviously had other salutary benefits as well: not only did Dos Passos manage to complete his massive three-volume trilogy on the first three decades of the American century; he also found himself uniquely positioned to take stock of the present and future state of the novel. When pressed to say what serious literary fiction could still accomplish in the time of cinema, Dos Passos seized upon a startling analogy: "[The novel] is the best possible moving picture machine contrived to focus the present moment on the screen of the future" (Foster 1986: 190).

Horace McCoy's *They Shoot Horses, Don't They?* (1935) and *I Should Have Stayed Home* (1938) both deal with, in Edmund Wilson's words, "the miserable situation of movie-struck young men and women who starve and degrade themselves in Hollywood" (Wilson 1950: 20). Like James M. Cain, McCoy was a contributor to *Black Mask* as well as a journalist. He arrived in Hollywood in 1931 hoping to become a movie star, not a writer, but in 1932, he took a job as a junior writer at Columbia for $50 per week. For the next 20 years he worked steadily in Hollywood, and his earnings rose to $1,000 per week by 1950 (Haut 2002: 54). During that time McCoy wrote five novels and nearly 100 screenplays (D. Fine 2000: 101). Hollywood was his primary employer and a precondition for the novels, as "McCoy borrowed heavily from his own Hollywood experiences" in his fiction (Springer 2000: 153). In *They Shoot Horses, Don't They?* Gloria Bailey comes from Dallas desperate for movie stardom, having read about Hollywood in fan magazines back home while in the hospital for an earlier suicide attempt. Robert Syverten wants to become, as he says immodestly, "the greatest director in the world" (McCoy 1935/1997: 20). Although he has not yet made a single picture, Robert offers her this unsolicited advice, "Why don't you quit the movies?" She replies, "Why should I? I may get to be a star overnight" (p. 23). Gloria enters a dance marathon contest in hopes that a producer or director might discover her and then give her "a start in a picture" (p. 24). Nothing of the sort happens, of course, and afterwards a despondent Gloria enjoins Robert to, as she puts it, "pinchhit for God" by killing her (p. 127). Now indicted for murdering his dance partner, Robert Syverten retrospectively narrates in typical hard-boiled style. He tries to exonerate himself by claiming it was assisted suicide, not murder. Simon & Schuster marketed *They Shoot Horses* as a hard-boiled novel like Cain's *The Postman Always Rings Twice*, which came out earlier that year (Haut 2002: 47). The two novels share a "confessional, flashback narrative" point of view, which "has the effect of implicating the reader as confidant and arousing some sympathy for the doomed men" (D. Fine 2000: 102). Whereas Cain does not reveal the outcome until the end, McCoy uses the murder trial as a narrative frame. The novel opens with the judge's words, printed alone on the page, "THE PRISONER WILL STAND" and ends with the judge's final words, "MAY GOD HAVE MERCY ON YOUR SOUL" (McCoy 1935/1997: 212).

McCoy wrote a more self-conscious Hollywood novel in *I Should Have Stayed Home*, which examines "the desperation of dream seekers who are chewed up and disgorged by the system," focusing on two movie extras, Mona Matthews and Ralph Carston (D. Fine 2000: 74). Near the beginning of the novel, the two characters pass a billboard that reads "ALL ROADS LEAD TO HOLLYWOOD," and there could hardly be a more fitting motto for the Hollywood novel as a genre (McCoy 1938/1996: 8). For Mona and Ralph the road leads not to "the Hollywood you read about," however, but to "a cheap town filled with cheap stores and cheap people" (p. 5). McCoy's novel measures the distance between a mythical Hollywood, "where today you are broke and unknown and tomorrow you are rich and famous," and the real Hollywood of disappointed actors like Ralph, who ends up "hating the place and all the celebrities in it (only because they were celebrities, something I was not)" (p. 6). "*I should have stayed home*," Ralph says bitterly at the end, voicing the phrase that gives the novel its title (p. 184). Perhaps because she is less resentful about not being a star herself, Mona is incisive in her critique of the discourse of celebrity, singling out fan magazines in particular for propagating "goddamn lies" about stars who "started at the bottom and rose to fame and fortune – what do you think that does for all the millions of other girls in this country – the millions of waitresses and small-town girls?" (pp. 44–5). "I'll tell you what it does," Mona declares emphatically, "It makes them discontented" (p. 45).

McCoy recognized that aspiring actors – with all their hopes and heartaches – were compelling subjects for literary fiction. One character in *I Should Have Stayed Home* even quits his job in the publicity department at Universal "to write a novel about extras in the movies. How they live, what they think – you know, there's a big field there" (McCoy 1938/1996: 73). Like the actual writers of Hollywood fictions, Johnny Hill plans to include "the tragedy and heart-break" of not making it in the film industry, as well as "the viciousness and cruelty" within it (p. 74). "That side of Hollywood's never been told," Hill claims. "All you ever read about Hollywood is the waitress who gets a test and turns out to be a big shot" (p. 74). American writers have "missed a good net," he says, by not writing about the nearly "twenty thousand extras" in Hollywood (p. 74).

That story *was* being told in a number of increasingly gloomy Hollywood novels in the late 1930s, and of course the most bitingly satirical Hollywood novel of all is Nathanael West's *The Day of the Locust* (1939), which according to none other than Edmund Wilson is "mostly occupied with extras and gives mere glimpses into the upper reaches" (Wilson 1950: 48). "Like McCoy's characters," David Minter points out, "West's come from the margins of Hollywood" (p. 238). These two writers also share the fact that they were "initially conspicuous failures in the mass market of American book publishing" (Springer 2000: 152). McCoy's only successful work was his later novel *Kiss Tomorrow Goodbye* (1948), which sold 1.6 million copies in paperback. By this point in his career, McCoy had capitulated to his publisher's desire to position him as a hard-boiled writer and thus tap into the pulp fiction market: a James Avanti cover illustration for *Kiss Tomorrow Goodbye* "depicts a cigarette-smoking man sitting on a bed, watching a semi-clad woman, who, with her back to him, assumes a provocative pose" (Haut 2002: 53). The blurb reads: "Love as hot as a blow-torch. Crime as vicious as the jungle" (p. 53).

As a Hollywood novel, *The Day of the Locust* has more in common with John O'Hara's *Hope of Heaven* (1938), published one year before, than with Fitzgerald's *The Last Tycoon* (1941), published two years later. For while Fitzgerald's last novel deals with a fictional studio boss named Monroe Stahr, O'Hara's novel, like West's, delves into what Edmund Wilson once called "the nondescript fringes of Hollywood" (Wilson 1950: 23). While working as a movie critic at the *New York Morning Telegraph* and as a publicist for Warner Brothers and RKO in New York, O'Hara harbored a "dream of going to Hollywood and making large sums there, but I don't suppose that will ever come true" (R. Fine 1993: 100). His dream did come true in 1934, when Paramount optioned his first novel *Appointment in Samara* and offered him a contract for ten weeks" (R. Fine 1993: 100). Edmund Wilson lambasted *Hope of Heaven*, charging that O'Hara "showed serious signs of suffering from Hollywood lightheadedness," even if he had not lost his "capacity for judgment" altogether (Wilson 1950: 24, 26). In contrast, Wilson was lavish with his praise of West for keeping his wits about him: "West has footed a precarious way and has not slipped at any point into relying on the Hollywood values in describing the Hollywood people" (p. 53). Anyone who has ever been to Hollywood, Wilson claims, "knows how the mere aspect of things is likely to paralyze the aesthetic faculty by providing no *point d'appui* from which to exercise its discrimination, if it does not actually stun the sensory apparatus itself" (p. 53). All the more remarkable, then, that West managed like some entomologist to have "stalked and caught some fine specimens of these Hollywood Lepidoptera and impaled them on fastidious pins" (p. 53).

Most prominent among West's specimens is the narrator Tod Hackett, a once promising painter who has taken a job as a set designer in Hollywood, "despite the arguments of his friends who were certain that he was selling out and would never paint again" (West 1962: 60–1). These so-called friends echo the reproach West received when he first went to Hollywood, and thus Hackett is a figure for the American novelist and in danger of becoming, as befits his name, a hack. Instead of writing an apologia for his involvement in a commercial medium, however, West subtly undermines the myth of selling out in Hollywood – the notion that writing for the movies "constitutes a deep betrayal of a writer's talents" (Dardis 1984: 167). Tod proves the prediction that he would never paint again premature, for instance, by completing his greatest artwork by the end of the novel, a painting titled *The Burning of Los Angeles*. Hollywood in fact acts as a spur to art, for "the strangeness of all he sees rekindles his desire to paint" (Dickstein 2002: 24). Only by coming to Los Angeles does Tod Hackett realize his full potential as an artist: "He had been in Hollywood less than three months and still found it a very exciting place," and "'The Burning of Los Angeles,' a picture he was soon to paint, definitely proved he had talent" (West 1962: 59–60). Hackett applies a lesson West had learned all too well: only by making it the subject matter of his fiction could Hollywood serve to spur rather than hinder his artistic efforts.

West's other lepidoptera include the "successful screen writer" Claude Estee, the morose automaton Homer Simpson (who later lends his name to Matt Groening's cartoon hero of *The Simpsons*), as well as the aspiring actress Faye Greener, who seems poised for movie stardom: she is not only "extremely beautiful" but "taut and vibrant" and "shiny as a new spoon" (West 1962: 94). Faye is "an affected actress" who is theatrical to the point of self-parody (p. 94). Tod admits, "Faye's affectations were so completely artificial that he found them charming" (p. 103). Nearly every male character promptly falls in love with her, and although she "enjoyed being stared at," she keeps all of them at a distance because they had "nothing to offer her" (pp. 67, 94). Faye has just appeared as "one of the dancing girls" in a B movie, and Tod "had gone all the way to Glendale to see her in that movie" (p. 67). Her screen persona is at once inviting and distancing: in one publicity still she "lay stretched out on the divan with her arms and legs spread, as though welcoming a lover" (p. 68). While Faye "reduces Homer to masochistic submission," she inspires in Tod an impulse to violence (Springer 2000: 163). "Her invitation wasn't to pleasure," the latter observes, "but to struggle, hard and sharp, closer to murder than to love" (West 1962: 68). Although Tod manages to laugh at his self-conscious parody of hard-boiled language here, there is nothing funny about the fact that West's otherwise sympathetic narrator fantasizes about raping Faye no less than three times (West 1962: 68). In the most brutal of these rape fantasies, Tod stalks Faye into a dark parking lot and "enacts" the following rape scenario in his mind:

> He knew what it would be like lurking in the dark vacant lot, waiting for her. . . . She would drive up, turn the motor off, look up at the stars, so that her breasts reared, then toss her head and sigh . . . then get out of the car. The long step she took would make her tight dress pull up so that an inch of glowing flesh would show above her black stocking. As he approached carefully, she would be pulling her dress down, smoothing it nicely over her hips. (West 1962: 174)

Tod's stalking fantasy appears to come straight out of a B-movie thriller, the kind West himself worked on at Republic Studios, which was nicknamed Repulsive Studios by writers. Indulging in the illicit images, clichéd language, and salacious content of so many Hollywood film noirs, the scene plays out both as a critique of sexual violence in the culture industry *and* as an example of it. Despite Tod's insistence that "she wasn't hard-boiled," Faye Greener is precisely hard-boiled, the kind of femme fatale who would hardly be out of place in a Raymond Chandler novel: "She was supposed to look drunk and she did, but not with alcohol" (pp. 67–8). In this scene, the novel is virtually indistinguishable in its language and visual imagery from hard-boiled detective fiction.

The Day of the Locust also represents the appeal of Hollywood for those who arrived by the thousands with hopes of achieving fame and fortune, only to realize that stardom would be more difficult to attain than the fan magazines and studio propaganda had led them to believe. According to Blaise Cendrars, "the human tide of interest and enthusiasm unleashed by the movies has become so threatening to Hollywood that Hollywood has had to take inhuman and lopsided defensive measures to hold back this frenzy fed by its own publicity" (Cendrars 1995: 98, 100). Whatever defensive measures Cendrars had in mind, his comments anticipate West's wry observation in his justly celebrated movie premiere scene that the "police force would have to be doubled when the stars started to arrive" to hold back the "frenzy" of the mob (West 1962: 176). Long viewed as a centerpiece of the novel, this scene captures the discontent that seethes beneath otherwise harmless celebrity worship. "They were savage and bitter," the narrator observes, "and had been made so by boredom and disappointment" (p. 176). Once the stars arrive, "the crowd would turn demoniac, . . . then nothing but machine guns would stop it" (p. 176). West envisions the riot as an eruption of pent-up disappointments and unfulfilled desires, pointing to the potential for collective protest against the adulation of stars. If the crowd spontaneously erupts into a collective protest of sorts, however, their protest is finally diffused by its own entropic energies as well as by the intervention of the police. Sitting alone in a police cruiser afterwards, Tod listens to sirens wailing outside, and he "began to imitate the siren as loud as he could" (p. 185). This crazed siren call resounds beyond the ending of *The Day of the Locust*, giving voice to a confused, unwitting recognition of the irrationality at the heart of the culture industry.

F. Scott Fitzgerald read *The Day of the Locust* while working on *The Last Tycoon* (1941) and felt that the novel "has scenes of extraordinary power": "Especially I was impressed by . . . the character and handling of the aspirant actress and the uncanny almost medieval feeling of some of his Hollywood background, set off by those vividly drawn grotesques" (Fitzgerald 1994: 395). Although left unfinished at his death in December 1941, *The Last Tycoon* is Fitzgerald's own contribution to the genre. "In this city that swarms with writers," Edmund Wilson observed, "none yet has really mustered the gumption to lay bare the heart and bowels of the moving-picture business," but at the time of his death, he reports, Fitzgerald "had written a considerable part of what promised to be by all odds the best novel ever devoted to Hollywood" (Wilson 1950: 48, 55). Fitzgerald wanted a narrator who was "*of* the movies but not *in* them," and he made Cecelia Brady a studio boss's daughter rather than a player herself: "My father was in the picture business the way another man might be in cotton and steel, and I look at it tranquilly" (Fitzgerald 1945: 138, Fitzgerald 1941/1994: 3). Twenty-year old Cecelia becomes infatuated with Monroe Stahr, "who led pictures way up past the range of theatre, reading a sort of golden age, before the censorship" (Fitzgerald 1941/1994: 28). Monroe Stahr is modeled on the maverick producer Irving Thalberg, whom Fitzgerald met in 1931 at MGM while working on a screen adaptation of Katharine Brush's novel *Redheaded Woman*. Although impressed with Thalberg, Fitzgerald took umbrage at being asked to adapt a novel he regarded as derivative of his own work and suffered the further humiliation of being assigned to collaborate with another writer. Fitzgerald was fired from the film after three weeks, and Anita Loos was assigned to rewrite his script (Springer 2000: 210). Fitzgerald always thought poorly of screenwriters (besides himself). He told Maxell Perkins that Hollywood was "a strange conglomeration of a few excellent overtired men making the pictures, and as dismal a crowd of fakes and hacks at the bottom as you can imagine" (R. Fine 1993: 137).

While publicly disdaining the culture industry, Fitzgerald seemed happy enough to reap its considerable financial rewards. He used whatever means necessary to profit from his writing: by placing his stories in the highest paying commercial magazines; by selling novels and short stories to Hollywood studios; and by signing on as a screenwriter himself. Fitzgerald had much success with his novels. He sold *This Side of Paradise* (1920) to Famous Players for $10,000, and he later associated the success of his first novel with the movies: "the presses were pounding out *This Side of Paradise* like they pound out extras in the movies" (Fitzgerald 1945: 88). Warner Brothers bought his next novel *The Beautiful and Damned* (1922) for $2,500, and in 1926 Fitzgerald sold film rights to *The Great Gatsby* (1925) for an astonishing sum of

$45,000. The next year he accepted a $3,500 advance to write an original screenplay and arrived in Hollywood with Zelda for the first of what would turn out to be many sojourns out West (Dixon 1986: 103, Springer 2000: 208). He returned in 1937 with a six-month contract at MGM for $1,000 per week, yet he managed only one screen credit during this final period in Hollywood (for *Three Comrades*), and he was fired for a second time by MGM two years later, when his literary fortunes were at an all-time low, with book royalties amounting to a mere $33 (Springer 2000: 211). Fitzgerald found *Esquire* to be his best source of income during these meager years; he wrote a series of short stories for the magazine about a Hollywood hack named Pat Hobby, a kind of fictional alter ego: "He had once known sumptuous living, but for the past ten years jobs had been hard to hold – harder to hold than glasses" (Springer 2000: 212). At one point, Fitzgerald even began signing telegrams to his editors as "Pat Hobby Fitzgerald," and the character clearly voices the author's frustrations with the factory-like studio system: "what people you sat with at lunch was more important in getting along than what you dictated in your office. This was no art, as he often said – this was an industry" (Fitzgerald 1962: 22).

Most Hollywood writers understood that their treatment by the studios was not likely to improve without unionization. Raymond Chandler observes in his essay "Writers in Hollywood," for instance, that a "salaried writer" in Hollywood has "little power or decision over the uses of his own craft," because the studios own all the copyrights, although he sounded a more hopeful note at the end of the essay, claiming that "the writers of Hollywood *are* winning their battle for prestige" (Chandler 1995a: 994, 1003). He meant that some writers – Preston Sturges comes to mind – were getting hired as "producers and directors of their own screenplays" (p. 1003). Meanwhile, efforts to create a union to represent the interests of all writers were underway, yet the studios predictably resisted these unionization efforts at every turn. While the Screen Writers Guild was founded in 1933, not until 1941 did the major studios begrudgingly accept the guild, and the intervening years witnessed what one critic has called a Hollywood writers war (Springer 2000: 179).

Budd Schulberg's novel *What Makes Sammy Run* (1941) chronicles the growing antagonism between writers and studios, as well as between writers themselves, such as when jokes about forming a writers guild went around the writers' table at the studio commissary: "Some of the laughter was automatic, some frightened, some reactionary" (Schulberg 1941/1990: 164). The son of a Paramount executive, Schulberg grew up in Hollywood but elected to become a novelist rather than a screenwriter. "I had chosen to live the free life of a novelist," he recalls, because "I resented the way writers – even the William Faulkners and Scott Fitzgeralds – were shuffled like cards in Hollywood" (Rapf 2003: xv). *What Makes Sammy Run* reflects this view of writers as pawns in the studio system; the narrator Al Manheim is a newspaper columnist who comes to Hollywood in hopes of becoming a screenwriter, only to find it inhospitable to writers.

In Steve Fisher's Hollywood crime novel *I Wake Up Screaming* (1941), a young screenwriter who is never identified by name reflects on a fledgling career that has taken him from Broadway to Hollywood Boulevard: "I was twenty-seven, had a play on Broadway, and now a studio contract with one of the majors. . . . Hell, I even had my Writer's Guild of America card!" (Fisher 1941: 3). The writer soon discovers that "desperate games were being played" behind the scenes (p. 21). At lunch one day, he notices a director sitting alone in the corner who had three weeks left on his contract "but whose option was being dropped": "He sat there like a ghost, nibbling at salad. No one wanted any part of him. No one could afford to be seen sitting with failure" (p. 22). This is just one example of "the rotten little jealousies, the screaming egos, the petty smugness" in an industry where you are only as good as your last hit film (p. 134). A novel that skillfully combines conventions of the Hollywood novel with those of hard-boiled detective fiction, *I Wake Up Screaming* attests to the fact that by 1941 Los Angeles had come to be seen not only as the nation's film capital but also as the "capital of American noir" (D. Fine 2000: x).

American hard-boiled detective fiction has most often been regarded as a popular genre, separate but equal to the mainstream US literary tradition. Segregation of literary forms is by no means as morally suspect as racial segregation, of course, but I use the term separate but equal advisedly to suggest that the classification of hard-boiled fiction, however appropriate in terms of generic considerations, was an invidious distinction under evaluative literary-critical paradigms. Because of their association with classic film noirs of the 1930s and 1940s, often directly adapted from them (as often as not by hard-boiled writers), American crime novels have always carried a taint of the popular in spite of their belated critical acceptance by scholars after the cultural turn in literary studies. The role of Hollywood as a cultural and economic force in the literary field during the 1920s and 1930s challenges this segregation of popular forms from the mainstream American literary tradition. While some writers conceived of themselves as serious literary authors, others were relegated – even against their wishes – to the restricted field of formula fiction. What these writers had in common, however, was their connection to Hollywood.

A shared connection to the film industry did nothing to prevent them from disparaging it, as if their resentment toward the invidious distinctions made in the literary field were displaced onto an undisguised disdain for the studio system. "There is no reward for aesthetic virtue here," James M. Cain once sneered, "no punishment for aesthetic crime" (D. Fine 1999: 124). Feigning nausea, Cain complained in his 1933 essay "Camera Obscura," what "makes a writer sick at his stomach when he walks on a movie lot" is the sense "that in some vague way he is a prostitute of the arts" (R. Fine 1993: 123). Like Faulkner, Cain advised fellow writers to compromise with Hollywood: "to have a clear idea of what his function is, and to discharge that function, instead of aspiring to functions which simply are not there" (R. Fine 1993: 155). He often boasted that he knew exactly what function he was expected to perform in Hollywood, and once he stopped writing fiction in later years, he consoled himself with the idea that, after all, "there are worse trades than confecting entertainment"

(R. Fine 1993: 156). In a sort of sequel to his Hollywood career, Cain played a major role in devising a plan to establish the American Authors' Authority, which he and other writers hoped would "revolutionize literary economics" (R. Fine 1992: 4).

Due to its initial reception as an indigenous popular genre, and no doubt owing as well to its reputation as a very masculine genre, hard-boiled detective fiction has a problematic status in the literary field. Certainly the changing fortunes of detective fiction over the years attests to the mutability of literary categories, if nothing else, yet even from the moment of its first appearance in the 1920s, the status of hard-boiled fiction was viewed as a problem. In the genre's infancy, crime fiction writers often wrote anonymously for the pulp magazines, thus occupying a much lower position in the spectrum of cultural forms than either serious novelists or journalist critics. But as detective fiction's status elevated after Dashiell Hammett and his hard-boiled descendants won over the critics, these writers found themselves adrift on a sea of shifting literary categories.

From the 1920s onward, Hollywood formed a link between literary and popular fiction, connecting hard-boiled writers Dashiell Hammett, James M. Cain, Raymond Chandler, and others to writers like Theodore Dreiser, William Faulkner, F. Scott Fitzgerald, and Ernest Hemingway, who staked their careers on the rather rarefied notion of the Great American Novel and produced a number of truly great novels in the process. Hard-boiled writers, meanwhile, suffered from an inferiority complex and often made desperate bids for literary respectability. Nearly every crime fiction writer started out in the pulp magazines that, as Sean McCann notes, "came to define a distinct subfraction of the American periodical marketplace – one at sharp ideological, aesthetic, and economic odds with both the era's elite journals of opinion and with the much larger realm of mass-market entertainment" (McCann 2000: 48). From the beginning, hard-boiled detective fiction arguably occupied a liminal or in-between status in the literary field, with one foot in the sea of mass culture and the other tentatively testing the waters of modernism.

The underlying connections between hard-boiled detective fiction and American literary modernism are all the more apparent when we consider that the same literary agent, H. N. "Swanie" Swanson, represented F. Scott Fitzgerald, William Faulkner, James M. Cain, Raymond Chandler, and Horace McCoy (Haut 2002: 29, 96). Moreover, many modernist writers, including T. S. Eliot, Gertrude Stein, and William Faulkner, were avid readers of American crime fiction (McGurl 2001: 158–9). In a kind of mutual admiration society, serious writers influenced hard-boiled fiction writers and vice versa.

When it was advantageous to look down his nose at screenwriting as a profession, Raymond Chandler could be as scathing as anyone. "Personally I think Hollywood is poison to any writer, the graveyard of talent. I have always thought so. But perhaps I have lived too close to it" (Chandler 1981: 6). Determined to make his living from writing literature, Chandler liked to think that he was not beholden to the studio system. If he could not make a living from his fiction, though, he knew he could always turn to what he called "the Hollywood slaughterhouse, ankle-deep in blood and screaming like a Saracen" (Chandler 1981: 112). Not a happy prospect. In his essay "Writers in Hollywood" (1945), he goes as far as to suggest that a writer simply cannot work in the studio system "without dulling the fine edge of his mind, without becoming little by little a conniver rather than a creator, a subtle and facile journeyman rather than a craftsman" (Chandler 1995a: 997). And finally, on a less serious note, Chandler once joked, "good original screenplays were almost as rare in Hollywood as virgins" (Chandler 1981: 70).

Such criticism betrays a slightly nervous undertone, as if Chandler could not help but worry about being further tainted by his association with Hollywood. Attuned to the nuances of prestige in a highly variegated culture industry, he already resented being relegated to the realm of popular culture even as he took credit for bolstering the status of detective fiction. "In this country," he wrote in a 1950 letter, "the mystery writer is looked down on as sub-literary merely because he is a mystery writer, rather than for instance a writer of social significance twaddle" (Chandler 1995a: 1042). By this point in his career, of course, it proved beneficial for him to be somewhat dismissive of prestige as the only measure of what he had accomplished as a writer. "What greater prestige can a man like me . . . have," he wondered, "than to have taken a cheap, slovenly, and utterly lost kind of writing and have made of it something that intellectuals claw each other about?" Sounding rather like French sociologist Pierre Bourdieu, he observes that "you cannot have art without a public taste, and you cannot have a public taste without a sense of style and quality throughout the social structure" (Chandler 1981: 48, 68). Besides, one could do little to determine one's position in the literary field in any case: "I do not know what the loftiest level of literary achievement is; neither did Aeschylus or Shakespeare" (Chandler 1995a: 986).

Saddled in later years with the charge that he was repeating himself as a writer, Chandler decided to take on a new challenge by tackling the Hollywood novel, a genre he ungenerously claimed "interests me because it has never been licked" (Phillips 2000: 119). "No doubt I have learned a lot from Hollywood," Chandler admitted. "Please do not think I completely despise it, because I don't. . . . It is a great subject for the novel – probably the greatest still untouched. But how to do it with a level mind, that's the thing that baffles me" (Chandler 1981: 64–5). To call Hollywood "still untouched" as a subject of fiction after the flurry of Hollywood novels between 1939 and 1941 seems more than a little disingenuous, yet Chandler's comment here interestingly echoes Edmund Wilson's pronouncement with which I began, to the effect that Hollywood was an untouchable subject because no writer could presume to have enough critical distance from it. Determined to succeed where his predecessors had failed, Chandler set out to write his own Hollywood novel, a project that, given his reputation as a detective fiction writer par excellence, nicely aligns the two literary genres I have been tracing in this essay.

The result was *The Little Sister* (1949), which describes Hollywood, "for all its surface glitter, as the dumping ground for failed dreams" (Phillips 2000: 123). At once a repository for the author's frustrations with the film industry and recognizably hard-boiled, *The Little Sister* improbably features Philip Marlowe, the now famous dick whom Chandler had created more than 10 years earlier. "I used to like this town," says the jaded Marlowe. "A long time ago. . . . Hollywood was a bunch of frame houses on the interurban line. Los Angeles was just a big dry sunny place with ugly homes and no style, but goodhearted and peaceful" (Chandler 1995a: 357). Marlowe's nostalgia harks back to a time before the postwar population boom was in full swing, when Los Angeles had fewer people and less crime. The city was also a haven for a small cadre of writers. "Little groups who thought they were intellectual used to call it the Athens of America," Marlowe tells us. "It wasn't that, but it wasn't a neon-lighted slum either" (p. 357). As intellectuals were absorbed into the culture industry, the place lost some of its luster. Marlowe concludes his little diatribe against Hollywood, "Los Angeles has Hollywood – and hates it" (p. 358). On a visit to the studio, Marlowe runs into the studio's top executive, Jules Oppenheimer, who appears in the novel apparently for no other reason than to give Chandler an opportunity to comment on the inefficiency of the studio system: "Save fifty cents in this business and all you have is five dollars worth of bookkeeping" (p. 306). Looking out on an expansive studio backlot with a dismissive wave of the hand, and denigrating all writers, directors, and actors in a single breath as the most "expensive talent in the world," Oppenheimer boasts that he could make a profit from virtually any product if only he controlled the distribution channels: "Doesn't matter a damn what they do or how they do it. Just give me fifteen hundred theaters" (p. 306).

Recognizing the potential for a monopoly that this vision of a vertically integrated film industry posed, the Supreme Court ruled in 1948 that the major Hollywood studios had to divest themselves of the theatre chains they controlled. That same year, the number of television sets in American households reached one million; and by 1950, there were 11 million (I. Hamilton 1990: 301). After movie attendance peaked in 1946, with more than 90 million tickets sold per week, box office fell by 40 percent over the next 10 years, while overall profits at the major studios declined by 50 percent (Rifkin 2000: 25). Studios faced challenges from other quarters as well. The motion picture industry suddenly came under more direct political scrutiny than ever before, an irresistible target of the government's rabid anti-Communist efforts. In October 1947, the House Committee on Un-American Activities (commonly referred to by the acronym HUAC) began nine days of hearings into alleged Communist influence in Hollywood. Led by new Committee Chair J. Parnell Thomas, the hearings were a sensation in the national press, with Thomas alleging that "90% of communist infiltration in Hollywood is to be found among screenwriters" (R. Fine 1992: 234). The committee summoned 24 so-called "friendly" witnesses to testify before Congress, including eventual Screen Actors Guild president and later US President Ronald Reagan, studio heads Jack Warner and Walt Disney, and a number of actors such as Robert Taylor and Gary Cooper. During the second week of hearings, 19 suspected Communists, labeled "unfriendly witnesses," were subpoenaed to testify before the committee. The first witness, John Howard Lawson, began the hearings by refusing to answer the infamous question, "Are you or have you ever been a member of the

Communist Party?" Among other unfriendly witnesses called to testify were the screenwriters Alvah Bessie, Lester Cole, Ring Lardner, Jr., and Dalton Trumbo, plus director Edward Dmytryk and producers Adrian Scott and Herbert Biberman. The 11th person to testify, German playwright Bertolt Brecht, "dissembled rather than defied the committee" (Doherty 2003: 21n). Following Brecht's testimony, Thomas abruptly suspended the hearings after only 11 of the 19 witnesses had taken the stand. Brecht fled to Europe the following day, and the remaining 10 witnesses who had already testified henceforth became known as the Hollywood Ten. In an unhappy denouement to the whole sorry affair, all 10 served short prison terms for "contempt of Congress" after the Supreme Court refused to hear their cases in 1950 (Belton 2004: 288–9).

Virtually no one involved in the HUAC hearings emerged unscathed; even the movie stars calling themselves the Committee on the First Amendment regretted their association with the hearings. Director John Huston, who was in Washington as part of the group lending support to the witnesses, summed up the disappointment felt by those who saw it as an opportunity to uphold the First Amendment: "You felt your skin crawl and your stomach turn. I disapproved of what was being done to the Ten but I also disapproved of their response. They had lost a chance to defend a most important principle" (I. Hamilton 1990: 293). Regarding what he privately dubbed the "Hollywood show in Washington," Chandler thought it worth considering that the Hollywood Ten "had very bad legal advice":

> They were afraid to say they were Communists or to say that they were not Communists; therefore they tried to raise a false issue. If they had told the truth, they would have had a far better case before the courts than they have now, and they would certainly have had no worse a case as regards their bosses in Hollywood. (Chandler 1981: 106–7)

Immediately after the HUAC hearings, studio executives met at the Waldorf-Astoria hotel in New York and emerged from two days of negotiations with the Waldorf Statement, a document that, according to Thomas Doherty, "asserted the determination of Hollywood to stand up to HUAC even as it knuckled under" (Doherty 2003: 22). Claiming that filmmaking "cannot be carried out in an atmosphere of fear," top executives nonetheless capitulated to the witch-hunt atmosphere, assuring the public that they would never "knowingly employ a communist" (p. 22). The fallout from the HUAC hearings was the blacklist, which contained the names of nearly 300 individuals who were subsequently denied work in the industry. Notwithstanding Billy Wilder's caustic remark, "Of the unfriendly Ten, only two had any talent; the other eight were just unfriendly," the blacklist effectively decimated the creative pool in Hollywood (Dick 1980: 10).

The HUAC hearings on Hollywood in 1947 and the Supreme Court ruling of 1948 together sounded the death knell of the studio system, even as they inadvertently heralded a new era for writers in the film industry. Billy Wilder's *Sunset*

Boulevard (1950) can be read as an elegy for old Hollywood (I. Hamilton 1990). The film's protagonist Joe Gillis (William Holden), a former newspaper journalist with two B pictures to his credit, is reduced to writing a vanity screenplay for faded silent film star Norma Desmond (Gloria Swanson), who accuses him of ruining movies with excess verbiage: "You made a rope of words and strangled this business." The movie ends with the writer floating face down in her swimming pool. "I always wanted a swimming pool," Gillis says in a voice-over from beyond the grave.

Despite the lingering pall cast over the film industry by the blacklist, writers were no longer part of a vertically integrated studio system controlling the filmmaking process from start to finish, but rather freelance writers hired on a per film basis. Chandler had predicted, in 1945, that the "cold dynasty" of the studio system "will not last forever," and he saw several reasons to hope for a better future for writers:

> There is hope that a decayed and make-shift system will pass, that somehow the flatulent moguls will learn that only writers can write screenplays and only proud and independent writers can write good screenplays, and that present methods of dealing with such men are destructive of the very force by which pictures must live. (Chandler 1995a: 1000–1)

Whether the freelance system that replaced the studio system Chandler decries here actually contributed to better movies is debatable, but one thing is clear: writers would henceforth be relatively unfettered. No longer under contract to a single Hollywood studio, they became free to ply their trade to any mogul, however flatulent, who was willing to take a chance on their scripts. Meanwhile, the expansion of higher education in the postwar period and the institutionalization of formalism in English departments helped to create a much larger market for modern novels, such that a William Faulkner, or Nathanael West for that matter, would very likely be astonished, if not a little bit wistful, to learn how many copies their novels have sold since their deaths.

References and Further Reading

Acker, Ally. (1991). *Reel Women: Pioneers of the Cinema, 1895 to the Present*. New York: Continuum.

Adorno, Theodor W. and Max Horkheimer. (1944/1989). *The Dialectic of Enlightenment*, trans. John Cumming. New York: Continuum.

Ames, Christopher. (2003). Pat Hobby and the fictions of the Hollywood writer. In Jackson R. Bryer, Ruth Prigozy, and Milton R. Stern (eds), *F. Scott Fitzgerald in the Twenty-first Century* (pp.

279–90). Tuscaloosa: The University of Alabama Press.

Ballard, W. T. (1942). *Say Yes to Murder*. New York: G. P. Putnam's Sons.

Barnard, Rita. (1995). *The Great Depression and the Culture of Abundance: Kenneth Fearing, Nathanael West, and Mass Culture in the 1930s*. New York: Cambridge University Press.

Belton, John. (2004). *American Cinema, American Culture*, 2nd edn. New York: McGraw Hill.

Benjamin, Walter. (1968). *Illuminations*, trans. Harry Zohn. New York: Schocken Books.

Bordwell, David, Janet Staiger, and Kristin Thompson. (1985). *The Classical Hollywood Cinema: Film Style and Mode of Production to 1960*. New York: Columbia University Press.

Botshon, Lisa. (2003). Anzia Yezierska and the marketing of the Jewish immigrant in 1920s Hollywood. In Lisa Botshon and Meredith Goldsmith (eds), *Middlebrow Moderns: Popular American Women Writers of the 1920s* (pp. 203–24). Boston: Northeastern University Press.

Bourdieu, Pierre. (1993). *The Field of Cultural Production*. New York: Columbia University Press.

Brooker-Bowers, Nancy. (1985). *The Hollywood Novel and Other Novels about Film, 1912–1982*. New York: Garland.

Bruccoli, Matthew J. (1977). *The Last of the Novelists: F. Scott Fitzgerald and* The Last Tycoon. Carbondale: Southern Illinois University Press.

Burroughs, Edgar Rice. (1924). *The Girl from Hollywood*. London: Methuen.

Cain, James M. (1934/1992b). *The Postman Always Rings Twice*. New York: Vintage Books.

Cain, James M. (1936/1992a). *Double Indemnity*. New York: Vintage Books.

Cain, James M. (1989). *Mildred Pierce*. New York: Vintage Books.

Campbell, Donna. (2004). Taking tips and losing class: Challenging the service economy in James M. Cain's *Mildred Pierce*. In Janet Galligani Casey (ed.), *The Novel and the American Left: Critical Essays on Depression-Era Fiction* (pp. 1–15). Iowa City: University of Iowa Press.

Casey, Janet Galligani (ed.). (2004). *The Novel and the American Left: Critical Essays on Depression-Era Fiction*. Iowa City: University of Iowa Press.

Cendrars, Blaise. (1995). *Hollywood: Mecca of the Movies*, trans. Garrett White. Berkeley: University of California Press.

Chandler, Raymond. (1949/1988). *The Little Sister*. New York: Vintage.

Chandler, Raymond. (1981). *The Selected Letters of Raymond Chandler*, ed. Frank MacShane. New York: Macmillan.

Chandler, Raymond. (1995a). *Later Novels and Other Writings*. New York: Library of America.

Chandler, Raymond. (1995b). *Stories and Early Novels*. New York: Library of America.

Chipman, Bruce L. (1999). *Into America's Dream-Dump: A Postmodern Study of the Hollywood Novel*. Lanham, MD: University Press of America.

Cooper, Stephen. (2000). *Full of Life: A Biography of John Fante*. New York: North Point Press.

Corrigan, Timothy and Patricia White. (2004). *The Film Experience: An Introduction*. Boston: Bedford Books.

Cowie, Elizabeth. (1993). Film noir and women. In Joan Copjec (ed.), *Shades of Noir* (pp. 121–32). New York: Verso.

Dardis, Tom. (1976). *Some Time in the Sun: The Hollywood Years of Fitzgerald, Faulkner, Nathanael West, Aldous Huxley, and James Agee*. New York: Charles Scribner's Sons.

Dardis, Tom. (1984). The myth that won't go away: Selling out in Hollywood. *Journal of Popular Film and Television* 11: 167–71.

Davis, Mike. (1992). *City of Quartz: Excavating the Future of Los Angeles*. New York: Vintage Books.

Denning, Michael. (1997). *The Cultural Front: The Laboring of American Culture in the Twentieth Century*. New York: Verso.

Dick, Bernard F. (1980). *Billy Wilder*. Boston: Twayne Publishers.

Dickstein, Morris. (2002). What price Hollywood? Dreams and nightmares of the Great Depression. *The Common Review* 1: 23–31.

Dixon, Wheeler Winston. (1986). *The Cinematic Vision of F. Scott Fitzgerald*. Ann Arbor, MI: UMI Research Press.

Doherty, Thomas. (1999). *Pre-Code Hollywood: Sex, Immorality, and Insurrection in American Cinema, 1930–1934*. New York: Columbia University Press.

Doherty, Thomas. (2003). *Cold War, Cool Medium: Television, McCarthyism, and American Culture*. New York: Columbia University Press.

Dos Passos, John. (1936/1969). *The Big Money*. New York: Signet.

Dos Passos, John. (1945). A note on Fitzgerald. In Edmund Wilson (ed.), *The Crack-Up* (pp. 338–43). New York: New Directions.

Dos Passos, John. (1973). *The Fourteenth Chronicle: Letters and Diaries of John Dos Passos*, ed. Townsend Ludington. Boston: Gambit.

Dos Passos, John. (1988). *The Major Nonfictional Prose*, ed. Donald Pizer. Detroit: Wayne State University Press.

Dreiser, Theodore. (1943). Myself and the movies. *Esquire* July 20: 159.

Faulkner, William. (1950/1977). *Collected Stories of William Faulkner*. New York: Vintage.

Fine, David M. (ed.). (1984). *Los Angeles in Fiction: A Collection of Original Essays*. Albuquerque: University of New Mexico Press.

Fine, David M. (1999). John Fante and the Los Angeles novel in the 1930s. In Stephen Cooper and David M. Fine (eds), *John Fante: A Critical Gathering* (pp. 122–30). Madison, WI: Fairleigh Dickinson University Press.

Fine, David M. (2000). *Imagining Los Angeles: A City in Fiction*. Albuquerque: University of New Mexico Press.

Fine, Richard. (1992). *James M. Cain and the American Authors' Authority*. Austin: University of Texas Press.

Fine, Richard. (1993). *West of Eden: Writers in Hollywood 1928–1940*. Washington: Smithsonian Institution Press.

Fisher, Steve. (1941). *I Wake Up Screaming*. New York: Dodd, Mead, & Company.

Fitzgerald, F. Scott. (1939–40/1962). *The Pat Hobby Stories*. New York: Scribner's.

Fitzgerald, F. Scott. (1941/1994). *The Love of the Last Tycoon: A Western*, ed. Matthew J. Bruccoli. New York: Scribner's.

Fitzgerald, F. Scott (1945). *The Crack-Up*. New York: New Directions.

Fitzgerald, F. Scott. (1994). *F. Scott Fitzgerald: A Life in Letters*, ed. Matthew J. Bruccoli. New York: Touchstone.

Foster, Gretchen. (1986). John Dos Passos' use of film technique in *Manhattan Transfer* and *The 42nd Parallel*. *Literature-Film-Quarterly* 14: 186–94.

Friedrich, Otto. (1986). *City of Nets: A Portrait of Hollywood in the 1940s*. New York: Harper & Row.

Gabler, Neal. (1988). *An Empire of Their Own: How the Jews Invented Hollywood*. New York: Doubleday/Anchor.

Godden, Richard. (1997). *Fictions of Labor: William Faulkner and the South's Long Revolution*. Cambridge, UK: Cambridge University Press.

Graham, Carroll and Garrett Graham. (1930/1976). *Queer People*. Carbondale: Southern Illinois University Press.

Guillory, John. (1993). *Cultural Capital: The Problem of Literary Canon Formation*. Chicago: University of Chicago Press.

Hallas, Richard. (1938). *You Play the Black and the Red Comes Up*. London: Cassell.

Hamilton, Cynthia S. (1987). *Western and Hard-Boiled Detective Fiction in America*. Iowa City: University of Iowa Press.

Hamilton, Ian. (1990). *Writers in Hollywood 1915–1951*. New York: Harper & Row.

Hammett, Dashiell. (1999). *Complete Novels*. New York: Library of America.

Harris, Oliver. (2005). Killing "the killers": Hemingway, Hollywood, and death. In David Seed (ed.), *Literature and the Visual Media* (pp. 74–95). Cambridge, UK: D. S. Brewer.

Haut, Woody. (2002). *Heartbreak and Vine: The Fate of Hardboiled Writers in Hollywood*. London: Serpent's Tail.

Hegeman, Susan. (1995). Taking *Blondes* seriously. *American Literary History* 7: 252–4.

Hughes, Rupert. (1922). *Souls for Sale*. New York: Harper & Row.

Huyssen, Andreas. (1985). *Across the Great Divide: Modernism, Mass Culture, Postmodernism*. Bloomington and Indianapolis: Indiana University Press.

Jameson, Fredric. (1990). *Signatures of the Visible*. New York: Routledge.

Latham, Aaron. (1972). *Crazy Sundays: F. Scott Fitzgerald in Hollywood*. New York: Pocket Books.

Lewis, R. W. B. (1975). *Edith Wharton: A Biography*. New York: Harper & Row.

Locklin, Gerald. (1984). The day of the painter, the death of the cock: Nathanael West's Hollywood novel. In David Fine (ed.), *Los Angeles in Fiction* (pp. 67–82). Albuquerque: University of New Mexico Press.

Loos, Anita. (1925/1927/1998). *Gentlemen Prefer Blondes* and *But Gentlemen Marry Brunettes*. New York: Penguin.

Loos, Anita. (1966). *A Girl Like I*. New York: Viking.

Loos, Anita. (1974). *Kiss Hollywood Good-By*. New York: Viking.

Loos, Anita. (1984). *Fate Keeps on Happening*. New York: Dodd, Mead.

Lurie, Peter. (2004). *Vision's Immanence: Faulkner, Film, and Popular Culture*. Baltimore: The Johns Hopkins University Press.

Marcus, Steven. (1983). Dashiell Hammett. In Glenn W. Most and William W. Stowe (eds), *The Poetics of Murder: Detective Fiction and Literary*

Theory (pp. 195–209). New York: Harcourt, Brace, Jovanovich.

Margolies, Alan. (2002). Fitzgerald and Hollywood. In Ruth Prigozy (ed.), *The Cambridge Companion to F. Scott Fitzgerald* (pp. 189–208). New York: Cambridge University Press.

Marion, Frances. (1926). *Minnie Flynn: The Story of a Film Star*. London: Chatto & Windus.

Marling, William. (1995). *The American Roman Noir: Hammett, Cain, and Chandler*. Athens: University of Georgia Press.

Martin, Jay. (1970). *Nathanael West: The Art of His Life*. New York: Farrar, Strauss, and Giroux.

Matthews, John T. (1992a). Gentlemen defer blondes: Faulkner, Anita Loos, and mass culture. In Waldemar Zacharasiewicz (ed.), *Faulkner, His Contemporaries, and His Posterity* (pp. 207–21). Tübingen, Germany: Francke Verlag.

Matthews, John T. (1992b). Shortened stories: Faulkner and the market. In Evans Harrington and Ann J. Abadie (eds), *Faulkner and the Short Story* (pp. 3–37). Jackson: University Press of Mississippi.

Matthews, John T. (1996). Faulkner and the culture industry. In Philip M. Weinstein (ed.), *The Cambridge Companion to William Faulkner* (pp. 51–74). Cambridge, UK: Cambridge University Press.

May, Elaine Tyler. (1980). *Great Expectations: Marriage and Divorce in Post-Victorian America*. Chicago: University of Chicago Press.

May, Lary. (1980). *Screening Out the Past: The Birth of Mass Culture and the Motion Picture Industry*. Chicago: University of Chicago Press.

May, Lary (ed.). (1988). *Recasting America: Culture and Politics in the Age of the Cold War*. Chicago: University of Chicago Press.

McCann, Sean. (2000). *Gumshoe Nation: Hard-Boiled Crime Fiction and the Rise and Fall of New Deal Liberalism*. Durham, NC: Duke University Press.

McCoy, Horace. (1935/1997). *They Shoot Horses, Don't They?* In *Crime Novels: American Noir of the 1930s and '40s* (pp. 97–214). New York: Library of America.

McCoy, Horace. (1938/1996). *I Should Have Stayed Home*. New York: Midnight Classics.

McEvoy, J. P. (1928). *Showgirl*. New York: Brentanos.

McEvoy, J. P. (1929). *Hollywood Girl*. New York: Simon & Schuster.

McGurl, Mark. (2001). *The Novel Art: Elevations of American Fiction after Henry James*. Princeton, NJ: Princeton University Press.

Minter, David. (2002). A Cultural History of the Modern American Novel. In Sacvan Bercovich (ed.), *The Cambridge History of American Literature: Volume 6: Prose Writing, 1910–1950* (pp. 3–281). Cambridge, UK: University of Cambridge Press.

Nabokov, Vladimir. (1996). *Novels 1955–1962*. New York: Library of America.

Ngai, Sianne. (2005). *Ugly Feelings*. Cambridge, MA: Harvard University Press.

Nickerson, Catherine Ross. (1998). *The Web of Iniquity: Early Detective Fiction by American Women*. Durham, NC: Duke University Press.

O'Hara, John. (1939/1969). *Hope of Heaven and Other Stories*. London: Panther.

Phillips, Gene D. (2000). *Creatures of Darkness: Raymond Chandler, Detective Fiction, and Film Noir*. Lexington: University of Kentucky Press.

Porter, Dennis. (2003). The private eye. In Martin Priestman (ed.), *The Cambridge Companion to Crime Fiction* (pp. 95–113). Cambridge, UK: Cambridge University Press.

Powdermaker, Hortense. (1950). *Hollywood, the Dream Factory: An Anthropologist Looks at the Movie-Makers*. Boston: Little, Brown.

Pratt, R. (2001). *Projecting Paranoia: Conspiratorial Visions in American Film*. Lawrence: University Press of Kansas.

Rabinowitz, Paula. (2002). *Black and White Noir: America's Pulp Modernism*. New York: Columbia University Press.

Rapf, Joanna E. (ed.). (2003). *On the Waterfront*. Cambridge, UK: Cambridge University Press.

Rhodes, Chip. (1998). *Structures of the Jazz Age: Mass Culture, Progressive Education, and Racial Discourse in American Modernism*. New York: Verso.

Rhodes, Chip. (2008). *Politics, Desire, and the Hollywood Novel*. Iowa City: University of Iowa Press.

Rifkin, Jeremy. (2000). *The Age of Access: How the Shift from Ownership to Access is Transforming Capitalism*. New York: Penguin Books.

Roach, Joseph. (2007). *It*. Ann Arbor: University of Michigan Press.

Ross, Steven J. (2001). How Hollywood became Hollywood: Money, politics, and movies. In Tom Sitton and William Deverell (eds), *Metropolis in the Making: Los Angeles in the 1920s* (pp. 255–76). Berkeley and Los Angeles: University of California Press.

Rosten, Leo. (1941). *Hollywood: The Movie Colony, the Movie Makers*. New York: Harcourt.

Rubin, Joan Shelley. (1992). *The Making of Middlebrow Culture*. Chapel Hill: University of North Carolina Press.

Rzepka, Charles J. (2005). *Detective Fiction*. Cambridge, UK: Polity Press.

Sale, Richard. (1942). *Lazarus #7*. New York: Simon & Schuster.

Schulberg, Budd. (1941/1990). *What Makes Sammy Run?* New York: Vintage.

Sklar, Robert. (1994). *Movie-Made America: A Cultural History of American Movies*, revised edn. New York: Vintage.

Sollors, Werner. (2002). *Ethnic Modernism*. In Sacvan Bercovitch (ed.), *The Cambridge History of American Literature: Volume 6: Prose Writing, 1910–1950* (pp. 355–556). Cambridge, UK: University of Cambridge Press.

Solomon, William. (2002). *Literature, Amusement, and Technology in the Great Depression*. Cambridge, UK: Cambridge University Press.

Springer, John P. (2000). *Hollywood Fictions: The Dream Factory in American Popular Literature*. Norman: University of Oklahoma Press.

St. Johns, Adela Rogers. (1925). *The Skyrocket*. London: Methuen.

Thomas, Ronald R. (1999). *Detective Fiction and the Rise of Forensic Science*. Cambridge, UK: Cambridge University Press.

Thorp, Margaret Farrand. (1939). *America at the Movies*. New Haven, CT: Yale University Press.

Ulin, David L. (ed.). (2002). *Writing Los Angeles: A Literary Anthology*. New York: Library of America.

Van Vechten, Carl. (1928). *Spider Boy: A Scenario for a Moving Picture*. New York: Knopf.

West, Nathanael. (1962). *Miss Lonelyhearts* and *The Day of the Locust*. New York: New Directions.

Whitfield, Raoul. (1931). *Death in a Bowl*. New York: Knopf.

Wilson, Edmund. (1950). *Classics and Commercials: A Literary Chronicle of the Forties*. New York: Farrar, Straus.

Wilson, Harry Leon. (1922). *Merton of the Movies*. New York: Doubleday.

Wodehouse, P. G. (1929). Slaves of Hollywood. *The Saturday Evening Post* December 7: 5.

25

The Belated Tradition of Asian-American Modernism

Delia Konzett

Introduction

While the first major Asian-American novels were still being written, the New Critics, a group of poets who were also English professors, were in the process of establishing its school as the dominant aesthetic paradigm of American modernism. In the post-World War II era, New Criticism would not only canonize high modernism, it would also, as Mark Morrisson writes, induce "the rise of university English departments and pedagogical anthologies as key sites of literary evaluation and canon formation" (Morrisson 2005: 28). Under the New Critics, notes Morrisson, the institution of the American university classroom (combined with that of the literary press) became the dominant way to establish aesthetic norms and a coexistent canon. Alternative modernisms, particularly that of the New Negro or Harlem Renaissance, were marginalized and obscured in the cultural administrative processes of the New Critics, and students in classrooms around the nation found themselves performing ahistorical and formal close analyses of exemplary poems by Eliot, Yeats, and Dickinson. And while the New Critics established a much-needed tradition of American modernism, their critical effort was still largely indebted to and following in the vein of a European modern literary tradition that emphasized formalist aesthetics.

Since the 1980s, however, it has become abundantly clear that American modernism is in essence diverse, promoting, says Daniel Singal, a "pluralist integration" of culture that challenges orthodox beliefs of religious, social, and racial uniformity (Singal 1987: 19). Indeed, critics now discuss modernism in the plural, referring to the many alternative and competing discourses once obscured by high modernism. Responding to the challenge of postmodernism and its stereotypical representation of modernism as functionalist style, recent modernist studies have instead stressed modernism's path-breaking commitment to cultural relativism. This reorientation of the national canon has led to new assessments and inclusion of alternative modernist cultures such as the Harlem Renaissance, as well as immigrant, feminist, postcolonial, working-class, regional, ethnic, and urban subcultural literatures. This essay will discuss the alternative modernism of Asian-American literature, focusing particularly on the novel.

The Evolving Concept of Asian-American Literature

Before discussing Asian-American modernism, a brief summary of Asian-American literature and its work of canon formation and production of a cultural legacy are in order. Though its evolving definition is hotly debated and in a continual process of revision, Asian-American literature is traditionally described as the body of creative works written by those of Asian ancestry living in North America (and more recently other parts of the Americas). A relative newcomer to American letters, Asian-American literature is highly significant as an indicator of America's national imagination, pointing to critical changes in mainstream cultural and sociopolitical perspectives particularly in the challenge that it poses to racial and cultural binary systems that now have to be rethought in the plural. As Amy Ling has argued, it is a critical mirror of America and "thus the study of Asian American literature is often a study of white America" (Ling 1985: 32). More importantly, however, Asian-American literature's multiple associations with ethnic, multicultural, women's, postcolonial, subaltern, diaspora, international, and other revisionary studies foreground the heterogeneous elements and complexity of cultural production and identity construction.

Depending on one's definition of "Asian-American," the timeline and history of its literature vary greatly. For example, playwright, author, and critic Frank Chin argues (in the Introduction to Chan, Chin, Inada, and Wong, 1974) that Asian-American literature begins with the classics of Carlos Bulosan's *America is in the Heart* (1946), John Okada's *No-No Boy* (1957), and Louis Chu's *Eat a Bowl of Tea* (1961), which establish the criteria of this alternative canon. According to Chin's restrictive definition of the term, Asian-American literature is limited to writing that originated in the earliest Asian immigrant communities, with Filipino and especially Japanese- and Chinese-American authors forming its core. He further stresses male genealogy and, above all, American nativity. Similarly, early Asian-American scholars Kai-yu Hsu and Helen Palubinskas (1972) rank Asian-American writers born and educated in the US as somehow more authentic than their immigrant counterparts. Such definitions not only exclude more recent immigrant Asian groups hailing from Cambodia or Vietnam, for example, but also perpetuate and reproduce hierarchies within the field. In contrast, Elaine Kim and Amy Ling incorporate migrants who were born and educated in Asia, putting forward a more fluctuating definition of Asian-American identity that enlarges its scope and pushes its literary origins back almost 60 years. Kim, for example, includes early "ambassadors of goodwill" who explained Asian customs and culture to mainstream US readers such as Lee Yan Phou (*When I Was a Boy in China*, 1887) and New II-Han (*When I Was a Boy in Korea*, 1928) (Kim 1982:

25). According to Ling, Winnifred Eaton, writing under the pen name Onoto Watanna, is the first Asian-American novelist (*Mrs. Nume of Japan*, 1899) and her older sister Edith Maud Eaton, more popularly known as Sui Sin Far, is the first Asian-American short fiction writer ("The Gamblers," 1896) (Ling 1992: 306). Born in Canada to an English father and a Chinese mother who was born in Shanghai and adopted by English missionaries, Winnifred Eaton deliberately staged her identity as a Japanese writer of exotic Japanese romances, at once avoiding the prevailing sino-phobia and catering to fashionable trends of Japonisme. Edith Eaton or Sui Sin Far, born in England to the same parents, chose to write about Chinese Americans in spite of sinophobia. The Eaton sisters, Ling argues, exemplify the fluidity of Asian-American identity, revealing that the concept of subject or self is not fixed, inflected instead by variable concepts of history, race, ethnicity, gender, sexuality, religion, and so forth. Kim and Ling's inclusive perspective represents a current trend in Asian-American literature; however, this all-encompassing definition celebrates an equally problematic pluralism and heterogeneity that potentially render the designa-tion of Asian American meaningless in its broad scope. Today it is now commonly paired with "Pacific Islander" and refers to a vast and rapidly increasing community of Asian immigrants (approximately 52 distinct cultures), including but not limited to Southeast Asians (Cambodians, Laotians, Vietnamese), South Asians (Pakistanis, Indians, Sri Lankans, Bhutanese), as well as a variety of Pacific Islanders (Hawaiian, Samoan, Tongan, Guamanian), not to mention East Asia (China, Korea, Japan, Mongolia) and the various Asian diasporas around the world.

Although the term Asian American was first used only in the 1960s by political activists to replace the derogatory term "Oriental," Asian-American consciousness was forcefully brought into focus in the World War II era and shaped by the ensuing Korean and Vietnam wars. In the early 1970s, the term would become standard usage in the academy. Also at this time, the first Asian-American anthologies and journals began appearing, including the controversial, if influential, *Aiiieeeee! An Anthology of Asian American Writers* (1974) which, taking its cue from the African-American, Third World, civil rights, and student protest movements, forcibly declared in its opening pages:

> Our anthology is exclusively Asian American. That means Filipino, Chinese and Japanese Americans, American-born and -raised, got their China and Japan from the radio, off the silver screen, from television, out of comic books, from the pushers of white American culture that pictured the yellow man as something that when wounded, sad, or angry, or swearing, or wondering, whined, shouted, or screamed, "Aiiieeeee!" Asian America, so long ignored and forcibly excluded from creative participation in American culture, is wounded, sad, angry, swearing, and wondering, and this is his AIIIEEEEE!!! (Chan, Chin, Inada, and Wong 1991: xi–xii)

Angry not only with the mainstream's exclusion of their culture, its polemic editors also took aim at Asian-American writers and novelists such as Jade Snow Wong (*Fifth*

Chinese Daughter, 1945) and C. Y. Lee (*The Flower Drum Song*, 1957) who they believed maintained offensive Asian stereotypes of humility and passivity and thereby promoted white supremacy and Americanization.

In 1976, Maxine Hong Kingston would make her astonishing entrance onto the American literary scene and garner mainstream attention for Asian-American writers and feminists, winning the 1976 National Book Critics Circle Award for *The Woman Warrior*. Kingston's memoir/novel has since become one of the most commonly taught works in college classrooms alongside Zora Neale Hurston's rediscovered *Their Eyes Were Watching God* (1937) and Toni Morrison's *Beloved* (1987). In 1979, the Association for Asian American Studies was founded "for the purpose of advancing the highest professional standard of excellence in teaching and research in the field of Asian American Studies." Elaine Kim's *Asian American Literature* followed in 1982, helping to transform the study of Asian-American literature into an acknowledged field in the academy. The first comprehensive study of Asian-American literature, Kim's work explored the historical and social "evolution of Asian American consciousness and self-image as expressed in the literature" and added as well a fourth constituency to Asian-American literature in the form of Korean-American writing (Kim 1982: xi). Further dramatic changes in student demographics, national and transnational perspectives, immigration laws and trends, Asia's economic expansion, and the continued publication of literary and scholarly works of consistently high quality help account for the field's recent popularity as demonstrated in the proliferation of Asian-American Studies programs within the academy. Today in the first decade of the twenty-first century, the field of Asian-American literature continues to grow, develop, and revise itself. Ongoing arguments about its boundaries and profiles are vigorously debated, informed particularly by the steady expansion of the corpus as new Asian immigrant groups enter the country, and by the field's problematic use of race, ethnicity, and national origin as an organizing and founding premise in an era of increasing transnationalism, internationalism, interculturalism, and diaspora.

The Question of Asian-American Modernism

While the Eaton sisters may represent idiosyncratic examples of Asian-American modernism, it is ultimately the movement's belated modernist project occurring in the World War II era that would give ample voice to the Asian-American experience. And yet, Asian-American writing is rarely discussed within the explicit context of modernism, due in part to this belatedness and an incomplete conceptualism of modernism as a cultural force (Chiu 1999: 1–2). Stressing only the formal dimension of modernism, for example, Amy Ling argues that Chuang Hua's *Crossings* (1968) is "Asian America's first modernist novel," due to its use of modernist experimental techniques that follow in the tradition of Faulkner, Hemingway, and imagist poets (Ling 1986: 1–2). In fact, I would argue that Hua's work is actually one of the last works of Asian-American modernism. Its supreme use of high modernist literary tools may mislead readers to overlook earlier modernist works where these techniques are evident but not deliberately foregrounded as a formal style. As will be discussed, modernist aesthetics reaches beyond mere formal and experimental techniques and is often reflected in agonistic narratives of migration and displacement. Indeed, the modernist works of Zora Neale Hurston, Anzia Yezierska, Jean Rhys, Sherwood Anderson, William Faulkner, Gertrude Stein, and T. S. Eliot, to name just a few, find strong correlatives and familial resemblances in works by Carlos Bulosan, Toshio Mori, Louis Chu, Monica Sone, and other Asian-American authors.

Asian-American literature is also often loosely aligned with postmodernism, since its institutionalization occurs roughly in the same period that thinkers such as Gilles Deleuze, Félix Guattari, Jacques Derrida, and Paul de Man begin to advance a poststructuralist program often understood as one of postmodernism's hallmarks. Moreover, Asian-American literature is perceived as having shared interests in the so-called postmodern agendas of multiculturalism, ethnicity, and identity politics, as well as in gender, queer, cultural, postcolonial, and interdisciplinary studies. Indeed, postmodernism has for the most part subsumed or incorporated modernism, reducing it to a functionalist aesthetics associated with high modernism. Similarly, the boundaries between the two paradigms are frequently blurred within the Asian-American canon. The result is that modernism's most productive political, social, and cultural expressions are ignored or presented ahistorically in the garb of postmodernism. However, revisionary modernist studies such as Houston Baker's *Modernism and the Harlem Renaissance* (1987), Paul Gilroy's *The Black Atlantic* (1993), Michael North's *The Dialect of Modernism* (1994), and Walter Benn Michaels' controversial *Our America* (1995) amply demonstrate the full force of modernism as a radical cultural and social revolution. Discussing Asian-American literature in a modernist context not only allows for a clearer sense of its historical contribution to the American literary canon, but also sharpens the internal distinction between these two significant aesthetic paradigms, namely modernism's bold advances into cultural relativism and postmodernism's concern with simulated and commodity identities as an intensification and ironic treatment of the modernist project.

In the arguments and readings of texts that follow, I would like to present in more detail the benefits of placing Asian-American literature (or at least aspects of it) squarely within the context of American modernism. Here modernism is loosely defined as the various aesthetic and cultural expressions that respond to, reflect upon, influence, and challenge the radically new conditions and sociocultural upheavals produced by modernity and modernization. Though modernism represents a considerable variety of artistic movements, projects, schools of thought, periods, genres, and media, its two common characteristics are: (1) a profound break with nineteenth-century traditions that stress classic bourgeois values upholding notions of refinement, stability, certainty, and continuity based on explicit or implicit metaphysical assumptions of authenticity and social hierarchy; and (2) an intense concern with aesthetic form and representation as the reflection of modern contextualized and constructed paradigms of reality in opposition to overarching and totalizing metaphysical paradigms. Modernism's critical tools of analysis provide in particular a theoretical base outside that of problematic biological or sociological definitions of race/ethnicity, allowing us to see identity formations of race, ethnicity, gender, nation, culture, and so forth as *constructed tropes of representation.* As guest editor of two issues of *Critical Inquiry* subsequently published as *"Race," Writing, and Difference,* Henry Louis Gates addresses the complexity of the term "race" as "a meaningful category in the study of literature and the shaping of critical theory." The term race (like all markers of identity) is not, as Gates reminds us, "an objective term of classification" but rather "a dangerous trope" that he places in quotation marks ("race" under erasure). As "a trope of ultimate, irreducible difference," race reveals not the ultimate difference between races but the arbitrariness of its representational logic as given in Saussurean modernist linguistics (Gates 1986: 5). While Gates explains the suspension of the term "race" using the critical vocabulary of deconstruction, this insight is already evident in the critical writings of the Harlem Renaissance, for whom the term meant something akin to a pliable mask and not a self-evident fact.

It is now of course commonplace to discuss identity markers as aesthetic constructs; consider, for example, Zora Neale Hurston's equation of race and fiction, or Benedict Anderson's influential term for nation as an imagined community. However, in reality it is exceedingly difficult to practice this theoretical suspension of race/ethnicity, especially in the context of ethnic literature. Race/ethnicity may be a constructed representation, but we know instantly that it would be absolutely wrong to place Hurston or Carlos Bulosan under the rubric of Native American or Jewish-American literature. Here, the tentative use of race/ethnicity as a heuristic device that mediates between theory or aesthetics and social praxis or experience becomes particularly significant. Literary scholar E. San Juan aptly depicts this creative process of self-discovery in his work on Bulosan as captured in his phrase, "on becoming Filipino" (San Juan 1995). Similarly, my own work on ethnic modernisms discusses how writers such as Anzia Yezierska, Hurston, and Jean Rhys use aesthetic tools of modernism, especially its stress on the performative present and the relativism of the linguistic sign, to stage self-determined and fluid versions of ethnic identities extracted from the contingent experiences of their everyday social and ethnic worlds (Konzett 2002). Thus in the case of Hurston the sociological and historical reality of skin color, the Jim Crow system of segregation, and America's history of slavery are turned into an aesthetics of defiance, a performative speech act captured in her well-known statement "But I am not tragically colored" (Hurston 1979: 153).

Not only does placing Asian-American literature/culture into a dialogue with American modernism foreground the literary and aesthetic aspects of identity production, it moreover allows for productive distinctions among the various types of modernisms, including diverse forms of Asian-American modernism. A case in point is that of sculptor, architect, craftsman, and designer Isamu Noguchi, an Asian American born in Los Angeles who came to prominence in the international movement of modernism. Noguchi's work is now generally seen as representative of

American modernist architecture and design, standing alongside that of Frank Lloyd Wright, Alexander Calder, and other naturalized peers such as Mies van der Rohe. Indeed, his works (particularly his furniture and lamps) are today perceived as classic icons of mid-century modernism. A detailed discussion of Noguchi's modernist work in the context of Asian-American studies could, for instance, explore the following questions: have Asian/Asian-American traditions significantly informed the organic and minimalist shapes of his modernist aesthetics? Have these traditions been obscured by the rubric of high modernism? Does his form of modernism share any similarity to the Asian-American vernacular literary modernisms of Louis Chu, Monica Sone, or John Okada operating outside of this high style and rooted instead in everyday traditions of Asian-American culture; or to other forms of modernism influenced by African cultures such as the works of Picasso and Gertrude Stein? Or along different lines, could we compare in meaningful ways say the vernacular agit-prop modernism of Carlos Bulosan and its experience of Filipino-American labor migration with the modernist abstract and experimental poetics of his immigrant compatriot Jose Garcia Villa? Would it be productive to see Bulosan also as a mass cultural modernist and not merely as a Filipino-American migrant writer? In its pluralistic engagement of diverse cultures, movements, classes, art forms, and history, American modernism since the 1980s can thus be understood as an aesthetics of critical self-reflexivity. It serves in the end to check hegemonic and/or simplified versions of monocultural modernism with a tendency towards Anglo-conformity, high modernism, exclusivist or essentialist paradigms, or a single linear genealogy. Indeed, this revisionary form of American modernism should be properly perceived as essentially ethnic, occurring at the intersection of cultural identities and their production.

The Modernist Aesthetics of Migration and Dislocation: Carlos Bulosan's *America Is in the Heart* and Louis Chu's *Eat a Bowl of Tea*

As Edward Said has pointed out, modern Western culture is in large part the production of exiles, émigrés, and refugees, especially in the United States where refugees from communism, fascism, and other oppressive regimes have significantly influenced and shaped academic, intellectual, and aesthetic thought (Said 1990: 357). Migration, as a fundamental experience that challenges the normative cultural perception of belonging, home, and settlement, is a profoundly modernist theme. In contrast to American colonial literature, in which conquest of the land redresses the displacement and loss incurred by migration, modernist literature knows of no such cure and instead settles into the condition of being unsettled. Once the traditional link between identity and homeland is severed, other beliefs and values built on the metaphysical composite of "being at home in the world" topple quickly. Modern migration thus acts like a prism, fracturing and dispersing light and laying bare its spectrum and foundation to analysis. In this sense, reading classic Asian-American texts by Bulosan and Chu as expressions of American modernism and cultural dislocation leads not as expected to a renewed search for roots and unity but to a deeper and more critical engagement with the evolving concepts of belonging, home, nation, and authenticity.

The experience of early Asian immigrants corresponds in certain ways to that of the great migration of Eastern European Jews and Italians to the US. Unlike the latter, however, Asian immigrants (specifically Chinese and Filipino) consisted of large numbers of single men compelled to live the life of bachelors or sojourners in various Chinatown or Manilatown ghettos. In addition, the legislative acts imposed upon Asian immigrants as nonwhite ethnics were much harsher, prohibiting miscegenation, property ownership, and citizenship. Not only were Asian (Chinese and Filipino) women restricted from entering the country, thereby preventing the formation of families, but also American citizens who married Asian immigrants were likewise stripped of citizenship. Whereas the rewards of assimilation seemed frustratingly just out of reach for Jewish and Italian-American immigrants, they were practically non-existent in the much harsher context that defines Asian immigration before World War II. As representatives of the unassimilable East, Asian immigrants can be described as the international counterpart to African Americans commonly portrayed as the unassimilable black Other of white America. And like African Americans, Asian Americans were rendered socially invisible through the implementation of laws and restrictions.

Based on his personal experience as a first-generation Filipino immigrant, Carlos Bulosan's autobiographic novel *America Is in the Heart: A Personal History* (1946) is considered the first significant treatment of Asian-American exile and migration. Set in the Depression Era 1930s and written during World War II, it was declared by *Look* to be one of the most important 50 American books ever published. All too often, however, *America* is seen primarily as a social and historical documentation of the plight of immigrants, which reduces the novel to a stereotypical narrative stressing the victimization and suffering of Asian minorities. This interpretation of Bulosan's work as an authentic record is encouraged in Carey McWilliams's introduction to the first edition, in which he dismisses critics who accused Bulosan of exaggeration or falsification:

> One may doubt that Bulosan personally experienced each and every one of the manifold brutalities and indecencies so vividly described in this book, but it can be fairly be said – making allowances for occasional minor histrionics – that some Filipino was indeed the victim of each of these or similar incidents. For this reason alone, *America Is in the Heart* is a social classic. (McWilliams 1996: vii)

Read within a modernist context, however, this text is not merely social documentation but demonstrates Bulosan's active appropriation of the migration experience and its creative transformation into a modernist aesthetics of dislocation and mobility.

Moreover, the modernist framework reveals its significance as an early articulation of a pan-Asian-American consciousness and solidarity centered not on the exclusive concepts of race, ethnicity, region, culture, or language but on the broader communal concerns of labor issues and political activism. Stressing the difficult and transitory lifestyle of migration not as an anomaly but rather as the norm of modern experience, Bulosan depicts exemplary lives lived under the duress of immigration and their radical challenge to tradition. While such stories may initially take on the character of victimization narratives, reflecting the experience of persecution and irrecoverable loss, Bulosan clearly emphasizes the dynamic nature of migration as a dislocating experience that challenges perceived essentialisms of nativism, soil and blood identity, and the naive myths of Anglo-conformity and Americanization. This severe disloca-tion of Asian immigrants finds its expression in a literature highly critical of the concept of America as the Promised Land, exploring instead the phantom constructs that lead to this profound deception.

Bulosan's novel, interestingly, begins with the depiction of farmers in the Philippines who are uprooted due to land speculation. America thus becomes not the point of entry for the experience of displacement and modernization but rather the continuation of its contingency. In this respect, the novel resembles Jewish immi-grant literature, which often takes its point of departure in the experience of pogroms that disenfranchised Jewish communities from their homeland. Similarly, colonialism, postcolonialism, and imperialism have forced a crippling condition of modernity onto the Philippines, dispossessing the native population of its land. And yet Bulosan's novel harbors little sentimentality for a lost homeland and instead attempts to come to terms with the modern condition. Aboard ship in steerage class, the novel's narrator encounters racism for the first time when a white woman from the first-class passenger section suddenly sees him, puts her "hand on her mouth and [says] in a frightened voice: 'Look at those half-naked savages from the Philippines, Roger! Haven't they any idea of decency?'" (Bulosan 1996: 98). This racialized moment, describing a cul-tural encounter between a "superior" Other and an "inferior" counterpart, is similar to Frantz Fanon's well-known experience of blackness summed up succinctly in phrases such as "Mama, see the negro! I'm frightened," "Dirty nigger!" or "Look, a Negro!" (Fanon 1967: 112, 109). For Bulosan's young protagonist, this encounter becomes a traumatic scene of instruction, violently fixing him into a subservient status in the racial hierarchy. As with displacement, racism is encountered before the narra-tor's arrival in the US, pointing once again to a condition of modernity facilitated in this case by the colonialism and postcolonialism that precedes immigration to America.

Upon landing in America, the novel's hero is subjected in a single chapter to repeated and accelerated displacements, making his journey more picaresque and quixotic and less realistic. Having survived a meningitis epidemic during the crossing of the Pacific, he disembarks moneyless in Seattle and is immediately sold and shipped to Alaska for hired labor in the fishing industry. Returning to Seattle after the seasonal labor is completed, the meager earnings are gambled away in one night, forcing the narrator into a new seasonal job of apple picking. The harsh law of modernization gradually impresses itself on the narrator: "I became as ruthless as the worst of them and I was afraid that I would never feel like a human being again" (Bulosan 1996: 109). The remainder of the novel can be construed as an attempt to depict the rehumanization of the narrator in a modern dehumanizing world. The novel, to be sure, does not seek to overcome the reality of displacement but simply seeks to deal with it constructively through the formation of alliances and solidarity.

Following the genre of the memoir, Bulosan's work provides the reader with a semiautobiographical account of migration not unlike works by Jewish immigrant writers such as Anzia Yezierska, Abraham Cahan, or Henry Roth who likewise thinly fictionalized their own experiences of immigration. Unlike the autobiography, the fictional memoir stresses the transformation that is achieved through revisiting scenes of displacement. What once may have presented itself in the light of contingency is now represented as a conscious act of self-determination in which respective heroes and heroines embrace a more sobered version of the Promised Land. As Bulosan's title tellingly suggests, "America is in the heart" and hence cannot be equated with a particular geography or a nativist tradition. Ontological concepts of nationhood and race are forsaken and reimagined in a nonessentialist struggle between contingency and freedom, between displacement and home. Here interesting comparisons could be drawn with other works of modernism, including John Steinbeck's *The Grapes of Wrath* (1939), which similarly depicts in the context of internal migration a quasi-metaphysical lapse from a too readily assumed entitlement to the land as well as the significance of an activist and political modernism.

Stylistically, Bulosan's novel retains an austere and stoic reticence typical of a detached modernist objectivity. The psychology of the subjective narrator is not so much based on bourgeois interiority and the accumulation of genealogical memory as on the objective modern condition that defines his life. Indeed, in a modernist spirit akin to T. S. Eliot, Bulosan's account offers a strange escape from personality, foregrounding instead a hero who becomes totally exteriorized and whose essence is found in the performative present. In this way, the narrator and his situation can be seen as a type of objective correlative that embodies and evokes the lifestyle of migration and displacement. Consider the following much-cited passage from the novel that read in this context can no longer be reduced to that of a mere social protest work but rather stunningly emerges as an expression of Asian-American modernism:

> I came to know afterward that in many ways it was a crime to be a Filipino in California. I came to know that the public streets were not free to my people: we were stopped each time these vigilant patrolmen saw us driving a car. We were suspect each time we were seen with a white woman. And perhaps it was this narrowing of our life into an island, into a filthy segment of American society, that had driven Filipinos like Doro inward, hating everyone and despising all positive urgencies toward freedom. (Bulosan 1996: 121)

Bulosan's description of social, cultural, and racial marginalization remains calmly and hauntingly objective, stripped of any self-indulgence. No outcry of emotion is permitted and denigrations are instead recorded merely as facts. Inwardness and interiority are seen as negative withdrawals from social contact and are in conflict with freedom and therefore not its expression. Linguistically, the passage stresses the speech act through the repetition of phrases "I came to know" and "we were" which gives it the character of a speech or oratory act performed in the present. The emphasis of the passage does not lie with a subjective expression of suffering but instead with an active moment of lucidity and self-recognition, including that of self-hatred that afflicts many of his immigrant peers. This passage is in fact an assured response to the initial race encounter on board the ship – "Look at those half-naked savages" – which in the course of the narrator's travails is transformed into a performative politics of knowledge and self-reflexivity.

Louis Chu's *Eat a Bowl of Tea* (1961) also takes a hard look at what Said (1990: 358) terms the "mutilations of exile" and migration; it does so however in an ironic and tragicomic fashion, using domestic melodrama and a Chinatown setting. As a late example of a migration novel, this work is more urbane and relaxed, enjoying the advantage of hindsight into an era that is quickly disappearing. It is set in the era immediately after World War II, when New York's Chinatown community was enjoying the benefits created by the lifting of severe immigration and naturalization restrictions. In an effort to remake itself into the democratic leader of the free world, the US government had passed a series of reforms aimed at discouraging racist treatment of African and Asian Americans. In 1943 the Chinese Exclusion Acts were repealed, particularly since China was a wartime ally, and a 1947 amendment to the War Brides Act allowed Asian Americans who had served in the military to bring home Asian spouses. Chu's novel captures this exciting time in Chinese-American society in which a predominantly male population comes to life as Asian women are finally allowed to enter the country. After years of living apart from wives and family and depending upon prostitutes to meet their sexual needs, the men look forward to a more settled and respectable middle-class life. However, for the young hero of Chu's novel, the pressure to grant his father's wishes for a grandchild and a respectable life or "big face" in New York's Chinatown becomes overwhelming. Reduced to a type of neurotic impotence, Ben Loy fails to father a child with his beautiful new Chinese bride Mei Oi and thereby draws ridicule in the community, which nicknames him "No Can Do." Lonely, confused, and an object of desire in this bachelor society, Mei Oi takes a lover and finally produces the desired male offspring but is eventually exposed to scandal as the community gets wind of the affair. In tragicomic fashion, the novel explores the obsession with genealogy particularly in light of the experience of displacement and demographic control created by immigration restrictions. The father and father-in-law's hopes for a more settled life for their offspring are disappointed and both fathers must leave New York as a result of the scandalous affair, an attempted murder, and their subsequent loss of face. The novel ends on a more positive note with the fathers and the young couple reconciling and resettling in different parts of the country. The biological stronghold of family is thus ironically broken and recovered in a modernist context through elective affiliation, mobility, and a spirit of forgiveness.

The novel's relaxed modernist charm lies in its ironic blending of the tragic and the comic and its playful use of fairy-tale conventions that work in the end to expose the question of identity and settlement to a thorough critique. Its hybrid tone in which old and new worlds must learn to coexist is underscored in its frequent use of the Anglo-Chinese idiom spoken in Chinatown, including the much used exclamation "Wow your mother!" As with Anzia Yezierska's Yinglish, this language takes on a metaphorical quality of its own, pointing to a world between Chinese as the language of heritage and English in its Anglo-normative sense. Similarly, the young couple have to simultaneously cure themselves of naive concepts of heritage and learn to live on their own, breaking with Chinese tradition and expectations of family. The novel ultimately challenges the law of the father and brings the woman into the foreground, as it remains unclear and, more significantly, unimportant as to who is the real father of her child. Yet the family eventually accepts this break with a clearly defined biological genealogy, redefining itself according to the laws of displacement and hybridity.

With its modernist redefinition of family that combines old and new world conventions and its sympathetic but critical treatment of tradition as embodied in the fathers and their bachelor society, *Eat a Bowl of Tea* breaks with earlier Chinese-American novels and autobiographies set in Chinatown aimed at introducing white mainstream readers to a Chinese-American family and its culture, especially that of gastronomy and foodways. Acting as tourist guides, works such as Pardee Lowe's *Father and Glorious Descendant* (1943), Lin Yutang's *Chinatown Family* (1948), Jade Snow Wong's *Fifth Chinese Daughter* (1950), and Chin Yang Lee's *The Flower Drum Song* (1957) garnered large reading audiences and commercial success at a time when mainstream America was interested in distinguishing among its various "Oriental" populations and learning about its Asian war allies, the Philippines, and particularly China. These works, however, as critics have noted, present a skewed version of Chinese-American culture in their desire to depict it as a legitimate ethnic subset of American culture. While they integrate Asian-American culture into the national lifestyle, these works still retain Anglo-American culture as the invisible but all-pervasive standard of Americanness and Asian-American characters are judged and hierarchized according to their proximity to these norms of whiteness. In an attempt to prove their Americanness, typically Chinese traits, dress, and customs are rejected or demeaned. Stereotypes (the tyrannical cold patriarch, the dragon lady, the humble servant, the china doll) are prevalent, and family life, though a rarity at this time due to restrictions, is treated as common in an attempt to normalize the presentation of the Chinese-American community and gloss over any form of dysfunctionality created by the immigrant lifestyle, especially that of the bachelor society. Nevertheless, these works are significant not only because they allow us to appreciate more fully the critical work done by Chu but also because they reveal the cultural and political production of American ethnicizing, that is, how a culture is transformed from an exotic Other into a familiar subset of American culture and given a place in the nation's cultural pluralist landscape.

World War II Orientalism and Modernism

The defining event that would trigger a modernist moment of self-awareness in Asian-American culture and literature is World War II, specifically the Japanese attack on Pearl Harbor on December 7, 1941. For mainstream Americans, this day of national infamy represents entry into war due to Japanese aggression. However, for Asian Americans it was a critical turning point, radically impacting their relation to the nation. Bulosan recalls how on a relaxing Sunday afternoon in San Francisco "the radio suddenly blared into [his] consciousness: JAPAN BOMBS PEARL HARBOR!" He runs to meet his brother and friends who cry to him "It has come, Carlos!" (Bulosan 1996: 315). Indeed, from this moment on, a type of absenteeist Asian-American identity, one that lived in spirit in Asia but in actuality resided in the US, is no longer possible. American Orientalism, which viewed Asians as the unassimilable foreign Other, encouraged in fact absenteeism and segregation up until 1941. With the start of World War II, America was forced to reconsider its racial policy of barring citizenship to its Asian immigrants who heretofore were viewed mainly as an anonymous mass to be used as an exploitable labor force. While anti-Asian sentiments certainly increased within the US during times of conflict with Asia, World War II challenged America to enter into a more complex process of differentiation among its Asian allies and enemies and thereby to question its monocultural and racial perceptions of Asians and its own Asian residents and citizens. Those once conveniently grouped under the single undiscerning rubric of Oriental now called for distinctions between America's Filipino and Chinese allies, between anti-Japanese Korean nationalists who were still considered by the US subjects of its conqueror Japan, and between pro- and anti-American Japanese immigrants. Similarly, the impact of World War II created, writes Ronald Takaki, a "crucial dividing line in the history of Asian American communities," forcing them "to determine more sharply than ever before their identities as Asians and as Americans" (Takaki 1989: 357). The doubt and suspicion cast on Asian Americans, especially Japanese Americans, forced Asian-American communities to produce and perform its identity as that of solid Americans and completely sever ties from ancestral countries.

World War II also changes the genre of the migration novel, which now acutely reflects the fact that tenuous settlement and integration can be quickly undone by political catastrophe. Due to the Gentlemen's Agreement of 1907, Japanese immigration (unlike that of the Filipino and Chinese) was diminished, but the act did allow wives, mothers, children, and other family members to join male resident immigrants.

Indeed, from 1908 through 1924, when the Immigration Act effectively halted entry of non-European immigrants, Japanese immigration was disproportionately female, consisting mainly of picture brides (wives selected by hired matchmakers based on pictures and family recommendations). Thus unlike the bachelor societies associated with Chinese-American and Filipino-American residents, Japanese immigrants led comparatively more settled and domestic lives in spite of severe restrictions, segregation, and racism. The attack on Pearl Harbor, however, would suddenly and completely transform its communities. Toshio Mori's *Yokohama, California* (1949) captures the prewar and precarious early war years of the Japanese community in the Oakland and San Francisco area. While Mori's episodic work and collection of short stories is not a novel in the strict sense, it is very much one in the modern sense of Sherwood Anderson's *Winesburg, Ohio* (1919), which is referenced in one key section. Like Anderson's work, it foregrounds a single location as the circumference of action for the work's various episodes, capturing the diversity and even fragmentation of modern life in a small community, but also framing and giving meaning to the work as a whole. As Lawson Fusao Inada writes in his insightful introduction to the book's 1985 edition, "Toshio acknowledges Anderson in the very title of his own book – a gesture of respect, of tradition – and though he also utilizes Anderson's concept of a centralized location, Anderson's work serves mainly as a point of departure" (Inada 1985: xv). In Bakhtin's sense of the novel, the work provides a heteroglossia of social voices, not only in its content and form but also in its deliberate gesture to Anderson and other modernist writers, thereby challenging monoglossia or hegemony of normative voices at several levels. Mori's work shares as well an important affinity with Gertrude Stein's experimental prose work *Three Lives* (1909) and its presentation of the obscured voices of ordinary women.

Mori's first episode or story, placed by the editor at the beginning of the collection when it was first published in 1949, begins in the manner of a fairy tale with the storyteller, the children's grandmother, recalling how she left Japan to join her husband in California:

> Long ago, children, I lived in a country called Japan. Your grandpa was already in California earning money for my boat ticket. The village people rarely went out of Japan and were shocked when they heard I was following your grandpa as soon as the money came.
>
> . . . One day his letter came with the money. . . . The neighbors rushed excitedly to our house. "Don't go! Live among us," they cried. "There will be war between America and Japan. You will be caught in mid-Pacific. You will never reach America." But I was determined. . . . "I have bought my ticket and my things are packed. I am going," I said. (Mori 1985: 15)

This segment, unlike most of the other installments, was written later during Mori's internment at Camp Topaz, Utah in 1942. The collection, accepted for publication in 1941, was originally scheduled to appear in 1943 but was not printed until the postwar era due to wartime anti-Japanese sentiment. Through its framing and strategic use of the fairy tale, the opening passage depicts Japan as inaccessibly remote, existing in a mythical, almost forgotten space. Similarly, America is equally remote as a utopian imaginary, a place, according to her neighbors, that she "will never reach." This emphasis on a space between an elusive somewhere else of the future and an irretrievable past places the immigrant narrator squarely into a present limbo that sets the modernist tone of the stories that follow. It likewise depicts the entire Japanese-American community in the limbo of a deracinated community. The present and daily activities of this community are in the modernist pragmatist sense its sole legitimate reason for existence and constitute a nontraditional type of settlement informed by modernity and displacement and not dependent upon established notions of assimilation and Americanization. By way of its retrospective view of the 1930s, when most of the stories were actually written, Mori defiantly grafts a Japanese cultural geography onto the American landscape, turning it into an irreversible Californian Yokohama in spite of the subsequent wartime expatriation and internment of West Coast Japanese Americans. In the spirit of Anderson's Winesburg, Ohio or Faulkner's Yoknapatawpha County, this imaginary community is at once real and utopian as indicated by the title of the story: "Tomorrow Is Coming, Children."

In this vein, Mori's work does not show us a homeless Japanese-American community but one determined to settle into daily habits within a life of dislocation. The curious inhabitants of this imaginary community, history's unremarkable and forgotten voices, are carefully revived by Mori and restored in all their human dignity fighting futile battles against commercial pressures, cultural invisibility, government racism, and dwindling numbers. The stories do not focus solely on a ghettoized community but show instead a quiet solidarity and heroic efforts to maintain a dignified life. In a telling episode, a young writer emulates Sherwood Anderson and persistently pursues his dream of becoming a published writer. His success is tragically short-lived, however, as the novel is not reviewed and goes unnoticed, relegating its author to obscurity. This story sadly anticipates Mori's own fate as an Asian-American writer whose work received little attention at the time and was only rediscovered in the 1970s by Asian-American scholars.

Many of the episodes have a similar bittersweet touch, drawing a memorable picture of an everyday history that rarely makes it into the official accounts of history. Stylistically the novel is characterized by a modernist self-effacement, containing little intrusive subjectivity or confessional elements and foregrounding rather an aesthetics of modern mass serialization. The characters are depicted objectively in their daily habits and interactions, including cooking, selling flowers, attending funerals, making doughnuts, writing, or conversing. The serialized nature of the work is thus not an anonymous mass construct but akin to Siegfried Kracauer's concept of the mass ornament, a performance by a mass or collective that enacts the coordination of the social body and reveals the many as one (Kracauer 1995: 75). Choreographed parades, dance numbers, and military formations are examples of the mass ornament aesthetic. It should be stressed that Mori's serialization is not an expression of the *e pluribus unum* of American nationalism in which democracy is merely an abstraction or metaphysical ideal removed from actual reality, considering Jim Crow, segregation, and other racial practices. Rather, Mori's serialized mass aesthetic of the many as one underscores a democratic solidarity rooted in a communal pragmatics of the everyday. As with Anderson, day-to-day activities, events, and the characters themselves are objective correlatives of the community, articulating its desires, needs, and feelings. Because of this modernist emphasis on the performative present, the stories do not lose any of their qualities by having been published almost a decade later and in a completely different historical context. They deal almost exclusively with the lives of Japanese Americans who often appear well versed and steeped in American culture in spite of their absenteeism in a hostile cultural environment. The community has its own baseball teams and their linguistic exchanges are rendered exclusively (and unrealistically) in English, thus making the community more familiar and accessible to the American reader in the face of common prejudices that view Asians as impenetrable and dissimulative. Additional references to American cultural figures such as Lincoln, Emerson, Dewey, and Anderson provide the intellectual framework on which this community is implicitly built, namely democracy, self-determination, pragmatism, and a poetic sense of the ordinary and the unremarkable.

Appearing in the latter part of the collection, "Slant-Eyed Americans" reflects upon the impossible situation of being Japanese and American. Set during the events of December 7, it pictures a shamed Japanese-American community just beginning to grasp the gravity of the situation and its members changing status from aspiring citizens to that of "enemy aliens." While the protagonist's brother is about to be shipped off to war as a Nisei soldier, the mother stands firm, believing in her entitlement to America: "We have stayed here to belong to the American way of life. Time will tell our true purpose. We remained in America for permanence – not for temporary convenience. *We common people need not fear*" (Mori 1985: 132, my emphasis). Read in the context of the government's (mis)treatment of "common people" or civilians, this story takes on an even more insidious tone. Indeed, the US interned approximately 120,000 Japanese-American civilians, of whom two thirds were native-born American citizens and 70,000 were children and infants, removing them under government threat from their homes, property, and businesses, and destroying their livelihoods. In its depiction of a Japanese-American community struggling for its existence within the national culture, and its pragmatic, secular rewriting of the many as one, Mori produces what Homi Bhabha calls a narration of nation, a counternarrative strategy that at once evokes and erases the nation's totalizing boundaries and reveals the nation as a rhetorical and cultural construct (Bhabha 1990).

Monica Sone's *Nisei Daughter* (1953) offers a striking contrast to Mori's *Yokohama, California*. Unlike Mori, who depicts the quiet lives of Japanese Americans as stubbornly resisting national norms, Sone instead exposes assimilation and its social rewards as a delusional fantasy that exists mainly in the minds of Japanese migrants aspiring to become Americans. The novel, a fictional autobiography, traces the life of its heroine and narrator Kazuko Monica from early childhood through adulthood, ending in the escalating events of the war and internment. These final events, of course, are already present at the beginning of the novel but are not noticed by its young, happy-go-lucky heroine. Superficially, Sone's work appears reminiscent of commercial "Orientalist" fiction such as Jade Snow Wong's *Fifth Chinese Daughter* (1950) in its embrace of anglonormative culture and discarding of traditional Japanese customs. However, the many carefully chosen settings and situations emphasize again and again the fantasy of becoming American and thereby radically break with the traditional mold of assimilative immigrant fiction and its rags-to-riches story of success and mobility.

The novel opens with six-year-old Kazuko's "shocking" discovery at the dinner table that she has "Japanese blood" (Sone 1995: 3). In the convention of the autobiography, she goes back to an earlier founding experience, namely that of her father's immigration to the US in 1904 and his subsequent marriage. She spends a significant amount of time describing their home, the Carrollton Hotel on Seattle's waterfront (mentioned in the very first sentence), detailing its purchase prior to her birth, and especially her parents' renovation of this former "flea-ridden" flophouse "for alcoholics and fugitives from the law" into a cleaner and more dignified hotel for hardworking and honest laborers (Sone 1995: 9). Her parents make an extra effort in renovating the old rooms and in selecting residents who will not destroy the reconstructed property. Metaphorically, they are preparing the home and residence for their children. If the novel had a different, or, more precisely, positive ending, this early episode could be understood as a fine example of immigrant mobility. However, keeping in mind the novel's date of publication (1953) and particularly the traumatic historical event of the internment, the reader becomes immediately suspicious of this all too fairy-tale entrance into American society. The setting of the hotel for transients thus resonates critically in the reader's mind, exposing these efforts of self-improvement and building a home as self-deceptive. The irony of this double-coded setting, hotel and home, will become evident once the daughter comes to inhabit it and thereby meets the parameters of her own life as a second-generation Japanese American or Nisei. What may initially appear to the reader as a shelter found in American society and its way of life will eventually revert to the modern homelessness of what Henry James called the "hotel society" (1994: 77–8), rendering the conventional concept of home outdated.

Upon being forced to enter a Japanese school after her integrated grammar school, Kazuko protests, crying into her bowl of rice and tea, and sees little use in a Japanese education that cannot be brought to bear in the world of the modern hotel environment. Yet, once again, the critical reader wonders why the young girl had to attend a segregated school if integration had been a realistic prospect. Indeed, the School Law of California (passed 1870) and its various amendments imposed segregation for children of African-American, Native American, and Asian descent. Important here is the 1921 amendment, calling for separate schools for children of Asian and Native American descent:

The governing body of the school district shall have power to exclude children of filthy or vicious habits, or children suffering from contagious or infectious diseases, and also to establish separate schools for Indian children and for children of Chinese, Japanese or Mongolian parentage. When such separate schools are established Indian children and children of Chinese, Japanese or Mongolian parentage must not be admitted into any other school. (Education Code, Section 1662)

Similarly, in Seattle, the home of our narrator, the school district voted on October 4, 1920 to segregate "foreign children," specifically Japanese Americans (who were native-born citizens) due to vociferous protests from "white American taxpayers" (Asato 2005: 103). While Sone discusses in detail how her family and other Japanese were excluded from renting summer homes, she surprisingly does not discuss administrative measures of segregation (with the exception of course of the internment). Here one begins to wonder whether the blindness to this system extends beyond the characters to the author herself. In any case, the novel's silences and omissions are significant as they reflect an entrenched national system of discrimination.

The heroine's quiet but continued rebellion against her Japanese descent is also expressed in her embrace of various forms of American popular culture such as dancing, dressing up in Mickey Mouse costumes, and detective stories (which appeal to her hope of catching criminals). In particular, the Disney commodities, which include a Disney wristwatch worn by the heroine, underscore that assimilation for the heroine is a mere fantasy. Kazuko's preference for American culture also points to the generational conflict between first-generation immigrants or Issei and second-generation native-born citizens or Nisei, as well as gender conflicts created by the different status of women in Japanese and American societies. Interspersed events such as the celebration of the birthday of the Japanese emperor, who is greeted with the traditional birthday greeting "Banzai!," one that Americans stereotypically associate with the World War II battle cry of kamikaze pilots, also add to the unease of the narrative. Indeed, the cry "Banzai!" is repeated later on the eve of the war, anticipating the destruction on December 7 of her Americanness:

I felt as if a fist had smashed my pleasant little existence, breaking it into jigsaw puzzle pieces. An old wound opened up again, and I found myself shrinking inwardly from my Japanese blood, the blood of an enemy. I knew instinctively that the fact that I was an American by birthright was not going to help me escape the consequences of this unhappy war. (Sone 1995: 145–6)

Her young Nisei friends too grasp this realization in an instant and when one asks, "Do you think we'll be considered Japanese or Americans?" another cynically but correctly responds: "We'll be Japs, same as always. But our parents are enemy aliens now, you know" (p. 146). As with Mori's work, Sone's autobiography is critically framed by the events of the war and internment, pointing to the inevitable double consciousness created by the national discourse on race. Like James Weldon Johnson's fictional autobiography *The Autobiography of an Ex-Coloured Man* (1912),

Sone's autobiography undoes and subverts the genre's traditional developmental structure and the reader's expectation of successful gained insight and closure.

A classic of Asian-American literature, John Okada's novel *No-No Boy* (1957)
effectively portrays the schizophrenic self of the Japanese American in the character
of Ichiro Yamada, a 25-year-old Nisei just released from prison for national disloyalty
at the end of the war. The novel follows Ichiro as he joins his recently disinterned
family and attempts to grapple with his conflicted hyphenated identity in a postwar
America unable to comprehend, much less abide by, the multiculturalism and democratic values it had broadcast so effortlessly during the war. Indeed, in an attempt to
represent the US as leader of the free world, the government (represented by the
Office of War Information) and Hollywood worked together to project democracy in
action as seen particularly in the popular and beloved image of the fighting combat
team. Born in the World War II era as a subgenre of the war film, the Hollywood
combat film (e.g., *Bataan, Guadalcanal Diary, Thirty Seconds Over Tokyo*) famously
introduced the world to the democratic multicultural combat team, consisting of
Americans of various descents and ethnicities (African, Jewish, Mexican, Irish, Polish,
Italian, etc.) as well as a few Chinese and Filipino ally soldiers. Ichiro's postwar and
precivil rights America, however, is a far cry from the popular Hollywood image of
nation.

Ichiro's defining act consists of his saying "no" to two questions on a War Department questionnaire circulated by the government in internment camps: (1) "Are
you willing to serve in the armed forces of the U.S. on combat duty, wherever
ordered?" and (2) "Will you swear unqualified allegiance to the U.S.A. and faithfully
defend the U.S. from any and all attack by foreign or domestic forces, and foreswear
any form of allegiance to the Japanese emperor, or any other foreign government,
power, or organization?" Ichiro answers no as he believes this act of negation is the
proper response to the internment of his family and his community. His "no,"
however, remains the product of a futile revolt against a perceived authority, paradoxically upholding it by this act of resistance. As with Sigmund Freud's "no" phase
in infancy, one cannot escape the vicissitudes of a binary system of authority through
the use of negation. In this system, an act of negation simply reaffirms the authority
in question and reduces a seemingly free choice to a contingent form of action. In
the novel, this fatal choice is shown to be an error not in content but in its systemic
dependence on the binary system of race discourse in America. Literally, Ichiro suddenly finds himself after the war hated by his own Japanese-American community
who misguidedly displace the racism they suffer as "Japs" onto no-no boys. Even
his own brother turns against him and betrays him to his Nisei peers who give
Ichiro a thorough beating, fulfilling thereby the grammar of racial discrimination
with an act of self-hatred. In his career pursuits, Ichiro is similarly haunted by his
choice and misses out on the postwar benefits granted to veterans. Yet when he does
find genuine sympathy for his conflicted situation and is offered a job, he turns it
down, remaining locked in his helpless quasi-infantile form of negation and
self-hatred.

A yes-yes boy who fought for the US, Okada exposes the narrow binary system that characterizes the relations between Asian Americans and the American mainstream. Indeed, like J. D. Salinger's coming-of-age hero Holden Caulfield in *The Catcher in the Rye* (1951), Ichiro faces a similar identity crisis that reflects the difficult coming of age of Asian-American identity. In its relentless exposure of crisis and impasse, Okada's novel is a plea for a different America where such binary oppositions no longer define cultural and national identity. As a modernist work, it is indebted to the avant-garde's critique of system, which calls into question not simply the work of art or genre but the entire institution of art. Similarly, Okada's work implicitly questions the institutional structure in which ethnic art performs. In its rejection of an overarching racial binary discourse and its exploration of a space beyond or between yes and no, the work shares a kinship with such path-breaking works as Ralph Ellison's *Invisible Man* (1952) or Richard Kim's *The Martyred* (1964). In these works, the heroes see through the system and begin to establish nonconventional and unorthodox stances (self-imposed invisibility in Ellison; a nonbeliever affirming Christianity in Kim) that allow them to retain some form of authenticity and existential freedom of action rather than becoming totally locked in an adversarial binary logic.

The Limits and Trajectories of Modernism

As I have tried to show in this discussion of Asian-American modernist literature, one cannot overlook this important formative period in Asian-American literature if one is to acknowledge its aesthetic achievements properly. In this approach to recover a forgotten Asian-American modernism, much work still needs to be done. Additionally, the complex voices and trajectories of transnational writers such as Chuang Hua, Diana Chang, and Bienvenido Santos need to be reassessed in their exact contribution to the field. Santos's collection of short stories *You Lovely People* (1955), published in Manila, for example, recalls the author's visit to the US during the wartime era. As with Hua and Chang, this work reflects an interesting transnational perspective on Asian migration and diaspora. The question to be asked is whether these works belong more properly to an international rather than American national modernism; or should they altogether be assigned to the global canon of colonialism and postcolonialism? Finally, it would help to establish in what ways more recent Asian-American literature parts with the modernist legacy. Acknowledging the growing sense that identity is an empty commodity that can be manipulated randomly, postmodernist discourse places a radical emphasis on the simulation of all identity. Here one has to ask whether postmodernism with its radical doubt still permits the subaltern to speak, as Gayatri Spivak has critically asked (Spivak 1988). As belated voices in the national public sphere, Asian-American writers appear at once enabled to speak only to discover that in a postmodernist paradigm such speech means little. Perhaps in the ongoing debate between modernism and postmodernism, the modernist emphasis on contextual and provisional worlds of communicative recognition can itself pose a challenge to an all too flippant dismissal of human agency on the part of postmodernism.

REFERENCES AND FURTHER READING

Asato, Noriko. (2005). Americanization vs. Japanese cultural maintenance: Analyzing Seattle's *Nihongo Tokuhon*. In Louis Fiset and Gail M. Nomura (eds), *Nikkei in the Pacific Northwest: Japanese Americans and Japanese Canadians in the 20th Century* (pp. 95–119). Seattle: University of Washington Press.

Baker, Houston A., Jr. (1987). *Modernism and the Harlem Renaissance*. Chicago: University of Chicago Press.

Bhabha, Homi (ed.). (1990). *Nation and Narration*. London: Routledge.

Bhabha, Homi. (1994). *The Location of Culture*. London: Routledge.

Bulosan, Carlos. (1996). *America Is in the Heart: A Personal History*. Seattle: University of Washington Press.

Chan, Jeffery, Frank Chin, Lawson Fusao Inada, and Shawn Wong (eds). (1974). *Aiiieeeee! An Anthology of Asian-American Writers*. Washington: Howard University Press.

Chan, Jeffery, Frank Chin, Lawson Fusao Inada, and Shawn Wong (eds). (1991). *The Big Aiiieeeee!: An Anthology of Chinese American and Japanese American Literature*. New York: Meridian.

Chang, Diana. (1994). *Frontiers of Love*. Seattle: University of Washington Press.

Chiu, Monica. (1999). Motion, memory, and conflict in Chuang Hua's modernist *Crossings*. *MELUS* 24, 4: 107–23.

Chiu, Monica. (2004). *Filthy Fictions: Asian American Literature by Women*. Walnut Creek, CA: AltaMira Press.

Chu, Louis. (1979). *Eat a Bowl of Tea*. Seattle: University of Washington Press.

Fanon, Frantz. (1967). *Black Skin, White Masks*. New York: Grove Press.

Gates, Henry Louis Jr. (1986). Introduction: Writing "race" and the difference it makes. In Henry Louis Gates (ed.), *"Race," Writing, and Difference* (pp. 1–20). Chicago: University of Chicago Press.

Gilroy, Paul. (1993). *The Black Atlantic: Modernity and Double Consciousness*. Cambridge, MA: Harvard University Press.

Hsu, Kai-yu and Helen Palubinskas (eds). (1972). *Asian American Authors*. Boston: Houghton.

Hurston, Zora Neale. (1979). How it feels to be colored me. In Alice Walker (ed.), *I Love Myself When I am Laughing . . .* (pp. 152–5). New York: The Feminist Press.

Inada, Lawson Fusao. (1985). Standing on Seventh Street: An introduction to the 1985 edition. In Toshio Mori, *Yokohama, California* (pp. v–xxvii). Seattle: University of Washington Press.

James, Henry. (1994). *The American Scene*. New York: Penguin.

Kim, Elaine. (1982). *Asian American Literature: An Introduction to the Writings and Their Social Context*. Philadelphia: Temple University Press.

Kingston, Maxine Hong. (1976). *The Woman Warrior: Memoirs of a Girlhood Among Ghosts*. New York: Vintage.

Konzett, Delia Caparoso. (2002). *Ethnic Modernisms: Anzia Yezierska, Zora Neale Hurston, Jean Rhys, and the Aesthetics of Dislocation*. New York: Palgrave Macmillan.

Kracauer, Siegfried. (1995). The mass ornament. In *The Mass Ornament: Weimar Essays* (pp. 75–86). Cambridge, MA: Harvard University Press.

Lee, C. Y. (1957). *The Flower Drum Song*. New York: Farrar Straus.

Ling, Amy. (1985). Asian American literature. *Association of Departments of English Bulletin* 80: 29–33.

Ling, Amy. (1986). Foreword. In Chuang Hua, *Crossings* (pp. 1–6). Boston: Northeastern University Press.

Ling, Amy. (1992). Creating one's self. In Shirley Geok-lin Lim and Amy Ling (eds), *Reading the Literatures of Asian America* (pp. 306–18). Philadelphia: Temple University Press.

Lowe, Pardee. (1943). *Father and Glorious Descendant*. Boston: Little, Brown.

McWilliams, Carey. (1996). Introduction. In Carlos Bulosan, *America Is in the Heart* (pp. vii–xxiv). Seattle: University of Washington Press.

Michaels, Walter Benn. (1995). *Our America: Nativism, Modernism, and Pluralism*. Durham, NC: Duke University Press.

Mori, Toshio. (1985). *Yokohama, California*. Seattle: University of Washington Press.

Morrisson, Mark. (2005). Nationalism and the modern American canon. In Walter Kalaidjian (ed.), *The Cambridge Companion to American Modernism* (pp. 12–35). Cambridge, UK: Cambridge University Press.

North, Michael. (1994). *The Dialect of Modernism: Race, Language, and 20th Century Literature*. Oxford: Oxford University Press.

Okada, John. (1979). *No-No Boy*. Seattle: University of Washington Press.

Okihiro, Gary Y. (1989). Fallow field: The rural dimension of Asian American studies. In Gail M. Nomura et al. (eds), *Frontiers of Asian American Studies: Writing, Research, and Commentary* (pp. 6–13). Pullman: Washington State University Press.

Said, Edward. (1990). Reflections on exile. In Russell Ferguson, Martha Gever, Trinh T. Minh-Ha, and Cornel West (eds), *Out There: Marginalized and Contemporary Cultures* (pp. 357–66). New York: The New Museum of Contemporary Art.

San Juan, E., Jr. (1995). Introduction. In E. San Juan, Jr. (ed.), *On Becoming Filipino: Selected Writings of Carlos Bulosan* (pp. 1–44). Philadelphia: Temple University Press.

Santos, Bienvenido N. (1955). *You Lovely People*. Manila: The Benipayo Press.

Singal, Daniel Joseph. (Spring 1987). Towards a definition of American modernism. *American Quarterly* 39, 1: 7–26.

Sone, Monica. (1995). *Nisei Daughter*. Seattle: University of Washington Press.

Spivak, Gayatri. (1988). Can the subaltern speak? In Cary Nelson and Lawrence Grossbert (eds), *Marxism and the Interpretation of Culture* (pp. 271–313). Urbana: University of Illinois.

Takaki, Ronald. (1989). *Strangers from a Different Shore: A History of Asian Americans*. New York: Penguin Books.

Wand, David Hsin-fu (ed.). (1974). *Asian American Heritage: An Anthology of Prose and Poetry*. New York: Washington Square.

Wong, Jade Snow. (1989). *Fifth Chinese Daughter*. Seattle: University of Washington Press.

Yutang, Lin. (1948). *Chinatown Family*. New York: J. Day Co.

26

Modernism and Protopostmodernism

Patrick O'Donnell

In a now classic essay on the relation between modernism and postmodernism, "Mapping the Postmodern," Andreas Huyssen writes: "In much of the postmodernism debate, a very conventional thought pattern has asserted itself. Either it is said that postmodernism is continuous with modernism; or, it is claimed that there is a radical rupture, a break with modernism, which is then evaluated in either positive or negative terms" (Huyssen 1986: 182). Huyssen goes on to argue that the relation between modernism and postmodernism is more of a shifting of sensibilities than a historical rupture – a shift wherein "modernism's relentless hostility to mass culture" is challenged by postmodernism's integrations of pop and high art (p. 188). Reiterations of this debate continue more than 20 years after Huyssen had announced the exhaustion of its possibilities, and Huyssen's own position has been vigorously challenged by new historical and cultural work in modernist studies that reveal the extent to which the relation of key modernist figures to mass culture is far from hostile. In this essay, I will focus on the relation between modernism and postmodernism primarily in terms of how temporality in modern writing reveals the ways in which "anticipatory" discourse – concerned with its own futurity *per se* – imbricates the postmodern within the modern.

For postmodernism, it would be redundant to claim that there are multiple narratives contending to govern the relationship between modernism and postmodernism, ranging from the assertion that postmodernism is merely the repetition-with-a-difference of modernism to that which views postmodernism as a radical break from modernism. Yet almost inevitably, and whether they are regarded as historical epochs, ideological fronts, or aesthetic formations, modernism and postmodernism are viewed, often contradictorily, as temporally contiguous, one leading to the other, as if the latter was the historical outcome of the former. Even the view that postmodernism is incipient in modernism, that it is already folded into modernism as the symptomatic kernel of modernism's limit and eventual rupturing, relies on the assumption that the relation between the two is that of "before-and-after." However, the temporal structure of this relation itself is troubled by modernism's investment in "the new" and postmodernism's investment in rupture and radical difference – investments that, when compared, undermine any notions of contiguity or sequence as figuring the relation between them.

In the Introduction to the seminal *Postmodernism*, Fredric Jameson remarks that "postmodern consciousness may . . . amount to not much more than theorizing its own condition of possibility, which consists primarily in the sheer enumeration of changes and modifications" (1991: ix), and later, that "postmodernism is not the cultural dominant of a wholly new social order . . . but only the reflex and the concomitant of yet another systematic modification of capitalism itself" (p. xii). Jameson goes on to complicate and critique these representations of postmodernism as just "another systematic modification of capitalism" (the economy of modernity), or merely the instantiation of its own possibility as the limit-condition of modernism, but these formulations underscore the perennial necessity of understanding the relation between modernism and postmodernism as temporal, but not periodic. That is, postmodernism is modernism's future, just as modernism is postmodernism's past, but the connection between the past of postmodernism and the future of modernism is neither causal nor sequential; rather, it is an overlapping that reveals the degree to which the modernist anticipation of postmodernism and the postmodernist recollection of modernism comprise modes of repetition-with-a-difference. As Tyrus Miller has suggested in his characterization of the "late modernism" of such writers as Wyndham Lewis, Djuna Barnes, and Mina Loy who reflect "a closure at the horizon of the future" and insist on "Sinking themselves faithlessly into a present devoid of future" (Miller 1999: 13), the relation between modernism and postmodernism, however each may be staged, is one that involves a troubling of temporality *per se* that puts the future at risk as a mode of distinguishable difference. The relation of the modern to the postmodern, then, is one in which each verges on the other, indicating the continued presence (posterior or anterior) and limits of the other. To consider "protopostmodernism" then is to consider, even before its advent, the presence and repetition of the postmodern within the modern.

To be sure, Jameson has significantly revised the imbricated relation between modernism and postmodernism in later work. In *A Singular Modernity*, for example, he proposes as one of four "theses of modernity" that "No 'theory' of modernity makes sense today unless it is able to come to terms with the hypothesis of a postmodern break with the modern," but that "If it does so come to terms, however, it unmasks itself as a purely historiographic category and thereby seems to undo all it claims as a temporal category and as a vanguard concept of innovation" (Jameson 2002: 94). Significantly, this notion of postmodernism as a "break" from modernism comes in the form of a hypothesis – one posited of necessity, as it were, by modernism itself in order to remain the viable site of change, innovation, and difference; thus once more the complicit relation between modernism and postmodernism must be viewed as a set of overlapping limits and aporias that, contradictorily, result in an apodictic rupture or break. In undertaking a consideration of the complex relation between modernism and postmodernism, I will focus on how representations of temporality, the performance of identity, and the deployment of reflexive narrative strategies comprise anticipatory gestures to be discerned in modernist works by Stein, Barnes, and Faulkner. These gestures at once open out upon and delimit a future (the future of postmodernism) that ensures the continued radicality of the modern.

The work of Gertrude Stein is often considered anomalous and historically transgressive in several regards: Ellen Berry's 1992 book-length study of Stein's "postmodernism" shows the degree to which she overtakes the Deleuzian "wanderings" of postmodern writing, concurring with Catharine Stimpson's remarkable statement in the mid-1980s, at a time when postmodernist experimentation in the United States was in its ascendancy, that "Stein is a modern and post-modern Medusa. Decades after her death, she is a freakish ghost that terrifies and frees us" (Stimpson 1984: 316). Stein's work, partaking of "high modernist" experiments in form and style, her fictions, plays, biographies, autobiographies, and essays can be seen as seeding the kernels of postmodernism within the formational crisis of modernism itself. Stein's linguistic play, her aggressive deconstruction of the laws of genre, her challenge to linearity both formally and in terms of strategies demanded of the reader, her capacity to alter the temporality of reading and writing in such a way as to proffer a radically new, performed and performative conception of identity and sexuality – all can be cited as occurring at the "origin" of modernism and as symptomatic of an incipient postmodernism.

The contemporary novelist and philosopher, William H. Gass, whose investments in the materiality of language, the necessity of form, and the half-life of objects mirror Stein's own, has said of Stein writings that:

> they became a challenge to criticism the moment they were composed and they have remained a challenge. The challenge is of the purest and most direct kind. It is wholehearted and complete. It asks for nothing less than a study of the entire basis of our criticism, and it will not be put off. It requires us to consider again the esthetic significance of style; to examine again the ontological status of the artist's vision, his medium, and his effect. (Gass 1970: 87)

In a note to this characterization of what he terms the "revolutionary" status of Stein's writing, Gass – often considered to be a postmodern heir to Stein, though he would utterly reject the term "postmodern" as applicable to his work – protests that "I am always calling for such a program . . . but I never do much more than cry out" (p. 87). At a stroke, Gass links the "ontological status" of Stein's vision with prophecy; he suggests that she produces a kind of writing that unsettles the basis of reality, overturns the transparent or communicative function of language, and – as a voice crying out in the wilderness – demands a reader who must have an eye and ear for a kind of writing that does not "fit" within the present moment. In the conclusion to his essay on Stein, Gass writes that she "was sometimes made to sound an utter idiot by present tense and Time" (p. 95). In other terms, for Gass, Stein's writing is a writing for and of the future; it is not anticipatory and predictive, but truly revolutionary in that it is incomprehensible within any available frameworks.

In a note prefacing "Melanctha" included as the selection from Stein's *Three Lives* (1909) in her *Selected Writings*, Carl Van Vechten cites Richard Wright judging Stein's early novella to be "the first long serious literary treatment of Negro life in the United States" (Van Vechten in Stein 1962/1990: 338). Van Vechten – Stein's great friend, advisor, and fellow writer whose involvement in fomenting the Harlem Renaissance is legendary – continues to quote Wright, who emerged from the Harlem Renaissance as the signal African-American modernist writer, as saying of "Melanctha" that "All of my life I had been only half-hearing, but Miss Stein's struggling words made the speech of the people around me vivid. From that moment on, in my attempts at writing, I was able to tap at will the vast pool of living words swirling around me" (p. 338). Wright, who emphasizes the "living word" of Stein's writing as a form of currency may seem at odds with Gass, who views her work breaking loose from the bondage of "present tense and Time." But Wright's emphasis on Stein's ability to capture and project voice, the "struggling" and "swirling" discourse of living people underscores the performative aspects of her writing as approaching the limits of vocalizations and speech acts occurring in a mutable and disincorporated present where self-knowledge is confronted with the instability of being in an indivisible temporality.

In "Melanctha," the second and longest of the *Three Lives*, whose protagonists are all proletarian women living and working as servants or companions in Bridgepoint, Melanctha Herbert is a "graceful, pale yellow, intelligent, attractive negress" (Stein 1909/1936: 86) (she is of mixed race heritage) who moves restlessly from job to job and who commences a complicated and turbulent relationship with a black doctor, Jeff Campbell. The novella charts the fluctuations of their doomed affair in terms of the conflict between "feeling" and "knowing," and the ever-shifting ratios between knowledge and affect present in each party individually as they converse about the intractable differences between them. To some degree these differences are marked as racial and gendered in the novella, but the weight of the language falls more heavily upon an abstraction of identity: how it is an admixture of knowing and being, speech and silence, declaration and repression.

Here, for example, is a fragment of conversation that takes place between Melanctha and Jeff:

> They sat together, very silent. "I certainly do wonder, Miss Melanctha," at last began Jeff Campbell, "I certainly do wonder, if we know very right, you and me, what each other is really thinking. I certainly do wonder . . . If we know at all really what each other seems by what we are always saying." "That certainly do mean, by what you say, that you think I am a bad one, Jeff Campbell," flashed out Melanctha. "Why no, Miss

Melanctha, why sure I don't mean any thing like that at all, but what I am saying to you. . . . I don't like to say to you what I don't know for very sure, and I certainly don't know for sure I know just all what you mean by what you are always saying to me, Miss Melanctha, that's what makes me say what I was just saying to you when you asked me." (1909/1936: 128–9)

The transcription of their conversation records the act of speaking as an ongoing process that evolves in relation to knowing the other, but it is clear in this "speaking" about "knowing" that the two elements are mismatched, that they do not follow a parallel trajectory. Here, Jeff Campbell reveals the insecurities that will sunder his affair with Melanctha – the judgmental attitude that Melanctha senses in his speech, his unwillingness to live with uncertainty – as performative issues that take place against the backdrop of the unknowable. The protagonists of "Melanctha" often talk of knowing nothing about each other, and often say nothing about what they do know. As the repetitions and ellipses of this conversation between Jeff and Melanctha disclose, there is an anxiety produced in the relationship between two identities always moving forward in time as that relationship is manifested in speech acts. For Stein, this anxiety rests upon the discordant relationship between ontology and epistemology, being and knowing, such that the erratic ratio of change in the personalities and identities of the two interlocutors in "Melanctha" is disjoined from their evolving self-knowledge and knowledge of each other. The frequent crises of knowing represented in their conversations gesture toward a fundamental instability in identity *per se* and its unfolding in speech. As Jeff complains at one point, "You see it's just this way, with me now, Melanctha. Sometimes you seem like one kind of girl to me, and sometimes you are like a girl that is all different to me, and the two kinds of girls is certainly very different to each other, and I can't see any way they seem to have much to do, to be together in you" (p. 188). The "problem," for Jeff Campbell, who sees knowledge as the quanta of reality, is that Melanctha's identity is multiple, dynamic, and indeterminate: she is a being made of differences that cannot be totaled up into a singularity.

In a certain sense, one could see the affair between the protagonists of "Melanctha" as a confrontation between the dominant of modernism and that of postmodernism, as Brian McHale charts this relation where, under postmodernism, the focus on representing "modes of being" replaces modernism's chief concern with "problems of knowing" (McHale 1987: 10–11). This, admittedly, is a heuristic and schematic designation of the relation between modernism and postmodernism that gives rise to the question of whether the relationship between them can be considered in terms of cultural dominants or paradigms in the first place. Nevertheless, it is a useful means of understanding how Stein's work is indicative of modernism's future as it exhibits a form of literary temporality that can be seen as both anticipating and recapitulating that "future" precisely through an exploration of the relation between temporality and identity.

In "Melanctha," this relation is posed in terms of differing conceptualizations of memory that Jeff and Melanctha discuss as they move toward the end of their affair:

> "You see Melanctha, it certainly is this way with you, it is, that you ain't ever got any way to remember right what you been doing, or anybody else that has been feeling with you. . . ." "It certainly is all easy for you Jeff Campbell to be talking. You remember right, because you don't remember nothing till you get home with your thinking everything all over, but I certainly don't think much ever of that kind of way of remembering right, Jeff Campbell. I certainly do call it remembering right Jeff Campbell, to remember right just when it happens to you so you have a right kind of feeling not to act the way you always been doing to me . . . No, Jeff Campbell, it's real feeling every moment when its needed, that certainly does seem to me like real remembering." (Stein 1909/1936: 181)

Almost framed as if a dialogue between body and soul, the conversation enacted here reflects upon two dramatically different versions of "right" remembering: one, oriented to the past, only recalls the event and its affect via a temporal delay and as a form of cognitive dissonance; the other constitutes (rather than recalling) the event *as* affect in the present instance of its conception and as it joins the stream of events, feelings, and thoughts always moving toward the vanishing horizon of the future.

I would not suggest that in representing these two forms of remembering one of many differences between Jeff and Melanctha that Stein is "choosing" between one or the other as "right," nor that the novella compels the reader to do so. Rather, this discourse of difference over memory and its relation to time and affect is symptomatic, in my view, of how Stein represents difference *per se* (the difference between feeling and reflection, female and male, being and knowledge, identity as form and identity as process) as at the foundation of speaking and living in time. Temporality is the issue in this climactic conversation between the novella's principals: it is either a form of spacing that allows for reflection and "knowing," from Jeff's perspective, or it is, in Melanctha's view, a nonspaced, epiphanic instancing that enables the merging of experience and identity. Nor are the two "times" of Jeff and Melanctha merely additive, their characters allegorical figures which, if joined, would constitute a whole or annealed temporality. The instillation of literary temporality in Melanctha reflected in this discourse of difference gestures toward a notion of the indeterminate that Marjorie Perloff has argued is fundamental to Stein's attempt to portray human change linguistically:

> Melanctha, Miss Furr and Miss Skeene, *The Making of Americans*, the Picasso portrait of 1909 – all these are examples of verbal compositions in which indeterminacy is created by repetition and variation, sameness and difference, a rhetorical pattern of great intricacy, which is set up so as to create semantic gaps. Gertrude Stein's syntax enacts the gradually changing process of human consciousness, the instability of emotion and thought. (Perloff 1981/1999: 98)

Perloff is concerned in this assessment to locate Stein in a continuous tradition that extends from Rimbaud's modernism to Cage's postmodernism – one in which language and speech are gauged for what they cannot say as much as for what they can. (But for a contrasting perspective on the "differences" of postmodernism celebrated by Perloff, see Sussman, who regards them as "structures and differences joyously celebrated and anxiously discovered by modernism [that] have ceased to make a difference," Sussman 1990: 177). Stein's "protopostmodernism" lies precisely in her capacity to portray the exfoliations of language and the extension of identity in and across time, as consonant with the ratio of change manifested through temporal processes. Writing in the present tense, she stands as the predicate for the writing that is to come.

If Stein's "Melanctha" charts the fluctuations of consciousness through differences in individual speech acts that temporalize being and identity and render them indeterminate, then Djuna Barnes's *Nightwood*, in T. S. Eliot's classic Introduction to the novel, presents us with "not simply a collection of individual portraits; the characters are all knotted together . . . by what we might call chance or destiny, rather than by deliberate choice of each other's company: it is the whole pattern they form, rather than any individual constituent, that is the focus of interest" (Eliot in Barnes 1937/2006: xx–xxi). Eliot's formalist view of the novel as the portrait of a cooperative brought together by contingency rather than choice, a clan of misfits whose identities are known only in terms of the "whole pattern" of their collective interactions unfolding within a destinal logic, contributes to the widely held view that *Nightwood* is a dream-novel, a Surrealist fantasy surveying the "modern scene" in all of its excess, grotesquerie, and desire unleashed. Indeed, both the published and original title of this novel (*Bow Down: Anatomy of Night*) which, as Miriam Fuchs (1993) has shown, was heavily influenced by Eliot, as well as the title of three of its eight parts ("La Somnambule," "Night Watch," and "Watchman, What of the Night?") are strongly indicative of its perceived status as an extended dream narrative, comparable to other modernist exemplars such as the "Nighttown" chapter in Joyce's *Ulysses* (1922) and the whole of *Finnegans Wake* (1939), Schnitzler's *Rhapsody: A Dream Novel* (1926), or Kafka's *The Castle* (1922).

Equally, *Nightwood* is an exploration of alterity and alternative sexualities in a world where difference is fetishized and the falsity of binary oppositions (human/animal, gay/straight, male/female, sacred/profane) is exposed. As a leading postmodern feminist novelist, Jeanette Winterson, writes in the Preface to the recent reissue of the novel, "*Nightwood* is a nano-text," implying that the novel has an internalized, germinal effect upon the reader over long reaches of time: "reading it is like drinking wine with a pearl dissolving in the glass. You have taken in more than you know, and it will go on doing its work. From now on, a part of you is pearl-lined" (Winterson in Barnes 1937/2006: ix). This concept of the reader is, to some degree, in alignment with the concept of identities in *Nightwood* knowable only as part of an assemblage (Eliot's "the whole pattern they form") that emerges over the time of the reading. Yet Winterson alternatively suggests that the novel is composed of individually fragmented hybrid assemblages who are strangers in the world and to themselves, ultimately only partially knowable through an infinite process of accretion that binds reader to character in the affective act of consumption. As Winterson continues, "*Nightwood* has neither stereotypes nor caricatures . . . Humans suffer and, gay or straight, they break themselves into pieces . . . crucify themselves on their own longings, and let's not forget, are crucified by a world that fears strangers" (p. xii).

The two prefatory comments on the novel offered in the current paperback edition of *Nightwood* reveal the novel's interesting status as a protopostmodern work. Eliot's Introduction, which appeared in the first American edition of the novel in 1937 and has been included in most editions of the novel since then, underscores the novel's formalistic qualities by circumspectly acknowledging its fragmentary aspects and identities as long as these are seen as part of a whole, a coherent pattern of dreamwork. This is to emphasize, coming from one often regarded as the high priest of modernism, the novel's functional aspect as a kind of transparent architecture that gives shape and form to its nightmarish content.

For Eliot, the important thing is that dangerous, unseemly, or hybridic content be contained by a "molar" narrative form ("molar" as used in physics, of a unit of matter perceived as a whole). Alongside this we can regard in Winterson's Preface, published nearly 70 years after Eliot's Introduction, the concept of *Nightwood* as "nano-text," a minuscule time-bomb that operates on the molecular level in such a way that the content becomes the form of the text as read or consumed, erratically and partially, by each idiosyncratic reader. The postmodern theorists Gilles Deleuze and Félix Guattari (1987) have posed the passage between "regimes of signs" that can be associated with modernism and postmodernism precisely in terms of a movement between the "molar" and the "molecular." (See especially "10,000 B.C.: The Geology of Morals," pp. 39–74, and "1730: Becoming-Intense, Becoming-Animal, Becoming-Imperceptible," pp. 232–309). This movement can be observed on many different planes in their thought, but for our purposes it can be read structurally out of Eliot's and Winterson's commentaries to figure a transition between modernism and postmodernism that involves viewing the relation between form, content, and reader as one of distance, containment, and total apprehension, compared to viewing that relation as one of proximity, disaggregation, and partial knowledge. On the level of language and image, *Nightwood* negotiates amidst these alternatives in relating the progress of is protagonist through a "surreal" world of temporal dislocation and ever-changing identities.

The novel traces the erratic progress of Robin Vote as she navigates across a series of modern metropolises (Vienna, Paris, Berlin, New York) and takes on a number of lovers, including Felix Volkbein, her voyeuristic husband whom she abandons along with their infant son; Nora Flood, formerly, like Robin, a circus performer in New

York; and Jenny Petherbridge, Nora's replacement in what appears to be, for Robin, a proliferating succession of liaisons with men and women, humans and – in the novel's climactic scene – animals. The odd figure of Dr Matthew O'Connor, a physician from San Francisco who hangs on the fringes of the cultural underworld that Robin inhabits, serves as a commentator upon and "conscience" for the unfolding phantasmagoria of the novel, albeit one who, as a closet transvestite, is caught up himself in the novel's play of mutating, alternating identities.

In a climactic conversation with Nora about Robin's affairs, perfidy, childishness, and innocence (or lack thereof), Dr O'Connor says of Robin that she is:

> Outside the "human type" – a wild thing caught in a woman's skin, monstrously alone, monstrously vain; like the paralysed man in Coney Island (take away a man's conformity and you take away his remedy) who had to lie on his back in a box, but the box was lined with velvet, his fingers jeweled with stones, and suspended over him where he could never take his eyes off, a sky-blue mounted mirror, for he wanted to enjoy his own "difference." Robin is not in your life, you are in her dream, you'll never get out of it. And why does Robin feel innocent? Every bed she leaves, without caring, fills her heart with peace and happiness. She has made her "escape" again. That's why she can't "put herself in another's place," she herself is the only "position" . . . You almost caught hold of her, but she put you cleverly away by making you the Madonna. (Barnes 1937/2006: 155)

This is one of numerous perspectives that Dr O'Connor offers on Robin – as child, doll, automaton, "Madonna," and harlot – where Robin becomes a performer of her own identity, in Judith Butler's sense of identity as "performatively constituted by the very 'expressions' that are said to be its results" (Butler 1990: 25). In formulating this conception of identity formation, Butler is expressly arguing for regarding gender as an ever-shifting performance that can take many shapes, and that cannot be confined to a "male/female" binary. The widely held view of postmodern identity as multiple, partial, self-contradictory, and mutable (see e.g., Lyotard 1993 and Hassan 1974) combined with Butler's notion of the performative is enunciated in Dr O'Connor's characterization of Robin. Dr O'Connor compares Robin to a circus performer paralyzed by his own narcissism, an accessorized and fetishized embodiment of utter self-reflexivity that is nothing but the objects that adorn him, a profusion of differences that are all the same in the mirror.

Here and elsewhere, the utter contradictions of Robin's identity are apparent. She is both self-centered and decentered, a seemingly homogeneous entity only visible as a singularity ("she herself is the only 'position' "). At the same time, she is a proliferation of differences, both human and animal ("a wild thing caught in a woman's skin"), male and female, only visible – in this paradoxical sense – as one who has escaped the confinements of a self-imposed narcissism by escaping the gaze of the other who would seek to know her. (Especially pertinent to this dimension of the novel is Justus Nieland's revealing commentary on performance, affect, animality, and public spectacle in Barnes and other modernists.) In her identity performances, she is the one who is equally constructed by those for whom she is a spectacle in Dr O'Connor's analogy, and self-fashioned as she arranges herself and the objects that she adorns herself with in the mirror. She is both dominating and submissive, as when Dr O'Connor compares her to a "doll":

> The last doll, given to age . . . the girl who should have been a boy, and the boy who should have been a girl! The love of that last doll was foreshadowed in that love of the first. The doll and the immature have something right about them, the doll because it resembles but does not contain life, and the third sex because it contains life but resembles the doll. The blessed face! It should be seen only in profile, otherwise it is observed to be the conjunction of identical cleaved halves of sexless misgiving! (Barnes 1937/2006: 157)

The rhetoric of this passage – characteristic of Dr O'Connor – is hyperbolic and prophetic; it veers wildly between tonal and symbolic registers as it depicts Robin as both old and young (elsewhere, the "blessed face" is portrayed as "ag[ing] only under the blows of perpetual childhood," p. 143), immature and yet part of a timeless succession "for the ages," self-identical yet "cleaved" as a member of the "third sex" which refers to someone who is neither of one sex or another in a binary gender system.

Notable in Dr O'Connor's commentary is his emphasis on the temporality of the performing subjectivity of Robin. She appears to be both quasi-mythical, primordial (her temples are like "young beasts cutting horns, as if they were sleeping eyes. And that look on a face we follow like a witch-fire," p. 143), and immature; she is the first and last doll of childhood, and seems to inhabit a temporality apart from the "structuring of contingency" that Mary Ann Doane suggests is characteristic of representational modernity. Doane writes that:

> the rationalization of time characterizing industrialization and the expansion of capitalism was accompanied by a structuring of contingency and temporality through emerging technologies of representation – a structuring that attempted to ensure their residence outside structure. Such a strategy is not designed simply to deal with the leakage or by-products of rationalization; it is structurally necessary to the ideologies of capitalist modernization. (Doane 2002: 11)

Nightwood and, particularly, the "character" of Robin Vote lie beyond such modernist temporalities; she is the "leakage" *per se*, and as such inhabits a temporality that fluctuates at random between the ancient and the modern, past and present.

Both ancient and modern, the protagonist of *Nightwood* peripatetically navigates a carnivalesque realm in a succession of present moments where she is simultaneously any one of a dozen different "molecular" identities, and where the "present" is constructed as a random series of instances that manifest the deep irrationality of the world as conceived by Barnes. To some degree, Barnes's protagonist is similar to Stein's: like Melanctha, Robin is a being-in-the-present whose experience is, in Giorgio Agamben's sense, "simply the name for a basic characteristic of consciousness: its essential nega-tivity, its always being what it has not yet become" (Agamben 1993: 33). Yet I would draw a critical distinction between the two in the quality of negativity they share as "protopostmodern" identities. For Stein, the process of being what one has not yet become is accretive, signified through the layerings of repetitious, overlapping phrases changing subtly over time that represent the affective life of her characters. To this degree, for Stein, character is a language with a future. For Barnes, the process of being what one has not yet become is centrifugal, as if the "self" is a kind of empty vortex around which whirl objects and narratives that are flung off and cast aside as Robin escapes the gravitational force of each exhausted relationship, each anachronis-tic version of the self to be discarded like a useless carapace. The multiplicity of identity, for Barnes's protagonist, is a kind of survival mechanism (as is her narcissism) that allows for continuance in a world where the present occurs with such instanta-neousness that it recedes before itself. Yet Barnes's more radical vision is the pretext for renegotiating a host of symbolic and cultural binaries that postmodern thought aggressively attempts to undo – those that exist, as I have suggested, as oppositions between male and female, dominant and submissive, empowered and colonized, para-noid and schizoid.

We thus foresee in Barnes a contradiction of postmodernity as such: the need to locate identity as "beyond" or "before" time, space, and the binary oppositions of language when it is only by means of these that identity can be known. It is a con-tradiction explored by a host of contemporary writers, especially those who explore the relation between language and gender. Kathy Acker, for example, in *Don Quixote, Which Was A Dream*, her experimental portrayal of a female knight-errant on a quest to destroy male-dominated power centers of Cold War America, everywhere chal-lenges the pieties attendant upon the alignments of identificatory binaries: male/ female, language/silence, power/enslavement. She does so by portraying selves in the novel as constantly mutating forms, in a language that veers wildly between the sacred and the profane. In one of many conversations with her dog-companion, Don Quixote states that "As long as you men cling to your identity of power-monger . . . as long as you cling to a dualistic reality which is a reality molded by power, women will not exist with you. . . . Women exist with the deer, the foxes of redness, the devious cats" (Acker 1986: 28). Acker echoes Barnes's vision of the (female) human merging with the animal; yet, beyond "dualistic reality" and the binaries that underlie the contem-porary world of power relations that excludes women, the only alternative for Acker is being which is nonbeing, language which is silence: "I'm your desire's object . . . be-cause I can't be the subject . . . I name 'nothingness.' I won't not be: I'll perceive and I'll speak," says "Medusa," one of the novel's hallucinatory apparitions (p. 28). In this state of contradiction, identity can only be an incomprehensible, unnamable assem-blage that is both singular and a monstrous hybrid: "Now a walrus-like head whose eyes are red . . . is sitting on the non-existent head of two fishy tales. . . . Two purple something-or-other's are, snakelike, wrapping themselves around the self, for each one is a self unto its one-ness or selfishness" (p. 95). We can look to other Acker contemporaries – Rikki Ducornet in *The Jade Cabinet* (1993), Carole Maso in *The American Woman in a Chinese Hat* (1994), or Winterson in *Sexing the Cherry* (1989) – to see experimental writing that attempts to articulate, at the limits of language and narrative, identities that are neither simply "imaginary" nor simply "real." In her fiction, Barnes makes it clear that such contradictions are an integral experience of a modern "world" always dissolving into its parts.

While the fiction of Gertrude Stein formulates and anticipates postmodernism's concern with the difference (that is not always a difference) between "knowing" and "being," and while Djuna Barnes's *Nightwood* portrays the mutability of identity in ways consonant with the postmodern philosophy of Deleuze and Guattari or the writing of Kathy Acker, the protopostmodernism of the novels of William Faulkner exists in their reflection on the capacity of narrative to transfer historical and personal knowledge through time in the telling and hearing of stories. The classic example of Faulkner's narrative reflexivity and his concern with the relation between "story" and "knowing" occurs in *Absalom, Absalom!*, perhaps his greatest novel, in which the story of the demonic patriarch and plantation owner, Thomas Sutpen, is told against the backdrop of the Civil War and its aftermath. As Mr Compson tells what he knows of the Sutpen story to his son, Quentin, he provides a rather cynical view of the efficacy of narrative:

> we have a few old mouth-to-mouth tales; we exhume from old trunks and boxes and drawers letters without salutation or signature, in which men and women who once lived and breathed are now merely initials or nicknames out of some now incomprehensible affection which sound to us like Sanskrit or Chocktaw; we see dimly people, the people in whose living blood and seed we ourselves lay dormant and waiting, in this shadowy attenuation of time possessing now heroic proportions . . . They are there, yet something is missing; they are like a chemical formula exhumed along with the letters from that forgotten chest . . . you bring them together again and again and nothing happens: just the words, the symbols, the shapes themselves, shadowy inscrutable and serene, against that turgid background of a horrible and bloody mischancing of human affairs. (Faulkner 1936/1986: 80)

At first glance, if one pursues McHale's modernist/epistemological, postmodernist/ontological divide that I have suggested Stein puts into question, it may appear that in this passage Faulkner is primarily interested in the modernist inquiry into the conditions of knowledge. (For a succession of discussions about Faulkner as modernist and/or postmodernist, see Moreland 1990, O'Donnell 1994, Weinstein 2002, Duvall 2002, and Kreiswrith 2002). Mr Compson suggests that historical truth – the truth behind the tragedies that have beset the Sutpen family from its origins, the "true story" of those origins – can be conveyed only as "through a glass, darkly" from generation unto generation; he views history as illegible and inscrutable because it is transferred via the highly unreliable human instruments of writing and voice and is subject to the distortions of interpretation. He is, of course, one of many idiosyncratic "voices" who speak in novels written by an author who typically distances himself from the enunciations of his characters, but at a further remove and throughout *Absalom, Absalom!*, Faulkner brings into play texts of all kinds (letters, the faded engravings on tombstones, diaries, business transactions, as well as the "text" we are reading in Faulkner's novel) and various forms of transcribed oral communication (gossip, rumor, conversations, confessions, proclamations, commands) in order to limn their truth-bearing or truth-distorting capacities in Compson-like gestures of reflexivity. (For a larger discussion of the epistemological uses of fiction in history, the uses of history in fiction, and the emergence of "historiographic metafiction" in modern and contemporary literature, see Hutcheon 1988.) In this regard, Faulkner is comparable to the Joseph Conrad of "Heart of Darkness" (1902) and *Lord Jim* (1900) or the Ford Madox Ford of *The Good Soldier* (1915), as "high modernist" writers who wish to test the limits of authenticity and skepticism in the transmission of knowledge via narrative.

A closer scrutiny of Mr Compson's reflection on the inadequacies of narrative, however, reveals Faulkner merging questions of epistemology with questions of genealogy, or, as John Irwin (1975) has shown, the mapping of how life and identity, as compared to the conveyance of narrative information, is passed on from one generation to another. Mr Compson is not just concerned with how "history" is handed down (even as he recounts the Sutpen history of betrayal and domination to his son), he is also concerned – obsessively so, as are his forebears, if one tracks the Compson family saga across *Absalom, Absalom!*, *The Sound and the Fury* (1929), and *Go Down, Moses* (1942) – with the transmission of identity via the passing on of stories and, in his pessimistic view, the degree to which both story and identity are contaminated, distorted, or destroyed over time. These concerns precisely replicate the lineaments of Sutpen's history, the anxieties besetting the telling of the story mirroring its contents in the narration of Sutpen's failed attempt to reduplicate himself in his heirs in the racist quest for an eternal dynasty, "uncorrupted" by racial mixing and the contingencies of history. Moreover, they reflect Mr Compson's fear – his racism equal in kind, if not in degree, to Sutpen's – that the Compson line is petering out, "the living blood and seed" of his ancestors now lying dormant, their epic grandeur diminished in the "shadowy attenuation of time" and through the "horrible and bloody mischancing of human affairs" commonly referred to as "history."

In Mr Compson's oratory, the conflation of apprehensions about maintaining the integrity of both "blood" and "story" over time reinforces twinned mythologized notions of identity as singular and unitary, and the now attenuated capacity of stories to be originary and truthful. Elsewhere in the novel, this view is countered by its opposite where stories and selves are portrayed as multiple and visible in their wandering from origins in a kind of writing that evinces "textuality," in Jacques Derrida's sense of the term, "constituted by differences and by differences from differences ... by nature absolutely heterogeneous" (Derrida 1981: 98). As John T.

Matthews has demonstrated, Derrida's conception of textuality is, in a sense, Mr Compson's view of what has happened to the Sutpen story turned inside out: seen positively, the "old mouth-to-mouth tales," the exhumed letters and ciphered figures from the past signify the inexhaustible possibilities of narrative once it is unleashed from its origins and recognized as a medium that, by endlessly deferring its own ultimacies, ensures its continuance.

Thus, in the late-night retellings of the Sutpen story that Quentin undertakes with his Harvard College roommate, Shreve McCannon, the proliferation of stories and identities results in the infamous "happy marriage of speaking and hearing" (Faulkner 1936/1986: 253), a conversion of partial narratives with multiple origins that allows Quentin to think:

> *Maybe nothing ever happens once and is finished. Maybe happen is never once but like ripples maybe on water after the pebble sinks, the ripples moving onwards, spreading the pool attached by a narrow umbilical water-cord to the next pool which the first pool feeds, has fed, did feed, let this second pool contain a different temperature of water, a different molecularity of having seen, felt, remembered, reflect in a different tone the infinite unchanging sky, it doesn't matter: that pebble's watery echo whose fall it did not even see moves across its surface too at the original ripple-space, to the old ineradicable rhythm* thinking *Yes, we are both Father. Or maybe Father and I are both Shreve, maybe it took Father and me both to make Shreve or Shreve and me both to make Father or maybe Thomas Sutpen to make all of us.* (Faulkner 1936/1986: 210, Faulkner's italics)

While this image – one of the most beautifully evocative in Faulkner's fiction – may be regarded on the one hand, especially for Quentin, as born of a short-lived youthful idealism, on the other it offers a stark alternative to the maniacal quest for genealogical purity and a singular, replicated identity sought by Sutpen. In Quentin's reflection, identities are multiple and converge, stories are molecular, only visible as a separation (a "ripple-space") from their origin; what is heard is an echo, what is seen is a movement outwards. Yet there is still in this image of the differences inherent in textuality and in and between identities as they move through time the notion of an origin and a "before" – the unseen fall of the pebble in the water, the "original ripple-space" that remains only in the form of its watery reverberations. Once again, there is an inversion of Mr Compson's mordant vision of stories and identities given over to time and history: in Quentin's reflection, a "different molecularity . . . doesn't matter," nor is it important where the origin of self or story temporally resides or begins, since identity is not one, but many, and made up by virtue of participation in a narrative that continues precisely because it is a divagation from erased or diminished origins.

Faulkner's anticipation of postmodernism partially resides in his bringing alongside, and into conversation, the narrative yearning for origin and monumentality with the heterogeneity of textuality, that is, in the propagation of narratives for the sake of their own difference in Derridean terms. Such proliferation for postmodern writers – for example, Borges's infinite self-mirroring, infinite libraries, or his labyrinths in which, for John Barth, "ideally, all the possibilities of choice . . . are embodied, and . . . must be exhausted before one reaches the heart" (Barth 1984: 75) – complicates notions of intention, authority, and linearity in the multiplication of paths and stories. At the same time, Faulkner's fiction situates this conflation of narrative drive and the formation of identity within specific, critical social and historical circumstances. Sutpen's obsession with singularity and genealogical purity is informed by a past replete with class exclusion and class embarrassment; attitudes toward (and fear of) "difference" of all kinds – racial, gendered, economic – are examined in this novel of textuality that portrays the transition of the South from plantation culture to industrialization, all under the shadow of slavery and its aftermath. For Faulkner, the labyrinth of differences to be negotiated by protagonists and readers involves both coming to terms with the indeterminacy of the past, and, in the key of the performative (the "happy marriage of speaking and hearing"), the ontic, construing identity amidst the "exhaustion of choices" that constitutes history.

In discussing the ways in which three modernist writers anticipate, incorporate, or supersede postmodernism, I have pursued but a few of the trajectories that arc across twentieth-century writing. The performative in Stein, which merges knowledge and affect; mutability in Barnes, which subverts the binaries of logocentric thought; and textuality in Faulkner, which both replicates and undoes narrative/genealogical origins and ends, all offer specific, prototypical anticipations of a highly selected array of postmodernism's dominant tendencies. Each of these protopostmodern strains reveals, as I mentioned at the beginning, a complex relationship between modernism and postmodernism that cannot be reduced to mere questions of succession or supersession. That relationship is one in which aesthetic strategies, social transformations, and the philosophical adventures of identity blend or conflict with countless other elements to produce sheer movement between ends constantly receding into the past and before the future.

A very short list of works and trajectories that would arise in a longer discussion might include John Dos Passos's *Manhattan Transfer* (1925) with its use of collage and cinematic techniques, an exploration continued in contemporary writers such as Robert Coover; Jean Toomer's *Cane* (1923), an assemblage of minor narratives that portray identities as heterogeneous and nomadic while engaging in questions of ethnicity, anticipatory of work by Amiri Baraka or Ana Castillo; or William Gaddis's *The Recognitions* (1955) which, to extend Miller's "late modernism" to the mid-1950s, stands between modernist encyclopedic monuments such as Joyce's *Ulysses* and contemporary novels such as Thomas Pynchon's *Gravity's Rainbow* (1973) or Richard Powers's *The Gold Bug Variations* (1991) that enfold multiple disciplines and discourses into novels encompassing a "world" in their density and range of reference. The list could be infinitely extended – ironically so because, of course, several points of contestation and collaboration between modernism and postmodernism revolve around issues of canon and proliferation. Because the movement from modernism to postmodernism is fundamentally historical (which, once more, does not mean that it is necessarily epochal or sequential), their relationality continues to evolve and change as the contours of the landscape change when new work appears, when "older" work attracts new forms of attention. The work of Stein, Barnes, and Faulkner, I have argued, exists in a continuum that cannot be understood chronologically or genealogically; their writing is a form of continuance whose effects can be observed in the specificities of postmodern writing as germinal, molecular. I have suggested that these effects are bidirectional, in that those writers who anticipate postmodernity do so as a consequence of producing work that is before its time, of the future. Such writing, one might argue, is what will survive.

References and Further Reading

Acker, Kathy. (1986). *Don Quixote, Which Was A Dream*. New York: Grove.

Agamben, Giorgio. (1993). *Infancy and History: Essays on the Destruction of Experience*, trans. Liz Heron. New York: Verso.

Barnes, Djuna. (1937/2006). *Nightwood*, preface Jeanette Winterson, intro. T. S. Eliot. New York: New Directions.

Barth, John. (1984). The literature of exhaustion. In *The Friday Book: Essays and Other Nonfiction* (pp. 62–76). New York: Putnam's.

Berry, Ellen E. (1992). *Curved Thought and Textual Wandering: Gertrude Stein's Postmodernism*. Ann Arbor: University of Michigan Press.

Butler, Judith. (1990). *Gender Trouble: Feminism and the Subversion of Identity*. New York: Routledge.

Deleuze, Gilles and Félix Guattari. (1987). *A Thousand Plateaus: Capitalism and Schizophrenia*, trans. and foreword Brian Massumi. Minneapolis: University of Minnesota Press.

Derrida, Jacques. (1981). *Dissemination*, trans. and intro. Barbara Johnson. Chicago: University of Chicago Press.

Doane, Mary Anne. (2002). *The Emergence of Cinematic Time: Modernity, Contingency, and the Archive*. Cambridge, MA: Harvard University Press.

Duvall, John N. (2002). Postmodern Yoknapatawpha: Faulkner as usable past. In John N. Duvall and Ann J. Abadie (eds), *Faulkner and Postmodernism* (pp. 39–56). Oxford, MS: University of Mississippi Press.

Faulkner, William. *Absalom, Absalom!* (1936). New York: Vintage, 1986.

Fuchs, Miriam. (1993). Djuna Barnes and T. S. Eliot: Authority, resistance, and acquiescence. *Tulsa Studies in Women's Literature* 12, 2: 288–313.

Gass, William H. (1970). Gertrude Stein: Her escape from protective language. In *Fiction and the Figures of Life* (pp. 79–96). New York: Knopf.

Hassan, Ihab. (1974). *The Dismemberment of Orpheus: Toward a Postmodern Literature*. New York: Oxford University Press.

Hutcheon, Linda. (1988). *A Poetics of Postmodernism: History, Theory, Fiction*. New York: Routledge.

Huyssen, Andreas. (1986). Mapping the postmodern. In *After the Great Divide: Modernism, Mass Culture, Postmodernism* (pp. 178–221). Bloomington, IN: Indiana University Press.

Irwin, John T. (1975). *Doubling and Incest/Repetition and Revenge: A Speculative Reading of Faulkner*. Baltimore: Johns Hopkins University Press.

Jameson, Fredric. (1991). *Postmodernism, or, the Cultural Logic of Late Capitalism*. Durham, NC: Duke University Press.

Jameson, Fredric. (2002). *A Singular Modernity: Essay on the Ontology of the Present*. New York: Verso.

Kreiswirth, Martin. (2002). Intertextuality, transference and postmodernism in *Absalom, Absalom!*: The production and reception of Faulkner's fictional world. In John N. Duvall and Ann J. Abadie (eds), *Faulkner and Postmodernism* (pp. 109–23). Oxford, MS: University of Mississippi Press.

Lyotard, Jean-François. (1993). *Libidinal Economy*, trans. Iain Hamilton Grant. London: Athlone Press.

Matthews, John T. (1982). *The Play of Faulkner's Language*. Ithaca, NY: Cornell University Press.

McHale, Brian. (1987). *Postmodernist Fiction*. New York: Methuen.

Miller, Tyrus. (1999). *Late Modernism: Politics, Fiction, and the Arts Between Two World Wars*. Berkeley: University of California Press.

Moreland, Richard C. (1990). *Faulkner and Modernism: Rereading and Rewriting*. Madison: University of Wisconsin Press.

Nieland, Justus. (2007). *Feeling Modern: The Eccentricities of Public Life*. Urbana: University of Illinois Press.

O'Donnell, Patrick. (1994). Faulkner and postmodernism. In Philip Weinstein (ed.), *A Faulkner Companion* (pp. 45–58). New York: Cambridge University Press.

Perloff, Marjorie. (1981/1999). *The Poetics of Indeterminacy: Rimbaud to Cage*. Evanston, IL: Northwestern University Press.

Stein, Gertrude. (1962/1990). *Selected Writings Gertrude Stein*, ed. and intro. Carl Van Vechten. New York: Vintage.

Stein, Gertrude. *Three Lives*. (1909/1936). New York: Vintage.

Stimpson, Catharine R. (1984). Gertrude Stein: Humanism and its freaks. *boundary 2* 12, 3: 301–19.

Sussman, Henry. (1990). *Afterimages of Modernity: Structure and Indifference in Twentieth-Century Literature*. Baltimore: Johns Hopkins University Press.

Weinstein, Philip. (2002). Postmodern intimations: Musing on invisibility: William Faulkner, Richard Wright, and Ralph Ellison. In John N. Duvall and Ann J. Abadie (eds), *Faulkner and Postmodernism* (pp. 19–38). Oxford, MS: University of Mississippi Press.

27

The Modern Novel in a New World Context

George B. Handley

Literary modernism's various and contemporaneous manifestations across many New World nations exhibit similar interests in racial, linguistic, and geographical distinctions, what is commonly known as "local color." This was true in the US West and South, and in the Harlem Renaissance, but also throughout the Caribbean basin and Latin America, where similar movements in the early twentieth century were afoot to affirm the value of memories and cultures that derived from African, indigenous, and rural sources. What motivated this interest and fostered an impatience for signs of national or regional exceptionality was a climate of postcolonial anxiety among nations seeking to deepen their claims to cultural autonomy, often in the wake of civil and racial conflict.[1] The allure of a local essence offered itself as a cure for these anxieties, but this literature's modernism is demonstrated by its self-conscious awareness of the seemingly inevitable failure to find and identify that essence. That is, New World literary modernism is a performance of a search for an essence, a search that remains as necessary as the essence is elusive. The forces of Western modernity pose the greatest threat to that alterity the authors seek, specifically the uneven advancement of modernization and its concomitant promises and disappointments regarding the liberation of the citizen subject through technology, globalization, economic opportunity, and democratization. Thus it is to those cultures, peoples, and places in the Americas defeated by European models of modernity that writers in the early decades of the twentieth century turn.

This is not to say that the various regionalist movements throughout the Americas were identical; they were inspired by different relationships to, and different versions of, modernity, but it is precisely the awareness of the differences that resulted from modernity's uneven arrival in the New World that inspires this transnational literary response (see Ramos 1989 on "modernización desigual" [uneven modernization], p. 12). That these modernisms nevertheless appear on the literary horizon with strikingly parallel anxieties and contradictions would seem to raise the question: if modern literature of the Americas probes the depths of local realities to perform a recovery of a lost essence, why has literary criticism assumed that its relevance can be determined only within the context of a particular national history? And when these modern works are placed in a comparative context, why has that so predominantly been a transatlantic one?

The transatlantic axis, of course, makes sense, given the great interest Europe, including Paris and Spain, held for a great number of US and Latin American writers, many of whom lived and traveled abroad and absorbed European influence. In the case of the United States, one thinks of Henry James, Gertrude Stein, F. Scott Fitzgerald, Ernest Hemingway, for example, and from Latin America and the Caribbean, Alejo Carpentier, Miguel Angel Asturias, Pablo Neruda, and Aimé Césaire. It should not be ignored, then, that it was in the give and take between the Old and New Worlds that New World modernism emerged. World War I, the rise of fascism, and the collapse of Europe in World War II helped to turn many writers back to their natal hemispheric origins in search of a national or regional alternative to Western modernity. The European context provided the impetus for New World critics to reconfigure the literary achievements of this emergent cosmopolitanism in the early decades of the century as significations of New World autonomy. When the modern novel treated New World themes, of course, this reconfiguration was a seemingly natural and straightforward process, but when the themes were overtly international, such as in Hemingway's *For Whom the Bell Tolls* about the Spanish Civil War, critics turned their attention to the formal achievements of the works. In those cases, it was the voice of the novel, not necessarily the geographical range of its themes, that determined the works' New World originality and modernism.

This was perhaps more true in the case of modernism's career in the United States than in Latin America. Chief among the distinctions between US and Latin American modernism is the fact that in the case of the US, critical reception was primarily interested in significations of national exceptionalism, whereas Latin American modernism saw itself primarily as a signification of transnationalism, albeit similarly self-conceived as exceptional (see Handley 2007). The formalism of the emergent Americanist critics helped to establish the belief in the exceptional nature of the US novel. Such an approach fashioned a literary genealogy of US modernism that understood it as descending exclusively from European precursors: James Joyce to William Faulkner, Virginia Woolf to Kate Chopin. The result is a transatlantic model of what Harold Bloom once famously described as an Anglo-American "anxiety of influence." The transatlantic anxieties of influence were far less worrisome for Latin American writers, and that partly had to do with an increasing awareness that a perhaps more threatening modernity existed to the north: that of the United States itself. Hence the story of Latin American modernism emerges as an expression of a collective spirit of a transnational region that stands over and against the United States as the most threatening manifestation of modernity. While Latin American writers of the early twentieth century were eventually seen to form a part of an emerging continental and transnational solidarity, the line that divided this community and the United States was clearly and unambiguously drawn.

The nationalist obsessions of early critics of US modernism notwithstanding, many of the writers of the early twentieth century were intent on resisting the call of Europe by discovering links of commonality with other American nations, a fact that suggests that perhaps axes of US modernity actually run in two directions: both East/West and North/South. This is certainly true of the writers of the Harlem Renaissance, such as Zora Neale Hurston and Langston Hughes, who sought reconnection with the larger African diaspora in the islands of the Caribbean. Southern writers who were not explicitly interested in the African diaspora, such as Charles Chesnutt, George Washington Cable, Kate Chopin, and William Faulkner, but who were concerned with racial relations, inevitably found their imaginations extending farther south beyond the nation's border. As Deborah Cohn (1999) has argued, it helped in their case that the Southern experience of modernity shared parallels with Latin America and the Caribbean because the US South had been similarly shaped by the history of slavery, the experience of civil conflict and military defeat, and by an awareness of anachronism, of having fallen out of time as kept by the drumbeat of Western cultural progress.

These parallels give reasons to doubt the exceptionality of the regional local colors of the United States. Such an axis opens the possibility that Chopin and Faulkner, for example, belong as much to the imaginary of a New World that extends south of the Gulf Coast as they do to a Euro-American literary trajectory, a crucible of sorts that alleviates the oedipal anxieties of US literature's transatlantic influence. In a time that saw the decline of European power and prestige and the rise of US imperialist activities in the Western hemisphere, it was important for Americanist critics that modern literature provide evidence that the US was not repeating the sins of the (European) father but was rather inaugurating a new chapter in Western history. Modern novelists, particularly those more willing to face the southward trajectory of modernity, might have begged to differ with this mission, but the construction of US literary history that resulted ensconced modern literature's ambivalence about American exceptionalism. While Americanists seem to have officially renounced the claims of exceptionalism, the persistence of the transatlantic literary history of the US modern novel tells a different story.

Understanding literary history as having crossed the Atlantic was one way of setting up an argument for "American" genealogical distinction vis-à-vis a literary parent. Despite the increasing traffic of literary influence across the Americas during the modern period, understanding New World literatures as having been shaped across an inter-American divide was of less interest. Even when they were written in response to one another across national boundaries, regionalist novels and the imagined community of onlookers they created seemed to offer a balm for the wounds of a community still striving to understand itself as such. As Carlos Alonso has argued regarding Latin American regionalism, this presents a paradox in which regionalist texts "propose to engage in an affirmation of cultural organicity, but through a discourse that has abandoned that presumed connectedness as a condition for its very existence" (Alonso 1990: 7). In other words, the very conditions of the uneven presence of modernity in the Americas has created an awareness of rupture, of a loss of an essence, that the literature seeks to breach, but the resultant expressions of essence rely on that rupture for the effect of a seemingly natural recovery. He asserts the paradox that "the essence of Latin American cultural production is the ever-renewed affirmation of having lost or abandoned an essence" (p. 15). He further explains that Latin American historical misfortune is not the result of Latin America's failed search for identity but rather of that which conditions Latin America's possibility:

> In this regard, Latin America's situation can be illuminated by comparing it to that of the United States. Born of modernity as well, the United States shared from the beginning the linguistic and historical difficulties attendant on the formulation of a cultural essence that has been identified in the case of Latin America. But in contrast to the latter, the ascendance of the United States to a position of historical hegemony has managed to invest with authority the myths of cultural identity that were generated by that country's intelligentsia. (Alonso 1990: 35–6)

The monomythic power of the so-called American Dream notwithstanding, awareness of an ironic slippage between US possibility and US reality would seem to be one of the most significant achievements of modern literature in the United States. We need only consider the work of such writers as Willa Cather, Katherine Anne Porter, Elizabeth Bishop, William Faulkner, and Zora Neale Hurston, to become aware of Alonso's simplification of US literature. Indeed, the myths of cultural identity that assured US ascendance had more to do with politically motivated readerly expectations and nonliterary narratives of the American story than with the aims of novelists and other artists. Alonso's critique of modernity in Latin America relies on a notion of categorical difference (which is one way, ironically given his argument, of imagining an essence) across the geopolitical boundaries in the Americas that does not correspond to the tale told by US modern literature. United States modernism exhibited many of the same contradictions Alonso highlights in Latin America, but because of its often exclusively intranational focus (especially in terms of its literary reception), US modern literature tended to be read as a signification of a merely local problem for which the nation was implicitly offered as the cure. That is to say, by ignoring the broader context of the Americas and its various transnational waves of diasporas from Africa, Asia, Europe and among the Americas themselves, US critics read local color as signifying national exceptionalism rather than for its echoes and parallels in a broader American hemisphere. Literature about New Orleans, for example, serves as a telling instance. Read in a broader New World context, modernism's attempted rescue of the local would appear more distinctly and self-consciously ironic.

Alonso makes nothing of the fact that Latin America's quest has historically involved a search for a broader transnational or continental entity from which distinct nations borrowed for their purposes. This belief in a shared New World identity facilitated the ascendance of Latin America's myths about itself, as the alternative space of modernity in the New World, characterized by interracial love, *mestizaje*, and hybridity. Central to this process was an almost universal exclusion of the United States from this hemispheric identity, a rhetoric that belied many Latin American writers' interest in drawing inspiration from such authors as Edgar Allan Poe, Walt Whitman, John Dos Passos, and of course William Faulkner. Even the most overtly nationalist programs in Latin America during the decades of modernism, such as that undertaken by Mexico's Minister of Education José Vasconcelos after the civil conflict of the Mexican Revolution, provided inspiration for countless writers and artists throughout Latin America who saw the achievements of the muralists, the composers, and novelists of Mexico as leading the way toward a more properly Latin American indigeneity. And this recovery of indigenous, African, and regional values, undertaken in the first half of the twentieth century throughout Latin America, sought independence not only from Europe but distinction from the growing threat of the United States and what was perceived to be its cultural essence: a utilitarian, xenophobic, Puritan and Anglo tradition. Such an image, though clearly evolved from the dominant self-image of US national culture (which, of course, was proposed in a kinder light), elided the regional qualities of the US South and the Southwest (consider George Washington Cable and Willa Cather respectively, for example) that were perhaps less distinct historically and culturally from Latin America than either US citizens or Latin Americans wanted to admit. In other words, if Randolph Bourne was correct in pointing to a US tendency toward negative protectiveness that ensconced the transnational character of most American experience, Latin America's transnational solidarity was limited by a similarly protective refusal to look north of the US geopolitical border for similar sites of countermemory to the march of modernity in the hemisphere.

And why this refusal? The United States's imperial growth and simultaneous racial struggles of the late nineteenth and early twentieth centuries provided a real threat to the survival of many of Latin America's cultures. However, the impatient rescue of these cultures was aided by a rhetorical and indispensable space of profoundly marked difference to the north. This difference has continually surfaced throughout the development of Latin Americanism. It was evident from the early articulations of Simón Bolívar, the writings of José Martí and Enrique Rodó at the conclusion of the nineteenth century, Alejo Carpentier's mid-century vision of the marvelous reality of Latin America, subsequent iterations of magical realism, and in Octavio Paz's (1985) argument regarding the differences between the United States and Mexico in the latter half of the century. This denial of commonality allowed Latin American cultural discourse to proceed on the basis of the problematic assumption that it could be the New World's categorical alternative to the Protestant North's legacies of racism, imperialism, and utilitarianism.

Cuba's voice of independence, José Martí, for example had insisted in the late nineteenth century that Cuba, and all of Latin America for that matter, must rise to the unique challenge of establishing a racial democracy in a way that would avoid the pitfalls of their northern neighbor. The US, according to Martí, had managed to establish democracy and champion equality on the basis, contradictorily, of an overt and often violent exclusion of Native and African Americans. Martí envisioned a Latin America founded on a respect for its deep indigenous past and radical racial equality. As laudable as his vision was, Martí never managed to articulate how this could happen without some backhanded exclusions of his own: Native Americans were not a significant portion of the Cuban population, and so his discussion of indigenous peoples generally relegated them to a past to be honored rather than a present population in need of full inclusion, a move that proved devastating to the millions of indigenous peoples in other Latin American nations where this rhetoric of Native-as-dead-ancestor was mimicked. Black Cubans were invited to be a part of the struggle for independence in extraordinary numbers, but ultimately Martí envisioned a society without races. After Martí's death and the establishment of Cuba's pseudo-independence, Martín Morúa Delgado, a mulatto Cuban novelist and senator, was inspired by Martí's raceless future and moved to outlaw political parties that had any racial basis. The law in effect squelched the continuing struggle for greater racial equality in Cuba (there is growing evidence that Cuba in the early decades of the twentieth century was not as different from the Jim Crow society of the US South as many have supposed) and cost some 5,000 lives of black Cubans in the race war of 1912 (see Ramos 1989, Guerra 2005, and Helg 1995). Cuba persists in concealing its ongoing struggles with racism by relying on a rhetorical stance in opposition to the racial shortcomings of the US, as do Brazil and other Latin American and Caribbean nations. This is not to suggest that there are no significant differences between the US and Latin America, racially, socially, or politically. Those differences are well known, but history demonstrates that categorical refusals to consider commonalities have often served to cloak local failures to eradicate racism.

A similar tendency to refuse any consideration of parallel experiences south of the US border has characterized racial discourse in the United States and with similar results. One of the most significant spaces of such denial is Haiti, where in 1804 a black and independent republic came into power after successfully overthrowing French colonial rule, thus forcing the United States as well as all other slave-owning nations to contemplate the possibility of such rebellions closer to home. It was especially disconcerting to US whites that this revolution had been fought under the banner of the ideals of the French Revolution – fraternity, equality, and liberty – that presumably echoed the most sacrosanct principles of US political philosophy. In order to continue to believe in its own Manifest Destiny, the US had not only to deny its own history of slavery but also the possibility of overturning slavery on the basis of such ideals. This was, of course, an impossible scenario, which is one reason why the Civil War was inevitable, but this denial of internal racial contradiction continued to inform US attitudes and diplomacy in the Caribbean and Latin America in its new-found hemispheric dominance at the dawn of the twentieth century. The US government isolated Haiti diplomatically from its independence until 1862 and occupied the island from 1915 to 1934. Hans Schmidt (1971) persuasively argues that US intervention in Haiti, and elsewhere in the Caribbean since 1898, was based on the precedent of the US's own internal struggles against alien races in the western and southern regions. It was not the adoption of the myths of the intelligentsia but rather this externalization of US internal contradictions that facilitated US political ascendance by providing a cleansed image of itself as a nation going about the business of promoting democracy.

The Caribbean had served as an imagined repository of the contradictions of US democracy and its practice of slavery ever since Thomas Jefferson and Abraham Lincoln had contemplated liberating the slaves and shipping them to the Caribbean. The Caribbean and Latin America were spaces of such profound imagined racial difference that it allowed the US to procrastinate its own reckoning with itself as a contradiction in terms. Such attitudes informed the Louisianan writer George Washington Cable's articulations of civil rights at the turn of the century. The worst legacy of slavery for Cable was miscegenation because it created a divergent and provincial cultural identity in the South. In his mind, if Southern whites could understand that the divisions between North and South and between the civil rights of blacks and whites were unnatural, regionalism *and* miscegenation would dissipate. In his famous "The Freedman's Case for Equity" he insists that if a clear line can be drawn between the freedoms of personal choice, which pertain so directly to marriage and family (and hence property) and the civil rights to which every citizen is entitled, the security of those rights will assure that the races do not mix and that family lines remain racially pure. He asserts that "the common enjoyment of equal civil rights never mixed two such races; it has always been some oppressive distinction between them that . . . has done it" (Cable 1890: 161). That is, the hierarchical legacies of colonialism have simply exacerbated the attractions between the races. Maintaining a "natural" separation of racial genealogies means that our "natural" repulsion toward racial mixing will reign and that Southern cultural expression will align itself with, rather than provincially diverge from, the Union.

The presence of people of mixed race, which he perceives to be threateningly prevalent across a racial border in the Caribbean and Latin America, signifies for Cable colonial oppression and lack of civilization. For this reason the South's only alternative to accepting its destiny as part of the Union is to be like Latin America. He urges that "when someone comes looking for Southrons, we can send them on to New Mexico, and say 'That is the New South. And make haste, friend, or they will push you on into South America, where we have reshipped the separate sort of books printed for the Southern market'" (Cable 1890: 48). In Latin America and the Caribbean, "Nationalization *by* fusion of bloods is the maxim of barbarous times and peoples. Nationalization *without* racial confusion is ours to profess and to procure . . . to make national unity without hybridity – the world has never seen it done as we have got to do it" (p. 130). Just as blacks and whites, civilization and barbarism, are "naturally" separate, Cable's "South" is naturally segregated from the Caribbean. This allows Cable to cast responsibility for the supposed barbarism of interracial mixing – and the real barbarism of slavery itself – within the US onto the lands beyond US borders. Cable's rhetoric concerning the barbarism of Latin America is, of course, not new to US cultural polemics. However, coming as it does in the last decades of the nineteenth century when the US begins to cast its imperialist eye towards the lands to the south, it is symptomatic of the globalization of plantation structures that would characterize the modern period in the wake of slavery. These symptoms of the plantation's globalization are both a product of US imperialism and the reason why the North, and US culture since the Civil War, has been blind to the truth of itself as the seat of imperial ambition. At no time was this more useful to a US self-image than in the first half of the twentieth century as the nation forged its self-image as the alternative to European imperialism and world defender of democracy.

The larger point here is that the imagined communities of the United States and of Latin America respectively have refused to consider how the greater Caribbean basin that includes the Gulf Coast of the US, the Caribbean coast of Mexico and Central America, and the northern reaches of Colombia, Venezuela, the Guyanas, and Surinam, shares the effects of a common history caused by the trauma of widespread slavery; indentured labor; transplantation of peoples, plants, and animals; and displacement and/or genocide of Native American populations. Even without the parallels created by the extraordinary international reach of the slave trade, other similarities connect the desert regions of Northern Mexico with the US Southwest and their overlapping mappings as outpost territories for aspiring New World neocolonial ambition. New World parallels need to be drawn not merely on the basis of neighboring geographies either. To cite just a few examples, Argentina modeled its relations with indigenous populations after the United States; Brazil's account of its three-part racial drama between Indians, subjects of the Africa diaspora, and European settlers deserves comparison to the work of William Faulkner; and the way Chile's southern frontier has figured so prominently in the national imagination has often been compared to the role of the Western frontier in US experience.

So what is the source of resistance to establishing transnational or even postnational comparative contexts for assessing the modern condition in the Americas? At its root, it is an intolerance for the ambiguity of being, an intolerance for circumstances that demand a simultaneous recognition of similarity and difference in the way that the past is remembered and passed on. The closer the neighbor and the more uncanny the similarities, the more threatening the prospect of recognizing the instability of the self. It is as if the self is unmade unless it can find reason for offense and differentiation in the political struggle over threatened memories that modernity has created. This is also an intolerance for the very ambiguity of "context," upon which any comparative study of "texts" must rely.[2] This ambiguity means that the claims of the self or of the collective community are never stable, of course, but it also means that in articulations of this ambiguity, we must tolerate the uneven and perhaps delayed political impact of critical assessment. Such anyway seems to be the patience of literature itself, representing the anxieties and their consequences without definitive ideological pronouncement of their ultimate meaning.

Given the way we continue to construct the story of US literature along national geopolitical borders, the modern novel, especially in the decades following the Spanish American War of 1898, showed particular interest in the larger scope of the Western hemisphere. For many writers – including, of course, major figures of the Harlem Renaissance such as Zora Neale Hurston, whose extensive anthropological work in the Caribbean inspired her fiction, Hemingway's unique relationship to Cuba, Katherine Anne Porter's years spent witnessing the Mexican Revolution of 1910, Faulkner's diplomatic tour of Latin America – the broader context of the Americas was arguably the fertile inter-American soil that inspired many of their most significant literary achievements. Amy Kaplan (2005) has urged a reading of US literature that considers the ways in which US international experience shaped the nation's domestic and national imagination, even when the literature is not linked by overt themes to US international imperialist projects. For example, Mark Twain's sharp critique of American imperialism or Charles Chesnutt's approbation of US expansion into Latin America cannot be dissociated from how their novels imagined racial relations.

The questions of national borders and a national imaginary are in dialectical relationship to the international, to be sure, but we must be careful not to reify the very boundaries between nations that such an approach is presumably aimed at breaking down. This can happen when we remain entrenched in a refusal to consider New World comparisons, which is another way of insisting that there is a clear line drawn between domestic and foreign, native and exotic. Such refusals have traditionally come from those convinced of US exceptionalism, as should be obvious, but more recently they have come from those who are convinced that such gestures will categorically result in a new and improved US hemispheric imperial dominance in the twenty-first century, a remapping of the one-time Good Neighbor Policy of Roosevelt on the brink of the Cold War. While this is no doubt a genuine risk, it would also seem to hamper the self-questioning that self-understanding requires if, as students of US literature, we refused to consider the possibility of shared commonalities with neighboring cultures. This would be like refusing to greet one's neighbor for fear of appearing self-absorbed.

If as readers of US literature we can at least suspend disbelief in the existence of historical parallels with other nations, commonly shared experiences, and experiences of individuals who have lived under diaspora in a broader transnational space, we might begin to break down the inflexible and impermeable boundaries of what we believe constitutes "American" experience and "American" literature. This is not to say that we should privilege fiction that treats the international cosmopolitan over the rural farmer as the exclusive means to bring us closer to an understanding of national, racial, religious, or regional communities. It simply means that failing to

consider possible parallels makes it more likely that we will overestimate the exceptionalism of local characteristics. Readings of American literature must be circum-
spect about simultaneous experiences elsewhere in neighboring geographical spaces
so that we can at least provide ourselves with reasons to suspect parallels that will
help to destabilize the rigidity of what we are aiming to call "American" literature.
And this won't have to be accomplished merely on the basis of imagining a dialectical
relationship between the so-deemed "other" spaces outside of US geopolitical borders,
as Kaplan's model implies, but will rather begin to disrupt the fixity of identities
both within and without particular geographical spaces.

There is a growing body of comparative criticism of modernity and modernism in
particular that stretches across national borders in the Americas, and this work has
done much to destabilize not only the coherence of national borders but of disciplines
and area studies.[3] The upshot of this criticism is that the binary between the dangers
of myopia and the dangers of facile transnationalism is fed by a dependence on the
persistence of the intact concept of nationalism itself, either as something worth
defending or something in need of critique. What is required is a more direct confrontation with the parallels of experience in the Americas informed by an awareness
of the persistence of amnesia that those experiences have facilitated. In other words,
the question of nationalism is pushed into the background and a new poetics of
reading emerges that worries less about diagnosing the contours and ills of the body
politic and stresses more the role our reading practices play in creating imagined
communities worth caring about and sustaining.

There are at least three historical reasons why it is true to claim, as Derek Walcott
has, that "amnesia is the true history of the New World" and why, therefore, this
poetics of reading comes to the fore as our primary responsibility as critics of modernity (Walcott 1998: 39). The first is the New World fact of widespread diaspora,
the violent transplantation and juxtaposition of peoples throughout the hemisphere.
The majority of the protagonists of regionalist literatures are themselves thrust into
their physical environments by means of the forces of modernity, which in the
Americas have resulted in an extraordinary spreading of peoples, voluntarily or violently moved, from Africa, Europe, and Asia. In the New World, assessing these
forces must begin with its history of slavery, since the subjects slavery brought to
the New World – African, of course, as well as the European settlers who came in
the wake of slavery's financial success or those who, along with millions of Asians,
came in the wake of slavery's collapse – were brought simultaneously to what already
were or would become distinct nations in the New World. Slavery's international
significance in the Americas has been neglected in our assessment of literature
throughout the New World. Amazingly, this is despite the fact that slavery "played
a major role in the discovery and economic exploitation" of the Americas (Solow
1987: 717); despite nearly four hundred years of its history stretching from the
Caribbean islands to Brazil and to the Caribbean coasts of South, Central, and North
America; despite the capture and scattering of an estimated 12 million Africans from
West African shores, the death of another estimated nine to ten million in the

Middle Passage, the death of countless others shortly after arrival in the New World, and a total slave population that reached six million in the 1850s; despite the centrality of slavery in international trade, the growth of industrialization and the struggle for empire involving six European nations; despite the obvious impact of the plantation system on the diaspora of European, African, and Asian peoples throughout the Americas; despite the fact that the slave trade "determined the living and dying patterns of the black communities that developed in the New World . . . and their ultimate cultural adaptation to the new American environment" (Klein 1978: xix); despite the impact of the slave trade on central features of modernity, including nationalism, the emergence of racialist conceptions of identity, of consumer culture, market economies, and others.

If it is true that by 1888, when Brazil abolished it, slavery was no longer legally practiced anywhere in the Americas, the legacies of slavery nevertheless predominated over the course of the next century. And it is arguably as soon as the late nineteenth and certainly by the early twentieth century that writers from the US, the Caribbean, Brazil, and other places where the plantation system thrived began to take stock of these legacies. It is no longer sufficient or fully fruitful to consider manifestations of this interest in, say, the Harlem Renaissance, without understanding the simultaneous emergence in the same decades of an interest in the African diaspora among black writers from the Caribbean and Latin America, many of whom had contact with the leading figures in Harlem (not to mention the fact that many Harlem writers, such as Claude McKay, were themselves of Caribbean descent). The rediscovery and re-evaluation of black diasporic experience in the New World was far from a nationalist project or relevant merely within the context of national critical discourse: manifestations of black themes were seen in Brazil, Venezuela, Colombia, Paraguay, the Caribbean islands, Central America, among others during the modern period, as of course they were in Northern US cities such as Harlem, following the migration to the North after slavery, and in the US South as well. The New World's history of slavery and postslavery necessitates that the assessment of the local demands a transnational perspective, even if only by implication or indirection.

A second important factor was Native American genocide and displacement, beginning with the horrific destruction of Native Americans in the wake of the conquest that left tens of millions dead, from Patagonia to Nova Scotia, as a result of the spread of disease and their violent mistreatment at the hands of European settlers. There is also the later phenomenon of forced relocation of tribes, the dispossession of their lands, and the threat to the survival of their cultures. In the context of Euro-American expansion, the indigenous presence and/or absence informs the meaning of virtually any act of imagining a New World home. Native Americans, of course, have never conceived of their communities in terms of contemporary geopolitical borders in the Americas, and this fact continues to be a source of tension for many nations in the Americas. Historically this is most compelling for my purposes here in the context of the region known as the Southwest, which is also a northwest to what was once Mexico, and before that New Spain and before that the Aztec empire. It is an area, in other words, that requires only a minimal scratch on the surface before overlapping histories make their competing claims on the root story of the land. This suggests that a national imaginary fed by its local color does so by means of deferment and erasure of a transnational, or perhaps more properly said, extranational presence within.

Indigenism flourished as a literary movement from the 1920s to the 1940s throughout Latin America, most significantly in Mexico, Central America, and in the Andean region. It was a movement characterized simultaneously by sympathy for the plight of indigenous peoples and by an attempt to tame the threats to nationalism that they posed. These are the contradictions of Latin American modernism described by Alonso, if not alone for the fact that the majority of the authors were not indigenous. It is undeniable that indigenous themes are much more prevalent in Latin American novels than in those of the US during this period, and that nations such as Mexico, Ecuador, Bolivia, and Peru could not resort to a policy of expulsion and the creation of reservations, as did the US, because of the challenge posed by large and concentrated numbers of indigenous people within the very metropolitan areas of political and cultural hegemony. Octavio Paz notes that for this reason Mexican memory is simultaneously indigenous *and* Spanish and that its particular struggles have emanated from its failure to reconcile these two parent stocks. He explains that in the US memory has always been European, that Native American experience has been expelled from the national imaginary (as Native Americans were expelled from their lands) and therefore has never played a significant role in the forging of the nation's identity. His account is compelling, but it is erroneous to imply that simply because of these broad differences between native populations in the US and Mexico, Native American experience is therefore irrelevant to the national imaginary of the United States. We must assume otherwise if for no other reason than because official memory forged modern nationalisms on the basis of the erasure of a native presence. If we would now revise US literary anthologies to include a growing list of Native American writers who stand ambiguously poised within and without US nationality, why are they not more aggressively compared to indigenous literatures elsewhere in the hemisphere?

It is a mistake to assume that the contradictions of indigenism throughout Latin America — nationalist projects of incorporation on the basis of paternalism and continued inequality — bear no resemblance to US experience. Indeed, Paz's description of the Mexican psyche, when highlighted against the backdrop of the broader North American context would seem to suggest the need to consider the ways in which US official identity was forged by means of a merely paternalistic recognition of the relevance of Native American experience. Certainly the early twentieth-century social criticisms of Willa Cather, Zitkala-Sa, Mourning Dove, Mary Austin, Charles Eastman, and even the overt sentimentality of Zane Grey would seem to demand our attention in this regard. If the majority of US writers have been "playing in the dark," as Toni Morrison (1992) provocatively once suggested in relationship to black/white racial difference, they have also been able to imagine their relationship to land, to home, and to community on the basis of an erasure of Native American presence. There is scarcely any work from the modern period that would not reveal some new insights by being placed in this New World context of indigenous experience.

A third facet of New World experience that must be applied to our understanding of the modern novel is that of environmental degradation. What is not frequently recognized is that lands suffered the same indignities as the "folk" in regional novels throughout the Americas. Wherever human populations spread and transplanted, so too did flora and fauna foreign to the Americas (it might serve to be reminded that diaspora literally refers to the spreading of seeds). Land itself, then, in most reaches of the New World where modernity has arrived, bears scars, vegetation, and animal life that all attest to its fundamentally changed character. While ecology tells the story of the land's changes, it also connects the local to a broader transnational geography; slavery traveled wherever the environment shared the needed climatic and environmental conditions for its various plantation products, and its effects on those environments was similarly devastating, facilitating what might be considered a kind of kinship among various environmental victims.

And yet these lands were invoked, as much as were the "folk," as symbols emptied of their diasporic and tragic history, to serve as nationalistic countermemories to European colonial dominance. This tended to obscure the staggering impact that the European arrival had on local ecologies throughout the hemisphere. The Old World settler acted as "a sort of botanical Midas changing the flora with his touch" because of the seeds borne intentionally or not along the routes of trade and migration (Crosby 1986: 160). Worse, animal husbandry of the Old World was the fertile ground for such devastating diseases as smallpox, the single most significant killer of indigenous populations from pole to pole in the Western hemisphere. But in addition to these broader phenomena, few environments in the world have been as drastically changed in such short order as were the lands affected by the plantation system. The plantation brought unprecedented levels of deforestation, soil erosion, crop and human disease, and radical transformation of flora and fauna. To understand the significance of region, particularly plantation regions, within the larger global picture, we can scarcely afford to focus myopically on human transplantation, let alone within a specific geopolitical space, and ignore the "biogeographical realities that underlay" and facilitated the New World's transition into modernity (Crosby 1986: 196).

Today what appear to us to be native biota often cover an indigenous environmental history hidden from immediate view. Despite the fact that New World biotic knowledge in the eighteenth century and beyond helped to nurture the growing awareness of national consciousness and yearnings for political autonomy and racial exceptionalism, the environmental histories within specific geopolitical borders were much more widely shared than the various mythologies of nationalism allowed (Dunlap 1999: 48). Such historical parallels and shared colonial legacies have paradoxically meant that the closer one observes the peculiar qualities of the local landscape, whether it be kudzu, the breadfruit, peach, or eucalyptus tree, the more one is drawn outward beyond the bounds of the nation or region and into an intricate web of human and natural historical parallels. As a result, frontiers between nations and regions, as well as the very dichotomy between natural and human histories, break down as useful distinctions.

Given the immeasurable shock of slavery's violence; Native American genocide and displacement; settlement from abroad; the fragmentation and mixing of cultures, languages, and beliefs on new soil; as well as the ongoing onslaught of environmental change that has accompanied the diaspora of peoples, understanding culture in the New World must begin with a reckoning of the reality of amnesia. This means, of course, that the countermemories provided by New World novels must be read as rhetorical performances that stand in relation to a shared but untraceable transnational history. One generalization made about the distinction between the US and Canada and their southern neighbors is that the northern version of New World culture is generally assumed to represent the Hegelian continuity of Western civilization in the Americas, whereas in the Caribbean and in Latin America we see a greater discontinuity and unpredictability, due largely to a more aggressive pattern of interracial marriage and the resultant transculturation and creolization of culture. Hegel, in fact, predicated his view of New World history on this distinction between patterns of racial mixing in Latin America and the US. There are, of course, a variety of historical factors that explain these differences, including the contrasting Protestant and Catholic heritages of the two regions and the differences they have created in social and economic realities; the more intensive reliance on the slave trade in the Caribbean and in Brazil; the more extensive and densely populated indigenous areas of Latin America; and so forth. But we have to be careful about the implications of these differences. Not all of American culture is characterized by a Protestant ethos, particularly when we consider the Spanish legacies in the Deep South and the Southwest and the Protestants' own history of miscegenation in the US South which extends back into the eighteenth century. Indigenous populations may not have been as dense as in areas of Mexico or the Andes, but they were highly relevant to social and political formations in early US history, and their absence or the denial of their relevance must not be ignored. Sugar plantations did not prove economically or environmentally viable in the US South, but arguments about the comparative violence of slavery in the US and elsewhere in the Americas have invoked more nationalist than rationalist rhetoric. The threat of amnesia, of discontinuity of family, belief, language, and custom, for slaves and their descendants was formidable regardless of particular national context. Even environmental differences between temperate and tropical zones can be used to overstate essential distinctions and ignore the common problems of the disappearance of native biota, a refusal on the part of Euro-American settlers to conform to local ecological reality, and the colonialism of transplanted seeds. Hurricanes Katrina and Rita only serve to remind us that nature ignores national borders and that clear lines of demarcation between the US and its southern neighbors are falsifications of a lived reality.

Edouard Glissant, a Caribbean author well acquainted with the Caribbean and the US, is a provocative and exemplary practitioner of a comparative poetics that I think tackles the reasons the Americas must be seen as sharing a history, as well as the reasons for this history's elusiveness. In other words, he provides a poetics of reading that enables the work of criticism to assess New World novels in a broader trans-national context while simultaneously recognizing the very ambiguity of the delinea-tions of context itself. In his essays, he argues that cultural differences cannot be explained by different histories alone; he insists that the Americas share a "concealed parallel in histories" and that this subterranean and submarine parallel is concealed precisely by each culture's approach to the New World past (Glissant 1989: 60). What has distinguished the Caribbean from the US is its willingness to embrace the ironies of its fragmentation and to reckon with the reality of amnesia by proceeding to forge continuity of community by means of a paradoxical "series of forgettings" (Glissant 1995: 273). That is, Caribbean identity is created self-consciously and poetically because it understands itself as a composite culture that does not have a single root story of origins; continuity can only be achieved on the basis of piecing together discontinuous fragments. Stories of origins cannot supply the myth of an indivisible and pure unity, so literary representations of "local color" are not read as signs of a root identity but rather as metonymic parts of a greater whole that is no longer accessible. Instead of uncanny similarities in neighboring nations causing anxieties that would push a national psyche into a state of denial about the compara-tive and ambiguous context in which it finds itself, the concealed parallels become justifications for the formation of a cross-cultural imagination that is synchronic, relational, and produced by the reader's imagination. This is because the awareness of partiality and fragmentation points the mind not back in time but across New World spaces in search of relations instead of local essences. Glissant reads himself and Caribbean reality into the regionalism of William Faulkner, for example, seeing Faulkner's opaque representations of black life in the South simultaneously as evidence of Faulkner's playing in the dark and as evidence of a parallel in New World histories forged by modernity that cannot be contained by a US literary imagination.

Glissant sees Faulkner's fiction as depicting the South as a manifestation of an enigmatic US American refusal to accept itself as a composite society. Composite cultures find themselves having to adopt myths from the fragments of atavistic cultures that have survived the violence of history. Consequently, composite cultures make claims to place, to legitimacy, and to originality that are more tentative, ironic, and self-conflicted. Their stories are open-ended and express, as he argues Faulkner's works do, a "suspension of identity" in their refusal to accept facile closure or restoration of social wholeness. They are cultures whose writers, like Faulkner, "are situated on the frontier, on the border between two apparent or actual possibilities" (Glissant 1998: 4). The danger is when a composite culture, such as the US, denies its composite nature and tries instead to stake its claim to legitimacy through filiation (p. 115). The result is what Faulkner saw as an unresolved suffering caused by the "torments of withdrawal into self and the damned solitude of a refusal that does not have to speak its name" (p. 31). Faulkner's fiction would seem to suggest that the US refusal to acknowledge this problem has fueled its expansion into southern territories (and by implication other territories where its imperialism has traveled) with which it then denies kinship. Reading modern novels in this light exposes US imperial self-fashioning and the ironies of US New World history that it ignores.

Faulkner, in other words, offers one reason for embracing what has already characterized Caribbean experience: that is, the "unpredictability [of creolization] that terrifies those who refuse the very idea, if not the temptation, to mix, flow together, and share" (Glissant 1998: 30). Glissant does not argue that there is anything exceptional about Faulkner's vision, since it already has parallels with a much longer history in the region (and much of Glissant's philosophy expressed in this book has already been well developed in his own Caribbean experience prior to his approach to Faulkner's fiction); his aim rather is to read the US South from an even deeper south and thus disrupt the nationalist and imperial vectors that have isolated regions of the US and elided their relevance to diasporic experience in the Americas. Significantly, this does not come at the cost of dismissing Faulkner for his limitations. Such readings provide a broader textual unconscious that informs a variety of creative, even if humanly and culturally limited, minds.

Placing modern novels in a New World context, then, means reading literature of region as a manifestation of a fragmented whole in a particular place and time. Literature as metonymy rather than metaphor of community has important advantages. It means that while we recognize the presence of a larger whole, we can only imagine its contours and cannot pretend to be able to subsume it. Identity remains potentially unstable and open to change by means of further iterations. Readers are thus induced to seek additional representations of identity from others and from elsewhere and to see other stories alongside their own as manifestations of a concealed parallel. United States stories do not present a depiction of origins but rather a picture of a possible relation to other Americans that can only be imagined by a poetics of reading. Reading, in other words, is the foundational moment of world-making, of building culture, which means all texts stand unstably in the interstitial moment before their next reading, their next iteration within new contexts, new worlds.

In our understandable hunger over the past several decades for stories of new identities that would disrupt the monomythic claims of an American sameness, we have often succumbed to the temptation of elevating literature to the status of documentary historiography, when it would be wiser to do the reverse: to poeticize historiography as just one among many rhetorical representations of the relationship between self and place in the Americas. It would seem to be one of the great aims of New World novels to thematize the literary imagination as archival countermemory to the various powers of knowledge production that have sought to contain or obliterate memory. Because it poses itself in opposition to history, New World fiction would appear to run the risk of illegitimacy, but that is only if we assume that historiography is somehow fully exempted from a similar opposition to history. Fiction's truths cannot be documented or verified, and in a world discourse so dominated by an epistemology of scientific certitude, we might look foolish holding up novels as mere imagination. Understanding nations, and particularly regions within nations, as shaped by the forces of diaspora indeed opens us to literature's force as a countermemory, as a means of recovering the shape of communities disrupted by modernity. This is not so much in the interest of constructing a new national family, however, but in the interest of reckoning with modernity's merciless deconstruction of family bonds. The point here is that we must tolerate the ironies and incompletion of our task to recover historical knowledge of what links the Americas, even if we cannot accept the stated reasons for New World nations to remain apart.

NOTES

1   I am in agreement here with Ramos (1989), Pollard (2004), Madureira (2005), Dash (1998) and others who have insisted on the need to understand New World modernisms as manifestations of a kind of New World postcoloniality. They are, in the words of Madureira, attempts to articulate "an incipient 'counter-discourse' of modernity" at the same time that they recognize the fact that the West is not a facile, monolithic entity to be resisted but is instead inherently contradicted by the "heteroglossic dimension of metropolitan discourses" (Madureira 2005: 215, 5).

2   Madureira argues that Derrida provides an important theoretical articulation of this problem of context that is useful when considering comparative modernisms in a New World context. Derrida's notion that every sign "carries with it a force of breaking with its context" means for Madureira that "the presuppositions underwriting a number of influential readings of nonwestern modernisms ought to be submitted to a thoroughgoing reevaluation" (Madureira 2005: 1–2). As a result, our understanding of the more commonly recognized metropolitan or transatlantic forms of modernism require similar re-evaluation.

3   What began with the work of a small number of scholars such as Lois Parkinson Zamora, Djelal Kadir, Earl Fitz, Vera Kutzinski, Doris Sommer, and others, has resulted today in an astonishing growth in bibliography. The academic framework of such organizations as the American Comparative Literature Association and the International American Studies Association have provided vital forums for the kind of inter-American work that seems now to be widespread. A new generation of scholars has grown the work exponentially. To name a few more recent cases, the last few years have seen the publication of Luis Madureira's study of *Cannibal Modernities*; Charles Pollard's *New World Modernisms*; Anita Patterson's *Race, American Literature and Transnational Modernisms*; Valerie Loichot's study of the plantation in the French Caribbean and the US, *Orphan Narratives*; Jessica Adams's edited volume (with Michael Bibler and Cécile Accilien) *Just Below South* and her critique of the southern plantation, *Wounds of Returning*; Monika Kaup and Debra Rosenthal's *Mixing Race, Mixing Culture*, which attacks its subject with diverse and challenging breadth across the Americas; Alexandra Isfahani-Hammond's edited volume, *The Masters and the Slaves*, which extends

Brazilian racial discourse into plantation cultures to the north; Silvio Torres-Saillant's sustained critique of Caribbean intellectual history, US ethnic formation, and the ambiguous case of the Dominican Republic; and Caroline F. Levander and Robert S. Levine's *Hemispheric American Studies*, a volume of ambitious and interdisciplinary explorations shaped by broad geographical contextualization. My own work in *Postslavery Literatures in the Americas* and *New World Poetics* are similarly aimed at furthering these discussions.

References and Further Reading

Adams, Jessica. (2007). *Wounds of Returning: Race, Memory, and Property on the Postslavery Plantation*. Chapel Hill: University of North Carolina Press.

Adams, Jessica, Michael P. Bibler, and Cécile Accilien (eds). (2007). *Just Below South: Performing Intercultures in the Caribbean and the Southern United States*. Charlottesville: University of Virginia Press.

Alonso, Carlos J. (1990). *The Spanish American Regional Novel: Modernity and Autochthony*. New York: Cambridge University Press.

Cable, George Washington. (1890). *The Negro Question*. New York: Scribner's.

Cohn, Deborah. (1999). *History and Memory in the Two Souths: Recent Southern and Spanish American Fiction*. Nashville, TN: Vanderbilt University Press.

Crosby, Alfred. (1986). *Ecological Imperialism: The Biological Expansion of Europe, 900–1900*. Cambridge, UK: Cambridge University Press.

Dash, J. Michael. (1998). *The Other America: Caribbean Literature in a New World Context*. Charlottesville: University of Virginia Press.

Dunlap, Thomas. (1999). *Nature and the English Diaspora: Environment and History in the United States, Canada, Australia, and New Zealand*. New York: Cambridge University Press.

Glissant, Edouard. (1989). *Caribbean Discourse: Selected Essays*, trans. J. Michael Dash. Charlottesville: University of Virginia Press.

Glissant, Edouard. (1995). Creolization in the making of the Americas. In Vera Lawrence Hyatt and Rex Nettleford (eds), *Race, Discourse, and the Origin of the Americas: A New World View* (pp. 268–75). Washington, DC: Smithsonian Institution Press.

Glissant, Edouard. (1998). *Faulkner, Mississippi*, trans. Barbara Lewis and Thomas C. Spear. New York: Farrar, Straus, and Giroux.

Guerra, Lillian. (2005). *The Myth of José Martí: Conflicting Nationalisms in Early Twentieth-Century Cuba*. Chapel Hill: University of North Carolina Press.

Handley, George B. (2007). *New World Poetics: Nature and the Adamic Imagination of Whitman, Neruda, and Walcott*. Athens: University of Georgia Press.

Handley, George B. (2000). *Postslavery Literatures in the Americas: Family Portraits in Black and White*. Charlottesville: University of Virginia Press.

Helg, Aline. (1995). *Our Rightful Share: The Afro-Cuban Struggle for Equality, 1886–1912*. Chapel Hill: University of North Carolina Press.

Isfahani-Hammond, Alexandra (ed.). (2005). *The Masters and the Slaves: Plantation Relations and Mestizaje in American Imaginaries*. New York: Palgrave.

Kaplan, Amy. (2005). *The Anarchy of Empire in the Making of U.S. Culture*. Cambridge, MA: Harvard University Press.

Kaup, Monika and Debra Rosenthal (eds) (2002). *Mixing Race, Mixing Culture: Inter-American Literary Dialogues*. Austin: University of Texas Press.

Klein, Herbert S. (1978). *The Middle Passage: Comparative Studies in the Atlantic Slave Trade*. Princeton, NJ: Princeton University Press.

Levander, Caroline F. and Robert S. Levine (eds). (2008). *Hemispheric American Studies*. New Brunswick, NJ: Rutgers University Press.

Loichot, Valerie. (2007). *Orphan Narratives: The Postplantation Literature of Faulkner, Glissant, Morrison, and Perse*. Charlottesville: University of Virginia Press.

Madureira, Luís. (2005). *Cannibal Modernities. Postcoloniality and the Avant-Garde in Caribbean and Brazilian Literature*. Charlottesville: University of Virginia Press.

Morrison, Toni. (1992). *Playing in the Dark; Whiteness and the Literary Imagination.* New York: Vintage Books.

Patterson, Anita. (2008). *Race, American Literature and Transnational Modernisms.* New York: Cambridge University Press.

Paz, Octavio. (1985). Mexico and the United States. In *The Labyrinth of Solitude: Life and Thought in Mexico,* trans. Lysander Kemp, Yara Milos, and Rachel Philips Belash (pp. 357–76). New York: Grave.

Pollard, Charles W. (2004). *New World Modernisms: T. S. Eliot, Derek Walcott, and Kamau Brathwaite.* Charlottesville: University of Virginia Press.

Ramos, Julio. (1989). *Desencuentros de la modernidad en America Latina: literatura y política en el siglo XIX.* Mexico: Fondo de Cultura Economica.

Schmidt, Hans. (1971). *The United States Occupation of Haiti 1915–1934.* New Brunswick, NJ: Rutgers University Press.

Solow, Barbara. (1987). Capitalism and slavery in the exceedingly long run. *Journal of Interdisciplinary History* 17, 4: 711–37.

Torres-Saillant, Silvio. (1998). *The Dominican Americans.* New York: Greenwood Press.

Torres-Saillant, Silvio. (2005). *An Intellectual History of the Caribbean.* New York: Palgrave Macmillan.

Walcott, Derek. (1998). *What the Twilight Says: Essays.* New York: Farrar, Straus, and Giroux.

28

Reheated Figures: Five Ways of Looking at Leftovers

Jani Scandura

The so-called "modern" novel appears to me to be a garbage-pail or ash-can which contains every cast-off remnant of living: old cloths, broken crockery, back numbers, stale food and decaying fish. (Oliver Gogarty, Rolling Down the Lea*)*

At the end of my time, when I die, I don't want to leave any leftovers. And I don't want to be a leftover. I was watching TV this week and I saw a lady go into a ray machine and disappear. That was wonderful, because matter is energy and she just dispersed. (Andy Warhol, The Philosophy of Andy Warhol (From A to B and Back Again)*)*

Thought waits to be woken one day by the memory of what has been missed. (Theodor Adorno, Minima Moralia*)*

No. 1: Remains

There is a passage in Joy Kogawa's 1981 novel, *Obasan*, that I can never shake. Naomi, a Japanese-Canadian Sansei (third-generation) who is coming to terms with her childhood memories of forced relocation from British Columbia and the unexplained loss of her mother during World War II, describes a visit with Obasan, the woman who raised her:

> Everyone someday dies, she [Obasan] is saying with a sigh as she clears the table. She takes half a piece of leftover toast and puts it away in a square plastic container. The refrigerator is packed with boxes of food bits, a slice of celery, a square of spinach, half a hard-boiled egg. She orchestrates each remainder of a previous dinner into the dinner to come, making each meal like every meal, an unfinished symphony. Our Lady of the Leftovers. There are some indescribable items in the dark recesses of the fridge that never see the light of day. But you realize when you open the door that they're there, lurking, too old for mold and past putrefaction.
> Some memories, too, might better be forgotten. (Kogawa 1981: 54)

The novel reminds us over and over again that even apparently vanquished memories are never entirely gone, they leave a reminder/remainder, something irrevocably transformed lurking in the dark. For Obasan, and within *Obasan*, the leftover serves as a kind of culinary anadiplosis, a repeated phrase that links one sentence to the next, literalizing the conjunction inherent in Mary Douglas's suggestion that the "meaning of a meal carries something of the meaning of the other meals" (Douglas 1997: 44). Each eating event becomes simultaneously retrospective and prospective, a temporal ligature between past and future.

Certainly, the novel's attention to leftovers alludes to its author's reliance on historical remains: Kogawa inserted slightly edited versions of the wartime letters and diaries of Muriel Kitagawa and other Japanese Canadians, which she had culled from the Canadian National Archives (see Lo 2001: 186 and Kitigawa 1985). Moreover, at first glance, the figurative work of Obasan's leftovers might even be said to perform what Marianne Hirsch calls postmemory, or a second-generational response to trauma (Hirsch 1997; see also Goldman 2005, Peterson 2001, Wong 1993, Cheung 1993). Descendants of victims of the Holocaust, Hirsch argues, use "leftovers" – old family photos of the dead, for instance – to simultaneously "affirm the past's existence and . . . signal its unbridgeable distance" (Hirsch 1997: 23). In *Obasan*, such "leftovers" do not solely take the form of photographs – although there are plenty of these – but letters hidden "in [a] gray cardboard folder" that describe the catastrophic aftermath of Nagasaki following the A-bomb attack and Grandma Kato's horrific encounter with Naomi's mother, her daughter, who was grotesquely disfigured as a result of the bombing (Kogawa: 281). For Naomi, the photos she saw as a child are poor substitutes for these letters, written in Japanese, and which she cannot read. She whispers to her dead mother after hearing the contents of the letters as an adult, "Obasan and Uncle hear your request [to not tell]. They give me no words from you. They hand me old photographs" (Kogawa 1981: 291).

As both a Canadian national narrative and a narrative of Japanese modernity, then, *Obasan* might indeed be said to perform some of the work of postmemory. It is one of the most popular Canadian novels of the twentieth century and is considered to have played a crucial role in the Japanese-Canadian redress movement, which was settled by the Canadian government in 1988 (Davidson 1994). Yet one cannot properly name Obasan's orchestral use of leftovers by that term. Her response is not second-generational. (Obasan is an Issei, a first-generation immigrant.) Strictly speaking, in fact, Obasan's response is not familial at all. Obasan means "Aunt," but it is also a universal honorific for older women that does not necessitate blood connection. Obasan's parentage of Naomi and her brother Stephen is, rather, situational: "When [Obasan] came to Canada, she worked as a music teacher and became close friends with Grandma Nakane," Naomi, the narrator, explains; eventually, Ayako – Obasan – marries Naomi's father's half brother (Kogawa 1981: 22). In September 1941, Naomi's mother and grandmother return to Japan to aid Naomi's great-grandmother, who is ill, and are unable to return to Canada after the Japanese attack on Pearl Harbor three months later. As a result of the Canadian War Measure Act, Naomi's father and

Uncle Isamu (Sam), are sent to a work camp, where Naomi's father dies from tuberculosis. Obasan is the only parent-figure left. With other Japanese Canadians, she, Naomi, and Stephen are forced to move from Vancouver to Slocan, a refurbished ghost town in British Columbia. Following the war, the three, rejoined by Uncle Isamu, are again "relocated" by the Canadian government to a beet farm on the Canadian plains. While Obasan's reminder of the ubiquitous nature of death ("everyone someday dies") refers to the traumatic experience of the impact of massive death on those who lived through the bombing of Nagasaki and whose friends and family perished there or in Hiroshima, they refer as well to Obasan's more quotidian (if not untraumatic) losses: her husband Isamu's death in old age at the beginning of the novel and the two stillborn babies she had in her youth, the first, a son, strangled by his "umbilical cord" (p. 22).

Where there is loss, there is the leftover. Where there is newness – New Worlds even – leftovers linger as well. Three decades ago, Robert Martin Adams observed that when "Joyce, Eliot, and Pound . . . set about creating a literature of modernism, [they] unanimously turned" to leftovers, "to a texture, if not a structure, of tags, allusions, quotations, misquotations, and phrases at second hand" (Adams 1976: 60). Leftovers are commonplace tropes in American modernist writing, particularly in that shaped by a multilingual immigrant experience. "Through his language, the [immigrant] writer is bound to the past," observed Isaac Bashevis Singer in 1943 of American Yiddish writers. But once in America, the writer who uses an "Old World" language "must, in a literary sense, dine on leftovers; only food prepared in the old world can nourish him in the new" (Singer 1989: 9, cited in Guzlowski 2001). For Asian Americans, Obasan's leftovers take on a specificity, according to Sau-ling Cynthia Wong, who reads the image of "stone bread" in *Obasan* "alongside the many other images of unpalatable food and strenuous eating found in Asian American literary works" in order to assume "the ethnic group-specific meaning of Necessity" (Wong 1993: 24).

Yet Obasan's respect for leftovers is not solely a by-product of immigrant necessity, but alludes to the more abstract Shinto belief in the sacred nature of natural objects no matter how lowly. The Japanese term for leftover, *nokorimono* (残り物), carries with it the sacred and embodied significance of "things left behind." As young children brought up in Obasan's Japan would know, to throw away leftovers or leave them on your plate is *mottainai* (勿体無い), an expression from Buddhism that means something like, "a regrettable situation in which something is wasted without its value being fully utilized" (Asaba 2001). Until recently, when the expression was adopted by environmental movements, *mottainai* was mostly recognized as the admonishment a mother (or, more likely, grandmother) might use to children to induce them to finish all the food on their plate.[1]

It goes without saying, in other words, that the leftover as term and concept is metaphorically rich. Consider, for instance, the lofty terms by which Byron MacFadyen describes leftovers in a 1930s article in *Good Housekeeping*: "Of course, every thrifty housekeeper has, or thinks she has, plans for each leftover she saves. She has faith in her ability to use them when she stows each dab and bite away," he writes.

Figure 28.1 Community Kitchen at Japanese-Canadian internment camp, ca. 1943, Greenwood, BC. National Film Board of Canada. Phototèque / Library and Archives Canada / C-024452.

"But speaking of faith, do you recall its definition? 'The substance of things hoped for.' Verily leftovers are often that – also 'the evidence of things not seen'" (MacFadyen 1930). Obasan's leftovers refer to *le reste* (the Derridean remainder) and *les restes* that, in French like the Japanese *nokorimono*, simultaneously suggest leftovers in all their culinary crudity as well as to the abject sacredness of bodily remains. One might even say that the leftover carries some of the messianic weight of the remnant, of "faintness faintly murmuring: what remains without remains" (Agamben 2002: 162). Maurice Blanchot calls this the fragment (Blanchot 1995: 33).

Because Obasan's food particles are called "leftovers," rather than remains or scraps, however, they are also marked as peculiarly modern. "Leftover" (or left-over) only began to be used as an expression in English to connote food waste in the 1890s. While Kogawa's novel is not modernist, then, Obasan's culinary composi-tions might nonetheless be seen as ambivalent memorials to the modern. Indeed, her leftovers, and leftovers more generally, offer a means through which to consider the figurative relationship between the modern and postmodern and even to ask: how may the contemporary deal with modernity's leftovers – *and* with its unused petrified bits?

Making do

Excerpt from the diary of Kaoru Ikeda, a Canadian Issei (first-generation), written at the Slocan "relocation camp" in southeastern British Columbia in December 1942 about the previous year:

> Now we are at the end of the year. In this wandering life of ours, there isn't much we can do to prepare for the New Year. Knowing that the children long for *kuri-kinton* [a chestnut sweet] I substituted peas for chestnuts and managed to make *mame-kinton*. I chopped fruit into the left-over gelatin which made for a nice dessert. I cooked the few black beans that we had received from Mrs. M. and had been saving for this occasion. Chisato baked some cupcakes and made *udon* noodles which took her a long time. (reprinted in Oiwa 1991: 134)

No 2: Restitution

There are, of course, two kinds of "remains" in *Obasan*: the decaying, but still useable, and that which is no longer "left-over" but simply over – dead, materially transformed. The food bits lurking in the recesses of Obasan's refrigerator have no use-value (or rather reuse-value), but neither are they utterly refused; "too old for mold and past putrefaction," they remain a shadow of their former selves. They are petrified, fossils – which refers not to the bone long ago buried in mud, but to its calcified absence. Not the artifact, but its impression made stone.

Obasan's leftovers might be seen as both a metaphor for and literal enactment of modernism's obsession with leftovers – for their preservation, aestheticization, commodification – and serve as a reminder for that which exceeds figurative language and the debt that figurative language demands. Julia Kristeva argues for a universal "ambivalence of residues"; she particularly remarks on food remainders, "as a precondition of all form" (Kristeva 1982: 77). For Kristeva, remainders (*les restes* or leftovers) are necessary by-products of nontotalizing thought (pp. 117–18).

If loss and trauma are associated with leftovers, however, so is literality. As Cathy Caruth observes, Freud's encounter with the dreams of shell-shocked World War I soldiers was startling because of their resistance to figuration. "Modern analysts as well have remarked on the surprising *literality* and nonsymbolic nature of traumatic dreams and flashbacks, which resist cure to the extent that they remain, precisely, literal," writes Caruth. "It is this literality and its insistent return which thus constitutes trauma and points toward its enigmatic core: the delay or incompletion in knowing, or even in seeing, an overwhelming occurrence that then remains, in its insistent return absolutely *true* to the event" (Caruth 1995: 4–6). It is the unassimilable nature of absolute literality, she insists, that "possesses the receiver and resists psychoanalytic interpretation and cure" (pp. 5–6). That is, the literal throws the subject into what Emmanuel Levinas calls the "menace of pure and simple presence, of the 'there is'" (Levinas 1978: 54). Stripped of the "consciousness of its own subjectivity," the subject becomes thing (Levinas 1978: 56). It is this quality of being thrown into thingness (the corpse?) in the presence of presence that is allegorized and negotiated – over and over – by the leftover.

Its connection to trauma does not endow the literal with a claim to moral superiority, authenticity, or even historicity in relation to figuration, however, as some have claimed in debates about "art after Auschwitz" (See Lang 1990. For critiques of a privileging of the literal in terms of morality or authenticity see Trezise 2001, Young 1988, and Van Alphen 1997.) Rather, the literal is that which resists identity and is thereby associated with a kind of absolute presencing and atemporality that implies not fantasies of truth, but fantasies of nonfiguration. Now. Here. This. "None but a vulgar idealist could believe, in order to compound his disdain for the detainee, that he is abject because he throws himself on a pail of leftovers and eats scrapings," writes Sarah Kofman in *Smothered Words*, her memoir-tinged critical philosophy of Auschwitz that includes a fragmentary history of her father's deportation and death in the camp (Kofman 1998: 63). Rather, within the context of Auschwitz, she explains, "what he experiences who feeds on peelings is one of the ultimate situations of resistance . . . the hungry man's invocation – as he struggles to eat enough to stay alive – of the highest of values" (Kofman 1998: 63, quoting Antelme 1992: 95).

Writing nearly 30 years after Auschwitz, yet with its specter still present, Roland Barthes meditated on the way that truth fantasies get narrated, observing that the "reality effect" of nineteenth-century realist narrative is undergirded by an overabundance of seemingly superfluous "details." The "effect" relies on exploiting both the reader's confusion between what *is/has been* (the unsignifiable Real), the figurative nature of language that must be used to describe it, and the reader's desire for an impossible direct access to presence. "The 'real' returns to [realistic narrative] as a signified of connotation," Barthes argues, "for just when these details are reputed to *denote* the real directly, all that they do – without saying so – is *signify* it" (Barthes 1989: 148). Yet if the narrative detail is mediated by a "referential illusion," leftovers harken up the undigestable literal, that "miserable little piece of the Real" that Slavoj Žižek sees as haunting modern narrative (Žižek 1989: 207). Indeed, Žižek argues that the price to be paid for preserving the gap between the Real and its symbolization is subjectivity itself (pp. 230–1).

In short, if Obasan's leftovers allegorize anything it is not memory *per se*, but the unstable dualism between the literal and the figurative that emerges in late modern narrative and, more broadly, the "troublesome" temporal tension between presence and deadness (particularly dead-metaphor and cliché) that Gertrude Stein observes as a condition of composition. "Now there is still something else the time-sense in the composition," writes Stein in her 1926 essay, "Composition as Explanation. "This is what is always a fear a doubt and a judgment and a conviction. The quality in the creation of expression the quality in a composition that makes it go dead just after it

Figure 28.2 Documentary, Our Mess Hall by Henry Sugimoto, 1942. Courtesy of Japanese American National Museum (Los Angeles, CA).

has been made is very troublesome" (Stein 1926/1993: 502). What Stein strives for, as we will see below, is the means to narrate a presence that might be reread, a narration that isn't always already elegiac, the resurrection and reburial of a corpse. This is part of what underlies the modernist quest for narrative newness, since the new – once it is recognized – is already remains. Leftovers haunt newness, are its necessary cohabitant and perpetual threat.

Cohabitation

From an interview with Harry Yoshio Ueno, who organized the Mess Hall Workers Union at Manzanar and was the principal figure in the Manzanar Riot of December 6, 1942, by Sue Kunitomi Embrey and Arthur A. Hansen for the Japanese American Oral History Project at California State University, Fullerton, San José, California, October 30, 1976:

> The people in Block 24 always ate the leftovers from the young people who had already eaten. On Thanksgiving Day, they had a big fuss because they had only so much turkey for each mess hall. By the time the rest of the people in Block 24

went in, they had only a few scraps, that's all. The turkey had been eaten by all the young people from other blocks, see. In Block 24, they then circulated a petition and tried to fire the chief, Tayama, but he wouldn't budge. So, finally, they came to my place. At that time I had already organized the Mess Hall Workers Union. So they asked me to talk to him. I went over and talked to Harry, but instead of talking, he threatened me – that's all. He practically pushed me out of the kitchen. (from interview available online at <http://www.calisphere. universityofcalifornia.edu>)

No. 3: Cleverness

Still, Obasan is frugal. She refuses to let go of the past. Her role is to preserve the continuity of the present with the past, literalizing the material continuity of the never wholly figurative trace – the recessive gene, the crumb – of previous generations within her own, within her niece. Yet because Obasan is also frugal with regard to the recent past – to yesterday's leftovers in relation to tomorrow's meals – her culinary practice cannot be subsumed exclusively into a discourse on immigration or even traumatic memory. Her serial remaking of leftovers is *situational* in Barthes's understanding (in contemporary French society of the 1960s and 1970s, he says, *"food has a constant tendency to transform itself into situation,"* Barthes 1979: 172). That is, Obasan's efforts make *place* when place is understood, on one hand, as a kind of happening and, on the other, as a kind of debt. Leftovers are connected etymologically to debt. In French, the expression for being indebted to someone is *être en restes de*. Obasan presents the past. That is, she makes the past present – she presences it. And she makes it *a present*, a gift still covered in wrapping. At the same time, by insisting upon a kind of redundancy in her culinary preparation, she presents the past as a bill past due. We might then see in this moment the leftover serving as a figure for the residual modern as an unpaid debt.

While Obasan's respect for leftovers no doubt calls forth the traditional imperative of *mottainai* and the figurative hold of modernist narrative, her cooking practice also mimics with an almost ironic literalism the modern tenets of North American domesticity (see Bhabha 1986: 88 on colonial mimicry). Even in the nineteenth century, Lydia Maria Child's popular 1829 text, *The American Frugal Housewife*, offered the advice to American women that, "With proper care, there is no need of losing a particle of bread, even in the hottest weather" (cited in Grover 1987: 98). Though frugality still underlay the North American discourse around leftovers into the twentieth century, by the late 1920s and 1930s, leftovers began to be discussed more often in terms of temporal longevity, taking on a tropic presence associated with the passage of time and preservation.

Mary Luce Girard argues that "doing cooking" is connected to "a multiple memory," one that is associated with "a memory of apprenticeship, of witnessed gesture, and of consistencies"; cooking also calls for "a programming mind," "sensory perception," and "creative ingenuity" (Girard 1998: 157). If Girard's first point suggests that Obasan's perpetual reuse of leftovers signifies a resistance to the persistent demands of the quotidian, to the daily chore of rechopping and repreparing food, Obasan's cooking practice exactly performs Girard's understanding of "cleverness," which the latter explains by asking as an example: "How can one make the most out of leftovers in a way that makes everyone believe that it is a completely new dish?" (pp. 157–8).

In this context, Obasan seems clever indeed. But the means through which she preserves food to be reused again and again owe as much to modern refrigeration as to ingenuity. By the late 1920s, descriptions of leftovers in North American women's magazines were largely shaped by the emergent marketing discourse that advocated domestic artificial refrigeration as the means to ward off disease. In an August 1929 article in *Collier's*, for example, Dr Royal S. Copeland, a US Senator, warns against overfrugality when it came to food and advocates the purchase of refrigerators as within reach of even "the average citizen" (Copeland 1929: 28). Although domestic refrigeration, mostly in the form of the icebox, became popular in the United States, Canada, and Europe after World War I, in 1929 electric refrigeration was still seen as a privilege of the rich. It was only after 1935, when Frigidaire began to market to middle- and lower-income housewives, that the electric refrigerator began to be considered a nonprestige appliance in the United States (see Nickles 2002). Susan Strasser remarks, "ten percent of American families owned refrigerators in 1930, fifty-six percent in 1940" (Strasser 1992: 19, citing Vaile 1937).

The intrusion of electric refrigeration into the culinary economy made visible issues associated with temporal progression – and its arrest. Refrigerators stop time, Dr John Harvey Kellogg admits in an article in *The Literary Digest* in November 1930; they arrest "the processes of fermentation and decay or putrefaction" ("Watch Your Refrigerator" 1929). More precisely, refrigeration *slows* temporal progression – the irrevocable putrefaction of once living matter that is no longer alive. Dr Kellogg vividly warns against the threat of improperly working refrigerators – and improperly refrigerated food: "When in good running order, an efficient refrigerator is a boon and a life-saving agency of great value. But what if the refrigerator stops? . . . There is a menace to health to which we desire to call attention, a danger that seems to be little understood and concerning which the public is unaware" (p. 38).

By the mid-1930s, with the boom in electric refrigerator sales coinciding with continued economic depression, women's magazines in the United States and Canada began to proliferate with recipes for remaking leftovers, shifting the discourse from frugality and health to creativity. "Economy has become the keynote of our life and a good housekeeper is one who can save money on her table without letting it show in the results," admits Leone B. Moats, sounding a good deal like Girard, in an August 1933 *House & Garden*. "For this reason leftover foods play an important role. They must be remarkable not only for their excellence but for the manner in which they are served. They must be so completely disguised that only the creator can possibly

Figure 28.3 United States Office of War Information, 1943. OWI Poster No. 35. Courtesy of the Minneapolis Public Library.

know that their base is something left over from another meal" (Moats 1933). "Leftovers are really a challenge," writes Louella G. Shouer in 1937 in *Ladies Home Journal*, but they are also "a stimulus to your imagination and ingenuity." A 1938 *American Home* article provides a photo-spread on "Left-over Meat in Fine Disguise"; a 1935 article in *Good Housekeeping* provides "Institute-tested and approved" recipes for remaking food "odds and ends" into something different using "imagination and ingenuity" (MacFadyen 1935).

With the onset of World War II, rationing and food shortages brought about a resurgence of the alarmist tone of 1920s advice about food safety in some articles. For instance, a 1943 article in the *Reader's Digest* cautions, "although no statistics are available, medical authorities believe (on the basis of newspaper reports and local experience) that food-poisoning cases are increasing alarmingly with war-time food shortages and the consequent greater use of leftovers" (de Kruif 1943). At the same time, there were government campaigns to make the use of leftovers a sign of patriotism – even for the president. "Leftovers from the White House table reappeared disguised as stew, ragout and hash," write the authors of a 1942 article in *Time* magazine.

"Scraps that could not be salvaged went to feed the pigs at Washington's six-acre, cooperative Self-Help Farm. White House trash had gone to the metals-salvage campaign, and a Treasury truck stopped weekly to collect old papers" (Citizen Roosevelt 1942).

In this more sophisticated age of consumption, women's magazines advocated the use of leftovers, but frequently shifted the vocabulary from culinary disguise to the production of a new modern art. "Be an artist with your leftovers!" enthuses a 1942 article in *Better Homes & Gardens*, providing recipes for those who might need instruction ("Serve Your Leftovers"). The more up-scale *House & Garden* titles a similar article, "The Art of Using Left-overs," advocating that the American woman sacrifice a bit of her "liberty" by borrowing the "useful" art of remaking leftovers from her European sisters, offering a series of French-sounding recipes such as, *Mousse au Jambon* and *Cornets à la Russe* for leftover ham (Markevitch 1942). In fact, those "square plastic" Tupperware containers that Obasan uses to store her leftovers were introduced in the 1940s and marketed to "young moderns," a low-key, yet design-savvy "new consumer group identified by postwar houseware editors" (Clarke 1999: 59). In 1956, curators at the Museum of Modern Art chose the minimalist splendor of Tupperware plastic for a display on modern design (Clarke: 37). While Obasan's use of leftovers is figurative, then, the means through which she saves food also literally marks her as a mid-century modern.

Oral history

Interview with June Igaue by Nancy Aweimrine on November 12, 1984 at 10:30 a.m. in Los Angeles for the Oral History Program at California State University, Fullerton:

> Later, the carpenters and plumbers made a little wash basin outside of each barracks so we didn't have to go clear to the latrine to get water. Sometimes when someone got sick from the food, we would all get sick, you know, eating from the same mess hall. Then you should have seen the latrine with everyone standing in line. That happened a lot of times because in those days the refrigeration wasn't that good. Also they tried to serve leftovers and that was bad because it was hot there and the food spoiled. Fortunately, not every block got sick at the same time, so we could run to another block at night and use their latrine. Real exciting, sometimes. (Igaue 1984: 21–2)

No. 4: Presence

Paul Valéry writes in his *Cahiers*, "Écrire pour publier, c'est chez moi l'Art d'accommoder les restes," of which Vincent Kaufmann observes in an essay on literary "drafts": Valéry was "so contemptuous of the completed work, [he] called publishing the art of accommodating leftovers" (Kaufmann 1996: 67, 74–5; Valéry 1973–4: 265). In vernacular speech, the "chez moi," imprecisely punctuated in Valéry's notes, most obviously refers to the writer's opinion and suggests a translation such as Kaufmann's: "Writing for publication is, *in my opinion*, the art of accommodating leftovers" (my emphasis). For Valéry, in this context, publishing houses are little more than "les bouchons," the lowest echelon of nineteenth-century Parisian restaurants, which scavenged (or bought) kitchen scraps and leftovers (dubbed, ironically, *bijoux* or jewels) from bourgeois kitchens and better restaurants and resold them, at times half-rancid, to the poor (De Certeau, Girard, and Mayol 1998, Aron 1979). Taken literally, however, the "chez moi" can be translated as "for me" or privately, in which case, it is *not* publishing that Valéry calls the art of accommodating leftovers, rather he refers to his own art – his writing for himself, the scribbles in his *Cahiers* – as the art of "using *up* leftovers" (emphasis mine; see the translation of "l'art d'accommoder les restes" in Armitage 1993). Still, translating "accommoder" with "using up" is also imprecise, since leftovers, as Valéry insisted, can't be *used up*. Moreover, "accommoder" might also be translated as "to make use of" or "to make room for." And, as noted earlier, "les restes" refers to both food remains and bodily or sacred remains. So we might also translate this as the art of "making room for" or "allowing for the use of" remains, without their concomitant *poubellication* (the pun is Lacan's), that is, without leftovers being turned into garbage (Kaufmann 1996: 71).

There is no doubt that Valéry is disdainful of print culture; he refers in a paradigmatically modernist fashion to the pressures of the market on art. In any translation, this disdain is clear. Yet Valéry's famous rejection of writing for publication is, more to the point, a rejection of writing as a recording of the past rather than as an exploratory mode of seeing, of becoming future. In another place in his *Cahiers*, he writes, "Je prends la plume pour l'avenir de ma pensée – non pour son passé" (I take the pen [to capture] the future of my thought – not its past.") (cited in Robinson 1961: 499). With this in mind, leftovers might be intolerable for their attachment to the past – or they might be interesting because of the way they anticipate their own future use.

Along the latter lines, we might also consider one of Joseph Cornell's diary entries from April 15, 1946: "Had a satisfactory feeling about clearing up debris on cellar floor – sweepings represent all the rich crosscurrents ramifications etc that go into the boxes but which are not apparent (I feel at least) in the final result," he writes (Cornell 1993: 128). Peter Schwenger recounts this passage in an essay about dreams and debris, noting Cornell's allusion to Freud's recuperation of "the residues of the day" in the psychoanalyst's theorization of dreamwork (Schwenger 2003: 75). Less obviously, Schwenger references another passage that Cornell had underlined in Jean Piaget's *The Language and Thought of the Child* that "characterized child narratives by 'an absence of order in the account given, and the fact that causal relationships are rarely expressed, but are generally indicated by a simple juxtaposition of the related terms'" (Schwenger 2003: 77,

Piaget cited in Keller 1987: 107). This, Schwenger observes, does not so much suggest an "anti-narrative" bias in Cornell's work, but rather a shift of narrative into a luminal space, the space of dreams. In fact, however, I would go further to suggest that this gesture alludes to a specific tension within modernist narrative: that of the *a posteriori* or "après-coup" that signifies a narrative resistance to presence, and which marks both narrative written under the sign of trauma and narrative leftovers, those elements of narrative that fail "to cohere" (Schwenger 2006: 144).

Thus we might say that modern narrative needs its leftovers in order to extricate it from its progressive momentum and give it presence and yet it is precisely those elements it also needs to discard. We might see Obasan's use (and preservation) of leftovers as performing, but also belying, a drive to newness associated with the historical avant-garde's future-driven impetus to "make it new" by remaking context. Therefore Obasan's cooking might be seen as modernist in the way that Cornell's constructions or Marcel Duchamp's "ready-mades" are modern: they make something new through a careful and innovative repositioning of leftovers of the immediate past. They make the past present, a *presence*.

Obasan cooks a cuisine of found objects, we might say. It is a cuisine subject to a cyclical, even sacred ("Our Lady of the Leftovers") temporality, disguised as reinvention. It is event-centered rather than object-centered, similar in this sense to the way that Octavio Paz describes Marcel Duchamp's work: "Duchamp denounced the superstition of the craft. The artist is not someone who makes things: his works are not pieces of workmanship – they are acts" (Paz 2002: 85). Yet Obasan's culinary constructions are devoid of Duchamp's sense of irony. For instance, the visual pun embodied in Duchamp's 1959 construction, *Sculpture-morte*, emphasizes the masking of decay (*la poubellication*) and thwarting of becoming-dead that is inherent to still-life painting or *la nature-morte* (literally, "dead nature"). If the still life aestheticizes the stoppage of time, Duchamp's *sculpture-morte* literalizes modernism's contradictory stance on progressive temporality. For Duchamp, what is most important is the material process of becoming-past, the erasure of the wounds of temporal progression. Forward-moving time is also a movement toward becoming-dead, decaying. Equally, for Duchamp, the eventuality of death is the least interesting part of temporal contiguity. "Death? There is no such thing as death," Hans Richter quotes Duchamp as saying. "When we no longer have consciousness then the world simply stops" (Richter 1969/2002: 148). Richter is distressed at Duchamp's earnestness and reassertion of the *cogito* and the primacy of the subject in world-making. But in terms of temporality, what Duchamp is suggesting is that it is not the continuity between past and future that interests him, but the ways that temporal discontinuity is produced. That is, he is less interested in a figure for the unseeable – death and decay – than for the *unforeseeable*, chance (see Hofmann 2002: 57–8). The leftover's relationship to chance makes it simultaneously future-directed and an eschewal of the future; the leftover is that which is unforeseeably left.

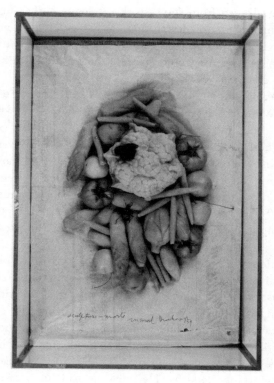

Figure 28.4 Sculpture-morte by Marcel Duchamp (1887–1968) © ARS, NY. Still-Life Sculpture. Summer 1959. Fruits and vegetables in marzipan, insects, paper mounted on a wooden box made of glass, 33.8 × 22.5 × 9.9 cm. Work done in Cadaqués, Inv.: AM1993–121. Photo: Jacques Faujour. Musée Nationale d'Art Moderne, Centre Georges Pompidou, Paris, France. CNAC//MNAM/Dist. Réunion des Musées Nationaux / Art Resource, NY. Image copyright © 2008 Artists Rights Society (ARS), New York / ADAGP, Paris / Succession Marcel Duchamp.

Therefore, an underlying tension of modernist narratives, particularly those associated with the work of memory and internal consciousness, is not that they demonstrate the transformation and decay inherent to the forward movement of time, but that they perform the imperfectibility of efforts to arrest it (see Adorno on progress, 1964: 126–7). Such narratives disguise *presence* as *the present*, through a simultaneous remembrance and forgetting of figuration. It is precisely this quality of narrative, this debt, the requirement of narrative to live only in the past and future that Stein comes up against in her artistic "autobiography," *A Novel of Thank You*, written in 1925–6, which asks the questions: what is left of a novel after you cut out characters and plot? What remains in writing when metaphor is left out? Or to take further the plaints of André Breton in his 1924 *Manifesto of Surrealism*: what can a novel do if it no longer informs and ceases to display a series of superimposed images taken from some stock catalogue – the author's "post cards" and clichés (dead metaphors) of description? What is left of a novel cluttered not with details, but with the leftovers of narrative after conscious figuration has been taken out? (In some ways, this would suggest the linguistic negative of Joyce's or Woolf's stream of consciousness.)

In his introduction to the Dalkey Archive edition of Stein's text, Steven Meyer observes, "Whatever it is that in writing isn't speech, whatever in a novel is not a story, in thought is not a conversation, in a human being is not character – these are both the means and ends of *A Novel*" (Meyer 1994: xxiii). In part, then, Stein is interested in the way the novel, and novel forms, absent themselves. "A novel returns at once," writes Stein slyly, referring to the "boomerang effect" of novelistic narrative, which requires both remembrance and the deferral of desire (Stein 1994: 239). Stein, for instance, attempts to explore ways of writing that might be associated with presence and the present: lists and the literal.

What is the difference, Stein's "novel" might be said to ask, between the novel and a list? If narrative necessitates waiting, a constant skittering between the future and the past, the list brings to bear on presence, offering the promise of identification, of relating the unrelated, of memorializing the extraconscious, the literal, not the drama of dying, but understanding what it means to already be dead, inert, stuff. "He knew he had his and this occasion and he was determined to understand lists," Stein writes, then repeats, "He knew he had his occasion and he was prepared to arrange lengths. He knew he had his occasion and very often it was the same one. The same one has the same sound at once and more than undoubted. How can he have both. There was a way after all of going there" (Stein 1994: 239).

The list is how one performs presence, according to Stein. She writes in "Composition as Explanation," written at the same time as *A Novel* (and sharing some of its language):

> It was all so nearly alike it must be different and it is different, it is natural that if everything is used and there is a continuous present and a beginning again and again if it is all so alike it must be simply different and everything simply different was the natural way of creating it then.
>
> In this natural way of creating it then that it was simply different everything being alike it was simply different, this kept on leading one to lists. Lists naturally for awhile and by lists I mean a series. (Stein 1926/1933: 499–500)

And, a few paragraphs later, she continues,

> So then I as a contemporary creating the composition in the beginning was groping toward a continuous present, a using everything a beginning again and again and then everything being alike then everything very simply everything was naturally simply

different and so I as a contemporary was creating everything being alike was creating everything naturally being naturally simply different, everything being alike. (Stein 1926/1993: 500–1)

What Stein suggests is most compelling – and inevitable – about the list is the way that in seeming to repeat, it remakes, and in this remaking brings one to – or one "gropes toward" – a continuous present. Presence.

The figure of the list, according to Tony Thwaites, is asyndeton, the omitting of conjunctions between words, phrases, or clauses. Associations are inevitable, but whether the effect of this omission conveys extemporaneity, vehemence, multiplicity, linearity, or perpetual presence is a matter of some speculation. "The asyndetic is not what is absent so much as what refuses to go away: the nagging possibility of connection beyond mere juxtaposition," Thwaites (1997) writes. And Michael André Bernstein, who notes that modernists were particularly fascinated by lists, observes: "Precisely because the rules governing the placement and sequence of a list's elements seem so strict, although never explicitly stated, lists compel their reader to work at divining the intention of the listmaker" (Bernstein 1998: 2). For Stein, however, the list is interesting not solely for the associations it forces one to make, but for its disassociations, for the mistakes. "To be mistaken literally mistaken to be literally mistaken, literally and listening, to be mistaken listening literally and listening and literally to be mistaken and listening," writes Stein in *A Novel of Thank You* (Stein 1994: 47). Even if metaphor is reinvented, the literal is left. And the literal always implies both forgetting and the mistake.

Packing list

"Instructions to All Japanese Living on Bainbridge Island," by J. L. DeWitt, Lieutenant General, US Army, Commanding, March 1942:

> Provisions have been made to give temporary residence in a reception center elsewhere. Evacuees who do not go to an approved destination of their own choice, but who go to a reception center under Government supervision, must carry with them the following property, not exceeding that which can be carried by the family or individual:

a. Blankets and linens for each member of the family;
b. Toilet articles for each member of the family;
c. Clothing for each member of the family;
d. Sufficient knives, forks, spoons, plates, bowls, and cups for each member of the family;
e. All items carried will be securely packaged, tied, and plainly marked with the name of the owner and numbered in accordance with instructions received at the Civil Control Office;
f. No contraband items may be carried. (Daniels 1989)

Figure 28.5 Relocation: Packing up, Manzanar Relocation Center, by Ansel Adams, 1943. Library of Congress, Prints & Photographs Division, Ansel Adams, photographer, LC-DIG-ppprs-00294 DLC.

No. 5: Gratitude

Another go, then. After the unthinkable can one go on living (Adorno 2000: 362–3)? After the A-bomb? After Auschwitz? After having survived? After after? There is no leftover as thing except as fetish, since in Adorno's words, "things are not simply so and not otherwise . . . they have to come to be under certain conditions. Their becoming fades and dwells within the things; it can no more be stabilized in their concepts than it can be split off from its own results and forgotten. Similar to this becoming is temporal experience" (Adorno 2000: 52). The solution, for Adorno, is to read things as a "text of their becoming," and we might say, as in the case of the leftover, as a text of becoming left, of becoming over.

Under the specter of Auschwitz and Manzanar, to talk about the discourse of leftovers seems vulgar. And yet, as I suggested above, the leftover *is* connected to the promise of a vulgar messianism that was inherent in modern art, which aspired to the literality of being extricated from figuration, to bridge the gap between "words and the thing they conjure" (Adorno 2000: 53). No ghosts, in other words, no remains.

The literal becomes the "dream of bringing back to life" *sui generis*. Jacques Derrida exclaims in *Archive Fever*:

> Freud seems himself obliged to let the phantoms speak for the duration of the archeo-logical digs but finishes by exorcising them in the moment he at last says, the work having been terminated (or supposed to have been), "Stones talk!" He believes he has exorcised them in the instant he lets them talk, provided that these specters talk, he believes in the figurative. Like stones, nothing but that . . . (Derrida 1995: 94–5)

Freud's is a phantomless fantasy from which *Obasan*'s Naomi has not yet escaped: "The word is stone," the prologue reads, and then continues: "I admit it. I hate the stillness. I hate the stone."

What we might read here is ambivalence – an ambivalence toward the "fratricidal war" between the literal and the figurative that produces metaphor, a submersion of the literal into the figurative, the necessary killing off of the literal in order for live metaphor to be resurrected (Johnson 1987). It cannot be an accident that Barbara Johnson's reading of this battle between the literal and the figurative is extracted from Baudelaire's story of two brothers fighting over a morsel of bread, renamed as a cake (Johnson 1987: 100). "Any sign *alone* appears dead," writes Wittgenstein, "What makes it come alive? It lives when it is in use. Does it then have living breath within? Or is the use its breath?" (cited in Hofmann 2002: 60).

Anthropologist Michael Taussig tells the story of the 1950 discovery of the Tollund Man, an Iron Age man found uncannily preserved thousands of years after his death in the acid-rich, air-deprived bog water of Denmark, in order to articulate the two-step "between literality and metaphor that makes language work" (Taussig 2004: 177). For Taussig language is "weird" like the bog, "so slippery yet firm . . . the provocation of meaning [is] created by the sliding back and forth between literality and metaphor . . . occurs, so to speak, as a process of depetrification, the very process we might now call miasmatic, remembering that both petrification and miasma owe their existence to the swamp" (p. 177). The bog man is an uncanny metaphor for language because it foregrounds and erases its violence: preserved along with the "majesty and gentleness" embossed on the Tollund Man's "lightly-closed eyes and half-closed lips," was the noose still clasped tightly around his neck (Glob 1969: 31).

So is the literal a miasma? A stone? A substitute – even metaphor – for the mistake? In her 1935 essay, "A Contribution to the Psychogenesis of Manic-Depressive States," Melanie Klein recounts two dreams of "patient C," the second of which she quotes as follows:

> He heard the frizzling sound of something which was frying in an oven. He could not see what it was, but he thought of something brown, probably a kidney which was frying in a pan. The noise he heard was like the squeaking or crying of a tiny voice and his feeling was that a live creature was being fried. His mother was there and he tried to draw her attention to this, and to make her understand that to fry something alive

was much the worst thing to do, worse than broiling or cooking it. It was more torturing since the hot fat prevented it from burning altogether and kept it alive while skin-
ning it. He could not make his mother understand this and she did not seem to mind.
This worried him, but in a way it reassured him, as he thought it could not be so bad
if she did not mind. The oven, which he did not open in the dream – he never saw the
kidney and the pan – reminded him of a refrigerator. In a friend's flat, he had repeatedly
mixed up the refrigerator door with the oven door. He wonders whether heat and cold
are, in a way, the same thing for him. The torturing hot fat in a pan reminds him of a
book about tortures he had read as a child; he was especially excited by beheadings and
by tortures by hot oil. (Klein 1986: 136)

With anxiety, Klein admits that she "has no space to quote all the important
associations given," and will "single out only the points bearing on the conclusions
arrived at in this paper," a paper that marks her shift from a developmental or
temporally progressive concept of ego formation to a spatially contingent or structural one (see Juliet Mitchell's introductory comments to the essay in Klein 1986:
116). She reads this dream alongside the patient's earlier one in order to demonstrate the process through which the child overcomes first the paranoid then the
depressive positions by recognizing that the good/loved/gratifying object and the
bad/hated/persecutory object are one and the same thing. In healthy development,
in addition to recognizing that the loved object is also the hated one, the child
comes to recognize that "real objects and the imaginary figures, both external and
internal, are bound up with each other" (p. 141). The healthy child comes to know,
identify with, and internalize a "more realistic" image of the mother as a "whole,
real and loved person" (p. 142). Through analysis, according to Klein, the patient
had begun to internalize (introject) his parents and shift from the paranoid position
to the depressive position, with all the attendant anxiety for his loved objects, his
"real parents," anxieties that became "internalized and thus multiplied, intensified
and, partly, altered in character," and thus were not wholly able to be worked
through (p. 138).

It was Klein's conception of the imago or internal object as a "body-phantasy,"
imagined as being "physically present within the individual's body," according to
Meir Perlow, that initiated a split in British psychoanalytic circles around the concept
of the object and came to demonstrate Klein's departure from Freud (Perlow 1995:
39). Klein was critiqued, in short, for being overly concrete (that is, literalist) and
blurring the distinctions between "internal objects . . . and perceptions, memories and
realistic images" (Perlow 1995: 42). But, Perlow argues, it is the "dual nature of
internal objects, combining aspects of both self and object" that is a crucial contribution of Kleinian thought (p. 43).

What Mary Jacobus calls the "corporeality of metaphor" in her reading of one of
Klein's defendants, Ella Freeman Sharpe, is a case in point. Sharpe, trained as a literary
scholar, maintained an interest in paying careful attention to the emergence of figurative language (and particularly metaphor) in the psychoanalytic process. While this
was something Freud also had done, Sharpe's insistence on the material nature of

metaphor is striking because, for Sharpe, metaphor holds not only a symbolic or phantasmatic function, but a literal one (Sharpe 1940: 202). Because children gain control over the sphincter and urethra at the same time as they acquire language, she argues, the activity of speaking becomes a substitute "outer-ance" for the now-restricted physical excretion; the words themselves come to serve as substitutes for bodily substances, faeces and urine. "Speech in itself is a metaphor," she writes, "metaphor is as ultimate as speech" (p. 203). The phantasy of incorporation, of maintaining and retaining the vivid sense-perceptions of early infancy in Sharpe's terms, is a nullification of figurative language, a retroactive "making literal" of the object set up to deny loss and preserve the status quo. There is no phantasy of incorporation, in other words, without the metaphor which first produces a sense of the object *as* lost. Metaphor, we might say, is its own leftover, a figure for its own production as well as a literal substitute for the faeces.

If we return to the dream that Klein recounts, keeping Sharpe's analysis in mind, we might see it as well as a dream about the anxiety of figuration. Just as Klein remarks that the "kidney burnt alive stood both for his father's penis – equated to faeces – and for the babies inside his mother's body (the stove which he did not open)" (p. 137), we can see that moment of excremental destruction coinciding with the emergence of "a tiny voice." The ambivalence that the patient feels about his confrontation with the screaming, frying kidney and his anxiety about the emergence of the voice as simultaneous with the killing off of the internal object (equated with faeces) can be seen as an ambivalence toward metaphor, an ambivalence that "calls out" and coincides with the recurrent emergence of the depressive position. Ironically, it is metaphor that becomes the means through which to reconcile the good and bad, part and whole objects, fantasy and reality.

What Klein does not mention – nor even allude to – in the many pages that follow is the patient's strange confusion between the oven and refrigerator. Yet this is a paper about anxiety and the making, compensating for, and rectifying of mistakes. The patient's perfectionism is part of what is at stake here, his incomplete internalization of his loved objects, his lingering at the moment when faced "with the psychical fact that [his] loved objects are in a state of dissolution – in bits" (Klein 1986: 124). The desire for perfection, according to Klein, is rooted in an anxiety the child feels in recognizing his simultaneous feelings of destruction/envy and love/gratitude toward his mother and his desire to protect and preserve the loved object, which he himself threatens to cannibalistically chew into bits (pp. 124–5). We might see this anxiety played out in the patient's confusion, his wondering whether "heat and cold are, in a way, the same thing for him" (p. 136).

Both cooking (heating) and refrigeration (cooling) are means of preserving objects that are to be eaten, that is, brought into the body – whole or in pieces. Yet the ways that the oven and refrigerator preserve are somewhat different: cooking causes an irreversible chemical change in food; it produces a new substance. Refrigeration or freezing, on the other hand, simply "slows" or eliminates putrefaction, the growth of microorganisms and oxidation within food, producing a physical change in the food, which is in most cases reversible. Figuratively, then, in Freudian terms, the former might be akin to introjection, which first implies a transformation of the ego in response to loss and later, in 1923, as an internalization of the parental figures that forms the superego; and the latter to melancholic incorporation, which staves off transformation by swallowing the object whole to preserve it from change. Since for Klein, however, the good and bad object are one and the same, an absolute split between incorporation and introjection cannot be sustained. In a later paper, "A Study of Envy and Gratitude," Klein remarks that an infant's eventual stability and capacity for love presupposes an early ability to separate the good from the bad object and "thus, in a fundamental way, [preserve] it" (Klein 1986: 217). At the same time, this cleft must not be too absolute or the depressive position cannot be worked through and "the all-important processes of ego integration and object synthesis, as well as mitigation of hatred by love, are impaired" (p. 217). In the integrated ego, gratitude to the good, giving object tempers hatred of the bad, persecutory one. Hatred, greed, and envy are mitigated by love, enjoyment, responsibility. It is only then, according to Klein, "step by step" that "gratitude becomes possible" (pp. 228–9). Klein sees infancy, the period before the splitting of objects, as a "perpetual present," a world without memory, metaphor, or conscious thought (see Juliet Mitchell in Klein 1986: 26). Gratitude emerges with an acceptance of one's ambivalence to figuration and the extrication of figuration from presence.

Within this context, it makes a certain sense that Stein's meaningful, meaningless novel is ultimately "A Novel of Thank You." She writes toward its end:

> It is very extraordinary that as long ago as three hundred years that they had second-hand chimney pieces put into their houses. It is undoubtedly true and just as if it were repeated to them repeated to this then to be sure. To very much regret not having waited to have that with this. After all one can enjoy meaning, I mean to be let alone and not to tell her that now there is no need for it. Thank you very much and thank you very much is not forgotten. (Stein 1994: 236–7)

It cannot be a surprise that the leftover (those second-hand chimney pieces) finds itself in this passage. Nor that it is here, finally, where we can recognize the ambivalence in Obasan's multiple uses of leftovers. Obasan's ambivalence is not just toward speech, not just toward narrative, but toward the retrospective component of meaning-production that masquerades in the figure as presence. It is only when Naomi can find presence without resurrecting the literal–figurative dichotomy that she can make peace with her lost mother. "I am thinking that for a child there is no presence without flesh," muses Naomi on the last page of the novel. "But perhaps it is because I am no longer a child I can know your presence though you are not here" (Kogawa 1981: 292). She is not accepting metaphoric presence here, nor is she insisting upon its literalization. Rather, she is finding a third way. Her rage at metaphoric substitution is mitigated by love. She is grateful. And this is something her mother might have taught her. There is a Japanese *kotowaza* (proverb), *Nokorimono ni wa fuku ga aru* (残り物には福がある), which means "there is good fortune in the *nokorimono*." That is, there is luck in accepting leftovers; even in bitterness and envy, one can be grateful for the presencing of remains.

NOTES

My thanks to Naomi Nakagawa for her help with the Japanese translations and to Maria Damon for her comments on an earlier draft.

1 In April 2001, in an attempt to reduce Japan's reliance on food imports, the Japanese Agriculture, Forestry and Fisheries Ministry passed a recycling law that required restaurants, food-processing and food-distribution companies, and other food-related businesses to recycle at least 20 percent of food that might have been thrown out. The 2004 Nobel Prize winner from Kenya, Wangari Muta Maathai, adopted the term and linked it to her Green Belt Movement, which in turn reintroduced it to Japan.

REFERENCES AND FURTHER READING

Adams, Robert Martin. (1976). Rags, garbage, and fantasy. *The Hudson Review* 29, 1: 54–68.

Adorno, Theodor A. (1964/2003). Progress. In Rolf Tiedemann (ed.), *Can One Live After Auschwitz: A Philosophical Reader* (pp. 126–7). Stanford, CA: Stanford University Press.

Adorno, Theodor W. (2000). *Negative Dialectics*, trans. E. B. Ashton. New York: Continuum.

Agamben, Giorgio. (2002). *Remnants of Auschwitz: The Witness and the Archive*. New York: Zone.

Antelme, Robert. (1992). *The Human Race*, trans. Jeffrey Haight and Annie Mahler. Malboro, VT: Malboro Press.

Armitage, Isabelle. (1993). La vie des mots. *The French Review* 66, 5: 800–1.

Aron, Jean-Paul. (1979). The art of using leftovers: Paris, 1850–1900. In Robert Forster and Orest Ranum (eds), *Food and Drink in History: Selections from the Annales Economies, Sociétés, Civilisation*, trans. Elborg Forster and Patricia Ranum (pp. 98–108). Baltimore: Johns Hopkins University Press.

Asaba, Masaharu. (2001). "Mottainai" holds key to food conservation. *The Daily Yomiuri*, April 8: 7.

Barthes, Roland. (1979). Toward a psychosociology of contemporary food consumption. In Robert Forster and Orest Ranum (eds), *Food and Drink in History: Selections from the Annales Econo-mies, Sociétés, Civilisations*, trans. Elborg Forster and Patricia Ranum (pp. 166–73). Baltimore: Johns Hopkins University Press.

Barthes, Roland. (1989). The reality effect. In *The Rustle of Language*, trans. Richard Howard (pp. 141–8). Berkeley: University of California Press.

Bernstein, Michael André. (1998). Making modernist masterpieces. *Modernism/Modernity* 5, 3: 1–17.

Bhabha, Homi K. (1986). Of mimicry and man. In *The Location of Culture* (pp. 85–92). London: Routledge.

Blanchot, Maurice. (1995). *The Writing of the Disaster*, trans. Ann Smock. Lincoln: University of Nebraska Press.

Caruth, Cathy. (1995). Trauma and experience: An introduction. In Cathy Caruth (ed.), *Trauma: Explorations in Memory* (pp. 3–12). Baltimore: Johns Hopkins University Press.

Cheung, King-kok. (1993). *Articulate Silences: Hisaye Yamamoto, Maxine Hong Kingston, Joy Kogawa*. Ithaca, NY: Cornell University Press.

Citizen Roosevelt. (1942). *Time* 39 (April 20). Available online at <http://www.time.com/time/magazine/article/0,9171,790318,00.html>.

Clarke, Alison. (1999). *Tupperware: The Promise of Plastic in 1950s America*. Washington, DC: Smithsonian Institution Press.

Copeland, Royal S., MD (1929). Eat, drink, but be wary. *Collier's* 84 (July 13).

Cornell, Joseph. (1993). *Joseph Cornell's Theatre of the Mind: Selected Diaries, Letters, and Files*, ed. Mary Ann Caws. New York: Thames & Hudson.

Daniels, Roger (ed.). (1989). *In American Concentration Camps: A Documentary History of the Relocation and Incarceration of Japanese Americans, 1942–1945. Volume 3: February 20, 1942–March 31, 1942*. New York: Garland.

Davidson, Arnold E. (1994). *Writing Against the Silence: Joy Kogawa's "Obasan."* Toronto: ECW Press.

De Certeau, Michel, Luce Girard, and Pierre Mayol. (1998). Plat du jour. In *The Practice of Everyday Life: Volume 2: Living & Cooking*, trans. Timothy J. Tomasik (pp. 171–4). Minneapolis: University of Minnesota Press.

de Kruif, Paul. (1943). Saboteur in the kitchen. *The Reader's Digest* 43 (July): 93–4.

De Man, Paul. (1979). *Allegories of Reading: Figural Language in Rousseau, Nietzsche, Rilke, and Proust*. New Haven, CT: Yale University Press.

Derrida, Jacques. (1995). *Archive Fever: A Freudian Impression*, trans. Eric Prenowitz. Chicago: University of Chicago Press.

Douglas, Mary. (1997). Deciphering a meal. In Carole Counihan and Penny Van Esterik (eds), *Food and Culture: A Reader* (pp. 36–54). New York: Routledge.

Girard, Luce. (1998). The nourishing arts. In Michel de Certeau, Luce Girard and Pierre Mayol. *The Practice of Everyday. Volume 2: Living & Cooking*, trans. Timothy J. Tomasik (pp. 151–69). Minneapolis: University of Minnesota Press.

Glob, P. V. (1969). *The Bog People: Iron-Age Man Preserved*, trans. Rupert Bruce-Mitford. Ithaca, NY: Cornell University Press.

Gogarty, Oliver St. John. (1950). *Rolling Down the Lea*. London: Constable.

Goldman, Marlene. (2005). Broken letters: *Obasan* as traumatic apocalyptic testimony. In *Rewriting Apocalypse in Canadian Fiction* (pp. 128–60). Montreal: McGill-Queen's University Press.

Grover, Kathryn (ed.). (1987). *Dining in America, 1850–1900*. Amherst: University of Massachusetts Press and Rochester, NY: Margaret Woodberry Strong Museum.

Guzlowski, John. (2001). Isaac Singer and the threat of America. *Shofar: An Interdisciplinary Journal of Jewish Studies* 20, 1: 21–35.

Hirsch, Marianne. (1997). *Family Frames: Photography, Narrative, and Postmemory*. Cambridge, MA: Harvard University Press.

Hofmann, Werner. (2002). Marcel Duchamp and emblematic realism. In Joseph Masheck (ed.), *Marcel Duchamp in Perspective* (pp. 53–66). Cambridge, MA: Da Capo Press.

Igaue, June. (1984). Interview with Nancy Aweimrine on November 12, 1984, Los Angeles. The Oral History Program at California State University, Fullerton. Available at <http://content.cdlib.org/xtf/view?docId=ft2j49n70p&doc.view=frames&chunk.id=d0e119&toc.depth=1&toc.id=&brand=oac>.

Johnson, Barbara. (1987). Disfiguring poetic language. In *A World of Difference* (pp. 100–15). Baltimore: Johns Hopkins University Press.

Kaufmann, Vincent. (1996). Valéry's garbage can. *Yale French Studies* 89: 67–81.

Keller, Marjorie. (1986). *The Untutored Eye: Childhood in the Films of Cocteau, Cornell, and Brackhage*. Rutherford, NJ: Farleigh Dickenson University Press.

Kestenbaum, David. (2007). Mottainai grandma reminds Japan, "Don't waste." National Public Radio. Available at <http://www.npr.org/templates/story/story.php?storyId=14054262>.

Kitagawa, Muriel. (1985). *This is My Own: Letters to Wes and Other Writings on Japanese Canadians, 1941–1948*, ed. Roy Miki. Talon Books.

Klein, Melanie. (1986). *The Selected Melanie Klein*, ed. Juliet Mitchell. New York: The Free Press.

Kofman, Sarah. (1998). *Smothered Words*, trans. Madeleine Dobie. Evanston, IL: Northwestern University Press.

Kogawa, Joy. (1981). *Obasan*. New York: Anchor.

Kristeva, Julia. (1982). *Powers of Horror: An Essay on Abjection*, trans. Leon Roudiez.. New York: Columbia University Press.

Lang, Berl. (1990). *Act and Idea in the Nazi Genocide*. Chicago: University of Chicago Press.

Left-over meat in fine disguise. (1938). *American Home* 20 (September): 49–50.

Levinas, Emmanuel. (1978). *Existence & Existents*, trans. Alphonso Lingis. Pittsburgh: Duquesne University Press.

Lo, Marie. (2001). *Obasan.* In Cynthia Wong Sauling and Stephen H. Sumida (eds), *A Resource Guide to Asian American Literature* (pp. 97–108). New York: Modern Language Association of America.

MacFadyen, Byron. (1930). Leftovers shouldn't be left over. *Good Housekeeping* 91 (September): 96–7.

MacFadyen, Byron. (1935). Leftovers made over and meals built around them. *Good Housekeeping* 101 (September): 86–7, 198.

Markevitch, Marie A. (1942). The art of using leftovers. *House & Garden* 81 (April): 73.

Meyer, Steven. (1994). The new novel: *A Novel of Thank You* and the characterization of thought. Introduction to Gertrude Stein *A Novel of Thank You* (pp. vii–xxvii). Normal, IL: Dalkey Archive Press.

Moats, Leone B. (1933). Today's left-overs – tomorrow's luncheon. *House & Garden* 33 (August): 18–19.

Nickles, Shelly. (2002). "Preserving women": Refrigerator design as social process in the 1930s. *Technology and Culture* 43: 693–727.

Nietzsche, Friedrich. (1999). On truth and lying in a non-moral sense. In *The Birth of Tragedy and Other Writings*, ed. Raymond Geuss and Ronald Speirs, trans. Ronald Speirs (pp. 139–53). Cambridge, UK: Cambridge University Press.

Oiwa, Keibo. (ed.). (1991). *Stone Voices: Wartime Writings of Japanese Canadian Issei.* Montreal: Véhicule Press.

Paz, Octavio. (2002). The ready-made. In Joseph Masheck (ed.), *Marcel Duchamp in Perspective* (pp. 139–53). Cambridge, MA: Da Capo Press.

Perlow, Meir. (1995). *Understanding Mental Objects.* London: Routledge.

Peterson, Nancy J. (2001). *Against Amnesia: Contemporary Women Writers and the Crisis of Historical Memory.* Philadelphia: University of Pennsylvania Press.

Piaget, Jean. (1959). *The Language and Thought of Children.* London: Routledge.

Richter, Hans. (1969/2002). In memory of Marcel Duchamp. In Joseph Masheck (ed.), *Marcel Duchamp in Perspective* (pp. 148–50). New York: Da Capo Press.

Robinson, Judith. (1961). The place of literary and artistic creation in Valéry's thought. *The Modern Language Review* 56, 4: 497–514.

Schwenger, Peter. (2003). The dream narratives of debris. *SubStance 100* 32, 1: 75–89.

Schwenger, Peter. (2006). *The Tears of Things: Melancholy and Physical Objects.* Minneapolis: University of Minnesota Press.

Serve your leftovers – here's how. (1942). *Better Homes & Gardens* 20 (March): 46.

Sharpe, Ella. (1940). Psycho-physical problems revealed in language: An examination of metaphor. *International Journal of Psycho-Analysis* 21: 201–13.

Shouer, Louella G. (1937). Return engagement. *Ladies Home Journal* 54 (October): 43, 71.

Singer, Isaac Bashevis. (1989). Problems of Yiddish prose in America, trans. Robert H. Wolf. *Prooftexts* 9, 1: 5–12.

Stein, Gertrude. (1926/1993). Composition as explanation. In *A Stein Reader*, ed. Ulla E. Dydo (pp. 493–503). Evanston, IL: Northwestern University Press.

Stein, Gertrude. (1994). *A Novel of Thank You*, ed. Steven Meyer. Normal, IL: Dalkey Archive Press.

Strasser, Susan. (1992). *Waste and Want: The Other Side of Consumption.* German Historical Institute. Annual Lecture Series. No. 5. Providence: Berg Publishers.

Taussig, Michael T. (2004). *My Cocaine Museum.* Chicago: University of Chicago Press.

Thwaites, Tony. (1997). Currency exchanges: The postmodern, Vattimo, et cetera, among other things (et cetera). *Postmodern Culture* 7, 2. <http://jefferson.village.virginia.edu/pmc/text-only/issue.197/thwaites.197>.

Trezise, Thomas. (2001). Unspeakable. *The Yale Journal of Criticism* 14, 1: 39–66.

Ueno, Harry Yoshio. (1976). Interview with Sue Kunitomi Embrey and Arthur A. Hansen. The Japanese American Oral History Project at California State University, Fullerton. San José, California. October 30.

Vaile, Roland S. (1937). Research memorandum on social aspects of consumption in the depression. *Social Science Research Council Bulletin* 35: 18–22.

Valéry, Paul. (1973–4). *Cahiers*, ed. Judith Robinson, vol. 1. Paris: Gallimard, Bibliothèque de la Pléiade.

Van Alphen, Ernst. (1997). *Caught by History: Holocaust Effects in Contemporary Art, Literature, and Theory.* Stanford, CA: Stanford University Press.

Warhol, Andy. (1977). *The Philosophy of Andy Warhol (From A to B and Back Again)*. San Diego, CA: Harvest Books.

Watch your refrigerator. (1929). *The Literary Digest* 103 (November 30): 38.

Wong, Sau-ling Cynthia. (1993). *Reading Asian American Literature: From Necessity to Extravagance*. Princeton, NJ: Princeton University Press.

Young, James E. (1988). *Writing and Rewriting the Holocaust: Narrative and the Consequences of Interpretation*. Bloomington: Indiana University Press.

Žižek, Slavoj. (1989). *The Sublime Object of Ideology*. London: Verso.

Index